CALIFORNIA DEPARTMENT OF CORRECTIONS
EUREKA

MISSOURI DEPARTMENT OF CORRECTIONS

COOS COUNTY SHERIFF'S OFFICE

DEPARTMENT OF JUVENILE JUSTICE
STATE OF FLORIDA

INDIANA DEPARTMENT OF CORRECTION

WASHINGTON STATE DEPARTMENT of CORRECTIONS

DEPARTMENT OF THE STATE OF TEXAS CRIMINAL JUSTICE

NEW YORK STATE EXCELSIOR CORRECTIONAL SERVICES

DEPARTMENT OF CORRECTIONS STATE OF KANSAS

SOUTH CAROLINA DEPARTMENT OF CORRECTIONS

Tuscolameta, inc
Walnut Grove Youth Correctional Facility

OFFICE OF SHERIFF The Bold New City of the South JACKSONVILLE CORRECTIONS

DEPARTMENT OF TENNESSEE COMMERCE CORRECTION

LEHIGH COUNTY DEPARTMENT OF CORRECTIONS

CORRECTIONS SHERIFF'S OFFICE MOBILE, ALABAMA

DEPARTMENT OF JUSTICE FEDERAL BUREAU OF PRISONS

OHIO DEPARTMENT OF REHABILITATION & CORRECTION

GEORGIA STATE OF GEORGIA 1776 CORRECTIONS

IMPORTANT:

HERE IS YOUR REGISTRATION CODE TO ACCESS
YOUR PREMIUM McGRAW-HILL ONLINE RESOURCES.

0-07-297553-9 T/A SCHMALLEGER: CORRECTIONS IN THE 21ST CENTURY, 2/E

MCGRAW-HILL
ONLINE RESOURCES

REGISTRATION CODE

ZSTK-B5BD-M66L-MZXC-YNZA

CORRECTIONS IN THE 21st Century

Brief Contents

▶ ▶ ▶ ▶ Expanded Contents

▶ PART 1 Introduction to Corrections 1

CHAPTER 1
Corrections: An Overview

CHAPTER 2
Punishments: A Brief History

CHAPTER 3

Sentencing: To Punish or to Reform?

▶ PART 2   Community Corrections   109

CHAPTER 4

Diversion and Probation: How Most Offenders Are Punished

CHAPTER 5
Intermediate Sanctions: Between Probation and Incarceration

CHAPTER 6
Jails: Way Stations Along the Justice Highway

CHAPTER 7
Prisons Today: Change Stations or Warehouses?

CHAPTER 8

Parole: Early Release and Reintegration

▶ **PART 4   The Prison World**   325

CHAPTER 9

The Staff World: Managing the Prison Population

CHAPTER 10
The Inmate World: Living Behind Bars

CHAPTER 11
The Legal World: Prisoners' Rights

CHAPTER 12
Special Prison Populations: The Elderly, HIV/AIDS, and the Mentally Challenged

Career Profile Boxes

Reflections on the Future Boxes

Preface

Corrections, when seen as the control and punishment of convicted offenders, has been an important part of organized society from the earliest days of civilization. It has not always had a proud past, however. In premodern times, atrocious physical punishment, exile, and unspeakable torture were the tools used all too often by those called upon to enforce society's correctional philosophies—especially the strongly felt need for vengeance.

Important changes in correctional practice began around the time of the American Revolution, when the purposes of criminal punishments were closely examined by influential reformers. More recently, corrections has become an important field of study in which scientific techniques are valued and reasoned debate is encouraged.

The best, however, is yet to come. It is only within the past 30 years that conscientious corrections practitioners have begun to embrace the notion of professionalism—wherein ethics, a sense of high purpose, a personal long-term career commitment, a respect for the fundamental humanity of those supervised, and widely agreed-upon principles and standards guide the daily work of correctional personnel. Corrections professionalism, while not yet as well-known as police professionalism, has garnered support from policymakers and is winning respect among the public. It serves as this textbook's organizing principle. *Corrections in the 21st Century*:

- provides an in-depth look at the past, present, and future of corrections;
- identifies the many *subcomponents* of modern-day corrections;
- highlights the *process* of modern-day corrections;
- focuses on the *issues* facing the correctional enterprise today;
- provides an appreciation for contemporary real-world correctional *practice;*
- examines the opportunities represented by new and developing corrections *technologies;* and

- points students in the direction of the still-emerging ideal of corrections *professionalism.*

It is our belief that a new age of corrections is upon us. It is an age in which the lofty goals of corrections professionalism will take their place alongside the more traditional components of a still-developing field. It is our hope that this textbook will play at least some small part in helping to bring about a new and better correctional enterprise—one that is reasonable and equitable to all involved in the justice process.

THE SECOND EDITION

The second edition of *Corrections in the 21st Century* has been extensively reorganized. The book's new table of contents illustrates that reorganization at a glance. All 16 chapters have been reordered to better reflect the corrections process, and chapters are now grouped into 5 parts, which are described in detail below. We have also added a chapter to this edition—Chapter 12, "Special Prison Populations: The Elderly, HIV/AIDS, and the Mentally Challenged"—to focus attention on correctional groups that require resources beyond those needed by the general population.

In addition to reorganizing material and including the new chapter on special-needs inmates, the second edition of *Corrections in the 21st Century* contains a number of new and exciting elements. Among these are feature articles provided by *Corrections Connection Network News* (CCNN) exclusively for this textbook, and *Reflections on the Future* essays written specifically for this edition by well-known corrections practitioners and scholars. (See pages xvi and xviii for a complete listing of these articles and essays.)

The new edition also contains updated material on the goals of punishment, the impact of terrorism on facility management, criminal sentencing, jails, prison classification systems, prison reform, professional credentialing, ethics, prisoner reentry, mentoring services for parolees, correctional technologies, prison security threat groups (gangs), social diversity in corrections (including the imprisonment of women and minorities), capital punishment, and faith-based correctional programs. The discussions dealing with sentencing reform and restorative and retributive justice have been significantly expanded.

High-profile events and cases taken from today's headlines are used to introduce each chapter, encouraging students to read on. Some of the cases incorporated are

- John Walker Lindh's trial and imprisonment for supporting militant Islamic fundamentalists during the 2002 U.S. war in Afghanistan;
- actor Charlie Sheen's drug convictions and resulting court-ordered probation;
- the arrest of actress Winona Ryder for shoplifting and the intermediate sanctions to which she was sentenced;
- boxer Mike Tyson's prison and parole time;
- young Mary Vincent's victimization at the hands of Larry Singleton that left her without arms; and
- the release from death row of Kirk Bloodsworth—the first person in the United States to be cleared of a capital murder charge after DNA testing proved his innocence.

A number of recent court decisions, especially those of the U.S. Supreme Court, have been incorporated into this new edition. A complete list of cases appears at the end of the text, but some of the most recent cases now covered are

- *Apprendi* v. *New Jersey* (U.S. Supreme Court, 2000), which brought into question the fact-finding authority of judges in making sentencing decisions;
- *Atkins* v. *Virginia* (U.S. Supreme Court, 2002), which held that executing mentally retarded people violates the Constitution's ban on cruel and unusual punishment;
- *Booth* v. *Churner* (U.S. Supreme Court, 2001), which upheld a requirement under the Prison Litigation Reform Act (PLRA) that state inmates must "exhaust such administrative remedies as are available" before filing a suit over prison conditions;
- *Correctional Services Corp.* v. *Malesko* (U.S. Supreme Court, 2001), which limited the ap-

plicability of federal civil liability standards to private corporations acting under color of federal law;
- *Ewing* v. *California,* (U.S. Supreme Court, 2003), a three-strikes case in which the Court found that a 25-year-to-life sentence following a conviction for felony grand theft of three golf clubs was not cruel or unusual punishment;
- *Gerber* v. *Hickman* (9th U.S. Circuit Court of Appeals, 2001), which held that a prison inmate does not have a constitutional right to procreate;
- *Lockyer* v. *Andrade* (U.S. Supreme Court, 2003), a three-strikes case in which the Court held that consecutive 25-year-to-life sentences following two petty theft with priors convictions did not violate the Eighth Amendment's proscription against cruel or unusual punishment; and
- *Porter* v. *Nussle* (U.S. Supreme Court, 2002), which held that the Prison Litigation Reform Act's "exhaustion requirement" applies to all inmate suits about prison life, whether they involve general circumstances or particular episodes and whether they allege excessive force or some other wrong.

ORGANIZATION

As mentioned, this book is organized into five parts. Part One, "Introduction to Corrections," provides an understanding of corrections by explaining the goals underlying the correctional enterprise and by describing the how and why of criminal punishments. Part One identifies professionalism as the key to managing successfully correctional personnel, facilities, and populations. Standard-setting organizations such as the American Correctional Association, the American Jail Association, the American Probation and Parole Association, and the National Commission on Correctional Health Care are identified, and the importance of professional ethics for correctional occupations and correctional administrators is emphasized.

Part Two, "Community Corrections," explains what happens to most convicted offenders, including diversion (the suspension of formal criminal proceedings before conviction in exchange for the defendant's participation in treatment), probation, and intermediate sanctions.

Part Three, "Institutional Corrections," provides a detailed description of jails, prisons, and parole. The reentry challenges that ex-inmates released from prisons face are explained. Education, vocational preparation, and drug treatment programs that are intended to prevent reoffending are also explored.

Part Four, "The Prison World," provides an overview of life inside prison from the point of view of both inmates and staff. Part Four also describes the responsibilities and challenges surrounding the staff role. A new chapter, Chapter 12, now focuses attention on special correctional populations, including the elderly, HIV/AIDS–infected inmates, and the mentally and physically challenged. We have chosen to integrate our coverage of women in corrections—including information about the important new NIC report entitled "Gender Response Strategies: Research, Practice, and Guiding Principles for Women Offenders"—throughout the body of the text rather than isolating it in Chapter 12.

Part Five, "Issues in Corrections," explores some of the most controversial topics in contemporary corrections. Prison crowding, capital punishment, the conditional rights of prisoners, and juvenile corrections can all be found in this section of the text. Victims' rights and the role that correctional authorities can play in protecting and advancing those rights are also explored.

PEDAGOGICAL AIDS

Working together, the authors and editor have developed a learning system designed to help students excel in the Corrections course. In addition to the many changes already mentioned, we have included a wealth of new photographs to make the book even more inviting and relevant for students. To this same end, our real-world chapter-opening vignettes give the material a fresh flavor intended to motivate students to read on; our photo captions, which raise thought-provoking questions, actively engage students in the learning process; and our marginal quotes spotlight intriguing details being discussed and draw students into those discussions. Redesigned and carefully

updated tables and figures highlight and amplify the text coverage. And chapter outlines, objectives, reviews, marginal definitions, and an end-of-book glossary all help students master the material.

The Schmalleger/Smykla learning system goes well beyond these essential tools, however. As mentioned, *Corrections in the 21st Century* offers a unique emphasis on corrections professionalism, an emphasis that has prompted us to create a number of innovative new learning tools that focus on the real world of corrections:

- *Reflections on the Future*—contributed essays from some of the field's most respected scholars and practitioners that offer insights into the future of sentencing, jails, parole, and other institutions in American corrections. See page xviii for a complete list of these essays.
- *Corrections Connection Network News*—exclusive feature articles from a popular website for corrections practitioners, that lend a real-world air to the text. See page xvi for a complete list of *Corrections Connection Network News* articles.
- *Career Profiles*—enlightening minibiographies of corrections professionals, such as a parole officer, a victim advocate, a corrections officer, a youth counselor, and a substance abuse manager. See page xvii for a complete list of *Career Profiles*.
- *Offender Speaks and Staff Speaks*—intriguing interviews with offenders and practitioners that provide a balance of perspectives and further expand on the text's real-world emphasis.
- *Ethical Dilemmas*—challenging issues confronted by corrections professionals on the job.
- *Appendix: Careers in Corrections*—an appendix which presents the steps involved in career planning, developing employability and job readiness, and finding the right job.

In addition to the features we have developed to further our goal of creating a uniquely practical, professionally oriented text, we have also included end-of-chapter review material to help students master the concepts and principles developed in the chapter:

- *Chapter Summary*—a valuable learning tool organized into sections that mirror the chapter-opening objectives exactly; the summary re-states all of the chapter's most critical points.
- *Key Terms*—a comprehensive list of the terms defined in margins of the chapter, complete with page references to make it easy for students to go back and review further.
- *Questions for Review*—objective study questions that allow students to test their knowledge and prepare for exams.
- *Thinking Critically About Corrections*—broad-based questions that challenge students to think critically about chapter concepts and issues and Internet-based exercises that are ideal for today's net-oriented learner.
- *On-the-Job Decision Making*—unique experiential exercises that enable students to apply what they have learned in the chapter to the daily work of correctional personnel.
- *Corrections on the Web*—Internet-based exercises that are ideal for today's web-oriented learner.

SUPPLEMENTS PACKAGE

As a full-service publisher of quality educational products, McGraw-Hill does much more than just sell textbooks. The company creates and publishes an extensive array of print, video, and digital supplements for students and instructors. This edition of *Corrections in the 21st Century* is accompanied by an extensive, comprehensive supplements package:

For the Student

- *Making the Grade CD-ROM*—a free electronic study guide packaged with every text that includes chapter quizzes with feedback indicating why each answer is right or wrong, an Internet guide, a study skills primer, and much more.
- *Online Learning Center Website*—an innovative, text-specific Website featuring PowerWeb (online access to articles from the popular and scholarly press, weekly updates, and daily newsfeeds) as well as flashcards that can be used to master vocabulary, quizzes with feed-

back that students can use to study for exams, downloadable state supplements, and more.

For the Instructor

- *Instructor's Resource CD*—a single CD with an easy-to-use interface providing access to a wide array of important ancillaries:
  - *Instructor's Manual/Testbank*—detailed chapter outlines, key terms, overviews, lecture notes, and a complete testbank.
  - *Computerized Testbank*—easy-to-use computerized testing program for both Windows and Macintosh computers.
  - *PowerPoint Slides*—complete, chapter-by-chapter slide shows featuring text, art, and tables.
- *Online Learning Center Website*—password-protected access to downloadable state supplements and other important instructor support materials and resources.
- *Videotapes*—access to a wide variety of videotapes from the *Films for the Humanities and Social Sciences* series.
- *Course Management Systems Cartridges*—whether you use WebCT, Blackboard, e-College, or another course management system, we can provide a cartridge that enables you to either conduct your course entirely online or to supplement your lectures with online material. If your school does not yet have one of these course management systems, we can provide you with PageOut, an easy-to-use tool that allows you to create your own course Web page and provide access to all material on the Online Learning Center.
- *Primis Online*—a unique database publishing system that allows instructors to create their own custom text from material in this text or elsewhere and deliver that text to students electronically as an e-book or in print format via the bookstore.

IN APPRECIATION

Writing a textbook requires a great deal of help and support. We would like to acknowledge and xxiii

thank the many individuals on whom we relied. Special thanks go to Dennis Stevens at the University of Massachusetts at Boston for his research on the special features, to Gordon M. Armstrong at Wayne State University for his useful critiques, to Jody Klein-Saffran at the Federal Bureau of Prisons and Gary Bayens at Washburn University for their contributions to our chapters on parole and juvenile corrections, respectively; and to the political science and criminal justice faculty and staff, the dean of the college of arts and sciences, and Nitra McClinton at the University of South Alabama for their encouragement and for the resources they made available. We also gratefully acknowledge the contributions of the following individuals who helped in the development of this textbook

Tom Austin
Shippensburg University
Shippensburg, Pennsylvania

Steve Abrams
California Department of Corrections
Santa Rosa, California

Ken Barnes
Arizona Western College
Yuma, Arizona

Kathy J. Black-Dennis
University of Louisville
Louisville, Kentucky

Robert Bohm
University of Central Florida
Orlando, Florida

Vicky Dorworth
Montgomery College
Rockville, Maryland

Robert Figlestahler
Eastern Kentucky University
Richmond, Kentucky

Lynn Fortney
EBSCO Subscription Services
Birmingham, Alabama

Donna Hale
Shippensburg University
Shippensburg, Pennsylvania

Homer C. Hawkins
Michigan State University
East Lansing, Michigan

Nancy L. Hogan
Ferris State University
Big Rapids, Michigan

Julius Koefoed
Kirkwood Community College
Cedar Rapids, Iowa

James L. Jengeleski
Shippensburg University
Shippensburg, Pennyslvania

Brad Johnson
Atlanta, Georgia

Walter B. Lewis
St. Louis Community College at Meramec
Kirkwood, Missouri

Jess Maghan
University of Illinois at Chicago
Chicago, Illinois

Alvin Mitchell
Delgado Community College
New Orleans, Louisiana

Etta Morgan
Pennsylvania State University
Capital College, Pennsylvania

Sarah Nordin
Solano Community College
Suisun City, California

Michael F. Perna
Broome Community College
Binghamton, New York

Scott Plutchak
University of Alabama at Birmingham
Birmingham, Alabama

John Sloan
University of Alabama at Birmingham
Birmingham, Alabama

Anthony C. Trevelino
Camden County College
Blackwood, New Jersey

Shela R. Van Ness
University of Tennessee at Chattanooga
Chattanooga, Tennessee

Gennaro F. Vito
University of Louisville
Louisville, Kentucky

John Vollmann
Florida Metropolitan University
Pompano Beach, Florida

Ed Whittle
Florida Metropolitan University at
   Tampa College
Tampa, Florida

Robert R. Wiggins
Cedarville College
Cedarville, Ohio

Dawn Zobel
Federal Bureau of Prisons
Alderson, West Virginia

We greatly acknowledge the assistance and support of the many dedicated professionals who provided original written contributions for the *Reflections on the Future* boxes in this edition. They include

Thomas J. Cowper, New York State Police

Richard S. Frase, University of Minnesota

Tara Gray, New Mexico State University

Edward Harrison, National Commission on Correctional Health Care

Herbert J. Hoelter, National Center on Institutions and Alternatives

Illinois Commission on Capital Punishment

Leslie W. Kennedy, Rutgers University

Ken Kerle, American Jail Association

Richard Kiekbusch, University of Texas Permian Basin

James W. Marquart, Sam Houston State University

William L. Tafoya, University of New Haven

Morris L. Thigpen Sr., National Institute of Corrections

Jeremy Travis, The Urban Institute

Mark Umbreit, University of Minnesota

Kathy Waters, Arizona Supreme Court

Alan C. Youngs, Lakewood, Colorado, Police Department

Finally, we want to acknowledge the special debt that we owe to the McGraw-Hill team, including publisher Philip A. Butcher for his encouragement and support; senior sponsoring editor Carolyn Henderson Meier for keeping the project on track; senior marketing manager Dan Loch for seeing value in this textbook; senior project manager Christina Thornton-Villagomez for her attention to the many day-to-day details; senior production supervisor Carol Bielski; development editor Roz Sackoff; design manager Laurie Entringer; editorial coordinator Julie Abodeely; photo researchers Nora Agbayani and David Tietz; media producer Shannon Gattens; and art editor Jennifer DeVere. The professional vision, guidance, and support of these dedicated professionals helped bring this project to fruition.

Frank Schmalleger
John Smykla

▶ ▶ **On January 29, 2003, John Walker Lindh,** known as the "American Taliban" for his support of militant Islamic fundamentalists during the 2002 U.S. war in Afghanistan, was transferred from a federal lockup in Virginia to the federal Bureau of Prisons medium security facility at Victorville, California. A few months earlier, Lindh, 21, had been sentenced to 20 years in prison after pleading guilty to supplying services to the Taliban and to carrying explosives in commission of a felony. Born in Maryland, Lindh is an American citizen who grew up in California. As a teenager, he became interested in Islam, became a Muslim, and traveled to the Middle East to learn more about the religion. He ended up as a Taliban conscript. Although Lindh apologized to Americans at his sentencing, the Judge who ordered him imprisoned told Lindh that forgiveness and punishment are two separate issues. "You were willing to give your life for the Taliban but not for your country," the judge said.[1]

Lindh, whose support of the Taliban apparently made him unpopular with fellow inmates, was attacked and slightly injured in March 2003 by another inmate as he was preparing for evening prayers in the Victorville prison chapel.[2] Lindh's story illustrates the fact that all **correctional clients**, as prison inmates, probationers, parolees, and those held in jails are called, are unique individuals. Nonetheless, the characteristics of the correctional population in the United States today can be described generally, as shown in Figure 1–1.

John Walker Lindh, known as the "American Taliban" for his support of militant Islamic fundamentalists during the 2002 U.S. war in Afghanistan, is imprisoned at the federal Bureau of Prisons medium security facility at Victorville, California. How have antiterrorism efforts impacted corrections?

correctional clients
Prison inmates, probationers, parolees, offenders assigned to alternative sentencing programs, and those held in jails.

The Corrections Explosion

Some years ago, Fox Butterfield, a staff writer for the *New York Times*, noted in an editorial, "It has become a comforting story: For five straight years, crime has been falling, led by a drop in murder. So why is the number of inmates in prisons and jails around the nation still going up? Last year [1996], it reached almost 1.7 million, up about 7 percent a year since 1990."[3]

The trends that Butterfield identified are still occurring today. One amazing fact stands out from all the information about corrections: While serious crime in the United States consistently declined throughout much of the 1990s, and while such declines continued into the first decade of the 21st century, the number of people under correctional supervision in this country—not just the number of convicted offenders sent to prison—has continued to climb. Crime rates are approximately 20 percent lower today than they were in 1980. They are at their lowest level in 20 years. But the number of people on probation is up almost 300 percent since 1980, the nation's prison population has increased by more than 400 percent, and the number of persons on parole has increased by almost the same proportion. Figure 1–2 illustrates these trends.

The question is, why? Why the steady increase in correctional populations in the face of declining crime rates? The answer to this question, like

4

▶ ▶ **Actress Winona Ryder rose to prominence** in 1988 with her role in *Beetle Juice*. She moved in a different direction on December 12, 2001, when she stole more than 20 high-fashion items worth $9,750 from Saks Fifth Avenue—a posh department store—in Beverly Hills, California. Store security officers observed Ryder trying to remove security tags affixed to socks, hair accessories, and a Gucci dress before hiding them in a large shopping bag she had brought into the store. At 7 P.M. she was arrested and charged with grand theft. By midnight she was released on a $20,000 bond. A year later, the two-time Academy Award nominee was convicted of felony grand theft and vandalism. On December 6, 2002, Superior Court Judge Elden Fox sentenced Ryder to a number of intermediate sanctions discussed in this chapter: three years' probation, a fine and court costs of $6,550, a restitution fee of $11,265 to Saks, 480 hours of community service within four months (240 hours at the City of Hope, a major medical center specializing in cancer treatment; 120 hours at the Foundation for the Junior Blind; and 120 hours at Caring for Babies with AIDS), and drug and psychological counseling. Because she had no prior convictions, prosecutors did not recommend incarceration.

At the sentencing hearing, Ryder's attorney told the Court that she would have to carry the scarlet letter "S" for shoplifting for the rest of her life. Judge Fox told Ryder, "It is not my intention to make an example of you." He added, "You have disappointed many people who have been entertained and inspired by your talents and also your acts of humanity. . . . There is going to be the need to confront certain issues that you have been unable, or refused, to confront and accept personal responsibility for what happened." Judge Fox told Ryder that he had been unable to explain to his 16-year-old son, Ryan, why someone who earned so much would shoplift. "You are the only person that's going to be able to answer my son's question." Judge Fox added, "If you steal again, you will go to jail. Understand that?" "Yes, Your Honor, I do," Ryder replied.

Ryder returned to court on December 15, 2003. Judge Fox commended her for abiding by the rules of her probation. Fox ordered Ryder to return to court May 26, 2004 for a six-month review and said he would decide then if she needs to continue probation supervision.

Ryder's story captures the essence of this chapter. Some offenders need punishment beyond regular probation but not incarceration. Today, judges have unlimited opportunities to order penalties that match the seriousness of a crime. In Ryder's case, three years' probation in addition to fines and restitution, community service, and counseling constitute what we call **intermediate sanctions**—punishment options that fill the gap between traditional probation and jail or prison and that better

In 2002, actress Winona Ryder was sentenced to three years' probation, ordered to pay $11,265 in restitution and $6,550 in fines and court costs, perform 480 hours of community service, and required to take drug and psychological counseling for stealing more than 20 high-fashion items worth $9,750 from Saks Fifth Avenue in Beverly Hills, California. Do you think intermediate sanctions teach offenders a lesson better than regular probation alone?

intermediate sanctions
New punishment options developed to fill the gap between traditional probation and traditional jail or prison sentences and to better match the severity of punishment to the seriousness of the crime.

158

Up-to-the-Minute Coverage

High-profile events and cases taken from today's headlines and recent Supreme Court decisions keep the book current and relevant for today's students.

:12
CHAPTER

Special Prison Populations:
The Elderly, HIV/AIDS, and the Mentally Challenged

CHAPTER OUTLINE

SPECIAL-NEEDS INMATES
Substance Abusing Inmates
HIV-Positive Inmates
Mentally Ill Inmates
Inmates with Tuberculosis
Older Inmates
DRUG TREATMENT PROGRAMS
Recidivism
Program Evaluation
Alcohol: The Biggest Culprit
Recommendations for Managing Substance-Abusing Offenders
DRUG COURTS
HIV AND AIDS IN CORRECTIONAL FACILITIES
Education and Prevention
SEXUALLY TRANSMITTED DISEASES IN JAIL
LEGAL ISSUES
Inmates with Disabilities
Inmates with HIV/AIDS
Inmates with Mental Illness

▶ ▶ **CHAPTER OBJECTIVES**

After completing this chapter you should be able to do the following:

1. Define the term *special-needs inmate*.
2. Report on the management needs of special population inmates.
3. Report on the impact of substance abusers on the corrections system.
4. Discuss the five essential elements of cost-effective management of HIV/AIDS inmates.
5. Explain why there are so many inmates with mental illnesses in prison.
6. Describe the ways that prisons may provide medical and mental health services.
7. List the cost and health issues associated with older inmates.
8. Discuss the rationale for drug treatment programs in prisons and jails.
9. Discuss why the future of drug court is promising.
10. Discuss why treating HIV in prison is difficult.
11. Review the legal issues surrounding special population inmates.

 The democratic principle that "all men are created equal" implies that persons with disabilities are entitled like everyone else to equal access and fair treatment appropriate to their context, whether the context is a prison, church, or place of employment. "

—Marca Bristo, Chairperson, National Council on Disability, letter to the editor of the *Washington Times*, July 27, 1998.

New Chapter on Special-Needs Inmates

Chapter 12, "Special Prison Populations: The Elderly, HIV/AIDS, and the Mentally Challenged," focuses student attention on correctional groups that require resources beyond those needed by the general population.

Unique *Reflections on the Future* Boxes

Written specifically for this text by some of the field's most respected scholars and practitioners, these essays offer insights into the future of sentencing, jails, parole, and more.

Restorative Justice
by Mark Umbreit, University of Minnesota

Restorative justice is a victim-centered response to crime that provides opportunities for those most directly affected by crime—the victim, the offender, their families, and representatives of the community—to be directly involved in responding to the harm caused by the crime. Restorative justice is based upon values that emphasize the importance of providing opportunities for more active involvement in the process of offering support and assistance to crime victims; holding offenders directly accountable to the people and communities they have violated; restoring the emotional and material losses of victims (to the degree possible); providing a range of opportunities for dialogue and problem solving among interested crime victims, offenders, families, and other support persons; offering offenders opportunities for competency development and reintegration into productive community life; and strengthening public safety through community building.

Restorative justice policies and programs are known to be developing in nearly every state, including a growing number of state and county justice systems that are undergoing major systemic change. Restorative justice is also developing in many other parts of the world, including numerous European countries, Australia, New Zealand, and South Africa. In recent years, restorative justice practices and/or policies have been endorsed by the American Bar Association (victim offender mediation and dialogue), the European Council, and the United Nations.

The principles of restorative justice draw upon the wisdom of many indigenous cultures throughout the world, most notably Native American culture within the United States and Aboriginal/First Nation culture in Canada. These principles are also deeply rooted in the ancient values of Judeo-Christian culture, which have emphasized crime as being a violation against people and families, rather than "the state." Many examples are found in the Old and New Testaments of the Bible of the responsibility of offenders to directly repair the harm they caused to individuals, representing a breach in the "Shalom community."

Specific examples of restorative justice include crime repair crews, victim intervention programs, victim offender mediation and dialogue, family group conferencing, peacemaking circles, victim panels that speak to offenders, sentencing circles, community reparative boards before which offenders appear, offender competency development programs, victim empathy classes for offenders, victim-directed and citizen-involved community service by the offender, community-based support groups for crime victims, and community-based support groups for offenders. As the oldest and most widely developed expression of restorative justice, with more than 25 years of experience and numerous studies in North America and Europe, victim offender mediation and dialogue programs currently work with thousands of cases annually through more than 300 programs throughout the United States and more than 1,200 in Europe.

There have been more than 60 empirical studies of restorative justice dialogue programs (primarily victim offender mediation but also a smaller number of studies of family group conferencing). Findings have included high levels of victim and offender satisfaction with the process and outcome, greater likelihood of successful restitution completion by the offender, greater perceptions of fairness, reduced fear among victims, and reduced frequency and severity of further criminal behavior.

ABOUT THE AUTHOR

Mark Umbreit, Ph.D., is a professor at the University of Minnesota, School of Social Work. He is the founding director of the Center for Restorative Justice & Peacemaking as well as the National Restorative Justice Training Institute. Dr. Umbreit has more than 28 years of experience as a mediator, trainer, and researcher and has authored four books and more than 140 articles, book chapters, and monographs in the field of restorative justice and mediation. His most recent book is *The Handbook on Victim Offender Mediation: An Essential Guide for Practice & Research* (San Francisco, Jossey-Bass, 2001).

Reflections on the Future

57

Chapter-Opening Previews

Detailed chapter-opening objectives and outlines combine with intriguing photographs, quotes, and vignettes to draw students in and help them focus on the chapter's most critical concepts.

> Changes in the institutions and the correctional system as a whole require that correctional officers be capable of interacting with offenders and with colleagues in a manner which reflects attitudinal change and a knowledge base different from that generally accepted in the past.
>
> —Paul H. Hahn, Xavier University

Corrections: An Overview

1
CHAPTER

CHAPTER OBJECTIVES

After completing this chapter you should be able to do the following:

1. Explain why correctional populations continue to rise even though the rate of serious crime in the United States has been declining.

2. Understand how rising correctional populations affect the costs of corrections.

3. List the kinds of crimes that cause people to enter correctional programs and institutions.

4. Describe how crime is measured in the United States and explain the differences between the two major crime reporting programs.

5. List and describe the various components of the criminal justice system.

6. List the major components of the corrections subsystem.

7. Describe criminal justice as a *system* and as a *process*.

8. Define the term *corrections*.

9. Explain the importance of professionalism in the corrections field.

10. Understand what is meant by *social diversity* and explain why issues of race, gender, and ethnicity are important in corrections today.

CHAPTER OUTLINE

THE CORRECTIONS EXPLOSION
Historical Roots of the Corrections Explosion
Correctional Expenditures

CRIME AND CORRECTIONS
Measuring Crime
The Crime Funnel

CORRECTIONS AND THE CRIMINAL JUSTICE SYSTEM
Entering the Correctional System
Prosecution and Pretrial Procedure
Judicial Procedures
Sentencing and Sanctions
The Correctional Subsystem

PROFESSIONALISM IN CORRECTIONS
Standards and Training
Basic Skills and Knowledge
Standard-Setting Organizations
Education

SOCIAL DIVERSITY IN CORRECTIONS

Plentiful Visuals

Photographs with complete, thought-provoking captions as well as figures and tables grace almost every page of the text and bring material to life.

Corrections Connection Network News Boxes

Exclusive feature articles from this popular website highlight practical issues facing corrections professionals in their daily work.

CAREER PROFILE

Zaira Tena
Correctional Officer   New Mexico Women's Correctional Facility   Grants, New Mexico

Zaira Tena is employed by Corrections Corporation of America (CCA) as a correctional officer at the New Mexico Women's Correctional Facility in Grants, New Mexico. She started working there 16 months ago. This is Zaira's first job in corrections. Zaira was attracted to CCA and a career in corrections because of the benefits that CCA offered her.

Zaira attended Laramie County Community College in Laramie, Wyoming, before joining CCA. The company provided additional training in interpersonal communication, special-needs inmates, crisis intervention, infectious diseases, suicide prevention, first aid, CPR, and firearms, giving her the skills she needs to ensure the health, welfare, and safety of prison employees and inmates. Since Zaira especially enjoys recreation, she coordinates the institution's recreation activities.

Zaira's enthusiasm for her own career and professional development shows in her advice to people thinking about a career in corrections. Wisely, Zaira is taking her own advice. She plans to stay in corrections and hopes one day soon to become assistant shift commander at the Grants women's facility.

❝ I like my job. I like working with people. What I learned and what I'd tell someone is, be very professional, firm, fair, and consistent at all times, and be able to work under a lot of pressure. ❞

discretionary power of judges, inconsistency and inequality in sentencing, the use of personal connections to obtain sentencing reductions, and the imposition of capital punishment for minor offenses.

Beccaria proposed that punishment could be justified only if it was imposed to defend the social contract—the tacit allegiance that individuals owe their society and the obligations of government to individuals. It is the social contract, said Beccaria, that gives society the right to punish its members.

Beccaria also argued that punishment should be swift, since swift punishment offers the greatest deterrence. When punishment quickly follows a crime, said Beccaria, the ideas of crime and punishment are more closely associated in a person's mind. He also suggested that the link between crime and punishment would be stronger if the punishment somehow related to the crime.

Finally, said Beccaria, punishments should not be unnecessarily severe. The severity of punishment, he argued, should be proportional to the degree of social damage caused by the crime. Treason, Beccaria said, is the worst crime, since it most harms the social contract. Below treason, Beccaria listed crimes in order of declining severity, including violence against a person or his property, public disruption, and crimes against property. Crimes against property, he said, should be punished by fines.

When his essay was translated into French and English, Beccaria became famous throughout much of Europe. Philosophers of the time hailed his ideas, and several European rulers vowed to follow his lead in the reform of their justice systems.

JEREMY BENTHAM

Philosopher and jurist Jeremy Bentham (1748–1832) was born in London. As a young child, he was considered a prodigy, having been found, at the age of two, sitting at his father's desk reading a multivolume history of

59

Career Profiles

Minibiographies of corrections professionals that can help prepare students for the meaningful careers in corrections.

Ethical Dilemmas

Marginal inserts pose challenging dilemmas faced by corrections professionals every day.

---

masterwork, *The Spirit of Laws*, was published in 1748. Montesquieu wrote that governmental powers should be separated and balanced in order to guarantee individual rights and freedom. He strongly believed in the rights of individuals. His ideas influenced leaders of both the American Revolution and the French Revolution.[38]

Another celebrated philosopher of the Enlightenment was the French writer Voltaire, who satirized both the government and the religious establishment of France. Voltaire twice served time in the Bastille and chose exile in England over prison for additional offenses. Voltaire deeply admired the English atmosphere of political and religious freedom.

A number of important thinkers influenced the justice systems of Western nations and the directions the correctional enterprise would take over the next 200 years. We will now turn our attention to those individuals.

WILLIAM PENN

William Penn (1644–1718), regarded as the founder of Pennsylvania, was the son of Sir William Penn, a distinguished English Admiral. During his youth, Penn traveled widely throughout Europe, served in the Royal Navy, and studied law. In 1667 he converted to the Quaker faith and by the next year found himself confined in the Tower of London as punishment for promoting the faith. While imprisoned he wrote a paper entitled "No Cross, No Crown." After release he was again imprisoned on a number of occasions, causing him to seek refuge in America. In 1682 Penn obtained a charter creating the Commonwealth of Pennsylvania and naming him governor. Gathering together hundreds of Quakers, Penn set sail for the New World. The colony he founded promoted religious tolerance, and it was soon attracting persecuted minorities from England, Germany, Holland, and Scandinavia.

Penn's influence on the criminal law of this country and on the coming age of imprisonment was most visible in the "Great Act" of 1682. Through that single piece of legislation, the Pennsylvania Quakers reduced capital offenses to the one crime of premeditated murder and abolished all corporal punishments as they had existed under English code.

JOHN HOWARD

John Howard (1726–1790) was born to a deeply religious English family. On a trip to Portugal as a young man, Howard was taken prisoner by pirates when the British merchant ship on which he was travelling was captured by a French privateer.[39] He and his fellow passengers were kept below deck in subhuman conditions. When they arrived in France, he was imprisoned in a French dungeon, but he was later released in exchange for a French naval officer.

In 1773, Howard was appointed High Sheriff of Bedfordshire. He was shocked at the abysmal conditions that existed in English jails of the time, and he set out on a quest for prison reform. He began arguing for the abolishment of spiked collars and chains, which prisoners were made to wear, and he argued against the common practice of paying jailers for release.

Ethical Dilemma

The United States has engaged in various forms of corporal punishment in the past, and many countries still engage in corporal punishment. What are the issues? What types of punishment are still being used in the 21st century? For more information go to Ethical Dilemma 2-2 at http://www.mhhe.com/schmalleger2.

Marginal Definitions and Glossary

Key terms are boldfaced and defined in the margin when they are first introduced, listed later at the end of the chapter, and collected in one comprehensive glossary at the end of the book.

---

counter performance
The defendant's participation, in exchange for diversion, in a treatment, counseling, or educational program aimed at changing his or her behavior.

true diversion
A form of diversion that keeps an offender out of the system and helps him or her avoid formal prosecution and labeling.

minimization of penetration
A form of diversion that keeps an offender from going further into the system.

definition we will use. **Counter performance** is the defendant's participation, in exchange for diversion, in a treatment, counseling, or educational program aimed at changing his or her behavior. The candidate for diversion is a person who has been or could be arrested for an alleged offense and who is or could become the defendant in a criminal matter pending the prosecution of a case is the hallmark of th

The overall goal of diversion is to reduce recidivism tion. In the criminal justice system, diversion is used i can be used to keep an offender out of the system a avoid formal prosecution and labeling. This is called tr ple, a person caught smoking marijuana by the po seled by the police and referred to TASC (Treatment A Crime) without the threat of arrest and prosecution TASC provides services to encourage diversion such problems, referring clients to community treatment pr toring progress.

The second way of using diversion is to keep an offe ther into the system. This is called **minimization of pen** ple, a man charged with possession and use of crac referred to TASC with the stipulation that, if he com program, the charge will be dropped. If he does not co he will be prosecuted for the crime. In this case, TASC back to criminal justice agencies.

The police, a prosecutor, a judge, or a probation officer may call for diversion probation officer practice *true diversion* by counseling youth caught smoki them to TASC. Do you think *true diversion* invites more law violation by allo prosecution?

---

citation A type of nonfinancial pretrial release similar to a traffic ticket. It binds the defendant to appear in court on a future date. (000)

civil liability A legal obligation to another person to do, pay, or make good something. (000)

classification The process of subdividing the inmate population into meaningful categories to match offender needs with correctional resources. (000)

clemency Kindness, mercy, forgiveness, or leniency, usually relating to criminal acts. (000)

client-specific plan (CSP) A privately prepared presentence report that supplements the PSR prepared by the probation department. (000)

cocorrections The incarceration and interaction of female and male offenders under a single institutional administration. (000)

coed prison A prison housing both female and male offenders. (000)

community corrections A philosophy of correctional treatment that embraces (1) decentralization of authority, (2) citizen participation, (3) redefinition of the population of offenders for whom incarceration is most appropriate, and (4) emphasis on rehabilitation through community programs. (000)

community corrections acts (CCAs) State laws that give economic grants to local communities to establish community corrections goals and policies and to develop and operate community corrections programs. (000)

community notification Notification to the community of the release or pending release of convicted offenders. (000)

community service A sentence to serve a specified number of hours working in unpaid positions with nonprofit or tax-supported agencies. (000)

commutation A change of a legal penalty to a lesser one; e.g., from death to life imprisonment. (000)

compensatory damages Money a court may award as payment for actual losses suffered by a plaintiff, including out-of-pocket expenses incurred in filing the suit, other forms of monetary or material loss, and pain, suffering, and mental anguish. (000)

concurrent sentences Sentences served together. (000)

conditional diversion Diversion in which charges are dismissed if the defendant satisfactorily completes treatment, counseling, or other programs ordered by the justice system. (000)

conditional release Pretrial release under minimum or moderately restrictive conditions with little monitoring or compliance. It includes ROR, supervised pretrial release, and third-party release. (000)

consecutive sentences Sentences served one after the other. (000)

consent decree A written compact, sanctioned by a court, between parties in a civil case, specifying how disagreements between them are to be resolved. (000)

constitutional rights The personal and due process rights guaranteed to individuals by the U.S. Constitution and its amendments, especially the first 10 amendments, known as the Bill of Rights. Constitutional rights are the basis of most inmate rights. (000)

contract system A system of prison industry in which the prison advertised for bids for the employment of prisoners, whose labor was sold to the highest bidder. (000)

convict lease system A system of prison industry in which a prison temporarily relinquished supervision of its prisoners to a lessee. The lessee either employed the prisoners within the institution or transported them to work elsewhere in the state. (000)

corporal punishments Physical punishments, or those involving the body. (000)

correctional clients Prison inmates, probationers, parolees, offenders assigned to alternative sentencing programs, and those held in jails. (000)

correctional econometrics The study of the cost-effectiveness of various correctional programs and related reductions in the incidence of crime. (000)

correctional officer personalities The distinctive personal characteristics of corrections officers including behavioral, emotional, and social traits. (000)

corrections All the various aspects of the pretrial and postconviction management of individuals accused or convicted of crimes. (000)

corrections professional A dedicated person of high moral character and personal integrity who is employed in the field of corrections and takes professionalism to heart. (000)

counter performance The defendant's participation, in exchange for diversion, in a treatment, counseling, or educational program aimed at changing his or her behavior. (000)

crime A violation of the criminal law.

crime index An annual statistical tally of major crimes known to law enforcement agencies in the United States. (000)

crime rate The number of index offenses reported for each unit of population. (000)

criminal justice The process of achieving justice through the application of the criminal law and through the workings of the criminal justice system. Also, the study of the field of criminal justice. (000)

criminal justice system The collection of all the agencies that perform criminal justice functions, whether these are operations or administration or technical support. The basic divisions of the criminal justice system are police, courts, and corrections. (000)

Offender Speaks and Staff Speaks Boxes

Interviews with offenders and practitioners provide a balance of perspectives and expand the book's real-world emphasis.

Well, here I am, about two and one-half years into my life sentence. The worst part so far for me has been the loneliness. I'm close to 3,000 miles away from my family. I really don't have anyone right now. I think my family is still digesting the fact that I'm in prison. I don't hear from them very often.

With all the time I have alone in my cell, my brain works overtime. I think about all the people I've hurt, whether physically, emotionally, or financially. I think about my crime every day of my life. I took a human life. What makes a man do that? I don't really know. All I can remember is the anger I felt and the hurt feelings. I can remember my heart hurting so bad that I couldn't function normally anymore. I cried all the time and I couldn't eat or sleep. At first it was all jealousy and then it was anger and pain. I guess it all came to a head that night. I had never felt that much rage before in my life. When it was over, I was holding a lifeless body in my arms. I couldn't speak or move. All I could feel was my soul leaving my body. It was an emptiness that I hope I never feel again. It was like I too had died that night.

I remember the day I was sentenced like it was yesterday. I know ahead of time what I was getting, but it didn't make it any easier. The tears, the stares, the looks, and the glares were all

directed in court from people who were once my friends. I was sentenced to life so I couldn't hurt anyone else ever again (or at least I thought so). I called home that afternoon to let my family know that it was all over and that I was going down for life. My father told me that my mom had tried to kill herself by putting a .38 in her mouth. By a miracle of God, my dad had called home at that very moment and talked her out of it. She was so depressed about me, plus she was addicted to painkillers because she had so many back operations. I wanted so much to comfort her, but I couldn't. I didn't know how.

I remember the time I saw my father cry. It was a day I'll never forget. It was a day or two after I was arrested and a week before I was extradited to Arizona when he came to visit me in the county jail in Pennsylvania. I was so nervous. We hadn't talked in years. He didn't like me much at all because I had disappointed him so many times over the years. I guess he blamed me. I was a failure in his eyes as well as mine. I walked down the hallway to where my father was sitting. I sat down in a chair and looked at him through the glass that separated us. He looked so broken and so sad. We picked up the phones and started to talk. The tears just started to run down his face. I had a lump in my throat so that I couldn't

swallow. My heart was bleeding inside and the pain was unbearable to see a rock of a man crumble before me because of what I had done. I wanted to end my life ri He tried so ha was strict bu for him. I wa my childhood like less than into my fathe he could hug cry too.

I guess I God for letting years. I tried so many time alcohol, and su way, prison h have died at alcohol, or m would have w just thankful demons in m now. I'm resp be kind. I gue up, and that's few years. I s but it's a star

George Killian,
ASPC-Eyman C
Florence, Ariz

I am a director and regional administrator for the state prison system, and I supervise nursing students in a locked ward with criminally insane clients. In addition, I'm a researcher for the National Commission on Correctional Health Care. The commission surveys prisons, jails, juvenile facilities, and immigration facilities all over the United States. I have directed teams in 29

states, in facilities ranging from 38 to 1,000 beds. Part of my job in prison is to consult and transport clients to other countries, which have in the past included Spain, Portugal, Canada, Panama, and Venezuela.

I love this field and encourage students who want a challenge and a career that is interesting to give corrections, especially work with the criminally

insane, a look. Every day and every interaction with our clients is different. No two days are alike, and no two situations are similar.

Source: Dr. Roger Childers
Supervisor
Psychiatric Unit for the
Criminally Insane
Bryce Hospital
Tuscaloosa, Alabama

Leandro Andrade, 37, had been in and out of state and federal prisons since 1982. In January 1982, Andrade had been convicted of a misdemeanor theft offense and was sentenced to six days in jail with 12 months' probation. He was arrested again in November 1982 for multiple counts of first-degree residential burglary. He pleaded guilty to at least three of those counts, and in April of the following year he was sentenced to 120 months in prison. In 1988, Andrade was convicted in federal court of transporting marijuana, and he was sentenced to eight years in federal prison. In 1990, he was convicted in state court for a misdemeanor petty theft offense and was ordered to serve 180 days in jail. In September 1990, he was again convicted in federal court for transporting marijuana and was sentenced to 2,191 days in federal prison. In 1991, he was arrested for a state parole violation—escape from federal prison. He was formally paroled from prison in 1993.

Before his case went to trial, Andrade admitted stealing the videotapes, telling police that he had been addicted to heroin since 1977 and wanted to sell the videos so that he could buy drugs. The prosecutor decided to charge Andrade with two counts of "petty theft with a prior conviction." In California, such a charge is called a "wobbler" because it can be punishable either as a misdemeanor or as a felony. The prosecutor chose to charge Andrade with a felony, and he was convicted, resulting in the two consecutive 25-year sentences. It was that conviction and sentence that, upon appeal, led to the Ninth Circuit Court's 2001 ruling on Andrade's behalf.

On March 5, 2003, however, the U.S. Supreme Court overturned the lower court's finding and ruled that Andrade's two consecutive 25-year-to-life sentences did not violate the Eighth Amendment's proscription against cruel or unusual punishment.[47] In effect, the Court held that it is *not* cruel and unusual punishment to impose a possible life term for a conviction of a nonviolent felony committed by a defendant with a history of serious or violent convictions.

In another 2003 case, *Ewing v. California*,[48] the U.S. Supreme Court upheld the conviction and sentence of Gary Ewing under California's three-strikes law. Ewing, who had a lengthy record of prior convictions, had received a 25-year-to-life sentence following his conviction for helping grand theft of three golf clubs. In writing for the Court, Justice Sandra Day O'Connor said that states should be able to decide when repeat offenders "must be isolated from society . . . to protect the public safety," even when nonserious crimes trigger the lengthy sentence.

A number of studies have claimed to show that incapacitating offenders through incarceration is cost-effective. Such studies conclude that imprisoning certain types of offenders (especially career or habitual offenders) results in savings by eliminating the social costs of the crimes offenders would be likely to commit if they were not imprisoned. Those social costs include monetary loss, medical costs of physical injury, and time lost from work.

One of the most frequently cited studies attempting to quantify the net costs of incarceration was by Edwin Zedlewski.[3] Zedlewski used a RAND Corporation survey of inmates in three states (Michigan, Texas, and California) to estimate the number of crimes each inmate would commit if not imprisoned. In the survey, the average respondent reported committing anywhere from 187 to 287 crimes annually just before being incarcerated. To calculate the cost associated with each crime, Zedlewski focus of most correctional programs and institutions. Harris also believed that the criminality of women was largely the result of their social roles and specifically their economic dependency upon men. As a result, Harris advocated training programs that would permit women prisoners to become financially independent upon release. At Alderson, Harris oversaw the development of programs designed to break the cycle of dependency. Her work became widely known and served as a model for women's prisons throughout the nation.

Before retiring in 1941, Harris wrote a number of books describing her experiences in corrections. Among them are *I Knew Them in Prison* (1936) and *The Pathway of Mattie Howard to and from Prison: The Story of the Regeneration of an Ex-Convict and Gangster Woman* (1937).

SUMMARY

1▶ Corporal, or physical, punishments were the most common response to crime for centuries before criminals began to be incarcerated.

2▶ Criminal punishments of the past generally consisted of flogging, branding, mutilation, exile, transportation, and public humiliation.

3▶ Many reformers based their ideas on Enlightenment principles, including the use of reason and deductive logic to solve problems. They laid the groundwork for the use of imprisonment as an alternative to traditional punishments.

4▶ Beginning in the mid-1700s, a number of correctional reformers fought the use of corporal punishments and sought to introduce more humane forms of punishment. Among those reformers were Cesare Beccaria, Jeremy Bentham, and John Howard.

KEY TERMS

corporal punishments, *p. 42*   utilitarianism, *p. 60*
bridewell, *p. 53*   hedonistic calculus, *p. 60*

QUESTIONS FOR REVIEW

1. What are corporal punishments? What has been the purpose of corporal punishments throughout history?

2. Which ancient civilization provided the earliest evidence that physical punishment is part of Western society tradition?

3. What were the Twelve Tables?

4. List and describe at least four corporal punishments used in the past for criminal offenders.

5. What were *theatrical punishments*?

6. What role did torture play in the application of corporal punishments? How was the use of torture justified?

QUESTIONS FOR REVIEW

1. What is *diversion*?

2. What are three objectives of diversion?

3. What are the four rationales for diversion?

4. Discuss three diversion policy issues.

5. What is *probation*?

6. How did probation originate in the United States?

7. What were some of the characteristics of adults on probation on January 1, 2003?

8. What are the four ways adult probation is administered? Which one is the most common?

9. What do we know about probation recidivism for misdemeanants? For felons?

10. What are some suggestions for implementing effective probation programs?

11. What is the presentence report? What are its purposes?

12. What are the elements of probation supervision?

13. What is the difference between technical and new offense violations?

THINKING CRITICALLY ABOUT CORRECTIONS

▶ ▶ ▶ **PSRs**

Critics of PSRs claim that the information in them is not always verified or reliable even though the trend today is toward limited disclosure of information to the defendant's attorney. Actually, much of the information in a PSR is hearsay. Although defendants or victims may object to the contents of a PSR or the way it characterizes their behavior, they have no right to have the PSR reflect their views. As a probation officer, how would you respond to these criticisms?

▶ ▶ ▶ **Probation Effectiveness**

Recidivism is one current measure of probation effectiveness. Others include the amount of restitution collected, the number of offenders employed, the amounts of fines and fees

collected, the number of hours of community service performed, the number of treatment sessions completed, the percentage of financial obligations collected, the rate of school enrollment, the level of educational attainment, the number of days employed, and the number of days drug free.

1. How important to you, as a taxpayer, is recidivism as a measure of program success?

2. Do you believe probation officers can really keep offenders from committing new crimes or violating the conditions of their probation?

3. If you were a probation officer today, by which outcome measures would you want to be judged? Why?

4. If recidivism is used as a measure of probation's effectiveness, how should it be defined?

ON-THE-JOB DECISION MAKING

▶ ▶ ▶ **Responding to Program Violations**

The new diversion program in your county was developed to help first-time misdemeanor drug offenders avoid incarceration and seek help in controlling their dependency. Your job as the new diversion officer is to set the conditions of the diversion program and then monitor and enforce compliance. One of your first clients fails the required weekly drug test.

1. Should you immediately remove that person from the program?

2. Why or why not?

▶ ▶ ▶ **Probation and Recidivism**

At a recent staff meeting, the chief PO reported that the department's recidivism rate exceeded the national average by 5 percent. The chief asks what can be done about it. You say, "Look at other measures besides recidivism." The chief asks you to explain. What do you say?

CORRECTIONS ON THE WEB

▶ ▶ ▶ **Probation Agency Web Pages**

Most probation agencies—whether administered by a state, a county, a state and county, or a court system—have Web pages. Using the information in Figure 4-5, try to find the Web page of one probation agency for each of the four methods of administration. What difference, if any, does the type of administration make in philosophy, mission, goals, structure, resources, and so forth? Visit the Web page of the Los Angeles County Probation Department (the largest probation department in the world) (http://probation.co.la.ca.us) as an example.

▶ ▶ ▶ **APPA**

The American Probation and Parole Association is an international association composed of individuals from the United States, its U.S. territories, and Canada actively involved with probation, parole, and community-based corrections in both adult and juvenile sectors at all levels of government. APPA is the voice for thousands of probation and parole practitioners including line staff, supervisors, and administrators.

APPA maintains an information clearinghouse at its Website, http://www.appa-net.org, listing free downloadable publications and resources and a list of frequently asked questions (FAQs). Use the free downloadable publications and FAQs to report in more detail on any of the topics covered in this chapter.

Easy-to-Use Chapter Reviews

Clear, concise chapter summaries, key terms lists, and review questions—tabbed along the side of the page for easy reference—provide students with essential study materials.

Unique End-of-Chapter Exercises

End-of-chapter critical thinking, experiential, and Internet activities challenge students to explore and think critically about corrections issues.

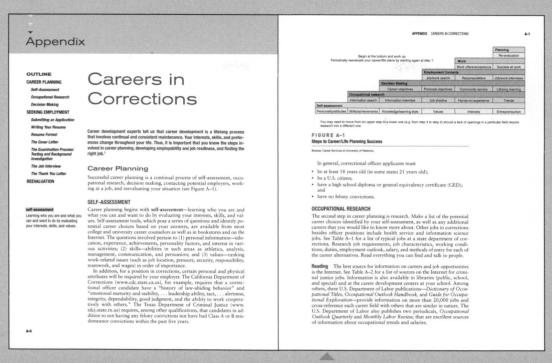

Unique *Careers in Corrections* Appendix

Helpful, step-by-step advice for students planning their careers, developing employability, and finding the right job.

Online Learning Center Website

Unique, book-specific website features a whole new set of chapter quizzes as well as online access to a wealth of popular press and scholarly articles, flashcards that can be used to master vocabulary, and many other chapter review tools.

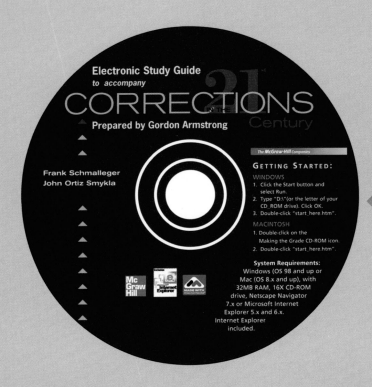

Free *Making the Grade* Electronic Study Guide

A CD-ROM packaged free with every text can help students study and improve their grades on exams.

Chapter-by-Chapter Quizzes

Multiple-choice quizzes with feedback explaining why responses are right or wrong help students master material.

And More...

In addition to 16 separate quizzes, the electronic study guide includes such important resources as an Internet guide, a study skills primer, and more.

Introduction to Corrections

Part One develops an understanding of corrections by examining the purposes of correctional punishments and by exploring how offenders have been punished throughout history.

Today, crime rates are falling but the number of people under correctional supervision (on probation or parole or in jail or prison) is increasing. Get-tough-on-crime attitudes, the War on Drugs, and the reduction in the use of discretionary parole board release explain this increase.

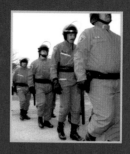

1

Professionalism is the key to managing the growth in the correctional population. Standard-setting organizations such as the American Correctional Association, the American Jail Association, the American Probation and Parole Association, and the National Commission on Correctional Health Care offer detailed sets of written principles for correctional occupations and correctional administrators.

Nevertheless, professional credentialing in corrections is new. The seed was planted during the Enlightenment when reformers such as Cesare Beccaria and the Philadelphia Quakers shifted the focus of punishment away from the body and toward the soul and human spirit. Correcting the soul and human spirit required understanding the causes of crime and new reforms. To that end, the National Prison Association (now known as the American Correctional Association) met in Cincinnati, Ohio, in 1870, to advance correctional theory and practice. The Assembly elected then–Ohio Governor and future U.S. President Rutherford B. Hayes as the first president of the Association. Today, the ACA remains the leader in advancing professionalism in corrections through education, training, and skills development.

2

The professional nature of corrections is also seen in the way sanctions are developed. From a time when theory and practice advocated indeterminate sentences to the legislatively mandated determinate sentences of today, correctional decision makers have had to use their knowledge of human behavior, philosophy, and law to construct sanctions that are fair and just. The correctional goals of retribution, desert, deterrence, incapacitation, rehabilitation, and restoration have produced the sanctions of probation, intermediate sanctions, jail, prison, and capital punishment.

3

What are the consequences of punishment? Choosing the best sanction means understanding the political, social, economic, human, and moral consequences of crime control. For that reason, corrections is a field in which complex decision making requires the skills of professional staff and administrators.

"Changes in the institutions and the correctional system as a whole require that correctional officers be capable of interacting with offenders and with colleagues in a manner which reflects attitudinal change and a knowledge base different from that generally accepted in the past."
—Paul H. Hahn, Xavier University

Corrections:
An Overview

▶ CHAPTER OBJECTIVES

After completing this chapter you should be able to do the following:

1. Explain why correctional populations continue to rise even though the rate of serious crime in the United States has been declining.

2. Understand how rising correctional populations affect the costs of corrections.

3. List the kinds of crimes that cause people to enter correctional programs and institutions.

4. Describe how crime is measured in the United States and explain the differences between the two major crime reporting programs.

5. List and describe the various components of the criminal justice system.

6. List the major components of the corrections subsystem.

7. Describe criminal justice as a *system* and as a *process*.

8. Define the term *corrections*.

9. Explain the importance of professionalism in the corrections field.

10. Understand what is meant by *social diversity* and explain why issues of race, gender, and ethnicity are important in corrections today.

On January 29, 2003, John Walker Lindh, known as the "American Taliban" for his support of militant Islamic fundamentalists during the 2002 U.S. war in Afghanistan, was transferred from a federal lockup in Virginia to the federal Bureau of Prisons medium security facility at Victorville, California. A few months earlier, Lindh, 21, had been sentenced to 20 years in prison after pleading guilty to supplying services to the Taliban and to carrying explosives in commission of a felony. Born in Maryland, Lindh is an American citizen who grew up in California. As a teenager, he became interested in Islam, became a Muslim, and traveled to the Middle East to learn more about the religion. He ended up as a Taliban conscript. Although Lindh apologized to Americans at his sentencing, the Judge who ordered him imprisoned told Lindh that forgiveness and punishment are two separate issues. "You were willing to give your life for the Taliban but not for your country," the judge said.[1]

Lindh, whose support of the Taliban apparently made him unpopular with fellow inmates, was attacked and slightly injured in March 2003 by another inmate as he was preparing for evening prayers in the Victorville prison chapel.[2] Lindh's story illustrates the fact that all **correctional clients,** as prison inmates, probationers, parolees, and those held in jails are called, are unique individuals. Nonetheless, the characteristics of the correctional population in the United States today can be described generally, as shown in Figure 1–1.

John Walker Lindh, known as the "American Taliban" for his support of militant Islamic fundamentalists during the 2002 U.S. war in Afghanistan, is imprisoned at the federal Bureau of Prisons medium security facility at Victorville, California. How have antiterrorism efforts impacted corrections?

correctional clients

Prison inmates, probationers, parolees, offenders assigned to alternative sentencing programs, and those held in jails.

The Corrections Explosion

Some years ago, Fox Butterfield, a staff writer for the *New York Times*, noted in an editorial, "It has become a comforting story: For five straight years, crime has been falling, led by a drop in murder. So why is the number of inmates in prisons and jails around the nation still going up? Last year [1996], it reached almost 1.7 million, up about 7 percent a year since 1990."[3]

The trends that Butterfield identified are still occurring today. One amazing fact stands out from all the information about corrections: While serious crime in the United States consistently declined throughout much of the 1990s, and while such declines continued into the first decade of the 21st century, the number of people under correctional supervision in this country—not just the number of convicted offenders sent to prison—has continued to climb. Crime rates are approximately 20 percent lower today than they were in 1980. They are at their lowest level in 20 years. But the number of people on probation is up almost 300 percent since 1980, the nation's prison population has increased by more than 400 percent, and the number of persons on parole has increased by almost the same proportion. Figure 1–2 illustrates these trends.

The question is, why? Why the steady increase in correctional populations in the face of declining crime rates? The answer to this question, like the answers to most societal enigmas, is far from simple. Pursuit of the answer is important, however. As Franklin Zimring, director of the Earl Warren Legal Institute at the University of California at Berkeley, points out, "The change in the number of inmates tells us . . . about our feelings about crime and criminals."[4]

The answer has a number of dimensions. First, it is important to recognize that get-tough-on-crime laws, such as the three-strikes (and two-strikes) laws that were enacted in many states in the mid-1990s, have fueled rapid increases in prison populations. The conservative attitudes that gave birth to those laws are still with us. Noted criminal justice scholar John P. Conrad summarizes today's mood this way: "There is an unprece-

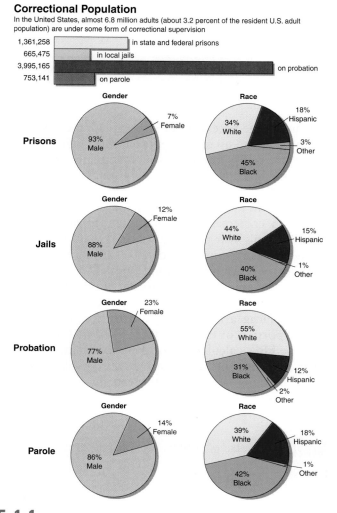

FIGURE 1-1

Characteristics of the Correctional Population

Sources: Paige M. Harrison and Allen J. Beck, *Prisoners in 2002* (Washington, DC: Bureau of Justice Statistics, August 2003); Lauren E. Glaze, *Probation and Parole in the United States, 2002* (Washington, DC: Bureau of Justice Statistics, August 2003); and Paige M. Harrison and Jennifer C. Karberg, *Prison and Jail Inmates at Midyear 2002,* Bureau of Justice Statistics Bulletin (Washington, DC: Office of Justice Programs, April 2003).

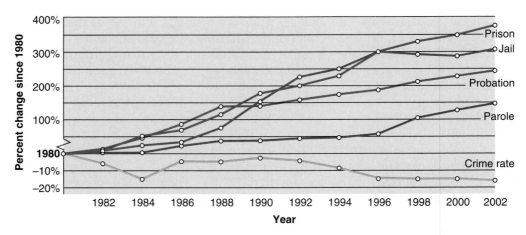

FIGURE 1-2
Trends in Corrections Since 1980

Sources: FBI, *Crime in the United States, 2002* (Washington, DC: U.S. Government Printing Office, 2003); Paige M. Harrison and Allen J. Beck, *Prisoners in 2002* (Washington, DC: Bureau of Justice Statistics, 2003); and Lauren E. Glaze, *Probation and Parole in the United States, 2002* (Washington, DC: Bureau of Justice Statistics, 2003).

dented consensus on the necessity for strengthening criminal justice. This consensus can be summed up in one sentence. Criminals must be locked up and kept off the streets."[5] Conrad goes on to explain, "The vast expansion of corrections today has not come about without good cause. For the citizen on the streets, there is only one reasonable response to the violence he or she fears. Lock them up, and hang the expense."[6]

A second reason correctional populations are rapidly increasing can be found in the nation's War on Drugs. The War on Drugs has led to the arrest and conviction of many offenders, resulting in larger correctional populations in nearly every jurisdiction (especially within the federal correctional system). In Table 1–1, compare the total number of individuals incarcerated for drug offenses with, for example, the total incarcerated for property offenses. Drug arrests continue to increase. Although they account for a large portion of the nation's correctional population, they do not figure into the FBI's calculations of the nation's rate of serious crimes. Hence, the War on Drugs goes a long way toward explaining the growth in correctional populations even while the rate of "serious crime" in the United States appears to be declining.

TABLE 1–1	Number of Prisoners by Offense (2002)		
Type of offense	**All**	**Male**	**Female**
Violent offenses	596,100	571,700	24,400
Property offenses	233,100	213,100	20,000
Drug offenses	246,100	222,900	23,200
Public-order offenses	129,900	121,600	8,300

Source: Adapted from Paige M. Harrison and Allen J. Beck, *Prisoners in 2002* (Washington, DC: Bureau of Justice Statistics, July 2003).

Third, parole authorities, fearing civil liability and public outcry, have become increasingly reluctant to release inmates. This has contributed to a further expansion of prison populations.

Fourth, as some observers have noted, the corrections boom has created its own growth dynamic.[7] As ever greater numbers of people are placed on probation, the likelihood of probation violations increases. Prison sentences for more violators result in larger prison populations. When inmates are released from prison, they swell the numbers of those on parole, leading to a larger number of parole violations, which in turn fuels further prison growth. Statistics show that the number of criminals being sent to prison for at least the second time has increased steadily, rising to 35 percent of the total number of admissions in 1995, from 17 percent in 1980.[8]

HISTORICAL ROOTS OF THE CORRECTIONS EXPLOSION

Seen historically, the growth of correctional populations may be more the continuation of a long-term trend than the result of recent social conditions. A look at the data shows that correctional populations have continued to grow through widely divergent political eras and economic conditions. Census reports show an almost relentless increase in the rate of imprisonment over the past 150 years. In 1850, for example, only 29 people were imprisoned in this country for every 100,000 persons in the population.[9] By 1890 the rate had risen to 131 per 100,000. The rate grew slowly until 1980, when the rate of imprisonment in the United States stood at 153 per 100,000. At that point, a major shift toward imprisonment began. While crime rates rose sharply in the middle to late

> Census reports show an almost relentless increase in the rate of imprisonment over the past 150 years.

U.S. correctional populations have grown dramatically over the past 25 years, as this photo of male arrestees sleeping in a crowded holding cell at Maricopa County (Arizona) Jail illustrates. What factors led to a substantial increase in the use of correctional options during the 1990s?

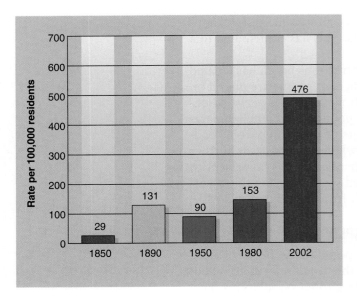

FIGURE 1-3
Rate of Imprisonment in the United States, 1850–2002

Sources: Margaret Werner Cahalan, *Historical Corrections Statistics in the United States, 1850–1984* (Washington, DC: U.S. Department of Justice, 1986); and Paige M. Harrison and Allen J. Beck, *Prisoners in 2002* (Washington, DC: Bureau of Justice Statistics, 2003).

1980s, the rate of imprisonment rose far more dramatically. Today the rate of imprisonment in this country is about 476 per 100,000 persons, and it shows no signs of declining.[10] Figure 1–3 illustrates changes in the rate of imprisonment over the past 150 years. Probation statistics—first available in 1935—show an even more amazing rate of growth. Although only 59,530 offenders were placed on probation throughout the United States in 1935, more than 3.9 million people are on probation today.[11]

CORRECTIONAL EXPENDITURES

Growing correctional populations also mean heightened costs. Budgetary allocations for corrections have grown in step with correctional populations. In 1965 the nation spent $1 billion on correctional services—including funding for juvenile institutions and programs. Thirty-five years later, at the start of 2000, a staggering $54 billion was allocated to federal, state, and local correctional budgets—with many additional dollars going to alternative programs for juveniles.[12] Most of the money spent on corrections today (about 75 percent) funds the day-to-day activities of correctional programs and institutions. Another 10 percent is allocated for the construction of new facilities—mostly prisons and jails.

As the trend continues toward ever greater use of correctional services, state and federal allocations are expected to continue to expand. The federal government alone spent $4.1 billion on correctional activities and services in 1999.[13] Federal expenditures on corrections are expected to exceed $5 billion by 2006,[14] and state correctional budgets are expected to rise proportionately.

The costs of running America's constantly expanding prison systems have begun to impose an enormous burden on government at all levels. Already, California and Florida spend more on incarceration than on higher education.[15]

On the flip side, growing correctional populations and increasing budgets have led to a dramatically expanding correctional workforce and to enhanced employment opportunities within the field. According to historical reports, persons employed in the corrections field totaled approximately 27,000 in 1950.[16] By 1975 the number had risen to about 75,000. The most current statistics available show that the number of uniformed correctional officers in adult prisons alone has grown to more than 215,000.[17] When juvenile detention facility personnel, probation and parole officers, correctional administrators, jailers, and other corrections professionals are added, the total number of persons employed in

Ethical Dilemma

In light of tight state budgets and overcrowded prisons, should governors use their authority to provide early release to some inmates? If so, under what circumstances? For more information go to Ethical Dilemma 1-1 at http://www.mhhe.com/schmalleger2.

corrections today stands at more than 716,000.[18] Table 1–2 shows some of the employment possibilities in corrections.

New prisons mean jobs and can contribute greatly to the health of local economies. Some economically disadvantaged towns—from Tupper Lake, in the Adirondack Mountains of upstate New York, to Edgefield, South Carolina—are cashing in on the prison boom, having successfully competed to become sites for new prisons. The competition for new prison facilities is reminiscent of the efforts states made some years ago to attract new automobile factories and other industries.

Crime and Corrections

The crimes that bring people into the American correctional system include felonies, misdemeanors, and minor law violations that are sometimes called *infractions*.

Felonies are serious crimes. Murder, rape, aggravated assault, robbery, burglary, and arson are felonies in all jurisdictions within the United States, although the names for these crimes may differ from state to state. A general way to think about felonies is to remember that a **felony** is a serious crime whose commission can result in confinement in a state or federal correctional institution for more than a year.

In some states a felony conviction can result in the loss of certain civil privileges. A few states make conviction of a felony and the resulting incarceration grounds for uncontested divorce. Others prohibit convicted felony offenders from running for public office or owning a firearm, and some exclude them from professions such as medicine, law, and police work.

Huge differences in the treatment of specific crimes exist among states. Some crimes classified as felonies in one part of the country may be misdemeanors in another. In still other states they may not even be crimes at all! Such is the case with some drug law violations and with social order offenses such as homosexual acts, prostitution, and gambling.

Misdemeanors, which compose the second major crime category, are relatively minor violations of the criminal law. They include crimes such as petty theft (the theft of items of little worth), simple assault (in which the victim suffers no serious injury and in which none was intended), breaking and entering, the possession of burglary tools, disorderly conduct, disturbing the peace, filing a false crime report, and writing bad checks (although the amount for which the check is written may determine the classification of this offense). In general, misdemeanors can be thought of as any crime punishable by a year or less in confinement.

Within felony and misdemeanor categories, most states distinguish among degrees, or levels of seriousness. Texas law, for example, establishes five felony classes and three classes of misdemeanor—intended to guide judges in assessing the seriousness of particular criminal acts. The Texas penal code then specifies categories into which given offenses fall.

A third category of crime is the **infraction.** The term, which is not used in all jurisdictions, refers to minor violations of the law that are less serious than misdemeanors. Infractions may include such violations of the law as jaywalking, spitting on the sidewalk, littering, and certain traffic violations,

felony
A serious criminal offense; specifically, one punishable by death or by incarceration in a prison facility for more than a year.

misdemeanor
A relatively minor violation of the criminal law, such as petty theft or simple assault, punishable by confinement for one year or less.

infraction
A minor violation of state statute or local ordinance punishable by a fine or other penalty but not by incarceration, or by a specified, usually very short term of incarceration.

TABLE 1–2	Careers in Corrections	
Academic teacher	Field administrator	Psychologist
Activity therapy administrator	Fugitive apprehension officer	Recreation coordinator
Business manager	Human services counselor	Social worker
Case manager	Job placement officer	Statistician
Chaplain	Mental health clinician	Substance abuse counselor
Correctional officer	Parole caseworker	Unit leader
Classification officer	Parole officer	Victim advocate
Clinical social worker	Presentence investigator	Vocational instructor
Children's services counselor	Probation officer	Warden/superintendent
Chemical dependency manager	Program officer	Youth services coordinator
Dietary officer	Programmer/analyst	Youth supervisor
Drug court coordinator	Program specialist	

including the failure to wear a seat belt. People committing infractions are typically ticketed—that is, given citations—and released, usually upon a promise to appear later in court. Court appearances may be waived upon payment of a fine, which is often mailed in.

MEASURING CRIME

Two important sources of information on crime for correctional professionals are the FBI's Uniform Crime Reports (UCR) and the Bureau of Justice Statistics' National Crime Victimization Survey (NCVS). Corrections professionals closely analyze these data to forecast the numbers and types of correctional clients to expect in the future. The forecasts can be used to project the need for different types of detention and rehabilitation services and facilities.

Uniform Crime Reports   The FBI's Uniform Crime Reports (UCR) are published annually. Individual reports are often referred to by their official title, *Crime in the United States*. The UCR contains information on eight major crimes: murder, forcible rape, robbery, aggravated assault, burglary, larceny-theft, motor vehicle theft, and arson. These major crimes are divided into two subcategories: **violent crime** and **property crime.** Violent crime consists of murder, forcible rape, robbery, and aggravated assault. Burglary, larceny-theft, motor vehicle theft, and arson fall into the property crime category. Table 1–3 summarizes the crimes reported to police in the eight index crime categories.

The data, gathered from police agencies across the country, include only the crimes known to the police. Unreported or undiscovered crimes, which might outnumber those reported to the police, are not included in the UCR.

The sum total of all major crimes provides a national **crime index,** useful in comparing the occurrence of major crimes over time. The UCR also reports a **crime rate** each year. The rate of crime is calculated by dividing the total number of major crimes by the population of the United States.

violent crime

Interpersonal crime that involves the use of force by offenders or results in injury or death to victims. In the FBI's Uniform Crime Reports, violent crimes are murder, forcible rape, robbery, and aggravated assault.

property crime

Burglary, larceny, automobile theft, and arson as reported in the FBI's Uniform Crime Reports.

crime index

An annual statistical tally of major crimes known to law enforcement agencies in the United States.

crime rate

The number of index offenses reported for each unit of population.

TABLE 1-3	Major Crimes Known to the Police, 2002		
Offense	**Number**	**Rate per 100,000**	**Clearance rate**
Violent crimes			
Murder	16,204	5.6	62.0%
Forcible rape	95,136	33.0	44.5%
Robbery	420,637	145.9	25.7%
Aggravated assault	894,348	310.1	56.5%
Property crimes			
Burglary	2,151,875	746.2	13.0%
Larceny-theft	7,052,922	2,445.8	18.0%
Motor vehicle theft	1,246,096	432.1	13.8%
Arson[1]	74,921	32.4	16.5%
U.S. total	**11,877,218**	**4,118.8**	**20.0%**

1. Only fires determined through investigation to have been willfully or maliciously set are classified as arsons.

Source: Adapted from FBI, *Crime in the United States, 2002* (Washington, DC: U.S. Government Printing Office, 2003).

The result is expressed as the number of crimes per 100,000 people. Crime rate comparisons provide a more realistic portrayal of changes in crime over time—and of the likelihood of victimization—than do simple comparisons of crime index totals.

The FBI reported that a total of 11.9 million major crimes occurred throughout the United States in 2002. The 2002 crime rate of 4,118.8 offenses per 100,000 U.S. inhabitants was the lowest since 1984.[19] Regionally, the crime rate was 4,722 offenses per 100,000 inhabitants in the South; 4,419 in the West; 3,883 in the Midwest; and 2,889 in the Northeast. The violent crime rate in 2002 was 495 per 100,000, while the rate of property crimes was 3,624 offenses per 100,000.

If we look at Table 1–3, we see that 16,204 murders were recorded in 2002. The murder rate was 5.6 offenses per 100,000 inhabitants. According to supplemental data in the UCR, 76.8 percent of murder victims in 2002 were male and 88.2 percent were 18 years old or older. Of victims whose race was known, 48.7 percent were white, and 48.5 percent were black. Slightly less than 90 percent of known murderers were male, and more than 90 percent were 18 or older. Of murderers whose race was known, 50 percent were black, and 47.7 percent were white.

The UCR includes supplemental data for each index crime. Such data, along with the crime index totals, offer corrections personnel a glimpse of the background, makeup, and motivation of the offenders who may eventually become clients of the correctional system.

The UCR also includes data on the numbers of arrests in the United States for all types of crimes. Offenses not included in the crime index are called *Part II offenses*. Law enforcement agencies made an estimated 13.7 million arrests in 2002 for all offenses except traffic violations. The highest arrest count for a specific crime category was 1.5 million arrests for drug abuse violations. Simple assaults registered 1.3 million arrests, while arrests for driving under the influence numbered 1.46 million. In 2002 the nationwide rate of arrest was 4,783 per 100,000 people.

Solving and Clearing Crimes   Most crimes reported to the police are not solved. Crimes that are solved are said to be *cleared*. For the UCR, a known offense is considered *cleared* or *solved* when a law enforcement agency has charged at least one person with the offense or when a suspect has been identified and located but circumstances have thus far prevented charging the suspect.

The *clearance rate* is the number of offenses cleared divided by the number of offenses known by police. Law enforcement agencies nationwide recorded a 20 percent crime index clearance rate in 2002. The clearance rate for violent crimes was 46.8 percent; for property crimes, 16.5 percent. Among crime index offenses, the clearance rate was highest for murder (62 percent) and lowest for burglary (13 percent). For many consensual crimes, such as prostitution, gambling, and drug abuse, rates of arrest are lower still. Table 1–3 shows the clearance rates for the index crimes reported in 2002. The clearance rates for individual index crimes help corrections professionals know the types and numbers of clients to expect in the correctional system.

National Incident-Based Reporting System (NIBRS)   The FBI is implementing a new crime reporting program called the *National Incident-Based Reporting System,* or NIBRS. Under the new system, many details will be gathered about each criminal incident. Included among them will be information on place of occurrence, weapon used, type and value of property damaged or stolen, personal characteristics of the offender and the victim, the nature of any relationship between the two, disposition of the complaint, and so on. The new reporting system gathers data on 22 general of-

Racial minorities are overrepresented among all segments of the correctional population in comparison with the ethnic makeup of America. What is the reason for this lopsided ethnic representation?

fenses: arson, assault, bribery, burglary, counterfeiting, vandalism, narcotic offenses, embezzlement, extortion, fraud, gambling, homicide, kidnapping, larceny, motor vehicle theft, pornography, prostitution, robbery, forcible sex offenses, nonforcible sex offenses, receiving stolen property, and weapons violations. Data will also be gathered on bad checks, vagrancy, disorderly conduct, driving under the influence, drunkenness, nonviolent family offenses, liquor law violations, "peeping Tom" activity, runaways, trespass, and a general category of all other criminal law violations.

The FBI began accepting crime data in NIBRS format in January 1989. Although NIBRS was intended to replace the old system by 1999, delays have been frequent. It will be a few more years before all police departments report their crime data to the FBI in NIBRS format.

National Crime Victimization Survey (NCVS)   The nation's second crime measuring tool is the National Crime Victimization Survey (NCVS).[20] The NCVS was begun by the Bureau of Justice Statistics (BJS) in 1973. It provides a detailed picture of crime incidents, victims, and trends. The survey collects detailed information on the frequency and nature of the crimes of rape, sexual assault, personal robbery, aggravated and simple assault, household burglary, theft, and motor vehicle theft. It does not measure homicide or commercial crimes (such as burglaries of stores).

To gather data for the NCVS, U.S. Census Bureau personnel each year interview all household members at least 12 years old in a national representative sample of approximately 49,000 households. The total sample contains about 101,000 persons. The NCVS collects information on crimes suffered by individuals and households, whether or not those crimes were reported to law enforcement agencies. It estimates the proportion reported for each type of crime covered by the survey, and it summarizes the reasons that victims give for reporting or not reporting.

For many types of offenses, the NCVS shows more crimes being committed than does the UCR. There are, however, some crimes—homicides and assaults—for which the police count more occurrences than does the NCVS. Table 1–4 shows total victimizations reported by the NCVS for 2002. Compare the totals for similar categories in Table 1–4 and Table 1–3. This comparison will help you understand the importance of knowing the source and the manner of compilation of the data you use to make corrections decisions.

The NCVS provides information about victims (age, sex, race, ethnicity, marital status, income, and educational level), offenders (sex, race, approximate age, and victim-offender relationship), and crimes (time, place, weapons, injuries, and economic consequences). Information also includes the experiences of victims with the criminal justice system, self-protective measures used by victims, and possible substance

TABLE 1–4	**Criminal Victimizations, 2002**
Type of crime	**Number of victimizations**
All crimes	**23,625,870**
Personal crimes[1]	**5,714,500**
Crimes of violence	5,542,620
Completed violence	1,790,690
Attempted/threatened violence	3,751,930
Rape/sexual assault	247,990
Robbery	571,590
Assault	4,723,040
Personal theft[2]	171,890
Property crimes	**17,911,370**
Household burglary	3,097,710
Motor vehicle theft	998,740
Theft	13,814,920

1. The NCVS is based on interviews with victims and therefore cannot measure murder.
2. Includes pocket picking, purse snatching, and attempted purse snatching.

Source: Adapted from Callie M. Rennison and Michael R. Rand, *Criminal Victimization, 2002* (Washington, DC: U.S. Department of Justice, September 2003), p. 3.

abuse by offenders. NCVS data are published annually under the title *Criminal Victimization in the United States.*

According to the most recent NCVS,[21] U.S. residents age 12 or older experienced approximately 23.6 million crimes in 2002. Seventy-six percent of those crimes, or 17.9 million, were property crimes, and 24 percent (5.7 million) were crimes of violence. NCVS findings show that, in 2002, Americans age 12 or older experienced fewer violent and property crimes than in any other year since 1973, when the NCVS began.

THE CRIME FUNNEL

Not all crimes are reported, and not everyone who commits a reported crime is arrested, so relatively few offenders enter the criminal justice system. Of those who do, some are not prosecuted (perhaps because the evidence against them is insufficient), others plead guilty to lesser crimes, and others are found not guilty. Some who are convicted are diverted from further processing by the system or may be fined or ordered to counseling. Hence, the proportion of criminal offenders who eventually enter the correctional system is small, as Figure 1–4 shows.[22]

Corrections and the Criminal Justice System

Corrections is generally considered the final stage in the criminal justice process. Some aspects of corrections, however, come into play early in the process. Keep in mind that although the term **criminal justice** can be used to refer to the justice *process,* it can also be used to describe our *system* of justice. Criminal justice agencies, taken as a whole, are said to compose the **criminal justice system.**

The components of the criminal justice system are (1) police, (2) courts, and (3) corrections. Each component, because it contains a variety of organizations and agencies, can be termed a *subsystem.* The subsystem of corrections, for example, includes prisons, agencies of probation and parole, jails, and a variety of alternative programs.

The *process* of criminal justice involves the activities of the agencies that make up the criminal justice system. The process of criminal justice begins when a crime is discovered or reported.

Court decisions based on the due process guarantees of the U.S. Constitution require that specific steps be taken in the justice process. Although the exact nature of those steps varies among jurisdictions, the description that follows portrays the most common sequence of events in response to serious criminal behavior. Figure 1–5, which diagrams the American criminal justice system, indicates the relationship among the stages in the criminal justice process.

ENTERING THE CORRECTIONAL SYSTEM

The criminal justice system does not respond to all crime because most crimes are not discovered or reported to the police.[23] Law enforcement agencies learn about crimes from the reports of citizens, through discovery by a police officer in the field, or through investigative and intelligence

criminal justice

The process of achieving justice through the application of the criminal law and through the workings of the criminal justice system. Also, the study of the field of criminal justice.

criminal justice system

The collection of all the agencies that perform criminal justice functions, whether these are operations or administration or technical support. The basic divisions of the criminal justice system are police, courts, and corrections.

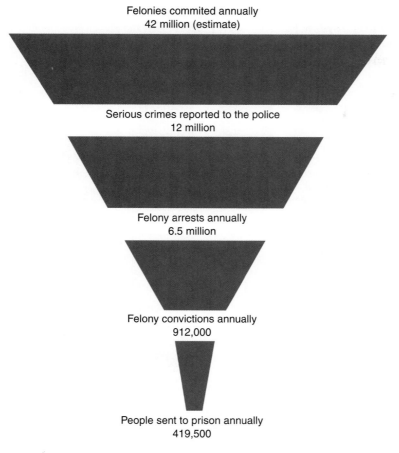

Felonies commited annually
42 million (estimate)

Serious crimes reported to the police
12 million

Felony arrests annually
6.5 million

Felony convictions annually
912,000

People sent to prison annually
419,500

FIGURE 1-4
The Crime Funnel

Sources: Statistics compiled from Bureau of Justice Statistics data. Felonies include violent crimes, attempted personal victimizations, selected property crimes (such as burglary and motor vehicle theft), and various drug offenses. The estimated number of felonies committed annually is calculated from NCVS data, FBI data on drug and other felonies, and general knowledge about unreported crimes. Also see Bureau of Justice Statistics, *Felony Sentences in the United States, 1996* (Washington, DC: BJS, 1999).

work. Once a law enforcement agency knows of a crime, the agency must identify and arrest a suspect before the case can proceed. Sometimes a suspect is found at the scene; sometimes, however, identifying a suspect requires an extensive investigation. Often no one is identified or apprehended—the crime goes unsolved. If an offender is arrested, booked, and jailed to await an initial court appearance, the intake, custody, confinement, and supervision aspects of corrections first come into play at this stage of the criminal justice process.

PROSECUTION AND PRETRIAL PROCEDURE

After an arrest, law enforcement agencies present information about the case and about the accused to the prosecutor, who decides whether to file formal charges with the court. If no charges are filed, the accused must

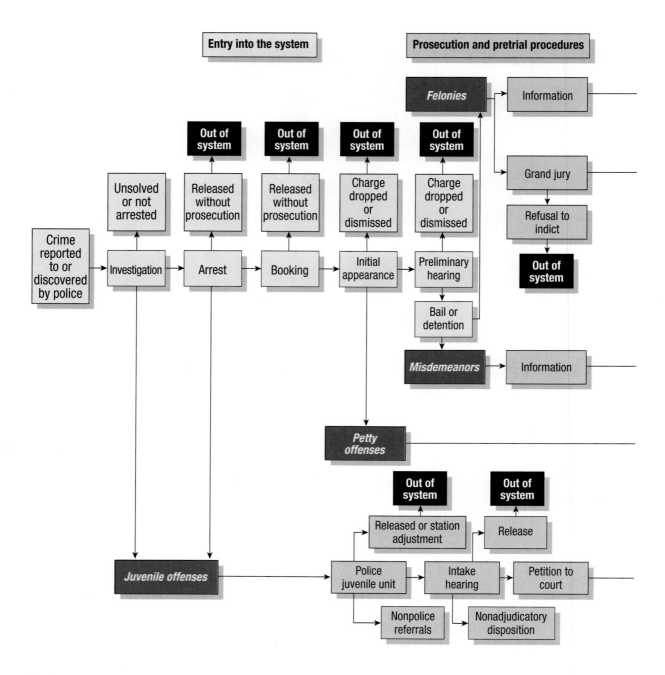

Procedures vary among jurisdictions

FIGURE 1-5
The Criminal Justice System

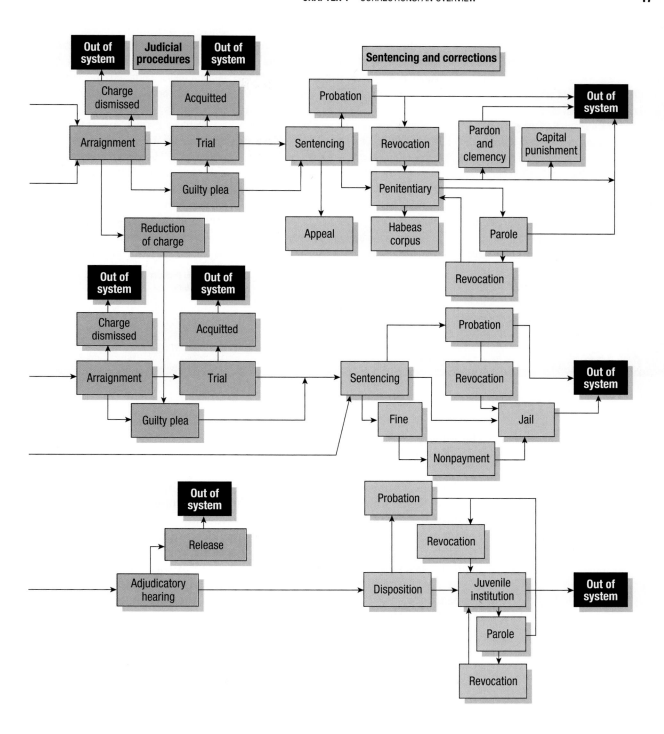

Very few of us do not think about beating the system. After all, the system deprives us of the freedom we cherish. It stands for all that we resent: lack of choice, restricted movement, denial of access to loved ones. We resent the walls, bars, uniforms, being told what to do, what programs we must take.

Moralists argue that we get exactly what we deserve, and many citizens believe that we are treated too well. Few of us can argue that we didn't know what we were getting into when we made the bad choices that landed us in prison. None of us arrived by accident, and if we are honest with ourselves, we'll acknowledge a whole series of destructive behaviors that preceded our committal to a "monastery of the damned."

In view of status and our chances of success upon release, the future doesn't look particularly bright. It's damn depressing to have to accept our collective reality. Hope is found in beating the system, the smart way. The smart way is not the path many of us have continually taken: defiance, conflict with "the man." AA members are familiar with the slogan "I can only change myself, not others." It is always easier to project blame for our inadequacies onto others. But until we come to terms with our individual reality; separate the crime from the man, decide that the "I am" is capable of much more than the label implies—we're doomed to failure.

The administration uses education statistics to create the illusion of massive programming. It is up to us to demand the delivery. Enroll in courses. Develop the thirst to learn. Ask for help from peer tutors. An education is the ultimate form of restorative justice. The entire population benefits when just one con becomes literate. Educated cons have reason to lift their heads in self-assurance. We are better able to articulate our needs, better able to negotiate collectively, better able to see a future for ourselves.

Whether "the man" wants to acknowledge it or not, educated prisoners get respect from everybody inside and outside the prison. Adult education and training at every level—whether basic literacy, high school, college, or university—are vital. The positive skills we learn in prison can't be taken away from us at the gate.

Joseph E. McCormick
—*A prisoner*

THE OFFENDER SPEAKS

be released. The prosecutor can also drop charges after filing them. Such a choice is called *nolle prosequi;* when it happens, a case is said to be "nolled" or "nollied."

A suspect charged with a crime must be taken before a judge or magistrate without unnecessary delay. At the initial appearance, the judge or magistrate informs the accused of the charges and decides whether there is probable cause to detain him or her. Often, defense counsel is also assigned then. If the offense charged is not very serious, the determination of guilt and the assessment of a penalty may also occur at this stage.

In some jurisdictions, a pretrial-release decision is made at the initial appearance, but this decision may occur at other hearings or at another time during the process. Pretrial release on bail was traditionally intended to ensure appearance at trial. However, many jurisdictions today permit pretrial detention of defendants accused of serious offenses and deemed dangerous, to prevent them from committing crimes in the pretrial period. The court may decide to release the accused on his or her own recognizance, into the custody of a third party, on the promise of satisfying certain conditions, or after the posting of a financial bond.

In many jurisdictions, the initial appearance may be followed by a preliminary hearing. The main function of this hearing is to determine whether there is probable cause to believe that the accused committed a crime within the jurisdiction of the court. If the judge or magistrate does not find probable cause, the case is dismissed. However, if the judge finds probable cause for such a belief, or if the accused waives the right to a preliminary hearing, the case may be bound over to a grand jury.

A grand jury hears evidence against the accused presented by the prosecutor and decides if there is sufficient evidence to cause the accused to be brought to trial. If the grand jury finds sufficient evidence, it submits an indictment to the court.

Not all jurisdictions make use of grand juries. Some require, instead, that the prosecutor submit an information (a formal written accusation) to the court. In most jurisdictions, misdemeanor cases and some felony cases proceed by the issuance of an information. Some jurisdictions require indictments in felony cases. However, the accused may choose to waive a grand jury indictment and, instead, accept service of an information for the crime.

JUDICIAL PROCEDURES

Adjudication is the process by which a court arrives at a decision in a case. The adjudication process involves a number of steps. The first is **arraignment.** Once an indictment or information is filed with the trial court, the accused is scheduled for arraignment. If the accused has been detained without bail, corrections personnel take him or her to the arraignment. At the arraignment, the accused is informed of the charges, advised of the rights of criminal defendants, and asked to enter a plea to the charges.

If the accused pleads guilty or pleads *nolo contendere* (accepts a penalty without admitting guilt), the judge may accept or reject the plea. If the plea is accepted, no trial is held, and the offender is sentenced at this proceeding or at a later date. The plea may be rejected if, for example, the judge believes that the accused has been coerced. If this occurs, the case may proceed to trial. Sometimes, as the result of negotiations between the prosecutor and the defendant, the defendant enters a guilty plea in expectation of reduced charges or a light sentence. *Nolo contendere* pleas are often entered by those who fear a later civil action and who therefore do not want to admit guilt.

If the accused pleads not guilty or not guilty by reason of insanity, a date is set for trial. A person accused of a serious crime is guaranteed a trial by jury. However, the accused may ask for a bench trial, in which the judge, rather than a jury, serves as the finder of fact. In both instances, the prosecution and defense present evidence by questioning witnesses, and the judge decides issues of law. The trial results in acquittal or conviction of the original charges or of lesser included offenses.

SENTENCING AND SANCTIONS

After a guilty verdict or guilty plea, sentence is imposed. In most cases the judge decides on the sentence, but in some states the sentence is decided by the jury, particularly for capital offenses, such as murder.

To arrive at an appropriate sentence, a court may hold a sentencing hearing to consider evidence of aggravating or mitigating circumstances. In assessing the circumstances surrounding a criminal act, courts often rely on presentence investigations by probation agencies or other designated authorities. Courts may also consider victim impact statements.

The sentencing choices available to judges and juries frequently include one or more of the following:

adjudication

The process by which a court arrives at a final decision in a case.

arraignment

An appearance in court prior to trial in a criminal proceeding.

nolo contendere

A plea of "no contest." A no-contest plea may be used by a defendant who does not wish to contest conviction. Because the plea does not admit guilt, it cannot provide the basis for later civil suits.

- the death penalty;
- incarceration in a prison, a jail, or another confinement facility;
- community service;
- probation, in which the convicted person is not confined but is subject to certain conditions and restrictions;
- fines, primarily as penalties for minor offenses; and
- restitution, which requires the offender to provide financial compensation to the victim.

In many states, laws mandate that persons convicted of certain types of offenses serve a prison term. Most states permit the judge to set the sentence length within certain limits, but some states have determinate sentencing laws (discussed in Chapter 3). Such laws specify the sentence that must be served, and these sentences cannot be altered by a parole board.

After the trial, a defendant may request appellate review of the conviction or the sentence. In many criminal cases, appeals of a conviction are a matter of right; all states with the death penalty provide for automatic appeal of cases involving a death sentence. However, under some circumstances in some jurisdictions, appeals are at the discretion of the appellate court, which may grant or deny a defendant's petition for a **writ of *certiorari***. Prisoners may also appeal their sentences through civil rights petitions and writs of *habeas corpus,* in which they claim unlawful detention.

writ of *certiorari*
A writ issued by an appellate court to obtain from a lower court the record of its proceedings in a particular case.

THE CORRECTIONAL SUBSYSTEM

After conviction and sentencing, most offenders enter the correctional subsystem. Before we proceed with our discussion, it is best to define the term *corrections*. As with most words, a variety of definitions can be found.

In 1967, for example, the President's Commission on Law Enforcement and Administration of Justice wrote that *corrections* means "America's prisons, jails, juvenile training schools, and probation and parole machinery. . . ." It is "that part of the criminal justice system," said the Commission, "that the public sees least of and knows least about."[24]

Years later, in 1975, the National Advisory Commission on Criminal Justice Standards and Goals said in its lengthy volume on corrections, "*Corrections* is defined here as the community's official reactions to the convicted offender, whether adult or juvenile."[25] The Commission noted that "this is a broad definition and it suffers . . . from several shortcomings."

We can distinguish between institutional corrections and noninstitutional corrections. A 1997 report by the Bureau of Justice Statistics (BJS) says that **institutional corrections** "involves the confinement and rehabilitation of adults and juveniles convicted of offenses against the law and the confinement of persons suspected of a crime awaiting trial and adjudication."[26] BJS goes on to say that "correctional institutions are prisons, reformatories, jails, houses of correction, penitentiaries, correctional farms, workhouses, reception centers, diagnostic centers, industrial schools, training schools, detention centers, and a variety of other types of institutions for the confinement and correction of convicted adults or juveniles who are adjudicated delinquent or in need of supervision. [The term] also includes facilities for the detention of adults and juveniles accused of a crime and

institutional corrections
That aspect of the correctional enterprise that "involves the incarceration and rehabilitation of adults and juveniles convicted of offenses against the law, and the confinement of persons suspected of a crime awaiting trial and adjudication."

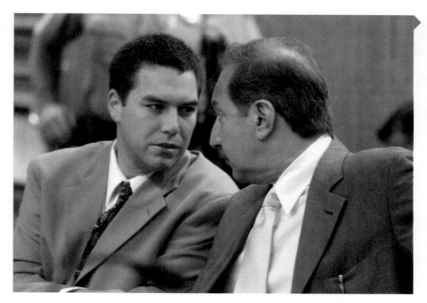

Murder defendant Scott Lee Peterson confers with his attorney during a pretrial hearing in Stanislaus (California) Superior Court in 2003. Correctional clients are those who have been found guilty of crimes in a court of law. Who decided what happens to defendants following conviction? After they enter the correctional system?

awaiting trial or hearing." According to BJS, **noninstitutional corrections,** which are sometimes called *community corrections,* include "pardon, probation, and parole activities, correctional administration not directly connectable to institutions, and miscellaneous [activities] not directly related to institutional care."

As all these definitions show, in its broadest sense the term *corrections* encompasses each of the following components, as well as the process of interaction among them:

- the *purpose* and *goals* of the correctional enterprise;
- jails, prisons, correctional institutions, and other *facilities;*
- probation, parole, and alternative and diversionary *programs;*
- federal, state, local, and international correctional offices and *agencies;*
- counseling, educational, health care, nutrition, and many other *services;*
- correctional *clients;*
- corrections *volunteers;*
- corrections *professionals;*
- fiscal appropriations and *funding;*
- various aspects of criminal and civil *law;*
- formal and informal *procedures;*
- effective and responsible *management;*
- community *expectations* regarding correctional practices; and
- the machinery of *capital punishment.*

When we use the word *corrections,* we include all of these elements. Fourteen elements, however, make for an unwieldy definition. Hence, for purposes of discussion, we will say that **corrections** refers to all the various aspects of the pretrial and postconviction management of individuals

noninstitutional corrections (also *community corrections*)

That aspect of the correctional enterprise that includes "pardon, probation, and parole activities, correctional administration not directly connectable to institutions, and miscellaneous [activities] not directly related to institutional care."

corrections

All the various aspects of the pretrial and postconviction management of individuals accused or convicted of crimes.

Eye On Corrections™

Developing New Leaders in Corrections

By Michelle Gaseau

Running a prison in the new millennium is like running a successful business. The days when corrections leaders only rose through the security ranks are long gone. The leaders needed to run today's prisons must be multifaceted and have a wealth of varied experience inside a prison's walls.

To that end, many corrections agencies are working feverishly to help develop new leaders who will be the next wardens and deputy secretaries. These agencies hope to fashion these new leaders in a modern role that stresses accountability and sensitivity to a "corporate culture" in addition to a clear understanding of corrections operations.

Kevin Wright, of the State University of New York—Binghamton, says that corrections leadership has changed over the years in a number of ways: "Most of the people I talk to say accountability is everything now. It dominates their lives. If you look at a manager 25 years ago, they could have been a good people person—they had to be good at working with people and motivating them. Today they have to be strategic managers. They need to have a vision of what they want the place to be, and they need to be able to collect the information about that, bring people on board, and do that within this environment of accountability."

Wright, who is the author of *Effective Prison Leadership*, says today's prisons are under increased scrutiny. Representatives from legislative offices and executive offices of the budget, attorneys for litigant inmates, as well as the press are all interested in the goings on behind bars. "[Previously] prisons became the little fiefdoms of wardens, and they often stayed for a long period of time and ran the place according to their own views. That has all changed now," says Wright.

PREPARING FOR THE FUTURE

Corrections officials in Oklahoma were forced to take a closer look at leadership development. We pulled the statistics on all of our upper and executive staff and looked at when they would be eligible for retirement. About 75 percent of those people [two years ago] would be eligible within five years. The feeling among the leadership at the time was that we did not have adequate numbers of people ready," says J'me Overstreet, Administrator for the Oklahoma DOC's Leadership Development Unit.

"Systems need to be able to find people who are people-people and identify folks that have good minds and are able to analyze complex problems," she adds. "Look for people who have an interest in leadership and who have demonstrated the ability to be leaders. Anticipating the future is really key. [The next leader] may not be someone like the present leader."

The next step is deciding how to train those potential leaders. Wright explains: "With [rapid] growth [in systems], that whole process has been accelerated. Sometimes the process is compressed into a couple of years."

In Oklahoma, officials had the talent and ability to create a leadership development program in house. In addition, they had a clear idea as to how new leaders would be trained.

OKLAHOMA PROGRAM TAKES A COMPREHENSIVE APPROACH

The Oklahoma leadership development program has classes in four levels including presupervisory preparatory, first line supervisory, middle management, upper-middle management and upper management preparatory, and upper management development and executive level preparatory. "We have people [participating] in security/prisons, administrative and clerical, medical, maintenance and computers," says Overstreet. She adds, "Each level progresses with regard to the criteria to attend, or employees may be accepted in concert with their levels of responsibility within the organization."

In the case of those employees starting the program at the first level, supervisors and participants fill out a questionnaire. Supervisors rate their staff members in basic management skills, such as communication, team building, vision, and delegation. The staff are asked to rate themselves as well, which gives the leadership development unit a chance to see any gaps in perception between the two.

"It provides, for many, the beginning of an ongoing dialogue between themselves and their supervisors as to what areas they need to improve in. They return to work with a developmental plan based on the identified gaps. They are encouraged to meet with their supervisors upon their return and discuss and refine those plans," says Overstreet.

The classes for all levels include leadership panels to increase the amount of exposure that new developing leaders have to current leadership. In addition, the DOC is working to develop on-the-job training structured developmental opportunities. Overstreet explains, "For example, we are meeting with wardens in October and will facilitate a process where they develop structured developmental opportunities for their deputy wardens to better prepare them to be wardens."

The leadership development unit plans to take some baseline statistics at the end of this year to begin tracking the careers and retention of program participants once they have completed two or more levels of the curriculum. "We hope to positively impact their retention, thus reducing turnover among this group," says Overstreet.

PENNSYLVANIA OPENS DOORS AND COMMUNICATION

The Pennsylvania DOC's leadership program encourages communication and discussion of the issues leaders face. According to John Shaffer, Deputy Secretary for the DOC, leaders today need to recognize cultural differences and understand that people may respond to one leadership style over another. "We teach our people situational leadership and contingency style," he says.

In the next phase of the program, participants discuss organizational culture and potential problems that they can identify. "That is more of a struggle because people are less willing to identify cultural problems in an institution for fear of retribution," says Shaffer.

He adds that participants are willing to open up after the DOC's executive leadership explains the importance of this exercise and working together as a team.

The final aspect of the program discusses the ethical and accountable leader. Case studies help class members identify problems for discussion, such as staff complacency.

Although the program is only four years old, Shaffer says the DOC has seen results: "We have seen fewer incidences of grievances from staff and inmates across the board. We use that as an indicator that they are appropriately managing their facilities. We have had good success in recruiting managers."

In addition, the program emphasizes mentoring for future leaders, which Shaffer says is an important part of their preparation to take over those roles. He adds, "There are a lot of people nearing retirement age. This management development program has brought along leaders to replace them. I would highly recommend a management development program."

Source: "Developing New Leaders in Corrections," Michelle Gaseau, The Corrections Connection Network News (CCNN). Eye on Corrections. www.corrections.com. October 1, 2001. Copyright © 2001, all rights reserved, The Corrections Connection Network News (CCNN), a division of J.S. Noonan, LLC. Reprinted with permission.

accused or convicted of crimes. Central to this perspective is the recognition that corrections—although it involves a variety of programs, services, facilities, and personnel—is essentially a management activity. Rather than stress the role of institutions or agencies, this definition emphasizes the human dimension of correctional activity—especially the efforts of the corrections professionals who undertake the day to day tasks. Like any other managed activity, corrections has goals and purposes. Exhibit 1–1 details the purpose of corrections as identified by the American Correctional Association (ACA).

The Societal Goals of Corrections   The ACA statement about the purpose of corrections is addressed primarily to corrections professionals. It recognizes, however, that *the* fundamental purpose of corrections "is to enhance social order and public safety." In any society, social order and public safety depend on effective social control. Some forms of social control take the form of customs, norms, and what sociologists refer to as *mores* (`mȯr-,āz). **Mores** are behavioral standards that embody a group's values. Violation of these standards is a serious wrong. They generally forbid such activities as murder, rape, and robbery. **Folkways,** in contrast, are time-honored ways of doing things. Although folkways carry the force of tradition, their violation is unlikely to threaten the survival of the group.

Societal expectations, whatever form they take, are sometimes enacted into law. The **criminal law,** also called **penal law,** is the body of rules and regulations that define public offenses, or wrongs committed against the state or society, and specify punishments for those offenses. Social control, social order, and public safety are the ultimate goals of criminal law.

The correctional subsystem is crucial in enforcing the dictates of the law because the rewards and punishments it carries out play a significant role in society's control of its members.

> The fundamental purpose of corrections is to enhance social order and public safety.

mores

Cultural restrictions on behavior that forbid serious violations—such as murder, rape, and robbery—of a group's values.

folkways

Time-honored ways of doing things. Although they carry the force of tradition, their violation is unlikely to threaten the survival of the social group.

criminal law
(also called *penal law*)

That portion of the law that defines crimes and specifies criminal punishments.

EXHIBIT 1–1   American Correctional Association

Purpose of Corrections

The overall mission of criminal and juvenile justice, which consists of law enforcement, courts, and corrections, is to enhance social order and public safety. As a component of the justice system, the role of corrections is to do the following:

1. Implement court-ordered supervision and, when necessary, detention of those accused of unlawful behavior prior to adjudication.

2. Assist in maintaining the integrity of law by administering sanctions and punishments imposed by courts for unlawful behavior.

3. Offer the widest range of correctional options, including community corrections, probation, institutions, and parole services, necessary to meet the needs of both society and the individual.

4. Provide humane program and service opportunities for accused and adjudicated offenders that will enhance their community integration and economic self-sufficiency and that are administered in a just and equitable manner within the least restrictive environment consistent with public safety.

Professionalism in Corrections

Only a few decades ago, some writers bemoaned the fact that the field of corrections had not achieved professional status. Happily, much has changed over the past few decades. By 1987, Bob Barrington, who was then the executive director of the International Association of Correctional Officers, was able to proclaim, in a discussion about prisons, that "correctional facilities . . . run smoothly and efficiently for one basic reason: the professional and forward-thinking attitudes and actions of the correctional officers employed."[27]

Some writers on American criminal justice have said that the hallmark of a true profession is "a shared set of principles and customs that transcend self-interest and speak to the essential nature of the particular calling or trade."[28] This definition recognizes the selfless and ethical nature of professional work. Hence, "professionals have a sense of commitment to their professions that is usually not present among those in occupational groups."[29] Work within a profession is viewed more as a "calling" than as a mere way of earning a living. "Professionals have a love for their work that is above that of employment merely to receive a paycheck."[30]

Although it is important to keep formal definitions in mind, for our purposes we will define a **profession** as an occupation granted high social status by virtue of the personal integrity of its members. We can summarize the *attitude* of a true professional by noting that it is characterized by the following:

- a spirit of public service and interest in the public good;
- the fair application of reason and the use of intellect to solve problems;
- self-regulation through a set of internal guidelines by which professionals hold *themselves* accountable for their actions;
- continual self-appraisal and self-examination;

profession

An occupation granted high-social status by virtue of the personal integrity of its members.

Offices of the American Correctional Association (ACA) in Lanham, Maryland. The ACA is a leading proponent of professionalism in corrections. What does corrections professionalism entail?

Agencies such as the Palm Beach (Florida) County Sheriff's Office understand that 40 hours of training every four years is not sufficient to maintain the proficiency of skills or the continuous development of staff. The Palm Beach County Sheriff's Office requires all certified correctional officers to participate in a minimum of 40 hours in-service training annually. This program is designed to develop not only technical skills but also the overall well-being of the officer.

In most training situations there is not the need, time, or resources to transfer detailed knowledge of theoretical concepts. Required outcomes must apply a practical balance between understanding the reason an action is done in a particular way and having the ability to apply procedures correctly.

It is important to define performance indicators and targets against these objectives, which are acceptable and practical expected levels of achievement.

Knowledge assessment techniques need to be integrated into training to enable assessment of whether adequate competencies have been achieved by each officer.

The Palm Beach County Sheriff's Office mandates the attendance and curriculum for 24 of the 40 hours. This 24-hour block attended by all officers consists of firearms, defensive tactics, first aid/CPR and blood-borne pathogens, and CJSTC (Criminal Justice Standards & Training Commission)—mandated courses. The remaining 16 hours are chosen by the individual officer from a training catalog compiled each year by the Bureau of Training. The available classes for selection by the officer range from yoga, nutrition, and retirement planning to advanced handgun and pressure point controlling techniques.

The presented materials in these in-service classes are not intended to be a comprehensive course in technical development and skills. Rather the lessons are meant to be a supplement that will give the officers an enhanced perspective on how to develop their skills and themselves. Not only do the lessons give the officers helpful tips and concepts, but they also are meant to provide them with insight on good methods to use

There is no such thing as a common knowledge of an unstated objective. Objectives need to be defined to ensure accountability. When determining the objectives of training, training managers should also define the indicators by which they can judge whether training programs are successful. This will make evaluation of training considerably more relevant.

Captain Alan Fuhrman
Palm Beach County Sheriff's Office
Planning & Research Unit
West Palm Beach, Florida

- an inner sense of professionalism (i.e., honor, self-discipline, commitment, personal integrity, and self-direction);
- adherence to the recognized ethical principles of one's profession; and
- a commitment to lifelong learning and lifelong betterment within the profession.

Most professional occupations have developed practices that foster professionalism among their members.

STANDARDS AND TRAINING

Historically, professional corrections organizations and their leaders have recognized the importance of training. It was not until the late 1970s, however, that the American Correctional Association (ACA) Commission on Accreditation established the first training standards. The commission did the following:

- specified standards for given positions within corrections;
- identified essential training topics;
- set specific numbers of hours for preservice (120) and annual inservice training (40); and
- specified basic administrative policy support requirements for training programs.[31]

Following ACA's lead, virtually every state now requires at least 120 hours of preservice training for correctional officers working in institutional settings; many states require more. Probation and parole officers are required to undergo similar training in most jurisdictions, and correctional officers working in jails are similarly trained.

Through training, new members of a profession learn the core values and ideals, the basic knowledge, and the accepted practices central to the profession. Setting training standards ensures that the education is uniform. Standards also mandate the teaching of specialized knowledge. Standards supplement training by doing the following:

- setting minimum requirements for entry into the profession;
- detailing expectations for those involved in the everyday life of correctional work; and
- establishing basic requirements for facilities, programs, and practices.

From the point of view of corrections professionals, training is a matter of personal responsibility. A lifelong commitment to a career ensures that those who think of themselves as professionals will seek the training needed to enhance their job performance.

BASIC SKILLS AND KNOWLEDGE

In 1990, the Professional Education Council of the American Correctional Association developed a model entry test for correctional officers. The test was intended to increase professionalism in the field and to provide a standard criminal justice curriculum.[32]

The council suggested that the test could act "as a quality control measure for such education, much as does the bar exam for attorneys." The standard entry test was designed to "reveal the applicant's understanding of the structure, purpose, and method of the police, prosecution, courts, institutions, probation, parole, community service, and extramural programs." It was also designed to "test for knowledge of various kinds of corrections programs, the role of punitive sanctions and incapacitation, and perspective on past experience and current trends."

More recently, Mark S. Fleisher of Illinois State University identified four core traits essential to effective work in corrections.[33] The traits are as follows:

- **Accountability:** "Correctional work demands precision, timeliness, accountability and strong ethics." Students may drift into patterns of irresponsibility during their college years. Once they become correctional officers, however, they need to take their work seriously.
- **Strong Writing Skills:** Because correctional officers must complete a huge amount of paperwork, they need to be able to write well. They should also be familiar with the "vocabulary of corrections."
- **Effective Presentational Skills:** "A correctional career requires strong verbal skills and an ability to organize presentations." Effective verbal skills help officers interact with their peers, inmates, and superiors.
- **A Logical Mind and the Ability to Solve Problems:** Such skills are essential to success in corrections because problems arise daily. Being able to solve them is a sign of an effective officer.

Does Corrections Need to Look Ahead?

by William L. Tafoya,
University of New Haven

Reflections on the Future

Two decades ago mathematician Olaf Helmer observed, "Traditional piecemeal approaches [to problem-solving] have proven to be sterile." He went on to note, "What is needed is a new type of massive, imaginative, and interdisciplinary effort" (1983: 372). Inspired by Helmer's admonition I penned a book chapter in which I argued the need to apply the methods of the field of Futures Research to criminal investigations (Tafoya 1990). Here I offer the same suggestion to corrections professionals. The extrapolation of current crime statistics and incarceration rates strongly suggests it is highly probable that—absent a new type of massive intervention—America will continue to construct rather than dismantle correctional facilities over at least the next two decades. The Bureau of Justice Statistics, for example, reports that the incarceration rate in America rose from 139 per 100,000 in 1980 to 470 per 100,000 in 2001 (USDOJ 2003). Perhaps it is time for a massive, multidisciplinary, imaginative approach to alternatives to incarceration? While this is not a new proposal, the alternatives previously attempted appear to have been largely unsuccessful. Why?

Overall the literature devoted to the future of criminal justice is quite sparse. The good news is that the portion dedicated to corrections is actually quite impressive. The bad news is that the majority of these publications tend to focus on identifying ways to increase the methodological precision of projecting incarceration rates rather than on forecasting ways to more effectively identify reliable alternatives to incarceration that do not put the public at risk from recidivists and career criminals (AP 2003; HRW 2003a; HRW 2003b). A notable exception is the work of Criminologist Gene Stephens who attributes the reduced crime, reduced fear, and revitalized communities of the 1990s to the combined efforts of imaginative and interdisciplinary efforts such as Community-Oriented Policing and the Restorative Justice movement (1999: 34). Practitioner-scholar Bernard Levin and his colleagues (2002) have endorsed this contention. What does the discipline of Futures Research offer to corrections that will contribute to a safer, saner society?

Futures Research, like other academic disciplines, is based on historical fact, scientific methods, and human values. To this mix, Futures Research adds vision, creativity, and innovation. Three essential ingredients set Futures Research apart from the traditional disciplines. Among its *principles* is the conviction of (1) the unity or interconnectedness of reality, (2) the crucial importance of time, and (3) the significance of ideas. Of the discipline's *premises*, consensus has solidified around three postulates: (1) the future is not predetermined, (2) the future is not predicable but can be forecast, and (3) future outcomes can be influenced by individual choice.

The *priorities* of Futures Research include three goals: (1) the *possible*, to form perceptions of the future; (2) the *probable*, to study likely alternatives; and (3) the *preferable*, to make choices to bring about particular events. Further, futurists subscribe to six planning time frames: the Immediate (present to 2 years), Short-term (2–5 years), Mid-level (5–10 years), Long-range (10–20 years), Extended (20–50 years), and Distant (50 years and beyond). Futurists do not cling to the status quo, the supposedly tried and true beliefs of the past. Futurists explore divergent ways to deal with old problems and constructing unprecedented ways to anticipate new paradigms.

The tools for looking ahead include an array of forecasting methodologies. The U.S. Army Corps of Engineers commissioned SRI International to compile *The Handbook of Forecasting Techniques* (SRI 1975). Of the *quantitative* methods, the Monte Carlo technique is excellent for probability distributions, sampling, and random number generation. The procedure has been used effectively in cost-benefit studies. The Markov Chain technique is used to describe a process in which a set of states moves through a sequence of steps observing probabilistic rather than deterministic laws. The procedure has been used successfully to delineate organizational growth and personnel administrative matters. Bayesian statistics enable a planner to utilize actual, realistic variables to anticipate the unexpected. Well suited to small sample sizes, it is arguably the best mathematical approach to problem solving in which uncertainty is a major factor. Finally, the Box-Jenkins method of Autoregressive Integrated Moving Averages (ARIMA) is designed to handle complex time-series data in which there is no apparent pattern. Unlike other quantitative techniques, the Box-Jenkins method does not require a clear definition of the trend.

Of the *qualitative* methods, several stand out. The Delphi technique is a structured group process that maximizes the likelihood of reaching consensus and identifying disagreement. The method involves anonymous structured exchanges between members of an expert panel. Iteratively the facilitator provides controlled feedback to the panel who remains anonymous to each other until the procedure is completed. One of the most well-known techniques, it has been widely heralded as well as vilified. It is a procedure that should be reserved for truly long-range planning, as the conventional administration requires more than a year to complete.

Also well known, Scenario Writing is intended to expand the plausible (known facts) to identify the possible, probable, and preferable. It consists of four essential elements: hypothetical, summarized, multifaceted, and factually based. It is an excellent tool for addressing the question "What if?" Cross-Impact Analysis is a means by which the probability of one forecast event can be adjusted as a function of its potential interaction with all other forecast events. Relevance Trees present a hierarchical structuring of detailed relationships. The method is ideal for analyzing situations in which distinct levels of complexity are involved. The discipline of Futures Research and its forecasting methodologies are discussed in greater detail in a number of sources, many conveniently available online from the World Future Society, such as the CD-ROM "The Knowledge Base of Futures Studies" (Slaughter 2001). The Society of Police Futurists International (PFI) also provides data mining assessments in its listserv discussions as well as its online and hard copy newsletter, *Police Futurist* (www.policefuturists.org).

Three decades ago renowned futurist and social critic Alvin Toffler observed, "If we do not learn from history, we shall be compelled to relive it. True. But if we do not change the future, we shall be compelled to endure it. And that could be worse" (1972: 3). There is ample evidence to demonstrate that most past correctional practices work only in limited fashion and only in the short term, if at all. We pour money down a well of desperation hoping that if we lock up offenders long enough they will be too old to recidivate once they are released. That belief has not been fully substantiated.

Will the present generation of corrections professionals learn from the history of their field and blaze new trails? Or will they ignore those lessons and follow the path of the past? Will those who read these words embrace the stale status quo, enduring the practices of the past? Or will they devise new, massive, imaginative, and interdisciplinary efforts to shape a brighter future for the field of corrections and American society? What if?

REFERENCES

Associated Press. 2003. "Incarceration rates of industrialized nations," www.zpub.com/un/prison1.html.

Helmer, Olaf. 1983. *Looking forward: a guide to futures research.* Beverly Hills, CA: SAGE Publications.

HRW. 2003a. "Punishment and prejudice: Racial disparities in the war on drugs." *Human Rights Watch World Report,* www.hrw.org/campaigns/drugs/war/adult-male.htm.

HRW. 2003b. "U.S. incarceration rates reveal striking racial disparities." *Human Rights Watch World Report,* www.hrw.org/press/2002/02/race0227.htm.

Levin, Bernard H., et al. 2002. "Social change, social policing: A consideration of trends." Presentation at the joint conference of the Society of Police Futurists International and the World Future Society, Philadelphia, PA, July 20–22.

PFI, Society of Police Futurists International. *Police Futurist,* www.policefuturists.org.

Slaughter, Richard A., ed. 2001. "The knowledge base of futures studies" CD-ROM. Bethesda, MD: World Future Society.

SRI. 1975. *Handbook of forecasting techniques.* Fort Belvoir, VA: U.S. Army Corps of Engineers.

Stephens, Gene. 1999. "Preventing crime: The promising road ahead," *The Futurist,* 33:9 (November): 29–34.

Tafoya, William L. 1990. "Futures research: implications for criminal investigations." In James N. Gilbert, ed. *Criminal investigation: Essays and cases.* Columbus, OH: Merrill Publishing, pp. 197–218.

Toffler, Alvin. 1972. "Probing tomorrow." In Alvin Toffler, ed. *The futurists.* New York: Random House, pp. 3–10.

USDOJ. 2003. "Incarceration rates trend chart." Bureau of Justice Statistics, www.ojp.usdoj.gov/bjs/glance/d_incrt.htm.

ABOUT THE AUTHOR

William L. Tafoya is professor of criminal justice at the University of New Haven. A retired special agent of the FBI, he spent 11 years on the faculty at the FBI Academy in Quantico, Virginia. His Ph.D. dissertation research (Criminology, University of Maryland) is entitled "A Delphi Forecast of the Future of Law Enforcement." He is founder of the Society of Police Futurists International (www.policefuturists.org).

CAREER PROFILE

Melanie Estes

Day Youth Counselor   United Methodist Family Services   Richmond, VA

Melanie Estes has been with the agency for only a few years and is currently one of two senior counselors. She completed a four-year degree in Criminal Justice in 1997 and is planning to attend graduate school in social work at Virginia Commonwealth University.

As a youth counselor, Melanie assists in developing, implementing, evaluating, and modifying individual and group treatment plans. She ensures that daily routine and expectations are followed in the residential home. It is also her responsibility to plan, oversee, and evaluate daily and weekly schedules of agency program activities. She is the liaison between the agency and the residents' social workers, probation officers, parents, and any others that may be involved in the youths' treatment. She keeps all parties informed of residents' progress.

As a staff member, Melanie's foremost duty is to act as a change agent for clients in the program. She believes that it is important that staffers learn that their interactions and interventions with one another are as crucial to the habilitative process as their interactions and interventions with youth. As a team member, she is asked to evaluate her coworkers' performance and to provide support, feedback, and training for other team members. Once a month, she is the chairperson and recorder for the weekly team meeting.

> " Working with troubled juveniles is challenging and rewarding, especially with abandoned and abused children. I'm not kidding anyone when I say that it is hard to maintain a healthy balance between friend and caretaker. But one of the greatest experiences I ever had is to help at risk youth. "

corrections professional

A dedicated person of high moral character and personal integrity who is employed in the field of corrections and takes professionalism to heart.

professional associations

Organizations of like-minded individuals who work to enhance the professional status of members of their occupational group.

In sum, we can say that a **corrections professional** is a dedicated person of high moral character and personal integrity who is employed in the field of corrections and takes professionalism to heart. He or she understands the importance of standards, training, and education and the need to be proficient in the skills required for success in the correctional enterprise. The corrections professional recognizes that professionalism leads to the betterment of society, to enhanced social order, and to a higher quality of life for all.

STANDARD-SETTING ORGANIZATIONS

A number of standard-setting **professional associations** in the field of corrections have developed models of professionalism. Among them are the American Correctional Association (ACA), the American Probation and Parole Association (APPA), and the American Jail Association (AJA).

Standard-setting organizations like these offer detailed sets of written principles for correctional occupations and corrections administration. The ACA, the APPA, and the AJA, for example, all have developed standards to guide training and to clarify what is expected of those working in corrections. Moreover, many professional associations have developed codes of ethics, outlining what is moral and proper conduct. Some of these codes will appear in later chapters.

Correctional associations also offer training, hold meetings and seminars, create and maintain job banks, and produce literature relevant to corrections. They sometimes lobby legislative bodies in an attempt to influence the development of new laws that affect corrections.

Future chapters will present ACA policies. The ACA policies are important because they guide the development of training and because they influence the work environment of many agencies and institutions.

In 1999, the ACA, through its national Commission on Correctional Certification, established a program for certifying correctional staff, from line officers to executive leaders. **Certification** is part of a process called *credentialing* that focuses specifically on the individual. Its counterpart is accreditation, a formal process that highlights the quality of a facility in an effort to ensure that it meets health, safety, and other correctional standards. Accreditation is discussed in more detail in Chapter 13. ACA certification began officially in January 2000 when the first CCE application was accepted by the ACA. The first CCE examination was administered in August 2000.[34]

Four ACA certification categories exist, extending from those who work at the highest organization levels to personnel employed at the line level, working directly with offenders. Those categories are (1) Certified Correctional Executive (CCE), (2) Certified Correctional Manager (CCM), (3) Certified Correctional Supervisor (CCS), and (4) Certified Correctional Officer (CCO). Applicants for certification must pass a 200-item multiple-choice examination, document their corrections experience, show compliance with the ACA's Code of Ethics (Exhibit 1–2), and meet minimum requirements for formal education. Educational requirements increase with each certification level. While a high school diploma or equivalent is required of those seeking COO certification, CCS and CCM certification-seekers are required to hold two-year college degrees (or the equivalent), while those applying for certification at the CCE level must hold four-year college degrees (or the equivalent). According to the ACA, the organization's certification program creates the opportunity for a lifetime of progressive professional achievement. Anyone successfully completing the certification process is designated a Certified Corrections Professional (CCP).[35]

The purpose of the ACA Professional Certification Program is "to uphold standards for competent practice." Moreover, certification provides an opportunity "for staff to be recognized as qualified correctional practitioners."

Like the American Correctional Association, the American Jail Association (AJA), through its five-member Jail Manager Certification Commission (JMCC), offers a program for the certification of jail administrators, managers, and supervisory personnel. The first Certified Jail Managers (CJMs) were recognized in 1997.[36]

EDUCATION

Education is another component, besides basic job skills and job-specific training, of true professionalism. Training, by itself, can never make one a true professional, because complex decision-making skills are essential for success in any occupation involving intense interpersonal interaction—and they can

certification
A credentialing process, usually involving testing and career development assessment, through which the skills, knowledge, and abilities of correctional personnel can be formally recognized.

> You are the warden of the only medium security prison in your state. Your nephew is sentenced to serve 10 years in your institution. Using the ACA Code of Ethics as a guide, determine what ethical issues you will face. For more information go to Ethical Dilemma 1-2 at http://www.mhhe.com/schmalleger2.

Ethical Dilemma

EXHIBIT 1-2   **American Correctional Association**

Code of Ethics

1. Members shall respect and protect the civil and legal rights of all individuals.

2. Members shall treat every professional situation with concern for the welfare of the individuals involved and with no intent to gain personally.

3. Members shall maintain relationships with colleagues to promote mutual respect within the profession and improve the quality of service.

4. Members shall make public criticism of their colleagues or their agencies only when warranted, verifiable, and constructive.

5. Members shall respect the importance of all disciplines within the criminal justice system and work to improve cooperation with each segment.

6. Members shall honor the public's right to information and share information with the public to the extent permitted by law subject to individuals' right to privacy.

7. Members shall respect and protect the right of the public to be safeguarded from criminal activity.

8. Members shall refrain from using their positions to secure personal privileges or advantages.

9. Members shall refrain from allowing personal interest to impair objectivity in the performance of duty while acting in an official capacity.

10. Members shall refrain from entering into any formal or informal activity or agreement that presents a conflict of interest or is inconsistent with the conscientious performance of duties.

11. Members shall refrain from accepting any gifts, services, or favors that are or appear to be improper or imply an obligation inconsistent with the free and objective exercise of professional duties.

12. Members shall clearly differentiate between personal views/statements and views/statements/positions made on behalf of the agency or Association.

13. Members shall report to appropriate authorities any corrupt or unethical behaviors for which there is sufficient evidence to justify review.

14. Members shall refrain from discriminating against any individual because of race, gender, creed, national origin, religious affiliation, age, disability, or any other type of prohibited discrimination.

15. Members shall preserve the integrity of private information; they shall refrain from seeking information on individuals beyond that which is necessary to implement responsibilities and perform their duties; members shall refrain from revealing nonpublic information unless expressly authorized to do so.

16. Members shall make all appointments, promotions, and dismissals in accordance with established civil service rules, applicable contract agreements, and individual merit, rather than furtherance of personal interests.

17. Members shall respect, promote, and contribute to a workplace that is safe, healthy, and free of harassment in any form.

Adopted by the Board of Governors and Delegate Assembly in August 1994.

be acquired only through general education. Education builds critical-thinking skills, it allows the application of theory and ethical principles to a multitude of situations that are constantly in flux, and it provides insights into on-the-job difficulties.

Correctional education that goes beyond skills training is available primarily from two-year and four-year colleges that offer corrections curricula and programs of study. The day will come when at least a two-year degree will be required for entry into the corrections profession.

Social Diversity in Corrections

The corrections profession faces a number of social issues that are of special concern to Americans today. Contemporary issues include questions about the purposes and appropriateness of punishment in general and the acceptability of capital punishment in particular; the usefulness of alternative or nontraditional sanctions; the privatization of correctional facilities; and the rights and overall treatment of prisoners. At the forefront of today's issues are those involving concerns about gender, race, ethnicity, and other forms of social diversity.

> At the forefront of today's (correctional) issues are those involving concerns about gender, race, ethnicity, and other forms of social diversity.

While a number of these issues are discussed in later chapters, this brief section provides definitions of some of the terms that will be discussed and suggests some structure for what is to follow.

Some terms, such as *race*, are not easy to define. Historical definitions of race have highlighted some supposed biological traits, such as skin color, hair type, or shape of the skull and face. Eighteenth-century European physical anthropologists distinguished among white, black, and Asian (or "yellow") races. The notion of race, however, is now generally recognized as a social construct and is not seen as an objective biological fact. Moreover, racial distinctions have blurred throughout American society, which has long been characterized as a melting pot. Nonetheless, when asked, the majority of Americans today still identify themselves as members of a particular racial group.

To say that race is a social construct means that racial distinctions are culturally defined. It does *not* mean, however, that such distinctions are without consequences. On the contrary, great social significance is often attached to biological or other indicators of race, and race plays a crucial role in social relations. *Racism*, which is also socially constructed, can be the result. **Racism** has been defined as social practices that explicitly or implicitly attribute merits or allocate value to members of racially categorized groups solely because of their race.[37] In the field of corrections, as in other social endeavors, it is racism (rather than race itself) that is the real issue because it can lead to forms of racial discrimination, including inequities in hiring and promotion for those working in corrections, and to unfairness in the handling of inmates or other correctional clients because of their race.

Considerable overlap exists between the concept of race and that of *ethnicity*. In contemporary usage, both terms imply the notion of lineage, or biological and regional as well as cultural background and inheritance. Of the two, however, ethnicity is most closely associated with cultural heritage.

racism
Social practices that explicitly or implicitly attribute merits or allocate value to individuals solely because of their race.

A female correctional officer at work. In recent years, the number of women working in corrections has increased significantly. Do you think that gender bias exists within the correctional career field?

Members of an ethnic group generally share a common racial, national, religious, linguistic, and cultural origin. Hence, from an ethnic perspective, a person might identify him- or herself as Hungarian, even though he or she has never lived in Hungary, does not speak Hungarian, and knows little of the history of the Hungarian nation. Ethnic differences can lead to serious consequences, as prison gangs built around ethnicity demonstrate.

At first blush, the term *gender* seems more straightforward than race or ethnicity because it relates to differences between the sexes. In fact, many critical issues that concern correctional administrators today reflect a rapid increase in the number of women entering correctional service.

For many years corrections was a male-dominated profession. Although the correctional process has always involved some women, historically most women in the profession have attended to the needs of the small number of females held in confinement. It wasn't until the 1970s that women began to enter the corrections profession in significant numbers. Many went to work in facilities that housed males where they soon found themselves confronting *gender bias* from an entrenched macho culture.

Today, women working in correctional facilities largely have been accepted, as evidenced by the fact that their proportion is more than double the proportion of female law enforcement officers: Twenty-six percent of sworn correctional officers in the United States are women, while only 13 percent of police officers are female. As Figure 1–6 shows, however, women working in corrections tend to be concentrated in the lower ranks and are underrepresented in supervisory positions. According to the National Center for Women in

Policing, women of color hold 12.9 percent of corrections positions, 9.7 percent of top command positions, and 9.1 percent of supervisory positions.[38]

Race, ethnicity, and gender are all aspects of social diversity—although diversity in society extends to many other areas as well, such as economics, religion, education, intellectual ability, and politics. Keep in mind, as you read through this textbook, that in the field of corrections diversity issues can be described from four perspectives: (1) as they impact individual correctional clients, (2) as they determine correctional populations and trends, (3) as they affect the lives and interests of those working in the field of corrections, and (4) as they change the structure and functioning of correctional institutions, facilities, and programs.

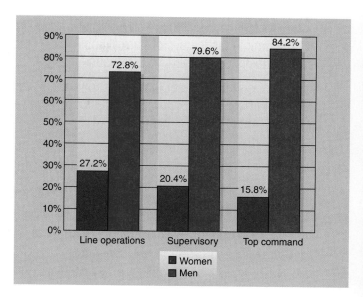

FIGURE 1–6
Corrections Personnel by Gender and Rank

Source: From Equality Denied: The Status of Women in Policing, 2001, p. 9. Copyright © National Center for Women and Policing. www.womenandpolicing.org Reprinted with permission.

SUMMARY

1 ▸ Although crime rates are at their lowest level in more than 20 years, correctional populations have been increasing because of get-tough-on-crime attitudes, the nation's War on Drugs, and the increasing reluctance of parole authorities, fearing civil liability and public outcry, to release inmates.

2 ▸ Growing correctional populations mean increasing costs. Budgetary allocations for corrections have grown in step with correctional populations. Growth in correctional populations and in spending has also led to a dramatically expanding correctional workforce and to enhanced employment opportunities within the field.

3 ▸ The crimes that bring people into the American correctional system include felonies, which are relatively serious criminal offenses; misdemeanors, which are less serious crimes; and infractions, which are minor law violations.

4 ▸ Two important sources of crime statistics are the FBI's Uniform Crime Reports (UCR), published annually under the title *Crime in the United States,* and the National Crime Victimization Survey (NCVS), published by the Bureau of Justice Statistics under the title *Criminal Victimization in the United States.* The UCR reports information on eight major crimes: murder, forcible rape, robbery, aggravated assault, burglary, larceny, automobile theft, and arson. The NCVS provides a detailed picture of crime incidents, victims, and trends. While UCR data are based upon crime reports made to the police, NCVS data are derived from annual nationwide surveys of American households.

REVIEW & APPLICATIONS

REVIEW & APPLICATIONS

5 ▶ Criminal justice agencies are said to make up the criminal justice system. The main components of the criminal justice system are (1) police, (2) courts, and (3) corrections. Each can be considered a subsystem of the criminal justice system.

6 ▶ The major components of the corrections subsystem are jails, probation, parole, and prisons. Jails and prisons are examples of institutional corrections, while probation and parole are forms of noninstitutional corrections.

7 ▶ The term *criminal justice* can be used to refer to our *system* of justice, or it can refer to the activities that take place during the justice *process.* Criminal justice agencies, taken together, make up the criminal justice system. Since the activities of criminal justice agencies routinely involve other agencies, the word *system* encompasses not only the agencies of justice, but also the relationships among those agencies. The justice *process,* on the other hand, refers to the events that unfold as a suspect is processed by the criminal justice system.

8 ▶ *Corrections* refers to all aspects of the pretrial and postconviction management of individuals accused or convicted of crimes.

9 ▶ Professionalism in corrections is important because it can win the respect and admiration of others outside the field. Moreover, professionals are regarded as trusted participants in any field of endeavor.

10 ▶ *Social diversity* encompasses differences of race, gender, and ethnicity. Social diversity is important in corrections today because it impacts individual correctional clients, influences correctional populations and trends, affects the lives and interests of those working in the field of corrections, and may help determine the structure and functioning of correctional institutions, facilities, and programs.

KEY TERMS

correctional clients, *p. 4*

felony, *p. 9*

misdemeanor, *p. 9*

infraction, *p. 9*

violent crime, *p. 10*

property crime, *p. 10*

crime index, *p. 10*

crime rate, *p. 10*

criminal justice, *p. 14*

criminal justice system, *p. 14*

adjudication, *p. 19*

arraignment, *p. 19*

nolo contendere, p. 19

writ of *certiorari, p. 20*

institutional corrections, *p. 20*

noninstitutional corrections, *p. 21*

corrections, *p. 21*

mores, *p. 24*

folkways, *p. 24*

criminal law, *p. 24*

penal law, *p. 24*

profession, *p. 25*

corrections professional, *p. 30*

professional associations, *p. 30*

certification, *p. 31*

racism, *p. 33*

QUESTIONS FOR REVIEW

1. Compare crime rates with correctional populations over time. What differences stand out? How might you explain them?

2. What three major categories of crime are discussed in this chapter? Explain the differences between them. Why is it important for corrections professionals to understand these differences?

3. Compare and contrast the Uniform Crime Reports and the National Crime Victimization Survey. What are the major differences? What are the similarities? What is the significance of these sources of information to the field of corrections?

4. What are the major components of the criminal justice system? Why may the term *criminal justice* be used to refer either to our system of justice or to the activities that take place during the justice *process*?

5. According to the ACA, what are the four fundamental purposes of corrections?

6. Explain how the UCR calculates its yearly crime rate.

7. According to the UCR, when is a crime considered *cleared* or *solved*?

8. What is the major difference between the original UCR system and the new system—NIBRS?

9. List four components of the corrections subsystem.

10. What is the function of a preliminary hearing?

11. Name and describe the first step in the adjudication process.

12. List at least five sentencing choices available to a judge or jury.

13. Based on the ACA statement defining corrections, what is the *fundamental* purpose of corrections?

14. Define *criminal law.*

15. List five characteristics of a true professional.

THINKING CRITICALLY ABOUT CORRECTIONS

▶ ▶ ▶ Vision

Dianne Carter, President of the National Academy of Corrections, once said, "Too often in corrections, only worker skills are targeted for training, and the organization misses a significant opportunity to communicate its vision and mission."[39] Do you agree or disagree with this statement? Why?

▶ ▶ ▶ Professionalism

Harold Williamson, a writer in the corrections field, has noted, "Higher levels of professionalization require greater amounts of training and usually involve increased specialization when compared to lesser professionalized activity. Higher levels of professionalization also involve the learning of more abstract knowledge and information."[40] Do you agree? Why or why not?

REVIEW & APPLICATIONS

ON-THE-JOB DECISION MAKING

▶ ▶ ▶ Training

Today is the first day of your job as a correctional officer. A severe statewide shortage of officers required you to begin work immediately before training, which you are scheduled to attend in three months. When you arrive at the facility, you are ushered into a meeting with the warden. He welcomes you and gives you a brief pep talk. He asks if you have any concerns. You tell him, "Well, I feel a little uneasy. I haven't gone through the academy yet." "Don't worry," he says, "all our new recruits get on-the-job experience before a slot in the academy opens up. You'll do fine!" He shakes your hand and leads you to the door. After you leave the warden's office, you are given a set of keys and a can of mace. The shift supervisor, a sergeant, gives you a brief tour of the prison. Then he tells you that, as you learn your job, you will spend most of your time with another officer; though pairing up will not always be possible.

The officer you are assigned to accompany is named Harold Gates. At first, you follow Officer Gates across the compound, getting more familiar with the layout of the facility. Then you spend an uneventful afternoon working with Officer Gates in the yard. At 4:30, Officer Gates instructs you to make sure that all inmates have left the classroom building in preparation for a "count." As you enter the building, you encounter a group of six inmates heading toward the door. Before you can move to the side, one of the inmates walks within an inch of you and stares at you. The others crowd in behind him. You can't move. You are pinned to the door by the men. The man directly in front of you is huge—over six feet tall and about 280 pounds. His legs look like tree trunks, and his arms are held away from his body by their sheer bulk. You're staring at a chest that could easily pass as a brick wall. With a snarl he growls, "What do you want?"

1. How do you respond? Would you feel more confident responding to a situation like this if you had had some training?

2. If you tell the inmates that it's time for a count and to move along, what will you do

next? Will you ask anyone for guidance in similar future situations or just chalk the encounter up to a learning experience? To whom might you talk about it?

3. Suppose you are a manager or supervisor at this facility. How would you handle the training of new recruits?

▶ ▶ ▶ Leadership

You are a correctional officer at the McClellan Correctional Facility. You and your coworkers have been following, with high interest, the events at Brownley, another correctional facility located approximately 35 miles away. Prisoner rioting at Brownley during the past four days has left four correctional officers and 19 prisoners seriously hurt. It now appears, though, that while tensions remain high, the riot has been contained, and the prisoners at Brownley are settling back down. The uneasy truce, however, mandates resolution of the issues that led to the riot in the first place.

The main issue leading to the riot was the prisoners' claims of mistreatment at the hands of certain members of the Brownley correctional staff. State correctional administrators have determined that an essential first step in preventing future riots is replacement of certain members of the correctional staff at Brownley. You are called to your supervisor's office, where she informs you that you are being reassigned temporarily to Brownley, with a possibility that the reassignment may become permanent.

This news does not make you happy. The logistical impact alone is irritating, because it will mean a significant commute each day. More important, though, is that you will be leaving a cohesive team of skilled and dedicated correctional officers with whom you have developed a close bond. You trust each other, and you trust your leaders. There's no telling what you will encounter at Brownley.

Your worst fears are realized when you report for your first shift and your new sergeant takes you aside. "We can't let them win on this," he says. "You know the drill. Stay on 'em hard, and don't cut 'em any slack. We need to let them know from the get-go that things haven't changed—we're still in charge, whether they like it or not, and we ain't gonna take any guff from the likes of them!"

It is immediately apparent to you that your sergeant has a strong "us-against-them" perspective. Your experience tells you that such an attitude at the leadership level likely induces similar, often stronger attitudes at the correctional officer level, and your common sense tells you that this is probably the root of the problem at Brownley.

1. How do you respond to your new sergeant?

2. If you elect to keep this information to yourself, how will you establish yourself with the Brownley inmates as a CO who does not subscribe to the other CO's practices without appearing weak or exploitable?

3. If you elect to bring this information to the attention of someone higher up in the supervisory chain, how will you deal with potential adverse reactions from your new coworkers?

CORRECTIONS ON THE WEB

▶ ▶ ▶ Associations

Access the websites of the following professional corrections organizations. For each one, determine the organization's mission, membership, services offered, and benefits of membership. Then, using the information you have gathered, decide whether you, as a correctional professional, should be a member of the organization and—if agency membership is available—whether the agency with which you are associated should be a member. Explain the reasons for your answers.

American Correctional Association
http://www.corrections.com/aca

American Jail Association
http://www.corrections.com/aja

American Probation and Parole Association
http://www.appa-net.org

National Sheriffs' Association (includes jailers)
http://www.sheriffs.org

Southern States Correctional Association
http://www.corrections.com/ssca

▶ ▶ ▶ Training

Revisit the websites of the organizations listed in the first Corrections on the Web assignment. Explore each website to learn what each organization offers in the area of correctional training. Use the information that you gather to describe the most comprehensive forms of training that are available. Do the same for the most specific forms of training that are offered.

REVIEW & APPLICATIONS

"No man shall be forced by Torture to confesse any Crime against him-selfe nor any other unlesse it be in some Capitall case, where he is first fullie convicted by cleare and suffitient evidence to be guilty. After which if the cause be of that nature, That it is very apparent there be other conspiratours, or confederates with him, Then he may be tor-tured, yet not with such Tortures as be Barbarous and inhumane."

—Massachusetts Body of Liberties of 1641, Section 45

Punishments:
A Brief History

CHAPTER OBJECTIVES

After completing this chapter you should be able to do the following:

1. Describe the types of punishment prevalent in ancient times.

2. List and describe the major criminal punishments used throughout history.

3. Explain the ideas that led to the use of incarceration as a criminal punishment and as an alternative to earlier punishments.

4. Explain the role of correctional reformers in changing the nature of criminal punishment.

▶ ▶ **Before the advent of prisons,** **corporal punishments** were often imposed for serious crimes. Some, although they were not regularly administered, were especially gruesome. In 1757 Robert-François Damiens was sentenced to be quartered publicly in Paris for attempting to kill King Louis XV. As the executioners took their places, it was announced that

corporal punishments
Physical punishments, or those involving the body.

THE STOCKS.

▼

An offender in the stocks in Colonial times. Early punishments were often both physical and public. What purposes did such punishments serve?

"the flesh will be torn from his breasts, arms, thighs, and calves with red-hot pincers, his right hand, holding the knife with which he committed said [crime], burnt with sulphur, and, on those places where the flesh will be torn away, poured molten lead, boiling oil, burning resin, wax, and sulphur melted together and then his body drawn and quartered by four horses and his limbs and body consumed by fire, reduced to ashes, and his ashes thrown to the winds."[1]

As it turned out, Damiens was a very muscular man. He remained conscious throughout the tortures, although a report tells us that he "uttered horrible cries." When it came time for him to be quartered, the four horses were unable to pull him apart—even after repeated attempts. Finally, six horses were used and, when they were still unable to disjoint the prisoner, his muscles had to be "cut through with knives."

Gruesome as this story may be, it illustrates the relative newness of our present system of corrections, which depends largely on the use of fines, probation, imprisonment, and parole. This chapter traces the historical and cultural roots of our present system.

Punishments in Ancient Times

Before the large-scale building of prisons began in 17th-century Europe, a variety of practices, based on the law and justice concepts of certain cultural groups, were used to punish wrongdoers and maintain civil order. We will briefly highlight some of these practices and the traditions that have influenced modern correctional practices.

ANCIENT GREECE

In the cultural history of punishments, the Greek city-states provide the earliest evidence that public punishment is part of the Western tradition—and that its roots are in ideas of law and justice. Of all the city-states, the practices of Athens are the best documented. This documentation, which ranges from the writings of orators and philosophers to plays and poetry, tell us that many early crimes were punished by execution, banishment, or exile. Greek poets described stoning the condemned to death, throwing them from high cliffs, binding them to stakes (similar to crucifixion), and cursing them ritually. In many cases, the bodies of executed criminals were regarded as dishonored and were prevented from being buried. Their bodies were left to scavengers and the elements, serving as a warning to anyone contemplating similar crimes.

Other punishments in ancient Athens included "confiscation of property, fines, and the destruction of the condemned offenders' houses."[2] Public denunciation, shaming *(atimia)*, imprisonment, and public display of the offender were also used. Criminal punishments in ancient Greece sometimes included civil penalties, such as loss of the ability to transfer property, to vote, and to marry.

ANCIENT ISRAEL

The chief record of ancient Hebrew history is the Bible. It describes the law and civilization of the ancient Hebrews, including their criminal law and penology. Punishments used by the Hebrews mentioned in the Old Testament included banishment, beating, beheading, blinding, branding and burning, casting down from a high place, crushing, confiscation of property, crucifixion, cursing, cutting asunder, drowning, exile, exposure to wild beasts, fining, flaying, hanging, imprisonment, mutilation, plucking of the hair, sawing asunder, scourging with thorns, slavery, slaying by spear or sword, use of the stocks, stoning, strangulation, stripes, and suffocation.[3] Michel Foucault, the French historian, says that the purpose of physical punishments was primarily revenge. "It was as if the punishment was thought to equal, if not to exceed, in savagery the crime itself," he writes.[4]

A stoning in pre-Christian times. How do ancient punishments and the philosophies that influenced them, contribute to today's understanding of the role of criminal punishment in society?

EARLY ROME

The Twelve Tables, the first written laws of Rome, were issued in 451 B.C. Conviction of some offenses required payment of compensation, but the most frequent penalty was death. Among the forms of capital punishment were burning (for arson), throwing from a cliff (for perjury), clubbing to death (for writing insulting songs about a citizen), hanging (for stealing others' crops), and decapitation. Not mentioned in the Twelve Tables were several other forms of capital punishment in vogue in ancient Rome. For killing a close relative, the offender was subjected to the *culleus,* which consisted of confining the offender in a sack with an ape, a dog, and a serpent and throwing the sack into the sea. Vestal virgins who had violated their vows of chastity were buried alive. As an alternative to execution, offenders might choose exile. Offenders who went into exile lost their citizenship, freedom, and immovable property. If they returned to Rome, they could be killed by any citizen.[5]

Physical Punishments

In western societies the practice of corporal punishment carried over into the Christian era. Physical punishments were imposed for a wide variety of

The purpose of punishment is for someone to learn from what they have done wrong. For example, when you were a child and you got caught sneaking a cigarette from your father's pack, the punishment was a spanking and getting sent to your room until told to come out. Well, most kids learn from this. Then you have the hard-headed ones such as myself who did not learn. I had to do this over and over and over again. Repeat the punishment until I got it right. I beat my head against the wall too many times and it ended up hurting too much.

If there were no punishment it would be one place I would not want to live. There would be total chaos throughout the world. Back to the wild, wild west days. I also believe that the punishment should fit the crime. Myself, I've spent 10 years 3 months in prison which I deserved to do. I did wrong, and this is my example of how the punishment should fit the crime. I was convicted of 11 armed robberies which I said I did over 10 years. I've met people in prison who did one armed robbery and they have been in since the early 1970s. I do not feel that is right.

Cary James Campbell
Palm Beach Detention Center, FL

THE OFFENDER SPEAKS

offenses during the Middle Ages. Physical punishments were also used in the American colonies: ". . . [T]he whole baggage of corporal punishments, as they existed in England, were brought to this country, and flourished, especially in New England where the precepts of Calvinism adorned them with pious sanctions."[6] The Puritans, for example, sometimes burned witches and unruly slaves; made wide use of the stocks, the pillory, and the ducking stool; branded criminal offenders; and forced women convicted of adultery to wear "scarlet letters."

As justice historian Pieter Spierenburg notes, many physical punishments during the Middle Ages and in "early modern Europe" were *theatrical punishments*.[7] That is, they were corporal punishments carried out in public. Spierenburg divides punishments that were both physical and public into five degrees of severity: (1) whipping or flogging; (2) burning of the skin; (3) mutilation, or "more serious encroachments on bodily integrity"; (4) a merciful instant death; and (5) a torturous and prolonged death.[8]

Michael Fay, the American teenager who was caned in Singapore in 1994. Corporal punishments like caning, which involves whipping with a bamboo rod, are still used in more than two dozen countries as criminal sanctions. Fay, who was 18 years old when caned, had spray painted some parked cars. Can corporal punishment be an effective criminal deterrent?

FLOGGING

Flogging (or whipping) has been the most common physical punishment through the ages.[9] The code established by Moses, for example, authorized flogging, and Roman law specified flogging as a punishment for certain forms of theft. Flogging was common in England during the Middle Ages as punishment for a wide variety of crimes. In England, women were flogged in private, but men were whipped publicly.[10]

The construction of flogging whips varied greatly, from simple leather straps or willow branches to heavy, complicated instruments designed to inflict a maximum of pain. A traditional form of whip was the cat-o'-nine-tails, consisting of nine knotted cords fastened to a wooden handle. The "cat" got its name from the marks it left on the body, which were like the scratches of a cat. One especially cruel form of the whip, the Russian knout, was made of leather strips fitted with fishhooks. When a prisoner was whipped, the hooks would dig into the body, ripping away a proverbial "pound of flesh" with each stroke. A thorough whipping with the knout could result in death from blood loss.

> Flogging (or whipping) has been the most common physical punishment through the ages.

Flogging was also widely used in the American colonies to enforce discipline, punish offenders, and make an example of "ne'er-do-wells" (shiftless and irresponsible individuals). As a mechanism for enforcing compliance with prison rules, flogging survived into the 20th century. As late as 1959, Harry Elmer Barnes and Negley K. Teeters were able to write, "Floggings have been prison practice down to our own times, and deaths have occurred due to over-severe whippings in southern prison camps and

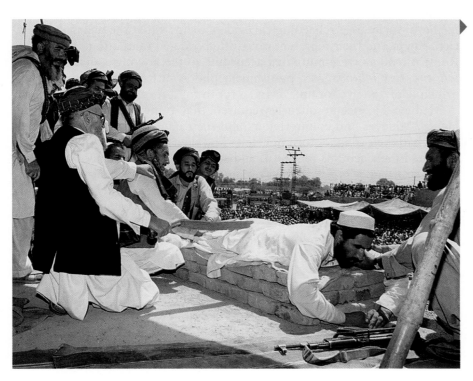

Convicted rapist Ghanat Khan, an Afghan refugee, being lashed at Bara near Pakistan's northwestern city of Peshawar. Kahn received 15 lashes in a public whipping as mandated by Islamic law. Why do some countries still impose physical punishments for crimes? Why are they sometimes carried out in public?

chain-gangs. Tying prisoners up by their hands and allowing them to hang suspended with their toes barely touching the floor or ground has been a common method of enforcing discipline."[11]

BRANDING

Branding, a type of mutilation, was practiced by Roman society. Criminals were branded with a mark or letter signifying their crimes. Brands, which were often placed on the forehead or another part of the face, served to warn others of an offender's criminal history.

The last documented incident of facial branding of English criminals occurred in 1699.[12] After that year, offenders were branded on the hand, since it was feared that more obvious marks would reduce employment possibilities. Branding was abolished in England during the last half of the 18th century.

The French branded criminals on the shoulder with the royal emblem. They later switched to burning onto the shoulder a letter signifying the crime of which the offender had been convicted.

Branding was also practiced in the early American colonies. The East Jersey Codes of 1668 and 1675, for example, ordered that burglars be branded on the hand with the letter *T* (for *thief*). After a second offense, the letter *R* (for *rogue*) was burned into the forehead. Maryland branded blasphemers with the letter *B* on the forehead. Women offenders were not branded but were forced to wear letters on their clothing.

MUTILATION

Mutilation was another type of corporal punishment used in ancient and medieval societies. Archaeological evidence shows that the pharaohs of ancient Egypt and their representatives often ordered mutilation.[13] In ancient Rome offenders were mutilated according to the law of retaliation, or *lex talionis*. *Lex talionis*, as a punishment philosophy, resembles the biblical principle of "an eye for an eye and a tooth for a tooth."

Medieval justice frequently required that punishment fit the crime. Hence, "thieves and counterfeiters had their hands cut off, liars and perjurers had their tongues torn out, spies had their eyes gouged out, sex criminals had their genitals removed, and so forth."[14] Blasphemers sometimes had their tongues pierced or cut out and their upper lips cut away.[15]

Mutilation had a deterrent effect; the permanently scarred and disfigured offenders served as warnings to others of what would happen to criminals. Sometimes, mutilation served merely as a prelude to execution. The right hand of a murderer, for example, was sometimes cut off before he was hanged.[16]

INSTANT DEATH

According to Spierenburg, beheading, hanging, and garroting (strangulation by a tightened iron collar) were the most common means of merciful or instant death.[17] Instant death was frequently reserved for members of the nobility who had received capital sentences (usually from the King) or

A 1786 German woodcut depicts a public execution by burning. What purpose did such public dispensing of justice serve for government authorities?

for previously honorable men and women who ran afoul of the law. Decapitation, especially when done by the sword, was regarded as the most honorable form of capital punishment—since a sword was a symbol that was both noble and aristocratic. Hanging, says Spierenburg, "was the standard nonhonorable form of the death penalty." For women, however, hanging was considered indecent. Garroting tended to replace hanging as a capital punishment for women.

LINGERING DEATH

The worst fate a criminal offender—especially one convicted of heinous crimes—might meet in medieval Europe was a slow or lingering death, often preceded by torture. Some offenders were burned alive, and others were "broken on the wheel." Breaking on the wheel was a procedure that broke all of the major bones in the body. A person who had been broken on the wheel and was still alive was often killed by an executioner's blow to the heart.

Offenders who were to be hanged sometimes had their arms and legs broken first; others were whipped or burned. Burning alive, a practice used in France until the 18th century, was undoubtedly one of the period's cruelest forms of capital punishment.

In the past, many corporal punishments were carried out in public, primarily to deter others. Some say the death penalty is a deterrent. Should we televise executions? For more information go to Ethical Dilemma 2-1 at http://www.mhhe.com/schmalleger2.

Ethical Dilemma

THE ROLE OF TORTURE

A variety of other corporal punishments were employed, some of which involved torture. Pain was central to retaliatory punishments, and it was used to extract confessions and get information. "Torture," said one source, "is the twisting (torsion) from its subjects of guilty secrets."[18] The use of torture in medieval England was based on a theory that knowledge of one's own guilt, or of the guilt of others, was an offense in itself. Moreover, the theory went, such knowledge was a kind of property that rightly belonged to the state. Hence, forcing an offender to relinquish such "property," by any means necessary, was a right of the government.

Tortures of all kinds were used during the Middle Ages in an effort to gain confessions from heretics. Heresy was considered a crime against the church and against God. At the time, there was no separation between church and state in many Western societies, and church courts were free to impose punishment as they saw fit. Believers were sure that the heretic's soul was condemned to eternal damnation and that confession would lead to salvation. As a result, torture flourished as a technique for saving souls. Some saw the suffering induced by corporal punishments as spiritually cleansing. Others compared it to the suffering of Jesus on the cross. They argued that physical pain and suffering might free the soul from the clutches of evil.

A common medieval torture was the rack—a machine that slowly stretched a prisoner until his or her joints separated. In another method of torture, red-hot pincers called *hooks* were used to pull the flesh away. Thumbscrews were used as their name implies. In *cording*, an offender's thumbs were tied tightly together behind the back by a rope that passed through a support in the ceiling. Weights were then tied to the ankles, and the person was hoisted into the air by his or her thumbs. Stones were used to crush confessions out of offenders: First a convict was covered with boards, and then suffer as one stone after another was placed on top of them.

Devil's Island, the infamous French prison where many political prisoners were held. What role did transportation play in the criminal punishments of times past?

EXILE AND TRANSPORTATION

In a number of early societies, exile, or banishment, sometimes took the place of corporal and capital punishment. The ancient Greeks permitted offenders to leave the Greek state and travel to Rome, where they might gain citizenship. Early Roman law also established the punishment of exile. Exile was regarded as akin to a death sentence, since the banished person could no longer depend on his or her former community for support and protection. He or she could generally be killed with impunity if attempting to reenter the area.

Exile was practiced in some European communities into the 1800s. One historical study, for example, revealed that, between 1650 and 1750, 97 percent of the noncapital sentences handed down in Amsterdam included banishment.[19]

Sentences of banishment drove petty offenders out of a municipality and kept known offenders out of town. But banished criminals resurfaced quickly in neighboring towns, and many communities in Europe confronted a floating population of criminals—especially petty thieves.

Though it was rarely practical to banish offenders from an entire province or nation, England practiced for more than 200 years a form of criminal exile known as *transportation*. An English law authorizing the transportation of convicts to newly discovered lands was passed in 1597. The law was intended primarily to provide galley slaves for a burgeoning English merchant fleet. Soon, however, public support grew for the transportation system as a way of ridding England of felons. As a result, large numbers of convicts were sent to America and other English colonies. One writer estimates that, by the beginning of the American Revolution, 50,000 prisoners had been sent to the New World. Most of them "were sold as indentured servants in the southern colonies, where their market value was greater than in New England."[20]

After the American Revolution, convicted felons began piling up in English jails with no place to go. Legislation was soon passed authorizing prisoners to be housed aboard floating prison ships called *hulks*. Many of these vessels were abandoned merchant ships or broken-down warships. Hulks were anchored in rivers and harbors throughout England. They were unsanitary, rat infested, and unventilated, and the keepers flogged the inmates to force them to work. Disease ran rampant in the hulks, sometimes wiping out all the prisoners on a ship, as well as the crew and nearby citizens. This "temporary" solution lasted about 80 years.

The system of hulks eventually proved impractical, and England soon began shifting its convict population to Australia, which Captain Cook had come upon in 1770. Convict transportation to Australia began in earnest in 1787,[21] with English convicts being transported to New South Wales, Norfolk Island, and Van Diemen's Land—now known as Tasmania. The journey was long and demanding, and conditions on prison ships were often ghastly. Many convicts did not survive the trip. Those who did were put to work at heavy labor when they reached their destinations, helping to develop the growing region.

In the late 18th century, the English government began turning broken-down war vessels and abandoned transport ships into *hulks* to house prisoners. What event caused the prison overcrowding that made these hulks necessary?

EXHIBIT 2–1   **Van Diemen's Land**

Van Diemen's Land, an island off the southern coast of Australia that is known today as Tasmania, served as a destination in the English system of convict transportation during the early 1800s. The paragraphs that follow, which were written in 1832, give some historical insight into the practice.

Van Diemen's Land was discovered so long ago as the year 1642, by the Dutch navigator Tasman, who gave it the name which it still bears, in honour of his employer Anthony Van Diemen, the then governor of the Dutch possessions in India. It was not, however, till the year 1804 that the country was taken possession of by England. In the early part of that year Colonel David Collins, having been appointed Governor of the projected settlement, arrived on the island with about four hundred prisoners in charge and a force of fifty marines under his command. He was accompanied also by several gentlemen, commissioned to fill the various situations on the new government. They fixed their headquarters on the site of the present capital, to which they gave the name of Hobart Town, after Lord Hobart, the then Secretary for the Colonies. The Colony . . . being thus founded, continued to take root, although at times suffering very great hardships. . . . No sheep or cattle were imported till three years after the settlement of the island. For some time after this, indeed, the colony was looked upon merely as a place of punishment for persons convicted of crimes in New South Wales, numbers of whom accordingly continued to be sent to it every year. Governor Collins died in 1810; and in 1813 Lieutenant-Colonel Davey arrived as his successor.

From about this time the colony began to be considered in a new light. The population consisted no longer merely of the convicts and the garrison; but, besides many persons who, having been originally crown prisoners, had obtained their freedom by servitude or indolence, embraced a considerable number of settlers who had arrived in successive small parties from the neighbouring colony of New South Wales. Hitherto the only places with which Van Diemen's Land was allowed to hold any communication had been New South Wales and England: That restriction was now done away with, and the two colonies were placed, in respect to foreign commerce, on precisely the same footing. . . .

In 1817 Colonel Davey was succeeded in the government by Colonel Sorell. The first object which engaged the attention of the new governor was the suppression of an evil under which the colony had for some years been suffering, the ravages of the bush-rangers, as they were called, or prisoners who had made their escape and roamed at large in the woods. The capture and execution of the principal leaders of these marauders in a short time put an end, for the present, to their destructive inroads.

About 1821 may be said to have begun the emigration from England, which has since proceeded almost with uninterrupted steadiness. . . . In December 1825, Van Diemen's Land was declared entirely independent of New South Wales; and an executive and legislative Council were appointed as advisers to the Governor, the members of both being named by the Crown. In 1827 the island was divided into eight police districts, each of which was placed under the charge of a stipendiary magistrate.

Source: The Society for the Diffusion of Useful Knowledge, *The Penny Magazine*, vol. I, no. 1, March 31, 1832.

Soon convicts who had served their sentences began to receive land grants. In 1791 the governor of New South Wales initiated a program to give released convicts up to 30 acres of land each, along with enough tools, seeds, and rations to last 18 months.

English transportation of criminals began to wane in 1853, when Parliament abolished transportation for prisoners with sentences of fewer than 14 years. Opposition to transportation was especially strong among the free settlers who had begun to populate Australia and nearby regions. In 1867 the practice of transportation officially ended, although England continued to send inmates from India to its penal colony in the Andaman Islands until World War II.

France also experimented with transportation. Beginning in 1791 French authorities sent prisoners in large numbers to Madagascar, New Caledonia, the Marquesas Islands, and French Guiana. Devil's Island, in the Caribbean Sea, off the coast of French Guiana, continued to function as a prison until 1951. The island was named for the horrors associated with imprisonment there. It was the site of an infamous penal colony that was used mostly for political prisoners. The island was also made famous by the Dreyfus Affair, which began in 1894 when French Captain Alfred Dreyfus (1859–1935) was convicted of treason by a court-martial, sentenced to life imprisonment, and sent to the island. Thirty-six years later, Dreyfus was exonerated after it was demonstrated that the original charges against him were the result of anti-Semitism in the French military and had no factual basis.

The only western nation to practice transportation into the 1990s was Russia, which sent prisoners to Siberia as late as 1990. Siberia is a cold and formerly desolate region in what is now central and eastern Russia. It stretches from the Ural Mountains to the Pacific Ocean. The extensive area was annexed by Russia in stages during the 16th and 17th centuries. It was used as a place of exile for political prisoners since the early 17th century. In 1741 the Russian Count Biron was found guilty of treason, but his sentence of death by quartering was changed to exile to Siberia.[22] Hard labor in Siberia became a common sentence for criminal offenders in Czarist Russia, and it is estimated that hundreds of thousands of vagrants, felons, political prisoners, and even voluntary exiles were sent to Siberia under the Czars to force settlement of the region and to develop its natural resources. During Joseph Stalin's rule (1928–1953), Siberian prison camps forced tens of millions of victims into a vast labor system. The brutal conditions in these camps resulted in millions of deaths and have been graphically described in the works of Aleksandr Solzhenitsyn.[23] After Stalin's death the camp population greatly decreased, although detention in remote and inhospitable parts of Siberia is still used to punish criminals and dissenters.[24]

PUBLIC HUMILIATION

Many corporal punishments were carried out in public, primarily to deter other potential lawbreakers. Some other forms of punishment depended on public ridicule for their effect. These included the stocks and the pillory.

Stocks held a prisoner in a sitting position, with feet and hands locked in a frame. A prisoner in the pillory was made to stand with his or her head and hands locked in place. Both devices exposed the prisoner to public scorn. While confined in place, prisoners were frequently pelted with eggs and rotten fruit. Sometimes they were whipped or branded. Those confined to the pillory occasionally had their ears nailed to the wood, and they had to rip them free when released. England abolished the pillory in 1834; according to at least one source, the pillory was still in use in Delaware in 1905.[25]

Found guilty of the offense of impiety in Athens in 399 B.C., Socrates chose poison over imprisonment. What was the goal of most early penalties for crimes?

CONFINEMENT

Confinement by chaining or jailing has been a punishment since ancient times. At times, confinement served functions other than punishment for crimes. In early Greece, for example, prisons were used to punish convicted offenders, to enforce the payment of debts, to hold those awaiting other punishments, and to detain foreigners who might otherwise flee before their cases could be heard.[26] Until the

1600s and the development of prisons as primary places of punishment, prisons were used to detain people before trial; to hold prisoners awaiting other punishments, such as death or corporal punishment; to force payment of debts and fines; and to hold and punish slaves.

Early European prisons were rarely called *prisons*. They went by such names as *dungeon, tower,* and *gaol* (from which we get the modern term *jail*). Some places used as prisons had been built for other purposes. The Tower of London, for example, was originally a fortified palace that had been used as an arsenal. The French Bastille began as a fortified city gate leading into Paris. Judicial proceedings were not necessary before imprisonment in such places; nor was a formal sentence. As a result, anyone thrown into a dungeon at the behest of authorities was likely to stay there until granted clemency or until death.

Incarceration as Punishment

According to Pieter Spierenburg, a Dutch justice historian, a form of punishment that emerged around the year 1500 was *penal bondage,* which included all forms of incarceration.[27] Spierenburg explained that "Courts came to use it almost as frequently as physical sanctions. Instead of being flogged or hanged, some offenders were incarcerated in workhouses or forced to perform labor in some other setting." According to Spierenburg, the word *bondage* means "any punishment that puts severe restrictions on the condemned person's freedom of action and movement, including but not limited to imprisonment."

Among the forms of penal bondage imposed on criminals, vagrants, debtors, social misfits, and others were forced labor on public works projects and forced conscription into military campaigns. Later, houses of correction also subjected inmates to strict routines.

One early form of incarceration developed in France. For at least 200 years, prisoners were regularly assigned to French warships as galley slaves. After the naval importance of galleys had declined, French naval officials continued to have custody of convicted offenders. By the mid-1700s, they had begun to put convicts to work in the shipyards of Toulon, Brest, and Rochefort. At night these prisoners were sheltered in arsenals, where they slept chained to their beds. As Spierenburg notes, "the arsenals were in fact labor camps where convicts had to remain within an enclosed space, so the penalty was more akin to imprisonment than to public works."

The public-works penalty, sometimes called *penal servitude,* became especially popular in Germany and Switzerland in the 1600s and 1700s. According to Spierenburg, "convicts dug ore in mines, repaired ramparts, built roads or houses, or went from door to door collecting human waste."[28]

THE HOUSE OF CORRECTION (1550–1700)

Midway between corporal punishments and modern imprisonment stands the workhouse or the house of correction. The development of workhouses was originally a humanitarian move intended to manage the unsettling social conditions of the late 16th and early 17th centuries in England. The feudal system had offered mutual protection for land-owning nobles and for serfs, who were tied to the land. By 1550 that system was breaking down in Europe. Hordes of former serfs roamed the countryside, unable to earn a living. Many flocked to the cities, where they hoped to find work in newly developing industries. The change from an agrarian economy to an industrial one displaced many persons, resulted in growing poverty, and increased the numbers of beggars and vagrants.

Vagrancy became a crime, and soon anyone unable to prove some means of support was imprisoned in a workhouse. The first workhouse in England was called Bridewell because it was located at St. Bridget's Well, near the town of Blackfriars. Soon, the word **bridewell** entered the language as a term for a workhouse. English Parliament ordered workhouses to be created throughout England. Parliament intended that those housed in workhouses be taught habits of industry and frugality and that they learn a trade.

bridewell

A workhouse. The word came from the name of the first workhouse in England.

At first, prisoners in workhouses were paid for the work they did. Work included spinning, weaving, clothmaking, the milling of grains, and baking. Soon, however, as the numbers of prisoners grew, the workhouse system deteriorated. As workhouses spread through Europe, they became catchall institutions that held the idle, the unemployed, the poor, debtors, the insane, and even unruly individuals whose families could not cope with them. According to one writer, imprisonment in a workhouse could serve "as a tool of private discipline. . . . The family drew up a petition explaining why the individual should be imprisoned, and the authorities decided whether or not to consent. Usually, private offenders were confined because of conduct considered immoral."[29]

Hence, workhouses served as informal repositories for people the community regarded as "inconvenient," irresponsible, or deviant—even if their behavior did not violate the criminal law. In the midst of this large population of misfits and unwanted persons could be found a core group of criminal offenders. In 1706 the British Parliament passed legislation "permitting judges to sentence felons to the house of correction for up to two years."[30]

Bridewells were penal institutions for social outcasts—ranging from vagrants to petty criminals—who were forced to work under strict discipline. What social conditions prompted governments to establish such houses of correction?

By the end of the 17th century, houses of correction had become mere holding cells with little reformative purpose. Nonetheless, because workhouses relied primarily on incarceration rather than corporal punishments, they provided a model for prison reformers bent on more humanitarian correctional practices.

THE EMERGENCE OF THE PRISON

Two main elements fueled the development of prisons as we know them today. The first element was a philosophical shift away from punishment of the body toward punishment of the soul or human spirit. By the late 1700s in Europe and America, a powerful movement was underway to replace traditional corporal punishments with deprivation of personal liberty as the main thrust of criminal sentencing. Michel Foucault explains the shift this way: "The punishment-body relation [was no longer] the same as it was in the torture during public executions. The body now serves as an instrument or intermediary: If one intervenes upon it to imprison it or to make it work, it is in order to deprive the individual of a liberty that is regarded both as a right and as property. The body, according to this penalty, is caught up in a system of constraints and privations, obligations and prohibitions. Physical pain, the pain of the body itself, is no longer the constituent element of the penalty."[31]

> Two main elements fueled the development of prisons as we know them today. The first element was a philosophical shift away from punishment of the body, toward punishment of the soul or human spirit. . . .The second element . . . was the passage of laws preventing the imprisonment of anyone except criminals.

The transition from corporal punishments to denial of liberties found its clearest expression in the work of the Philadelphia Society for Alleviating the Miseries of Public Prisons. The society, established by the Pennsylvania Quakers in 1787, had as its purpose the renovation of existing prisons and jails and the establishment of the prison as the basic form of criminal punishment. Thanks largely to the widely publicized works of the society, Pennsylvania became in April 1794 the first state to abolish permanently the death penalty for all crimes except first-degree murder, and it adopted a system of fines and imprisonment in place of corporal punishments.[32] The new Pennsylvania criminal code was important because it "marked the first permanent American break with contemporary juristic savagery, was the forerunner of the reform codes of other American states, and was the essential basis of Pennsylvania criminal jurisprudence until the next systematic revision in 1860."[33]

The second element fueling the development of modern prisons was the passage of laws preventing the imprisonment of anyone except criminals. Civil commitments to prison ended, and a huge class of social misfits were removed from prisons and dealt with elsewhere. Primary among this group were debtors, who historically had been cast into jails as a result of civil rulings against them. John Howard's study of English jails found 2,437 debtors among the 4,084 prisoners he encountered.[34] Many others were vagrants who had committed no "intentional" crime.

According to Pieter Spierenburg, the Dutch were the first Europeans to segregate serious criminals from vagrants and minor delinquents, and Dutch courts were the first European courts to begin substituting imprisonment for corporal punishments.[35] The workhouse in Amsterdam, which opened in 1654, "represented the first criminal prison in Europe," says Spierenburg. By the start of the 1700s, Dutch "courts frequently imposed sentences of imprisonment. During the third quarter of the seventeenth century, the Amsterdam court did so in one-fifth of its criminal cases; a century later, it did so in three-fifths. By the 1670s the court of Groningen-City imposed imprisonment in two-fifths of criminal cases." Even so, the imprisonment of debtors persisted in Holland for another hundred years, and Dutch prisons of the period held both criminal and civil "convicts."

These ideas—that "doing time" was often the most appropriate punishment for criminal activity and that incarceration should be imposed only on criminal offenders—soon combined with a burgeoning emphasis on reformation as the primary goal of criminal sentencing. Reformation, argued many prison advocates of the time, could best be achieved by enforced solitude.

In 1776 the British philanthropist Jonas Hanway published a book entitled *Solitude in Imprisonment*. Hanway's work appears to have had a significant influence on prison advocates. Hanway argued that the interruption of transportation provided a much-needed opportunity to re-examine prevailing policies for dealing with prisoners. He suggested that reformation should be the primary goal of criminal sentencing and said that it was plainly not being met by sentencing practices then in existence. Solitary confinement, said Hanway, would force the prisoner to face his or her conscience—leading to reformation: "The walls of his prison will preach peace to his soul, and he will confess the goodness of his Maker, and the wisdom of the laws of his country."[36]

The Reformers

Prisons, as institutions in which convicted offenders spend time as punishment for crimes, are relatively modern. They came about largely as a result of growing intellectualism in Europe and America and as a reaction to the barbarities of corporal punishment.

The period of Western social thought that began in the 17th century and lasted until the dawn of the 19th century is known as the Age of Enlightenment. One author explains that "The phrase was frequently employed by writers of the period itself, convinced that they were emerging from centuries of darkness and ignorance into a new age enlightened by reason, science, and a respect for humanity."[37] The Enlightenment, also known as the Age of Reason, was more than a set of fixed ideas. Enlightenment thought implied an attitude, a method of knowing based on observation, experience, and reason.

One of the earliest representatives of the Enlightenment was the French social philosopher and jurist Charles de Montesquieu (1689–1755) whose

> Prisons, as institutions in which convicted offenders spend time as punishment for crimes, are relatively modern.

masterwork, *The Spirit of Laws,* was published in 1748. Montesquieu wrote that governmental powers should be separated and balanced in order to guarantee individual rights and freedom. He strongly believed in the rights of individuals. His ideas influenced leaders of both the American Revolution and the French Revolution.[38]

Another celebrated philosopher of the Enlightenment was the French writer Voltaire, who satirized both the government and the religious establishment of France. Voltaire twice served time in the Bastille and chose exile in England over prison for additional offenses. Voltaire deeply admired the English atmosphere of political and religious freedom.

A number of important thinkers influenced the justice systems of Western nations and the directions the correctional enterprise would take over the next 200 years. We will now turn our attention to those individuals.

WILLIAM PENN

William Penn (1644–1718), regarded as the founder of Pennsylvania, was the son of Sir William Penn, a distinguished English Admiral. During his youth, Penn traveled widely throughout Europe, served in the Royal Navy, and studied law. In 1667 he converted to the Quaker faith and by the next year found himself confined in the Tower of London as punishment for promoting the faith. While imprisoned he wrote a paper entitled "No Cross, No Crown." After release he was again imprisoned on a number of occasions, causing him to seek refuge in America. In 1682 Penn obtained a charter creating the Commonwealth of Pennsylvania and naming him governor. Gathering together hundreds of Quakers, Penn set sail for the New World. The colony he founded promoted religious tolerance, and it was soon attracting persecuted minorities from England, Germany, Holland, and Scandinavia.

Penn's influence on the criminal law of this country and on the coming age of imprisonment was most visible in the "Great Act" of 1682. Through that single piece of legislation, the Pennsylvania Quakers reduced capital offenses to the one crime of premeditated murder and abolished all corporal punishments as they had existed under English code.

JOHN HOWARD

John Howard (1726–1790) was born to a deeply religious English family. On a trip to Portugal as a young man, Howard was taken prisoner by pirates when the British merchant ship on which he was travelling was captured by a French privateer.[39] He and his fellow passengers were kept below deck in subhuman conditions. When they arrived in France, he was imprisoned in a French dungeon, but he was later released in exchange for a French naval officer.

In 1773, Howard was appointed High Sheriff of Bedfordshire. He was shocked at the abysmal conditions that existed in English jails of the time, and he set out on a quest for prison reform. He began arguing for the abolishment of spiked collars and chains, which prisoners were made to wear, and he argued against the common practice of paying jailers for release.

Ethical Dilemma

The United States has engaged in various forms of corporal punishment in the past, and many countries still engage in corporal punishment. What are the issues? What types of punishment are still being used in the 21st century? For more information go to Ethical Dilemma 2-2 at http://www.mhhe.com/schmalleger2.

Restorative Justice

by Mark Umbreit,
University of Minnesota

Reflections on the Future

Restorative justice is a victim-centered response to crime that provides opportunities for those most directly affected by crime—the victim, the offender, their families, and representatives of the community—to be directly involved in responding to the harm caused by the crime. Restorative justice is based upon values that emphasize the importance of providing opportunities for more active involvement in the process of offering support and assistance to crime victims; holding offenders directly accountable to the people and communities they have violated; restoring the emotional and material losses of victims (to the degree possible); providing a range of opportunities for dialogue and problem solving among interested crime victims, offenders, families, and other support persons; offering offenders opportunities for competency development and reintegration into productive community life; and strengthening public safety through community building.

Restorative justice policies and programs are known to be developing in nearly every state, including a growing number of state and county justice systems that are undergoing major systemic change. Restorative justice is also developing in many other parts of the world, including numerous European countries, Australia, New Zealand, and South Africa. In recent years, restorative justice practices and/or policies have been endorsed by the American Bar Association (victim offender mediation and dialogue), the European Council, and the United Nations.

The principles of restorative justice draw upon the wisdom of many indigenous cultures throughout the world, most notably Native American culture within the United States and Aboriginal/First Nation culture in Canada. These principles are also deeply rooted in the ancient values of Judeo-Christian culture, which have emphasized crime as being a violation against people and families, rather than "the state." Many examples are found in the Old and New Testaments of the Bible of the responsibility of offenders to directly repair the harm they caused to individuals, representing a breach in the "Shalom community."

Specific examples of restorative justice include crime repair crews, victim intervention programs, victim offender mediation and dialogue, family group conferencing, peacemaking circles, victim panels that speak to offenders, sentencing circles, community reparative boards before which offenders appear, offender competency development programs, victim empathy classes for offenders, victim-directed and citizen-involved community service by the offender, community-based support groups for crime victims, and community-based support groups for offenders. As the oldest and most widely developed expression of restorative justice, with more than 25 years of experience and numerous studies in North America and Europe, victim offender mediation and dialogue programs currently work with thousands of cases annually through more than 300 programs throughout the United States and more than 1,200 in Europe.

There have been more than 60 empirical studies of restorative justice dialogue programs (primarily victim offender mediation but also a smaller number of studies of family group conferencing). Findings have included high levels of victim and offender satisfaction with the process and outcome, greater likelihood of successful restitution completion by the offender, greater perceptions of fairness, reduced fear among victims, and reduced frequency and severity of further criminal behavior.

ABOUT THE AUTHOR

Mark Umbreit, Ph.D., is a professor at the University of Minnesota, School of Social Work. He is the founding director of the Center for Restorative Justice & Peacemaking as well as the National Restorative Justice Training Institute. Dr. Umbreit has more than 28 years of experience as a mediator, trainer, and researcher and has authored four books and more than 140 articles, book chapters, and monographs in the field of restorative justice and mediation. His most recent book is *The Handbook on Victim Offender Mediation: An Essential Guide for Practice & Research* (San Francisco, Jossey-Bass, 2001).

Within a few years, Howard had visited almost every county in England, Wales, and Scotland, traveling no fewer than 7,000 miles in 1779 alone.

Howard's greatest legacy was his 1777 book, *The State of the Prisons*,[40] in which he described clean and well-run institutions, prisons in which the sexes were separated, and jails in which inmates were kept busy at productive work, and in which he promoted the notion that the fundamental business of corrections should be to reform rather than to punish. Howard's *The State of the Prisons* argued that every citizen must accept responsibility for the criminal justice system of the society in which he or she lives. *The State of the Prisons* appealed to policymakers looking for alternatives to existing systems, and it fueled the efforts of prison reformers in both Europe and America. Many of the principles described in Howard's book later became the foundation for the English Penitentiary Act of 1779.

As Randall McGowen, corrections historian at the University of Oregon, explains, "Howard's contribution was to make the prison the center of focus, shifting all other forms of punishment to the margins. He fostered a vital change of perspective at the very time that judges were sentencing greater numbers of felons to confinement. Howard's book created the impression that the prison was the natural and inevitable shape of punishment."[41]

Howard died of the plague in Russia in 1790. At the time, he was in the midst of his sixth tour of European prisons and was about to leave on a trip to study prisons in Turkey and Asia. On his tomb are engraved these words:

> Whosoever Thou Art
> Thou Standest at the
> Grave of Thy Friend

CESARE BECCARIA

Cesare Beccaria (1738–1794) was born in Italy, the eldest son of an aristocratic family. By the time he reached his mid-20s, Beccaria had formed, with his close friends Pietro and Alessandro Verri, an intellectual circle called the Academy of Fists.[42] The academy took as its purpose the reform of the criminal justice system. Through the Verri brothers, Beccaria became acquainted with the work of French and British political writers such as Montesquieu, Thomas Hobbes (1588–1679), Denis Diderot (1713–1784), Claude-Adrien Helvetius (1715–1771), and David Hume (1711–1776).

In 1764 Beccaria published an essay titled *On Crimes and Punishments*. Although the work was brief, it was, perhaps, the most exciting essay on law of the 18th century. In the essay, Beccaria outlined a utilitarian approach to punishment, suggesting that some punishments can never be justified because they are more evil than any "good" they might produce. The use of torture to obtain confessions falls into that category, said Beccaria. Beccaria also protested punishment of the insane, a common practice of the times, saying it could do no good because insane people cannot accurately assess the consequences of their actions. Beccaria said that *ex post facto* laws, or laws passed after the fact, imposed punishment unfairly, since a person could not calculate the risk of acting before a law against a specific action was passed. He also argued against the use of secret accusations, the

Cesare Beccaria (1738–1794), an Italian jurist and criminologist, was one of the first to argue against capital punishment and inhumane treatment of prisoners. What writing by Beccaria influenced the criminal justice systems of Western Europe?

CAREER PROFILE

Zaira Tena

Correctional Officer   *New Mexico Women's Correctional Facility*   *Grants, New Mexico*

Zaira Tena is employed by Corrections Corporation of America (CCA) as a correctional officer at the New Mexico Women's Correctional Facility in Grants, New Mexico. She started working there 16 months ago. This is Zaira's first job in corrections. Zaira was attracted to CCA and a career in corrections because of the benefits that CCA offered her.

Zaira attended Laramie County Community College in Laramie, Wyoming, before joining CCA. The company provided additional training in interpersonal communication, special-needs inmates, crisis intervention, infectious diseases, suicide prevention, first aid, CPR, and firearms, giving her the skills she needs to ensure the health, welfare, and safety of prison employees and inmates. Since Zaira especially enjoys recreation, she coordinates the institution's recreation activities.

Zaira's enthusiasm for her own career and professional development shows in her advice to people thinking about a career in corrections. Wisely, Zaira is taking her own advice. She plans to stay in corrections and hopes one day soon to become assistant shift commander at the Grants women's facility.

> " I like my job. I like working with people. What I learned and what I'd tell someone is, be very professional, firm, fair, and consistent at all times, and be able to work under a lot of pressure. "

---

discretionary power of judges, inconsistency and inequality in sentencing, the use of personal connections to obtain sentencing reductions, and the imposition of capital punishment for minor offenses.

Beccaria proposed that punishment could be justified only if it was imposed to defend the social contract—the tacit allegiance that individuals owe their society and the obligations of government to individuals. It is the social contract, said Beccaria, that gives society the right to punish its members.

Beccaria also argued that punishment should be swift, since swift punishment offers the greatest deterrence. When punishment quickly follows a crime, said Beccaria, the ideas of crime and punishment are more closely associated in a person's mind. He also suggested that the link between crime and punishment would be stronger if the punishment somehow related to the crime.

Finally, said Beccaria, punishments should not be unnecessarily severe. The severity of punishment, he argued, should be proportional to the degree of social damage caused by the crime. Treason, Beccaria said, is the worst crime, since it most harms the social contract. Below treason, Beccaria listed crimes in order of declining severity, including violence against a person or his property, public disruption, and crimes against property. Crimes against property, he said, should be punished by fines.

When his essay was translated into French and English, Beccaria became famous throughout much of Europe. Philosophers of the time hailed his ideas, and several European rulers vowed to follow his lead in the reform of their justice systems.

JEREMY BENTHAM

Philosopher and jurist Jeremy Bentham (1748–1832) was born in London. As a young child, he was considered a prodigy, having been found, at the age of two, sitting at his father's desk reading a multivolume history of

England.[43] He began to study Latin at the age of three. When Bentham was 12, his father, a wealthy attorney, sent him to Queen's College, Oxford, hoping that he would enter the field of law.

After attending lectures by the leading legal scholar of the day, Sir William Blackstone (1723–1780), young Bentham became disillusioned with the law. Instead of practicing law, he decided to criticize it, and he spent the rest of his life analyzing the legal practices of the day, writing about them, and suggesting improvements.

Bentham advocated **utilitarianism,** the principle that the highest objective of public policy is the greatest happiness for the largest number of people. Utilitarianism provided the starting point for Bentham's social analysis, in which he tried to measure the usefulness of existing institutions, practices, and beliefs against a common standard. Bentham believed that human behavior is determined largely by the amount of pleasure or pain associated with a given activity. Hence, he suggested, the purpose of law should be to make socially undesirable activities painful enough to keep people from engaging in them. In this way, said Bentham, "good" can be achieved

Bentham's idea, that people are motivated by pleasure and pain and that the proper amount of punishment can deter crime, became known as **hedonistic calculus.** Bentham's hedonistic calculus made four assumptions:

1. People by nature choose pleasure and avoid pain.
2. Each individual, either consciously or intuitively, calculates the degree of pleasure or pain to be derived from a given course of action.
3. Lawmakers can determine the degree of punishment necessary to deter criminal behavior.
4. Such punishment can be effectively and rationally built into a system of criminal sentencing.

Bentham is also known as the inventor of the *panopticon* (from a Greek word meaning "all-seeing")—a type of prison he proposed building in England as early as 1787. The panopticon was intended to put utilitarian ideas to work in the field of penology.

Key to the panopticon was its unique architecture, which consisted of a circular, tiered design with a glass roof and with a window on the outside wall of each cell.[44] The design made it easy for prison staff, in a tower in the center of the structure, to observe each cell (and its occupants). Within the wheel-like structure, walls separated the cells to prevent any communication between prisoners. Speaking tubes linked cells with the observation platform so that officers could listen to inmates.

The panopticon, also called an *inspection house,* was intended to be a progressive and humanitarian penitentiary. Bentham thought of it as a social experiment. The design was touted as being consistent with the ideals of utilitarianism because only a few officers would be subject to the risks and unpleasantness of the inspection role, while many prisoners would benefit from this enlightened means of institutional management.

After years of personally promoting the concept, Bentham saw his idea for an innovative penitentiary die. The panopticon was never built in England, and in 1820 government officials formally disavowed it. The concept may have fallen victim to the growing emphasis on transportation, which

utilitarianism

The principle that the highest objective of public policy is the greatest happiness for the largest number of people.

hedonistic calculus

The idea that people are motivated by pleasure and pain and that the proper amount of punishment can deter crime.

Jeremy Bentham (1748–1832), an English philosopher and social reformer, spent his life trying to reform the law. His innovative plan for a prison, called the *panopticon,* consisted of a huge structure covered by a glass roof. A central tower allowed guards to see into the cells, which were arranged in a circle. Although the British government did not use Bentham's plan, several U.S. prisons did, including one in Stateville, Illinois. What is the name given to Bentham's principle that the highest object of public policy is the greatest happiness for the greatest number of people?

delayed all prison construction in England. Another significant factor in the demise of the panopticon ideal, however, was Bentham's insistence that panopticons be built near cities to deter crime among the general population. Although a number of sites were chosen for construction, nearby residents always protested plans to build any sort of prison in their neighborhoods. Despite Bentham's failure ever to construct a facility completely true to his panopticon plan, he will always be remembered for his idea that order and reform could be achieved in a prison through architectural design.

SIR SAMUEL ROMILLY

Sir Samuel Romilly (1757–1818) was an English legal reformer who worked ceaselessly to lessen the severity of existing criminal law in his home country. Romilly, once described as "the flower of the English reform movement,"[45] attacked laws that authorized capital punishment for a host of minor felonies and misdemeanors.

Romilly's dedication to his cause drew the admiration from a number of reformers. M. Dumont, once described as "the leading orator of the French Revolution," said of Romilly, "[He is] always tranquil and orderly yet has an incessant activity. He never loses a minute; he applies all his mind to what he is about. Like the hand of three watches, he never stops. . . ."[46] Another contemporary said of Romilly that "in the House of Commons he looked like Apollo surrounded by crowds of satyrs and goats. . . . This man

Eye On Corrections™

Predictions for Corrections in the 21st Century: A Compilation of Thoughts, Trends, and Predictions for the Corrections Industry

By Michelle Gaseau

As we enter the next century, The Corrections Connection polled leaders from several aspects of corrections to find out where the profession is headed, where the challenges lie, and what workers in the field should pay attention to in the coming years, from staffing issues to the growth of professionalism to changes in how society looks at punishment. What follows are excerpts from some of their feedback.

BILL KISSEL, HEALTH DIRECTOR, GEORGIA DEPARTMENT OF CORRECTIONS

Our biggest challenges are going to be the challenges that any organization or agency that has a health care responsibility will face: handling the budgetary impact of scientific advancements especially in the area of pharmaceuticals, mental health medications, and Hepatitis C. As these scientific advancements, which are outstanding, hit us, we in correctional health care are then forced to figure out how to pay for that. It's a good guesstimate that it will only continue as new treatments become the community standard. What we're having to do is determine whether they are community standard.

Then, of course, we'll be challenged with an older population that we'll face because of mandatory sentencing. We've established within our medical prison a chronic care unit here. We have consolidated our inmates system-wide who frequently would have to be sent to a free world hospital.

For the future, in Georgia our goal is to better integrate folks into the community, especially for mental health, Hepatitis C, and HIV. We're working with other agencies so when folks are on discharge or probation in Georgia. We can connect them to resources. We're trying to do that from a vocational perspective as well.

Then of course we'll be challenged with recruiting qualified health care professionals in physical, mental, and dental health. With a strong economy people don't want to work in prisons. My vision would be we develop partnerships with other agencies and teaching facilities where we increase opportunities for students to train in the prison environment. Hopefully some would gain interest in working in this environment.

DAVID PARRISH, COMMANDER, HILLSBOROUGH, FLORIDA, COUNTY SHERIFF'S DEPARTMENT

The most significant thing is the continuing difficulty in hiring and keeping qualified people. There's an old saying that "If only I had the right staff I could run a good prison in an old red barn." We're building lots of new facilities nationwide but if we don't have the staff we'll be in serious trouble.

I'm seeing a trend in some jurisdictions where the solution to recruiting difficulties is to lower standards. We've worked so hard to improve standards for selection and employment in this profession, I can't see going backwards. I chaired the American Jail Association's Jail Manager Certification process, and I always thought that was a significant step. That was started for jails, and now the American Correctional Association is developing a similar program for correctional staff working in prisons primarily.

If you don't set some standards for yourself no one else will appreciate that you are professional.

BRIAN DAWE, OFFICER, CORRECTIONS USA

One of the first things we'll see is the end of prison privatization as it relates to medium and maximum security facilities. It has become pretty evident they don't save money, and they cause more problems than anything else.

We're also going to need to see some changes in the level of training and staffing numbers. We're going to need to see mandatory staffing principles.

These inmates have all day long to think up schemes. They deal nationally and internationally. Intelligence has to be shared, and it all comes down to training. We're required by law that part of our training is in firearms, we should have it, but it's rare that we use it. With physical defense [tactics], we get that once, but we see it every day.

One thing we will have to see in the system is alternative sentencing programs. We cannot continue to have some of these individuals behind the walls. There are a great number who would be better served and we would be better served by them being in community resource centers.

Also, there will be changes in laws and eventually a turn back of mandatory sentencing. There's a movement among the judiciary to restore some of the decision-making process to them. That's where you need the discretion back in the process. There has to be discretion. You can't build your way out of a crime problem.

ART LEONARDO, FORMER WARDEN, GREEN CORRECTIONAL INSTITUTION, NEW YORK STATE, AND CORRECTIONS CONSULTANT

In my opinion, the most important task we face in the year 2000 is to pay more attention to the men and women who work in the correctional field. The pay in most jurisdictions is still very poor; we constantly lose good people to better status and higher benefits. Training in the field is very much improved, but we can't rest on our laurels. We all need to work on the public, legislative, and governmental perception of our workforce. They are good people doing a tough job.

Continued on page 68

Not adequately compensating our people leads to constant turnover, poor security and higher real costs. Unions, wardens, commissioners, professional organizations all need to work together to improve the overall status of our people.

In corrections you need experienced people and you need something to keep them working. It's not the easiest job in the world. My experience has been in New York where the pay and the benefits are good. Technology is fine, but people are the ones who run all of that, and consistent people are very important.

it was who led the fight to get the gentleness of the English character expressed in its laws."[47]

Romilly entered Parliament in 1806, and in 1810 he proposed a reexamination of the Penitentiary Act of 1779. As a result, the government appointed the Holford Committee to examine issues associated with penal reform. Until his early death in 1818, Romilly fought to reduce the number of English capital crimes. He succeeded in getting passed a bill abolishing the death penalty in cases of "private stealing from the person," and he won the abolition of the death penalty in cases of soldiers and sailors found absent without leave. At the time of his death, 200 offenses were still punishable by sentence of death. The movement he began, however, continued to flower. By 1840 the number of capital crimes in England had been reduced to 14, and by 1861 the number fell to 4 (treason, murder, piracy, and setting fire to arsenals).

Romilly's work and the results it produced led others to recognize the need for alternatives to capital punishment as a means of dealing with the large majority of offenders.

SIR ROBERT PEEL

Sir Robert Peel (1788–1850) was a British Parliamentary leader bent on seeing the ideas of Romilly, Bentham, and others incorporated into English law. Peel is best known in the history of criminal justice for establishing a police force that influenced the development of policing throughout much of the rest of the world. His force, the London Metropolitan Police, became known as the Met.

Prior to Peel's time, agents of law enforcement often meted out "justice" as they saw fit, sometimes apprehending the offender and punishing him or her on the spot. Peel and other legal reformers of the day worked to identify the fundamental function of the police as the investigation of crime and the apprehension of criminals. Peel insisted that the police should be responsible for investigation and arrest only, while the trial, defense, and conviction phase of the justice process should reside entirely in the hands of another body, the judiciary.[48] Punishment, he said, should not be imposed by the police, but by specialists in the field of penology. In Peel's words, it is necessary for the police "to recognize always the need for strict adherence to police executive functions and to refrain from even seeming to usurp the powers of the judiciary or avenging individuals or the state and of authoritatively judging guilt and punishing the guilty."

In effect, while working to formalize police administration, Peel pointed out the need for other specialists in the administration of justice such as attorneys, magistrates, and correctional personnel. Peel was also primarily responsible for legislation, Peel's Gaol Act of 1823, aimed at reforming British jails. The Gaol Act required that men and women be segregated while in jail and mandated the supervision of female prisoners by female correctional personnel.[49]

ELIZABETH FRY

Elizabeth Fry (1780–1845), a strict Quaker committed to religious and philanthropic work, campaigned during the early 1800s to "expose the plight of women in prison and to promote better conditions for them."[50]

While most Enlightenment era thinkers had been influenced by a belief in utilitarian principles, Fry's reformist activities grew out of her religious faith.

Fry had been strongly influenced by a delegation of American Quakers who visited London's notorious Newgate jail in 1813. Their report said that they had been horrified to find "blaspheming, fighting, dram-drinking, half-naked women," occupying part of the facility. A few months later, Fry visited the jail herself and found that women were being held in what she described as "filthy" conditions. From then on Fry campaigned for reform of the conditions under which women were confined, arguing that women should be treated "tenderly" and "with gentleness and sympathy so that they would submit cheerfully to the rules and cooperate willingly in their own reform."[51]

Mary Belle Harris (1874–1957), the first warden of the Federal Institution for Women at Alderson, West Virginia. What historical role have women played in the development of the field of corrections?

Fry formed the Ladies Association for the Reformation of Female Prisoners in Newgate and, later, the British Ladies Society for the Reformation of Female Prisoners. Fry's influence was also felt in the United States where concerned women banded together under the banner of prison reform in order to draw attention to the welfare of women prisoners.

Fry and her followers, including American feminist leader Dorothea Dix, believed that women are more likely than men to change and that appeals "to the heart" would be more effective with women offenders than with men. In her 1825 publication, *Observations on the Siting, Superintendence, and Government of Female Prisoners*, Fry provided concrete ideas on how women's prisons should be run. "Especially important for women, "she argued," were cleanliness, plain decent clothing, and warm, orderly surroundings."[52]

MARY BELLE HARRIS

Another American woman reformer who was influenced by Fry was Mary Belle Harris (1874–1957). Harris, who was born in Pennsylvania, eventually became the first warden of the Federal Institution for Women in Alderson, West Virginia, when it opened in 1927. Harris had turned to a career in corrections only after already having worked as a teacher, social worker, and archaeologist.

Harris came to Alderson after serving as superintendent of the Women's Workhouse on Blackwell Island (New York), as superintendent of the State Reformatory for Women at Clinton, New Jersey, and as assistant director of the section on Reformatories and Detention Homes for the U.S. War Department.

Known as a vocal advocate of correctional reforms and as an avid supporter of the reformation ideal, Harris believed that reformation and not punishment should be the primary

▶ Throughout history, reformers have made significant contributions to the corrections field. What current reform movement would you champion? What obstacles do you expect to encounter? For more information go to Ethical Dilemma 2-3 at http://www.mhhe.com/schmalleger2.

Ethical Dilemma

focus of most correctional programs and institutions. Harris also believed that the criminality of women was largely the result of their social roles and specifically their economic dependency upon men. As a result, Harris advocated training programs that would permit women prisoners to become financially independent upon release. At Alderson, Harris oversaw the development of programs designed to break the cycle of dependency. Her work became widely known and served as a model for women's prisons throughout the nation.

Before retiring in 1941, Harris wrote a number of books describing her experiences in corrections. Among them are *I Knew Them in Prison* (1936) and *The Pathway of Mattie Howard to and from Prison: The Story of the Regeneration of an Ex-Convict and Gangster Woman* (1937).

SUMMARY

1 ▶ Corporal, or physical, punishments were the most common response to crime for centuries before criminals began to be incarcerated.

2 ▶ Criminal punishments of the past generally consisted of flogging, branding, mutilation, exile, transportation, and public humiliation.

3 ▶ Many reformers based their ideas on Enlightenment principles, including the use of reason and deductive logic to solve problems. They laid the groundwork for the use of imprisonment as an alternative to traditional punishments.

4 ▶ Beginning in the mid-1700s, a number of correctional reformers fought the use of corporal punishments and sought to introduce more humane forms of punishment. Among those reformers were Cesare Beccaria, Jeremy Bentham, and John Howard.

KEY TERMS

corporal punishments, *p. 42*
bridewell, *p. 53*
utilitarianism, *p. 60*
hedonistic calculus, *p. 60*

QUESTIONS FOR REVIEW

1. What are corporal punishments? What has been the purpose of corporal punishments throughout history?

2. Which ancient civilization provided the earliest evidence that physical punishment is part of Western society tradition?

3. What were the Twelve Tables?

4. List and describe at least four corporal punishments used in the past for criminal offenders.

5. What were *theatrical punishments?*

6. What role did torture play in the application of corporal punishments? How was the use of torture justified?

7. What purpose did the branding of criminals serve?

8. What two important thinkers discussed in this chapter adapted principles born of the Enlightenment and applied them to the field of law and corrections? Describe the contributions each made to the field.

9. What was the original intent of a 1597 English law authorizing transportation of criminals to the New World?

10. What factors led to the abolition of transportation to Australia?

11. Describe the house-of-correction movement. How did it develop? What kinds of "offenders" were housed in such institutions?

12. What two elements contributed to the development of modern prisons?

THINKING CRITICALLY ABOUT CORRECTIONS

▶ ▶ ▶ Corporal Punishment

In 1994 Michael Fay, an American teenager convicted of spray painting parked cars, was flogged in Singapore. The flogging (called *caning* because it was done with a bamboo rod) sparked an international outcry from opponents of corporal punishment. In this country, however, it also led to a rebirth of interest in physical punishments—especially for teenagers and vandals.

The last official flogging of a criminal offender in the United States took place in Delaware on June 16, 1952, when a burglar was tied to a whipping post in the state's central prison and was given 20 lashes. Since then, no sentencing authority in this country has imposed whipping as a criminal punishment, and most jurisdictions have removed all corporal punishments from their statutes. Amnesty International, however, reports that whipping is still in use in parts of the world for certain kinds of prisoners.

After the Fay flogging, lawmakers in eight states introduced legislation to institute whipping or paddling as a criminal sanction. Mississippi legislators proposed paddling graffitists and petty thieves, Tennessee lawmakers considered punishing vandals and burglars by public caning on courthouse steps, the New Mexico Senate Judiciary Committee examined the feasibility of

caning graffiti vandals, and Louisiana looked into the possibility of ordering parents (or a correctional officer if the parents refused) to spank their children in judicial chambers. So far, none of the proposals has become law.

1. Would a return to corporal punishments, in the form of whipping or paddling, be justified for some offenders? Why or why not?

2. Might paddling be appropriate for some juvenile offenders? Why or why not?

3. Do you think that any state legislatures will eventually pass legislation permitting the paddling or whipping of criminal offenders? Why or why not?

▶ ▶ ▶ Capital Punishment

Proponents frequently cite deterrence as a benefit of the death penalty. Some studies refute this contention. When confronted with such studies, proponents sometimes respond that execution "will definitely deter the executed offender." They also argue that death is the only thing that the offender really "deserves."

1. How would you respond to proponents' first argument?

2. How would you respond to proponents' second argument?

REVIEW & APPLICATIONS

ON-THE-JOB DECISION MAKING

▶ ▶ ▶ **Counseling**

You are a parole officer for the state corrections system. You are so burdened with paperwork that you rarely get out of the office to see any of your 200 clients—even though you are supposed to make regular home visits.

While you are shuffling papers one day, one of your clients, Bob Boynton, knocks at your door. It is time for him to make his monthly report. You tell him to have a seat, and you ask him the usual questions: "Have you been in trouble with the law since I saw you last?" "Are you still working?" "Are you paying your bills on time?"

Before you finish the interview, Boynton says, "You know, I'm never going to get anywhere this way. I need a better education. The time I spent in prison was wasted. They didn't teach me anything. I need to learn a skill so that I can make more money. If I can't earn better money I won't be able to pay my bills—and I'm afraid that I'll be tempted to get into the drug business again. I don't want to do that!"

You tell Boynton that there are a number of training schools in the area that can teach him a skill. Some of the computer classes offered at the local community college, you've heard, can lead to jobs paying decent wages. Boynton says, "I don't have a high school diploma. I can't get into the college. I'll never learn computers. I'm just too old. Besides, I need to work with my hands."

You go through the list of schools and training centers in the area, but Boynton raises an objection to each one. You sense that Boynton is trying to transfer responsibility for his success or failure to you. What should you do to get him to take responsibility for himself, yet provide support and guidance for his efforts?

▶ ▶ ▶ **Dispute Resolution**

As a newly assigned assistant warden, you are responsible for discipline within your correctional facility. During your initial meeting with the warden, he said that your predecessor had a well-earned reputation among the inmate population as one who unfailingly sided with the correctional staff in all disputes between staff and inmates, no matter how egregious the staff member's behavior. Warden Cowen specifically asked you to establish yourself as a fair and impartial arbiter so as to reduce inmate concerns about injustice in dispute resolution.

An incident on your second day on the job presents you with a dilemma that even Solomon might be at a loss to resolve. Correctional Officer Tim Dashe is a six-year veteran with absolutely no record of abusive behavior toward inmates. In fact, during your transitional briefing into this job, your predecessor cited Dashe as one of the stalwarts on your staff, particularly praising his professionalism, maturity, good judgment, and reliability.

Inmate Deon Kussick has been incarcerated for 13 years without a single blemish on his record. Quiet, mature, and intelligent, Kussick is considered one of the "go-to" guys when the administration needs cooperation from the prisoners to resolve a problem.

Inexplicably, Dashe and Kussick get into a fight. A real knock-down-drag-out, the fight is now the buzz of conversation among both the prisoner population and the correctional staff. Not surprisingly, tension is rising between the prisoners and the staff as both elements back "their" man and claim that the other was responsible for the fight.

While it is clear that something is amiss, both Dashe and Kussick are closemouthed about the reason or reasons behind the fight. Their vague explanations are of the "It was just one of those things" variety. Obviously, though, there is a significant point of contention between the two men that, unless resolved, might lead to another confrontation. You can't resolve it, however, if you can't figure out what it is.

For you, the situation is particularly delicate, and the stakes are high. The correctional staff is waiting to see if you will back their fellow officer, the inmates are watching to see if you will be impartial in your handling of the incident, and the warden is evaluating your ability to handle a crisis. What you do will establish your reputation for loyalty (among the staff) and fairness (among the inmates) and serve as an indicator (to the warden) of your reliability and judgment.

One of the old-timers among the inmates sidled up a few minutes ago and, with a casual-

ness that belied his intense interest, asked this simple question: "Watcha gonna do, chief?"

1. What are you going to do?
2. Why?

CORRECTIONS ON THE WEB

▶ ▶ ▶ Prison History

Visit the Website of the British Home Office and read about the history of prisons in Britain (http://www.homeoffice.gov.uk/docs/prishist.html). Learn how British prisons developed during the 1800s and 1900s. Be sure to read about the Gladstone and Mountbatten Reports, the May Inquiry, and the development of the Borstal system.

▶ ▶ ▶ The Bentham Project

Visit the Bentham Project Website (http://www.ucl.ac.uk/Bentham-Project) and read about Jeremy Bentham and his panopticon. Be sure to click on "The Auto-Icon" link to learn about the preservation and display of Bentham's physical remains into the present day.

REVIEW & APPLICATIONS

“ We will not punish a man because he hath offended, but that he may offend no more; nor does punishment ever look to the past, but to the future; for it is not the result of a passion, but that the same thing be guarded against in time to come.

—Seneca, the younger, Roman Philosopher, 3 B.C.–A.D. 65 ”

3

CHAPTER

Sentencing: To Punish or to Reform?

▶ CHAPTER OBJECTIVES

After completing this chapter you should be able to do the following:

1. Describe sentencing philosophy and identify the central purpose of criminal punishment.

2. Name the six goals of criminal sentencing.

3. List and explain the sentencing options in general use today.

4. Explain what a model of criminal sentencing is and identify models in use today.

5. Describe three-strikes laws and their impact on the correctional system.

6. Identify and explain some major issues related to fair sentencing.

▶ ▶ **On June 7, 2002, a jury** of six women and six men found 41-year-old Michael Skakel guilty of the October 31, 1975, murder of his childhood neighbor, Martha Moxley.[1] Skakel was convicted of beating Moxley to death with his mother's golf club in a fit of sexual rage. Both were 15 years old at the time of the crime.

Although rumors had long circulated about Skakel's involvement in Moxley's murder, his conviction came 26 years after her death. Some attributed the long delay to police deference because Skakel is a cousin of the politically powerful Kennedy clan. After he was convicted, Skakel faced Judge John F. Kavanewski Jr., who sentenced him to 20 years to life in prison. By following the requirements of Connecticut's 1975 criminal law—the law that was in place at the time the crime was committed—Skakel's sentencing highlighted the changes in sentencing practices that have occurred over the past quarter century throughout much of the United States. Under that law, Judge Kavanewski could have chosen a sentence of between 10 years to life in prison; current law would have required a sentence of at least 25 years.[2]

The Skakel case also highlights the role of sentencing in the justice process. **Sentencing** is a court's imposition of a penalty on a convicted offender. A **sentence** is the penalty imposed.

This chapter concerns itself with the nature, history, purpose, and philosophy of criminal sentencing. One of the most crucial issues surrounding sentencing is whether to punish or to reform. The punish-or-reform debate has a long history and continues to concern many people today. We turn now to an examination of the history of sentencing philosophy.

sentencing
The imposition of a criminal sanction by a sentencing authority, such as a judge.

sentence
The penalty a court imposes on a person convicted of a crime.

Michael Skakel (left) and Martha Moxley. In 2002 Skakel, 41, was found guilty of beating Moxley to death in 1975—when both were 15 years old. Should offenders be held responsible for crimes they committed 25 years earlier?

Sentencing: Philosophy and Goals

PHILOSOPHY OF CRIMINAL SENTENCING

Western society has a long tradition of punishing criminal offenders. Historically, offenders were banished, exiled, killed, or tortured. Corporal, or physical, punishments became common during the Middle Ages, replacing executions as the preferred penalty. Physical punishments such as flogging and mutilation, though severe in themselves, deterred rampant use of the death penalty. Eventually, as we shall see in later chapters, imprisonment and a variety of other sentencing alternatives replaced corporal punishments as criminal sanctions.

Contemporary sentencing of offenders is still intimately associated with historical notions of punishment. Crimes are frequently seen as *deserving* of punishment. We often hear it said that the criminal must "pay a debt to society" or that "criminals deserve to be punished." John Conrad puts it another way: "The punishment of the criminal is the collective reaction of the community to the wrong that has been done."[3] Conrad goes on to say, "It is the offender's lot to be punished."

Philosophers have long debated *why* a wrongful act should be punished. Many social scientists suggest that criminal punishment maintains and defends the **social order.** By threatening potential law violators and by making the lives of violators uncomfortable, they say, punishments reduce the likelihood of future or continued criminal behavior.

Still, one might ask, instead of punishing offenders, why not offer them psychological treatment or educate them so that they are less prone to future law violation? The answer to this question is far from clear. Although criminal sentencing today has a variety of goals, and educational and treatment programs are more common now in corrections, punishment still takes center stage in society's view. Some writers, such as Conrad, have suggested that society will always *need* to punish criminals because punishment is a natural response to those who break social taboos.[4] Others disagree, arguing that an enlightened society will choose instead to reform lawbreakers through humanitarian means.

social order

The smooth functioning of social institutions, the existence of positive and productive relations among individual members of society, and the orderly functioning of society as a whole.

THE GOALS OF SENTENCING

In April 1999, 22-year-old Nushawn Williams was sentenced to 4 to 12 years in prison for statutory rape and two counts of reckless endangerment. Williams, a convicted drug dealer from Chautauqua County, New York, had been accused of infecting as many as 103 teenage girls and young women with the AIDS virus in a series of drugs-for-sex encounters.[5] At trial, prosecutors were able to show that Williams had sex with the women while knowing he was HIV positive. Williams, who kept a journal of his many "conquests," was originally charged with one count of reckless endangerment for each sexual encounter and with first-degree assault for each partner who subsequently became infected. The statutory rape conviction stemmed from his having had sex with a 13-year-old girl who later tested positive for the AIDS virus. During trial, prosecutor James Subjack told jurors, "It takes an individual with no regard for human life to do something like this." Denied parole in late 2001, Williams is still in a New York prison as this book goes to press.[6]

A crowded city street. Many social scientists say that criminal punishments help maintain social order. What would a society without order be like?

revenge

Punishment as vengeance. An emotional response to real or imagined injury or insult.

retribution

A sentencing goal that involves retaliation against a criminal perpetrator.

just deserts

Punishment deserved. A just-deserts perspective on criminal sentencing holds that criminal offenders are morally blameworthy and are therefore *deserving* of punishment.

The Williams case demonstrates a crucial component of contemporary sentencing philosophy: that people must be held accountable for their actions and for the harm they cause. From this perspective, the purpose of the criminal justice system is to identify persons who have acted in intentionally harmful ways and (where a law is in place) to hold them accountable for their actions by imposing sanctions. Seen this way, our justice system is primarily an instrument of retribution.

Sentencing, however, also has a variety of other purposes. As shown in Table 3–1, the goals of sentencing are (1) revenge, (2) retribution, (3) desert (or the fact of deserving punishment), (4) deterrence, (5) incapacitation, (6) rehabilitation or reformation, and (7) restoration.

Revenge   One of the earliest goals of criminal sentencing was revenge. **Revenge** can be described as both an emotion and as an act in response to victimization. Victims sometimes feel as though an injury or insult requires punishment in return. When they act on that feeling, they have taken revenge.

While we think of vengeance as a primitive need, it can still play an important role in contemporary societies and even in modern justice systems. The "tit-for-tat" exchange of terrorist attacks for military incursions between the Palestinians and Israelis that is taking place as this book goes to press is one example of a highly charged emotional situation where calls for revenge seem to play an important—and sometimes guiding—role. Similarly, had the terrorists who perpetrated the 9/11 attacks been captured (instead of dying in the suicide attacks), there can be but little doubt that many Americans would have sought revenge on the perpetrators through our justice system.

Retribution   **Retribution** involves the payment of a debt to both the victim and society and, thus, atonement for a person's offense. Historically, retribution was couched in terms of "getting even," and it has sometimes been explained as "an eye for an eye, and a tooth for a tooth." *Retribution* literally means "paying back" the offender for what he or she has done. Retribution is predicated on the notion that victims are *entitled* to reprisal.

Because social order suffers when a crime occurs, society is also a victim. Hence, retribution, in a very fundamental way, expresses society's disapproval of criminal behavior and demands the payment of a debt to society. It is not always easy to determine just how much punishment is enough to ensure the debt is paid.

Desert   Retribution is supported by many sentencing schemes today—although the concept is now often couched in terms of **just deserts** even though there is a difference between retribution and desert. The concept of just deserts deemphasizes the emotional component of revenge by claiming that criminal acts are *deserving* of punishment, that offenders are *morally blameworthy,* and that they must be punished. In this way, desert restores the moral balance to a society wronged by crime.

TABLE 3–1	Goals of Criminal Sentencing
Goal	**Rationale**
Revenge	Punishment is equated with vengeance and involves an emotional response to criminal victimization.
Retribution	Punishment involves a "settling of scores" for both society and the victim. Victims are entitled to "get even."
Desert	Offenders are morally blameworthy and deserving of punishment. Punishment restores the moral balance disrupted by crime.
Deterrence	Punishment will prevent future wrongdoing by the offender and by others. Punishment must outweigh the benefits gained by wrongdoing.
Incapacitation	Some wrongdoers cannot be changed and need to be segregated from society. Society has the responsibility to protect law-abiding citizens from those whose behavior cannot be controlled.
Rehabilitation or Reformation	Society needs to help offenders learn how to behave appropriately. Without learning acceptable behavior patterns, offenders will not be able to behave appropriately.
Restoration	Crime is primarily an offense against human relationships and secondarily a violation of a law. All those who suffered because of a crime should be restored to their previous sense of well-being.

Andrew von Hirsch, who identified the rationales underlying criminal punishment, says that when someone "infringes the rights of others . . . he deserves blame [and that is why] the sanctioning authority is entitled to choose a response that expresses moral disapproval: namely, punishment."[7] Hence, from a desert point of view, justice *requires* that punishments be imposed on criminal law violators.

Of all the purposes of punishment that are discussed here, only retribution and desert are past oriented. That is, they examine what has already occurred (the crime) in an effort to determine the appropriate sentencing response.

Deterrence   A third goal of criminal sentencing is **deterrence**. Deterrence is the discouragement or prevention of crimes similar to the one for which an offender is being sentenced. Unlike retribution and desert, deterrence is future oriented in that it seeks to prevent crimes from occurring. Two forms of deterrence can be identified: specific and general.

Specific deterrence is the deterrence of the individual being punished from committing additional crimes. Long ago, specific deterrence was achieved through corporal punishments that maimed offenders in ways that precluded their ability to commit similar crimes in the future. Spies

deterrence

The discouragement or prevention of crimes through the fear of punishment.

specific deterrence

The deterrence of the individual being punished from committing additional crimes.

had their eyes gouged out and their tongues removed, rapists were castrated, thieves had their fingers or hands cut off, and so on. Even today, in some countries that follow a strict Islamic code, the hands of habitual thieves are cut off as a form of corporal punishment.

general deterrence

The use of the example of individual punishment to dissuade others from committing crimes.

General deterrence occurs when the punishment of an individual serves as an example to others who might be thinking of committing a crime—thereby dissuading them from their planned course of action. The **pleasure-pain principle**, which is central to modern discussions of general deterrence, holds that actions are motivated primarily by the desire to experience pleasure and avoid pain. According to this principle, the threat of loss to anyone convicted of a crime should outweigh the potential pleasure to be gained by committing the crime.

pleasure-pain principle

The idea that actions are motivated primarily by a desire to experience pleasure and avoid pain.

For punishment to be effective as a deterrent, it must be relatively certain, swiftly applied, and sufficiently severe. *Certainty, swiftness,* and *severity* of punishment are not always easy to achieve. The crime funnel,

> For punishment to be effective as a deterrent, it must be relatively certain, swiftly applied, and sufficiently severe.

described in Chapter 1, demonstrates that most offenses do not end in arrest, and most arrests do not end in incarceration. Although it may not be easy for all offenders to get away with crime, the likelihood that any individual offender will be arrested, successfully prosecuted, and then punished is far smaller than deterrence advocates would like it to be. When an arrest does occur, an offender is typically released on bail, and, because of an overcrowded court system, the trial, if any, may not happen until a year or so later. Moreover, although the severity of punishments has increased in recent years, modern punishments are rarely as severe as those of earlier centuries. Arguments over just how much punishment is enough to deter further violations of the criminal law rarely lead to any clear conclusion.

incapacitation

The use of imprisonment or other means to reduce an offender's capability to commit future offenses.

Incapacitation   Many believe that the huge increase in the number of correctional clients has helped lower the crime rate by incapacitating more criminals. Many of these criminals are behind bars, and others are on supervised regimens of probation and parole. **Incapacitation** restrains offenders from committing additional crimes by isolating them from free society. A recent report by the National Center for Policy Analysis, for example, observed that a "major reason for [the] reduction in crime is that crime has become more costly to the perpetrators. The likelihood of going to prison for committing any type of major crime has increased substantially."[8]

The report claims that "the best overall measure of the potential cost to a criminal of committing crimes is *expected punishment.*" Expected punishment, says the report, "is the number of days in prison a criminal can expect to serve for committing a crime." The center calculated expected punishment by multiplying the median sentence imposed for each crime by the probabilities of being apprehended, prosecuted, convicted, and sentenced. Crime rates are declining, says the report, because expected prison stays are significantly longer today than two decades ago for every category of serious crime.

According to the center, "Between 1980 and 1995, expected punishment more than doubled for murder and nearly tripled for rape. It increased by about three-fourths for burglary and larceny/theft and increased 60 percent for motor vehicle theft."

Well, here I am, about two and one-half years into my life sentence. The worst part so far for me has been the loneliness. I'm close to 3,000 miles away from my family. I really don't have anyone right now. I think my family is still digesting the fact that I'm in prison. I don't hear from them very often.

With all the time I have alone in my cell, my brain works overtime. I think about all the people I've hurt, whether physically, emotionally, or financially. I think about my crime every day of my life. I took a human life. What makes a man do that? I don't really know. All I can remember is the anger I felt and the hurt feelings. I can remember my heart hurting so bad that I couldn't function normally anymore. I cried all the time and I couldn't eat or sleep. At first it was all jealousy and then it was anger and pain. I guess it all came to a head that night. I had never felt that much rage before in my life. When it was over, I was holding a lifeless body in my arms. I couldn't speak or move. All I could feel was my soul leaving my body. It was an emptiness that I hope I never feel again. It was like I too had died that night.

I remember the day I was sentenced like it was yesterday. I knew ahead of time what I was getting, but it didn't make it any easier. The tears, the stares, the looks, and the glares were all directed in court from people who were once my friends. I was sentenced to life so I couldn't hurt anyone else ever again (or at least I thought so). I called home that afternoon to let my family know that it was all over and that I was going down for life. My father told me that my mom had tried to kill herself by putting a .38 in her mouth. By a miracle of God, my dad had called home at that very moment and talked her out of it. She was so depressed about me, plus she was addicted to painkillers because she had so many back operations. I wanted so much to comfort her, but I couldn't. I didn't know how.

I remember the time I saw my father cry. It was a day I'll never forget. It was a day or two after I was arrested and a week before I was extradited to Arizona when he came to visit me in the county jail in Pennsylvania. I was so nervous. We hadn't talked in years. He didn't like me much at all because I had disappointed him so many times over the years. I couldn't blame him. I was a failure in his eyes as well as mine. I walked down the hallway to where my father was sitting. I sat down in a chair and looked at him through the glass that separated us. He looked so broken and so sad. We picked up the phones and started to talk. The tears just started to run down his face. I had a lump in my throat so that I couldn't swallow. My heart was bleeding inside and the pain was unbearable to see a rock of a man crumble before me because of what I had done. I wanted to end my life right there. My father didn't deserve what I was putting him through. He tried so hard to be a good father. He was strict but fair. I know it wasn't easy for him. I was his stepson. All through my childhood, he never treated me like less than his own son. As I looked into my father's eyes, I wished that he could hug me and I could cry too.

I guess I should thank God for letting me live for 31 years. I tried to destroy myself so many times with drugs, alcohol, and suicide attempts. In a way, prison has saved my life. I would have died at a young age from drugs or alcohol, or maybe the suicide attempts would have worked sooner or later. I'm just thankful I was able to overcome the demons in my life. I'm a better person now. I'm responsible, caring, and able to be kind. I guess that's all part of growing up, and that's what I've done the past few years. I still have a long way to go, but it's a start.

George Killian, #82256
ASPC-Eyman Complex, Meadows Unit, Florence, Arizona

A number of studies have claimed to show that incapacitating offenders through incarceration is cost-effective. Such studies conclude that imprisoning certain types of offenders (especially career or habitual offenders) results in savings by eliminating the social costs of the crimes offenders would be likely to commit if they were not imprisoned. Those social costs include monetary loss, medical costs of physical injury, and time lost from work.

One of the most frequently cited studies attempting to quantify the net costs of incarceration was done by Edwin Zedlewski.[9] Zedlewski used a RAND Corporation survey of inmates in three states (Michigan, Texas, and California) to estimate the number of crimes each inmate would commit if not imprisoned. In the survey, the average respondent reported committing anywhere from 187 to 287 crimes annually just before being incarcerated. To calculate the cost associated with each crime, Zedlewski

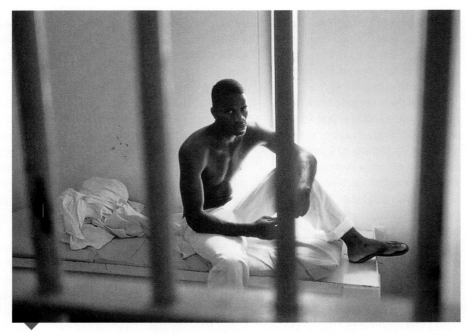

As a goal of sentencing, incapacitation restrains offenders from committing more crimes by isolating them from society. Does this threat of isolation from society encourage law-abiding behavior?

divided the total criminal justice expenditures in the United States by the total number of crimes committed in the United States. From this he concluded that the average crime "costs" $2,300. Multiplying $2,300 by the 187 crimes estimated to be committed annually by a felon, Zedlewski calculated that society saves $430,100 per year for each felon who is incarcerated. Figuring that incarceration costs society about $25,000 per prisoner per year, he concluded that prisons produce a cost-benefit return to society of 17 to 1 ($17 saved for every $1 spent)—leading him to strongly support increased incarceration.

Three years after Zedlewski's work, well-known criminologist John DiIulio performed a cost-benefit analysis using a survey of Wisconsin prisoners. The study, called "Crime and Punishment in Wisconsin," led to the conclusion that prisons saved taxpayers in Wisconsin approximately $2 for every dollar they cost.[10]

correctional econometrics

The study of the cost-effectiveness of various correctional programs and related reductions in the incidence of crime.

Studies such as those by Zedlewski and DiIulio are part of the growing field of correctional econometrics. **Correctional econometrics** is the study of the cost-effectiveness of various correctional programs and related reductions in the incidence of crime.

Not everyone agrees with the conclusions reached by Zedlewski and DiIulio. Critics include Franklin Zimring, Gordon Hawkins,[11] (1988), and David F. Greenberg.[12] Criticisms include (1) the fact that the RAND survey used by Zedlweski included data from three states, and those states had crime rates well above the national average; (2) the possibility that inmates may overreport criminal activity in order to impress their peers; and (3) the generally recognized fact that a particular inmate may not represent the general criminal population but may be the "worst of the worst."

Rehabilitation or Reformation The goal of **rehabilitation** or reformation is to change criminal lifestyles into law-abiding ones. Rehabilitation has been accomplished when an offender's criminal patterns of thought and behavior have been replaced by allegiance to society's values. Rehabilitation focuses on medical and psychological treatments and on social skills training, all designed to "correct" the problems that led the individual to crime.

A subgoal of rehabilitation is **reintegration** of the offender with the community. Reintegrating the offender with the community means making the offender a productive member of society—one who contributes to the general well-being of the whole.

Rehabilitation, which became the focus of American corrections beginning in the late 1800s, led to implementation of indeterminate sentencing practices (soon to be discussed), probation, parole, and a separate system of juvenile justice. During the 1970s, however, rehabilitation came under harsh criticism. As American society experienced disruptions brought about by economic change, the decline of traditional institutions, and fallout from the war in Vietnam, conservatives blamed the rehabilitative ideal for being too liberal, and liberals condemned it for providing an unfair basis for coercive action against disenfranchised social groups.[13] About the same time, an influential and widely read study by Robert Martinson, which evaluated rehabilitation programs nationwide, reported that few, if any, produced real changes in offender attitudes.[14] Dubbed the "nothing works doctrine," Martinson's critique of rehabilitation as a correctional goal led some states to abandon rehabilitation altogether or to de-emphasize it in favor of the goals of retribution and incapacitation. In other states, attempts at rehabilitation continued but were often muted.

Today, some governments and private organizations are re-embracing rehabilitation, emphasizing treatment and education. According to Francis T. Cullen and Paul Gendreau, it is time to give the rehabilitative ideal a second chance. They call for *reaffirming rehabilitation.* "Many [rehabilitative] programs fail to work," say Cullen and Gendreau, "because they either are ill-conceived (not based on sound criminological theory) and/or have no therapeutic integrity (are not implemented as designed)." "We would not be surprised," they write, "if young children turned out to be illiterate if their teachers were untrained, had no standardized curriculum, and met the children once a week for half an hour."[15] Until recently, contend Cullen and Gendreau, many correctional treatment programs were in such a state.

Other writers hold that continued efforts at rehabilitation are mandatory for any civilized society. "In order to neutralize the desocializing potential of prisons," says Edgardo Rotman, "a civilized society is forced into rehabilitative undertakings. These become an essential ingredient of its correctional system taken as a whole. A correctional system" with no "interest in treatment," says Rotman, "means . . . de-humanization and regression."[16]

Rehabilitation typically implies the notion of treatment, in the belief that offenders who receive appropriate counseling, psychological treatment, psychiatric intervention, or drug therapy will be less prone to repeat criminality. California's Proposition 36, officially known as the Substance Abuse Crime Prevention Act of 2000 (SACPA), is indicative of the return to rehabilitation now occurring. Passed by the state's voters in 2000, it

rehabilitation

The changing of criminal lifestyles into law-abiding ones by "correcting" the behavior of offenders through treatment, education, and training.

reintegration

The process of making the offender a productive member of the community.

CAREER PROFILE

Erich Parsons
Deputy Sheriff   Palm Beach County, FL

Erich Parsons is Deputy Sheriff with the Palm Beach County Sheriff's Department in West Palm Beach, Florida. A 44-year-old Army veteran and grandfather of five, he attended Johnson Bible College in Knoxville, Tennessee, where he received a Bachelor of Arts degree, and has been an ordained minister since 1986. He has been with the department since 2000, working the midnight to 8 A.M. shift.

Sheriff Parsons had no educational background in law enforcement. While working in his family's business in the late 1990s (as a glazier in the family glass factory), he tore his rotator cuff, and he says that during his stay in the hospital he became interested in the job.

"Part of my desire to move on to something of this caliber was the need for significance. I felt that even though I was comfortable where I was and who I was, I like challenges. I'm a kid from the streets—grew up fast. So my penchant was to reach youth, and the training I took in theology was youth ministry–specific. I felt that my greater outreach perhaps would be those individuals in the county level as opposed to the state level, that the street kids needed more than just the church setting."

On a typical day, Sheriff Parsons will handle unresolved issues from the previous shift; handle new arrests, fingerprints, and photographs; "and try to maintain order as we're doing all that," he says.

"I love my job," he says. "My satisfaction is to know that I've done my job the best I was able to do, with what was available to me."

---

became effective on July 1 of that year. The law's purpose, stated in Section 3(c), is to "enhance public safety by reducing drug-related crime and preserving jails and prison cells for serious and violent offenders, and to improve public health by reducing drug abuse and drug dependence through proven and effective drug treatment strategies." It seeks to accomplish that goal by mandating probation for any person convicted of a nonviolent drug possession offense, and requires participation in, and completion of, proven and effective community-based treatment programs as a condition of probation. According to some estimates, approximately 37,000 offenders will be diverted from the California correctional system and into treatment programs as a result of the new law.[17]

Restoration   In recent years, a new goal of criminal sentencing, known as **restoration,** has developed. **Restorative justice** is based on the belief that criminal sentencing should involve restoration and justice for all involved in or affected by crime.

Advocates of restorative justice (or, as some agencies refer to it, *community justice* or *reparative justice*) believe that crime is committed not just against the state but also against victims and the community. Restorative justice is especially concerned with repairing the harm to the victim and the community. Harm is repaired through negotiation, mediation, and empowerment rather than through retribution, deterrence, and punishment. A restorative justice perspective allows judges and juries to consider **victim-impact statements** in their sentencing decisions. These are descriptions of the harm and suffering that a crime has caused victims and their survivors.

restoration
The process of returning to their previous condition all those involved in or affected by crime—including victims, offenders, and society.

restorative justice
A systematic response to wrongdoing that emphasizes healing the wounds of victims, offenders, and communities caused or revealed by crime.

victim-impact statement
A description of the harm and suffering that a crime has caused victims and survivors.

Eye On Corrections™

Reflections on Restorative Justice in Corrections

By Keith Martin

With the shift in corrections moving more toward community involvement and inclusion, restorative justice initiatives are becoming more commonplace in agencies both in the United States and internationally. By working with citizens to take a more positive role in halting the ripple effect of crime, agencies are turning to methods that focus more on making things right than on making people pay.

"It boils down to the fact that when people see [restorative justice], they recognize it as the right thing to do and common sense," says Ron Claassen, codirector of the Center for Peace-making and Conflict Studies at Fresno State University. "I think that when [others] look at the idea of restoration versus retribution and think about what makes people change and makes a better community, it is obvious that restoration is the way to go."

Claassen adds that there are some misunderstandings about the true nature of restorative justice endeavors in corrections. For example, if individuals think of it as purely "a victim's program," then they are missing the bigger picture. While the victim's needs and concerns are a large piece of restorative justice, they are just one aspect.

"[Restorative justice approaches] should also address the larger community concerns," he says. "I think if [it] is labeled as a 'victim's program,' it's true—it is for the victim *and* for the community *and* for offenders."

Considering restorative justice as purely a program with the victim in mind is just one of many misconceptions in corrections, however.

KEEPING IN MIND PRINCIPLES, NOT ACTIONS

While the heart of any restorative justice initiative lies in aiding the community, the offender, and the victim, it is the principles behind the initiative, not the activity itself, that sets it apart from other approaches in corrections.

"The question is, 'Is it being done to repair damage and make right, or is it being done to punish?'" says Claassen. "Inmates can do community service, for example, as a way to make them miserable or to help [themselves], the victim, and the community. Also, [the question should be asked] 'Does it establish or reestablish dignity and reintegrate those harmed?'"

If the answer to the latter question is yes, he adds, then it is a restorative approach. If the activity is to punish and have others see the punished in a negative light, then the answer is no. Sometimes correctional agencies will label an activity "restorative justice" because it gives back to the community but does not take into account the true principles that should be at the heart of such an initiative.

The reason for this mislabeling is not deliberate, says Kay Pranis, restorative justice planner for the Minnesota Department of Corrections. In her opinion, it is because the level of information on the subject can vary, so people assume something like community service is restorative, when it is only if it looks past the practice itself and to the philosophy.

Also among the efforts being introduced on behalf of victims and their survivors are victim assistance and victim compensation programs.

Advocates of restorative justice believe not only that the victim should be restored by the justice process but also that the offender and society should participate in the restoration process. To this end, efforts at restoration emphasize, as well as victims' rights and needs, the successful reintegration of offenders into the community. Another aspect of involving offenders in restoration is having them actively address the harm they have caused. The system strives to accomplish this by holding them directly accountable and by helping them become productive, law-abiding members of their community.[18] Restorative justice programs try to personalize crime by showing offenders the consequences of their behavior.

Restorative justice is based on the premise that since crime occurs in the context of the community, the community should be involved in addressing it. Particular restorative justice or community justice programs might make use of any of the following: (1) victim-offender mediation, (2) victim-offender reconciliation, (3) victim impact panels, (4) restorative justice panels, (5) community reparative boards, (6) community-based courts, (7) family group conferences, (8) circle sentencing, (9) court diversion programs, and (10) peer mediation.

Restorative justice seeks to restore the health of the community, repair the harm done, meet victims' needs, and require the offender to contribute to those repairs. Thus, the criminal act is condemned, offenders are held accountable, offenders and victims are involved as participants, and repentant offenders are encouraged to earn their way back into the good graces of society. Restorative justice principles, developed by the Restorative Justice Consortium in 1998 and modified in 2002, are shown in Table 3–2.

Not only is restorative justice having an impact on U.S. sentencing practices, but it is also becoming influential internationally. A 2002 United Nations report on the international acceptance of restorative justice principles in 35 member countries, for example, found that the concept has received considerable international attention by both practitioners and policymakers who view it as an alternative approach to more common criminal justice practices. According to the report, restorative justice is seen as offering promising concepts and options if taken as a supplement to established criminal justice practices. In general, says the report, restorative justice principles are seen as a complement to established justice systems and practices but not as a replacement for existing systems.[19]

Sentencing Options and Types of Sentences

OPTIONS

Legislatures establish the types of sentences that can be imposed. The U.S. Congress and the 50 state legislatures decide what is against the law and define crimes and their punishments in the jurisdictions in which they have control. Sentencing options in wide use today include the following:

- fines and other monetary sanctions;
- probation;

TABLE 3-2 **Restorative Justice Principles**

The following principles were developed by the Restorative Justice Consortium in order to provide a working basis for particular settings involved in the practice of restorative justice, including adult criminal justice, youthful offenders, schools, the workplace, prisons, and communities.

1. Principles relating to the interests of all participants
   a. Voluntary participation based on informed choice
   b. Avoidance of discrimination, irrespective of the nature of the case
   c. Access to relevant agencies for help and advice
   d. Ongoing access to various established methods of dispute resolution
   e. Processes that do not compromise the rights under the law of the participants
   f. Commitment not to use information in a way that may prejudice the interests of any participant in subsequent proceedings
   g. Protection of personal safety
   h. Protection of and support for vulnerable participants
   i. Respect for civil rights and the dignity of persons

2. Principles relating to those who have sustained harm or loss
   a. Respect for their personal experiences, needs, and feelings
   b. Acknowledgment of their harm or loss
   c. Recognition of their claim for amends
   d. Opportunity to communicate with the person who caused the harm or loss, if that person is willing
   e. Entitlement of victim to be the primary beneficiary of reparation

3. Principles relating to those who caused the harm or loss to others
   a. The opportunity to offer reparation, including before any formal requirement
   b. Reparation appropriate to the harm done and within the person's capacity to fulfill it
   c. Respect for the dignity of the person making amends

4. Principles relating to the interests of local community and society
   a. The promotion of community safety and social harmony by learning from restorative processes and the taking of measures that are conducive to the reduction of crime or harm
   b. The promotion of social harmony through respect for cultural diversity and civil rights, social responsibility, and the rule of law
   c. Opportunity for all to learn mediation and other methods of nonviolent resolution of conflict

5. Principles relating to agencies working alongside the judicial system
   a. Settlement outside the judicial system, except when this is unworkable due to the level of harm done, the risk of further harm, issues of public policy, or disagreement about the critical facts
   b. Avoidance of unfair discrimination by ensuring that rights under the law are not compromised
   c. Provision of a wide and flexible range of opportunities to enable those who have caused loss or harm to make amends

6. Principles relating to the judicial system
   a. A primary goal of repairing harm
   b. Restorative requirements that are fair, appropriate, and workable
   c. Opportunities for community reparation or reparation to others who have suffered harm or loss when a restorative requirement is appropriate but victims decline to participate
   d. Enforcement of community reparation when a restorative requirement is appropriate but those who have caused harm or loss decline to participate

Continued on page 86

TABLE 3-2   Restorative Justice Principles—*concluded*

  e. Valuing of voluntary offers to repair harm or loss by those who have caused it

  f. Privileged status of content of restorative meetings, subject to public interest qualifications

7. Principles relating to restorative justice agencies

  a. Commitment to needs-based practice

  b. Safeguarding of legal human rights

  c. The participation of restorative justice practitioners who are seen to be neutral

  d. The participation of restorative justice practitioners who act impartially

  e. Maintenance of neutrality and impartiality by restorative justice practitioners who play no other role in the case

  f. Commitment of restorative justice agencies to keep confidential the content of restorative meetings, subject to the requirements of the law

  g. Participant commitment to confidentiality about the contents of restorative meetings

  h. Facilitation of the engagement of weaker parties in negotiation

  i. Upholding of respectful behavior in restorative processes

  j. Upholding of equality of respect for all participants in restorative processes, separating this from the harm done

  k. Engagement with good practice guidelines within the restorative justice movement

  l. Commitment by the agency to the use of constructive conflict resolution in general and of internal grievance and disciplinary procedures in specific

  m. Commitment to the accreditation of training, services, and practitioners

  n. Commitment to continually improved practice

Source: Restorative Justice Principles. Copyright © Restorative Justice Consortium. Used with permission.

- alternative or intermediate sanctions such as day fines, community service, electronic monitoring, and day reporting centers;
- incarceration; and
- death penalty.

As punishment for unlawful behavior, fines have a long history. By the fifth century B.C., Greece, for example, had developed an extensive system of fines for a wide variety of offenses.[20] Under our modern system of justice, fines are usually imposed as punishment for misdemeanors and infractions. When imposed on felony offenders, fines are frequently combined with another punishment, such as probation or incarceration.

Fines are only one type of monetary sanction in use today. Others include the court-ordered payment of the costs of trial, victim restitution, various fees, forfeitures, donations, and confiscations. **Restitution** consists of payments made by a criminal offender to his or her victim as compensation for the harm caused by the offense. While fines are usually paid to the government, restitution may be paid directly to the victim (or paid to the court which turns it over to the victim). Some innovative courts have ordered offenders to donate specified amounts to specified charities in lieu of a fine.[21] Restitution is an example of a restorative justice sentencing option.

With a sentence of probation, the convicted offender continues to live in the community but must comply with court-imposed restrictions on his or her activity and freedom of movement. Alternative sanctions or intermedi-

restitution

Payments made by a criminal offender to his or her victim (or to the court, which then turns them over to the victim) as compensation for the harm caused by the offense.

ate sentencing options (which are discussed in detail in Chapters 4 and 5) usually combine probation with some other punishment, such as community service or house arrest with electronic monitoring. A sentence of incarceration, or total confinement away from the community, is used when the community needs to be protected from further criminal activity by an offender. The death penalty, or capital punishment, is the ultimate sentence. Figure 3–1 displays recent trends in fuor sentencing options.

> Sentencing structures vary from state to state. Is this fair? How might we address disparities in sentencing? For more information go to Ethical Dilemma 3-1 at http://www.mhhe.com/schmalleger2.
>
> **Ethical Dilemma**

TYPES OF SENTENCES

A sentence is generally imposed by a judge. Sentencing responsibility can also be exercised by a jury or a group of judges, or it may be mandated by statute. **Mandatory sentences** are those that are required by law under certain circumstances—such as conviction of a specified crime or of a series of offenses of a specified type. Mandatory sentences may add prison time to sentences for offenders who carried weapons during the commission of their crimes, who used or possessed illegal drugs, or who perpetrated crimes against elderly victims. Such sentences allow judges no leeway in sentencing.

Even when there is no mandatory sentence, judges cannot impose just any sentence. They are still limited by statutory provisions. They also are guided by prevailing sentencing goals. A judge usually considers a **presentence report,** sometimes called a **PSR**. This report, prepared by the probation department attached to a court, is a social and personal history as well as an

mandatory sentences

Those that are required by law under certain circumstances—such as conviction of a specified crime or of a series of offenses of a specified type.

presentence report (PSR)

A report, prepared by the probation department of a court, that provides a social and personal history as well as an evaluation of a defendant as an aid to the court in determining a sentence.

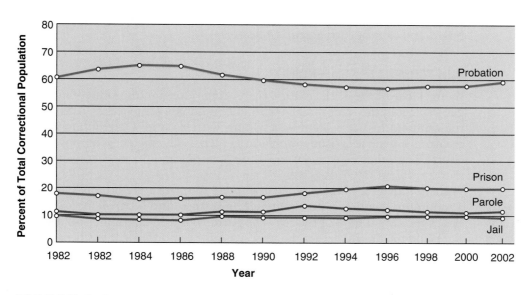

FIGURE 3-1
Adults on Probation, in Jail, in Prison, or on Parole

Source: Adapted from Kathleen Maguire and Ann L. Pastore (eds.), *Sourcebook of Criminal Justice Statistics 2002* (Washington, DC: Bureau of Justice Statistics, 2003) and other years. See also http://www.ojp.usdoj.gov/bjs/pub/pdf/ppus00.pdf.

evaluation of the offender. Finally, judges' sentencing decisions are influenced by their own personal convictions and characteristics.

Once the sentence is chosen, the judge must decide how it will be served, especially if more than one sentence is being imposed. Sentences can be consecutive or concurrent. **Consecutive sentences** are served one after the other. When a person is convicted of multiple offenses, a judge might impose, for example, a sentence of 10 years for one offense and 20 years for another. If the sentences are to run consecutively, the offender will begin serving the second sentence only after the first one expires. **Concurrent sentences** are served together. If the sentences in the example are to run concurrently, the 10-year sentence will expire when the offender has served one-half of the 20-year sentence. The offender will then need to serve the remainder of the 20-year sentence before being released.

Sentencing Models

A **model of criminal sentencing** is a strategy or system for imposing criminal sanctions. Sentencing models vary widely (see Table 3–3). Over the past 100 years, a shift has occurred from what might be called a judicial model of sentencing to an administrative model. Judges generally have far less discretion in sentencing decisions today than they previously did. The majority of sentences imposed in American courts today follow legislative and administrative guidelines.

Sentencing in 19th-century America involved mostly fines, probation, and "flat" prison sentences. **Flat sentences** specify a given amount of time to be served in custody and allow little or no variation from the time specified. A typical flat sentence might be stated as "five years in prison." Flat sentences generally mean that an offender has to complete the sentence imposed and cannot earn an early release.

INDETERMINATE SENTENCING

By the close of the 19th century, sentencing reform in the United States began replacing the flat sentence with indeterminate sentences.[22] At the time, the criminal justice system was coping with a rapidly expanding and increasingly diverse prison population, increased efficiency of police and courts, and other factors. Overcrowded prisons and the warehousing of inmates resulted.[23]

In an **indeterminate sentence**, the judge specifies a maximum length and a minimum length, within limits set by statute, and a parole board determines the actual time of release. The parole board's determination depends on its judgment of whether the prisoner has been reformed, has been cured, or has simply served enough time. An example of an indeterminate sentence is "5 to 10 years in prison." A second form of indeterminate sentencing requires the judge to specify only the maximum sentence length, with the associated minimum set by statute. Some states, for example, require an offender to serve as little as one-quarter of the sentence before becoming eligible for parole.

With an indeterminate sentence, discretion is distributed, not only among the prosecutor, defense counsel, and judge, but also to prison offi-

consecutive sentences
Sentences served one after the other.

concurrent sentences
Sentences served together.

model of criminal sentencing
A strategy or system for imposing criminal sanctions.

flat sentences
Those that specify a given amount of time to be served in custody and allow little or no variation from the time specified.

indeterminate sentence
A sentence in which a judge specifies a maximum length and a minimum length, and an administrative agency, generally a parole board, determines the actual time of release.

TABLE 3-3	**Sentencing Models**

DETERMINATE SENTENCING

Sentencing to a fixed term of incarceration that may be reduced by good time. Usually, explicit standards specify the amount of punishment and a set release date, with no review by a parole board or other administrative agency. Postincarceration supervision may be part of the sentence.

INDETERMINATE SENTENCING

Sentencing in which an administrative agency, generally a parole board, has the authority to release an incarcerated offender and to determine whether an offender's parole will be revoked for violation of the conditions of release. In one form of indeterminate sentencing, the judge specifies only the maximum sentence length (a fixed term); the associated minimum is automatically implied but is not within the judge's discretion. In the more traditional form of indeterminate sentencing, the judge specifies maximum and minimum durations within limits set by statute. The judge has discretion over the minimum and maximum sentences.

PRESUMPTIVE GUIDELINES SENTENCING

Sentencing that meets all the following conditions: (1) the appropriate sentence for an offender in a specific case is presumed to fall within a range authorized by guidelines adopted by a legislatively created sentencing body, usually a sentencing commission; (2) judges are expected to sentence within the range or provide written justification for departure; and (3) the guidelines provide for review of the departure, usually by appeal to a higher court. Presumptive guidelines may employ determinate or indeterminate sentencing structures.

VOLUNTARY/ADVISORY GUIDELINES SENTENCING

Recommended sentencing policies that are not required by law. They serve as a guide and are based on past sentencing practices. The legislature has not mandated their use. Voluntary/advisory guidelines may use determinate or indeterminate sentencing structures.

MANDATORY MINIMUM SENTENCING

A minimum sentence that is specified by statute for all offenders convicted of a particular crime or a particular crime with special circumstances (e.g., robbery with a firearm or selling drugs to a minor within 1000 feet of a school). Mandatory minimums can be used in both determinate and indeterminate sentencing structures. Within an indeterminate sentencing structure, the mandatory minimum requires the inmate to serve a fixed amount of time in prison before being eligible for release with the approval of a parole board. Under a determinate sentence, the offender is required to serve a fixed amount of time in prison before being eligible for release.

cials and the parole board, which have considerable influence over an offender's length of stay. Prison officials have discretion over the amount of **good time** an inmate earns, which can affect parole eligibility, the discharge date, or both. The parole board decides the actual release date for most inmates. The result is a system of sentencing in which few people understand or can predict who will be imprisoned and for how long.

good time

The number of days or months prison authorities deduct from a sentence for good behavior and for other reasons.

Under indeterminate sentencing, punishments are made to fit the criminal rather than the crime. Proponents of indeterminate sentences assume that crime is a product of individual deviation from the norm and that rehabilitation can be achieved within a prison system designed to punish and not treat inmates. They also assume that prison personnel have the knowledge to impose treatment or to predict recidivism accurately enough to justify their discretion over when an inmate should be released. The use of indeterminate sentences has prompted numerous accusations of disparity in sentencing as well as protests from inmate groups, penologists, and other critics of the penal system. These protests have spurred a movement for sentencing reform.

> Under indeterminate sentencing, punishments are made to fit the criminal rather than the crime.

DETERMINATE SENTENCING

**determinate sentence
(also called *fixed sentence*)**

A sentence of a fixed term of incarceration, which can be reduced by good time.

A **determinate sentence** (also known as a *fixed sentence*) specifies a fixed period of incarceration, which can be reduced for "good time" served. The term is generally used to refer to the sentencing reforms of the late 1970s. Determinate sentences are generally based on the incapacitation and deterrence goals of sentencing. The theory behind determinate sentencing is that criminals will be off the streets for longer periods of time. The other advantage, supporters say, is that prisoners know when they will be released. In most determinate-sentencing models, parole is limited or is replaced by the use of good-time credits. With good time, inmates are able to reduce their sentences by earning credits. The amount of the reduction depends on the number of credits earned. Good-time credits can be earned by demonstrating good behavior and not being "written up" for violating prison rules. It can also be earned by participating in educational programs, community service projects, or medical experiments. The procedure for earning credits and the number that can be earned vary from state to state. Prison administrators generally favor determinate sentencing and good-time credits because they aid in controlling prison populations.

GUIDELINE SENTENCING

As we have seen, the sentences that judges impose are regulated by law. As part of the movement to eliminate sentencing disparities, some states, as well as the federal government, have enacted sentencing guidelines for judges to follow. The guidelines fall into two categories.

Voluntary/Advisory Sentencing Guidelines   Among the earliest guided-sentencing innovations in the United States was the experiment with voluntary guidelines, also called *advisory guidelines*. These are recommended sentencing policies that are not required by law. Usually, they are based on past sentencing practices and serve as a guide to judges. Voluntary or advisory guidelines have had disappointing results, because they are often not enforced and are sometimes ignored. More important, the guidelines are voluntary; judges can simply ignore them. A review of all the major studies conducted on voluntary and advisory guidelines reveals low compliance by judges and, hence, little reduction in disparity.[24]

sentencing commission

A group assigned to create a schedule of sentences that reflect the gravity of the offenses committed and the prior record of the criminal offender.

Presumptive Sentencing Guidelines   By the early 1980s, states had begun to experiment with the use of presumptive sentencing guidelines. (See Table 3–4 for a summary of sentencing practices by state.) These models differ from determinate sentences and voluntary or advisory guidelines in three respects. First, the guidelines are developed, not by the legislature, but by a **sentencing commission** that often represents diverse interests, including private citizens as well as all segments of the criminal justice system. Second, the guidelines are explicit and highly structured, relying on a quantitative scoring instrument. Third, the guidelines are not voluntary or advisory. Judges must adhere to the sentencing system or provide a written rationale for departure.

The forces stimulating presumptive sentencing guidelines were the same as those that had driven the moves to determinate sentencing and voluntary or advisory guidelines: issues of fairness and prison crowding. These

TABLE 3-4	Sentencing Practices by State, 2002			
State	**Determinate sentencing**	**Indeterminate sentencing**	**Guideline sentencing by type**	**Mandatory minimum sentencing**
Alabama[a]		☐		☐
Alaska		☐		☐
Arizona	☐			☐
Arkansas		☐	Voluntary/advisory	☐
California	☐			☐
Colorado		☐		☐
Connecticut		☐		☐
Delaware	☐		Presumptive	☐
District of Columbia		☐		
Florida	☐		Presumptive	☐
Georgia		☐	Under study	☐
Hawaii		☐		☐
Idaho		☐		☐
Illinois	☐			☐
Indiana		☐		☐
Iowa		☐		☐
Kansas		☐	Presumptive	☐
Kentucky		☐		☐
Louisiana		☐	Voluntary/advisory	☐
Maine	☐			☐
Maryland		☐	Voluntary/advisory	☐
Massachusetts		☐	Under study	☐
Michigan		☐		☐
Minnesota	☐		Presumptive	☐
Mississippi	☐			☐
Missouri		☐	Voluntary	☐
Montana		☐	Under study	☐
Nebraska		☐		☐
Nevada		☐		☐
New Hampshire		☐		☐
New Jersey		☐		☐
New Mexico	☐			☐
New York		☐		☐
North Carolina	☐		Presumptive	☐
North Dakota		☐		☐
Ohio	☐		Presumptive	☐
Oklahoma		☐	Voluntary/advisory	☐
Oregon	☐		Presumptive	☐
Pennsylvania		☐	Presumptive	☐
Rhode Island		☐		☐
South Carolina		☐		☐
South Dakota		☐		☐
Tennessee[b]		☐	Presumptive	☐
Texas		☐		☐
Utah		☐	Voluntary/advisory	☐
Vermont		☐		☐
Virginia	☐		Voluntary/advisory	☐
Washington	☐		Presumptive	☐
West Virginia		☐		☐
Wisconsin[b]		☐		☐
Wyoming		☐		☐
Total	**14**	**37**	**17**	**51**

Source: Bureau of Justice Assistance, *1996 National Survey of State Sentencing Structures* (Washington, DC: U.S. Department of Justice, September 1998), updated June 2002 with information from Adam Gelb, executive director, the Governor's Commission on Certainty in Sentencing (Georgia).

a   The Alabama Legislature created the Alabama Sentencing Commission in 2000, and the state is currently transitioning to determinate sentencing.

b   Tennessee and Wisconsin continue to have sentencing guidelines; the sentencing commissions were abolished in 1996.

concerns provided the impetus for states to adopt guidelines, replace indeterminate sentencing with determinate sentencing, and abolish or reduce discretionary parole release. The first four states to adopt presumptive sentencing guidelines were Minnesota (1980), Pennsylvania (1982), Washington (1981), and Florida (1983).

The state of Washington's Sentencing Reform Act of 1981 (as amended), for example, is based on a determinate sentencing model. The law mandated creation of a Sentencing Guidelines Commission, which developed a set of sentencing guidelines "to ensure that offenders who commit similar crimes and have similar criminal histories receive equivalent sentences."[25] The state's presumptive sentencing schedules, which apply to all felonies committed in the state after June 30, 1984, are structured "so that offenses involving greater harm to a victim and to society result in greater punishment." According to the Sentencing Guidelines Commission, "The guidelines apply equally to offenders in all parts of the state, without discrimination as to any element that does not relate to the crime or to a defendant's previous criminal record."

As is typically the case in presumptive sentencing states, Washington's guidelines specify a standard sentence range based on the seriousness of an offense combined with an offender's criminal history "score." In Washington state, a defendant's criminal history includes his or her prior adult felony convictions in any state or federal court or in another country and dispositions in juvenile court. Misdemeanors are not counted except when related to current convictions of felony traffic offenses (i.e., driving under the influence of alcohol or drugs may figure into a defendant's criminal history when felony convictions for crimes such as vehicular assault occur). Judges make use of forms provided by the state's sentencing commission in calculating an offender's score for sentencing purposes. Crimes representative of each "seriousness level" are shown in Table 3–5.

As in other presumptive sentencing states, in Washington judges may sentence offenders outside of the standard ranges found in the state's sentencing grid. When doing so, however, they must provide a written reason for such variation.

States continue to create sentencing commissions, generally with the intention of adopting the guidelines those commissions are likely to recommend. In 1999, for example, the newly established Governor's Commission on Certainty in Sentencing in Georgia recommended that "the introduction of voluntary sentencing guidelines would provide a rational, consistent, and planned approach to sentencing in Georgia."[26] In 2000, Alabama became the most recent state to establish a sentencing commission. In creating the commission, the Alabama legislature identified its central functions as "Establish[ing] an effective, fair, and efficient sentencing system for Alabama adult and juvenile criminal offenders which provides certainty in sentencing, maintains judicial discretion and sufficient flexibility to permit individualized sentencing as warranted by mitigating or aggravating factors, and avoids unwarranted sentencing disparities among defendants with like criminal records who have been found guilty of similar criminal conduct." "Where there is disparity," the legislature noted, "it should be rational and not related . . . to geography, race, or judicial assignment."[27] While Table 3–4 classifies Alabama as an indeterminate sentencing

TABLE 3-5	State of Washington: Representative Crimes by Level of Seriousness

Level of seriousness	Representative offense	Level of seriousness	Representative offense
XVI	Aggravated Murder in the First Degree[a]	V	Third Degree Child Molestation
XV	First Degree Murder		First Degree Custodial Sexual Misconduct
	Homicide by Abuse		Domestic Violence Court Order Violation
	First Degree Malicious Explosion		First Degree Extortion
XIV	Second Degree Murder		Persistent Prison Misbehavior
XIII	Second Degree Malicious Explosion		Possession of a Stolen Firearm
	First Degree Malicious Placement of an Explosive		Stalking
XII	First Degree Assault	IV	Second Degree Arson
	First Degree Rape		Second Degree Assault
XI	First Degree Manslaughter		Bribing a Witness
	Second Degree Rape		Counterfeiting
X	First Degree Child Molestation		Knowingly Trafficking in Stolen Property
	Indecent Liberties (with Forcible Compulsion)		Threats to Bomb
	First Degree Kidnapping	III	Third Degree Assault
	Leading Organized Crime		Second Degree Burglary
IX	Controlled Substance Homicide		Communication with a Minor for Immoral Purposes
	Inciting Criminal Profiteering		Criminal Gang Intimidation
	First Degree Robbery		Harassment
	Sexual Exploitation		Intimidating a Public Servant
	Vehicular Homicide, by Being Under the Influence of Intoxicating Liquor or Any Drug		Maintaining a Dwelling or Place for Controlled Substances
VIII	First Degree Arson		Manufacture, Deliver, or Possess with Intent to Deliver Marijuana
	Deliver or Possess with Intent to Deliver Methamphetamine		Patronizing a Juvenile Prostitute
	Hit and Run—Death		Possession of Incendiary Device
	Second Degree Manslaughter		Possession of Machine Gun or Short Barreled Shotgun or Rifle
	First Degree Promoting Prostitution		Tampering with a Witness
	Vehicular Homicide, by the Operation of Any Vehicle in a Reckless Manner	II	First Degree Computer Trespass
VII	First Degree Burglary		Create, Deliver, or Possess a Counterfeit Controlled Substance
	Drive-by Shooting		Health Care False Claims
	Indecent Liberties (without Forcible Compulsion)		Theft of Rental, Leased, or Lease-Purchased Property (Valued at $1,500 or More)
	Involving a Minor in Drug Dealing		Unlicensed Practice of a Profession or Business
	Use of a Machine Gun in Commission of a Felony	I	Attempting to Elude a Pursuing Police Vehicle
VI	First Degree Incest		False Verification for Welfare
	Intimidating a Judge		Forged Prescription
	Intimidating a Juror/Witness		Taking a Motor Vehicle Without Permission
	Theft of a Firearm		Unlawful Use of Food Stamps

a   Aggravated murder in the first degree is first degree murder under certain circumstances. Among them are (a) the victim was a law enforcement officer or fire fighter performing his or her official duties; (b) the defendant was serving a term of imprisonment in a state institution at the time of the homicide; (c) the defendant solicited another person to commit the crime for pay; etc. To learn the statutory elements of each of the offenses listed here view Title 9 of the Revised Code of Washington (the state's criminal law) online at http://www.mrsc.org/rcw.htm. Visit the state of Washington Sentencing Guidelines Commission at http://www.sgc.wa.gov where you can read the state's online adult sentencing guidelines manual. The manual contains a comprehensive list of all felonies defined by state law along with their location in the sentencing grid.

America's Sentencing Future

by Richard S. Frase,
University of Minnesota

Reflections on the Future

Predicting the future is always a risky business, especially in the field of sentencing. Consider the revolutionary changes that have occurred in American sentencing during recent decades. Michael Tonry observes that if a group of judges from the 1970s were able to time-travel to a national sentencing conference 25 years later, most "would be astonished at a quarter century's changes."[1] Thirty years ago, sentencing generated little controversy or attention. There was almost universal agreement that judges and correctional authorities should have broad discretion in the imposition and execution of sentences, making highly individualized decisions based largely on assessments of the offender's need for, amenability to, and progress toward rehabilitation. By the early 1990s, political, media, legislative, and academic interest in sentencing had dramatically increased; rehabilitative goals had been abandoned or greatly de-emphasized, with sentencing based much more on the severity of the conviction offense; judicial and correctional discretion had been considerably reduced by means of sentencing guidelines, mandatory penalties, and parole abolition; and sentencing severity levels had increased dramatically.

What changes will the next quarter century bring? Although the particulars of future sentencing systems are difficult to predict, we can foresee changes in the fundamental elements of sentencing policy and practice that will determine—through complex interactions—each jurisdiction's sentencing future. These basic elements involve sentencing purposes, alternatives, structures, and severity. There is good reason to expect further change in each of these areas based on past changes, current trends, and the inevitable pendulum shifts in public, academic, and official thinking: We try one thing, get tired of it, and look for something new—or recycled.

Sentencing purposes will probably evolve into a hybrid approach combining elements of our current offense-based approach with greater attention to case- and offender-specific factors—in particular, (re)habilitation and (re)integration efforts, offender risk factors, and restorative justice goals. Community-based rehabilitation programs never disappeared, and the public never stopped believing that offenders can and should be helped not to reoffend. There has recently been much greater awareness of the critical importance of integrating offenders into a stable, law-abiding life in the community—and, in particular, facilitating re-entry of the huge number of incarcerated offenders released into the community every day. Offender risk assessment and management (in lieu of massive overincarceration) will be facilitated by steadily improving prediction tools and behavior controls. Victim- and community-restorative justice programs will continue to enjoy broad public support. Nevertheless, offense-based sentencing goals—just deserts, general deterrence and norm-reinforcement, and sentencing uniformity—will also remain popular. The inherent conflict between offense- and offender-based or restorative goals will be reconciled by hybrid models such as Norval Morris's theory of Limiting Retributivism: Just deserts and other offense-based values set outer limits on maximum and minimum allowable sentencing severity, within which courts may pursue case-specific sentencing goals.[2]

Thirty years ago, there were really only two *sentencing alternatives:* incarceration in prison or a local jail and probation (with few major conditions other than avoiding further crime). Since the late 1980s, more and more jurisdictions have experimented with "intermediate" sanctions such as intensive probation, day reporting centers, home detention, community service, and day fines. Since these measures are cheaper than incarceration and provide more control and punishment than probation, they are likely to be more and more heavily used. The pace of this growth will depend on whether states are willing to invest in staffing and other infrastructure to run these programs; many local jurisdictions do not have sufficient tax base and/or foresight to fund them. The specific types of intermediate sanctions used will depend in part on the development of new technologies and our willingness to employ them—not only predictive tools (including biological as well as traditional predictors), but also electronic monitoring and the blocking of chemical abuse and violence through medication or surgery.

Sentencing structures will continue to evolve. At present, most states still use some form of indeterminate sentencing, often combined with various mandatory penalty provisions and limited or no parole release discretion ("truth in sentencing").[3] More and more states have successfully implemented guidelines (despite the unpopularity of the federal version); states have done so not only to bring greater fairness and rationality to sentencing policy and practice, but also because the increased uniformity of guideline sentencing allows states to better predict future prison populations, avoid overcrowding, and set priorities in the use of limited resources. Most guidelines systems implement some form of the Limiting Retributivism theory already noted, maintaining a degree of sentencing uniformity and proportionality while still leaving room, within the recommended sentence ranges or by departure or charging discretion, for sentences to reflect unusual offense details, offender characteristics, and the needs of victims and the community. Since no other existing or proposed sentencing system accommodates all of these important goals and values, it is likely that more and more states will create sentencing commissions to draft and implement guidelines.

Will American *sentencing severity* levels remain high? Adoption of a Limiting Retributive model, broader use of intermediate punishments, or the implementation of sentencing guidelines often leads to stable or reduced overall severity levels, but this result is not guaranteed—the upper limits of desert can still be very severe, and intermediate sanctions can be targeted at low-level offenders (thus *increasing* severity); federal prison rates under guidelines have risen even faster than state prison rates. At the close of the 20th century, the United States had the most punitive criminal justice system of any developed nation. But at least at the state level, prison population increases are slowing, and in many states they are stable or declining. More and more citizens and officials are recognizing that, particularly for nonviolent drug and property offenders, the punitive binge of the 1980s and 1990s went too far. Unlike the federal government, states must balance their budgets; moreover, correctional expenses represent a large portion of a state's budget and compete directly with popular state programs (such expenses are hardly even visible in the huge federal budget). As states continue to struggle with budget crises (and gain little help from the deficit-ridden federal government), they will look for ways to reduce correctional expenditures and make better use of available resources. States will find they can achieve these goals through sentencing guidelines that reserve prison for violent and repetitive crimes, while encouraging broader use of intermediate sanctions for midlevel offenders.

NOTES

[1]Michael Tonry, *Sentencing Matters* (New York: Oxford University Press 1996), p. 6.
[2]Richard S. Frase, "Sentencing Principles in Theory and Practice," 22 *Crime & Justice: A Review of Research* 363 (1997).
[3]Kevin R. Reitz, "Sentencing: Allocation of Authority," *Encyclopedia of Crime and Justice*, 2 ed., Vol. 4 (New York: MacMillan Reference, 2002), p. 1400.

ABOUT THE AUTHOR

Richard S. Frase is the Benjamin N. Berger professor of criminal law at the University of Minnesota Law School. He is the author or editor of six books and over 40 articles and is a frequent contributor to local and national news stories and programs related to issues of contemporary criminal justice. His principal research interests are in the areas of sentencing and comparative criminal procedure.

jurisdiction, the state is in the midst of a transition and can be expected to move toward presumptive sentencing once the new commission makes its report on recommended changes in sentencing practices to the legislature.

Federal Sentencing Guidelines   In the early 1980s, the U.S. Congress focused its attention on disparity in sentencing.[28] Congress concluded that the sentencing discretion of federal trial judges needed boundaries. The resulting legislation, termed the Sentencing Reform Act of 1984,[29] created the United States Sentencing Commission. The nine-member commission, first organized in October 1985, is a permanent body charged with formulating and amending national sentencing guidelines. The commission's guidelines apply to all federal criminal offenses committed on or after November 1, 1987.

Federal sentencing guidelines take into account a defendant's criminal history, the nature of the criminal conduct, and the particular circumstances surrounding the offense. Congress has mandated that all federal trial judges must follow the guidelines in their sentencing decisions. Deviations from the guidelines are permitted only when a judge provides a written justification setting forth specific reasons as to why a sentence outside of the range specified by the guidelines was appropriate.

Federal sentencing guidelines are subject to change, and the commission may submit guideline amendments to Congress each year between the beginning of the regular congressional session and May 1. Suggested amendments automatically take effect 180 days after submission unless Congress rejects them.

Early challenges to the constitutionality of federal sentencing guidelines were resolved by the 1989 case of *Mistretta* v. *United States*, in which the U.S. Supreme Court upheld the 1984 Sentencing Reform Act and ruled that Congress had acted properly in delegating authority to the United States Sentencing Commission in the creation of sentencing guidelines.

In addition to creating the United States Sentencing Commission, the Sentencing Reform Act abolished parole for federal offenders sentenced under the guidelines. As a consequence, sentences imposed on convicted federal offenders today are essentially the sentences that will be served. Under federal law, however, inmates may earn up to 54 days of credit (time off their sentences) each year for good behavior.

The Legal Environment and Sentencing Guidelines   A number of U.S. Supreme Court cases have focused on the authority that judges retain in deciding to depart from sentencing guidelines and on the application of **sentencing enhancements.** Most of these decisions have involved federal law, although some state-level cases have been especially significant. In 1994, in the case of *Nichols* v. *United States*, the Court held that "an uncounseled misdemeanor conviction," because no prison term was imposed, is valid when used to enhance punishment at a subsequent conviction. (An "uncounseled conviction" is one in which the defendant was not represented by an attorney.)

In 1997, in the case of *United States* v. *Watts*, the Court found that "a jury's verdict of acquittal does not prevent the sentencing court from considering conduct underlying the acquitted charge, so long as that

sentencing enhancements
Legislatively approved provisions that mandate longer prison terms for specific criminal offenses committed under certain circumstances (such as a murder committed because of the victim's race or a drug sale near a school) or because of an offender's past criminal record.

conduct has been proved by a preponderance of the evidence." In other words, even when a person has been acquitted of previous criminal charges, the criminal conduct that was alleged when those charges were brought might provide an acceptable basis for an enhanced sentence in guideline jurisdictions.

In the 1998 case of *Edwards* v. *United States*, the Court ruled that federal sentencing guidelines require the sentencing judge, not the jury, to determine both the amount and kind of drugs at issue in a drug conspiracy. In *Edwards*, the justices wrote that the federal sentencing guidelines "require the judge to determine whether the 'controlled substances' at issue—and how much of those substances—consisted of cocaine, crack, or both."

In the potentially far-reaching case of *Apprendi* v. *New Jersey* (2000), however, the Supreme Court limited the fact-finding authority of judges in sentencing decisions. The case involved Charles Apprendi, a New Jersey defendant who had pleaded guilty to unlawfully possessing a firearm—an offense that carried a prison term of 5 to 10 years under state law. Prior to imposing sentence, however, the judge found that Apprendi had fired a number of shots into the home of an African American family living in his neighborhood. The judge further determined that Apprendi had done so to frighten the family and to convince them to move. Statements made by Apprendi, said the judge, classified the shooting as a hate crime. The judge then applied a sentencing enhancement provision under New Jersey's hate crimes statute and sentenced Apprendi to 12 years in prison—two years beyond the 10-year maximum authorized by statute for the weapons offense to which he had confessed. Significantly, the sentence was imposed without the benefit of a jury-based fact-finding process and with the judge alone making the determination that a hate crime had taken place. In overturning the state court's finding, the Supreme Court reasoned that Apprendi's due process guarantees were violated when the judge—and not a jury—made a factual determination that did not require proof beyond a reasonable doubt. In the words of the Court, "Under the Due Process Clause of the Fifth Amendment and the notice and jury trial guarantees of the Sixth Amendment, any fact (other than prior conviction) that increases the maximum penalty for a crime must be charged in an indictment, submitted to a jury, and proven beyond a reasonable doubt."

The *Apprendi* case is likely to result in more court challenges to sentencing practices in guideline jurisdictions for years to come because it raises the question of whether judges can legitimately deviate from established guidelines or apply sentence enhancements that deviate from those guidelines—especially when such deviations are based on judicial findings of fact that might otherwise be made by a jury.[30]

MANDATORY MINIMUM SENTENCING

Mandatory minimum sentencing refers to the imposition of sentences required by statute for those convicted of a particular crime or a particular crime with special circumstances, such as robbery with a firearm or selling drugs to a minor within 1,000 feet of a school, or for those with a particular type of criminal history. By 1994, all 50 states had enacted one or more mandatory minimum sentencing laws,[31] and Congress had

mandatory minimum sentencing
The imposition of sentences required by statute for those convicted of a particular crime or a particular crime with special circumstances, such as robbery with a firearm or selling drugs to a minor within 1,000 feet of a school, or for those with a particular type of criminal history.

enacted numerous mandatory sentencing laws for federal offenders. Mandatory minimum sentencing rationales dominated the 1980s and early 1990s.

Many states have adopted sentence enhancements, usually the mandating of longer prison terms for violent offenders with records of serious crimes. Mandatory sentence enhancements aim to deter known and potentially violent offenders and to incapacitate persistent criminals through long-term incarceration.[32] These sentence enhancements have come to be known as *three-strikes laws* (and, in some jurisdictions, *two-strikes laws*).

Three-strikes laws vary in breadth. Some stipulate that both the prior convictions and the current offense must be violent felonies; others require only that the prior felonies be violent. Some three-strikes laws count only prior adult convictions; others permit consideration of juvenile adjudications for violent crimes. Under California's three-strikes law, an offender who is convicted of a qualifying felony and has two prior qualifying felony convictions must serve a minimum of 25 years. The law also doubles prison terms for offenders convicted of a second violent felony.[33]

Rationales   Mandatory sentences have two goals—deterrence and incapacitation. The primary purposes of modest mandatory prison terms (e.g., three years for armed robbery) are specific deterrence, for already-punished offenders, and general deterrence, for prospective offenders. If the law increases the imprisonment rate, it also serves the goal of incapacitation, leaving fewer offenders free to victimize the population at large. The intent of three-strikes (and even two-strikes) laws is to incapacitate selected violent offenders with very long terms—25 years or even life.

Mandatory sentencing laws have become highly politicized. By passing mandatory sentencing laws, legislators can convey that they deem certain crimes especially grave and that people who commit these crimes deserve, and can expect, harsh sanctions. Such laws typically are a rapid and visible response to public outcries following heinous or well-publicized crimes.

Impact   Mandatory sentencing has had significant consequences that deserve close attention. Among them are its impact on crime and the operations of the criminal justice system. The possibility that the consequences will be different for different groups of people also bears examination.

Crime   Evaluations of mandatory minimum sentencing have focused on two types of crimes—those committed with handguns and those related to drugs (the offenses most commonly subject to mandatory minimum penalties in state and federal courts). An evaluation of the Massachusetts law that imposed mandatory jail terms for possession of an unlicensed handgun concluded that the law was an effective deterrent of gun crime, at least in the short term.[34]

However, studies of similar laws in Michigan[35] and Florida[36] found no evidence that crimes committed with firearms had been prevented. An evaluation of mandatory sentence enhancements for gun use in six large cities (Detroit, Jacksonville, Tampa, Miami, Philadelphia, and Pittsburgh) indicated that the laws deterred homicide but not other violent crimes.[37] An assessment of New York's Rockefeller drug laws was unable to support their claimed efficacy in deterring drug crime in New York City.[38]

Mandatory sentencing laws are often passed in reaction to public outcries against especially violent or well-publicized criminal acts. Does mandatory sentencing fulfill the goals of deterrence and incapacitation?

The Criminal Justice System The criminal courts rely on a high rate of guilty pleas to speed case processing and thus avoid logjams. Officials can offer inducements to defendants to enter these pleas. At least in the short term, mandatory sentencing laws may disrupt established plea-bargaining patterns by preventing a prosecutor from offering a short prison term (less than the new minimum) in exchange for a guilty plea. However, unless policymakers enact the same mandatory sentences for several related crimes, prosecutors can usually shift strategies and bargain on charges rather than on sentences.

Michael Tonry, a criminal justice scholar, has summarized the findings of research on the impact of mandatory sentencing laws on the criminal justice system. He concluded that mandatory sentencing laws:

- do not achieve certainty and predictability because officials circumvent them if they believe the results are unduly harsh;
- are redundant in requiring imprisonment for serious cases because the offenders in such cases are generally sentenced to prison anyway;
- are arbitrary in the sentences they require for minor cases; and
- may occasionally result in an unduly harsh punishment for a marginal offender.[39]

Most two- and three-strikes laws leave judges no discretion to deviate from the sentences dictated by legislatures. Another central feature of such laws is the extraordinary length of the prison terms they require. Offenders serving life sentences in California and North Carolina under such legislation, for example, become eligible for parole only after serving 25 years, those in New Mexico after 30 years, and those in Colorado after 40 years. Three-strikes laws in some states mandate life without the possibility of parole. Two- and three-strikes laws came about in response to public concerns about crime and the growing belief that many serious offenders were being released from prison too soon.[40] Proponents view such legislation as

habitual offender statute

A law that (1) allows a person's criminal history to be considered at sentencing or (2) makes it possible for a person convicted of a given offense and previously convicted of another specified offense to receive a more severe penalty than that for the current offense alone.

the best way to deal with the persistent, serious violent offender—the proverbial three-time loser.

Two- and three-strikes laws are a form of **habitual offender statute.** Although habitual offender laws have been on the books in a number of jurisdictions since at least the 1940s, the older laws were often geared to specific types of prior offenses, such as crimes of violence, sex offenses, or crimes perpetrated with guns. Moreover, most early habitual offender laws allowed enhanced sentences but did not make them mandatory as does two- and three-strikes legislation.[41]

Three-Strikes Models—Washington and California

During the 1990s, 26 states and the federal government enacted new habitual offender laws that fell into the three-strikes category.[42] Washington State was the first of those to do so.[43] California soon followed with a considerably broader version of the three-strikes law. As those laws were being implemented, people debated the impact they would have on the criminal justice systems of those states. Proponents predicted the laws would curb crime and protect society by warehousing the worst offenders for a long time. Opponents argued that defendants facing lengthy mandatory sentences would be more likely to demand trials, slowing the processing of cases, and that more offenders would serve long terms of incarceration, ballooning prison populations already at crisis levels in many states.[44]

Although they were enacted within months of each other, amid the same "three strikes and you're out" rallying cry, and they count many of the same offenses as strikes, the Washington and California laws differ in three important ways. First, in Washington all three strikes must be for felonies specifically listed in the legislation. Under the California law, only the first two convictions must be from the state's list of "strikeable" crimes (which include most violent offenses and many drug offenses); *any* subsequent felony can count as the third strike. Second, the California law contains a two-strikes provision, by which a person convicted of any felony after one prior conviction for a strikeable offense is to be sentenced to twice the term he or she would otherwise receive. There is no two-strikes provision in the Washington law. Third, the sanctions for a third strike differ. The Washington statute requires a life term in prison without the possibility of parole for a person convicted for the third time of any of the "most serious offenses" listed in the law. In California a "third-striker" has at least the possibility of being released after 25 years.[45]

California's law came under attack for the seeming ease with which offenders who commit relatively minor crimes can be sentenced to prison for a long time. The law, however, found a powerful ally in the Supreme Court. In 2001, for example, the Ninth U.S. Circuit Court of Appeals ruled in *Andrade* v. *Attorney General of the State of California*[46] that two consecutive 25-year-to-life sentences imposed on a California man who was twice caught shoplifting videotapes from a Kmart constituted cruel and unusual punishment under the Eighth Amendment to the U.S. Constitution. The offender,

Ethical Dilemma

What's wrong with "three strikes" laws? For more information go to Ethical Dilemma 3-2 at http://www.mhhe.com/schmalleger2.

Leandro Andrade, 37, had been in and out of state and federal prisons since 1982. In January 1982, Andrade had been convicted of a misdemeanor theft offense and was sentenced to six days in jail with 12 months' probation. He was arrested again in November 1982 for multiple counts of first-degree residential burglary. He pleaded guilty to at least three of those counts, and in April of the following year he was sentenced to 120 months in prison. In 1988, Andrade was convicted in federal court of transporting marijuana, and he was sentenced to eight years in federal prison. In 1990, he was convicted in state court for a misdemeanor petty theft offense and was ordered to serve 180 days in jail. In September 1990, he was again convicted in federal court for transporting marijuana and was sentenced to 2,191 days in federal prison. In 1991, he was arrested for a state parole violation—escape from federal prison. He was formally paroled from prison in 1993.

Before his case went to trial, Andrade admitted stealing the videotapes, telling police that he had been addicted to heroin since 1977 and wanted to sell the videos so that he could buy drugs. The prosecutor decided to charge Andrade with two counts of "petty theft with a prior conviction." In California, such a charge is called a "wobbler" because it can be punishable either as a misdemeanor or as a felony. The prosecutor chose to charge Andrade with a felony, and he was convicted, resulting in the two consecutive 25-year sentences. It was that conviction and sentence that, upon appeal, led to the Ninth Circuit Court's 2001 ruling on Andrade's behalf.

On March 5, 2003, however, the U.S. Supreme Court overturned the lower court's finding and ruled that Andrade's two consecutive 25-year-to-life sentences did not violate the Eighth Amendment's proscription against cruel or unusual punishment.[47] In effect, the Court held that it is *not* cruel and unusual punishment to impose a possible life term for a conviction of a nonviolent felony committed by a defendant with a history of serious or violent convictions.

In another 2003 case, *Ewing* v. *California*,[48] the U.S. Supreme Court upheld the conviction and sentence of Gary Ewing under California's three-strikes law. Ewing, who had a lengthy record of prior convictions, had received a 25-year-to-life sentence following his conviction for felony grand theft of three golf clubs. In writing for the Court, Justice Sandra Day O'Connor said that states should be able to decide when repeat offenders "must be isolated from society . . . to protect the public safety," even when nonserious crimes trigger the lengthy sentence.

IMPACT ON LOCAL COURTS AND JAILS

When three-strikes laws were first passed in Washington and California, some analysts projected a much greater impact on local criminal justice systems in California, because the California law had a much broader scope.[49] They predicted that California courts would be overwhelmed as defendants facing enhanced penalties demanded jury trials. The added time to process cases through trials and the reluctance of courts to grant pretrial release to defendants facing long prison terms, they said, would cause jail populations to explode as the number of jail admissions and the length of jail stays grew.

Early evidence from California supported these predictions. A review of 12,600 two- and three-strikes cases from Los Angeles, for example, showed that two-strikes cases took 16 percent longer to process and three-strikes cases 41 percent longer than nonstrike cases.[50] In addition, strikes cases were three times as likely to go to trial as nonstrike felonies and four times as likely as the same types of cases before the law took effect. This effect led to a 25 percent increase in jury trials as well as an 11 percentage-point rise in the proportion of the jail population awaiting trial, from 59 percent before the law was enacted to 70 percent. Furthermore, a survey of sheriff's departments showed that the pretrial detainee population in the state had grown from 51 percent of the average daily population before the three-strikes law to 61 percent by January 1, 1995.[51]

According to more recent data, however, at least some California counties are learning how to handle the changes brought about by the law. A recent survey of eight California counties with populations of more than 1 million identified several that were successfully disposing of two- and three-strikes cases early in the process.[52] In addition, data from the Los Angeles County Sheriff's Department suggest that the pace of strikes cases coming into that system may be slowing.[53]

IMPACT ON STATE PRISON SYSTEMS

The impact of the Washington and California laws on state corrections departments has not been as severe as projected. Planners in Washington had expected that 40 to 75 persons would be sentenced under three-strikes provisions each year. The actual numbers, however, have been much lower. During the first three years the law was in effect, only 85 offenders—not the 120 to 225 projected—were admitted to the state prison system under the three-strikes law.[54]

A similar overestimate was made of the impact the California law would have on prisons there. As of May 2001, 6,721 prisoners had been admitted to the California Department of Corrections (CDC) under the state's three-strikes law, and another 43,800 were serving time for second-strike convictions.[55] Even though the sheer number of cases affected by the law is significantly higher than for any other state, the numbers are not as great as originally projected. Still, according to some experts, three-strikes laws may be having a real, but subtle, impact on the California prison system. Such laws, they say, funnel increasingly older persons into correctional institutions and ensure that they will remain there for a very long time.

Between 1994 and 1999, for example, new felony admissions to California prisons of persons over 40 years in age increased from 15.3 percent to 23.1 percent.[56] The result is an inmate population that is getting older. The aging of America's inmate population, which has begun to concern policy-makers across the country, is discussed in more detail in Chapter 12.

The Current Applicability of Three-Strikes Laws and Habitual Offender Statutes According to the Washington, D.C.–based Sentencing Project, only a handful of states have convicted more than a hundred individuals using two- and three-strikes statutes—even though more than half of all states have such laws on the books. The Sentencing Project says that only Georgia (with 942 inmates sentenced under the law in mid-1998), South Carolina (825), Nevada (304), Washington (121), and Florida (116) are actually using three-strikes legislation "to any significant extent."[57]

There is also evidence of a movement away from mandatory minimum sentences in a number of jurisdictions where such sentences have been blamed for prison crowding and budgetary problems. In Louisiana, for example, where prison populations increased from 25,260 to 38,000 in the six years following the state's 1995 implementation of mandatory sentences, the legislature recently eliminated mandatory prison time for crimes such as residential burglary, Medicaid fraud, prostitution, theft of a firearm, and possession of small amounts of controlled substances. "This [was] an attempt to bring under control a system that was bankrupting the state and was not reducing crime," said state Senator Donald R. Cravins.

In similar legislative action, other states, including Connecticut, Indiana, and North Dakota, have eliminated some laws that required certain offenders to serve long prison terms without the possibility of parole. Likewise, in 2001, Mississippi passed a law establishing parole eligibility for nonviolent first-time offenders who have served only 25 percent of their sentences—reducing the figure from what had been a required 85 percent under previous law.[58]

The economic problems that have caused some states to use habitual offender statutes less frequently or to release repeat offenders early are present in almost all regions of the country. In 2002, for example, New York Governor George Pataki proposed releasing 1,300 nonviolent drug offenders from the state's prisons. The governor said that the proposed releases would save the state of New York $28.7 million over the next fiscal year.[59] Some states have moved to release nonviolent and relatively minor drug offenders in order to address budgetary shortfalls in their correctional systems but have refused to shorten the sentences of habitual felons.

Issues in Sentencing

Many sentencing reforms have been an attempt to reduce disparity in sentencing and make the process more fair. The term **fair sentencing** or *fairness in sentencing,* has become popular in recent years. Although fair sentencing today often refers to fairness for *victims,* many suggest that any truly fair sentencing scheme must incorporate fairness for both victims and offenders. These are the issues related to fairness in sentencing:

fair sentencing

Sentencing practices that incorporate fairness for both victims and offenders. Fairness is said to be achieved by implementing principles of proportionality, equity, social debt, and truth in sentencing.

- proportionality;
- equity;
- social debt; and
- truth in sentencing.

PROPORTIONALITY

proportionality

The sentencing principle that the severity of punishment should match the seriousness of the crime for which the sentence is imposed.

Proportionality is the sentencing principle that the severity of punishment should match the seriousness of the crime for which the sentence is imposed. To most people today, the death penalty would seem grossly disproportional to the offense of larceny—even if the offender had a history of such violations. However, this was not always the case. Larceny *was* punishable by death in medieval England. On the other hand, probation would seem disproportional to the crime of murder—although it is occasionally imposed in homicide cases.

EQUITY

equity

The sentencing principle that similar crimes and similar criminals should be treated alike.

Equity is the sentencing principle that similar crimes and similar criminals should be treated alike. The alternative to equity is *disparity*, in which similar crimes are associated with different punishments in different jurisdictions or in which offenders with similar criminal histories receive widely differing sentences. Disparity can also result from judicial discretion when judges hold widely different sentencing philosophies. In a jurisdiction with wide leeway for judges to determine sentences, one judge might treat offenders very harshly while another may be lenient. Under such circumstances, now largely eliminated by sentencing reform, one burglar, for example, might receive a sentence of 30 years in prison upon conviction, but his partner in crime is merely put on probation simply because he appears before a more lenient judge.

As this book goes to press, the United States Sentencing Commission has recommended a change in federal sentencing practices because of what it perceives as a disparity in existing mandatory minimum sentences for crack and powdered cocaine.[60] Under current law, anyone convicted of possession with intent to sell five grams of crack cocaine receives a five-year mandatory minimum term of imprisonment—the same as someone convicted of the sale of 500 grams of cocaine powder. The federal Drug Abuse Act of 1986 created the basic framework of statutory mandatory minimum penalties currently applicable to federal drug trafficking offenses and established a 100-to-1 drug quantity ratio between powder and crack cocaine offenses for sentencing purposes. That ratio was based on beliefs that crack cocaine sales and use are associated with violent crime, that crack cocaine is highly addictive, and that children and young teens are especially attracted to crack cocaine use. Not everyone, however, agrees with those beliefs, and some point out that the 1986 law created a sentencing disparity that weighs more heavily on African Americans than other ethnic groups because African Americans are more likely to be involved in small-scale crack dealing.

To reduce what it perceives as existing disparities, the commission currently recommends increasing the drug quantity threshold for the five-year

Ethical Dilemma

Our criminal justice system sometimes fails. What are the causes and remedies of wrongful convictions? For more information go to Ethical Dilemma 3-3 at http://www.mhhe.com/schmalleger2.

statutory minimum sentence for crack cocaine offenses from 5 grams to *at least* 25 grams. The change, if approved, would likely impact over 90 percent of crack cocaine offenders.

The commission's recommendations are controversial. Although such political heavyweights as President George W. Bush and Senators Orrin Hatch and Jeff Sessions have proposed making sentences for dealing in crack and powder more similar, the U.S. Department of Justice and Attorney General John Ashcroft remain opposed to the change. The Department of Justice continues to argue that crack cocaine is more dangerous than the powder form of the drug, that it is associated with urban crimes of violence, and that it is more addictive than powdered cocaine. The department also suggests that dealers in crack cocaine do more damage to society than those selling cocaine in powder form.[61]

SOCIAL DEBT

Social debt is the sentencing principle that the severity of punishment should take into account the offender's prior criminal behavior. As we have seen, a number of laws designed to recognize social debt have recently been passed. Among them are three-strikes and two-strikes laws. Although there is considerable variation in such laws among states, the primary characteristic of these laws is that they "call for enhanced penalties for offenders with one or more prior felony convictions."[62] They require a repeat offender to serve several years in prison in addition to the penalty imposed for the current offense.

social debt
The sentencing principle that the severity of punishment should take into account the offender's prior criminal behavior.

TRUTH IN SENTENCING

Until the sentencing reforms of the 1970s, the laws of many states enabled convicted offenders to be released from prison long before they had served their full sentences. Inmates frequently had good time deducted from their sentences or time off for good behavior. *Gain time* could be earned for going to school, learning a trade, or doing volunteer work. Moreover, many states mandated routine parole eligibility after inmates had served one-quarter or even one-fifth of their sentences.

Recent truth-in-sentencing laws have changed such practices by requiring offenders to complete sentences very close to the ones they are given. **Truth in sentencing** requires an offender to serve a substantial portion of the sentence and reduces the discrepancy between the sentence imposed and actual time spent in prison. (The results of a recent study, comparing actual time served in prison with sentences imposed, can be seen in Figure 3–2.) The Violent Crime Control and Law Enforcement Act of 1994 includes a truth-in-sentencing provision. To qualify for federal aid under the act, a state must amend its laws so that an imprisoned offender serves at least 85 percent of his or her sentence before being released. Parole eligibility and good time credits are generally restricted or eliminated in truth-in-sentencing laws.

truth in sentencing
The sentencing principle that requires an offender to serve a substantial portion of the sentence and reduces the discrepancy between the sentence imposed and actual time spent in prison.

By 1998, 27 states and the District of Columbia had met the 85 percent federal truth-in-sentencing requirement. Another 13 states had adopted truth-in-sentencing laws requiring certain offenders to serve a specified portion of their sentences.[63] Three states—Idaho, Nevada, and New

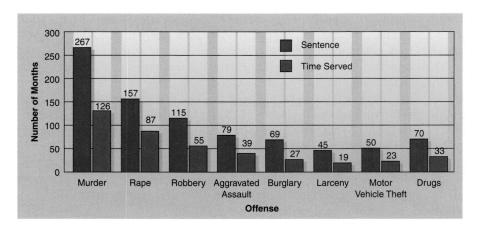

FIGURE 3–2
Time Served in State Prisons Compared with Court Sentences

Source: Paula M. Ditton and Doris J. Wilson, *Truth in Sentencing in State Prisons* (Washington, DC: Bureau of Justice Statistics, 1999), p. 7.

Hampshire—require inmates to serve 100 percent of the minimum sentence they receive before they become eligible for release.

BROADER ISSUES

Today's two main sentencing initiatives—guideline-based determinate sentencing and restorative justice—represent different attempts to achieve sentencing fairness. The two, however, appear to be inherently at odds with one another. That is because determinate sentencing requires a top-down approach in which an authoritative decision-making body imposes strict limits on the sentencing process, whereas restorative justice emphasizes community involvement at the grassroots level. "All this," say some experts, "suggests that, at its philosophical core, restorative justice appears to be incompatible with sentencing guidelines."[64]

One way of addressing the differences between these two approaches would be to seek greater community involvement in the development of sentencing guidelines. In fact, many states have encouraged local participation in the guideline-development process. Similarly, some guideline states encourage the use of local sentencing options such as community-based sanctions (which are discussed in more detail in Chapters 4 and 5. For example, North Carolina, a guideline state, assigns county officials the responsibility for developing and recommending local community sentencing options for certain categories of offenders.

Still, community sentencing may be appropriate only for relatively minor offenders, and traditional grid-based guidelines offer little leeway for sentencing offenders convicted of serious crimes. Some authors have suggested creation of a hybrid system of "restorative sentencing guidelines" to resolve the problem. Under the system, a new restorative sentencing option would be created and made applicable to less serious offenders. For such offenders, the traditional guideline grid, based on severity of offense and prior record, would not apply.

SUMMARY

1 ▶ The philosophy underlying criminal sentencing is that people must be held accountable for their actions and the harm they cause. Western society has a long tradition of sentencing criminal offenders to some form of punishment. Many social scientists suggest that the central purpose of criminal punishment is to maintain social order.

2 ▶ The goals of criminal sentencing today are (1) revenge (2) retribution, (3) desert, (4) deterrence, (5) incapacitation, (6) rehabilitation or reformation, and (7) restoration.

3 ▶ Sentencing options in use today include fines and other monetary sanctions, probation, alternative or intermediate sentences, incarceration, and capital punishment.

4 ▶ A model of criminal sentencing is a strategy or system for imposing criminal sanctions. Sentencing models vary widely among the jurisdictions in the United States. These models include indeterminate sentences, determinate sentences, voluntary or advisory sentencing guidelines, presumptive sentencing guidelines, and mandatory minimum sentencing.

5 ▶ Recent laws have increased penalties for criminal offenses, particularly violent crimes, and for repeat offenders. Many such laws are three-strikes laws. The rationale for such laws is simple: Offenders convicted repeatedly of serious offenses should be removed from society for long periods of time. Many three-strikes laws mandate a life sentence for the third violent-felony conviction. Analysts of three-strikes laws predicted that courts would be overwhelmed as more defendants, facing enhanced penalties, demanded jury trials. The added time to process cases and the reluctance to grant pretrial release to defendants facing long prison terms, said analysts, would cause jail populations to explode as the number of admissions and the length of jail stays grew. The actual effects of the laws have been similar to the effects predicted but to a lesser extent.

6 ▶ *Fair sentencing* often refers to fairness for *victims.* Fair sentencing advocates, however, suggest that any truly fair sentencing scheme must incorporate fairness for both victims and offenders. Issues related to fairness in sentencing are proportionality, equity, social debt, and truth in sentencing.

KEY TERMS

sentencing, *p. 72*
sentence, *p. 72*
social order, *p. 73*
revenge, *p. 74*
retribution, *p. 74*
just deserts, *p. 74*
deterrence, *p. 75*
specific deterrence, *p. 75*
general deterrence, *p. 76*
pleasure-pain principle, *p. 76*
incapacitation, *p. 76*

correctional econometrics, *p. 78*
rehabilitation, *p. 79*
reintegration, *p. 79*
restoration, *p. 80*
restorative justice, *p. 80*
victim impact statement, *p. 80*
restitution, *p. 84*
mandatory sentences, *p. 85*
presentence report (PSR), *p. 85*

consecutive sentences, *p. 86*
concurrent sentences, *p. 86*
model of criminal sentencing, *p. 86*
flat sentences, *p. 86*
indeterminate sentence, *p. 86*
good time, *p. 87*
determinate sentence, *p. 88*
sentencing commission, *p. 88*
sentencing enhancements, *p. 94*

REVIEW & APPLICATIONS

mandatory minimum
    sentencing, *p. 95*
habitual offender
    statute, *p. 98*

fair sentencing, *p. 101*
proportionality, *p. 102*
equity, *p. 102*

social debt , *p. 103*
truth in sentencing, *p. 103*

QUESTIONS FOR REVIEW

1. Define *sentencing*.
2. What are the modern goals of criminal sentencing?
3. Describe the two forms of deterrence.
4. Define *incapacitation*.
5. What is *correctional econometrics*?
6. When has rehabilitation been accomplished?
7. Restorative justice is based on what beliefs?
8. What are the five sentencing options in wide use in the United States today?

9. Differentiate between *fines* and *restitution*.
10. Give some examples of intermediate sanctions.
11. How have American models of criminal sentencing changed over the past 100 years?
12. What consequences might three-strikes (and two-strikes) laws have for the criminal justice system and for the corrections subsystem?

THINKING CRITICALLY ABOUT CORRECTIONS

▶ ▶ ▶ Rehabilitation

Edgardo Rotman says, in *Beyond Punishment*, "Rehabilitation . . . can be defined tentatively and broadly as a right to an opportunity to return to (or remain in) society with an improved chance of being a useful citizen and staying out of prison."[65] Do you agree that offenders have a right to rehabilitation? Why or why not?

▶ ▶ ▶ Mandatory Sentencing

Mandatory sentencing laws for drug possession offenses were initially hailed as the best method for toughening the government's response to the growing drug problem. Critics now complain that, in practice, mandatory sentencing rules lead to excessive punishments for many low-level offenders and to unwarranted leniency for the high-volume dealers who were the original targets of the new laws.

Further, critics contend that plea-bargaining is the culprit. Faced with lengthy prison terms, many arrested big-time dealers readily provide the names of numerous "little fish" in the drug distribution chain to prosecutors who are too quick to abandon prosecution of a single high-volume dealer in favor of procuring numerous convictions of low-level dealers.

Should mandatory sentencing laws be amended to prohibit plea bargaining in cases where the accused is charged with trafficking in quantities exceeding an established volume?

In view of the dramatic impact mandatory sentencing has had on prison population growth, should the sentences of current inmates be reviewed with an eye toward reducing, where appropriate, the sentences of the previously mentioned "little fish?"

ON-THE-JOB DECISION MAKING

▶ ▶ ▶ **Sentencing Fairness**

Federal judge Max Hamlin frets over two sentences he is about to impose. Standing in front of him is Jack Edmunds. Edmunds has been convicted in federal court of selling five grams of crack cocaine, and federal sentencing guidelines require that he receive a mandatory minimum five-year prison sentence. Also awaiting sentencing is Richard Doggart, a defendant who has been convicted of selling 500 grams of powdered cocaine. Hamlin knows that the federal guidelines also require a minimum five-year prison term for Doggart. The judge is concerned, however, because he does not want to sentence Doggart to any more time than the mandatory minimum. However, Doggart sold 100 times as much cocaine (by weight) as Edmunds did, and the requirements of the federal sentencing law seem unfair to the judge. He knows that pharmacologists have said that there is no difference between crack and powdered cocaine. Hamlin is aware, however, that the U.S. Department of Justice says that crack is more dangerous than powder because it easily can be broken down and packaged into very small quantities—which dealers then sell to the most vulnerable members of society. Hamlin also knows that any deviation from the sentencing guidelines will require him to write a lengthy justification, and he has little time for any more writing. What should Judge Hamlin do?

▶ ▶ ▶ **Recidivism**

You have spent the past six years as a counselor at a minimum-security state correctional facility. Your effectiveness has earned you a strong reputation throughout the Department of Corrections as a specialist in prerelease counseling, a program designed to prepare inmates for their return to society upon parole or completion of their sentence.

Lately, a series of highly publicized violent crimes has been committed by former inmates of the state's super-maximum security facility. All were released recently upon completion of their sentences, and all had moved almost directly from their cell back to the criminal lifestyle that originally landed them in prison.

Hard-line correctional officers insist that because those incarcerated in the "Super-Max" are the worst of the worst, they cannot be trusted to behave during prerelease counseling. The safety risks such inmates represent, they say, make leaving them in their cells until the law requires they be set free the only sensible course of action. What happens after that, in the hard-liners' opinions, is both the decision and responsibility of the former inmate.

Reformers insist that immediate recidivism is the likely outcome of releasing inmates directly from a harsh, totally controlled lockdown environment. They call for significant transitional counseling as essential for helping the inmate adjust to free society and also for defusing their angry urge to make society pay for the harsh life from which they are being released.

Both the governor and the commissioner of corrections face daily media demands to explain what the administration is going to do about this problem. In particular, the governor is under the gun because his opponent in the upcoming and hotly contested gubernatorial race has seized on this as an issue that demonstrates "this governor's inability, or unwillingness, to take the tough steps necessary to protect the good citizens of our state."

You have been asked to speak at a meeting to develop potential courses of action to address this problem. The meeting will be chaired by the corrections commissioner, and various wardens, assistant wardens, and senior correctional specialists from throughout the state will attend. It is likely but not yet confirmed that the governor will also attend.

1. What issues will you address?

2. How might you resolve the conflict between the need to protect counselors and staff from the often violent behavior of Super-Max inmates and the need to provide this critical prerelease counseling to these troubled inmates?

3. How would you respond to hard-line COs who contend that what happens after release is not their problem?

CORRECTIONS ON THE WEB

▶ ▶ ▶ The Sentencing Project

The Sentencing Project, based in Washington, D.C., is a nonprofit organization that promotes decreased reliance on incarceration and increased use of more effective and humane alternatives.

Access the Sentencing Project at http://www.sentencingproject.org. Determine whether the group is prosecution based or defense based. Then read the information you find about the Sentencing Project and the National Association of Sentencing Advocates. Write a paragraph summarizing the information.

▶ ▶ ▶ The U.S. Sentencing Commission

The United States Sentencing Commission is an independent federal agency in the judicial branch of government charged with formulating and amending national sentencing guidelines.

Visit the United States Sentencing Commission at http://www.ussc.gov. Explore the areas of interest to you. Then use the link to the state sentencing commissions and go to the NASC Contact List. If your state is listed, contact its commission to find out who serves on the commission and what the basic sentencing philosophy of the commission is. Write a few paragraphs summarizing the information you find.

REVIEW & APPLICATIONS

Community Corrections

Part Two examines what happens to convicted offenders, which includes diversion, probation, and intermediate sanctions. Diversion is the suspension of formal criminal proceedings before conviction in exchange for the defendant's participation in treatment, counseling, or other programs. Diversion recognizes that not all offenders should be formally prosecuted and subjected to the stigma of formal arrest, trial, and conviction.

As you will learn, diversion has its supporters and critics. Supporters believe diversion is the first opportunity to give offenders individualized assistance before they get too far down the path of crime and to resolve problems that lead to offending behavior. Critics argue that diversion tends to force people to give up some of their freedom without being tried and convicted, it violates the safeguard of due process, and it might actually produce more crime.

4

If diversion is not warranted or if an offender fails diversion, probation is often the next step in the correctional process. Probation is the conditional release of *convicted* offenders under community supervision. The degree of supervision depends on an offender's risk level. Some offenders pose no risk to the community. For them, checking in monthly at an automated probation kiosk may be all that is necessary. On the other hand, high-risk offenders require intensive face-to-face supervision and sometimes random drug testing, community service, and home confinement with remote-location monitoring.

5

Sanctions more punitive than probation but not as restrictive as incarceration, are called *intermediate sanctions.* Drug court, economic sanctions, community service, day reporting centers, remote-location monitoring, residential centers, and boot camps are some intermediate sanctions.

Today, almost 45,000 probation officers investigate and supervise over 3.9 million adults under probation and intermediate sanctions. Probation officers are faced with enormous case investigation and supervision challenges that include increasing caseloads without new resources, deciding on what information to include in a presentence report, figuring out how to structure the report so it is read, and incorporating novel forms of technology into their day-to-day jobs.

Whether supervision is low level or intense, many probationers will violate its technical conditions. Others will commit new crimes. Tightening the offender's supervision without resorting to using an already overburdened system of incarceration is a challenge that probation officers face. The decision to revoke probation and incarcerate the offender is influenced by legal, social, political, and economic issues.

COUNTY OF ORANGE
PROBATION
DEPARTMENT
SUITE 1 909

" If all law violations were processed officially as the arrest-conviction-
imprisonment model calls for, the system obviously would collapse
from its voluminous caseloads and from community opposition. "
—1976 National Advisory Commission on Criminal Justice Standards and Goals

CHAPTER

Diversion and Probation: How Most Offenders Are Punished

▶ ▶ ▶ **CHAPTER OBJECTIVES**

After completing this chapter you should be able to do the following:

1. Define *diversion* and know its objectives.

2. Explain the rationales for diversion.

3. Give examples of stages at which diversion occurs in the criminal justice process.

4. Discuss diversion policy issues.

5. Define *probation* and know its goals.

6. Explain the reasons for using probation.

7. Describe some of the characteristics of adults on probation.

8. Explain the different ways that probation is administered.

9. Describe the measures used to evaluate probation.

10. Describe the investigation and supervision functions of probation officers.

11. Explain revocation hearings.

Charlie Sheen, star of the TV sitcoms *Two and a Half Men* and *Spin City*, and the movies *Platoon, Wall Street,* and *Money Talks*, is a convicted misdemeanant. In June 1997, Sheen was accused of beating his girlfriend, slamming her to the floor, which left a gash on her lip that required seven stitches, and threatening to kill her if she told anyone what happened. Sheen pleaded "no contest" to the charge of battery in the Malibu courtroom of Judge Lawrence Mira. Under California law, "no contest" is the equivalent of a conviction without admitting guilt. Mira gave the actor a one-year suspended prison sentence and placed him on probation for two years. Mira also ordered Sheen to pay $2,800 in fines and restitution, perform 300 hours of community service, and attend eight counseling sessions. "You will not see me back in this courtroom," Sheen told the judge. One year later, however, Sheen was back in a Malibu courtroom for volunteering information that he used drugs while on probation. Noting that the actor had voluntarily divulged information about his drug use and had voluntarily entered a drug rehab clinic in Los Angeles, the judge extended Sheen's probation until June 2000.

In 1997 actor Charlie Sheen pled "no contest" to charges of battery with serious bodily injury. The charges stemmed from an incident involving his former girlfriend, Brittany Ashland. Sheen allegedly beat her and then threatened to kill her if she told anyone about what had happened. He received a one-year suspended prison term that required him to serve two years on probation. A year later, however, Sheen admitted that he used drugs while on probation, and his probationary term was extended. Is probation an effective criminal sanction?

Overview of Diversion and Probation

Charlie Sheen's case demonstrates a number of points covered in this chapter. A majority of offenders are sentenced to probation. Conditions of probation routinely include paying fines, restitution, and performing community service. Drug use is frequently connected with offending behavior, and rather than revoke a person's probation and order the person incarcerated, judges are willing to use a range of options to help offenders overcome their problems.

On January 1, 2003, 3,995,165 adults—1 of every 54 adults—were on probation in the United States.[1] The number of people on probation is equivalent to the population of South Carolina.

The typical probationer is a Southern white male who has never married and has either completed high school or earned a general equivalency diploma (GED). He has been convicted of a felony and has at least one prior sentence, to probation or confinement. He has five or more probation conditions and pays an average of $34 monthly in supervision fees plus monetary restitution to his victim. At least 40 percent of probationers are ordered to undergo substance abuse treatment.

However, the face of probation is changing. Using new laws that prohibit people from maintaining a building where drugs are sold or used, judges are ordering probation for companies found guilty of violating federal law. On June 13, 2001, a company called *Barbecue of New Orleans* pleaded guilty to violating federal crack-house laws. The company had leased a building known as the State Palace Theater for raves, or dance parties that feature extensive use of Ecstasy and other drugs. Since 1995, federal investigators had linked the raves held at the State Palace Theatre to numerous overdoses and to the death of a 17-year-old girl in 1998. Drug Enforcement Administration (DEA) agents bought 13 grams of Ecstasy at eight raves at the theater in 2001. The court did not shut down the raves but ordered that the Barbecue of New Orleans be placed on probation. The company was also fined $100,000 and ordered to stop the distribution of drug paraphernalia, including pacifiers, inhalers, and dust masks, at raves on its premises.

This chapter introduces you to two areas of corrections that most offenders first experience—diversion and probation. Diversion occurs *before* trial. Probation occurs *after* a person has been convicted. Figure 4–1 shows how these two processes can occur in the criminal justice system. Because offenders can be diverted one or more times before they are tried, convicted, and sentenced to probation, we discuss diversion first.

Diversion

Diversion has been defined as "the halting or suspension, before conviction, of formal criminal proceedings against a person, [often] conditioned on some form of counter performance by the defendant,"[2] and this is the

diversion

"The halting or suspension, before conviction, of formal criminal proceedings against a person, conditioned on some form of counter performance by the defendant."

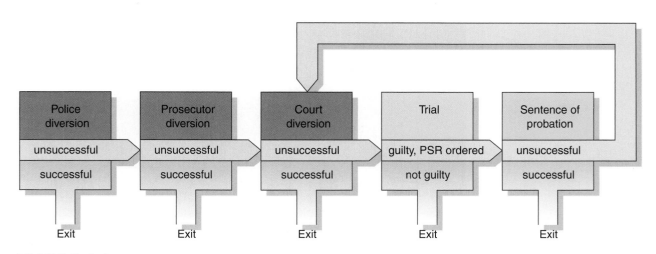

FIGURE 4-1
Case Flow Model for Diversion and Probation

counter performance

The defendant's participation, in exchange for diversion, in a treatment, counseling, or educational program aimed at changing his or her behavior.

definition we will use. **Counter performance** is the defendant's participation, in exchange for diversion, in a treatment, counseling, or educational program aimed at changing his or her behavior. The candidate for diversion is a person who has been or could be arrested for an alleged offense and who is or could become the defendant in a criminal prosecution. Suspending the prosecution of a case is the hallmark of the diversion process.

The overall goal of diversion is to reduce recidivism through rehabilitation. In the criminal justice system, diversion is used in two ways. First, it can be used to keep an offender out of the system and help him or her avoid formal prosecution and labeling. This is called **true diversion.** For example, a person caught smoking marijuana by the police could be counseled by the police and referred to TASC (Treatment Alternatives to Street Crime) without the threat of arrest and prosecution for not attending. TASC provides services to encourage diversion such as diagnosing drug problems, referring clients to community treatment programs, and monitoring progress.

true diversion

A form of diversion that keeps an offender out of the system and helps him or her avoid formal prosecution and labeling.

minimization of penetration

A form of diversion that keeps an offender from going further into the system.

The second way of using diversion is to keep an offender from going further into the system. This is called **minimization of penetration.** For example, a man charged with possession and use of crack cocaine could be referred to TASC with the stipulation that, if he completes the treatment program, the charge will be dropped. If he does not complete the program, he will be prosecuted for the crime. In this case, TASC reports information back to criminal justice agencies.

The police, a prosecutor, a judge, or a probation officer may call for diversion. Here the police and a probation officer practice *true diversion* by counseling youth caught smoking marijuana and referring them to TASC. Do you think *true diversion* invites more law violation by allowing offenders to avoid prosecution?

Across the United States today, TASC is one of the major approaches to the diversion of drug-abusing offenders. A rigorous study of five TASC diversion programs in 1999 found that TASC was effective in delivering to offenders treatment services such as drug counseling, urinalysis to detect drug use, and AIDS education. However, there was no clear evidence of reductions in either new arrests or *technical violations* (technical violations are discussed later in this chapter). The research also found that the hardcore offenders benefit from TASC more than those who pose the least threat or seem the easiest to treat.[3]

> Across the United States today, TASC is one of the major approaches to the diversion of drug-abusing offenders.

Most diversion programs share three objectives:

1. Prevent future criminal activity by diverting certain defendants from criminal justice processing into community supervision and service. This goal is based on the belief that diversion programs are more effective ways to control criminal behavior than taking offenders to court, convicting them, and sentencing them.
2. Save prosecution and judicial resources for serious crimes by offering, for less serious crimes, alternatives to the usual prosecution process. Defendants eligible for diversion are given the opportunity to avoid arrest or prosecution and to obtain medical services, counseling, and educational and vocational training.
3. Provide, where appropriate, a vehicle for restitution to communities and victims of crime.

RATIONALES FOR DIVERSION

Diversion has four rationales. First, the experience and the stigma of being formally arrested, tried, and convicted can actually encourage more criminal behavior. For example, having a criminal record might restrict a person's educational, vocational, and social opportunities, making the person more apt to turn to crime to survive. In addition, as a result of time spent in jail or prison, an offender may be more likely to associate with other offenders.

A second rationale for using diversion is that it is less expensive than formally processing an offender through the criminal justice system. The expense of arrest, trial, conviction, and sentence is easily justified for serious crimes. In most cities and counties across the United States today, however, police are overworked, courts are overloaded, jails and prisons are overcrowded, and probation and parole officers have caseloads that are unmanageable. Diversion is a way to reduce or at least contain these burdens, reserving formal criminal justice processing for the cases that need it the most.

A third rationale for diversion is that the public may think formal processing through the criminal justice system is inappropriate for crimes without perceived victims. These offenses involve a willing and private exchange of illegal goods or services. Examples include prostitution, certain forms of sexual behavior, gambling, and drug sales. Such offenses are called *victimless crimes* because the participants do not feel they are being harmed. Prosecution is justified on the grounds that these offenses harm society as a whole by threatening the moral fabric of the community. Since formal prosecution of these offenses is costly, offenders are often diverted to health clinics and treatment programs.

A final rationale for using diversion is to give the typical diversion client a better chance in life. Our nation's jails, lockups, prisons, and probation and parole caseloads are filled with people who are economically disadvantaged, belong to minority groups, and are young, undereducated, and chronically unemployed or underemployed. Diversion offers such persons help with some of the challenges they face, without adding to their difficulties the stigma of formal arrest, trial, and conviction.

THE PROCESS OF DIVERSION

Diversion may occur at any point in the criminal justice process after a criminal complaint has been filed or police have observed a crime. The police, a prosecutor, or a judge may call for diversion. The accused participates voluntarily and has access to defense counsel before deciding whether to participate.

Most diversion programs use an assessment process to determine a defendant's needs. Then an intervention plan for that defendant is developed. The diversion program then contracts with the defendant, and all parties agree on the requirements of the plan and the criminal justice consequences of succeeding or failing in the plan. Figure 4–2 shows the conditions of pretrial diversion used by the TASC program in Alabama. Similar conditions are used by diversion programs in many other states. In some states, the diversion process is established by law; in other states, local agreements with prosecutors are the basis for the process.

Diversion programs offer a variety of remedial responses to defendants' problems. Such responses can include drug and alcohol treatment, mental health services, employment counseling, and education and training. They may involve agencies in or outside of the criminal justice system. The variety of responses often reflects a community's unique criminal justice population.

Diversion is also used for persons who are classified as mentally ill or incompetent and either are not equipped to stand trial or need a form of incarceration and treatment other than imprisonment. Such persons may be referred to an agency for voluntary treatment or civil commitment to an institution in lieu of prosecution and a prison sentence.

DIVERSION POLICY ISSUES

Diversion has its supporters and critics. Supporters believe diversion is the first opportunity to give offenders individualized assistance before they get too far down the path of crime. Diversion may thus resolve problems that lead to offending behavior. Critics argue that diversion tends to force people to give up some of their freedom without being tried and convicted. They argue that it violates the safeguard of due process. Other critics believe that diversion is "nonpunishment" and might actually produce more crime. To these and other issues about diversion we now turn our attention.

STATE OF ALABAMA

- STATE OF ALABAMA
- JEFFERSON COUNTY
- <u>District</u> COURT
- BOND $ <u>$5,000.00</u>
- CASE NO. <u>DC04-6342917</u>

vs

<u>Brett Gould</u>

CONDITIONS OF RELEASE

1. Defendant must appear to answer and must submit to the orders and process of the court having jurisdiction of this case as directed.

2. Defendant must refrain from committing any criminal offense.

3. Defendant must refrain from any contact with prosecutor's witness(s) /the complainant's victim(s). Specifically: <u>Karen Koch</u>.

4. Defendant must continue to reside at <u>2055 2nd. Ave., Birmingham</u> with <u>son</u>, and may not leave the state of Alabama or change residence without written permission of the Court having jurisdiction of this case.

5. Defendant must obtain and/or maintain full-time employment or schooling. Written verification of employment attendance or attempts to secure employment/enrollment will be presented to the TASC case manager.

6. Defendant must report to the TASC Office within 72 hours after release, at 401 Beacon Parkway West, for an evaluation by a case manager.

7. Defendant must submit to random urinalysis for drug screening. Defendant must pay the $20 fee for each month. If drug abuse is indicated, appropriate treatment will be required.

8. Defendant must attend AA/NA/CA meetings <u>3</u> times per week and provide case manager with written verification of that attendance.

9. Defendant must abide by a curfew requiring presence in house of residence between hours of <u>6</u> p.m. and <u>7</u> a.m.

10. Defendant must seek and accept drug and/or alcohol treatment within <u>7</u> days of release date.

11. Defendant must appear in this court on the next scheduled court date, <u>March 20, 2004</u>.

Done this <u>13th</u> day of <u>March</u>, 20 <u>04</u>

<u>Carl Stephan</u>
Judge

INSTRUCTION TO DEFENDANT

You have agreed to appear in court whenever ordered. Your responsibility to the above conditions is to remain until either the case is ended or you are released. If you do not appear whenever ordered, you may be required to pay the bond amount.

<u>Brett Gould</u>
DEFENDANT

<u>Terry Williams</u>
WITNESSED

FIGURE 4-2
Pretrial Release Bond Agreement

Legal and Ethical Issues   There is agreement that a diversion program should protect a defendant's rights. Protections include requiring an informed waiver of the right to a speedy trial, the right to a trial by jury, the right to confront one's accusers, the privilege against self-incrimination, and informed consent to the conditions of a diversion program. For supporters, the risk of violating rights is outweighed by the chance diversion gives defendants to avoid the stigma of a criminal record and by the possibility of resolving problems that might result in future criminal behavior.

unconditional diversion

The termination of criminal processing at any point before adjudication with no threat of later prosecution. Treatment, counseling, and other services are offered and use is voluntary.

Unconditional diversion is the termination of criminal processing at any point before adjudication with no threat of later prosecution. It affords the best protection for a defendant's legal rights because dismissal of charges does not require any counterperformance. In effect, the defendant has everything to gain and nothing to lose. In unconditional diversion, treatment, counseling, and other services are offered on a voluntary basis. Many corrections leaders regard voluntary treatment as more likely than coerced treatment to have beneficial effects.

conditional diversion

Diversion in which charges are dismissed if the defendant satisfactorily completes treatment, counseling, or other programs ordered by the justice system.

Conditional diversion means that charges are dismissed if the defendant satisfactorily completes treatment, counseling, or other programs ordered by the justice system. Conditional diversion at or after arraignment, with judicial participation, affords greater protection against prosecutorial overreach and more assurance of informed voluntary decisions by the defendant than does diversion by the police or the prosecutor. In diversion programs run by the police and prosecutor, some participants may not have been prosecuted at all or might have been exonerated (cleared of blame) if they had been prosecuted. Conditional diversion does not eliminate the possibility of more severe penalties for divertees who fail the program.

Law Enforcement Issues   Does diversion weaken law enforcement? Does diversion invite more widespread violation of laws by allowing offenders to avoid conviction? There is no particular evidence one way or the other. Certainly, if unconditional diversion were practiced extensively, there might be increases in violations. However, if unconditional diversion is limited to the first or second charge, then increases in violations are less likely. Conditional diversion requiring supervision and counter performance does not seem more likely to encourage crime than the dispositions it most often replaces—fines, suspended sentences, and probation.

Economic Issues   How cost-effective is diversion? What is the least costly method of diversion that will yield acceptable results? What are the trade-offs among different kinds of diversion programs? How does diversion compare in cost and effectiveness with traditional prosecution and sentencing practices?

Some argue that, in the long run, diversion can protect the community better than traditional processing can. Consider that, with diversion, treatment starts promptly after the criminal act, the social handicap of a criminal record is avoided, and exposure to criminal influences is minimized.

Presumably, diversion is less conducive to recidivism than is traditional processing. However, efforts to compare diversion with what would have happened without it have been unsuccessful. It seems safe to say that the community protection that diversion affords is at least comparable to the traditional measures that would most likely be used if prosecution were not suspended. The economic question, then, is which approach costs less?

The costs of both diversion and its alternatives include the costs of arriving at a decision; the costs of implementing decisions; and the costs of undesired consequences of decisions, such as reinstatement of prosecution, leveling of new charges, or revocation of probation or parole because of a new charge or violation.

Diversion is not always the appropriate response to criminal behavior. When diversion fails to bring about the desired changes in an offender's behavior, probation is often the next step in the corrections process.

Probation

Probation has long been one of the most popular and most frequently used forms of criminal punishment (see Figure 4–3). It is a way to keep the offender at home in the community, avoid incarceration, and carry out sanctions imposed by the court or the probation agency. **Probation** is the conditional release of a convicted offender into the community, under the supervision of a probation officer. It is conditional because it can be revoked if certain conditions are not met. The judge or the probation department usually imposes a set of restrictions on the offender's freedom. Almost all probationers have at least one special condition on their release.[4] Among such conditions are paying fines or restitution; submitting to electronic monitoring, house arrest, or drug tests; obeying a curfew; and keeping a log of daily activities. More than 80 percent of probationers have three or more conditions on their sentences. The most common (84 percent) condition is the payment of fees, fines, or court costs. If the probationer violates any of the technical conditions of her or his probation or commits a new crime, the judge may order that the entire sentence be served in prison.

Under probation, the offender lives at home but is monitored in some way, such as by meeting with a probation officer a specified number of

probation
The conditional release of a convicted offender into the community, under the supervision of a probation officer. It is conditional because it can be revoked if certain conditions are not met.

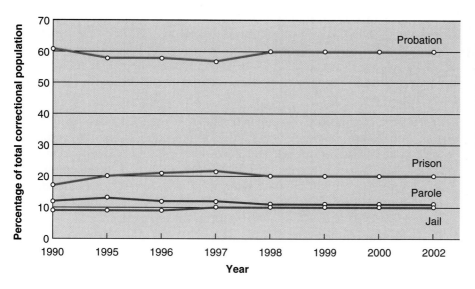

FIGURE 4-3
Adults on Probation, on Parole, in Jail, or in Prison

Source: Lauren E. Glaze, *Probation and Parole in the United States, 2002* (Washington, DC: Bureau of Justice Statistics, August 2003) and Lauren E. Glaze, *Probation and Parole in the United States, 2001* (Washington, DC: Bureau of Justice Statistics, August 2002).

times per month. According to the Bureau of Justice Statistics, three out of every four probationers were under active supervision on January 1, 2003, and were required to report regularly to a probation authority in person, by mail, or by telephone. The percent of probationers required to report regularly has dropped steadily, from 83 percent in 1990 to 75 percent in 2003.

REASONS FOR AND GOALS OF PROBATION

Probation is used for at least four reasons. First, probation permits the offender to remain in the community for reintegration purposes. Offender reintegration is more likely to occur if social and family ties are not broken by incarceration.

Second, probation avoids prison institutionalization and the stigma of incarceration. Prison institutionalization is the process of learning and adopting the norms and culture of institutional living. Living in the artificial environment of an institution does not teach prisoners how to live in the free world. Probationers do not experience prison institutionalization, nor do they have to worry about the negative effects of being treated like a prisoner, which decrease even further their ability to function as law-abiding citizens when released.

The third reason for probation is that it is less expensive than incarceration, more humanitarian, and at least as effective as incarceration in reducing future criminal activity.

The final reason for probation is that it is fair and appropriate sentencing for offenders whose crimes do not merit incarceration. Furthermore, probation is the base on which more severe punishments can be built. Not all crimes deserve incarceration, nor do all crimes deserve probation. Probation is preferred when the offender poses no threat to community safety, when community correctional resources are available, and when probation does not unduly minimize the seriousness of the offense. The probation risk-needs assessment and statutory sentencing guidelines help identify which offenders deserve community-based punishment and which deserve institutional punishment.

The goals of probation reflect society's values. In the 1960s, when society showed a strong interest in social welfare and offender rehabilitation, probation work reflected that emphasis. Today, probation emphasizes offender control. Most probation programs share five goals:

1. Protect the community by preparing the presentence report (PSR) to assist judges in sentencing and supervising offenders. The PSR indicates the degree of risk an offender poses to the community. It also identifies the offender's special needs. Offenders posing a threat to the community are then given secure placement, usually incarceration. Offenders who do not pose a threat to the community are given probation supervision. (We will return to the PSR later in this chapter.)

2. Carry out sanctions imposed by the court. Probation officers accomplish this by educating offenders about the orders of the court,

Ethical Dilemma

Does gender or celebrity status play a role in who gets probation? For more information go to Ethical Dilemma 4-1 at http://www.mhhe.com/schmalleger2.

supervising offenders, and removing them from the community when they violate the conditions of their probation.

3. Conduct a risk-needs assessment to identify the level of supervision and the services probationers need.

4. Support crime victims by collecting information that describes the losses, suffering, and trauma experienced by a crime victim or by the victim's survivors. This information is reported to the court in a written document called the victim-impact statement. The judge considers it when sentencing the offender. The information is particularly valuable for sentences that include restitution.

5. Coordinate and promote the use of community resources. Probation officers refer offenders to community agencies and programs that serve the offenders' needs. Such programs include drug and alcohol treatment, job training, vocational education, anger management, and life skills training.

Not all probation agencies achieve these objectives in the same way. A probation department's orientation is a function of many factors, including department philosophy, leadership, the community served, and the offenders supervised. Some departments lean more toward treating the offender; others lean more toward offender control. It is likely that the majority of probation departments do both, depending on the need and the situation. The American Correctional Association Policy on Probation is found in Exhibit 4–1.

HISTORY OF PROBATION

Probation in America developed during the 19th century. What started as a charitable and volunteer movement took almost 125 years to become available to adults in every state across the country.

Probation Begins in America   It was in the Boston courtroom of Municipal Court Judge Peter Oxenbridge Thatcher, in 1830, that the groundwork for probation was laid. Searching for a new way to exercise leniency and to humanize the criminal law—sentencing goals that still dominate corrections —Judge Thatcher made the first recorded use of *release on recognizance* in America, in sentencing Jerusa Chase.

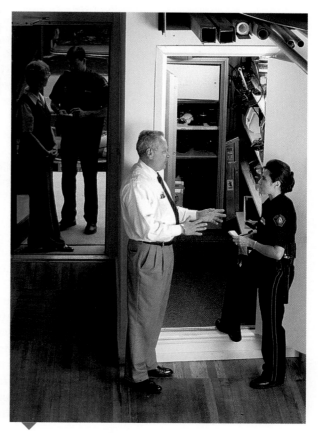

A house is burglarized and the owners call the police to describe their losses, suffering, and trauma. Judges consider the report when sentencing the offender. What kind of information do you think would be important to include in such a statement?

> The indictment against Jerusa Chase was found at the January term of the court. . . . She pleaded guilty to the same and would have been pronounced at that time, but upon the application of her friends, and with the consent of the attorney of the Commonwealth, she was permitted, upon her recognizance for her appearance in this Court whenever she should be called for, to go at large.[5]

EXHIBIT 4-1 American Correctional Association

Policy on Probation

Probation is a frequently used and cost-effective sanction of the court for enhancing social order and public safety. Probation may be used as a sanction by itself or, where necessary and appropriate, be combined with other sanctions such as fines, restitution, community service, residential care, and confinement. Agencies responsible for probation should do the following:

1. Prepare disposition assessments to assist the court in arriving at appropriate sanctions. The least restrictive disposition consistent with public safety should be recommended.

2. Establish a case management system for allocating supervisory resources through a standardized classification process.

3. Provide supervision to probationers and, with their input, develop a realistic plan to ensure compliance with orders of the court.

4. Monitor and evaluate, on an ongoing basis, the probationer's adherence to the plan of supervision and, when necessary, modify the plan of supervision according to the changing needs of the offender and the best interests of society.

5. Provide access to a wide range of services to meet identifiable needs, all of which are directed toward promoting law-abiding behavior.

6. Assure any intervention in an offender's life will not exceed the minimal amount needed to assure compliance with the orders of the court.

7. Initiate appropriate court proceedings, when necessary, if the probationer fails to comply with orders of the court, the supervision plan, or other requirements, so the court may consider other alternatives for the protection and well-being of the community.

8. Oppose use of the probation sanction for status offenders, neglected or dependent children, or any other individuals who are neither accused of nor charged with delinquent or criminal behavior.

9. Establish an educational program for sharing information about probation with the public and other agencies.

10. Evaluate program efficiency, effectiveness, and overall system accountability consistent with recognized correctional standards.

Chase's release had many of the characteristics of present-day probation: suspension of sentence, freedom to stay in the community, conditions on that freedom, and the possibility of revocation of freedom for violation of the conditions.

In 1841 when John Augustus,[6] a wealthy Boston shoemaker, became interested in the operation of the courts, the practice of probation began to emerge. Augustus was particularly sensitive to the problems of persons charged with violating Boston's vice or temperance laws. He was a member of the Washington Total Abstinence Society, an organization devoted to the promotion of temperance. By posting bail in selected cases, he had the offenders released to his care and supervision, and so began the work of the nation's first probation officer, an unpaid volunteer. Augustus carefully screened the offenders he sought to help. Here is an entry from his journal:

> In the month of August, 1841, I was in court one morning . . . in which [a] man was charged with being a common drunkard. The case was clearly made out, but before sentence was passed, I conversed with him for a few moments, and found that he was not yet past all hope of reformation. . . . He

told me that if he could be saved from the House of Corrections, he never again would taste intoxicating liquors; there was such an earnestness in that one, and a look of firm resolve, that I determined to aid him; I bailed him, by permission of the Court. He was ordered to appear for sentence in three weeks; at the expiration of this period of probation, I accompanied him into the courtroom. . . . The Judge expressed himself much pleased with the account we gave of the man, and instead of the usual penalty—imprisonment in the House of Correction—he fined him one cent and costs, amounting in all to $3.76, which was immediately paid. The man continued industrious and sober, and without doubt has been by this treatment, saved from a drunkard's grave.

John Augustus (1785–1859) was a Boston shoemaker who invented probation in 1841, and became the first "unofficial" probation officer. He is called the Father of Probation. Which aspects of Augustus' probation system are still in use today?

Augustus criticized the police, judges, and others who did not share his views. His "helping" role was not universally accepted. Law enforcement officials of the day wanted offenders punished, not helped. A newspaper of the time described him as someone who "seems to have a great itching for notoriety, and dollars . . . and takes more airs upon himself than all the judges and officers . . . and unless he conducts himself henceforth with a great deal more propriety, we shall take it upon ourself [*sic*] to teach him decency."

Still, Augustus persisted and, by the time of his death in 1859, he had won probation for almost 2,000 adults and several thousand children. Several aspects of his probation system are still in use. Augustus investigated the age, character, and work habits of each offender. He identified persons he thought redeemable and "whose hearts were not fully depraved, but gave promise of better things." He made probation recommendations to the court. He developed conditions of probation and helped offenders with employment, education, and housing. And he supervised offenders during their probation, which lasted, on the average, about 30 days. Until 1878, probation continued to be the work of volunteers—individuals and agencies.

Early Probation Statutes   In 1878, the Massachusetts legislature passed the first statute authorizing probation. The law applied only to Suffolk County (Boston). It required the mayor of Boston to appoint a probation officer from the police department or citizenry. In 1880, a new law authorized probation as an option in all cities and towns in Massachusetts. But because the law remained voluntary and the probation concept was still new, few cities and towns exercised the power. In 1891, the power to appoint probation officers was transferred from the mayor to the court, in response to criticism that the mayor's appointments were influenced by political considerations. The second state to pass a probation statute was Vermont, in 1898.

As more and more states passed laws authorizing probation, probation became a national institution. On March 4, 1925, President Calvin Coolidge signed the National Probation Act. The act authorized each federal district court to appoint one salaried probation officer with an annual income of $2,600.[7]

The early laws had little in common. Some authorized probation for adults only. Others authorized it for juveniles only. (In fact, the spread of probation was accelerated by the juvenile court movement.) Some laws restricted the crimes for which probation could be granted. Still others provided for the hiring of probation officers but neglected to provide for paying them. Training for probation officers was brief or nonexistent. Appointments were often based on politics rather than merit, and salaries were typically even lower than those of unskilled laborers. By 1925, probation was available for juveniles in every state; by 1956, it was available for adults in every state.

CHARACTERISTICS OF ADULTS ON PROBATION

On January 1, 2003, 3,995,165 adults were on federal, state, or local probation, an increase of 1.6 percent (63,434) over January 1, 2002.[8] One of every 54 persons age 18 or older is on probation. The average length of probation is 27 months.[9] Table 4–1 shows that the majority of adults on probation are in regular caseloads, they have one face-to-face contact with their probation officers per month, and the cost of their supervision is $2.11 per day. By contrast, offenders who pose a higher risk of re-offending or who might otherwise be incarcerated are placed in intensive supervision caseloads. Each caseload averages 29 offenders, with seven face-to-face contacts with their probation officers per month, and costing approximately $9.66 per day. Without probation, the cost of jail incarceration is $56.72 per day, and the cost of prison incarceration is $57.92 per day. Probation is cost-effective, providing it can protect the community by matching the level of supervision with the level of risk an offender poses.

Figure 4–4 presents selected characteristics of the 3.9 million adults on probation in 2003. For example, women made up 23 percent of the probation population. Blacks represented a third of probationers, while Hispanics, who may be of any race, made up 12 percent of probationers. Less than 1 percent of probationers are on federal probation. Other interesting

TABLE 4-1	Probation Statistics		
Case type*	Average caseload per officer	Average number of face-to-face contacts between probationer and officer per month	Average cost per day per probationer
Regular	139	1	$2.11
Intensive	29	7	$9.66
Electronic	6	3	$8.71
Special	45	4	$4.27

*Regular supervision: Supervision of a probationer according to normal/average number of visits, contacts, or reports with a probation officer. Intensive supervision: Supervision of a probationer that includes a greater number of visits, contacts, or reports to or from a probation officer than exists under regular supervision. Offenders who pose a higher risk of re-offending or who might otherwise be incarcerated are candidates for placement under intensive supervision. Electronic supervision: Supervision of a probationer that includes the use of an electronic monitoring device such as an ankle bracelet, pager, or voice verification telephone that assists probation officers in ascertaining an offender's whereabouts. Special supervision: Supervision of a probationer that includes special programming such as boot camp, substance abuse treatment programs, sex offender treatment, or other programs or services. More about intensive, electronic, and special supervision programming is discussed in Chapter 5.

Source: Adapted form Camille Graham Camp and George W. Camp, The Corrections Yearbook 2000, pp. 170, 172, 176, 177, and 187. Copyright © 2000 Criminal Justice Institute. Used with permission.

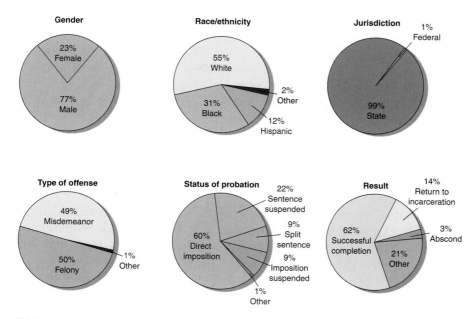

FIGURE 4-4
Selected Characteristics of Adults on Probation, January 1, 2003

Source: Lauren E. Glaze, *Probation and Parole in the United States, 2002* (Washington, DC: Bureau of Justice Statistics, August 2003).

findings about probationers are that one-half were sentenced for felony convictions, 49 percent for a misdemeanor, and 1 percent for other infractions. Twenty-four percent were on probation for drug law violations and 17 percent for driving while intoxicated.

The Bureau of Justice Statistics also reported that 60 percent of probationers had a direct sentence to probation; 22 percent received a sentence to incarceration that had been suspended; and 9 percent received incarceration followed by probation an arrangement sometimes called a *split sentence.* As Figure 4–4 shows, 62 percent of probationers successfully completed their terms of supervision during 2002, with *successful* meaning the satisfaction of all requirements of supervision (that is, completing all proscribed visits, passing substance abuse tests, receiving counseling, and meeting other requirements that may have been in place), up 2 percent from the previous year.

Recently, researchers at the Department of Justice learned from hour-long interviews with active probationers that 9 percent of male probationers and 28 percent of female probationers had been physically or sexually abused before their sentences and before age 18.[10] (Prevalence estimates of child abuse in the general population are 5 to 8 percent for males and 12 to 17 percent for females.) Abused probationers told DOJ researchers that the abuser was either a family member or someone they knew intimately. Researchers are just beginning to study the link between child abuse and offending.

On January 1, 2003, 1,854 adults were on probation for every 100,000 persons aged 18 and older in the United States, up from 1,297 a decade earlier and 1,537 in 1996. The Bureau of Justice Statistics also reports that the southern U.S. states generally have the highest per capita ratio of probationers—reporting 2,105 probationers per 100,000 adults. In terms of sheer numbers of probationers, Texas has the largest adult probation population (about 434,493), followed by California (358,121). The smallest adult probation populations are in New Hampshire (3,102) and North Dakota (3,199). Only 31,326 persons were on federal probation on January 1, 2003.

The five states that use probation the most are Washington (3,819), Delaware (3,328), Idaho (3,263), Minnesota (3,237), and Rhode Island (3,168). The five states that use probation the least are New Hampshire (387 per 100,000 adult population), West Virginia (446), North Dakota (669), Utah (677), and Virginia (730).

If probation were being used primarily as an alternative to incarceration, one might expect to find that the states that imposed more probationary sentences would have lower than average incarceration rates and vice versa. This is not the case. Southern states generally place more persons on probation at a high rate, and they generally incarcerate more than the rest of the nation, as we shall see in Chapter 7. The main reason is that there are no national guidelines for granting probation or limiting its use. The court is supposed to grant probation when the defendant does not pose a risk to society and if the granting of probation would not underrate the seriousness of the offense. Only recently have states begun to define categories of offenses that render offenders ineligible for probation. Mandatory sentencing now limits judicial discretion and the court's ability to grant probation to repeat offenders.

WHO ADMINISTERS PROBATION?

As probation spread throughout the United States in the late 19th and early 20th centuries, its organization and administration depended on local and state customs and politics. Currently, probation in the 50 states is administered by more than 2,000 separate agencies, reflecting the decentralized and fragmented character of contemporary corrections. The agencies have a great deal of common ground, but because they developed in different contexts, they also have many differences in goals, policies, funding, staffing, salaries, budgets, and operation. In 2000, the average budget for probation agencies across the United States was $56 million, an increase of only 1 percent ($600,000) from 1992. The number of persons on probation, however, increased 36 percent from 1992 to 2003, from 2.8 million to 3.9 million. Probation supporters argue that resources for probation have not kept pace with the increase in the number of persons sentenced to probation.

> Probation supporters argue that resources for probation have not kept pace with the increase in the number of persons sentenced to probation.

Probation is commonly considered a part of the correctional system, although it is technically a function of the court system. Figure 4–5 gives a state-by-state breakdown of how probation is administered. The map shows that in most (31) states the responsibility for adult probation rests with the state department of corrections. This means that one statewide agency administers a central probation system for adult offenders and provides services throughout the state. The second most common way of administering adult probation is through the court system. In 10 states and the District of Columbia, the responsibility for adult probation lies with the state judiciary. In eight states, the responsibility is shared by the state and the counties. In one state, counties provide adult probation services. Federal probation is administered through the Administrative Office of the U.S. Courts. Federal probation officers, like most state adult probation officers, also carry adult parole caseloads. Juvenile probation is generally organized and administered at the county court level, although variations exist. Understanding how adult and juvenile and state and federal probation are organized is important for finding out about career opportunities in probation and applying for jobs.

Ms. Kathy Waters, immediate past president of the American Probation and Parole Association and author of this chapter's Reflections on the Future feature, has worked in both executive and judicial branches of government that have the jurisdiction and responsibility for probation. She says there's nothing magical about where probation services are organized and administered.[11]

> There are difficulties in both jurisdictions. . . . Probation and parole continue to change as each matures. . . . Whether under the executive branch of government (which, for some jurisdictions, works well) or under the judiciary (which seems like the only natural place for probation to be in some states), the system will have problems and frustrations that will need to be addressed. . . . Both branches provide leadership, policy establishment, and the resources to fulfill their mission.

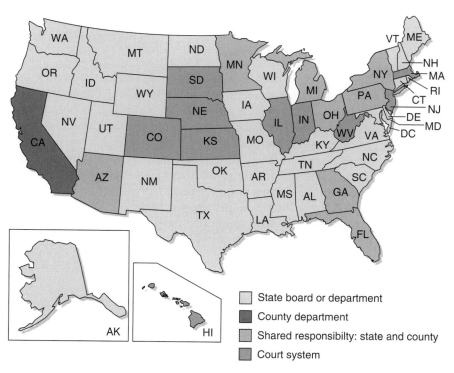

FIGURE 4-5
Administration of Adult Probation in the States

CAREER PROFILE

Mechael Dedeian

Senior Probation and Parole Officer (CSAC)   District 29 Adult Probation and Parole   Fairfax, Virginia

Mechael Dedeian is a senior probation and parole officer with District 29 Adult Probation and Parole in Fairfax, Virginia. She has worked there for the past 15 years, in a senior position for the past three. Prior to that, she worked as both a jails auditor and a CDI case manager. She earned her Bachelor's of Science degree in elementary education from Longwood College in Farmville, Virginia. She later went on to acquire her CSAC (Certified Substance Abuse Counselor) certification.

Mechael says she fell in love with probation while working with the CDI program, and it was also in her blood to start with—her father was a juvenile probation officer. She specializes in substance abusers and individuals with mental health problems, so on any given day she sees a wide variety of challenges—getting relapsed individuals into detox, placing people in the right programs, deciding when to have someone arrested, and working with jails and others within the system. With a laugh, she describes her days as "rough . . . never-ending."

"I wear many hats, and that's the one thing with a probation officer," she says. "Sometimes I'm the jailer, sometimes I get them off the street, sometimes I try to get them into the treatment program that they need. I just have to decide which hat to put on—am I the police officer? Am I the counselor? It's a case by case basis."

Although the job is tough, Mechael loves what she does. She recalls her first parolee, when she started the job at age 24—he still calls her every now and then to tell her he's doing well. "So there are some successes," she says. "But it's not a job where you get a lot of pats on the back—you have to be a self-motivator, and you have to know that what you're doing is making a difference, even if you don't see it all the time."

> " There are days where all you do is put out a fire— sometimes they're huge fires. But when you're dealing with people that don't follow rules, this is what you get. "

Privatizing Probation   Today there is also a movement to let the private sector administer probation supervision. Two states—Connecticut and Colorado—have successfully privatized probation supervision. In both states, the impetus for privatizing probation was similar: Staffing and resources were not keeping pace with increasing caseloads. Community supervision officials felt they had exhausted the use of interns and volunteers, and funding for new staff was not possible. They used risk management principles to assign staff and resources in direct proportion to the risk levels of cases. Both states partnered with the private sector to monitor the low-risk offender population, people who generally have few needs, whose past records reflect little or no violence, and who successfully complete probation about 90 percent of the time.

In Connecticut, the privatization initiative to monitor low-risk offender populations by the private sector allowed scarce resources to be used to better monitor offenders with higher levels of risk. Private case management responsibilities in Connecticut included sending an introductory letter to the probationer, monitoring restitution payments and compliance with conditions of probation, responding to probationer's inquiries, preparing standardized reports for probation officers, providing verification of condition compliance, and providing statistical reports. Robert J. Bosco, director of Connecticut's Office of Adult Probation, says that the "success" of this privatization initiative "is in the agency's ability to use its resources to control recidivism of the highest-risk offender population."[12]

The situation in Colorado was similar. When Colorado officials adopted risk management and looked at how treatment and supervision were matched with levels of risk, they found more probation officers were needed than the Colorado General Assembly would fund. The result was a directive that allowed probation departments to contract with private agencies for the supervision of low-risk probationers. Thirteen of Colorado's 22 judicial districts have entered into such contracts. The private agencies directly bill the probationers for their supervision, eliminating public expenditures for community supervision. According to Suzanne Pullen, management analyst with Colorado's Judicial Department in the Office of Probation Services, "The diversion of these low-risk offenders allows local probation departments to focus more clearly on the supervision and case management of medium- and high-risk offenders that are burdening their caseloads."[13]

A probation officer involves an offender's spouse to help with rehabilitation. Probation officers also refer offenders to community agencies to help them overcome the problem that led to their offending behavior. What obstacles might a probation officer face in making referrals to a community agency and involving the family in offender rehabilitation?

A number of researchers and organizations have expressed reservations about turning over probation to the private sector. The American Probation and Parole Association (APPA) does not support the wholesale privatization of probation, parole, or community-based corrections, but it does recognize that the private sector offers new tools—such as expertise, specialized services, and advanced technologies with which the jurisdiction has had little experience or involvement—to assist probation departments in supervising offenders. Carl Wicklund, executive director of APPA, cautions that private companies need to be held to the same standards as public agencies. "It's not enough to do it because it is cheaper," he argues. Government jurisdictions and their representatives are ultimately accountable for the quality and care of private sector services delivered under contractual agreements. By operating within established parameters, standards, regulations, and laws, private probation providers can contribute to the ability of a probation department to protect the public and supervise offenders under its jurisdiction.

DOES PROBATION WORK?

The most common question asked about probation is "Does it work?" In other words, do persons granted probation refrain from further crime? **Recidivism**—generally defined as *rearrest*—continues to be the primary outcome measure for probation, as it is for all corrections programs. Summaries of probation effectiveness usually report the recidivism rates of felons as if felons represented the total adult probation population, instead of just 52 percent of it. Some researchers tell us that recidivism rates are

recidivism

The repetition of criminal behavior; generally defined as *rearrest*. It is the primary outcome measure for probation, as it is for all corrections programs.

low for misdemeanant probationers but high for felony probationers. RAND researchers found that over three-fourths of offenders on probation for a misdemeanor successfully complete their probation, but almost two-thirds of felony probationers are rearrested.[14] Recently, however, a study of the recidivism of male property offenders on felony probation showed just the opposite: a success rate of 67.7 percent; in essence, the antithesis of RAND's findings.[15] According to the Department of Justice, however, the percentage of all offenders successfully completing their probation terms is falling. In 1986, 74 percent of those who exited probation successfully completed their terms; by 2001, the figure had dropped to 60 percent.

Recidivism rates vary greatly from place to place, depending on the seriousness of offenses, population characteristics, average length of probation, and the amount and quality of intervention, surveillance, and enforcement. A summary of 17 studies of adult felony probationers found that felony rearrest rates ranged from 12 to 65 percent. John Gondles Jr., Executive Director of the American Correctional Association, argues that, by the time offenders reach probation, other institutions of social control have failed. If the offending behavior could have been controlled, families, neighborhoods, schools, and other social institutions would have controlled it. Offending behavior is not easy to correct, and for that reason Gondles believes that probation systems across the United States need help:

> [Probation officers] are often held accountable for the failures of other elements of the criminal justice community. Therefore, all of us in corrections must help them by doing our own jobs better, to escape the perception that they are ineffective. We must work together to ensure that all elements of the criminal justice system receive adequate funding and that all elements of the criminal justice system work closer together to provide offenders with the services they require.[16]

The APPA, representing U.S. probation officers nationwide, argues that recidivism rates measure just one probation task while ignoring others. The APPA has urged its member agencies to collect data on other outcomes, such as the following:

- amount of restitution collected;
- number of offenders employed;
- amounts of fines and fees collected;
- hours of community service performed;
- number of treatment sessions attended;
- percentage of financial obligations collected;
- rate of enrollment in school;
- number of days of employment;
- educational attainment; and
- number of days drug free.

Advocates of measures other than recidivism tell us that probation should be measured by what offenders do while they are in probation programs, not by what they do after they leave.

The American public understands that not all criminals can be locked up. Doubts are being raised about allocating a significant proportion of tax dollars to prisons. The cost of prison construction and housing now totals nearly $40 billion annually.[17] Seeing no reduction in crime will slowly move the public to reassess attitudes toward punishment.

Research also shows that citizens are less punishment oriented than many political leaders believe. For example, in surveys conducted in Alabama, Delaware, and Pennsylvania, the Public Agenda Foundation of New York City found that "when the public is made aware of the possible range of punishments, and given information about how and with whom they are used, they support alternatives to incarceration—including punishments administered in the community—for offenders considered nonviolent and low risk."[18]

To implement credible and effective probation programs, several steps appear necessary. Joan Petersilia offers us five suggestions.[19]

1. Implement High-Quality Programs and Enforce Them

Experienced probation officers tell us that besides using the techniques and strategies of coercion and threats of incarceration to induce offenders to comply with the conditions of probation supervision, we should not neglect to reward cooperative behavior and compliance. When offenders respond favorably to supervision, praise and tangible rewards sustain favorable behavior. Reclassifying offenders, reducing their level of supervision (e.g., face-to-face contacts and drug testing), and advocating early termination are used to encourage offenders to comply and cooperate.

2. Invest Adequate Resources in Treatment *and* Surveillance

When probationers receive *both* surveillance (e.g., unannounced contact and random drug tests) and treatment, recidivism can decline by one-third.[20] Probation can become more effective by giving some offenders more intensive supervision and treatment and others less and by targeting the effort to offer precise services and meet objectives by using a standardized assessment of probationer risks and needs. This approach can help probation staff determine more reliably which clients need intensive supervision, special services, or routine probation. When appropriate interventions (e.g., residential drug treatment, outpatient treatment, urine monitoring) are used with drug-involved clients, scarce treatment resources are utilized more effectively to reduce recidivism and relapse. However, treatment, surveillance, and classifying probationers to appropriate levels of supervision cost money. Adequate funding will be available only if the public believes that new supervision conditions are punitive as well as effective in reducing crime.

3. Demonstrate That Probation Is Tough on Crime

Policymakers say they send large numbers of people to prison because the public wants to be tough on crime. But there is a groundswell of evidence that tough punishment may no longer equate with prison.[21] Some offenders see probation as more punitive and restrictive than prison. For example, researchers in Texas and Oregon gave offenders the choice of serving a prison term or serving probation with mandatory drug testing, community service, employment, counseling, and frequent visits with a probation officer. In Oregon, 25 percent of those eligible for probation chose prison. In Texas, many offenders described common prison terms as less punitive than even only three to five years on probation. Prison was more attractive than the pressures of close supervision. The public must be convinced that probation sanctions can be just as punitive as prison. Of course, the choice of probation or prison should be for the judge to make, not the offender.

4. Target Drug Offenders Drug offenders are prime candidates for tough probation programs. Research has revealed the different risks and needs of traffickers, addicts, and low-level users.[22] Even if drug offenders are coerced into treatment by the court, there is evidence that the treatment can reduce both later drug use and later crimes. The largest study of drug treatment outcomes found that criminal justice clients stayed in treatment longer than clients without involvement in the justice system and had higher than average success rates.[23] Indeed, offenders in outpatient drug treatment programs have significantly lower rates of rearrest and relapse if they stay in treatment for more than three months than if they drop out earlier.[24]

The new knowledge is resulting in different laws and punishment strategies for different kinds of drug offenders. Many Americans prefer prison sentences for drug traffickers but are willing to accept something other than prison for other drug offenders. Nationally, 17 states have either reformed their drug laws or are considering it. In 1996, the people of Arizona led the way in drug reform by passing the Drug Medicalization, Prevention and Control Act. The centerpiece of the Act is the diversion of persons convicted of possession or use of a controlled substance. The Act requires drug offenders to be placed on probation and participate in appropriate drug treatment. In the second year of operation, 62 percent of the probationers complied with treatment. Probation supervision and community treatment cost approximately $1.1 million. Based on prison costs of almost $53 per day, Arizona saved an estimated $6.7 million in incarceration. Four years later, 61 percent of California voters passed Proposition 36—the Substance Abuse and Crime Prevention Act. The Act offers first- and second-time nonviolent drug offenders convicted of possession, use, or transportation of drugs substance abuse treatment instead of incarceration. As of February 2002, of the 4,329 defendants sentenced to drug treatment in Los Angeles County from July 1, 2001, to December 31, 2001, 69 percent were still receiving treatment. Judges and county officials say they are pleased with the program, and preliminary reports are that the program is working. Similar ballot initiatives are being considered across the country.

5. Make Probation Research a Priority With more than 3.9 million adults under probation supervision today, probation research should be a priority. The suggestion is to incorporate research on causes and effective interventions into local probation programs. Furthermore, local probation departments need to conduct research into their programs to see what works best in reducing recidivism.

It would be useful for probation research to assess the value of revoking probation for persons who commit technical violations (which are failures to fulfill the conditions of probation—attending counseling, paying restitution, contacting the probation officer) instead of committing new offenses. Judges need assurance that probationers will be held accountable for their behavior, and the public needs assurance that probation sanctions are punitive. More research is also needed on the relationship of technical violations to criminal behavior. For example, what types of conditions are imposed? How do those conditions manage offenders, encourage rehabilitation, and protect the community? What are the trends in the number of technical violators and the effect on jails and prisons? What innovative programs, policies, and statutes have emerged in other jurisdictions to deal with technical violators?

What Probation Officers Do

Probation officers are more extensively involved with offenders and their cases—often starting at arrest—than any other criminal justice professionals, and for that reason probation officers must be aware of cultural differences between themselves and their probationers if they are to build rapport and help change offending behavior. Recall from our earlier discussion that the majority of probationers are male and almost half are members of minority groups. Slightly more than half of the probation officers are female, and three-fourths of all POs are white. These demographic differences raise questions on how probation officers can build rapport across gender, race, and ethnicity. Without rapport, experts believe there is more likelihood that probationers will miss scheduled appointments, not follow through on referrals, violate the conditions of probation, reoffend, and end up back in the system. Racial and cultural tensions that exist in society at large can also be present between the probationer and probation officer. To lessen this tension and mistrust, experts suggest five strategies to build rapport between the probationer and probation officer.[25]

1. Sincerity is one thing that allows probationers to forgive probation officers who violate a cultural norm such as by saying the wrong thing.

2. High service energy sends a message to the probationer that the probation officer is in his or her corner. The probationer may think that less service energy has something to do with ethnic differences.

3. Knowledge of the probationer's culture increases empathy in the cross-cultural counseling relationship. For example, if the probationer speaks English as a second language, it would be helpful in building rapport for the officer to learn key words and phrases in the probationer's native language.

> **Ethical Dilemma**
>
> Should probation officers be advocates for sentencing reform? Why or why not? What are the issues? For more information go to Ethical Dilemma 4-2 at http://www.mhhe.com/schmalleger2.

4. A nonjudgmental attitude increases the officer's credibility.

5. Helping probationers with needed resources facilitates rapport building and officer credibility.

On January 1, 2000, there were 16,768 state adult probation officers, 21,466 state adult probation and parole officers, and 6,750 federal probation and parole officers in the United States. There were more female (54 percent) than male probation officers. By race and ethnicity, 72 percent were white, 21 percent were African American, 4.2 percent were Hispanic, 1.1 percent were Asian, and 0.5 percent were Native American/Native

Alaskan and 1.2 percent were other races and ethnicities. Probation officers completed an average of 31 hours of in-service training in 2000 and earned over $36,000. In 22 states and the federal government, probation officers are also peace officers.[26]

Probation officers interact with many criminal justice agencies and influence many decisions affecting offenders. They do this in two major ways: through case investigation and client supervision.

CASE INVESTIGATION

Investigation includes the preparation of a presentence report (PSR), which the judge uses in sentencing an offender. The PSR is a report prepared by the probation department of a court, that provides a social and personal history as well as an evaluation of a defendant as an aid to the court in determining a sentence. The PSR is an integral part of the sentencing process in many jurisdictions despite the growth in mandatory sentencing laws, three strikes laws, and truth-in-sentencing legislation, as well as the increased use of sentencing guidelines. While a PSR is required for sentencing purposes in many states, it remains discretionary in others. During 1999, more than 538,000 state and federal PSRs were written. Probation staff in Texas wrote the most (89,000), and staff in South Carolina wrote the fewest (26).

Purposes of the Presentence Report   The PSR has two main purposes. First, and most important, the PSR assists the court in reaching a fair sentencing decision. The specific content areas of the PSR vary from jurisdiction to jurisdiction, but common areas include (1) information regarding the current offense; (2) the offender's past adult and juvenile criminal record; (3) family history and background; and (4) personal data about education, health, employment, and substance abuse history. In addition, some state statutes dictate content areas such as victim impact statements. It is not uncommon for jurisdictions to include a sentencing recommendation in the PSR. However, sentencing reforms are limiting judicial sentencing discretion, so the PSR recommendation is much less important than it once was. Still, research on the relationship between the sentencing recommendation and actual sentencing outcomes is very clear: Judges follow the recommendation over 80 percent of the time when probation is recommended and over 60 percent of the time when prison is recommended.

A recent study of 227 Utah judges, prosecutors, public defenders, and probation/parole officers found significant opposition (86 percent) to the notion of removing the sentencing recommendation from the PSR altogether.[27] Critics of the PSR have asserted that judges do not bother to read the entire report, so the Utah study asked respondents their approach to reading the PSR. The study asked, Do you (a) start at the beginning and read the entire report by section, (b) skip over most of the report and focus on the evaluative summary and sentence recommendation, or (c) skim and scan the entire report? Ninety percent of judges claimed to read the entire report from the beginning, but only 55 percent of all respondents (judges, prosecutors, public defenders, and probation/parole officers) indicated that they started at the beginning and read the entire report section by section.

The rest would either skim and scan the entire report or ignore most of it and focus on the sentencing recommendation and evaluative summary sections. The authors of the study conclude, "While this finding might surprise some, we believe that it is consistent with other communications research on selective reading. As a result of time constraints, working professionals skim and scan documents and read only what they deem important. Given the pressure and time limitations confronting the various PSR user groups, there was no reason for us to assume that they would behave any differently."[28]

The second purpose of the PSR is to outline a treatment plan for the offender. During the investigation, besides determining the degree of risk the offender poses to the community, the probation officer identifies treatment needs so that the offender can receive appropriate services (counseling, treatment, education, community service, restitution, employment, and some form of supervision) during probation or in jail or prison.

In most cases, the court orders the PSR after conviction but before sentencing. The defendant reports to the probation department if released on bond pending sentencing. Otherwise, the probation officer visits the defendant in jail.

Client-Specific Plans The defendant or defense counsel may hire a private agency to prepare a PSR in addition to the one ordered by the court. A privately prepared PSR is sometimes called a **client-specific plan (CSP)**. CSPs accomplish three things. First, they are an alternative source of information for judges. Second, they generally favor the defendant, encouraging greater use of treatment, counseling, education, community service, restitution, employment, and supervision. They may, however, call for the offender to pay a greater share of the cost of treatment. Third, they balance the information in the PSRs prepared by government agencies.

client-specific plan (CSP)

A privately prepared presentence report that supplements the PSR prepared by the probation department.

Creating a Presentence Report The PSR starts with an interview between the probation officer (PO) and the defendant. The interview follows a structured format for obtaining information about the offense and the offender. The PO is expected to verify, clarify, and explore any information to be presented in the PSR. Recently, researchers in Utah found that POs frequently made no attempt to verify the accuracy of the information supplied by the defendant because of the large volume of presentence reports and the time limitations placed on the POs. How widespread this situation may be in other jurisdictions is unknown because the research is unavailable.

In the PSR, the PO is also expected to estimate the offender's degree of risk to the community. The estimate is based on the offender's lifestyle, prior criminal involvement, and experience with the criminal justice system. The PO summarizes the information gathered and, in most jurisdictions, makes a sentence recommendation. If the sentence recommended is incarceration, in most jurisdictions the length must be within guidelines set by statute (see Chapter 3). However, if the sentence recommended is probation or some other intermediate sanction (see Chapter 5), few jurisdictions have guidelines for sentence length. Only recently have some states (e.g., Delaware, North Carolina, and Pennsylvania) begun to design sentencing guidelines for nonprison sentences such as probation. Copies of the PSR are filed with the court and made available to the judge, the prosecutor, and the defense attorney. Exhibit 4–2 is an example of a short-form federal PSR.

Disclosure of Presentence Reports   One of the most important questions about the PSR is whether the defendant has a constitutional right to see it and challenge the statements contained in it. Judges and probation officers generally oppose disclosure for several reasons. First, they fear that persons having knowledge about the offender will refuse to give information if the defendant knows they have given information about him or her. Second, they believe that, if the defendant challenges information in the PSR, court proceedings may be unduly delayed. Third, opponents believe disclosure to the defendant of some kinds of information, such as psychological reports, might be harmful to that defendant. And fourth, they argue that the PSR is a private and confidential court document. On the other hand, advocates of disclosure argue that fundamental fairness and due process demand that convicted persons should have access to the information in the PSR on which their sentence is based so they can correct inaccuracies. However, the U.S. Supreme Court has held, in *Williams* v. *Oklahoma* (1959), that unless disclosure is required by state law or court decisions, there is no denial of due process of law when a court considers a PSR without disclosing its contents to the defendant or giving the defendant an opportunity to rebut it.

The trend today is toward limited disclosure of information to the defendant's attorney. The American Bar Association favors disclosure of the factual contents and conclusions of the PSR (not the sources of confidential information) and the defendant's opportunity to rebut them.[29] Federal courts require that the PSR be disclosed to the defendant, his or her counsel, and the attorney for the government, except in three instances: when disclosure might disrupt rehabilitation of the defendant, when information disclosed in the PSR was obtained on the promise of confidentiality, and when disclosure might result in harm to the defendant or any other person. Observers note that jurisdictions that practice limited disclosure have not encountered the problems anticipated by opponents of disclosure.[30] Limited disclosure has led probation departments to analyze the offense and the offender more objectively, increase the court's reliance on the PSR, and develop a closer relationship between the offender and probation officer.

Technology and Case Investigations   Today, technological innovations are affecting where and how POs do their job. Software packages can generate PSRs from data from official records and interviews entered by probation officers. The software programs can also calculate risk assessment scores. A PO can edit the report before submitting it to the court.

The trend toward telecommuting is also affecting probation officers' case investigations. Telecommuting is usually defined as working at home or at another telework facility for at least one day a week during regularly scheduled business hours, supported by the necessary hardware and software. Today, between 30 and 40 million people either telecommute or work strictly from their homes.[31] Some jurisdictions are finding that presentence officers are successful telecommuters. The U.S. Probation Office in the

EXHIBIT 4–2 **Sample Presentence Report**

IN THE UNITED STATES DISTRICT COURT
FOR THE NORTHERN DISTRICT OF ALABAMA

UNITED STATES OF AMERICA	)	
	)	PRESENTENCE
v.	)	REPORT
	)	
EDDIE PALMER	)	Docket No. CR 03-H-248-S

Prepared For: Honorable Casandra Phillips
                 U.S. District Judge

Prepared By: Noelle Koval
                 U.S. Probation Officer
                 Birmingham, AL
                 (205)555-0923

Offense: Count One: Possession With Intent to Distribute a
                                           Schedule II Controlled Substance (Cocaine
                                           Base), not less than 10 Years and not more
                                           than Life and/or $4,000,000 Fine. With
                                           Enhancement, Mandatory Life and/or
                                           $8,000,000 Fine.

Release Status: Released on $25,000 unsecured bond on 8/26/03
                                           Remanded to custody on 12/14/03

<u>Identifying Data</u>

Date of Birth:	1/9/71
Age:	32
Race:	B
Sex:	M

<u>Charge(s) and Conviction(s)</u>

Eddie Palmer was indicted on two counts by the September 2003 Grand Jury for the Northern
District of Alabama. Count One charged that on June 12, 2003, the defendant unlawfully possessed
with intent to distribute approximately 500 grams of a mixture or substance containing a detectable
amount of cocaine, Schedule II controlled substances, in violation of 21 USC § 841(a)(1). Count
Two charged that on June 12, 2003, the defendant carried a firearm during the commission of a
drug trafficking crime in violation of 18 USC § 924(c)(1). The October 2003 Grand Jury returned a
superseding indictment in which the defendant was charged in two counts. Count One charges that

EXHIBIT 4-2   **Sample Presentence Report—continued**

on June 12, 2003, the defendant intentionally possessed with intent to distribute approximately 100 grams of a mixture or substance containing a detectable amount of cocaine base and approximately 240 grains of a mixture or substance containing a detectable amount of cocaine, Schedule II controlled substances, in violation of 21 USC § 841(a)(1). Count II charges that on June 12, 2003, the defendant carried a firearm during the commission of a drug trafficking crime in violation of 18 USC § 924(c)(1). On December 14, 2003, Palmer pled guilty to Count One, and Count Two was dismissed on motion of the government. Sentencing was continued generally to a later date.

Pretrial Adjustment

Mr. Palmer was released on a $25,000 unsecured bond on 8/26/03 with special conditions. One drug urinalysis was taken which was negative. Mr. Palmer ceased reporting in person on 10/6/03. He stated that people were looking for him and he was afraid to go out. The defendant had given information on a public corruption case. He was allowed to telephone report. On 12/14/03 Palmer was taken into custody following his plea of guilty pursuant to 18 USC § 3143.

Substance Abuse

Mr. Palmer relates that he started using marijuana and cocaine around the age of 24. He quit using it for one year while he was in the TASC program. He went to TASC as a special condition of state probation from 1/3/95 to 2/14/96. He was considered to be making minimal effort to comply with TASC and was terminated after he completed his probation term.

Education and Vocational Skills

Mr. Palmer attended El Camino Community College, Torrance, California, from 2/7/93 to 6/15/94. His scholastic standing was average. He was in the Vocational School and took courses in Cosmetology.

Employment Record

Mr. Palmer states that he opened SimplyClean AutoWorks, Inc., in 1997. He is the owner and has a monthly gross income from $1,200 to $2,000 per month. This company washes, details, and repairs automobiles. Mr. Palmer lists his home address as the address of the company.

Mr. Palmer reports that when he initially moved to Alabama from L.A., he worked as a hairdresser out of his mother's home and was paid in cash. While in L.A., he worked for Simply Raw Beauty Salon in 1994 for approximately six months as a cosmetologist. He states that he worked for the L.A. County Art Museum, Beverly Hills, California, as a laborer earning minimum wage from April through July 1994. The Art Museum could find no record of Mr. Palmer ever working for them. Mr. Palmer states that he often did odd jobs and fixed hair to earn an income.

EXHIBIT 4-2 **Sample Presentence Report—continued**

Mr. Palmer joined the U.S. Army on 9/30/92. He was discharged under honorable conditions on 1/13/94 as a Private, 2nd Class. The discharge was for misconduct which included frequent incidents of a discreditable nature with civil or military authorities.

Financial Condition: Ability to Pay

The following information was verified through a credit report, the Tax Assessor's office, reviewing some household bills, and DEA, who verified values of automobiles and other equipment and is proceeding on forfeiture.

Assets:

Unencumbered Assets:

1995 CB1000 Honda motorcycle, fair market value:	$ 4,070.00

Equity in Other Assets:

Residence	21,000.00
1994 Chevrolet Lumina	4,025.00

Total Assets: $29,095.00

Unsecured Debt:

Attorney Fees	$10,000.00
Medical Center East	4,000.00

Total Unsecured Debt: $14,000.00

NET WORTH: $15,095.00

Monthly Cash Flow:

Income:

New Profit from Business	$ 1,200.00
Spouse's Salary	400.00

Total Income: $ 1,600.00

—3—

EXHIBIT 4-2   Sample Presentence Report—continued

Necessary Monthly Living Expenses:

Mortgage	$ 634.00
Electricity	80.00
Gas	50.00
Water	14.00
Telephone	150.00
Groceries and Supplies	200.00
Life Insurance	50.00
Transportation	50.00
Medical	300.00
Clothing	200.00
Child Support	400.00
Monthly Installment Payments	250.00

Total Expenses: $2,378.00

Monthly Cash Flow: ($ 778.00)

The above information represents the defendant's version of income and expenses. The mortgage payment and utilities were verified. Other expenses and income were not verified although verification was requested. The defendant claims to have filed income tax returns and stated that the information was with his attorney, Warren Skinner. Mr. Skinner was contacted about financial information but was not forthcoming. In fact, he prohibited the family from talking with me after the defendant pled guilty. Therefore, information may not be complete and is possibly inaccurate based on this lack of cooperation.

The bottom line is that it is very difficult to give an accurate reflection of the defendant's financial status. Based on his purported income from illegal activity, it is quite likely that there are other assets available to him. This cannot be stated as fact because it is frankly unknown.

Respectfully submitted,

Noelle Koval

Noelle Koval
U.S. Probation Officer

Approved:

Frank Medina   12/23/03

Frank Medina   DATE
Supervising U.S. Probation Officer

EXHIBIT 4-2   Sample Presentence Report—concluded

SENTENCING RECOMMENDATION

UNITED STATES DISTRICT COURT
FOR THE NORTHERN DISTRICT OF ALABAMA

UNITED STATES V. EDDIE PALMER   DOCKET NO. CR 03-H-248-S

TOTAL OFFENSE LEVEL: 29
CRIMINAL HISTORY CATEGORY: III

	Statutory Provision	Guideline Provisions	Recommended Sentence
CUSTODY:	Mandatory Life	Mandatory Life	Life
PROBATION:	N/A	N/A	N/A
SUPERVISED RELEASE:	Not Less Than 10 Years	10 Years	10 Years
FINE:	$8,000,000	$15,000 to $8,000,000	$15,000
RESTITUTION:	N/A	N/A	N/A
SPECIAL ASSESSMENT:	$50	$50	$50

Justification

The sentence of life is mandatory. Supervised release must be ten years. A $15,000 fine is recommended because it is incumbent upon the defendant to demonstrate that he does not have the financial ability to pay a fine. He and his attorney have not cooperated in providing information, and it appears that he does have the ability to pay the minimum fine based on his purported monthly income from trafficking in illegal drugs.

Voluntary Surrender

The defendant is in custody.

Respectfully submitted,

Noelle Koval

Noelle Koval
U.S. Probation Officer

—5—

My first PO was a man who had years of experience. He was cynical. He took his job too seriously. I cooperated and soon he trusted me. His requirements were few. I was rarely asked to report at his office, and he would call to let me know he was coming to my home for a visit.

After several months, I was assigned a female PO. I was required to give urine samples under her observation. That bothered me, because I had no history of substance abuse. The purpose of these samples seems to have been to humiliate me. I wondered why the feds wanted to be in the business of humiliating people!

Being on supervised release was no big deal, as long as I sent in my monthly reports and got permission to travel outside the district (which meant 10 miles to the north and 12 miles to the west). At my request, my second PO processed the forms for my release from supervision one year ahead of schedule. My cooperation paid off.

I don't know if federal probation reduces crime. But I do think that probation should be used more often, instead of incarceration, with community service. I think most prison sentences are too long and disruptive to families. I also think that all efforts should be made to support an offender's attempts to straighten out his or her life. The entire "justice" system needs to become caring and compassionate, putting more people into treatment and job programs than into prison.

Did probation disrupt my life? Yes. But I committed a crime and accepted probation willingly. Still, I think that it was wasteful, since once the feds realized that I had paid my fine off early, had no drug problems, kept a stable work record, and was cooperative, they might have saved us all some money by letting me off even sooner than they did.

Anonymous female, formerly on federal probation

THE OFFENDER SPEAKS

Middle District of Florida found that presentence officers reported an increase in job satisfaction and a higher level of productivity. They reported to the office to interview defendants, meet with attorneys, attend court hearings, and perform other routine office duties. They spent the remainder of their time at their residences working on their investigations. The officers averaged 2.5 to 3.0 days a week telecommuting. Their work was transmitted electronically through a secure Intranet mailing system. Telecommuting was not effective for supervision officers, however, who were needed in the probation office to handle the needs of their offenders and who had to travel in the field to meet their probationers.

SUPERVISION

supervision

The second major role of probation officers, consisting of intervention, surveillance, and enforcement.

The second major role of probation officers is client supervision. Probation **supervision** has three main elements: intervention, surveillance, and enforcement. *Intervention* means providing offenders access to a wide variety of services, such as job development, substance abuse treatment, counseling, and education. *Surveillance* means monitoring the activities of probationers through office meetings, home and work visits, drug and alcohol testing, and contact with family, friends, and employers. *Enforcement* means making probationers accountable for their behavior and making sure they understand the consequences of violating the conditions of probation.

Caseload The average PO in the United States supervises approximately 139 offenders. On January 1, 2000, probation officers in Rhode Island had the largest probation caseload (311), followed by Georgia (279). Such large caseloads do not allow probation officers time for adequate intervention, surveillance, or enforcement. A number of jurisdictions are experimenting with Probation Automated Management (PAM). The PAM kiosk is similar to an ATM at which low-risk probationers can report in 24 hours a day,

When I started as a probation officer in West Virginia, Martinson's "Nothing Works" study supported the philosophy that, since rehabilitation and probation failed, the real answer to crime control was to "lock 'em up" for long periods of time. Nothing-works philosophy translated to the "truth in sentencing" perspective and widespread spending in the construction of new federal, state, and local prisons and jails. Probation and rehabilitation advocates were afraid that, if they challenged the new philosophy, they would find themselves unemployed. In the 1970s, I helped develop the West Virginia Association of Probation Officers to improve the professionalism of probation in West Virginia. One of our aims was to consolidate probation under the West Virginia Supreme Court instead of having it under the Department of Welfare, the Department of Corrections, and the local courts. Today, probation comes under the West Virginia Supreme Court. Nationally, the American Probation and Parole Association has enhanced probation and community-based programs that have proved to be successful.

Juvenile programs administered by our department include mediation and arbitration for juveniles in which volunteers help resolve conflicts among juvenile offenders, their families, victims, and others. Alternative Learning Center programs provide education for violent juvenile offenders in off-school settings. Volunteers in Probation programs provide a mentor for every juvenile placed on probation. Adult programs include community probation officers for supervision and treatment and the supervision of community service work by offenders. I can honestly say that after 27 years as a probation officer, I am more energized than I have ever been, thanks to our success in the community. And I know that the 21st century will confirm that probation and its community-based programs are an effective way to reduce crime, rehabilitate offenders, and bring peace to many households and communities.

James R. Lee
Chief Probation Officer
First Judicial Circuit
Wellsburg, West Virginia

THE STAFF SPEAKS

seven days a week, with their fingerprints as biometric identifiers. PAM is an attempt to deal with the increasing workload of probation officers.

What is the ideal caseload size for probation? This issue has been discussed for as long as there have been professionals in the field. Because probation and parole are pluralistic, highly decentralized, and used by hundreds of departments at the federal, state, county, and municipal levels across the United States, the APPA adopted the position that the search for a "magic number" is futile and counterproductive. Instead, the APPA recommends that probation agencies adopt a "workload or case management model" that focuses on the amount of time that is required to supervise a particular case up to standards. Assuming one PO has 120 hours available for supervision each month, a caseload can be made up of 30 high-risk cases (each receiving four hours of supervision a month), 40 close-risk cases (each receiving three hours of supervision a month), 60 intermediate-risk cases (each receiving two hours of supervision a month), or 120 low-risk cases (each receiving one hour of supervision per month).

At probation automated monitoring (PAM) kiosks, probationers check in by handprint or ID card to answer questions about their progress. These machines are used in some areas to supervise low-risk offenders who do not require face-to-face contact with a probation officer. What advantages and disadvantages do you see in this approach?

High risk supervision	Close risk supervision	Intermediate risk supervision	Reduced risk supervision
2 face-to-face contacts each day	1 face-to-face contact each day	1 face-to-face contact each week	1 face-to-face contact each month
2 drug tests each week	2 drug tests each week	1 drug test each week	no drug tests

FIGURE 4-6
Extent of Supervision by Assessed Risk Level

In all four instances, the officer would have a full caseload/workload; that is, one in which the number of hours needed to fulfill the minimum requirements on all the cases (demand) was equal to the amount of hours available to the officer (supply). Figure 4–6 shows typical supervision plans (number of face-to-face contacts and drug tests each day, week, or month) matched to risk level (high, close, intermediate, or reduced).

Regardless of their level of supervision, all probationers are subject to "general" conditions of supervision. These include reporting to a probation officer as directed, paying court-ordered monies, working, obeying all laws, and being "of general good behavior." Figure 4–7 presents, as an example, the general conditions for all probationers in Georgia. The court may also order "special conditions" that relate directly to the offender's particular crime or history. For example, a person convicted of cybercrime might be subject to the special conditions shown in Figure 4–8.

Technology and Supervision   As in case investigation, there are now software programs to help POs in client supervision. Computer programs can track fine and probation payments, alert POs when their clients are behind on payments, and help them track whether probationers have satisfied the conditions of their sentences.

A probation officer interviews a crime victim. Case investigation is one of a probation officer's most important tasks. What questions would you ask a crime victim as part of the investigation?

The court shall determine the terms and conditions of probation and may provide that the probationer shall:

(1)   Avoid injurious and vicious habits;

(2)   Avoid persons or places of disreputable or harmful character;

(3)   Report to the probation supervisor as directed;

(4)   Permit the supervisor to visit him at his home or elsewhere;

(5)   Work faithfully at suitable employment insofar as may be possible;

(6)   Remain within a specified location;

(7)   Make reparation or restitution to any aggrieved person for the damage or loss caused by his offense, in an amount to be determined by the court. Unless otherwise provided by law, no reparation or restitution to any aggrieved person for the damage or loss caused by his offense shall be made if the amount is in dispute unless the same has been adjudicated;

(8)   Make reparation or restitution as reimbursement to a municipality or county for the payment for medical care furnished the person while incarcerated pursuant to the provisions of Article 3 of Chapter 4 of this title. No reparation or restitution to a local governmental unit for the provision of medical care shall be made if the amount is in dispute unless the same has been adjudicated;

(9)   Repay the costs incurred by any municipality or county for wrongful actions by an inmate covered under the provisions of paragraph (1) of subsection (a) of Code Section 42-4-71;

(10) Support his legal dependents to the best of his ability;

(11) Violate no local, state, or federal laws and be of general good behavior; and

(12) If permitted to move or travel to another state, agree to waive extradition from any jurisdiction where he may be found and not contest any effort by any jurisdiction to return him to this state.

FIGURE 4-7
State of Georgia, General Conditions of Probation

Source: Georgia Department of Corrections, Probation Division, General Conditions of Probation, Code Section 42-8-35.

Another technological innovation, one of the more interesting strategies for managing the three elements of probation supervision, is mapping technology or GIS (geographic information systems). Mapping has helped law enforcement locate hot spots of crime. Police departments used to map with pins on a "point map." Today, mapping is done electronically, which affords complex and instant analyses. Probation departments use mapping as a tool for the management of offenders in the community. Mapping helps ensure that probation and parole officers are dispersed in areas with high concentrations of them.

Agencies in Wisconsin and New York are using probation mapping to enhance offender supervision. Mapping can show what kind of crime problem an area has (e.g., drug or theft) and deploy probation staff and resources appropriately. Services can be moved to areas that need them most. For example, the Wisconsin Department of Corrections found through mapping that "if you have an area with a drug usage problem, we would bring drug programming to that area. Really, our experience was we got better attendance and better completion rates with that."[32] The Center for

(A=Internet Access Permitted, B=Limited or No Access to Internet)	A	B
You shall consent to your probation officer and/or probation service representative conducting periodic unannounced examinations of your computer(s) equipment which may include retrieval and copying of all memory from hardware/software to ensure compliance with this condition and/or removal of such equipment for the purpose of conducting a more thorough inspection; and consent at the direction of your probation officer to having installed on your computer(s), at your expense, any hardware or software systems to monitor your computer use or prevent access to particular materials. You hereby consent to the periodic inspection of any such installed hardware or software to insure it is functioning properly.	X	X
You shall not possess encryption or steganography software.	X	X
You shall provide your probation officer accurate information about your entire computer system and software; all passwords used by you; and your Internet Service Provider(s).	X	X
You shall possess only computer hardware or software approved by your probation officer. You shall obtain written permission from your probation officer prior to obtaining any additional computer hardware or software or Internet Service Provider(s).	X	X
You shall refrain from using a computer in any manner that relates to the activity in which you were engaged in committing the instant offense or violation behavior, namely _____.	X	X
You shall provide truthful information concerning your identity in all Internet or E-Mail communications and not visit any "chat rooms" or similar Internet locations/sites where minors are known to frequent.	X	
You shall maintain a daily log of all addresses you access via any personal computer (or other computer used by you), other than for authorized employment, and make this log available to your probation officer.	X	
You shall not create or assist directly or indirectly in the creation of any electronic bulletin board, Internet Service Provider, or any other public or private network without the prior written consent of your probation officer. Any approval shall be subject to any conditions set by the U.S. Probation Office or the Court with respect to that approval.	X	X
You shall not possess or use a computer with access to any "on-line" computer service at any location (including employment or education) without prior written approval of the U.S. Probation Office or the Court. This includes any Internet Service Provider, bulletin board system, or any other public or private computer network. Any approval shall be subject to any conditions set by the U.S. Probation Office or the Court with respect to that approval.		X
You shall not purchase, possess, or receive a personal computer which utilizes a modem, and/or an external modem.		X
You will have an occupational condition that you can not be employed directly or indirectly where you are an installer, programmer, or "trouble shooter" for computer equipment.	X	X

FIGURE 4-8

Specific probation conditions for computer crime

Source: Arthur L. Bowker and Gregory B. Thompson, "Computer Crime in the 21st Century and Its Effect on the Probation Officer," *Federal Probation*, vol. 65, no. 2 (September 2001), p. 21.

Alternative Sentencing and Employment in New York uses mapping to monitor employment rates in areas where ex-offenders will reside and, with the assistance of community agencies, helps them find a job link upon leaving prison.

Revocation of Probation   If the offender willfully violates the conditions of his or her probation, a **revocation hearing** is usually the next step. A revocation hearing is a due process hearing that must be conducted by the court, probation, or probation authority to determine whether the conditions of probation (or parole as we will see in Chapter 8) have been violated before probation can be revoked and the offender removed from the community. **Revocation** is the formal termination of an offender's conditional freedom. During 1999, states averaged 4,400 probation revocation hearings.

Revocation is a serious matter for four reasons. First, the offender might lose his or her freedom to remain in the community. Second, the handling of probation violators by supervision agencies and courts consumes a significant portion of the court's time, energy, and resources. One jurisdiction estimated that, in addition to using the equivalent of more than two full-time probation officers, the various stages of the probation violation process use the equivalent of a full-time judge, prosecutor, and courtroom staff.[33] Third, the cost of keeping an offender under probation supervision is much lower than that required for care and treatment in prison or jail. For example, we saw in Table 4–1 that the per day cost of probation ranges from $2.11 to $9.66, depending on the level of supervision and risk an offender poses, but it costs $56.72 per day to keep an offender in jail and $57.92 per day to keep an offender in prison. And fourth, imprisoning offenders who otherwise would have been placed on probation may force their families to go on welfare or make greater demands on community resources.

Still, revocation is the only way to protect the community from some offenders who refuse to abide by the conditions of probation. A group of leading officials in the field of probation and parole, called the Reinventing Probation Council, recently concluded that the reason probation has not been able to protect the public is lax enforcement of the probation rules. Others agree. Joan Petersilia, a criminologist at the University of California, Irvine, notes, "The result is that probationers quickly learn that failing a drug test or violating other court-ordered conditions has little consequence."[34] The council stresses, "All conditions of a probation sentence must be enforced. The response must be swift and sure. This does not mean that each violation will result in the revocation of probation but rather the imposition of graduated sanctions."[35]

A number of jurisdictions now recognize that revoking even a small percentage of the probation population can have a dramatic effect on the prison population. In some states (e.g., California, Oregon, and Texas), over two-thirds of prison admissions are probation or parole violators. While it is important to take action when violations are discovered, prison may not be the best response. State legislatures in Georgia,

revocation hearing
A due process hearing that must be conducted to determine whether the conditions of probation have been violated before probation can be revoked and the offender removed from the community.

revocation
The formal termination of an offender's conditional freedom.

> A number of jurisdictions now recognize that revoking even a small percentage of the probation population can have a dramatic effect on the prison population.

Eye On Corrections™

Effective Ways to Manage Parole and Probation Violations

By Meghan Fay

Parole and probation officers have enormous caseloads. A lack of sufficient guidelines to help them deal with violators consistently and in a timely fashion only adds to their already overflowing plate. While parole and probation violations are common, the response to technical violations often varies.

VIOLATION RESPONSES

Technical violations can encompass such things as a positive drug test, a loss of a job, or a failure to stay in treatment. In response to these violations, agencies that do not have a specific violation policy must go through a formal court hearing. A more informal procedure addressing specific violations will allow a probation or parole officer to handle an offender's positive drug test quickly and place an offender in a program to tackle his or her substance abuse relapse rather than on the court docket.

SOUTH CAROLINA'S MODEL

The South Carolina Department of Probation, Parole, and Pardon Services was named in the *American Correctional Association's Best Practices* for having one of the best methods for managing probation and parole violations. In the early 1990s, the agency reviewed its existing policies. South Carolina officials found that their violation system was filled with misunderstandings, the process was inefficient, the policy objectives had several interpretations, and judges often disagreed with the sanction recommendations.

The agency laid out a plan. The improvements the staff suggested were as follows:

- Empower the department's internal administrative hearing officers so that they can impose intermediate sanctions and community options.
- Ensure that response to violations reflects the severity of the violation and the risks posed to the community.
- Give greater authority to probation and parole agents and their supervisors to impose sanctions and to become proactively involved in the resolution of violation behavior. This will lead to prompt and appropriate results for violations.
- Issue citations in some cases rather than warrants to eliminate the need for many offenders to be housed in jails to await disposition of their violations.
- Create a method to evaluate the progress of these initiatives.

Some sanctions that agents and frontline supervisors can impose are placing an offender in a halfway house for up to 60 days, placing an offender in a treatment facility, placing offenders on home detention, and increasing reporting or drug testing. If, even with these alternatives, an agent cannot resolve a violation case, the case goes to an administrative hearing, which is the last step before it goes to the court or parole board.

Mississippi, and Washington are trying to reserve prison space for violent offenders by structuring the courts' response to technical violations. Georgia and Mississippi use 90-day boot camp programs for probation and parole violators. Oregon and Washington use short jail stays (two to three days). Corrections officials and researchers make two observations about these new responses to probation and parole violators. First, these programs increase the certainty of punishment. The offender will find the term disruptive to normal living and be deterred from further violations. Second, there is no evidence that technical violators go on to commit new offenses; therefore, commitment to prison is a wasted resource.

Violations That Trigger Revocation   Revocation is triggered in one of two ways. Either offenders willfully violate the *technical* conditions of their probation, or they commit *new offenses*.

A **technical violation** is failure to comply with conditions of probation. It is not a criminal act. Most revocations are the result of technical violations. According to a report published by the National Institute of Corrections in 2001, the most likely reason for prison incarceration of probation (and parole) violators is a technical violation.[36] In 1999, technical violators accounted for 68 percent of all prison admissions. The most commonly committed technical violations are positive urinalysis, failure to participate in treatment, **absconding** (fleeing without permission the jurisdiction in which the offender is required to stay), and failure to report to the probation officer. Most probation officers do not ask the court to revoke probation for an occasional technical violation. They understand that technical violations are supervision issues and best handled by program or treatment referrals. One analyst in the National Institute of Corrections report commented, "If our jails and prisons are filled with offenders who are merely noncompliant, there will be no room for the dangerous offender." To ensure compliance, probation officers can tighten the offender's supervision with a reprimand, increase reporting requirements, limit travel or other privileges, increase drug/alcohol testing, treatment/education referrals, restructure payments (for probationers who demonstrate an inability to pay in accordance with the court-established payment plan), or extend the terms of probation. A probationer who says he or she did not understand the conditions of probation could be required to spend a Friday evening attending a "reorientation" meeting at the local halfway house. The possibilities are limitless. The key to creating these types of violation responses is understanding that a violation may be the manifestation of a supervision issue. If a circumstance is discovered early enough, the need to impose sanctions may not arise. Repeated serious technical violations, however, may lead to revocation.

The revocation process is also predicated on the offender committing a *willful* or *intentional* violation. In this case it is guided by a body of court decisions. For example, if a probationer made a real effort to pay his or her court-ordered supervision fees and/or victim restitution but was unable to do so because of minimal education, few job skills, job loss, and so forth, probation may not be revoked unless alternate measures are inadequate to meet the state's interest in deterrence and punishment. However, the courts have held that, where there may be a risk to public safety, probation can be

technical violation
A failure to comply with the conditions of probation.

absconding
Fleeing without permission the jurisdiction in which the offender is required to stay.

Reflections on the Future

In the future, probation professionals must have a clear mission and must define for all involved, including the public, what the expectations of probation will be. We must stop telling the public, legislatures, and other criminal justice professionals that we are responsible for public safety and for changing offenders' behavior. What we need to tell them is that our efforts—holding offenders accountable and enforcing court orders—contribute to the safety of the community and also help change offenders' behavior. We are enforcement agents and, it is hoped, assist offenders in changing their behavior. We do not change offenders; they change themselves with our assistance and with the help of many other professionals and the support systems in their lives.

Unless we communicate and reestablish our goals and the purpose of probation, we will continue to exist in a shadow cast from considerable doubt about the effectiveness of probation and the future use of community supervision. Today, probation is the most widely used judicial sanction and disposition that encompass elements of both community protection and offender rehabilitation. It is a status, a system, and a process.

We continue to struggle with the ability to present grounded and credible research as to the outcomes of probation and community supervision. We talk about "what works," but do we really know? Are we able to back up these statements about our programs with facts? Evidence-based practices will need to be a requirement. We must establish ourselves as a viable sanction, and we must agree about what is the true purpose of probation. We must enlist the community to help develop and accept outcome measures that are supported by credible research.

Finding people with the right attitudes and knowledge must drive hiring practices. Staff must demonstrate the knowledge and skills to produce effectively the outcomes we are trying to achieve. The ability of a probation officer effectively to monitor and assist an offender while enforcing the orders of the court will demand ongoing training and skill development. Resources must be available to ensure this training is available.

In summary, as prison overcrowding continues, probation has an opportunity to demonstrate its worth in the criminal justice system. We must take advantage of the current situation and focus on the core values and basics of what probation supervision was intended to be. If we do not, we will be seen as an ineffective cog in a larger failing criminal justice system.

ABOUT THE AUTHOR

Kathy Waters is immediate past president of the American Probation and Parole Association and director of Adult Services, Administrative Office of the Courts, Arizona Supreme Court. Ms. Waters received the Bachelor of Science and Master of Science in criminal justice from Northeastern State University, Tahlequah, Oklahoma.

revoked even if the offender is not responsible for his or her inability to complete the conditions of probation. For example, if a sex offender is unable to complete a sex offender treatment program through no fault of his or her own, the court noted that, without treatment, the offender would present public safety risks because of the likelihood of reoffending, and it thus supported revocation.

new offense violation

The arrest and prosecution for the commission of a new crime.

A **new offense violation** is the arrest and prosecution for the commission of a new crime. In 1999, 32 percent of adults sentenced to prison were admitted for probation violations as well as new felonies. In 2001, the National Institute of Corrections conducted a study of how jurisdictions respond to probation violators in Macomb County, Michigan, and Suffolk County, New York.[37] The researchers found that 12 percent of the violations for which probation officers filed motions to revoke probation were for new felonies, and 4 percent were for new misdemeanors. The point to remember is that a substantial percentage of the prison population each year is probation (and parole) violators.

Revocation Hearings   Revocation hearings usually begin with a violation report prepared by the probation officer. They are governed by the 1973 U.S. Supreme Court decision known as *Gagnon* v. *Scarpelli*. In this case, the Court said that there was no difference between probation and parole revocation because both of them resulted in loss of liberty. The Court extended the same rights to probationers that it granted to parolees a year earlier in *Morrissey* v. *Brewer*. The Court ruled that probation cannot be revoked without observing the following elements of due process:

1. written notice of the charge;
2. disclosure to the probationer of the evidence;
3. the opportunity to be heard in person and present evidence as well as witnesses;
4. the right to confront and cross-examine witnesses;
5. the right to judgment by a detached and neutral hearing body;
6. a written statement of the reasons for revoking probation; and
7. the right to counsel under "special circumstances," depending on the offender's competence, case complexity, and mitigating circumstances.

SUMMARY

1▶ Diversion is the official halting or suspension, before conviction, of formal criminal proceedings against a person, often conditioned on some form of counter performance, such as participation in a treatment, counseling, or educational program. Diversion is intended to (1) prevent future criminal activity by diverting certain defendants from criminal justice processing into community supervision and service, (2) save prosecution and judicial resources for serious crimes by offering alternatives to the usual prosecution process for less serious ones, and (3) provide, where appropriate, a vehicle for restitution to communities and victims of crime.

2▶ There are four rationales for diversion: (1) Formal processing can encourage more criminal behavior; (2) diversion is cheaper than formally processing an offender through the criminal justice system; (3) formal processing may seem inappropriate for crimes without perceived victims; and (4) formal arrest, trial, and conviction add to the burdens of certain disadvantaged groups.

3▶ Diversion may occur at any stage in the criminal justice process after a criminal complaint has been filed or police have observed a crime. The police, a prosecutor, or a judge may call for diversion.

4▶ Issues concerning diversion include (1) the legal and ethical issues of protecting a defendant's rights; (2) the law enforcement question about whether diversion encourages violation of the law; and (3) the economic question of diversion's cost-effectiveness.

REVIEW & APPLICATIONS

5 ▶ Probation is the conditional release of a convicted offender into the community, under the supervision of a probation officer. Most probation programs are designed to (1) protect the community by assisting judges in sentencing and supervising offenders, (2) carry out sanctions imposed by the court, (3) help offenders change, (4) support crime victims, and (5) coordinate and promote the use of community resources.

6 ▶ Probation is used for four reasons: (1) It permits offenders to remain in the community for reintegration purposes, (2) it avoids institutionalization and the stigma of incarceration, (3) it is less expensive than incarceration and more humanitarian, and (4) it is appropriate for offenders whose crimes do not necessarily merit incarceration.

7 ▶ On January 1, 2003, federal, state, and local probation agencies supervised 3.9 million adult U.S. residents, with felony convictions accounting for one-half. Twenty-three percent of all probationers were women, and 55 percent of probationers were white. Sixty percent of adults had a direct sentence to probation.

8 ▶ In 31 states, adult probation services are administered by the state department of corrections. In 10 states and the District of Columbia, the responsibility for adult probation lies with the state judiciary. In eight states, the responsibility is shared by the state and the counties. In one state, counties provide adult probation services.

9 ▶ Corrections professionals urge evaluators to collect data on outcomes other than recidivism, such as amount of restitution collected, number of offenders employed, amounts of fines and fees collected, hours of community service, number of treatment sessions completed, percentage of financial obligations collected, rate of enrollment in school, number of days employed, educational attainment, and number of days drug free.

10 ▶ Case investigation and client supervision are the two major roles of probation officers. Investigation includes the preparation of a presentence report (PSR), which the judge uses in sentencing an offender. Supervision includes the functions of intervention, surveillance, and enforcement.

11 ▶ A revocation hearing is a due process hearing that must be conducted to determine whether the conditions of probation have been violated before probation can be revoked and the offender removed from the community. Probation can be revoked when offenders fail to comply with the technical conditions of probation or commit new crimes.

KEY TERMS

diversion, *p. 113*
counter performance, *p. 114*
true diversion, *p. 114*
minimization of penetration, *p. 114*
unconditional diversion, *p. 118*

conditional diversion, *p. 118*
probation, *p. 119*
recidivism, *p. 129*
client-specific plan (CSP), *p. 135*
supervision, *p. 142*
revocation hearing, *p. 147*

revocation, *p. 147*
technical violation, *p. 149*
absconding, *p. 149*
new offense violation, *p. 150*

QUESTIONS FOR REVIEW

1. What is *diversion*?
2. What are three objectives of diversion?
3. What are the four rationales for diversion?
4. Discuss three diversion policy issues.
5. What is *probation*?
6. How did probation originate in the United States?
7. What were some of the characteristics of adults on probation on January 1, 2003?
8. What are the four ways adult probation is administered? Which one is the most common?
9. What do we know about probation recidivism for misdemeanants? For felons?
10. What are some suggestions for implementing effective probation programs?
11. What is the presentence report? What are its purposes?
12. What are the elements of probation supervision?
13. What is the difference between technical and new offense violations?

THINKING CRITICALLY ABOUT CORRECTIONS

▶ ▶ ▶ **PSRs**

Critics of PSRs claim that the information in them is not always verified or reliable even though the trend today is toward limited disclosure of information to the defendant's attorney. Actually, much of the information in a PSR is hearsay. Although defendants or victims may object to the contents of a PSR or the way it characterizes their behavior, they have no right to have the PSR reflect their views. As a probation officer, how would you respond to these criticisms?

▶ ▶ ▶ **Probation Effectiveness**

Recidivism is one current measure of probation effectiveness. Others include the amount of restitution collected, the number of offenders employed, the amounts of fines and fees collected, the number of hours of community service performed, the number of treatment sessions completed, the percentage of financial obligations collected, the rate of school enrollment, the level of educational attainment, the number of days employed, and the number of days drug free.

1. How important to you, as a taxpayer, is recidivism as a measure of program success?
2. Do you believe probation officers can really keep offenders from committing new crimes or violating the conditions of their probation?
3. If you were a probation officer today, by which outcome measures would you want to be judged? Why?
4. If recidivism is used as a measure of probation's effectiveness, how should it be defined?

REVIEW & APPLICATIONS

REVIEW & APPLICATIONS

ON-THE-JOB DECISION MAKING

▶ ▶ ▶ Responding to Program Violations

The new diversion program in your county was developed to help first-time misdemeanor drug offenders avoid incarceration and seek help in controlling their dependency. Your job as the new diversion officer is to set the conditions of the diversion program and then monitor and enforce compliance. One of your first clients fails the required weekly drug test.

1. Should you immediately remove that person from the program?

2. Why or why not?

▶ ▶ ▶ Probation and Recidivism

At a recent staff meeting, the chief PO reported that the department's recidivism rate exceeded the national average by 5 percent. The chief asks what can be done about it. You say, "Look at other measures besides recidivism." The chief asks you to explain. What do you say?

CORRECTIONS ON THE WEB

▶ ▶ ▶ Probation Agency Web Pages

Most probation agencies—whether administered by a state, a county, a state and county, or a court system—have Web pages. Using the information in Figure 4–5, try to find the Web page of one probation agency for each of the four methods of administration. What difference, if any, does the type of administration make in philosophy, mission, goals, structure, resources, and so forth? Visit the Web page of the Los Angeles County Probation Department (the largest probation department in the world) (http://probation.co.la.ca.us) as an example.

▶ ▶ ▶ APPA

The American Probation and Parole Association is an international association composed of individuals from the United States, its U.S. territories, and Canada actively involved with probation, parole, and community-based corrections in both adult and juvenile sectors at all levels of government. APPA is the voice for thousands of probation and parole practitioners including line staff, supervisors, and administrators.

APPA maintains an information clearinghouse at its Website, http://www.appa-net.org, listing free downloadable publications and resources and a list of frequently asked questions (FAQs). Use the free downloadable publications and FAQs to report in more detail on any of the topics covered in this chapter.

CERTIFICATE OF COMPLETION

PRESENTED TO

DEE CLINEBELL

CONGRADULATIONS ON YOUR COMPLETION
OF
THE CENTRAL NEBRASKA DRUG COURT
PROGRAM

“ Crime and bad lives are the measure of a State's failure; all crime in the
end is the crime of the community. ”

—H. G. Wells, father of modern science fiction, 1866–1946

Intermediate Sanctions: Between Probation and Incarceration

▶ **CHAPTER OBJECTIVES**

After completing this chapter you should be able to do the following:

1. Define *intermediate sanctions* and describe their purpose.

2. Define *net widening.*

3. Describe how intensive supervision probation works.

4. Explain what drug courts are.

5. Explain how day fines differ from traditional fines.

6. Describe what a sentence to community service entails.

7. Explain what day reporting centers are.

8. Describe how remote-location monitoring works.

9. Explain what residential community centers are.

10. Identify the major features of boot camps.

11. Distinguish between a policy-centered approach and a program-centered approach to planning intermediate sanctions.

12. Define *community corrections.*

13. Explain what community corrections acts are.

▶ ▶ Actress Winona Ryder rose to prominence in 1988 with her role in *Beetle Juice.* She moved in a different direction on December 12, 2001, when she stole more than 20 high-fashion items worth $9,750 from Saks Fifth Avenue—a posh department store—in Beverly Hills, California. Store security officers observed Ryder trying to remove security tags affixed to socks, hair accessories, and a Gucci dress before hiding them in a large shopping bag she had brought into the store. At 7 P.M. she was arrested and charged with grand theft. By midnight she was released on a $20,000 bond. A year later, the two-time Academy Award nominee was convicted of felony grand theft and vandalism. On December 6, 2002, Superior Court Judge Elden Fox sentenced Ryder to a number of intermediate sanctions discussed in this chapter: three years' probation, a fine and court costs of $6,550, a restitution fee of $11,265 to Saks, 480 hours of community service within four months (240 hours at the City of Hope, a major medical center specializing in cancer treatment; 120 hours at the Foundation for the Junior Blind; and 120 hours at Caring for Babies with AIDS), and drug and psychological counseling. Because she had no prior convictions, prosecutors did not recommend incarceration.

In 2002, actress Winona Ryder was sentenced to three years' probation, ordered to pay $11,265 in restitution and $6,550 in fines and court costs, perform 480 hours of community service, and required to take drug and psychological counseling for stealing more than 20 high-fashion items worth $9,750 from Saks Fifth Avenue in Beverly Hills, California. Do you think intermediate sanctions teach offenders a lesson better than regular probation alone?

At the sentencing hearing, Ryder's attorney told the Court that she would have to carry the scarlet letter "S" for shoplifting for the rest of her life. Judge Fox told Ryder, "It is not my intention to make an example of you." He added, "You have disappointed many people who have been entertained and inspired by your talents and also your acts of humanity. . . . There is going to be the need to confront certain issues that you have been unable, or refused, to confront and accept personal responsibility for what happened." Judge Fox told Ryder that he had been unable to explain to his 16-year-old son, Ryan, why someone who earned so much would shoplift. "You are the only person that's going to be able to answer my son's question." Judge Fox added, "If you steal again, you will go to jail. Understand that?" "Yes, Your Honor, I do," Ryder replied.

Ryder returned to court on December 15, 2003. Judge Fox commended her for abiding by the rules of her probation. Fox ordered Ryder to return to court May 26, 2004 for a six-month review and said he would decide then if she needs to continue probation supervision.

Ryder's story captures the essence of this chapter. Some offenders need punishment beyond regular probation but not incarceration. Today, judges have unlimited opportunities to order penalties that match the seriousness of a crime. In Ryder's case, three years' probation in addition to fines and restitution, community service, and counseling constitute what we call **intermediate sanctions**—punishment options that fill the gap between traditional probation and jail or prison and that better

intermediate sanctions

New punishment options developed to fill the gap between traditional probation and traditional jail or prison sentences and to better match the severity of punishment to the seriousness of the crime.

match the severity of punishment to the seriousness of the crime. Intermediate sanctions fulfills important sentencing goals: retribution, deterrence, desert, incapacitation, rehabilitation, and restoration. Because intermediate sanctions are administered outside prison or jail and generally in the offender's community, they are a form of **community corrections.** After considering the principal intermediate sanctions in use in the United States, we will turn our attention to community corrections in general.

community corrections

A philosophy of correctional treatment that embraces (1) decentralization of authority, (2) citizen participation, (3) redefinition of the population of offenders for whom incarceration is most appropriate, and (4) emphasis on rehabilitation through community programs.

Intermediate Sanctions

Sanctions less restrictive than prison but more restrictive than probation are not new. Variations of intermediate sanctions like many of those discussed later in this chapter (restitution, fines, and community service) were used as sentences in ancient Israel, Greece, and Rome.[1] Other intermediate sanctions—such as drug court, remote-location monitoring, boot camps, and day fines—started in the 1980s. What is new today is the effort to bring all these sanctions together into a comprehensive sentencing system like the one suggested in Figure 5–1, which provides judges with an expanded menu of corrections options. Relatively less intrusive interventions proportional to the severity of a violation and the risk of the offender are to the left in Figure 5–1; more intrusive ones are to the right. Figure 5–1 is also multidimensional, creating depth for each step on the continuum. For example, if an offender on intensive supervision probation (ISP) fails to report as scheduled (whether to an ISP officer or via an automated probation machine as described in Chapter 4) and is relatively low risk, it may be appropriate to require more frequent reporting for a period of time within ISP than to move to the next higher level of intervention.

Advocates for intermediate sanctions include the American Jail Association (see Exhibit 5–1). This organization calls for a range or continuum of sanctions with graduated levels of supervision and harshness. Simple probation is at one end, traditional incarceration is at the other, and a variety of intermediate sanctions bridge the middle ground. This type of sentencing enables criminal justice officials to reserve expensive prison and jail space for violent offenders. It gives nonviolent offenders less restrictive intermediate sanctions and restitution-focused sentences while teaching them accountability for their actions and heightening their chances for rehabilitation. This approach to sentencing treats prisons as the backstop, not the backbone, of the corrections system.

Intermediate sanctions are most often used for offenders considered nonviolent and low risk. They usually require the offender to lead a productive life in the community by working (finding work if unemployed) or learning new job skills; to perform unpaid community service; to pay restitution to victims; to enroll in a treatment or educational program; or sometimes to do all of these.

> You have been victimized by an offender, causing you great personal stress. You are asked by the court to consider "intermediate sanctions" for the offender. How do you respond? For more information go to Ethical Dilemma 5-1 at http://www.mhhe.com/schmalleger2.
>
> Ethical Dilemma

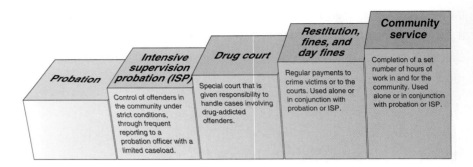

FIGURE 5-1
A Three-Dimensional Continuum of Intermediate Sanctions

front-end programs

Punishment options for initial sentences more restrictive than traditional probation but less restrictive than jail or prison.

back-end programs

Sanctions that move offenders from higher levels of control to lower ones for the final phase of their sentences.

net widening

Increasing the number of offenders sentenced to a higher level of restriction. It results in sentencing offenders to more restrictive sanctions than their offenses and characteristics warrant.

Intermediate sanctions are sometimes referred to as *front-end programs* or strategies. **Front-end programs** are options for initial sentences that are more restrictive than traditional probation but less restrictive than jail or prison. They are usually designed to limit the number of people who go to prison. In front-end programs, judges commonly sentence offenders directly to one or a combination of intermediate sanctions before requiring incarceration. **Back-end programs** are reduced restrictions for offenders who have made progress in compliance and treatment. In back-end programs, offenders are moved from higher to lower levels of control to complete the final phase of their sentences. For example, the state department of corrections may move an offender from prison to remote-location monitoring.

Front-end programs tend to apply more to offenders who would otherwise receive less restrictive sentences than to those who would otherwise go to jail or prison. In that way, they contribute to **net widening.** Net widening is increasing the number of offenders sentenced to a higher level of restriction. As a result, many offenders may receive more restrictive sentences than their offenses and characteristics warrant. Community service,

---

EXHIBIT 5-1   American Jail Association Resolution

Intermediate Punishments

WHEREAS, the American Jail Association (AJA) recognizes the detrimental impact that crowding places on local jails; and

WHEREAS, many of those who are incarcerated in jails do not pose a known danger to themselves or to society;

THEREFORE BE IT RESOLVED THAT AJA supports the expansion of intermediate punishments in states and localities throughout America for offenders who do not pose a known danger to public safety. AJA believes that intermediate punishments address real concerns of constituents.

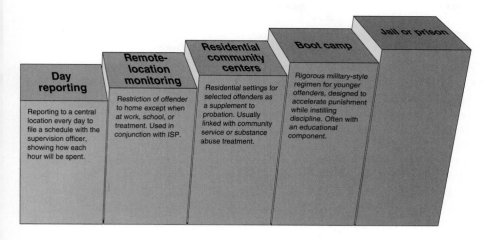

for instance, might be added to probation in a front-end program. The downside of such intermediate sanctions that provide discipline and structure for disruptive individuals is that large numbers of people will receive sanctions that will not be suitable.

VALUE OF INTERMEDIATE SANCTIONS

At midyear 2002, the nation's jail and prison population exceeded two million inmates for the first time. From the end of 1995 to mid-2002, the number of people confined in state and federal prisons and local jails increased 27 percent from 1,585,586 to 2,019,234, an annual increase of 3.8 percent.[2] This level of increase in the nation's prisons and jails places a heavy economic burden on taxpayers. That burden includes the cost of building, maintaining, and operating prisons and jails, as well as the loss of offenders' contributions and the cost of caring for the destabilized families left behind. In addition, overcrowded jails and prisons are hard to manage and staff, and they invite disorder.

During the same period, new intermediate-sanction programs expanded rapidly across the United States, and the number of persons sentenced to them increased. The result has been an explosion in the number of persons under correctional supervision. Many intermediate sanctions were started with the goal of reducing the prison population. Though there has been no decline in the number of people sentenced to prison since these new intermediate sanctions appeared, proponents argue that, without the new programs, the number would be even larger. Other supporters say that, by increasing the surveillance, punishment, and treatment of offenders under community supervision, intermediate sanctions achieve other correctional goals.

Intermediate sanctions are valuable for a number of reasons. First, they provide a means for offenders who are not dangerous to repay their victims and their communities. Second, intermediate sanctions promote rehabilitation—which most citizens want, but most prisons and jails find difficult to

Intermediate Sanctions: Quality Programs or Stepchildren of the Correctional and Judicial Systems

by Herbert J. Hoelter, National Center on Institutions and Alternatives

Reflections on the Future

When asked to write some introductory comments on the future of intermediate sanctions, I accepted the task with enthusiasm, welcoming the opportunity to share the wisdom of my 25 years of experience in alternative and community corrections. Being an inveterate optimist, I was confident that I could put forth a piece that might enlighten and encourage those in the field of community corrections, as well as those hoping to enter the field.

However, upon reflecting on how to address most accurately the issue of the future in this field, my optimism waned. I came to realize that to be able to address the future of a particular topic, there is an inherent assumption that there is a past, or at minimum a present, in a given field. On the issue of intermediate sanctions, that assumption is misguided. Truth be known, the use of intermediate sanctions in the prison and correctional system in the United States is much more of a *concept* than a reality.

In order to begin to understand this, it is incumbent to remember how the term "intermediate sanctions" entered the field of community corrections. It was during the early 1980s, when conservatives were arguing that rehabilitation was a failure and worthless, and the liberal advocacy organizations decided that in order to "win" the argument for community corrections, rehabilitation should be downplayed (and in some cases abandoned) in favor of punishment and deterrence. The theory was that successful arguments could be made to legislators and judges that programs such as house arrest, community sanction centers, rigorous community service, ankle bracelets, global positioning tracking, drug testing, and shameful sentencing could be effective "intermediate sanctions," bridging the gap between traditional probation and prisons, particularly for nonviolent offenders. In theory, perhaps it was an interesting idea; in practice, it has become an albatross. Probation officers have turned into foot soldiers for the prison system, and many programs originally designed to help offenders in the community turned into mini correctional facilities.

This is not to suggest that all of the intermediate sanction programs currently in operation are somehow failures; on the contrary, there are hundreds of successful programs doing intensive supervision, effective monitoring, valuable community service, and restitution and providing treatment in the community. The point is that these are isolated, individual programs on the fringes of the prison system. They are not now, nor have they ever been, viewed as an integral part of any state or federal correctional system. Additionally, they are subject to the political ideology and budget priorities of the day.

If there is to be a future to intermediate sanctions, the challenge is to find a method and political will to move these programs firmly into the correctional and judicial systems, rather than be the stepchildren of those systems. In my view, and in looking at lessons learned from the past, there are three fundamental issues to address in order to move the concept of intermediate sanctions into accepted practice.

The first issue is that we must be strong in our conviction that rehabilitation of offenders is an acceptable and worthwhile process. Rehabilitation can and does work, and everybody deserves the opportunity to change.

Second, we must recognize that intermediate sanctions deserve the financial resources to do the difficult task of working with offenders in the community. We must advocate that some or all of the $22,000 spent on keeping a person incarcerated for a year gets recommitted to the intermediate sanction serving that person.

Finally, unpopular as it may sound, we must develop a philosophy that we handle offenders in the community with the same care, concern and commitment we would expect if they were our own sons or daughters, fathers or mothers. We must insist on developing quality programs that have respect for the individuals they serve and maintain a certain dignity for all of our populations, even those that seem "undeserving."

Intermediate sanctions can and should have a future—but it must be on these terms, not those defined by the failing prison system.

ABOUT THE AUTHOR
Mr. Hoelter is cofounder and CEO of the National Center on Institutions and Alternatives. He is recognized as one of the country's leading experts in developing alternative programs to incarceration. Mr. Hoelter holds a Master of Social Work degree from Marywood College in Pennsylvania and a Bachelor of Arts degree from the University of Buffalo. Mr. Hoelter is coeditor of *The Real War on Crime*.

provide—and the reintegration of the offender into the community. And third, once the programs are in place, they can do these things at a comparatively low cost. Compare the lower costs of intermediate sanctions with jail and prison in Table 5–1. In California alone, officials estimate that 2,120 people are serving prison time for petty theft. Sentencing them to intermediate sanctions would save the state $14 million.[3]

Intermediate sanctions should not be haphazardly planned or implemented. High-quality intermediate sanctions must be thoughtfully conceived, effectively targeted, well planned, and well staffed. Most important, intermediate sanctions must be incorporated into sentencing guidelines to achieve reasonable consistency in sentencing while allowing judges to consider meaningful differences between cases. (Delaware, North Carolina, and Pennsylvania are on the vanguard of incorporating intermediate sanctions into their sentencing guidelines.[4]) Perhaps the most important lesson learned from 20 years' experience with intermediate sanctions is "they are seldom likely to achieve their goals unless means can be found to set and enforce policies governing their use. Otherwise, the combination of officials' risk aversion and practitioners' preferences to be guided solely by their judgments about appropriate penalties in individual cases is likely to undermine program goals."[5]

> Some people view intermediate sanctions as an "easy out" from punishment. Do you agree? Read what two communities have done in this area. For more information go to Ethical Dilemma 5-2 at http://www.mhhe.com/schmalleger2.
>
> **Ethical Dilemma**

[Intermediate sanctions] are 'seldom likely to achieve their goals unless means can be found to set and enforce policies governing their use.'

VARIETIES OF INTERMEDIATE SANCTIONS

The specific varieties of intermediate sanctions discussed in the following subsections include intensive supervision probation, drug court, fines, community service, day reporting centers, remote-location monitoring

TABLE 5–1	Average Annual Cost of Correctional Options
Correctional option	**Cost per year per participant**
Boot camp	$32,119
Prison	21,140
Jail	20,702
Halfway house	18,074
Remote-location monitoring	4,102
Intensive supervision	3,551
Day reporting	2,781
Community service	2,759
Drug court	2,500
Probation/parole	1,222
House arrest	402

Source: Adapted from *Seeking Justice: Crime and Punishment in America* (New York: Edna McConnell Clark Foundation, 1977), p. 34; Camille Graham Camp and George M. Camp, *Adult Corrections* (Middletown, CT: Criminal Justice Institute, 2001), pp. 87, 125, 188, 198; Camille Graham Camp and George M. Camp, *Jails* (Middletown, CT: Criminal Justice Institute, 2001), p. 42; and the Website of the National Association of Drug Court Professionals, http://www.nadcp.org/whatis/.

In January of 2001, I pled guilty to fifth-degree assault. It was a domestic-type thing. Instead of jail time, I wore a home monitor, which I wore around my ankle. I had to wear it 24/7, and I couldn't take it off until my time was up—and if you do try to tamper with it, it gives a signal and they know right away and come to arrest you. There is a little bit of discomfort—it weighed maybe a half-pound. It's not torturous by any means, but you look forward to getting the darned thing off.

I was allowed to leave for work on certain hours, so between 8 A.M. and 4 P.M. I was allowed to be gone, but I had to be home at 4 P.M. and couldn't leave after that. Could you walk out to the garage from your house? I didn't—I always called and got permission, because I didn't want to set that thing off.

You don't think it's a big deal at first, but it really makes you feel like you're a prisoner in your own home. There is some punitive feeling that you get from

having to wear it. It takes away some of your freedom. So I think it's very, very effective. It's a better alternative than going to jail, but it's still not like "Oh, you didn't do anything, you can go home." You are being punished. It's a good alternative to crowded jails—it's a great idea. Not that I liked it. I hated it. I couldn't wait to get it off.

Mike Schoffman
Spicer, Minnesota

THE OFFENDER SPEAKS

(formerly known as *house arrest* and *electronic monitoring*), residential community centers, and boot camps.

Intensive Supervision Probation   Probation with frequent contact between offender and probation officer, strict enforcement of conditions, random drug and alcohol testing, and other requirements is known as **intensive supervision probation (ISP)**. On January 1, 2000, 5 percent (122,938) of the adult population on probation or parole was on ISP.[6]

As a technique for increasing control over offenders in the community, ISP has gained wide popularity. It allows offenders to live at home but under more severe and more punitive restrictions than those of conventional probation. The primary purpose of such program restrictions and surveillance is to protect the community and deter the offender from breaking the law or violating the conditions of release. Requirements of ISP usually include performing community service, attending school or treatment programs, working or looking for employment, meeting with a probation officer (or team of officers) as often as five times a week, and submitting to curfews, employment checks, and tests for drug and alcohol use. Because of the frequency of contact, subjection to unannounced drug tests, and rigorous enforcement of restitution, community service, and other conditions, ISP is thought more appropriate for higher-risk offenders.

ISP was initially the most popular intermediate sanction. It emerged in the 1960s as an effort to improve offender rehabilitation by reducing probation and parole caseloads from 100 or more to 30. However, researchers soon discovered that small caseloads led to enhanced supervision and control (and more violations) but not necessarily to enhanced treatment.[7] It wasn't until ISP combined supervision and control with treatment components and skill development programs and reinforced clearly identified behaviors that it became effective.[8] Today, ISP programs exist in every state. They may be state or county programs and may be administered by parole, probation, or prison departments. As a result, it is not easy to estimate the number of ISP programs in the United States.

In general, evaluators of ISP have concluded that offenders sentenced to ISP commit new crimes at about the same rate as comparable offenders receiving different sentences. Also, technical violation and revocation rates

intensive supervision probation (ISP)

Control of offenders in the community under strict conditions, by means of frequent reporting to a probation officer whose caseload is generally limited to 30 offenders.

are typically higher for ISP participants because more frequent contact makes misconduct more likely to be discovered. Early proponents of ISP argued that ISP would reduce recidivism rates, rehabilitate offenders, and save money and prison resources. However, most evaluations suggest that the combination of net widening, high revocation rates, and costs of processing revocations makes savings unlikely.[9]

There is one tantalizing positive finding about ISP: It increases participants' involvement in counseling and treatment programs. There is evidence that rearrests are reduced when offenders receive treatment in addition to the increased surveillance and control of ISP programs. The literature demonstrates that participation in drug treatment, whether

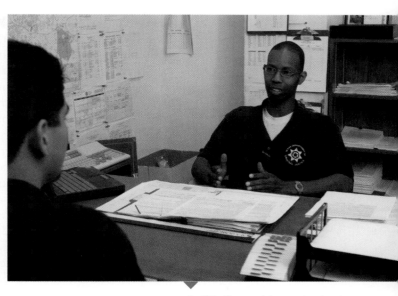

An ISP officer explains court-ordered sanctions to a probationer. Frequent face-to-face contact is a condition of ISP. What other controls are used to monitor offenders on ISP?

voluntary or compelled, can reduce both drug use and crime by drug-using offenders. Data indicate that in many cities, one-half to three-fourths of arrested felons are drug abusers; ISP holds promise as a device for getting addicted offenders into treatment and keeping them there.[10] Evaluation of the Florida Community Control Program (FCCP) by the National Council on Crime and Delinquency concluded that ISP graduates commit new crimes at a lower rate than a comparable group of offenders released from prison and that each FCCP participant saved the state $2,750.[11]

To reap the benefits of ISP, what must be done is straightforward. Because recidivism rates for new crimes are no higher for ISP participants than for comparable imprisoned offenders, ISP is a cost-effective alternative to prison for offenders who do not present unacceptable risks to public safety. Cost savings are likely to depend, however, on using ISP only for offenders who would have received appreciable prison time. And technical violations require a range of responses, not a rush to incarcerate the violator. Incarcerating all violators cancels out the initial savings of ISP.

Drug Courts **Drug court** is a special court that is given responsibility to handle cases involving drug-addicted offenders.[12] It is a new intermediate sanction that uses the power of the court to treat, sanction, and reward drug offenders with punishment more restrictive than regular probation but less severe than incarceration. In testimony before the Senate Judiciary Subcommittee on Youth Violence, John S. Goldcamp of Temple University's Department of Criminal Justice told the panel of senators, "The effect of the drug court movement on courts and the justice system over the last 11 years may turn out—with more historical distance—to have been one of the major justice reforms of the last part of the 20th century in the United States."[13]

In 1989, troubled by the devastating impact of drugs and drug-related crime on Dade County (Florida) neighborhoods and the criminal justice system, Miami judge Herbert M. Klein developed the nation's first drug court and proactively oversaw an intensive, community-based treatment,

drug court

A special court that is given responsibility to treat, sanction, and reward drug offenders with punishment more restrictive than regular probation but less severe than incarceration.

rehabilitation, and supervision program for felony drug defendants. By April 2002, nearly 700 drug courts were operating in all 50 states, the District of Columbia, Puerto Rico, Guam, and two federal district courts. Of this number, there were 483 adult drug courts, 167 juvenile drug courts, 37 family drug courts, and 10 combination drug courts. Another 427 drug courts were in the planning stages.[14] In these jurisdictions, coalitions of judges, prosecutors, attorneys, substance abuse treatment professionals, probation officers, community-based service organization staff, law enforcement officials, and others use the coercive power of the court to force abstinence from drugs and alter the behavior of substance-abusing offenders.

In comparison with the aims of other types of courts, those of the drug court are much less punitive and more healing and restorative in nature. This new approach integrates substance abuse treatment, sanctions, incentives, and frequent court appearances with case processing to place drug-involved defendants in judicially supervised rehabilitation programs. Successful completion of the treatment program results in dismissal of the charges, reduced or set-aside sentences, lesser penalties, or a combination of these. Drug court provides a new alternative to traditional methods of dealing with the devastating impact of drugs and drug-related crime and a way to eliminate the revolving-door syndrome of substance abuse in the criminal justice system. Figure 5–2 is a sample drug court participation agreement.

Drug courts vary from one jurisdiction to another in terms of structure, scope, and target populations. Because drug courts are developed at the local level, their design and structure reflect the unique strengths, circumstances, and capabilities of each community. Still, all drug courts share three primary goals: (1) to reduce recidivism, (2) to reduce substance abuse among participants, and (3) to rehabilitate participants. The key components of drug court that work together to achieve these goals are the following:

- incorporating drug testing into case processing;
- creating a nonadversarial relationship between the defendant and the court;
- identifying defendants in need of treatment and referring them to treatment as soon as possible after arrest;
- providing access to a continuum of treatment and rehabilitation services;
- monitoring abstinence through frequent, mandatory drug testing;
- establishing a coordinated strategy to govern drug court responses to participants' compliance;
- maintaining judicial interaction with each drug court participant;
- monitoring and evaluating program goals and gauging their effectiveness;
- continuing interdisciplinary education to promote effective drug court planning, implementation, and operations; and
- forging partnerships among drug courts, public agencies, and community-based organizations to generate local support and enhance drug court effectiveness.

STATE OF ALABAMA   )   IN THE SIXTH JUDICIAL CIRCUIT COURT
)   DRUG COURT DIVISION
vs.   )   TUSCALOOSA COUNTY, ALABAMA
)
_____   )   CASE NO. _____

DRUG COURT TREATMENT PROGRAM
PARTICIPATION AGREEMENT

I agree to the following as conditions of my participation:

1. Following assignment by the Tuscaloosa County Drug Court Judge to the Drug Court
    Program, I will be treated by Indian Rivers Treatment Facility. (Treatment only).

2. An assessment will be conducted to determine whether my participation in the Drug Court
    Treatment Program is clinically appropriate.

3. If treatment is indicated, I will begin attendance the following day or as instructed.
    Treatment will continue for approximately two (2) years.

4. Treatment will be in four (4) phases:
    Phase I: Attend four IOP Groups per week for two weeks and one Saturday Family Group
    Phase II: Attend three IOP Groups per week plus one Saturday Family Group <u>or</u> Thursday
                  Family Group for 12 weeks, attend three (3) 12-step meetings a week (or
                  equivalent court-approved program).
    Phase III: Attend one weekday Alumni Group per week and one Thursday Family Group
                  (if qualified) <u>or</u> One Saturday Alumni Group per week for 12 weeks, attend four
                  (4) 12-step meetings a week (or equivalent court approved program).
    Phase IV: Attend one weekday Alumni group per week for seventy-eight weeks, attend four
                  (4) 12-step meetings a week for 78 weeks (Or equivalent court-approved
                  program).

5. I agree to provide a urine specimen to be tested for the presence of drugs as follows:
    Phase I: Twice a week (minimum)
    Phases II and III: Once per week (minimum)
    Phase IV: When requested by the Court or Treatment

6. I agree to sign an individualized plan for treatment with my case manager and to participate in the
    accomplishment of goals and objectives as designated.

7. The Tuscaloosa County Drug Court Judge and the Case Manager will be informed of my attendance
    in counseling, results of urinalysis and progress in the program

8. Failure to attend counseling, remain drug and alcohol free or demonstrate progress in treatment
    will result in a review of my case by the Tuscaloosa County Drug Court Judge to determine my
    continued participation in the Drug Court Program or the imposition of interim legal consequences,
    including incarceration.

9. I understand and accept the contents and ramifications of this form which I have read or have
    had read to me.

_____   _____
Attorney for Defendant   Defendant

FIGURE 5-2
Sample Drug Court Participation Agreement

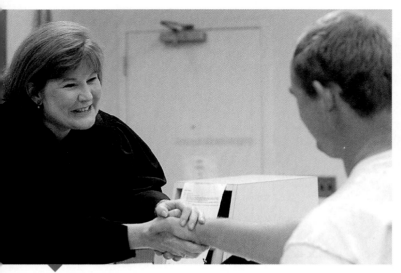

Judge Sarah Smith congratulates drug court participant Bronco Anderson in her Tulsa, Oklahoma, courtroom for completing phase one and moving to phase two of the drug court program. Drug courts treat, sanction, and reward drug offenders with punishment more restrictive than regular probation but less severe than incarceration. What are the key components of drug court?

Because drug courts are relatively new, the body of research concerning them is still growing. Still, researchers agree that the thrust of findings from assorted studies is generally supportive of drug courts and points to positive results. After conducting drug court research for more than a decade, Goldcamp told the Senate Judiciary Subcommittee on Youth Violence that "drug courts can and do have an important impact on substance abuse and offending and represent an important new direction in criminal justice, drug treatment, and health."[15] In a study of two of the nation's oldest and longest operating drug courts, Goldcamp reported that drug court graduates were rearrested less frequently during one-, two-, and three-year follow-up periods than nongraduates overall and during each year studied.[16]

The National Association of Drug Court Professionals produced other positive findings:

- Drug courts provide more comprehensive and closer supervision of the drug-using offender than do other forms of community supervision.
- Drug use and criminal behavior are substantially reduced while clients are participating in drug court.
- Criminal behavior is lower after program participation, especially for graduates.
- Drug courts generate cost savings ($10 for every $1 spent on drug court) from reduced jail/prison use, reduced criminality, and lower criminal justice system costs.
- Drug courts are successful in bridging the gap between the court and the treatment/public health systems and spurring greater cooperation among the various agencies and personnel within the criminal justice system, as well as between the criminal justice system and the community.[17]

In 1998, Columbia University's National Center on Addiction and Substance Abuse provided the first major academic review and analysis of drug courts and concluded that "drug courts provide closer, more comprehensive supervision, and much more frequent drug testing and monitoring during the program than other forms of community supervision. More importantly, drug use and criminal behavior are substantially reduced while offenders are participating in drug court."[18]

However, the debate over the effectiveness of drug court continues because reported rates of recidivism from individual drug courts vary widely. The variation reflects the diversity across drug courts in the characteristics of participants (for example, in the severity of addiction, the types of drugs used, and criminal history) and in how drug courts operate (for example, program eligibility, treatment availability and quality, and court monitoring polices).

In July, 2003, the National Institute of Justice and the Drug Court Program Office produced the first estimate of recidivism among a nationally representative sample of drug court graduates.[19] Researchers identified all drug courts funded by the Drug Court Program Office that had been in operation for at least one year as of January 1, 1999, and had at least 40 program graduates. From a population of 17,000, FBI records of 2,021 drug court graduates from 95 drug courts were analyzed.

Researchers defined recidivism as any arrest and charge that carried a sentence of at least one year upon conviction. Within one year after graduation, 16.4 percent of drug court graduates had been arrested and charged with a serious offense (a success rate of 83.6 percent). Within two years, re-arrests increased to 27.5 percent, lowering the success rate to 72.5 percent.

Researchers also estimated the number of serious offenses committed by drug court graduates. In the first year after graduation, drug court graduates averaged 0.23 serious crimes per person and 0.50 serious crimes per person in the first two years after graduation. Among those drug court graduates that did commit a serious crime, the average was 1.42 in the first year and 1.83 in the second year.

Researchers discovered other interesting findings about drug court. When they compared drug court recidivism to the severity of the population admitted to drug court, they found that drug courts with the highest recidivism rates tended to accept offenders who were primarily cocaine and heroin users, and who were classified by the drug courts as having "moderate" or "severe" drug problems. Researchers also found that recidivism was related to the size of the drug court. Graduates of the largest drug courts (defined as having more than 832 total graduates) had a two year recidivism rate of 30.8 percent, compared with a two year recidivism rate between 22.5 percent and 24 percent for drug courts with fewer graduates. The reason, the authors suggest, is large drug courts are located in the largest metropolitan areas, and accept clients with the most severe drug problems.

With these national benchmark estimates, the future of drug courts is promising. More than 220,000 adults and 9,000 juveniles have enrolled in drug courts, and 73,000 adults and 1,500 juveniles have graduated. The retention rate is 70 percent. Over three-fourths of drug court participants were previously incarcerated, a finding that lessens the problem of net widening. More than 1,000 drug-free babies have been born, and 3,500 drug-free parents have regained custody of their children. Child support payments are being made by more than 4,550 drug-free parents. And almost three-fourths of drug court graduates have obtained employment. These results, federal funding for planning, implementing, and enhancing drug courts through the U.S. Department of Justice Drug Courts Program Office, and the support of national, state, and local leaders who recognize that traditional criminal justice policies have little impact on substance abuse suggest that drug courts will play an increasingly visible role in the nation's response to drug-related crime.

Fines   A **fine** is a financial sanction requiring a convicted person to pay a specified sum of money. The fine is one of the oldest forms of punishment. It is, in practice, the criminal justice tool for punishing minor misdemeanors, traffic offenses, and ordinance violations. To be effective, fines should be

fine
A financial penalty used as a criminal sanction.

proportionate to the seriousness of an offense and should have roughly similar economic impacts on persons with differing financial resources who are convicted of the same offense. In the United States, fines are rarely regarded as a tough criminal sanction. They are not taken seriously, for at least four reasons. First, judicial, legislative, and prosecutorial attitudes restrict their use to traffic offenses, minor misdemeanors, and ordinance violations. Second, a judge seldom has enough reliable information on an offender's personal wealth to impose a just fine. Third, mechanisms for collecting fines are often ineffective. Far too often the responsibility for collecting fines has been left to probation officers, who are already overburdened and have no interest in fine collection. As a result, fines are seldom paid. Fourth, many believe that fines work hardship on the poor, while affluent offenders feel no sting.

day fine

A financial penalty scaled both to the defendant's ability to pay and the seriousness of the crime.

A **day fine** is a financial penalty based on the seriousness of the crime and the defendant's ability to pay. It is called a *day fine* because it is based on the offender's daily income. Day fines, also called *structured fines*, have been common in some northern and western European countries for many years. They were introduced in Sweden in the 1920s and were quickly incorporated into the penal codes of other Scandinavian countries. West Germany adopted day fines as a sentencing option in the early 1970s. Today, Sweden and Germany have made day fines the preferred punishment for most criminal cases, including those involving serious crimes. In Germany, for example, day fines are the only punishment for three-quarters of all offenders convicted of property crimes and two-thirds of offenders convicted of assaults.[20] Recently, the day fine of a Nokia executive made international headlines. Anssi Vanjoki of Finland, Nokia's vice president for Africa and Europe, drove his Harley-Davidson 17 miles per hour above the speed limit on a Helsinki street and was fined $103,600.[21] Vanjoki appealed the fine. He argued that the fine was assessed on his 1999 income of $5.2 million instead of his 2000 income of only $609,000. The Helsinki district court agreed and reduced Vanjoki's speeding ticket to $5,245. Others have been similarly fined in Finland. Nokia's president, Pekka Ala-Pietila, paid $31,200 for driving through a red light, and dot-com millionaire Jaakko Rytsola was fined $71,000 for zigzagging through Helsinki in his Ferrari, but his fine was later reduced to $119 because his wealth had fallen.

Day fines have been tried experimentally in some areas of the United States, including New York, Arizona, Connecticut, Iowa, and Oregon. Figure 5–3 is a sample notification of a structured fine program. The notice may be mailed to a defendant along with the summons or handed to the defendant when he or she appears in court.

To be effective, a day fine program must have the support of a cross-section of criminal justice professionals in a jurisdiction, as well as others who have a stake in the operation of the criminal justice system. According to a Bureau of Justice Assistance report[22] on day fines, the following officials should be involved in planning a county day fine program:

- a prosecutor;
- a public defender;
- a representative of the private defense bar;
- a court administrator;
- the presiding judges of the general and limited-jurisdiction courts;

A PRELIMINARY COMPLAINT
HAS BEEN FILED CHARGING YOU WITH
AN INDICTABLE OFFENSE

IF CONVICTED, THE COURT <u>MAY</u> IMPOSE ONE OR MORE OF
THE FOLLOWING SANCTIONS:
1.   JAIL OR PRISON
2.   PROBATION
3.   A FINE

If a fine is imposed, the Court may <u>structure</u> the level of the fine
partly according to the seriousness of the offense and partly in
relation to your means or ability to pay the fine. This method of
computing the amount of a "structured fine" is an effort by the Court
and the Polk County Attorney's Office to <u>equalize</u> the impact of
criminal sanctions and to <u>reduce</u> the number of persons who are
sentenced to prison, jail, or formal probation.

In order for the County Attorney's Office to consider recommending
a structured fine to the Court at the time of sentencing, you or your
attorney must schedule an interview with a Structured Fines Officer
at 555-1234, IMMEDIATELY. If you intend to secure an attorney to
represent you on this charge, please make these arrangements prior
to calling the Structured Fines Program.

Your ability to pay a structured fine as well as the length of time
needed to pay the fine are based on the information you provide in
the attached AFFIDAVIT OF FINANCIAL CONDITION. It is
required that you and/or your attorney complete this form prior to
meeting with a Structured Fines Officer. It is also required that you
take to your meeting with the Structured Fines Officer verification of
your income in the form of paycheck stubs, income tax returns, etc.

POLK COUNTY ATTORNEY'S OFFICE
STRUCTURED FINES PROGRAM
POLK COUNTY COURTHOUSE, ROOM B-40
DES MOINES, IOWA 50309
555-1234

Appointments with a Structured Fines Officer are available
Monday through Friday, from 1:30 P.M. to 4:30 P.M.

FIGURE 5-3
Sample Notification of a Structured Fine Program

- the director of a pretrial services agency;
- the chief probation officer or the director of a community corrections agency;
- the sheriff or another jail administrator; and
- representatives of county government.

The planning process for introducing day fines is unique for each jurisdiction, depending on its organizational structure, traditions, personalities, and legal culture. Every jurisdiction, however, addresses similar issues: current sentencing patterns, current fine collection operations and their effectiveness, goals and priorities for the day fine program, and potential legal challenges to the program.

Once a system for imposing day fines is put in place, the next step is to develop a structured process for setting fines. This structured process is the feature that distinguishes day fines from traditional fines. The process usually has two parts: (1) a unit scale that ranks offenses by severity and (2) a valuation scale for determining the dollar amount per unit for a given offender.

The first step in setting a day fine is to determine the number of fine units to be imposed. A portion of the unit scale used in a Staten Island, New York, day fine experiment is shown in Figure 5–4. The number of

Penal Law Charge*	Staten Island Day Fine Unit Scale (Selected Offense Categories)	Number of Day Fine Units Discount - PRESUMPTIVE - Premium
	Type of Offense**	
120.00 AM	Assault 3: Range of 20-95 DF	
	A. Substantial Injury *Stranger-to-stranger; or where victim is known to assailant, he/she is weaker, vulnerable*	81 - **95** - 109
	B. Minor Injury *Stranger-to-stranger; or where victim is known to assailant, he/she is weaker, vulnerable; or altercations involving use of a weapon*	59 - **70** - 81
	C. Substantial Injury *Altercations among acquaintances; brawls*	38 - **45** - 52
	D. Minor Injury	17 - **20** - 23
110/120.00 BM	Attempted Assault 3: Range of 15-45 DF	
	A. Substantial Injury *Stranger-to-stranger; or where victim is known to assailant, he/she is weaker, vulnerable*	38 - **45** - 52
	B. Minor Injury *Stranger-to-stranger; or where victim is known to assailant, he/she is weaker, vulnerable; or altercations involving use of a weapon*	30 - **35** - 40
	C. Substantial Injury *Altercations among acquaintances; brawls*	17 - **20** - 23
	D. Minor Injury *Altercations among acquaintances; brawls*	13 - **15** - 17

*AM = Class A Misdemeanor; BM = Class B Misdemeanor
**DF = Day Fines

FIGURE 5-4

Example of a Day Fine Unit Scale

Source: Bureau of Justice Assistance, *How to Use Structured Fines (Day Fines) as an Intermediate Sanction* (Washington, DC: Bureau of Justice Assistance, 1996), p. 59.

units ranges from a low of 5 to a high of 120, for the most serious misdemeanors handled by the court. For example, the presumptive number of
units for the offense of assault with minor injury and aggravating factors is
70; the range is from 59 to 81 units. The presumptive number is the starting point. Negotiation and consideration of individual circumstances may
raise or lower the number. There is no magic in the unit scale established.
What is important is to establish a scale broad enough to cover the full
range of offenses handled by the courts that will use structured fines.

Once the unit scale is established, the second step is to create a valuation
table. The purpose of the valuation table is to establish the dollar amount
of each fine. A portion of the valuation table used in the Staten Island experiment is shown in Figure 5–5. Net daily incomes run down the left side,
and numbers of dependents run across the top. Net daily income is the
offender's income (after-tax wages, welfare allowance, unemployment
compensation, etc.) divided by the number of days in a payment period.
Staten Island planners also adjusted the net daily income downward to account for subsistence needs, family responsibilities, and incomes below the
poverty line.

Suppose a defendant convicted of assault, with minor injury and aggravating factors, has a net daily income of $15 and supports four people, in-
cluding herself. Find the row for her net daily income. Move across the row
to the column for the number of dependents. The figure there is the value
of one structured fine unit for that defendant. Multiply the number of fine
units to be imposed (70) by the value of a single fine unit (3.38). The product, $236.60, is the amount of the day fine to be imposed.

Staten Island, New York, Valuation Table
Dollar Value of One Day Fine Unit, by Net Daily Income and Number of Dependents

Net Daily Income($)	Number of Dependents (Including Self)							
	1	2	3	4	5	6	7	8
3		1.05	0.83	0.68	0.53	0.45	0.37	0.30
4	1.70	1.40	1.10	0.90	0.70	0.60	0.50	0.40
5	2.13	1.75	1.38	1.13	0.88	0.75	0.62	0.50
6	2.55	2.10	1.65	1.35	1.05	0.90	0.75	0.60
7	2.98	2.45	1.93	1.58	1.23	1.05	0.87	0.70
8	3.40	2.80	2.20	1.80	1.40	1.20	1.00	0.80
9	3.83	3.15	2.48	2.03	1.58	1.35	1.12	0.90
10	4.25	3.50	2.75	2.25	1.75	1.50	1.25	1.00
11	4.68	3.85	3.03	2.47	1.93	1.65	1.37	1.10
12	5.10	4.20	3.30	2.70	2.10	1.80	1.50	1.20
13	5.53	4.55	3.58	2.93	2.28	1.95	1.62	1.30
14	7.85	4.90	3.85	3.15	2.45	2.10	1.75	1.40
15	8.42	5.25	4.13	3.38	2.63	2.25	1.87	1.50

FIGURE 5-5
Example of Day Fine Valuation Table

Source: Bureau of Justice Assistance, *How to Use Structured Fines (Day Fines) as an Intermediate Sanction* (Washington, DC: Bureau of Justice Assistance, 1996), p. 64.

The National Institute of Justice (NIJ) sponsored an evaluation of the Staten Island experiment. That evaluation showed that judges used day fines for many offenses for which they had formerly used fixed fine amounts—including some property crimes, drug possession, and assault.[23] Most judges cooperated with the new, voluntary scheme throughout the yearlong experiment. Research showed that the average fine increased by 25 percent, from $206 before the experiment to $258 during the year day fines were used. If day fines had not been held low by state law, the average day fine would have been $440. The news on collections was also good. Eighty-five percent of the defendants in the day fine program paid their fines in full, compared with 71 percent in a control program using routine collection processes. Furthermore, when full payment was not made, partial payment was much more likely in the day fine cases than in cases from before the experiment or in the control group. Thus, the higher fines levied in the day fine cases did not make collection more difficult, and the new enforcement procedures independently improved collection rates.

There has been little research on the effectiveness of fines in reducing recidivism rates. However, since the use of fines could reduce the costs of courts and corrections and since day fines address problems of inequality, fines are a promising intermediate sanction. At present, most Western justice systems, except the United States, rely heavily on financial penalties. In the 21st century, U.S. jurisdictions are likely to continue their experiments with monetary penalties and to assign them even greater importance.

community service

A sentence to serve a specified number of hours working in unpaid positions with nonprofit or tax-supported agencies.

Community Service   Community service is a sentence to serve a specified number of hours working in unpaid positions with nonprofit or tax-supported agencies.[24] Community service is punishment that takes away an offender's time and energy. Community service is sometimes called a "fine of time." Requiring offenders to compensate victims with their time or money was customary in ancient civilizations. The desire for compensation in time or money was probably at least as common then as the urge to retaliate. In colonial Boston, drunkards were sentenced to chop wood. During World War II, youths were given the choice of going to detention or going to war.[25]

Community service as a criminal sanction began in the United States in 1966 in Alameda County, California. Municipal judges there devised a community service sentencing program for indigent women who violated traffic and parking laws. Too poor to pay fines, these women were likely to be sentenced to jail. But putting them behind bars imposed a hardship on their families. Community service orders (CSOs) increased sentencing options, punished the offenders, lightened the suffering of innocent families, avoided the cost of imprisonment, and provided valuable services to the community. As Alameda judges gained experience with the new sentencing option, they broadened the program to include male offenders, juveniles, and persons convicted of crimes more serious than traffic or parking violations.

The Alameda County community service program received international attention. England and Wales developed pilot projects in the 1970s, using community service as a midlevel sanction between probation and prison and as an alternative to prison sentences up to six months. By 1975,

Offenders sentenced to community service landscape and maintain public parks. Community service as a criminal sanction is valuable to the community, the victim, and the offender. How does each benefit?

community service had become a central feature of English sentencing. The approach swept throughout Europe, Australia, New Zealand, and Canada.

However, what had begun as an American innovation atrophied in the United States.[26] Today in the United States, community service is seldom used as a separate sentence. Instead, it may be one of many conditions of a probation sentence. Nor is it viewed as an alternative to imprisonment in the United States, as it is in other countries. Generally speaking, in the United States, public officials do not consider any sanction other than imprisonment punitive enough. Substituting community service for short prison sentences is not accepted. This is unfortunate because community service is a burdensome penalty that meets with widespread public approval,[27] is inexpensive to administer, and produces public value. Also, it can be scaled to the seriousness of the crime.

Community service can be an intermediate sanction by itself or used with other penalties and requirements, including substance abuse treatment, restitution, or probation.[28] Offenders sentenced to community service are usually assigned to work for government or private nonprofit agencies. They paint churches; restore historic buildings; make baby blankets; maintain parks; clean roadways, public parks, and county fairgrounds; remove snow from around public buildings; perform land and river reclamation; and renovate schools and nursing homes. Offenders who are doctors may be ordered to give medical service to persons who might otherwise lack it. Traffic offenders may be ordered to serve in hospital emergency rooms to learn about the injuries they risk for themselves and others. Drug offenders who are prominent sports figures may be ordered to lecture in high schools on the dangers of drugs. The service options are limited only by the imagination of the sentencing judge and the availability of personnel to ensure that the offender fulfills the terms of the sentence. To become and remain a tough criminal sanction, community service must have credible and efficient enforcement mechanisms.

CAREER PROFILE

Megan Hill

Case Manager   *Day Reporting Center*   *Boston, Massachusetts*

While an undergraduate at Northeastern University, Megan Hill participated in several co-op programs, including spending six months at a day reporting center in Boston. Shortly after her experience ended, the day reporting center advertised for a case manager and hired Hill for the job. Hill credits Northeastern's co-op program with giving her the qualifications to be hired full-time before earning her degree and with providing her the opportunity to explore different aspects of the criminal justice field.

Each day, Hill's responsibilities include approving day reporting clients' daily itineraries, monitoring clients' call-in times, and visiting her clients at home and work. Daily contact, she says, helps her know her clients better, understand what they're going through, and know how to assist them. She also believes it's important to respect clients. "The more respect you give your clients, the more respect and honesty you get in return."

Hill's advice to people interested in working in corrections is to do an internship or participate in a co-op to find out if they like the work. For Megan Hill, the most important thing is to be happy with your job and to feel that you're making a difference.

> " Probably the best part about my job is working with individuals who are truly dedicated to their recovery and reintegration back into society. The feeling you get from seeing a client start with all the frustrations of job rejections and discrimination to seeing them attain their first legal job and actually enjoy it is pretty satisfying. I am actually helping people put their lives back together. "

By the late 1980s, some form of community service sanction was in use in all 50 states. When Congress passed the Comprehensive Crime Control Act and Criminal Fine Enforcement Act of 1984, it mandated that felons who receive a sentence (except for class A or B felony—the most serious) must be ordered to pay a fine, make restitution, and/or work in community service. The Bureau of Justice Statistics estimates conservatively that 6 percent of all felons in the United States are sentenced to perform community service, often in conjunction with other sanctions.[29]

The state of Washington has made the most extensive use of community service. At least one-third of its convicted felons receive sentences that include community service. Washington State sentencing guidelines permit substitution of community service for incarceration at a rate of 8 hours of work for 1 day of incarceration, with a limit of 30 days. Most jurisdictions recognize 240 hours as the upper limit for community service. Washington State also is breaking new ground in sentencing reform with the idea of *interchangeable sentences* for nonviolent or not very violent crimes against strangers. The actual sentence depends on the offender and the purposes to be served. For those with little or no income, community service may substitute for a fine. Before offenders are sentenced to community service in Washington, they complete a community service order questionnaire (see Figure 5–6). The questionnaire helps the state Department of Corrections

STATE OF WASHINGTON
DEPARTMENT OF CORRECTIONS

**COMMUNITY SERVICE WORKER QUESTIONNAIRE
AND RELEASE OF INFORMATION**

Name _____   DOC Number _____

By action of the Superior Court, or an administrative Department of Corrections action, you have been ordered to perform community service work. This work must be performed within an approved unit of government or non-profit agency. To help us find the best assignment for you, and ensure reasonable accommodation for any sensory, physical or mental limitations or disabilities that you may have, please supply the following information. You are not obligated to disclose conditions that do not relate to your ability to perform community service.

1. List your job skills.

2. Do you have a preference for a certain agency or a particular type of work that you would like to perform?
   If yes, describe:

3. List the hours and days you are available for work.
   Monday _____   Wednesday _____   Friday _____   Sunday _____
   Tuesday _____   Thursday _____   Saturday _____

4. What means of transportation do you have to get to and from the work site?

5. Do you wear contacts or glasses?   Yes   No   N/A   (circle one)

6. Are you pregnant?   Yes   No   N/A   (circle one)

7. Are you currently taking any prescription medications that have side effects that may affect your ability to perform
   community service work (i.e., drowsiness, slurred speech, etc.)?   Yes   No   (circle one)
   If "Yes," describe side effects:

8. Note whether you have been diagnosed as having any of the following problems:

	Yes	No		Yes	No		Yes	No
Severe Allergy Reactions			Heart Problems			Epilepsy		
Breathing Disorders			Hearing Loss			Uncorrected Vision Problems		
Balance Problems			Diabetes			Other		

   If "Yes," please describe:

9. Is there any activity or motion that is difficult for you to do (i.e., crawling, climbing, bending, lifting, etc.)?
   Yes   No   (circle one)   If "Yes," please describe:

10. Do you have any other sensory, physical and/or mental limitations or disabilities that may affect your ability to do
    community service?   Yes   No   (circle one)   If "'Yes," please describe:

11. You are required to provide to your Community Corrections Officer, a clearance from your health care provider, documenting any sensory/physical/mental limitations or disabilities which impact your ability to perform community service hours. This documentation is required within 30 days of today's date, and will be at your expense. Release of information is on the reverse side.

Distributions: ORIGINAL-Community Service Worker, COPY-Worksite, Community Service Coordinator, File

DOC 05-103 (REV 10/97) OCO   COMMUNITY SERVICE PROGRAM

FIGURE 5-6
Sample Community Service Order Questionnaire

match the offender's abilities and limitations with community service work. A community corrections officer then makes sure the offender performs the required community service.

Georgia reported that in 2001, offenders worked 1.6 million hours of community service. Their work was worth $8.6 million to the state.[30] For offenders who do not present unacceptable risks of future violent crimes, a punitive intermediate sanction such as community service—which costs much less than prison, can save other state monies, promises comparable recidivism rates, and presents negligible risks of violence by those who would otherwise be confined—has much to commend it.

day reporting center (DRC)

A community correctional center to which an offender reports each day to file a daily schedule with a supervision officer, showing how each hour will be spent.

Day Reporting Centers A **day reporting center (DRC)** is a nonresidential community correctional center to which an offender reports each day to file a daily schedule with a supervision officer. The schedule shows how each hour will be spent—at work or looking for work, in class, at a support group meeting, and so on.[31] Aiming primarily to provide treatment and reduce prison crowding, DRCs typically offer numerous services to address offenders' problems, and they strictly supervise offenders in a setting that is more secure than probation but less inhibiting than incarceration. DRCs differ from other intermediate sanctions by a marked concentration on rehabilitation. Staff members assess the offender's needs and offer her or him various types of in-house treatment and referral programs, including substance abuse treatment, education, vocational training, and psychological services. DRCs have an aura of rigor that appeals to those wanting punishment and control of offenders, and it appeals to those advocating more access to treatment for offenders.[32]

Day reporting centers first developed in Great Britain in 1972. British officials noted that many offenders were imprisoned, not because they posed a risk to the public but because they lacked basic skills to survive lawfully. Frequently, such offenders were dependent on drugs and alcohol. In 1985, officials in Connecticut's Department of Corrections learned about British day reporting centers and came to believe that such centers might alleviate the state's prison crowding problem. Ten years later, a National Institute of Justice survey identified 114 DRCs in 22 states.[33] Most had opened after 1990. Many of the programs were concentrated in just a few states, including Connecticut, Kansas, Oregon, Texas, and Wisconsin.

DRCs provide rehabilitation for offenders through intensive programming, while retaining a punishment component by maintaining a highly structured environment. DRCs commonly require offenders to obey a curfew, perform community service, and undergo drug testing twice a week. Participants check in at the center in person once a day and telephone periodically. They are responsible for following a full-time schedule that includes a combination of work, school, and substance abuse or mental health treatment. Programs range in duration from 40 days to nine months, and program content differs. Most programs require hour-by-hour schedules of participants' activities. Some are highly intensive, with 10 or more supervision contacts per day, and a few include 24-hour remote-location or other electronic monitoring.[34] Some centers refer clients to service agencies; others provide services directly. Some focus on monitoring; others emphasize support.

There have been few evaluations of DRCs. Early evaluations were favorable, but they were based on impressions rather than validated findings. The NIJ-sponsored survey showed generally high failure rates, averaging 50 percent. A study conducted on DRCs in North Carolina in 2000 compared the outcome of offenders sentenced to DRCs *plus* intensive supervision probation to that of offenders sentenced to intensive probation alone.[35] The researchers found that the addition of a DRC to ISP did not significantly reduce the rate of rearrest. In fact, they suggested that any rehabilitative effect that DRCs may have is counterbalanced by increased surveillance. "The 'piling up' of sanctions increases the likelihood of the offender's exposure to numerous forms of control and scrutiny culminating in frequent violations of the terms of the sentence."[36] On the positive side, however, the researchers found that DRCs empower the individual offender through literacy courses, a general equivalency diploma (GED), substance abuse counseling, and anger management classes. Reasons for the lack of evaluation are, first, that the DRC is still relatively new and, second, that DRCs vary greatly in terms of target population, eligibility criteria, services offered, monitoring procedures, and termination policies.

As DRCs move into the 21st century, a number of policy issues will influence their development and implementation. Those issues are (1) ensuring offenders' access to services, (2) responding to violations of DRC regulations in ways that will not add to jail and prison crowding, and (3) conducting evaluation of DRC programs. Charles Bahn and James Davis conclude that, "since most offenders are ultimately going to be released from incarceration, it is essential that we experiment with and evaluate innovative community-based programs [such as day reporting centers] that will enable offenders to reintegrate into society."[37]

Remote-Location Monitoring Technologies that probation and parole officers use to monitor remotely the physical location of an offender are known as **remote-location monitoring.** For example, home-based electronic monitoring (EM) is often used by officers to monitor remotely offenders who are restricted to their homes. It is estimated that from 1994 to 1998, the number of EM programs jumped from 400 to 1,500, and the number of offenders on EM rose from 12,000 to 95,000.[38] (While it is commonplace to refer to home confinement as EM, the acronym actually refers to a technological tool for monitoring a participant's compliance with some of the rules of the overall home confinement program.)

Remote-location monitoring uses technological systems such as EM, voice verification, and other tracking systems to verify a person's physical location, either periodically or continuously, 24 hours a day. An offender's compliance with the conditions of supervision may require him or her to schedule appointments, conduct a job search, and maintain regular employment. Location monitoring systems provide a tool to verify—in real time—a person's whereabouts for specific risk issues or court-ordered release conditions. In this way, technology aids the officer in effectively satisfying specific supervision functions.

A major benefit of remote-location monitoring is that it costs significantly less than incarceration. Another is that it allows defendants and offenders to continue to contribute to the support of their families and pay

remote-location monitoring
Technologies, including global positioning system (GPS) devices and electronic monitoring (EM), that probation and parole officers use to monitor remotely the physical location of an offender.

Kentucky Militia leader, Charles "Charlie" N. Puckett, 55, from Lancaster, Kentucky. Puckett was ordered confined to his home in November 2001, following his arrest on a nine-count indictment that included obstruction of justice and weapons charges. A few months later, he slipped off his electronic bracelet and disappeared. He was later rearrested when he turned himself in to authorities. What are the pros and cons of remote-location monitoring as a probationary strategy?

taxes. Moreover, courts may order program participants to pay all or part of the costs. Depending on the type of equipment used, the cost of remote-location monitoring ranges from $5 per day for traditional EM ankle or wrist bracelets to $25 per day for the global positioning system (GPS) tracking unit.

Remote-location monitoring can be categorized into three risk-related areas: random/programmed contact systems, hybrid systems, and GPS or terrestrial-based systems.[39] Random/programmed contact systems are either active or passive. Active systems are typically comprised of automated telephone contact systems that require the offender to call in or receive a telephone call, followed by a process of identification and location, usually through voice verification methods that compare the spoken words or phrases to a voice template created during the system enrollment. Passive systems monitor the offender's location through a series of radio frequency signals emitted usually every 10 to 15 seconds by a tamper-resistant transmitter worn on the ankle to a receiver unit connected to the home phone. Normally, the participant must stay within a prescribed distance of the receiving unit. The supervising officer sees the results of active and passive systems on a computer screen. Program participants who do not comply with the conditions of their supervision may face sanctions ranging from reprimand to loss of privileges to revocation proceedings. An alternative passive system is referred to as "drive-by" interrogation. Here, a hand-held portable receiver can be used by the supervision officer to determine that a subject is within the prescribed premises.

Hybrid systems combine EM and a programmed contact method such as voice or video verification. EM verifies the person's location while at home, and the programmed contact system periodically verifies the location when away from home. The programmed voice contacts substitute for the officer's telephone calls or in-person field visits to monitor the person's compliance with an approved schedule and location. Video verification calls are placed to the offender, who has a video camera in his or her home with a telephone line video adaptor. The offender is told to perform an action, such as holding up two fingers, and the picture is transmitted to the central station, where it is date and time stamped. Some hybrid systems can measure an offender's breath alcohol content. A breath alcohol analyzer is connected to the in-home receiver/dialer. Periodically, or on demand from a telephone call from the officer, the offender blows into a straw, and his or her breath alcohol level is recorded. The technology uses voice verification to ensure that it is the offender providing the sample. Other technologies take a photograph of the offender as he or she provides the sample. The sample is then reported immediately through the offender's phone line to the supervision officer.

Today, researchers are in the developmental phase of designing a ground-based tracking technology that is expected to be more accurate and cost-effective than GPS. This system is called *terrestrial-based monitoring*. The biggest difference between GPS and terrestrial-based monitoring is that the latter does not require the use of a satellite to transmit signals. Terrestrial-based systems can use existing cell phone or radio towers to send and receive signals to pinpoint the location of an offender. The offender wears a small bracelet that interacts continuously with the receiving towers. Advocates of terrestrial-based systems contend that they are better than GPS for dealing with the congestion of tall inner-city buildings and that they work better inside buildings and parking systems. Terrestrial-based systems are also more accurate and can locate an offender within 200 feet as compared to the 300-foot range of GPS. Advocates also say that terrestrial-based systems will cost less than GPS because many cell phone and radio towers already exist. Towers would have to be built only in remote areas where they do not exist. In addition, the equipment being designed is smaller and weighs less than the tracking unit an offender must use with GPS.

In theory, remote-location monitoring satisfies three correctional goals. First, it incapacitates the offender by restricting him or her to a single location. During the pretrial phase, remote-location monitoring is an alternative to detention used to ensure that individuals appear in court. In the postsentence phase, it is used as punishment, viewed as more punitive than regular probation but less restrictive than imprisonment. Second, remote-location monitoring is punitive because it forces the offender to stay home when not at work, school, counseling, or community service. Third, it contributes to rehabilitation by allowing the offender to remain with his or her family and continue employment, education, or vocational training.

The growing popularity of remote-location monitoring is due in large part to prison and jail overcrowding, the need to supervise more offenders, and concerns about the ability of standard probation to protect the community. Recently, a review of the performance of 17,000 participants in the federal home confinement program from 1988 through 1996 showed positive results.[40] Eighty-nine percent of the participants successfully completed home confinement without incident. The success rate for postsentence offenders was slightly higher than for pretrial defendants in the home confinement program (89 percent vs. 77 percent). The main reasons for unsuccessful termination included testing positive for illegal substances or incurring unauthorized leave violations. Only 0.7 percent of prerelease participants and 4.8 percent of postsentence participants were arrested or charged with new offenses, including misdemeanor offenses, such as driving under the influence (DUI) or shoplifting, or with more serious offenses such as theft, fraud, or drug possession.

Advocates of remote-location monitoring point to a number of advantages. Since the offender often pays to use the system, it usually pays for itself. In fact, it often generates profits for the supervising agency. Some hypothesize that, if only 10 percent of inmates were transferred to any of the three categories of remote-location monitoring, the savings would be nearly $4 billion.[41] It's tougher than routine probation. And since offenders can remain at home, keep working, maintain ties to the community, and avoid the negative influence of incarceration, it is more humane. The

Eye On Corrections™

Global Positioning System: A New Surveillance Tool

By Diana Rodriguez

New satellite technology is enabling probation officers to keep better track of offenders in the community and increase public safety. This technology is called the SMART system, and it consists of a portable tracking device containing a global positioning system (GPS) receiver. The device is worn around an offender's ankle and receives radio signals from the 24 GPS satellites orbiting the earth. These signals determine the location of an offender. Using specialized mapping software, the data center can track the activity of an offender 24 hours a day, seven days a week. This is a significant improvement over the prior system which could only monitor for a portion of the day and could only tell whether or not the offender was at home.

"We know if he's driving, at which intersection, and at what speed," said Richard Nimmer, the Director of Program Services in the Florida DOC. "With other systems, we only know that an offender is supposed to be at work. But instead of going to work he could have gone out, committed a murder, and returned home at the same time. The parole officer would think everything's fine."

Also, with the GPS system, parole officers can set boundaries around areas the probationer is forbidden to go. This is specifically useful for sex offenders, who can be restricted from schools, parks, and playgrounds. In addition, a victim's home and office can be set out of bounds; this enforces protection orders for the victims and allows them to be notified if the offender is in the area.

HOW IT IS USED

Bill Kimberland, the Chief Parole Officer in Sandusky, Ohio, said that the department reserves the GPS system for "high risk offenders." Wearing the GPS receiver is not voluntary but is a condition stipulated in the offender's probation. It can also be used as a method to track offenders who have managed to post bond. "Without this technology, we could set guidelines but we wouldn't have the manpower to follow [the offender] around," said Kimberland.

In addition to providing surveillance and security, the GPS system also can help prevent released offenders from committing future crimes. "Sex offenders are typically smart offenders. But with GPS, they know they're being watched and they know they'll get caught. To commit a crime you need motive and opportunity; this system takes away their opportunity," said Nimmer.

COMPARING COSTS

Currently, the GPS SMART system costs around $15 per day for each released offender, but the price decreases when it is bought in volume. However, considering the average $55 per day cost at a correctional facility, the GPS price appears more economical. In addition, according to Kimberland, offenders in Sandusky, Ohio, pay their own bill. "If an offender is convicted, he can sometimes plea bargain. As part of the plea, he would have to agree to wear the bracelet and pay for its cost. We pass the cost right along to them. If it costs $15 a day, then they have to pay for it, and for a lot of them that's a couple hours of work. But their only other alternative is jail."

Officials in both the Florida DOC and the Probation Office in Sandusky, Ohio, said that the GPS system was a very effective monitoring tool. It helps to control overpopulation in correctional facilities while maintaining accurate 24-hour surveillance. And one sex offender on the system commented, "This technology stalked me more intensely than I stalked [my victim]." *This article has been reprinted in part from CCNN. To read this article in its entirety go to www.corrections.com.*

American Probation and Parole Association supports remote-location monitoring to assist probation and parole officers in achieving their prescribed goal of community protection.

Critics argue that when the innovation of remote-location monitoring is tested with sophisticated research designs involving comparison groups matched for offender risk, it shows no connection to program completion or recidivism, and it has a net-widening effect.[42] They also tell us that the requirement to have a telephone and pay for the monitoring equipment keeps remote-location monitoring out of reach for many offenders who would benefit from it. In addition, traditional home confinement with or without EM does not guarantee that crimes will not occur in the house. Vice crimes, domestic violence, and assaults—to name a few—occur during electronic house arrest. (House arrest is an intermediate sanction that requires an offender to remain in his or her house except for approved absences, such as going to work, school, or treatment programs.) And electronic monitors intrude on the privacy of the family and increase family stress.

Despite these concerns, remote-location monitoring has grown enormously throughout the United States since electronic surveillance technology was introduced in 1969. Not only is the number of offenders on remote-location monitoring increasing, but the offenders are also becoming more diverse. Initially, remote-location monitoring targeted only the traditional clients of house arrest: low-risk probationers, such as those convicted of DUI. More recently, however, it has expanded to include people awaiting trial or sentencing, offenders released from institutional and community corrections facilities, and juvenile offenders. Furthermore, whereas electronic house arrest initially gained acceptance as a response to property crimes, advances in remote-location monitoring can be used with selected offenders whose crimes are more serious (e.g., stalking).

Residential Community Centers   A residential community center (RCC) is a medium-security correctional setting that resident offenders are permitted to leave regularly—unaccompanied by staff—for work, for educational or vocational programs, or for treatment in the community. Initially, such centers were called *halfway houses* and were for offenders who either were about to be released from an institution or were in the first stages of return to the community. However, as the number of halfway houses grew and new client groups (divertees, pretrial releasees, and probationers) were added, the umbrella term *residential community center* was adopted.

Halfway houses, prerelease and work release centers, and restitution centers are examples of RCCs. Some RCCs specialize in a type of client or treatment—for example, in drug and alcohol abuse, violent and sex offenders, women, abused women, or prerelease federal prisoners. The type of population served varies from community to community and from RCC to RCC. On January 1, 2000, more than 1,000 RCCs involving almost 27,000 adult residents were in operation across the United States,[43] and there is substantial diversity among them.[44] Some are public and some private. There are RCCs at all levels of government. The federal Bureau of Prisons (BOP) has the largest number of inmates (6,987) in RCCs, almost 6 percent of the BOP's total population. The largest number of programs

residential community center (RCC)

A medium-security correctional setting that resident offenders are permitted to leave regularly—unaccompanied by staff—for work, for education or vocational programs, or for treatment in the community.

(about 40 percent) are operated by private nonprofit agencies. Those in the next largest group (about 35 percent) are run by state government. Then come those run by county government (almost 20 percent), for-profit corporations (less than 10 percent), and other agencies (less than 5 percent). RCCs range from fewer than 10 beds to more than 200 beds. More than half are small, with fewer than 50 beds; almost 30 percent are classified as medium in size, with 50 to 100 beds; and 20 percent are large, with more than 100 beds. More than half of RCCs serve only men, 40 percent serve both men and women, and fewer than 10 percent serve only women.

Texas operates 17 restitution style RCCs with a combined bed capacity of more than 700 residents.[45] The primary purpose of the program is to serve as a cost-effective form of punishment. Residents' activities are monitored by the center's staff and by the probation department. Residents work in the community and return to the center after work. They use their wages to pay for room and board, transportation, court and probation costs, victim restitution, and child support. They also perform community service. One review of the Texas Restitution Center Program reported the following:

- An average of 61 percent of the residents successfully completed the program.
- Twelve percent are discharged for technical violations; 2 percent are discharged for new crimes, mostly misdemeanors that do not threaten public safety.
- Seventy-five percent were employed upon successful completion.
- Residents perform almost 97,000 hours of community service each year.
- Each year center residents pay approximately $96,000 in victim restitution: $75,000 for court costs, fines, and fees; $74,000 for probation fees; almost $200,000 to support dependents and into personal savings; and almost $75,000 to other financial obligations in the community.

According to Lawrence, "Considering the incarceration costs in the Texas Department of Corrections, the restitution center program is a success. The operating cost for Texas prisons is reported to be $37.50 per day per inmate. This figure includes only operating expenses, not the more than $50,000 per cell for new prison construction. Cost to the Texas Adult Probation Commission for operating the Restitution Center Program averages $30 per day per bed space. In addition to lower operating costs, the monetary restitution paid by the residents helps make a strong case for the program."[46]

The objectives of RCCs are community protection and offender reintegration. Community protection is achieved by screening offenders; setting curfews; administering drug or polygraph tests; confirming that when residents leave the center they go directly to work, school, or treatment; and providing a medium-security correctional setting. Reintegration is achieved by giving residents opportunities to learn and use legitimate skills, thereby reducing their reliance on criminal behavior. Staff members determine the obstacles to each resident's reintegration, plan a program to overcome those obstacles, and provide a supportive environment to help the resident test, use, and refine the skills needed.

The benefits of RCCs are many. RCCs benefit offenders by providing them with the basic necessities of food, clothing, and shelter while they find housing and employment. RCCs also offer residents emotional support to deal with the pressures of readjustment and help them obtain community services. Benefits to the community include a moderately secure correctional setting in which residents' behavior is monitored and controlled, as well as an expectation that opportunities for offenders to get on their feet will reduce postrelease adjustment problems and criminal behavior. For the criminal justice system, an RCC offers a low-cost housing alternative to incarceration of nonviolent offenders. An RCC can control offenders in the community at less cost than building and operating more secure facilities. It may also serve as an enhancement to probation and an option for dealing with probation and parole violators.

There has not been much research on the effectiveness of RCCs. An early General Accounting Office (GAO) report proposed that extensive planning and coordination of information were greatly needed for halfway houses to reach their objectives.[47] More recently, the state of Colorado conducted a statewide study of recidivism of halfway house clients.[48] The Colorado Office of Research and Statistics analyzed information on all offenders ($n = 3,054$) who terminated from 25 halfway houses during fiscal year 1997–1998 and explored why some clients failed while others succeeded. The study tracked cases for 24 months. It reported that 69 percent had no arrest within 24 months. Of the 31 percent who recidivated within 24 months, the majority of cases were drug/alcohol related. Only 3.4 percent were for violent offenses. High-risk, prior criminal history, young age, and lack of postrelease supervision predicted future offending. The report recommended that intensive treatment, therapeutic community models, and multidisciplinary approaches to deal with drug and alcohol addiction should be replicated across the state. The report stated that the criminal justice system alone cannot manage the problem of addiction and that programs following halfway house models yielded high success rates. The report also called for specific aftercare services to enhance offenders' likelihood of success, maximize public safety, and reduce recidivism. Offenders who did not receive postrelease supervision were almost twice as likely to fail as those who did (45 percent compared to 26 percent).

Some researchers have concluded that "adopting more realistic outcome measures may make it possible to bridge the wide gap between public expectations for the justice system and what most practitioners recognize as the system's actual capability to control crime. By documenting what corrections programs can accomplish, we can move toward integrating programs like work release [as part of a residential community center program] into a more balanced corrections strategy. Such a strategy would successfully return low-risk inmates to the community, thereby making room to incarcerate the truly violent offenders."[49]

Boot Camps   In 1983, in an effort to alleviate prison crowding and reduce recidivism, the departments of corrections in Oklahoma and Georgia opened the first adult prison programs modeled after military boot camps.

Since then, boot camp, or *shock incarceration*, has become an increasingly popular intermediate sanction.

boot camp

A short institutional term of confinement that includes a physical regimen designed to develop self-discipline, respect for authority, responsibility, and a sense of accomplishment.

Boot camp is a short institutional term of confinement, usually followed by probation, that includes a physical regimen designed to develop self-discipline, respect for authority, responsibility, and a sense of accomplishment. According to the NIJ, four characteristics distinguish boot camps from other correctional programs: (1) military drill and ceremony, (2) a rigorous daily schedule of hard labor and physical training, (3) separation of boot camp participants from the general prison population, and (4) the idea that boot camps are an alternative to long-term confinement.[50] On January 1, 2000, a partial listing of boot camps revealed that 69 camps involving more than 8,000 adult inmates were in operation by state departments of corrections, jails, and probation and parole agencies.[51] Women represented 9 percent (723) of the adult boot camp population.

Although all boot camps involve a short period of imprisonment in a military atmosphere, the specific components of boot camp programs vary widely. Boot camps differ in whether their activities include work, community services, education, and counseling and in whether they provide aftercare support and monitoring for community reintegration. There is some consistency, however, in their goals: reducing prison crowding and changing offenders' behavior and thus their future involvement in crime.

Most boot camps target young, first-time offenders who have been convicted of such nonviolent crimes as drug possession, burglary, or theft and who seem more open to changing their attitudes and behavior than older offenders. Most participants are males who do not have extensive criminal histories and are physically and psychologically able to complete the strict

The military-style training and drill that characterize boot camps are frequently supplemented with substance abuse education and vocational training. What aftercare programs might contribute to the effectiveness of boot camp strategies?

We opened the Fresno County Boot Camp on December 5, 1997. We're out in a rural area, so it took us a year to pass all the red tape to open up the facility.

The main mission of our facility is to decrease the number of victims in the community, and to prepare these young men for a crime-free life. I take the things that the military model teaches, then add programs on top of that. We teach the kids to achieve and be successful. The kids that come to use are not acquainted with success—they're not acquainted with walking across the school stage and getting awards.

Our famous quote is "Do what you're told when you're told; do more than what's asked." That's the formula for success for employment. So although we come across in a very tough way, they have to have those skills to be employed. Kids don't know how to listen. So teaching them to focus on what somebody is telling them is very, very important. So we do it by setting them up for success, teaching them to listen, and teaching them how to function socially in a very appropriate manner.

Our other motto is it's a "no-fail program." Do we have kids who fail?

Absolutely. But we maintain a very high standard, and the kids rise to it. When you set a low standard—when you say, "We need to relate to them on their level" —that's the best way to keep them there.

Our ages go from 14 to 18, boys. Fourteen to 16 is our least successful population—junior high kids have problems all their own. They're not mature enough for the long-lasting effect you're looking for. Our program runs from six to eight months, and they've done a lot to get here—they may have gotten into the system at 10 or 11, so they can be pretty dysfunctional young men. Our most successful is the more mature population, 16 to 18. Most of these kids have a three-years-plus deficit in their education and usually not because they're stupid—it's because they don't go to school and haven't for years.

If a program is done right and if you're working to build experiences with kids, you can't buy that. Coming in here, these kids only know one way to be— with their gang emphasis, their bad attitude, and the way they've related to people all their lives. They come out of here a different way. Now, the challenge is, are they going to use it?

We have our kids out all over the county doing projects—they're working with the community, painting, planting trees, and these people just eat it up. They have good manners, saying, "Yes ma'am, yes sir." They go out and do color guards, they're in parades, and people come up and shake their hands and congratulate them. You can't buy that in any rehab program. We put them in all kinds of social situations, because that builds character.

Our goal is "no new victims." So even though we might have some young men not doing very well in the community, if they're not committing a crime, they're a success. But we have a tremendous number of kids going on to college. We're teaching them "How do I get myself through the day; what am I responsible for?" Right now we're running about an 82 percent success rate.

Commander Leslie Knobel
Assistant Director
The Elkhorn Correctional Facility
Fresno County, California

THE STAFF SPEAKS

military exercise requirements. Disabled offenders or those with nondisabling medical conditions that limit their physical performance (e.g., being overweight) are typically excluded.

States differ in their age requirements for boot camp eligibility. For example, in California, participants must be 40 or younger; in Illinois, 17 to 29; in Kansas, 18 to 25; in Maryland, under 32; in New York, 30 or younger; in Oklahoma, under 25; and in Tennessee, 17 to 29.

Several researchers have examined boot camp programs for women.[52] Some programs integrated women with male inmates. Others were completely separate female programs. The researchers found that when boot camps combined men and women, few women were in the camps, and those women faced serious problems. They were supervised more intensely than the men, and their activities were restricted to protect them from abuse and harassment and to prevent sexual relations with male drill instructors. Combined programs did not take into consideration women inmates' physical stamina, nor did they offer therapeutic programs for the problems that many of these women faced, such as how to survive sexual assault or battering, make a successful transition into the community, or obtain job skills. Combined programs also failed to take into consideration the importance of children to women in boot camps.

Women in separate programs fared better. The separate camps were more likely to offer therapeutic programs suited to women's needs. Visitation policies were less restrictive, so the women had more opportunities to see their children while in boot camp. The researchers concluded that women should not be combined with men in boot camps designed for men. If boot camps are developed for women, they should be compatible with the needs and characteristics of women offenders.

The emergence of juvenile boot camps has been a recent and explosive trend. In 1995, MacKenzie and Rosay identified 37 juvenile boot camps operating across the United States.[53] The typical juvenile boot camp inmate was a nonviolent male between the ages of 14 and 18. Unlike most adult boot camps that exclude violent offenders from participating, however, half of the juvenile boot camps accepted offenders convicted of violent crimes. Juvenile boot camps were more likely than adult boot camps to spend more time on education and counseling. Still, when recidivism was examined in four high-quality studies involving random assignment of subjects to groups, there were no significant differences between the boot camp youths and the control groups. In one site, the youths released from the boot camp recidivated more than those in the control group. Recently, the NIJ released the findings from an evaluation of the Los Angeles County Drug Treatment Boot Camp, one of the longest continuous-running boot camps in the United States since its inception in 1990.[54] The researchers found no difference in rearrests or convictions between juvenile boot camp graduates and a comparison group. The only significant difference they reported was that juvenile boot camp graduates were more likely to have probation revocations than the comparison group. They concluded, "The findings from this project support the conclusion from the existing literature that juvenile boot camps as a treatment model are probably not any more effective than most existing juvenile programs."

Critics have raised questions about using boot camps as a correctional tool. They note that correctional boot camp programs are built on a model of military basic training that the military itself has found lacking and in some cases has revised.[55] Critics also argue that the military model was designed to produce a cohesive fighting unit, and after military boot camp, there is further specialized training and career planning. That is not a goal of corrections. One analyst wrote, "If an offender can't read [or] write and is drug-involved, sending him to a 90-day boot camp that does not address his job or literacy needs will only have a short-term effect, if any, on his behavior."[56]

There is reason for both optimism and skepticism about boot camps. Although boot camps are promoted as a means of reducing recidivism rates, there is no evidence that they significantly reduce recidivism or promote socially desirable activities. A multisite evaluation of boot camps in Texas, South Carolina, and Florida showed no significant differences in reoffending rates among the different groups of offenders.[57] Research on Oklahoma's boot camp program, called the Regimented Inmate Discipline (RID) program, revealed that even when the researchers controlled for type of offense, age, and race on recidivism, boot camp graduates recidivated more frequently than either traditionally incarcerated inmates or probationers.[58] Research published in 2001 on a county-based boot camp in Florida shows similar results. The likelihood of an offender being rearrested was unaffected by his or her being sent to boot camp. Eighty-one percent of the boot camp graduates were rearrested, averaging 271 days before rearrest. Seventy-three percent of the comparison group was rearrested, averaging 290 days before rearrest.[59] The body of literature in this area suggests that recidivism is no better for boot camp graduates than it is for comparison groups.

Some researchers have reported that boot camp graduates have higher self-esteem, have better attitudes toward family, are less likely to see themselves as victims of circumstances, and are more likely to feel in control of their future. However, the research does not always compare boot camp graduates with other groups. Research into what boot camp participants say they'll do is less conclusive than research into what they've actually done.

Also disappointing is that the recidivism rates of boot camp graduates are very similar to those of other parolees.[60] One-third to one-half of front-end boot camp participants fail to complete their programs and are sent to prison as a result. In most programs, close surveillance of graduates after release leads to technical violation and revocation rates that are higher than those of comparable offenders in less intensive programs.

Boot camps are also promoted as a means of reducing prison crowding and corrections costs. Here the news is not all bad. Back-end programs, to which imprisoned offenders are transferred by corrections officials, do save money and prison space. Although they often experience high failure, technical violation, and revocation rates, those rates are no higher than those for offenders who have been kept in prison longer. If enough offenders complete boot camp and are released early from prison, the programs can reduce prison crowding. However, a number of researchers have found that most boot camps have not reduced prison crowding, because the programs are designed for offenders who would otherwise be on probation, not those who would otherwise have received prison terms.[61] MacKenzie and her colleagues found in a multisite evaluation of boot camps that only two of the five boot camp programs examined appeared to save prison beds. The remaining three boot camp programs appeared to increase the need for prison beds.[62] Crowding can be reduced only if boot camp participants are selected from inmates already incarcerated and only if their participation substantially reduces their overall sentence lengths.

A number of researchers and policymakers have pointed out that the most successful boot camp programs are those that emphasize treatment over military regimen and increase postrelease supervision and support for graduates. Participants should benefit from earning a GED or learning job skills to make them more employable in the future or to encourage them to continue their education or vocational training. Successful boot camp programs also offer intensive postrelease supervision and support that helps graduates bridge the program to their neighborhood. Support is needed because boot camp graduates return to their previous environments with the same problems, such as unemployment, poverty, racial discrimination,

> It is one thing to make noble commitments under closely controlled custody; it is quite another to maintain those commitments in reality.

dysfunctional families, lack of opportunities, and criminal temptations. Stinchcomb and Terry put it this way: "It is one thing to make noble commitments under closely controlled custody; it is quite another to maintain those commitments in the reality of a world where drill instructors are often replaced by drug dealers, where secure confinement is replaced by self-control, and where marching in straight lines is replaced by hanging out on street corners."[63] The programs that include continuing supervision and support are the ones that help boot camp graduates make more successful transitions back into the life of the community.[64]

POLICY-CENTERED APPROACH TO DEVELOPING INTERMEDIATE SANCTIONS

A policy is a statement of intent. It expresses *why* we are engaging in a particular set of activities. It also tells *how* we are to carry out these activities. Policy can be very general, very specific, or in between.

In recent decades, sanction options have proliferated, increasing the choices available to judges at sentencing and to governmental agencies moving offenders from higher levels of control to lower ones. As we take stock of the contributions and limitations of the movement toward intermediate sanctions, it is important to think about such sanctions, not as punishments developed in isolation from one another, but rather as parts of a system of policy-driven responses to criminal behavior.

The **policy-centered approach** to intermediate sanctions emphasizes the *policy* that spells out the sentencing scheme and the place of each sentencing option as much as the sanctions and programs themselves. This approach draws together stakeholders from inside and outside the corrections

policy-centered approach

A method of thinking about and planning for intermediate sanctions that draws together key stakeholders from inside and outside the corrections agency that will implement the sanction.

In Anoka County, Minnesota, a policy team of key stakeholders inside and outside the corrections agency developed a day reporting center for high-risk probationers as one of six intermediate sanctions designed to save jail space for serious offenders. What are the advantages of using a policy-centered approach to devise intermediate sanctions?

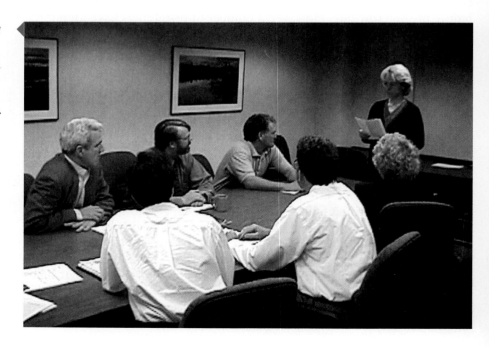

agency that will implement the proposed sanction. The planning group often includes decision makers from all three branches of government (judicial, executive, and legislative) and all three subsystems of criminal justice (police, courts, and corrections). The group examines the overall context within which the proposed new sanction will be used and analyzes data on offenses and offenders to form sound policy. Public hearings may also be held. The policy that emerges is a statement of intent. It expresses why the group has decided to provide a particular set of sanctions and explains how those sanctions should be implemented. A good example of a policy-centered approach in intermediate sanctions is found in the experience of North Carolina and Pennsylvania. These two states developed comprehensive sentencing guidelines that incorporated confinement and nonconfinement punishment sanctions, including intermediate sanctions, for the courts to follow. The legislatures in these states drew together panels of stakeholders from law enforcement, courts, executive branches of government, and community groups to form the policies.

PROGRAM-CENTERED APPROACH TO DEVELOPING INTERMEDIATE SANCTIONS

Unfortunately, most intermediate sanctions are discrete local programs, devised and implemented without the participation of the decision makers who will use them. In such a **program-centered approach,** planning for an intermediate-sanction (e.g., remote-location monitoring) program is usually undertaken by a single agency, which develops and funds the program. The program staff then tries to inform judges, prosecutors, defense counsel, and other corrections agencies about the program, its potential benefits, and the target population for which it is best suited.

program-centered approach
A method of planning intermediate sanctions in which planning for a program is usually undertaken by a single agency, which develops and funds the program.

The program-centered approach has serious limitations and often results in disappointment. It makes nationwide comparison and evaluation difficult because there is no coordination among the programs of different jurisdictions. Programs that are established this way are seldom evaluated because most local agencies lack the resources and the understanding of evaluation research. The program-centered approach often leads to many new programs that pursue multiple goals, sometimes even conflicting ones. When that happens, ambiguous and inconsistent operating policies develop. Finally, the program-centered approach tells us very little about how intermediate sanctions affect a jurisdiction's overall sentencing and imprisonment practices, very important information for most intermediate-sanction programs.

Community Corrections

So far in this chapter, we have been discussing intermediate sanctions as strategies to control crime. Now we turn our attention from the *strategies* to the *goal* they are designed to achieve. That goal is community corrections. There is no consensus in the field of criminal justice on the definition of *community corrections.* Sometimes the term refers to noninstitutional programs. Sometimes it refers to programs administered by local government rather than the state. Other times, it indicates citizen involvement.

We define *community corrections* as a philosophy of correctional treat-ment that embraces (1) decentralization of authority from state to local levels; (2) citizen participation in program planning, design, implementa-tion, and evaluation; (3) redefinition of the population of offenders for whom incarceration is most appropriate; and (4) emphasis on rehabilita-tion through community programs.

Community corrections recognizes the importance of partnership with the community in responding to crime. In short, our communities not only have a *right* to safe streets and homes but also bear *responsibility* for mak-ing them safe. All the major components of the criminal justice system have alliances today with the community. The field is experiencing many changes, including the following:

- *community policing*—a law enforcement strategy to get residents in-volved in making their neighborhoods safer by focusing on crime pre-vention, nonemergency services, public accountability, and decentralized decision making that includes the public;
- *community-based prosecution*—a prosecution strategy that uses a com-bination of criminal and civil tactics and the legal expertise, resources, and clout of the prosecuting attorney's office to find innovative solu-tions to a neighborhood's specific problems;
- *community-based defender services*—a defender strategy that provides continuity in representation of indigent defendants and helps defen-dants with personal and family problems that can lead to legal trou-bles; and
- *community courts*—a judicial strategy of hearing a criminal case in the community that is most affected by the case and including that com-munity in case disposition.

Debate and innovation continue to reflect these themes. The Vermont Department of Corrections leads the nation in giving local citizens decision-making authority about punishment and supervision issues that directly affect the offender, the victim, and community safety. The Vermont DOC established a network of 44 "community-based reparative boards" composed of more than 300 citizen volunteers. In just under one year (May 1999 through March 2000), these boards handled more than 3,000 cases. After conviction and referral by a judge, offenders meet with their local reparative board to review their offense and learn how it harmed the com-munity. They must then accept the terms of what is usually a multifaceted, community-based sanction, including apologies, restitution, and commu-nity service. An evaluation of Vermont's community reparative boards was published in 2000 under a grant from the NIJ.[65] The researchers used focus groups; in-depth interviews with board members, crime victims, and of-fenders; and telephone surveys with randomly selected Vermonters. They found that Vermonters had more confidence in the criminal justice system after the establishment of community reparative boards than they did be-fore the reparative boards existed. Thus, what began as an attempt to make the major components of the criminal justice system more community based now involves citizen volunteers as they strive to reinvent a super-vision system to manage offender harm and repair effectively.

COMMUNITY CORRECTIONS ACTS

This spirit of correctional collaboration and community partnership has led 28 states to pass **community corrections acts (CCAs)** (Figure 5–7). CCAs are state laws that give economic grants to local communities to establish community corrections goals and policies and to develop and operate community corrections programs. Most CCAs transfer some state functions to local communities, decentralizing services and engaging communities in the process of reintegrating offenders. Along with the transfer of correctional responsibility from the state to the community, CCAs provide financial incentives for counties, private citizens' groups, and private agencies to participate. The financial incentives help communities manage more of their own correctional cases. With the money, local communities design, implement, and evaluate a complete range of local sentencing options. (The intermediate sanctions discussed earlier in this chapter, for example, can be funded through a CCA.) Locally designed sanctions have a better chance of succeeding because they are based in the community where offenders' families, friends, and other social supports are. Although CCAs authorize and allow funding for a range of sanctions, including intermediate sanctions, they do more than that. CCAs implement community corrections philosophy by providing statewide structures that specify government and citizen roles and responsibilities in the planning, development, implementation, and funding of community sanctions.

community corrections acts (CCAs)

State laws that give economic grants to local communities to establish community corrections goals and policies and to develop and operate community corrections programs.

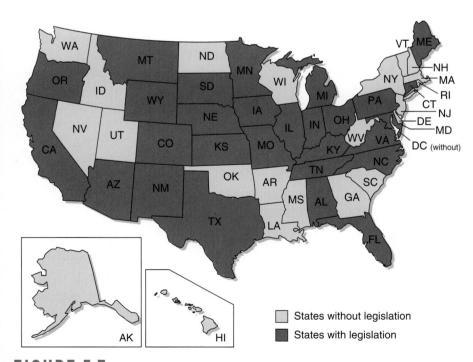

FIGURE 5-7
States with Community Corrections Legislation

In 1973, Minnesota became the first state to adopt a CCA. Minnesota officials wanted to reduce fragmentation in criminal justice service delivery, to control costs, and to redefine the population of offenders for whom state incarceration was most appropriate. Communities throughout Minnesota were willing to assume greater correctional responsibility for less serious offenders, as long as the communities were also given state subsidies and significant control over planning and service delivery. The huge success of Minnesota's CCA can be seen in Minnesota's incarceration rate, one of the lowest in the United States today. While the crime rate is not much different from those of other states, the incarceration rate is only 141 persons for every 100,000 residents. The U.S. average on January 1, 2003, was 476 per 100,000 residents. The majority of Minnesota's offenders are handled under the CCA.

There are tremendous differences among the CCAs in the United States. The most common goal, held in 14 states, is expansion of sanction choices. Twelve states cite the promotion of state and community partnerships as the goal. Some CCAs focus on nonviolent offenders; others merely include them. Some CCAs help communities move offenders out of local jails and into correctional programs that are less expensive and that offer reasonable community protection.

Simply having correctional programs in a community does not mean that a community corrections program exists. Consistent goals and consistent approaches to achieving those goals are the backbone of successful community corrections. Community corrections legislation can help accomplish that consistency.

SUMMARY

1▶ *Intermediate sanctions* is the term given to the range of new sentencing options developed to fill the gap between traditional probation and traditional jail or prison sentences, better match the severity of punishment to the seriousness of the crime, reduce institutional crowding, and control correctional costs. Punishments typically identified as intermediate sanctions include intensive supervision probation (ISP), drug courts, fines, community service, day reporting centers, remote-location monitoring, residential community centers, and boot camps.

2▶ *Net widening* means increasing the number of offenders sentenced to a higher level of restriction. As a result, many offenders receive more restrictive sanctions than their offenses and characteristics warrant.

3▶ Intensive supervision probation (ISP) is control of offenders in the community through strict enforcement of conditions and frequent reporting to a probation officer with a reduced caseload. ISP programs exist in all 50 states. They may be state or county programs and may be administered by parole, probation, or prison departments.

4▶ Drug courts are special courts that are given responsibility to handle cases involving drug-addicted offenders.

5 ▶ A day fine is a financial punishment scaled to the seriousness of the offense and the offender's ability to pay. A traditional fine is based on a fixed amount, without regard to the offender's ability to pay.

6 ▶ Community service is a sentence to serve a specified number of hours working in unpaid positions with nonprofit or tax-supported agencies. Research suggests that, for offenders who do not present unacceptable risks of future violent crimes, community service costs much less than prison, has comparable recidivism rates, and presents negligible risks of violence by those who would otherwise be confined.

7 ▶ A day reporting center (DRC) is a community correctional center to which an offender reports each day to file a daily schedule with a supervision officer, showing how each hour will be spent. DRCs aim to provide strict surveillance over offenders and, depending on their resources, provide treatment services, refer offenders to community social service agencies, or arrange to have community agencies offer services on site.

8 ▶ *Remote-location monitoring* refers to technologies that probation and parole officers use to monitor remotely the physical location of an offender. For example, home-based electronic monitoring (EM) is often used by officers to monitor remotely offenders who are restricted to their homes.

9 ▶ Residential community centers (RCCs) are medium-security correctional settings that resident offenders are permitted to leave regularly—unaccompanied by staff—for work, for educational or vocational programs, or for treatment in the community.

10 ▶ Boot camp is a short institutional term, usually followed by probation, that includes a physical regimen designed to develop self-discipline, respect for authority, responsibility, and a sense of accomplishment.

11 ▶ A policy-centered approach draws together diverse stakeholders to think about and plan for an intermediate sanction. A program-centered approach, on the other hand, is usually undertaken by a single agency, which develops and funds the program in isolation from other programs.

12 ▶ Community corrections is a philosophy of correctional treatment that embraces decentralization of authority from state to local levels; citizen participation in program planning, design, implementation, and evaluation; redefinition of the population of offenders for whom incarceration is most appropriate; and emphasis on rehabilitation through community programs.

13 ▶ Community corrections acts (CCAs) are state laws that give economic grants to local communities to establish community corrections goals and policies and to develop and operate community corrections programs. CCAs decentralize services and engage communities in the process of reintegrating offenders by transferring correctional responsibility from the state to the community and by providing financial incentives for communities to manage more of their own correctional cases.

REVIEW & APPLICATIONS

REVIEW & APPLICATIONS

KEY TERMS

intermediate sanctions, *p. 158*
community corrections, *p. 159*
front-end programs, *p. 160*
back-end programs, *p. 160*
net widening, *p. 160*
intensive supervision
  probation (ISP), *p. 164*
drug court, *p. 165*

fine, *p. 169*
day fine, *p. 170*
community service, *p. 174*
day reporting center
  (DRC), *p. 178*
remote-location
  monitoring, *p. 179*
residential community center
  (RCC) *p. 183*

boot camp, *p. 186*
policy-centered
  approach, *p. 190*
program-centered
  approach, *p. 191*
community corrections acts
  (CCAs), *p. 193*

QUESTIONS FOR REVIEW

1. What are intermediate sanctions?
2. What are the purposes of intermediate sanctions?
3. Define *front-end programs, back-end programs,* and *net widening.* How do these three terms relate to intermediate sanctions?
4. What is ISP? How is it more punitive than standard probation?
5. What are the three primary goals of all drug courts?
6. What are four reasons fines are not taken seriously as punishment in the United States? Might enforced collection change that perception?
7. Distinguish between *fixed fines* and *day fines.*
8. Describe community service. Where, when, and why were community service orders first used in the United States?

9. What is a day reporting center (DRC), and how widespread is the use of DRCs in the United States?
10. What is remote-location monitoring? What correctional goals does it satisfy?
11. What are boot camps? How are they different from other correctional programs? What criticisms are there of boot camps?
12. What problems do boot camps pose for women offenders?
13. Describe the differences between a policy-centered approach and a program-centered approach to the development and implementation of intermediate sanctions.
14. What is *community corrections?*
15. What are community corrections acts?

THINKING CRITICALLY ABOUT CORRECTIONS

▶ ▶ ▶ **Fines**

Summarizing the results of a national survey of judges' attitudes toward fines, researchers noted that "at present, judges do not regard the fine alone as a meaningful alternative to incarceration or probation."[66] What could you tell such judges to convince them that day fines, or structured fines, are a viable sentencing option?

▶ ▶ ▶ **Policy-Centered Approach to Intermediate Sanctions**

Supporters of the policy-centered approach to devising intermediate sanctions cite three advantages: (1) It avoids wasting scarce resources on the wrong category of offender; (2) it draws the support of judges, prosecutors, and defense counsel outside the sponsoring agency; and (3) it helps develop consensus on specific goals for a program. Do you agree that these are advantages of the approach? Explain.

ON-THE-JOB DECISION MAKING

▶ ▶ ▶ **Why Day Fines?**

Your state legislature recently passed a bill authorizing day fines as an intermediate sanction. Part of the bill requires each probation department to send one or more probation officers to a workshop to prepare for implementing the bill. The chief probation officer designates you. Before the workshop, you are given two questions: (1) Why are day fines a good idea? (2) What would you do with offenders who don't pay? Write a response to bring to the workshop.

▶ ▶ ▶ **Are Drug Courts Working?**

Imagine you are Herbert M. Klein, founder of the nation's first drug court in Miami, Florida, in 1989. Experience tells you that drug courts provide closer, more comprehensive supervision and much more frequent drug testing and monitoring than other forms of community supervision. Yet some researchers are finding that there is no difference in arrest rates between drug court offenders and comparison group members, and if there is, it's difficult to say which of the ten components of drug court or combinations of features are the most important for determining success. The media asks you to respond. What do you say? [Recall in Chapter 4 we talked about outcome measures other than recidivism. You might consider searching the links on the home page of the National Association of Drug Court Professionals at http://www.nadcp.org/home.html for additional information.]

CORRECTIONS ON THE WEB

▶ ▶ ▶ **National Institute of Corrections**

The National Institute of Corrections (NIC) provides training, technical assistance, information services, and assistance in policy and program development to federal, state, and local corrections agencies. NIC's Web page at http://www.nicic.org provides full-text articles on community corrections issues. Click on *Community* and then *Publications*. Choose an article that interests you. Prepare a one-page report to present in class.

▶ ▶ ▶ **National Criminal Justice Reference Service**

Go to the home page of the National Criminal Justice Reference Service at http://www.ncjrs.org. Locate Michael Tonry's *Intermediate Sanctions in Sentencing Guidelines* (NCJ # 165043). Read Chapter 5. Discuss the four approaches states are using to incorporate intermediate sanctions into sentencing guidelines. Which do you believe has the most promise and why?

REVIEW & APPLICATIONS

Institutional Corrections

Part Three examines jail, prison, and parole. These three correctional components account for almost 2.8 million offenders daily.

How much have jail inmates, facilities, and staff changed since the country's first jail officially opened in Philadelphia in 1776? As you will learn, many of today's jails are large and some are quickly adapting high technology to their purposes. Even though only 3 percent of the nation's 3,365 locally operated jails are "mega" jails (having 1,000 or more cells), they hold over 45 percent of the jail population. And why is it that with only 90 percent of all jail capacity occupied nationwide, jail staff perceive that jails are overcrowded? Staffing has not kept up with the increase in the jail population. Are privatization and accreditation solutions? You will decide.

Prisons also first developed in Pennsylvania. In 1790, a wing of the Walnut Street Jail was devoted to long-term incarceration and served as a model for the world's first prison, the Eastern State Penitentiary, in 1829. The architecture of jails and prisons changed over the years from linear to podular. Prisoner supervision approaches also changed, from indirect to direct. Regardless of all the changes, overcrowding remains a problem.

Each day, 1,400 people will leave prison. How prepared are they to reenter society? Did they receive the educational and vocational preparation and drug treatment they need to minimize their likelihood of reoffending? Unfortunately, probably not. Prisons simply do not have the resources to rehabilitate all inmates under their care. Even after release, one of five prisoners will have no supervision because he or she served a full sentence, as a result of legislation that abolished discretionary parole board release completely or for certain violent offenses. Has the pendulum swung too far?

Why is it that, in spite of the enormous amount of money that is spent on incarceration, the majority of inmates leave prison with very little reentry preparation, few marketable skills, and a high probability of returning? To counter such problems, states are experimenting with reentry courts, community partnership councils, and reintegration programs. Never before in the history of this country has there been such an emphasis on reentry preparation.

6

7

8

" It is with the unfortunate, above all, that humane conduct is necessary. **"**

—Fyodor Dostoyevski, Russian writer, 1821–1881

6

CHAPTER

Jails:
Way Stations Along
the Justice Highway

▶ **CHAPTER OBJECTIVES**

After completing this chapter you should be able to do the following:

1. List the purposes of jails and understand how jail populations are different from prison populations.

2. Trace briefly the development of jails in history.

3. Explain how first-, second-, and third-generation jails differ in design and in method of inmate management.

4. Outline the characteristics of jail inmates, facilities, and staff.

5. Outline the arguments for and against privatization.

6. Discuss ways to reduce jail crowding.

7. Describe how jail vocational and educational programs affect inmate behavior and recidivism.

8. Discuss how faith-based organizations and a jail chaplain can influence jail inmates and help jail staff.

9. Discuss why jail accreditation is important.

10. Explain why it is important for jail staff to conduct themselves as professionals.

▶ ▶ Darryl Strawberry is a baseball legend. He was the most sought-after senior high school baseball player in the country. He was MVP by the end of his second year in the minor leagues. In 1983 he was named National League Rookie of the Year. In 1988 he was the National League's Home Run Champion. He has four World Series Championship rings, and he was selected for the National League's All-Star team for eight consecutive seasons beginning in 1984. His doesn't sound like the background of a jail inmate, but on April 14, 1999, Hillsborough County Jail (Tampa, Florida) named Strawberry jail inmate 99019528 for cocaine possession, solicitation for prostitution (Strawberry solicited sex from an undercover officer and offered her $50), and violation of probation. He was released on a $6,000 bond.[1] This was not Strawberry's first brush with the law, nor would it be his last.

In March 2000, Strawberry voluntarily entered a drug rehabilitation clinic for the third time in 10 years, but citing his need to support his wife and children, Strawberry left the program a month later. After a car crash in September 2000, he entered another treatment program but continued to test positive for cocaine. He spent 21 days in jail, and in late November 2000 he was sentenced to a year's probation and 50 hours of community service, ordered to wear an electronic monitor, and ordered to serve the sentence concurrently with house arrest at a Tampa drug-treatment center.

Baseball legend Darryl Strawberry, has repeatedly been in trouble for drug law violations. In 2000, Strawberry was jailed for 21 days after failing a drug test. He was also ordered to wear an electronic monitor as part of a sentence that included house arrest at a Florida drug-treatment center. Can short jail terms be effective in changing someone's behavior?

In April 2001, Strawberry committed a technical violation of his probation when he left the drug treatment center without his probation officer's permission and attempted to obtain a Florida driver's license. He disappeared for four days. When he was arrested, he tested positive for cocaine and antidepressants and was sent to another drug treatment center for two years, followed by a year's probation and 100 hours of community service. Strawberry subsequently violated the rules at Phoenix House, a substance abuse rehabilitation center in Citra, Florida, by sneaking cigarettes, not taking his medication, and having sex with a female patient, and he was kicked out. A month later, Hillsborough County Judge Ralph Steinberg told Strawberry, "You've been given several opportunities to avoid incarceration. You've squandered those opportunities. It is now time for you to face the consequences." For repeated violations of probation, Steinberg sentenced Strawberry to serve 18 months at the Gainesville Correctional Institution, a minimum-medium security facility 135 miles north of Tampa. The prison houses a substance abuse program. Strawberry was released on April 8, 2003, after serving 11 months. He told reporters,

"I needed to be incarcerated. I wouldn't wish it on anybody, but certain people have to go through certain channels to be able to come to grips with themselves—and that was me."

It's hard to tell what the future holds for Darryl Strawberry (besides his struggles with addiction, he has battled colon and stomach cancer). Maybe jail and prison made a crucial difference in Strawberry's fight against substance abuse.

Darryl Strawberry isn't much different from the thousands of men and women who enter our nation's jails each day, many with substance addictions. Most are not as economically fortunate or as athletic as Strawberry, but the offense similarities are surprising. As you'll read in this chapter, jails are often disparaged in corrections, but that image is changing. Today's jails have opportunities that were unheard of just a decade ago. Citizen advocates, community linkages, judicial oversight, and jail professionalism are changing the ways jails are operating. These windows of opportunity can leverage jails to successfully perform their functions.

Purpose of Jails

Jails are locally operated correctional facilities that confine people before or after conviction. Jails are different from prisons (the subject of Chapter 7) in a number of ways that you will learn about as you read. The fundamental difference between jail and prison is the nature of their populations.[2]

Total admission is the total number of persons admitted to jail each year, which falls between 10 million and 13 million. The **average daily population (ADP),** on the other hand, is the number of persons confined on a specific day. Jail ADP at midyear 2002 was 737,912. Prison total admission is currently estimated at 500,000 a year, and prison ADP on January 1, 2003, was 1,440,655 adults (see Chapter 7). The *daily* population of jails is lower than that of prisons, but the *annual* total of people incarcerated in jails is higher. Put another way, it takes two years for the nation's state and federal prison population to turn over once; the jail population turns over almost 20 times each year. The jail population is, thus, dynamic, and the prison population is static. The changing nature of jail populations raises significant issues and problems that form the core of this chapter.

On June 28, 2002, local jail authorities held or supervised 737,912 offenders, an increase of almost 5.4 percent from midyear 2001, the largest annual increase since 1977.[3] Jail authorities supervised 10 percent of these offenders (72,437) in alternative programs outside jail facilities (see Figure 6–4). A total of 665,475 were housed in local jails. Inmates sentenced to jail usually have a sentence of one year or less, but jails also incarcerate persons in a wide variety of other categories.

jails

Locally operated correctional facilities that confine people before or after conviction.

total admission

The total number of people admitted to jail each year.

average daily population (ADP)

The number of people confined on a specific day.

> It takes two years for the nation's state and federal prison population to turn over once, while the jail population turns over almost 20 times each year.

Jails are used to do the following:

- Receive persons awaiting court action on their current charge—60 percent at midyear 2002.
- Readmit probation and parole violators and bail-bond absconders.
- Detain juveniles until custody is transferred to juvenile authorities— 7,248 at midyear 2002.
- Hold mentally ill persons until they are moved to appropriate health facilities.
- Hold individuals for the military.
- Provide protective custody.
- Confine persons found in contempt.
- Hold witnesses for the courts.
- Hold inmates about to be released after completing a prison sentence.
- Transfer inmates to federal, state, or other authorities—71,256 on January 1, 2003.
- House inmates for federal, state, or other authorities because of crowding of their facilities.
- Operate some community-based programs as alternatives to incarceration.
- Hold inmates sentenced to short terms (generally under one year) of incarceration.

For all their important roles and responsibilities, jails have been a disgrace to every generation.[4] Many of the nation's 3,365 locally operated jails are old, overcrowded, poorly funded, scantily staffed by underpaid and poorly trained employees, and given low priority in local budgets. Yet a strong groundswell of support is rising for the nation's jails. Tomorrow's jail professionals have tremendous opportunities to continue that momentum. Progress is being made because of new emphases on jail education, staff selection and training, professional associations, standards, technology, accountability, and laws, among other things. Groups such as the American Jail Association (AJA) are advancing jail professionalism through training, information exchange, technical assistance, publications, and conferences. Members of the AJA include sheriffs, jail administrators, judges, attorneys, educators, correctional staff, jail inspection officials, health care providers, and clergy. The AJA mission statement is shown in Exhibit 6–1. This chapter will explore the problems of jails of the past and present and discuss direction for the 21st century.

Almost one-half of the nation's jails like the one pictured above are small (less than 50 cells), holding only 4 percent of the jail population. Most small jails were built in the early part of the 20th century. What management style does this jail suggest?

I've been on the job 15 years, and it's been wonderful—it's been an excellent career. I would tell anybody to step into it. It's so rewarding—it can be so stressful, but there are so many rewards. I'm a hands-on person; I enjoy working with people. We don't always see people coming into jail pretty—you see them at their lowest—and if you can help that person to move up, I guess that's where the reward comes in.

Prior to this, I worked at the state hospital, so I worked with the mentally challenged and the handicapped. Then I had my second child and went into day care, and I baby-sat the sheriff's grandson. I always told him, "If there's ever an opening, keep me in mind," so I went for an interview and got a position.

I have never been afraid of my position; I've never been afraid of working with individuals. I've had a wonderful captain—he always trained in the adage "Treat them as you'd like to be treated if you were behind bars." I've always used

that as my outlook with the individuals that I come into contact with here. You never know; you could be falsely charged with something—it could be you behind bars.

People in the community do not know what it is like to be locked up. And in a sense, I'm locked up for eight hours a day, or if I have to stay longer. When we work the floor, we're basically prisoners too. We don't realize what it's like for somebody to be away from their family —sure, they've messed up. But if we can give them a TV or send them to a GED class or a religious class, that is taking their minds off of thoughts of suicide, thoughts of "I'm worthless." I've been through I don't know how many attempted suicides, and it's not a pretty sight. You have to step into a prisoner's eyes and see where they're at but not step down to their level.

Some people say that we're just glorified babysitters, but if you feel that way, you're in the wrong position. We're not

here to find these people guilty—we're here to meet their needs while they're incarcerated.

Right now I'm in charge of the transport area—I deal a lot with probation and courts and see to it that people are transported to where they need to be. So I've got to keep the rapport good and open with probation and the court. That's one area that I really work hard at. But my work ethic is maybe different than some—because when I'm here, I'll do whatever I can to help anybody out. I love my job, and you don't hear too many people say that after so many years. You can always find something good in a person.

Terrie Butterfield
Sergeant
Kandiyohi County Jail
Wilmer, Minnesota

Jails in History

It is believed that King Henry II of England ordered the first jail built, in 1166. The purpose of that jail was to detain offenders until they could be brought before a court, tried, and sentenced. From that beginning, jails spread throughout Europe but changed in scope and size over time.

With the development of workhouses and poorhouses in the 15th and 16th centuries in England, sheriffs took on the added responsibility of supervising vagrants, the poor, and the mentally ill. These institutions, despite their distinct names, were indistinguishable from jails. Their squalid, unhealthy conditions and the sheriffs' practice of demanding money from persons under their charge caught the attention of 18th-century Enlightenment reformers. One such reformer was the English sheriff John Howard. In 1779, England's Parliament passed the four jail reforms that Howard proposed: secure and sanitary structures, jail inspections, elimination of fees, and an emphasis on reforming prisoners. To this day, the John Howard Association and *Howard Journal* carry Howard's ideas forward.

FIRST JAIL IN AMERICA

The first jail in America was the Walnut Street Jail in Philadelphia, built in 1776. The jail housed offenders without regard to sex, age, or offense. Following the jail's opening, conditions quickly deteriorated. According to

---

EXHIBIT 6-1   American Jail Association

Mission Statement

To band together all those concerned with or interested in the custody and care of persons awaiting trial, serving sentences, or otherwise locally confined; to improve the conditions and systems under which such persons are detained.

To advance professionalism through training, information exchange, technical assistance, publications, and conferences.

To provide leadership in the development of professional standards, pertinent legislation, management practices, programs, and services.

To present and advance the interests, needs, concerns, and proficiency of the profession as deemed appropriate by the membership and their representatives.

---

some, the jail became a "promiscuous scene of unrestricted intercourse, universal riot, and debauchery."[5] The Philadelphia Quakers had wanted the Walnut Street Jail to be a place where inmates reformed themselves through reflection and remorse. In 1790 the Philadelphia Society for Alleviating the Miseries of Public Prisons and the General Assembly of Pennsylvania designated a wing of the Walnut Street Jail a penitentiary. Implementing Quaker beliefs, the penitentiary emphasized prisoner reform through reflection and penitence and rehabilitation through good conduct. Sixteen solitary cells were added to the facility and workshops were built. Alcohol and prostitution were prohibited; prisoners were segregated by sex, age, and offense; diets were monitored; guardians were appointed to care for minors; and religious, health care, and educational services were provided. Debtors were housed separately from the general inmate

The Walnut Street Jail, started in Philadelphia in 1776, originally housed offenders without regard to sex, age, or offense. Following its redesignation as a penitentiary in 1790, it housed only convicted felons. Which religious group's principles influenced correctional institutions in Pennsylvania?

population and had no such privileges. Their prison conditions were piti-
ful, and many debtors starved.[6]

In 1798 a fire destroyed the workshops at Walnut Street. The destruction brought about disillusionment and idleness. Rising costs crippled the
jail's budget. Disciplinary problems rose with overcrowding, and escape
and violence increased. The number of inmates who were destitute vagrants or debtors soared as did the incidence of disease. There were political conflicts between the religious Quakers and the non-Quaker prison
board members. Prisoners rioted on March 27, 1820, and on October 5,
1835, the Walnut Street Jail closed. State prisoners were transferred to the
new Eastern State Penitentiary in Philadelphia, the first institution of its
kind in the world (see Chapter 7). County inmates and those awaiting trial
were transferred to a new county jail.

By the close of the 19th century, most cities across the United States had
jails to hold persons awaiting trial and to punish convicted felons. The
sheriff became the person in charge of the jail. As crime increased and urban centers expanded, jails grew in importance, as did the sheriffs' control
over jails.

AMERICAN JAILS IN THE 20TH CENTURY

On any given day, America's jails serve a variety of functions. They detain
people awaiting arraignment or trial, 60 percent at midyear 2002. They
confine offenders serving short sentences for less serious offenses. Jails also
serve as surrogate mental hospitals. They frequently detain people with
drug or alcohol dependency. They are the first stop on the social services
highway for the homeless, street people, and some with extremely poor
physical health, especially those with HIV, AIDS, and tuberculosis (TB).

Some historians refer to America's jails as the "poorhouse of the twentieth century," the dumping grounds for society's problems.[7] Jails in 20th-
century America evolved into institutions of social control, not only for
people who committed criminal acts, but also for those who made up the
underclass in American society.

John Irwin (in 1986) called the purpose of jails **rabble management;** that
is, the control of persons whose noncriminal behavior is offensive to their
communities.[8] The central purpose of the 20th-century jail was to detain
the most disconnected and disreputable persons, who were arrested more
because they were offensive than because they had committed crimes. They
were individuals of whom all were aware yet whom society ignored: public
nuisances, derelicts, junkies, drunks, vagrants, the mentally ill, and street
people. The purpose of America's 20th-century jails must be understood in
relation to the composition of the jail population. Jails not only confined
people before and after conviction, but also held those who did not fit into
the mainstream of American society. Moreover, since jails housed society's
outcasts, there was no incentive to improve jail conditions.

rabble management
Control of people whose noncriminal behavior is offensive to their
communities.

ARCHITECTURE AND INMATE MANAGEMENT

In an attempt to better manage and control inmate behavior, jails have progressed through three phases of architectural design. Each design is based
on a particular philosophy of inmate management and control.

first-generation jail

Jail with multiple-occupancy cells or dormitories that line corridors arranged like spokes. Inmate supervision is intermittent; staff must patrol the corridors to observe inmates in their cells.

First-Generation Jails   First-generation jails were built in a linear design that dates back to the 18th century. In a typical **first-generation jail**, inmates live in multiple-occupancy cells or dormitories. The cells line corridors that are arranged like spokes. Inmate supervision is sporadic or intermittent; staff must patrol the corridors to observe inmates in their cells. Contact between jailers and inmates is minimal unless there is an incident to which jailers must react. See Figure 6–1.

The design of such linear jails reflects the assumption that inmates are violent and destructive and will assault staff, destroy jail property, and try to escape. The facility is designed to prevent these behaviors. Heavy metal bars separate staff from inmates. Reinforced metal beds, sinks, and toilets are bolted to the ground or wall. Reinforced concrete and razor wire surround the facility.

The biggest problem with first-generation jails is the inability of an officer to see what is going on in more than one or two cells at a time. That limitation gave rise to the second-generation jails of the 1960s.

Second-Generation Jails   Second-generation jails emerged in the 1960s to replace old, rundown linear jails and provide officers the opportunity to observe as much of the housing area as possible from a single vantage point.

Second-generation jails adopted a different philosophical approach to construction and inmate management. In a **second-generation jail**, staff remain in a secure control booth overlooking inmate housing areas, called *pods* (see Figure 6–2). Although visual surveillance increases in such jails, surveillance is remote, and verbal interaction with inmates is even less frequent than in first-generation jails. Property destruction is minimized because steel and cement continue to define the living areas. Outside, fences and razor wire continue to discourage escapes as well as unauthorized entry.

second-generation jail

Jail where staff remain in a secure control booth surrounded by inmate housing areas called *pods* and surveillance is remote.

FIGURE 6-1
First-Generation Jail—Intermittent Surveillance

Cells line corridors in first-generation jails. Unable to observe all inmate housing areas from one location, prison staff must patrol inmates' living areas to provide surveillance. What are the consequences of first-generation jails?

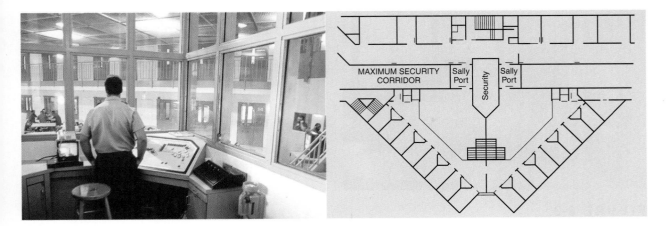

FIGURE 6-2
Second-Generation Jail—Remote Surveillance
Inmate living areas are divided into pods, or modules, in which cells are clustered around dayrooms that are under remote observation by staff in a secure control room. What are the consequences of second-generation jails?

While staff can observe activity in common areas, or *dayrooms,* they are unable to respond quickly to problems or even to interact effectively with inmates because of the intervening security control booth. In both the first- and second-generation jails, the biggest problem is that staff and inmates are separated. As David Parrish, detention commander for the Hillsborough County Sheriff's Department (Tampa, Florida) puts it, ". . . staff managed the hallways and control rooms, generally about 10 percent of the facility, while inmates ran the housing areas, roughly 90 percent."[9]

Third-Generation Jails Third-generation jails, also known as direct-supervision jails, emerged in the 1970s. The housing unit design of such jails is podular. Inmates' cells are arranged around a common area, or dayroom. There is no secure control booth for the supervising officer, and there are no physical barriers between the officer and the inmates. The officer may have a desk or table for paperwork, but it is in the open dayroom area.

In a third-generation jail the inmate management style is direct supervision. An officer is stationed in the pod with the inmates. The officer moves about the pod and interacts with the inmates to manage their behavior. The pod contains sleeping areas, dayroom space, all necessary personal hygiene fixtures, and sufficient tables and seats to accommodate unit capacity. Officers are not separated from inmates by a physical barrier. Officers provide frequent, nonscheduled observation of and personal interaction with inmates (see Figure 6–3). Furnishings are used to reduce inmate stress caused by crowding, excessive noise, lack of privacy, and isolation from the outside world. Bars and metal doors are absent, reducing noise and the dehumanization common in first- and second-generation jails.

Direct-supervision jails facilitate staff movement, interaction with inmates, and control and leadership over pods. By supervising inmate activities directly, the staff can help change inmate behavior patterns, rather than

third-generation jail

Sometimes called a *direct-supervision jail,* a jail where inmates are housed in small groups, or pods, staffed 24 hours a day by specially trained officers. Officers interact with inmates to help change behavior. Bars and metal doors are absent, reducing noise and dehumanization.

FIGURE 6-3
Third-Generation Jail—Direct Supervision
Cells are grouped in housing units, or pods. Each pod has a central dayroom. Prison staff are stationed inside the housing unit to encourage direct interaction between inmates and staff. What are the consequences of direct-supervision jails?

simply react to them. Staff control inmate behavior through the enforcement of boundaries of acceptable behavior and the administration of consequences for violating the boundaries. Observing unacceptable behavior and administering consequences is less likely to occur in first- and second-generation jails where staff supervision is sporadic and remote.

Researchers tell us that pods and direct supervision provide a safer and more positive environment for inmates and staff than do first- and second-generation jails.[10] Still, there's an element of resistance to the concept of direct supervision, especially with local law enforcement agencies. Reasons for the skepticism include the short history of direct supervision, little supporting data, and the belief among sheriffs and jail administrators that direct supervision facilities are not as "safe" or "strong" as remote supervision facilities because of distance and physical separation from inmates.[11] Simply put, many agencies are not comfortable removing the "barriers" between "us and them," especially if the jail becomes overcrowded. However, one sheriff's captain with over 25 years of experience working in overcrowded remote supervision and overcrowded direct-supervision jails recently wrote ". . . it is clear to me that the direct-supervision jail is superior when it comes to safety, security, and overall operations in overcrowded conditions. . . . [T]hose who maintain their commitment to the direct-supervision principles will maintain better control and ownership of their facilities. With the current or future reality of overcrowding in our facilities, it is difficult for me to understand why anyone would choose lack of control over more control."[12] Yellowstone (Montana) County Sheriff's Captain, Dennis McCave, explained that, when his direct supervision facility became overcrowded and the sheriff's budget was too tight to build more beds or hire more staff, his agency "Hot Poded." Inmates shared hours out of their cell in the pod dayroom—only one-half of the inmates were allowed out at a time. "I've been there and I'm convinced," wrote Captain McCave. "Managing by the principles and philosophy of direct supervision is by far the superior alternative in the 'best of times and the worst of times.'"[13]

> Managing by the principles and philosophy of direct supervision is by far the superior alternative in the 'best of times and the worst of times.'

The first direct-supervision county jail in the United States was the Martinez Detention Facility in Contra Costa, California. It opened in January 1981. Today, an estimated 300 of the 3,365 local jails use direct supervision.[14] Almost 100 have opened since 1995.

Characteristics of Jail Inmates, Facilities, and Staff

Who is in jail? Why are they there? How many jails are there? How many people work in jail? What do we know about the operation and administration of jail facilities? To these and related questions we now turn our attention.

JAIL INMATES

The characteristics of jail inmates changed slightly from mid-2001 to mid-2002. In June 2002, local jail authorities held or supervised 737,912 offenders—an increase of 5.4 percent from June 2001. Ten percent of these offenders (72,437) were supervised outside jail facilities (see Figure 6–4). Of those offenders supervised outside jail facilities, 44 percent were

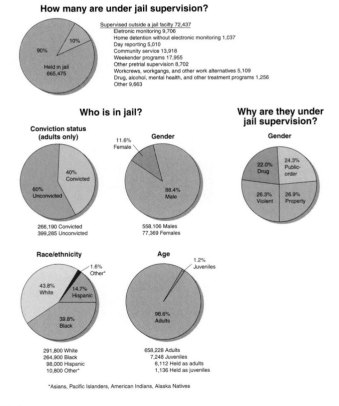

FIGURE 6-4
Persons Under Jail Supervision, Mid-2002

Source: Paige M. Harrison and Jennifer C. Karberg, *Prison and Jail Inmates at Midyear 2002,* (Washington, DC: Office of Justice Programs, April 2003); and Caroline Wolf Harlow, *Profile of Jail Inmates, 1996* (Washington, DC: Bureau of Justice Statistics, April 1998).

involved in community service or weekend programs. The remaining 90 percent (665,475) were held in local jails.

Since 1970, when the first national jail statistics were collected, the number of inmates held in locally operated jails has almost quadrupled. During the 1970s the growth was very modest—13 percent—but during the 1980s it was more than 120 percent, consisting of more than 220,000 inmates. Since 1995 the nation's jail population has increased an average of 4.0 percent a year.

The Bureau of Justice Statistics has compiled a profile of inmates in local jails. That profile is shown in Table 6–1. Note that at the time of arrest:

TABLE 6-1	**Profile of Jail Inmates**			
Categories	**Percentage of jail inmates**		**Categories**	**Percentage of jail inmates**
Criminal justice status at arrest			**Physical or sexual abuse (females)**	
None	46.4%		Ever	47.5%
Status[1]	53.6%		Before age 18	36.6%
On probation	31.7%		Age 18 or after	26.7%
On parole	13.7%		Physical abuse	37.2%
On bail-bond	12.7%		Sexual abuse	37.1%
On other pretrial release	4.4%		Rape	32.2%
Criminal history			**Employment status**	
None	27.3%		Employed	64.3%
Priors	72.7%		Full-time	49.3%
Probation	63.0%		Part-time	10.4%
Jail/prison	58.4%		Occasionally	4.6%
Prior drug use				
Never	17.6%		Not employed	35.8%
Ever[1]	82.4%		**Person(s) lived with most**	
Regular	64.2%		**of the time**	
In month before the offense[2]	55.0%		Both parents	39.7%
At the time of the offense[2]	35.6%		Mother only	43.3%
Alcohol at time of offense[2]			Father only	4.9%
Not under the influence	59.5%		Grandparents	7.0%
Under the influence	40.5%		Other	5.2%
Substance abuse treatment			**Perceived safety of jail**	
Never	57.7%		**compared to that of streets**	
Ever[1]	42.3%		Jail safer	20.9%
Since admission to jail	10.3%		Streets safer	43.3%
Reported disability			About the same	35.8%
Any disability	36.5%			
Physical, mental, or other health problem	20.7%			
Difficulty seeing newsprint	9.2%			
Learning disability	9.1%			
Difficulty hearing	6.1%			
Speech disability	3.7%			

1. Detail may add to more than total; inmates may fit more than one category.
2. Based on convicted jail inmates only.

Source: Caroline Wolf Harlow, *Profile of Jail Inmates, 1996* (Washington, DC: Bureau of Justice Statistics, April 1998).

- More than half of the inmates were under supervision by the courts or corrections.
- Almost one-third were on probation and almost one-eighth were on parole.
- Seven of every 10 had prior sentences.
- Almost two-thirds used drugs regularly.
- More than one-third were disabled.
- One-third of the women had been physically or sexually abused or raped.
- One-third were unemployed at the time of arrest.
- Two-thirds grew up in homes without both parents.
- Four of every 10 believed that the streets were safer than jails.

Another way to look at the nation's jail population is to consider the rate of incarceration. Jail populations give us a count of the total number incarcerated (e.g., 737,912 offenders held or supervised in mid-2002). Because of differences in total population, however, such counts do not allow for accurate comparison of jurisdictions. Rates of jail incarceration, expressed as the number of jail inmates per 100,000 residents aged 18 and older, provide for a more meaningful and useful analysis of trends in incarceration. With rate data, we can compare changes over time. Figure 6–5 shows changes in the jail incarceration rate from 1990 through 2002. Note that the incarceration rate increased 42 percent, from 163 jail inmates per 100,000 adults in 1990 to 231 jail inmates per 100,000 adults in 2002. Relative to the numbers of male and female U.S. residents, the incarceration rate of men was nearly eight times that of women (417 per 100,000 adult population for men compared to 53 per 100,000 adult population for women) in mid-2002. The incarceration rate of blacks was five times the incarceration rate of whites (740 versus 147 per 100,000 adult population, respectively) and two and one-half times the incarceration rate of Hispanics (740 versus 256 per 100,00 adult population).

Gender and Jail Populations   There has been an enormous surge in the number of women incarcerated in the United States. The number of women in jail has almost quadrupled over the past 25 years, from 19,000 in 1985 to 77,369 in mid-2002, representing 11.6 percent of the local jail inmate population in mid-2002. On average, the adult female jail population has grown 5.9 percent annually since 1995, while the adult male population has grown 3.8 percent.

The typical female jail inmate is poor, is a high school dropout with low skills, has held mainly low-wage jobs, is young (25 to 29), is unmarried with one to three children, and belongs to a racial minority. Almost twice as many women as men in jail are first time offenders (42 versus 28 percent).[15] Before incarceration, 40 percent used drugs daily. Forty percent had members of their immediate families sentenced to prison. One of three grew up in a home where one or both parents abused drugs, alcohol, or both. And one of three had been physically or sexually abused before she was 18 years old.

This profile raises troubling concerns about the children of jailed mothers. Two-thirds of women in jail are mothers with children under age 18

FIGURE 6-5

**Jail Incarceration Rate,
1990–2002**

Source: Adapted from Paige M. Harrison
and Jennifer C. Karberg, *Prison and Jail Inmates at Midyear 2002,* (Washington, DC:
Office of Justice Programs, April 2003).

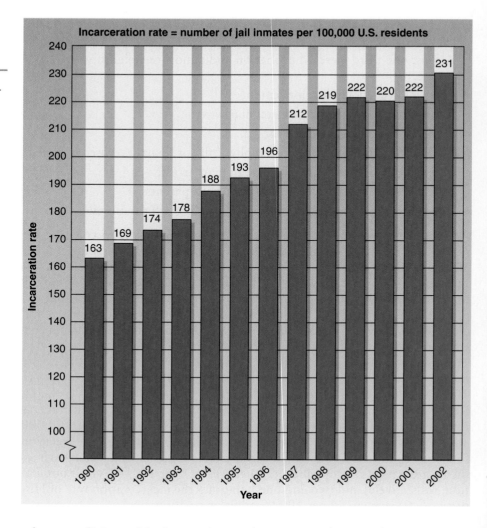

who were living with them prior to detention. When mothers go to jail,
children become silent victims. The children may already have been victims
if their mothers used drugs during pregnancy. Young children, not yet
capable of understanding why their mother is gone, where she has gone,
and if or when she will return, may develop depression and
feelings of abandonment. Even children who are fortunate
enough to be placed with emotionally supportive caregivers
must cope with seeing their mother only through a glass
barrier and hearing her voice only over the phone. Studies
have shown that children of incarcerated mothers have more
behavioral problems at home and in school and are four times
as likely to become juvenile delinquents as children from similar socioeconomic backgrounds with parents at home. Maintaining bonding with children and family is the most difficult
female inmate experience.[16] Recognizing that children should
not be made to suffer for the poor choices of their parents
and recognizing that support for family maintenance is a societal value, some jails are establishing visitation and parenting

Ethical Dilemma

Female offenders have an average of
2.5 children. Rising numbers of incarcerated, pregnant and/or parenting women being sentenced to jail
have resulted in many more children
being separated from their mothers.
Should jail administrators concern
themselves with providing services
for families of jail inmates? For more
information go to Ethical Dilemma
6-1 at http://www.mhhe.com/
schmalleger2.

programs that accommodate this need. Through such programs, jail administrators have the opportunity to become leaders in preserving families and reducing crime.

Some scholars believe that many women in jail do not pose a threat to public safety but are jailed because they do not have the financial resources to make bail. Less than 15 percent are charged with violent offenses.[17] Most are charged with property offenses (32 percent), drug offenses (34 percent), and public order offenses (19 percent). This suggests some differences are needed in women's facility bed space and program space from men's facility space (for example, there may need to be less high-security bed space and more substance abuse programming space).

The increase in the number of women in jail has required that local officials identify and try to meet the needs of female inmates, yet severe limitations in resources often impede the provision of programs and services for women in jail. Jails are not prepared to house and treat rapidly rising female populations. They have difficulty providing appropriate housing, bed space, programs, jobs, mental health care, and other services. Women in jail have high needs for education, job training, health care, mental health care, alcohol and drug abuse counseling, and parenting skills development. Properly classifying women according to their risks and needs is beyond the scope of most jails in the United States.[18] In 1993, the National Institute of Justice surveyed 54 jails and found that the same classification instrument was used for both male and female inmates in 50 jails. The survey found no effort to gauge women inmates' different needs, circumstances, and risk profiles.[19]

Ignoring problems relating to women in jail increases a jail's exposure to litigation and liability. The National Institute of Corrections argues against doing nothing: ". . . the 'get tough on inmates' mood, combined with decreasing levels of accountability for maintaining some level of minimum standards, raises the specter of decreased funding for jails, corresponding cutbacks in staff and training, and the rebirth of the sorts of very brutal, barbaric, and often dangerous conditions that led to the initial wave of court intervention in the early 1970s."[20]

Women are normally housed in a "women's unit," often an afterthought built inside facilities designed for men or simply a replica of the men's facility design. Such design fails to take into account the different needs of women. For example, the traditional jail bunks and fixed-seating arrangements in the jail's dayroom or at dining room tables may present safety and comfort issues for women who are pregnant in jail. In addition, jailed women seldom have access to programs and services provided to male inmates. Special programming designed specifically for their unique needs as women and mothers is not offered.[21]

Another deficiency affecting women in jail is jail staffing. Either there are no female correctional officers or there are too few to ensure around-the-clock supervision of women in jail. The result too often is that women inmates are exploited and abused by male staff. In 1975, a North Carolina jury found Joan Little, then 20 years old, not guilty of the murder of 62-year-old Clarence Alligood, a correctional officer in the Beaufort County Jail. Alligood had entered Little's cell and sexually attacked her. She argued that she killed him in self defense with the ice pick he had brought into her cell. Dr. Ken Kerle, managing editor of *American Jails* and author of this chapter's Reflections on the Future, argues that the best defense for a jail against female inmates' allegations of sexual harassment by male staff is to have a female officer present at all times.[22]

Ethnicity and Jail Populations   From 1990 through mid-2002, the majority of local jail inmates were black or Hispanic. By mid-2002, whites made up 44 percent of the jail population; blacks, 40 percent; Hispanics, 15 percent; and other races (Asians, Pacific Islanders, American Indians, and Alaska Natives), 1 percent (see Figure 6–4). Relative to percentages of the U.S. population, the proportion of blacks in local jails by mid-2002 was 5 times that of whites, nearly 3 times that of Hispanics, and almost 10 times that of people of other races.

In May 2002, the Bureau of Justice Statistics published its third report on jails in Indian country in the United States.[23] (*Indian country* is a statutory term that includes all lands within an Indian reservation; dependent Indian communities; and Indian trust allotments, or lands held in trust for tribes or their members.) The Bureau reported that 2,030 inmates were held in 68 Indian country facilities by mid-2001, up 10 percent from 2000 and up 37 percent from mid-1998. Seven of the 10 largest jails in Indian country are in Arizona. Together they held in 2001 almost 29 percent of the total inmate population

Whites comprise nearly 70 percent of the U.S. population but only 44 percent of the jail population. In the general population, Hispanics make up almost 13 percent, and blacks make up 12.7 percent, but in jail their populations are 15 percent and 40, respectively.

Explanations for the overrepresentation of minorities in jail abound, not the least of which is how the U.S. Census Bureau defines *race*. The decennial Census measures race and ethnicity differently than did the previous Census. First, the census item on *race* (on which people identify themselves as white, black, or of other races and ethnicities) and the item on Hispanic identity are separate. This means that one can be both black and Hispanic. Second, for the first time in 2000, Census respondents could check more than one race, an attempt by the Census Bureau to identify multiracial people. One result is that blacks and Hispanics are not two distinct groups. In 2000, about 1.7 million blacks were also estimated to be Hispanic. How does one determine which group is larger? Should blacks be deducted from the Hispanic population or the other way around? Does one grouping take precedence over the other?

Another explanation for minority overrepresentation in jail has to do with the function of jails as pretrial detention centers. The jail population is heavily influenced by bail decisions. A number of researchers have found that judges impose higher bail—or are more likely to deny bail altogether—if the defendant is a racial minority.[24] Still another reason is the impact of the war on drugs and on law enforcement strategies of racial profiling. Other researchers have argued that the war on drugs has had a particularly detrimental effect on black males.[25] Across the past two decades, more black males than white males have been detained for drug offenses. Researchers at the University of Nebraska argue that police are *reactive* in responding to crimes against persons and property, but they are *proactive* in dealing with drug offenses. "There is evidence," they write, "to suggest that they [police] target minority communities—where drug dealing is more visible and where it is thus easier to make arrest—and tend to give less attention to drug activities in other neighborhoods."[26]

Juveniles and Jail Populations   Over the past 25 years, there has been a dramatic reversal in the theory and practice of punishing juveniles. In the mid-1970s, juvenile offenders were deemed to have special needs. The Juvenile Justice and Delinquency Prevention Act provided federal money to states and cities that agreed not to hold juveniles in jails where they might have regular contact with adults. By 1996, however, in the face of pressure to increase punishment for juvenile offenders, new legislation allowed cities and states to detain juvenile offenders for up to 12 hours in an adult jail before a court appearance and made it easier to house juveniles in separate wings of adult jails. That shift in philosophy and policy has increased the number of juveniles held in adult jails. By mid-1993, 4,300 juveniles were held in jail, making up 0.9 percent of the jail population. By mid-2001, that number and percentage had increased to 7,613 (1.2 percent). By mid-2002, 84 percent (6,112) of these young inmates had been convicted or were being held for trial as adults. The remaining 1,136 (16 percent) were held as juveniles (see Figure 6–4).

The incarceration of juveniles in adult jails is criticized for a number of reasons. Holding juveniles in adult jails places young people at greater risk of being physically, sexually, and mentally abused by adult offenders. Juvenile girls are especially vulnerable to sexual assault. Juveniles in adult jail are almost eight times more likely to commit suicide than are juveniles in juvenile detention centers. One explanation is that juveniles are held in isolated parts of adult jails where they receive less staff support and supervision. Another is that jail staff are not trained to recognize depression in juveniles.

So why does the practice continue? Perhaps it is because there is a lack of alternatives. Or maybe it is because smaller counties believe separate facilities are cost prohibitive. Perhaps society does not know or believe there is a problem. Or maybe the public believes that jailing juveniles is necessary for public safety and to reduce crime.

JAIL FACILITIES

The capacity to house jail inmates has kept pace with the jail population. In the 12 months ending June 28, 2002, fewer beds (14,590) than inmates (34,235) were added to the nation's jails for the first time since 1997. By mid-2002, 93 percent of jail capacity was occupied, down from 104 percent in 1990. Between 1995 and 2002, the average annual increase in the number of new beds at the nation's jails was 24,019, whereas the average annual increase in the number of persons held in jail was 19,803. The occupied percentage of jail **rated capacity**, which is the number of beds or inmates a rating official assigns to a correctional facility, has remained below 100 percent since 1995. (The other ways to measure capacity are discussed in Chapter 7.) Jails that on average held between 500-999 inmates reported the highest occupancy rates (94 percent), compared to those with 1,000 or

rated capacity
The number of beds or inmates a rating official assigns to a correctional facility.

more inmates (92 percent). In 2002, the nation's 25 largest jail jurisdictions accounted for 23 percent of all inmates. Eight of them operated at over 100 percent of their rated capacity (see Table 6–2).[27]

Of the nation's 3,365 jails, 47 are privately operating under contract to local governments.[28] Texas leads the nation in private jail operations with approximately one-fifth of its inmates (3,469) and facilities (eight). (We will discuss jail privatization later in this chapter.) Tennessee has the second-largest number of inmates (2,278) in privately operated jails, followed by Florida (1,931). Across the country, another 15 percent of jails are under federal court order or consent decree (most often for crowding or other confinement conditions). Another 11 percent have been ordered to limit populations.

TABLE 6–2	The 25 Largest Local Jail Jurisdictions, Mid-2002		
Jurisdiction	**Number of inmates held**	**Average daily population[1]**	**Rated capacity[2]**	**Percentage of capacity occupied at midyear[3]**
---	---	---	---	---
Los Angeles County, CA	19,867	19,258	24,440	81
New York City, NY	14,201	13,952	20,793	68
Cook County, IL	10,990	10,888	9,798	112
Maricopa County, AZ	7,919	8,008	5,201	152
Philadelphia City, PA	7,383	7,221	5,600	132
Dade County, FL	6,746	6,680	8,179	82
Harris County, TX	7,153	6,641	8,721	82
Dallas County, TX	6,805	6,567	8,187	83
Orleans Parish, LA	6,482	5,875	7,477	87
Broward County, FL	5,053	5,116	5,198	97
San Bernardino County, CA	5,049	4,977	4,957	102
San Diego County, CA	4,656	4,872	4,634	100
Shelby County, TN	4,627	4,835	6,216	74
Orange County, CA	5,086	4,561	5,410	94
Santa Clara County, CA	3,884	3,915	3,629	107
Alameda County, CA	3,719	3,886	3,811	98
Orange County, FL	3,759	3,792	3,426	110
Bexar County, TX	3,742	3,638	4,294	87
Baltimore City, MD	3,721	3,637	3,861	96
Hillsborough County, FL	3,406	3,501	3,373	101
Sacramento County, CA	3,295	3,293	3,885	85
Riverside County, CA	3,282	3,283	3,005	109
Tarrant County, TX	3,043	3,119	4,739	64
Milwaukee County, WI	2,973	3,105	3,790	78
Jacksonville City, FL	2,895	2,965	3,137	92

Note: Jurisdictions are ordered by their average daily population in 2002.
1.   The average daily population is the sum of the number of inmates in jail each day for a year, divided by the number of days in the year (for the year ending June 30).
2.   Rated capacity is the number of beds or inmates assigned by a rating official to all the facilities within a jurisdiction.
3.   The number of inmates, divided by the rated capacity and multiplied by 100.

Source: Paige M. Harrison and Jennifer C. Karberg, *Prison and Jail Inmates at Midyear 2002* (Washington, DC: Bureau of Justice Statistics, April 2003).

Almost one-half (47 percent) of the nation's jails are small (fewer than 50 cells), holding only 4 percent of the jail population. In contrast, 3 percent of the nation's jails, referred to as *megajails,* have 1,000 or more cells.[29] Megajails hold over 45 percent of all jail prisoners.[30] Typically these large facilities are located in major metropolitan and urban areas. Jail operating budgets are highest in New York (almost $1.1 billion) and lowest in North Dakota ($3.5 million).[31]

JAIL STAFF

Twenty years ago, staffing was cited as the number-one concern in a survey of 2,452 jails.[32] The managing editor of *American Jails,* Ken Kerle, says this is still a major problem.[33] Today, an estimated 297,600 people work in the nation's jails.[34] Women comprise one-third of all jail employees (one-fourth of all corrections officers). Sixty-six percent of all jail corrections officers are white, 24 percent are black, 8 percent are Hispanic, and 2 percent are of other races. Minority employees are underrepresented relative to their proportion among inmates.

From 1993 to 1999, the number of jail inmates increased 32 percent, but the size of jail staff grew only 25 percent. In spite of the fact that there are more jail beds than inmates, as noted earlier, jail staff perceive that jails are overcrowded because there are not enough staff on shift to handle the workload properly. Jail staff think of a jail as overcrowded if, due to staff shortages, inmate counts, bed checks, and cell searches are not performed and inmate programs such as visitation and outdoor recreation are postponed.[35] Because most jails are locally funded, local politics determine how much staff a county government allocates to operate the county jail. How much is the county willing to spend on the jail compared to other county agencies such as roads, police and fire?

Most jails spend 75 to 90 percent of their budgets on salaries. One jail post operating 24 hours a day, seven days a week requires five officers when sick time, vacation, and other leaves are factored in. This partially explains why county officials are reluctant to increase staffing to correspond with an increase in inmate population. Yet understaffing poses a threat to inmate and staff security and safety. Too often inadequate staffing leads to inmate lockdowns to prevent escape and ease the handling of prisoners. Further, without appropriate staff supervision, little can be done to protect inmates from one another in multiple-occupancy cells.

Other problems of jail staff include substandard pay compared to that of other employees in the criminal justice system, low job prestige, high turnover, and inadequate systems for recruitment, selection, and training. The National Sheriff's Association (NSA) believes that too often "warm bodies are taken off the street, put into uniform, given a set of keys, and told to go to work."[36] Concerning salaries, the NSA wrote, "Jail officer careers will never achieve the status they deserve so long as counties continue to pay jail officers less money than the officers assigned to law enforcement. . . . No person wants to make a career where the reward is lousy wages. You can't attract the people who have the potential to be the best officers by paying them wages in the poverty range."[37]

Although the Palm Beach County Sheriff's Department starts jail corrections officers at $32,952, not all jails can do this. Nevertheless, most jails

Eye On Corrections™

Children Among Men: The Issue of Juveniles in Adult Jails

By Keith Martin

While the legislation that called for the separation between juveniles and adults in jails is nearly 20 years old, such separation is still not being accomplished everywhere in the nation. While the guidelines are clear, meeting them in some localities is a challenge, causing juveniles to be held alongside adults for short periods. In some cases, such exposure to adult criminals in a jail environment may cause more damage than the offense that brought young people to jail in the first place. "[Research shows that] kids in adult facilities are much more likely to commit suicide and be assaulted, including sexually, than those in juvenile facilities," says Rasheed Newson of the Coalition for Juvenile Justice. "They are 'children among men' and don't physically stand a chance."

In order to provide better treatment and safer environments for young people, the Federal Juvenile Justice and Delinquency Prevention Act (JJDPA) was created in 1974. The Act has four main requirements for nationwide improvements in the juvenile justice system: (1) deinstitution-alization of status offenders, (2) removal of juveniles from adult jails and lockups (with some exceptions), (3) addressing disproportionate minority confinement, and (4) separation of juveniles from adult offenders.

This last requirement calls for "sight and sound" segregation of juveniles from adults being held in the jail, not only to maintain the physical well-being of young people, but also to minimize any influence that a criminal environment may have. "One reason the [JJDPA] requires sight and sound separation is so young people are not tormented, but also so they are not in a place to find mentors and bond with those around them," says Newson. "Children are still highly impressionable and those that leave impressions are those around them. If they are around criminals, they might become better criminals."

LOCATING THE PROBLEM

While states that receive funding from the JJDPA must comply with the requirements, there are still incidences of juveniles being held in adult jails. According to Newson, this predominantly occurs in rural communities that have neither a juvenile detention center where they can bring young offenders nor the means to transport them in a timely manner to another nearby county that does.

"[What happens is] they get a kid and need to get them to a juvenile facility which takes time and effort," says Newson. "In the meantime, they keep [a young person] in the adult jail and hope nothing goes wrong. They are gambling with kids' lives and with public safety. If it is inconvenient [to transfer that youth], they should work on the resources to make it happen."

Newson recognizes that most jail administrators don't want to lock kids up with adults and that the issue is that they have nowhere else to put them and a lot of other problems to deal with. The Coalition for Juvenile Justice hopes to persuade these administrators to move toward implementing a procedure to get a young person to a juvenile detention center as soon as possible, before an incident can take place.

The problem at most rural jails is that they are not getting one young person per day; instead they process maybe one every six months or so, explains Newson. Therefore, it may not seem like a problem that is in dire need of a fix, yet when a juvenile does walk through the front door, the facilities are completely unprepared.

"If you ask most jail administrators, they are trying to get through the next 24 hours, so the thought of asking for more money or resources for an infrequent problem is hard," says Newson.

DOES THE JJDPA JEOPARDIZE PUBLIC SAFETY?

Some jail administrators have argued that the JJDPA requirements prevent them from protecting the public. In 1997, a small group of rural sheriffs testified before the Senate in favor of the Violent and Repeat Juvenile Offender Act, which would have loosened the restrictions on holding juveniles in adult jails. Their main argument was that the JJDPA prohibited them from holding especially dangerous young offenders, who they felt belonged in their facilities.

According to Jason Ziedenberg, Deputy Director for the Center on Juvenile and Criminal Justice, although a handful of communities had a significant increase in juvenile crime and homicides in the late 1980s and early 1990s, the nation as a whole has not had a problem with serious juvenile crime. "The extent to which juvenile crime is a problem is that when it is a problem in even a handful of communities, as a nation we get into 'tough on crime,'" says Ziedenberg. "If we were smart, we'd focus on those areas [with the problems] and give them the resources [rather than have a nationwide focus]."

Ziedenberg adds that statistics show that, although juvenile crime is at a point at which both serious and rudimentary crimes are equal to what they were in the 1970s and even 1960s in some areas, the public still perceives it as a problem. A 1999 "Building Blocks for Youth" poll showed that 63 percent of the public thought juvenile crime was on the rise when in fact it had been dropping for seven years prior, he says.

A report co-authored by Ziedenberg in 1997, entitled *The Pods of Elmore County,* reinforced the fact that, across the nation, the majority of juvenile arrests were for nonviolent offenses. Such juveniles should be leaving the jail in a few hours to go to elsewhere, including to alternatives to incarceration. In rural areas where officials were fighting for lightened restrictions under the JJDPA, local resources could be used to curb problems, obviating the need to call for wholesale change. "I'm not saying that it isn't harder in rural areas [to deal with juvenile offenders] because of [fewer] resources, but if all the data says that a vast majority of arrested juveniles are nonviolent, why can't they be quickly moved through the jail versus changing *all* juvenile legislation that protects kids in contact with adults?" says Ziedenberg.

KENTUCKY'S REMARKABLE TURNAROUND

The state of Kentucky is mostly a rural state that focused its energy on fixing problems in its own backyard instead of lobbying for exemptions in detaining juveniles. Until two years ago, Kentucky was one of two states in the nation out of compliance with the JJDPA. Large numbers of status and nonoffender youth were being held in juvenile detention and sections of adult jails, and at one point, the state led the nation in the number of youth wasting away in pretrial custody.

In 1998, the Kentucky General Assembly authorized and financed the Statewide Detention Plan, calling for the state's newly created Department of Juvenile Justice (DJJ) to assume responsibility for all juvenile detention throughout the state, thus taking the physical and financial burden out of county hands. The plan called for the creation of 10 regional juvenile detention centers operated by the DJJ throughout the state.

As of April first, six of these regional locations are operational. They focus on the unique needs of juveniles, offering a range of services from a complete school day to group and individual therapy sessions.

"Obviously, when you have kids in a standalone facility [versus an adult jail], you can do better things for them," says Vicki Reed, director of the DJJ's Division of Placement Services. "For adult jailers, running a juvenile section [of the jail] is what I call 'a hobby.' For us, this is what we do, and we do it well." *This article has been reprinted in part from CCNN. To read the article in its entirety, go to www.corrections.com.*

Source: "Children Among Men: The Issue of Juveniles in Adult Jails," Keith Martin, The Corrections Connection Network News (CCNN). Eye on Corrections. www.corrections.com. April 4, 2002. Copyright © 2002, all rights reserved, The Corrections Connection Network News (CCNN), a division of J.S. Noonan, LLC. Reprinted with permission.

CAREER PROFILE

Quentin X. Escott
Deputy Sheriff   Jefferson County   Birmingham, Alabama

Quentin X. Escott has been a deputy sheriff for 1½ years. He is currently assigned to the county jail booking area. His responsibilities include searching incoming prisoners, using the computer imaging system to take inmate photographs and fingerprints, recording personal property, exchanging civilian clothes for jail clothes, and assigning prisoners to housing areas based on their charge classifications.

Deputy Escott has completed almost two years at Lawson State College. He is transferring to the University of Alabama at Birmingham, where he will major in criminal justice.

His advice to persons interested in working in a jail? "Treat people like you want to be treated. Yeah, they're prisoners and they broke the law. For that they're in here for punishment. But if I'm going to like my job I have to get along with everybody, prisoners and staff. That means treating everyone with respect and hopefully getting it back in return." For Deputy Escott, the most gratifying part of the job is helping an inmate who really wants help.

> " When I work with an inmate and help him change his life, it's extremely gratifying. But the inmate has to want to change. He has to want help. I can't force it. A lot of prisoners want to know you'll help them and give them a chance. That's all. "

can help officers find satisfaction in their work by setting clearly defined goals, identifying the officer's job obligations and performance expectations, and providing jail officers adequate organizational resources to perform their jobs. These are the same factors that contribute to employee satisfaction whether in education, health care, or insurance.

Jail Issues

Jail administration and staff will face many important issues in the 21st century. We will now consider some of these issues and their effects on corrections professionals.

PRIVATIZATION

privatization

A contract process that shifts public functions, responsibilities, and capital assets, in whole or in part, from the public sector to the private sector.

Privatization is defined as a contract process that shifts public functions, responsibilities, and capital assets, in whole or in part, from the public sector to the private sector. We expand on the issue of *correctional* privatization in Chapter 13. Our focus here is on *jail* privatization.

Jails can be privatized in one of three ways: through private management, private sector development, or private services provision. In private management, private firms have total responsibility for the operation of a facility. This is the most common application of the term *privatization* and the most controversial aspect of the private sector's involvement in corrections.

In private sector development, the private sector develops, designs, and finances or arranges for the financing of jails. This often involves owning the jail and leasing it back to the jurisdiction through a lease/purchase contract, which serves as an alternative to a public bond issue or outright tax increase.

In private services provision, jails contract with private vendors to run services such as health and dental care, alcohol and drug treatment, mental health services, food service, training, and programming. This is the most familiar privatization model and the least controversial.

The debate between proponents and opponents of jail privatization surfaced early and continues today. Pressures for privatization come from escalating costs and crowded jails as well as from general dissatisfaction with county government. Jail privatization is sometimes seen as a practical option when a jurisdiction needs to update facilities quickly in response to a court order for additional capacity. Advocates of privatization claim that private operators can operate facilities more efficiently and cost-effectively.

Opponents of jail privatization dismiss cost comparisons—dispute them altogether. Some insist that the fundamental point is that it is the responsibility of local governments to operate jails, not to delegate power and liability. Opponents believe that the administration of justice is a basic function of government and a symbol of state authority and should not be delegated. From this perspective, jails are, as John J. DiIulio Jr., University of Pennsylvania professor of Politics, Religion, and Civil Society put it, "a public trust to be administered on behalf of the community and in the name of civility and justice."[38]

Opponents also fear that if we privatize jails, we risk enabling private corporations to use their political influence to continue programs not in the public interest. For example, would private contractors keep jail occupancy rates high to maintain profit? Might private contractors accept only the best inmates, leaving the most troublesome for public facilities to handle?

Turning a jail over to a private corporation also raises questions about accountability. Who is responsible for monitoring the performance of the private contractor? Who will see that local laws and regulations are followed? As jail incarceration rates continue to rise, the debate over privatizing jails and the competition for new contracts will continue.

After reviewing the pros and cons of jail privatization, Chang and Tillman concluded, "It is good to have private management as a viable alternative that plays the role of checking and balancing the public sector management. Whether county jails should be privatized depends on how well jails are managed in keeping costs of operation low and preparing inmates for their after-release adaptation to mainstream society. As Kerle stated, 'A badly run jail . . . would be an inviting target for privatization.'"[39]

Professional associations have addressed jail privatization through policy statements that range from cautious (American Corrections Association) to negative (American Jail Association and the National Sheriff's Association). The American Federation of State, County and Municipal Employees has been opposed from the beginning, and the American Bar Association has urged a moratorium until more information is available.

OVERCROWDING

Even though by mid-2002, only 93 percent of jail capacity was occupied, overcrowding is the most critical problem in large urban jails. As already mentioned, one-third of the largest 25 jails in the United States were operating at over 100 percent of their rated capacity in 2002.

Reflections on the Future

Betting people who worked in the world of American local corrections in the year 1990 probably would have been lost if asked to predict the number of jail inmates in the United States over the next decade. Who would have guessed that 200,000 jail inmates would be added in the ensuing 10 years! This 1990's growth occurred despite a drop in crime and arrests, the slowing of the inmate population increase, and failing jail occupancy rates. A knowledgeable corrections statistician writing about growth in the first 10 years of this new century posited four different patterns, spanning the continuum of rapid growth to small growth.[1] Jails still receive Bureau of Citizenship and Immigration Services (formerly INS) prisoners from the Department of Homeland Security and the U.S. Marshals, which helps to fill some of the empty beds after a decade of jail expansion.

California voters passed proposition 36 in November 2000, mandating the sentencing of non-violent substance abusers into community punishment/treatment programs.[2] This will cause a substantial decline in the number of California jail inmates who use drugs recreationally. Coincident with this change has been the decision of the U.S. Supreme Court to review two cases under the California sentencing "three strikes" laws. Twenty-five other states also passed three strikes legislation in the mid-1990s.[3] A hotly debated topic of the California law is whether prosecutors have the discretion to charge certain third offenses as felonies rather than misdemeanors, which results in mandatory lengthy sentences for those so convicted.[4] The three strikes law impacted jails when people who were arrested (and facing their third strike) refused to plea bargain and demanded a jury trial, resulting in a lengthy jail stay, which crowded the jails.[5]

Good news for jail staff is the American Jail Association's collaboration with a state university in Kansas to offer a college degree based on the distance learning concept. Jail officers can do their course studies on the computer on their own time and avoid the difficulty of shift scheduling to attend classes on campus. More women are now jail administrators. The 1990 first edition of *Who's Who in Jail Management* identified 150 female jail administrators; by the 3d edition (1999) the number had increased to 500.[6]

NOTES
1. Allen J. Beck, "Jail Population Growth: National Trends and Predictors of Future Growth," *American Jails* (May/June 2002): 9.
2. William Booth, "California Drug Users Get Treatment, Not Jail," *The Washington Post* (August 13, 2001,): A-1.
3. J. W. Barbrey and Keith E. Clement, "An Investigation into the Hybridization of State Sentencing Schemes," Parts I and II, *American Jails* (July/August 2001): 23 and (September/October 2001): 27.
4. Charles Lane, "Court to Review 'Three Strikes,'" *The Washington Post* (April 2, 2002): A-2.
5. *Pretrial Reporter* (December 1995): 11–12.
6. American Jail Association, *Who's Who in Jail Management* (Hagerstown, MD).

ABOUT THE AUTHOR
Ken Kerle has been managing editor of *American Jails,* a publication of the American Jails Association, since 1986. He has visited over 900 jails and prisons in the United States and 21 foreign countries. Kerle is author of *Exploring Jail Operations* (American Correctional Association, 2004). He received his Ph.D. from American University.

Jail crowding has a number of causes, including mandatory arrests and sentences, overcrowding at state and federal prisons, and an overall increase in the arrest rate as politicians "get tough" on crime. Crowded jails have serious health and safety consequences for staff and inmates, including decreased quality of life; overloaded educational, vocational, and recreational programs; insufficient medical services and supplies; increased discipline problems; spread of disease; and staff and inmate assaults.

WAYS TO REDUCE JAIL OVERCROWDING

Practices that can reduce crowding include creating an analytical process for the collection, analysis, and discussion of jail data, financial and nonfinancial pretrial release, diversion, and new jail construction.

THE OFFENDER SPEAKS

Create an Analytical Process   In 2002, the National Institute of Corrections raised the bar on ways to control jail crowding, from nuts and bolts approaches to analytical thinking.[40] According to NIC, the key to prevent crowding is continuously to collect, monitor, and analyze admission and length-of-stay information and then to share the results with other justice officials and with officials in leadership positions in general government such as the judiciary, the mayor, and county commissioners. Collectively, these officials control the policies and practices that determine jail admissions and length of stay. Jail administrators and sheriffs can exert a great deal of influence on the decision making of other agencies. However, only if they have the facts can they competently answer questions about how the jail population is changing and clearly demonstrate how changes in admission rates or lengths of stay can improve the administration of justice. As Mark Cunniff writes, "A county must ascertain changing jail usage and the forces at play in its jail system before it can implement effective programs and measures to alleviate jail crowding, including the construction of new jail beds."[41]

> A county must ascertain changing jail usage and the forces at play in its jail system before it can implement effective programs and measures to alleviate jail crowding, including the construction of new jail beds.

Financial Pretrial Release   Financial pretrial release programs are one alternative to the pretrial detention of accused offenders. Releasing a person upon that person's financial guarantee to appear in court is known as **release on bail.** The Eighth Amendment to the United States Constitution reads, "Excessive bail shall not be required, nor excessive fines imposed, nor cruel and unusual punishments inflicted." The Constitution does not guarantee defendants an automatic right to bail—only protection from excessive bail. The defendant has the option to post the full amount of the bail, secure the amount privately through a bail bondsman, or deposit a percentage (usually 10 percent) with the court.

release on bail
The release of a person upon that person's financial guarantee to appear in court.

Nonfinancial Pretrial Release   An alternative form of pretrial release requires only the defendant's promise to appear in court as required. This release without a cash guarantee is called **release on own recognizance (ROR).** Generally, information about defendants is gathered and verified to determine the appropriateness of nonfinancial pretrial release.

release on own recognizance (ROR)
Pretrial release on the defendant's promise to appear for trial. It requires no cash guarantee.

citation

A type of nonfinancial pretrial release similar to a traffic ticket. It binds the defendant to appear in court on a future date.

supervised pretrial release

Nonfinancial pretrial release with more restrictive conditions (for example, participating in therapeutic or rehabilitative programs, reporting to a pretrial officer, and checking in regularly).

conditional release

Pretrial release under minimal or moderately restrictive conditions with little monitoring of compliance. It includes ROR, supervised pretrial release, and third-party release.

Another type of nonfinancial pretrial release is a **citation.** Similar to traffic tickets, citations are issued by police in some jurisdictions for misdemeanors such as disorderly conduct. A citation binds the defendant to appear in court on a future date. It places no conditions on the released person's behavior and requires no payment to guarantee the court appearance.

In the 1960s and 1970s, a new form of nonfinancial pretrial release emerged. Called **supervised pretrial release,** it imposes more restrictive conditions on defendants. The conditions often include participating in therapeutic or rehabilitative programs, reporting to a pretrial officer, and checking in regularly. During the same period, a third-party release option developed. A third party—such as the defendant's lawyer, family, or employer or a social service agency—assumes responsibility for the defendant's appearance in court.

Programs such as ROR, supervised pretrial release, and third-party release are all forms of **conditional release.** They impose minimal or moderately restrictive conditions with little monitoring of compliance. In a number of jurisdictions across the United States today, electronic monitoring is also being used as part of conditional release.

Diversion Another way jail crowding can be reduced is through the expanded use of diversion. Diversion, as we learned in Chapter 4, means referring defendants to non–criminal-justice agencies for services instead of processing them through the criminal justice system. For example, people with substance abuse problems can be diverted to treatment centers. Jail inmates with mental disorders can be referred to mental health clinics, where they receive both treatment and custodial supervision. After accepting diversion, a defendant is required to cooperate and participate in treatment, whether or not he or she feels it is necessary. Failure to show progress may lead to reinstatement of charges.

New Construction New construction is another way to reduce jail crowding. Proponents of new construction argue that jail incarceration is here to stay. Because the public supports jails, we have a responsibility to build them. Opponents argue that if we continue to add new beds to the nation's jails, we will fill up all the space we create. In other words, some believe that availability drives up occupancy. They also claim that most nonviolent pretrial detainees and convicted offenders do not need to be in jail and that it wastes resources to house them there.

EDUCATIONAL AND VOCATIONAL PROGRAMS

Many jail inmates have poor reading skills. National studies show that more than 40 percent of all jail inmates have less than a ninth-grade education.[42] They also have substance abuse problems and few job skills. They frequently cannot find jobs after they are released or can find only low-paid or temporary work. As a result, in part, they often return to a life of crime.

Too many jails simply warehouse inmates and care little about education or job skills. It costs taxpayers money to provide educational services to jail inmates—the same people who already have financially and psychologically burdened society through their crimes. Education does not guarantee that an offender will remain free of crime upon release. However, consider the alternative: More than 40 percent of defendants on pretrial release have one or more prior convictions. The cost of keeping one inmate in jail for one year ranges from $20,000 to $40,000. Studies also show that inmates who earn their GEDs while incarcerated are far less likely to return to crime. Educational and vocational programs help offenders help themselves, they boost self-esteem, and they encourage legitimate occupations upon release. Overall, it costs less to educate offenders and teach them job skills than to do nothing to change their attitudes, abilities, and outlooks. Ignoring an offender's educational and vocational deficiencies leaves the offender with fewer marketable skills or qualifications when released, increasing the chance of a return to crime.

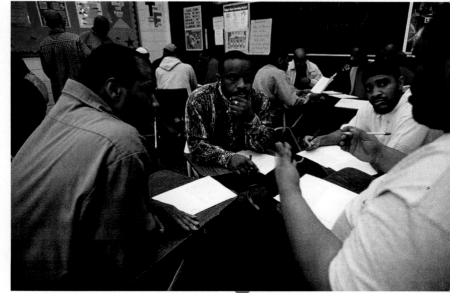

Small groups of jail inmates discuss job interviews. Educational and vocational programs help offenders help themselves, boost self-esteem, and encourage legitimate occupations upon release. What do you believe will happen if educational and vocational programs are not available for jail prisoners?

Recently, the Orange County, Florida, Jail—one of the largest in the nation, with 3,300 beds—began an innovative strategy.[43] The entire jail—the operation, budget, and architecture—now revolves around its educational and vocational programs. The jail offers inmates a wide range of structured educational and vocational programs designed to fit inmates' short stays. The jail provides job readiness and placement services. It offers inmates valuable incentives to participate in programs and to avoid misconduct. And it uses the design and philosophy of third-generation jails, discussed earlier in this chapter, to manage inmates in a way that contains costs, promote inmate responsibility, and create classrooms in open areas. According to the National Institute of Justice, "Each of these features is part of a comprehensive corrections strategy that enables programming to flourish at the same time that it saves the county money, keeps inmates occupied and out of trouble, and (it is hoped) reduces recidivism."[44]

The principal steps in the Orange County Jail's educational and vocational programs are presented in Figure 6–6. The jail provides unusually intensive educational and vocational opportunities to most of its inmates. Five features are very important to the success of the programs: incentives for participation, direct supervision, active support by corrections officers, cooperation from schools, and programs tailored to short jail stays.

> ▶ Sometimes administrators must make hard decisions when faced with budget cuts. As a jail administrator, you must cut one position, either a correctional officer or teacher. Which position will you cut? Why? For more information go to Ethical Dilemma 6-2 at http://www.mhhe.com/schmalleger2.
>
> **Ethical Dilemma**

RELIGIOUS PROGRAMS IN JAIL

Very little is written about the use and effects of religion in jail. Too often the topic is looked at skeptically by outsiders, who believe that inmates pretend to "find God" as a convenient way to obtain release or forgiveness.

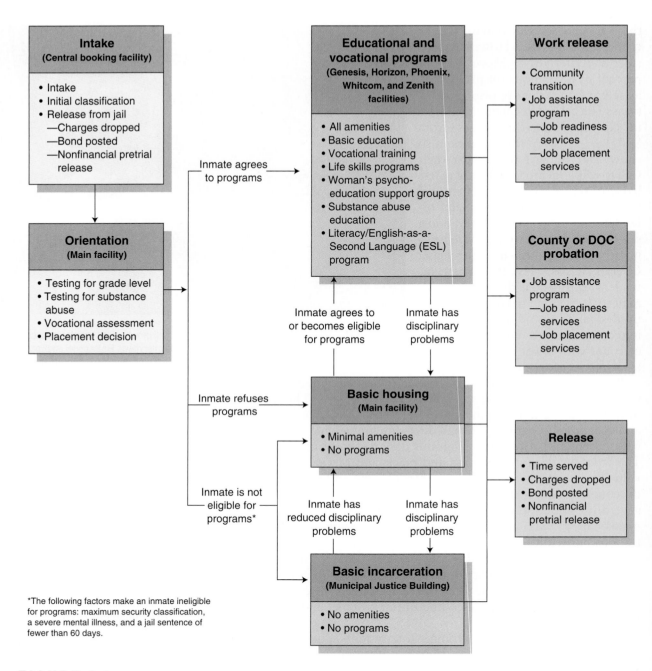

FIGURE 6-6
Orange County, Florida, Jail Educational and Vocational Programs

Source: National Institute of Justice, *The Orange County, Florida, Jail Educational and Vocational Programs* (Washington, DC: U.S. Department of Justice, 1997).

Getting into trouble and then turning to religion is supported by the "coping" literature, which links major life events to a greater tendency to turn to spirituality or religion. However, what we will explore here is not the research supporting the veracity of inmates' claims of conversion but instead the partnership between government and faith-based organizations to meet the nation's corrections needs. We will also consider the experiences of those who minister to jail inmates.

Religious belief can make a difference in people's lives and can assist in tackling social problems. Much crime is the result of people making the wrong moral choices. Churches and religious organizations can provide the moral and spiritual aspects to correctional programs. There are not enough correctional officers, probation or parole officers, or police to prevent every ex-offender from committing another crime, and help from other partners is needed. As President George W. Bush said, "Government cannot be replaced by charities, but it can and should welcome them as partners." Pat Nolan, vice president of Prison Fellowship Ministries writes, "The way society will be able to reduce crime is if during their time of incarceration, offenders have been transformed and internalized a moral code that allows them to exercise self-restraint and be good citizens after they are released. . . . It will be helpful to look upon local churches as partners to help teach inmates these important lessons during their incarceration and to act as mentors as they re-enter their communities."[45]

Recently researchers conducted a study to investigate the impact of religious programs on two matched groups of adult male prisoners in New York.[46] They found that inmates most actively involved in Bible studies (meaning they attended 10 or more classes over the course of one year) were less likely than inmates who attended fewer classes (or none) to commit institutional infractions, or if they did, the infractions were not as serious as the infractions of those who attended fewer classes (or none); and inmates most actively involved in Bible studies were less likely than inmates who attended fewer classes (or none) to be arrested during a one-year follow-up.

A faith-based organization encourages jail inmates to form a circle and ask their victims for forgiveness. Major life events like incarceration are linked to a greater tendency to turn to spirituality or religion. What do you think is the role of religion in jail?

The researchers tell us that religion and spirituality can be empowering to prisoners who find themselves alone and in trouble. Others agree, noting that participation in religious activities can inhibit adult crime.[47]

Those who minister to jail inmates tell us there are at least five benefits of jail chaplaincy. First, most jail chaplains believe that the cycle of crime can only be broken one life at a time. Jail inmates must experience an inner conversion before they change their behavior. Jail chaplains can assist in that conversion. Second, jail chaplains can help jail staff with their emotional and family problems. An on-site chaplain can help staff deal with problems daily, as they develop. Third, jail chaplains are in a unique position to mediate and moderate tensions and conflicts between inmates and staff before they get serious. Pleading for nonviolence is a chaplain's strong tool. Inmates usually see a jail chaplain as neutral—not as "one of them." The chaplain has the unique opportunity to speak his or her mind and be seen as someone who cares enough to confront and comfort. Fourth, the public perceives ministering to the disadvantaged as legitimate, and so such ministry helps the community remember those they would just as soon forget (recall the concept of inmates as "rabble," discussed earlier in this chapter). In the role as community liaisons, chaplains help raise the awareness about and sensitivity to jail issues and interests. The ability of chaplains to involve the public as jail volunteers is an added benefit. And fifth, jail chaplains can help inmates confront the truth about themselves and reverse the "everything is relative" attitude that offenders develop to justify their crimes.

In the following excerpt, a chaplain shares some thoughts about his two years on the job:[48]

> A chaplain occupies a unique place in an inmate's thinking. She or he is not seen as "one of them"; we are not associated so much with the institution or judicial system. That gives us unique opportunities to speak openly and be viewed not as someone who has a sinister hidden agenda, but as someone who cares enough to confront.

JAIL ACCREDITATION

accreditation
Process through which correctional facilities and agencies can measure themselves against nationally adopted standards and through which they can receive formal recognition and accredited status.

jail accreditation
Formal approval of a jail by the American Correctional Association (ACA) and the Commission on Accreditation.

Accreditation is a process through which correctional facilities and agencies can measure themselves against nationally adopted standards and through which they can receive formal recognition and accredited status. We will expand on the issue of correctional accreditation in Chapter 13. The focus here is on jail accreditation.

Jail accreditation is the formal approval of a jail by the American Correctional Association (ACA) and the Commission on Accreditation. The ACA and the commission have developed standards for the services, programs, and operations they consider essential to good jail management. The standards cover administrative and fiscal concerns, staff training and development, the physical plant, safety and emergency procedures, sanitation, food service, and rules and discipline. Standards are divided into two categories. To be accredited, a jail must have 100 percent compliance with mandatory standards and 90 percent compliance with nonmandatory standards. Accreditation is valid for three years. Then the jail may apply for reaccreditation and receive another on-site audit by ACA staff and an accreditation hearing.

Very few jails followed established standards or policies before the 1960s. Several reasons for this have been suggested, including the traditional independence of sheriffs, who operate the jails in most jurisdictions, and the tendency of most sheriffs to focus on law enforcement rather than on corrections.

Although jails were slow to respond to the standards movement, their response has picked up in recent years. On April 29, 1986, and then again on May 19, 1993, the American Jail Association passed a resolution urging all jails to become involved in the accreditation process. Today, 3 percent of the nation's jails are ACA accredited. The Mecklenburg County Jail (Charlotte, North Carolina), with 1,850 inmates and 850 detention and civilian staff, became the latest jail (and the only jail in North Carolina) to receive accreditation by ACA on January 13, 2003. Mecklenburg County Sheriff Jim Pendergraph told the audience at the accreditation ceremony, "Achieving accreditation within one year of starting the process speaks volumes to the professionalism of the Sheriff's Office staff and the willingness of the taxpayers to support our vision of being recognized as a leading and professional organization. Having accredited facilities means that buildings last longer, staff and inmates remain safe, and employees stay longer with the Sheriff's Office. All this leads to more efficient use of the tax dollars entrusted to us. Again, Mecklenburg County leads the way for other communities around the country."[49]

There are several reasons jails have been slow to adopt national standards or seek national accreditation. First, accreditation is expensive and time-consuming. Many jails do not have the resources to commit to it. This is especially true of small jails that are already overburdened. Approximately 2,000 U.S. jails are designed to hold fewer than 50 inmates. Second, jails hold relatively few long-term inmates. Few inmates are in a jail long enough to file a successful legal action regarding poor conditions in the jail. Knowing this, some jail administrators may not be willing to undergo the expense and burden of seeking accreditation. Third, some states have their own standards that jails must meet.

There are, however, at least four reasons for jails to have national accreditation:

1. Accreditation by the ACA and the Commission on Accreditation indicates that a jail adheres to strict standards to protect the health and safety of staff and inmates.

2. Being accredited may help a jail defend itself against lawsuits over conditions of incarceration. For example, in 1999, Thelma Grayson filed suit in Federal Court after her client, Gerald Collins, was found dead the day after he was arrested and transported to the Fairfax County (Virginia) Adult Detention Center. Grayson alleged that the arresting officer, the sheriff in charge of the detention center, and Fairfax County had violated Collins's constitutional rights. However, the Court found that Grayson's own expert penologist conceded that the sheriff's policies met the standards of both the Virginia Board of Corrections and the American Correctional Association. At the time of the incident, the Adult Detention Center had been accredited for more than 10 years by both the American Correctional Association and the National

Commission on Correctional Health Care, two organizations whose training requirements often surpass minimal constitutional standards.

3. In preparing for the accreditation review, the sheriff's office may evaluate all operations, procedures, and policies, leading to better management practices.

4. With accreditation come professional recognition and status, greater appreciation by the community, and a sense of pride in the achievement and in the hard work that went into it.

JAIL STAFF AS PROFESSIONALS

Jail staff assume enormous responsibility, and we expect them to conduct themselves as professionals. Before 1970, training and education for jail officers were virtually nonexistent, for several reasons. Jail officers often aspired to be law enforcement officers, or they were using jail work as their last stop on the road to retirement. Many people also believed that education and training for jail staff were unnecessary because the work was unsophisticated and could be learned on the job.

Since 1970, however, the image of jail staff has changed. Thanks to organizations such as the American Jail Association and the American Correctional Association, national, state, and local commissions on jail issues, and studies by practitioners, consultants, and academic researchers, jail work is now recognized not only as difficult but also as a career path that is different from law enforcement and requires different attitudes and skills. Jail staff perform work that is vital, complex, and potentially hazardous, even under the best of circumstances.

To conduct themselves as professionals, jail staff must have strong communication skills, knowledge of the psychology of behavior, multicultural sophistication, ethnic and racial tolerance, human management expertise, endurance, and fitness. Even more important, they must, for their own mental well-being, be able to understand and tolerate the stress of a potentially explosive environment. The American Jail Association's Code of Ethics for Jail Officers is shown in Exhibit 6–2.

The trend toward better educated and trained jail staff is evident across the United States. There are tougher entrance requirements. Applicants must have a higher level of education, increased basic training, more experience, other related skills, and the appropriate personality. Jail staff also learn to conduct themselves as professionals.

Many departments require applicants to have completed a correctional officer training and education program. There are a number of advantages to the policy. First, a department can hire certified correctional officers without paying for training. Second, the department can ask training program staff about applicants' abilities, reliability, and other relevant issues. And third, new jail officers will have the needed skills and an essential understanding of the job.

In 1978, the American Correctional Association pioneered correctional accreditation. In 1999, it embarked on another milestone in the process of bringing professionalism into corrections by developing a national Commission on Correctional Certification.

EXHIBIT 6-2 American Jail Association

Code of Ethics for Jail Officers

As an officer employed in a detention/correctional capacity, I swear (or affirm) to be a good citizen and a credit to my community, state, and nation at all times. I will abstain from questionable behavior which might bring disrepute to the agency for which I work, my family, my community, and my associates. My lifestyle will be above and beyond reproach, and I will constantly strive to set an example of a professional who performs his/her duties according to the laws of our country, state, and community and the policies, procedures, written and verbal orders, and regulations of the agency for which I work.

On the job I promise to

KEEP the institution secure so as to safeguard my community and the lives of the staff, inmates, and visitors on the premises.

WORK with each individual firmly and fairly without regard to rank, status, or condition.

MAINTAIN a positive demeanor when confronted with stressful situations of scorn, ridicule, danger, and/or chaos.

REPORT either in writing or by word of mouth to the proper authorities those things which should be reported and keep silent about matters which are to remain confidential according to the laws and rules of the agency and government.

MANAGE and supervise the inmates in an evenhanded and courteous manner.

REFRAIN at all times from becoming personally involved in the lives of the inmates and their families.

TREAT all visitors to the jail with politeness and respect and do my utmost to ensure that they observe the jail regulations.

TAKE advantage of all education and training opportunities designed to assist me to become a more competent officer.

COMMUNICATE with people in or outside of the jail, whether by phone, written word, or word of mouth, in such a way so as not to reflect in a negative manner upon my agency.

CONTRIBUTE to a jail environment which will keep the inmate involved in activities designed to improve his/her attitude and character.

SUPPORT all activities of a professional nature through membership and participation that will continue to elevate the status of those who operate our nation's jails. Do my best through word and deed to present an image to the public at large of a jail professional, committed to progress for an improved and enlightened criminal justice system.

Adopted by the American Jail Association Board of Directors on November 10, 1991. Revised May 19, 1993.

Just as accreditation provides an opportunity for facilities to be recognized, certification is an opportunity for jail staff to be recognized as qualified correctional practitioners. The ACA certification process requires applicants to meet the educational requirements of the category within which they seek certification (for example, the category of correctional executive requires a college degree; correctional managers and supervisors require an associate degree; correctional officers require a high school diploma). Next, applicants must pass a national examination developed by the National Institute of Corrections for the job tasks and related competencies associated with the job category. Third, applications enter into "candidacy status," a two-year period during which they must pass a certification examination. Those who pass the certification exam become Certified Correctional Professionals for three years. Maintaining that status involves becoming recertified and obtaining a specified number of continuing education credits. Through the efforts of the ACA's Commission on Correctional Certification, jail personnel are on the road to upgrading their public image and professional stature and achieving the status of other professions that rely on universal compliance with a self-imposed credentialing process.

SUMMARY

1▶ There are 3,365 locally operated jails in the United States. Besides incarcerating people who have sentences of a year or less, jails serve a number of purposes. They hold people awaiting trial, probation and parole violators, adults and juveniles awaiting transfer, and prison inmates about to be released. Sometimes they operate community-based programs. The jail population is different from the prison population in terms of total admissions and average daily population.

2▶ Jails emerged in Europe in the 12th century to detain offenders for trial. In the 15th and 16th centuries, the poor and unemployed were detained alongside criminals. The first jail in America was the Walnut Street Jail. Quakers designed it according to their principles of religious reflection and penance. It fell short of reaching its goals and closed in 1835.

3▶ American jails have progressed through three phases of architecture and inmate management: first-generation jails (linear design and sporadic supervision), second-generation jails (pod design and remote supervision), and third-generation jails (pod design and direct supervision).

4▶ By mid-2002, jails held or supervised 737,912 offenders, an increase of 5.4 percent from mid-2001. An estimated 266,190 (40 percent) of jail inmates are convicted offenders. Women represent 12 percent of the jail population; nonwhites, 56 percent; and juveniles, 1.1 percent. By mid-2002, 93 percent of jail capacity was occupied. Jails that hold between 500-999 inmates reported the highest rates of occupancy. Forty-seven jails are privatized. The most (eight) are in Texas. Almost 300,000 people work in jails. The increase in the jail population is outpacing the growth in jail staff. The problems of jail staff include low pay and prestige, high turnover, and inadequate systems for recruitment, selection, and training.

5▶ Advocates of privatization claim they can build and operate jails more efficiently than government. Opponents argue they cannot, or they dismiss the cost issues altogether. For them, operating a jail is a basic function of government and a symbol of state authority and should not be delegated.

6 ▶ Jail crowding can be reduced by creating a process for the collection, analysis, and discussion of jail data, through financial and nonfinancial pretrial release, through diversion, and through new jail construction.

7 ▶ Jail vocational and educational programs are important avenues for managing inmates and reducing recidivism. They keep inmates occupied, they boost self-esteem, and they help inmates find jobs after release.

8 ▶ Jails are partnering with faith-based organizations to meet the needs of jail inmates. Jail chaplaincy can influence jail inmates in five ways. First, chaplains can help inmates with the inner conversion needed to break the cycle of crime. Second, a jail chaplain can help staff deal with day-to-day problems. Third, a jail chaplain can mediate and moderate tensions and conflicts between inmates and staff. Fourth, jail chaplaincy can involve the public as jail volunteers and remind people that inmates exist. And fifth, chaplains can help inmates confront the truth about themselves.

9 ▶ Jail accreditation is important for four reasons. First, accreditation indicates that a jail adheres to strict standards. Second, accreditation may help a jail defend itself against lawsuits over conditions of incarceration. Third, through accreditation, the sheriff's office may evaluate all jail operations, procedures, and policies, leading to better management practices. And fourth, accreditation generates professional recognition and status, greater appreciation by the community, and a sense of pride.

10 ▶ It is important for jail staff to conduct themselves as professionals because jail work is difficult and carries enormous responsibility. It requires a special attitude, communication skills, knowledge of the psychology of behavior, multicultural sophistication, endurance, and fitness. Together, college education and jail training prepare jail staff to work as professionals. In 1999, the American Correctional Association established the Commission on Correctional Certification (CCC). The purpose of the CCC is to recognize jail staff as qualified correctional practitioners using a self-imposed credentialing process.

KEY TERMS

jails, *p. 203*
total admission, *p. 203*
average daily population (ADP), *p. 203*
rabble management, *p. 207*
first-generation jail, *p. 208*
second-generation jail, *p. 208*

third-generation jail, *p. 209*
rated capacity *p. 217*
privatization, *p. 222*
release on bail, *p. 225*
release on own recognizance (ROR), *p. 225*
citation, *p. 226*

supervised pretrial release, *p. 226*
conditional release, *p. 226*
accreditation, *p. 230*
jail accreditation, *p. 230*

REVIEW & APPLICATIONS

QUESTIONS FOR REVIEW

1. Explain the difference between *total admission* and *average daily population*. Why is the distinction important in understanding the difference between jail and prison?
2. How many people did jails hold and supervise in 2002?
3. What are the main purposes of jails?
4. How many jails are there in the United States?
5. When and where was the first jail built? What was the purpose of this jail?
6. Who was John Howard?
7. What was the first jail in America, and when was it built?
8. Explain what John Irwin meant by *rabble management*.
9. Describe how first-, second-, and third-generation jails differ in terms of architecture and philosophy of inmate management.
10. As of 2002, how many women, minorities, and juveniles were in jail and why?
11. What is *rated capacity*, and how much jail capacity was occupied in 2002?
12. Why is staffing a problem in jail, and what can be done about it?
13. List some arguments against jail privatization.
14. Outline some strategies to reduce jail crowding.
15. Why are educational and vocational programs for inmates important for jail management?
16. How can faith-based organizations and jail chaplaincy be positive forces in the jail environment?
17. What are the advantages and disadvantages of jail accreditation?
18. List some characteristics of a professional jail employee and explain what the American Correctional Association is doing to help jail staff upgrade their public image and professional stature.

THINKING CRITICALLY ABOUT CORRECTIONS

▶ ▶ ▶ **Pretrial Release**

When deciding whether to grant pretrial release, a judge looks at the offense, the evidence, and the defendant's family ties, employment, financial resources, character, mental condition, length of residence in the community, and criminal record. To which of these do you think the judge should give the greatest weight? Why?

▶ ▶ ▶ **Faith-Based Organizations**

President Bush has said that faith-based organizations can help meet the nation's needs. What needs can they meet in jail and how?

ON-THE-JOB DECISION MAKING

▶ ▶ ▶ Promoting a Third-Generation Jail

You are the administrator of a new county jail with the architecture and philosophy of direct supervision. The new jail replaced a jail built in 1912. Some of the senior staff have begun complaining to you about direct supervision. They say they don't like to interact with inmates. They talk about "the good old days" when inmates were "on the other side" of the reinforced glass and steel bars. There's even been a letter to the editor in the local newspaper complaining that the new jail doesn't "look like a jail."

1. What could you tell the senior staff about third-generation philosophy and architecture that might ease their concerns?

2. What strategies might you use to educate the public about the benefits of direct supervision?

▶ ▶ ▶ Reducing Jail Crowding

Jail crowding is a problem across the country. Imagine you are the sheriff of a large urban county with a megajail (more than 1,000 beds), and your jail is overcrowded. Since you are an elected official and would like to be re-elected, you don't want to appear "soft on crime," yet you know you can't build your way out of the crowding problem. There's simply not enough money to expand the jail or build a new one. How do you argue in favor of reducing jail crowding?

CORRECTIONS ON THE WEB

▶ ▶ ▶ Jail Web Pages

Carefully read the mission statement on the Niagara County Sheriff's Department Web page (http://www.ncsd.com). What emphasis does the mission statement give to jail operations? If possible, look at the Web pages of other jail facilities and review their mission statements. What do you think the ideal mission statement should say about jail operations?

▶ ▶ ▶ American Correctional Association Accreditation

Visit the Website of the American Correctional Association at http://www.aca.org. Click on *Accreditation and Standards*. Learn more about correctional accreditation by reading the FAQs, benefits of accreditation, and agency testimonials. Search the site for accredited facilities and programs in your area.

REVIEW & APPLICATIONS

Within the image (signage):

NO CAMERAS
BEYOND
THIS POINT.

NO FIREARMS
ALLOWED
BEYOND THIS
POINT

YOU ARE ENTERING
A TOBACCO FREE
ENVIRONMENT. THE
USE OF TOBACCO
OR TOBACCO
RELATED PRODUCTS
IS PROHIBITED.

USTED ESTA
ENTRANDO A UN
AMBIENTE LIBRE DE
TABACO. EL USO
DE TABACO O
PRODUCTOS DE
TABACO ES
PROHIBIDO.

3205

"When society places a person behind walls and bars, it has an obligation—a moral obligation—to do whatever can reasonably be done to change that person before he or she goes back into the stream of society."

—Warren Burger, Former United States Supreme Court Chief Justice, 1981

7

Prisons Today: Change Stations or Warehouses?

▶ CHAPTER OBJECTIVES

After completing this chapter you should be able to do the following:

1. Explain the differences between the Pennsylvania and Auburn prison systems.

2. Outline the nine eras of prison development.

3. Describe the characteristics of today's prisoners and discuss reasons for the incarceration of women and minority prisoners.

4. Explain prisoner classification and its purposes.

5. Explain the three types of prison work programs.

6. Report on the availability of education, recreation, and health care programs for prisoners.

7. Compare state and federal prison organization and administration.

8. Discuss the question "Does incarceration work?"

For nine days beginning October 25, 1994, the nation was riveted by the account of a 23-year-old mother that a black car jacker had abducted her two sons, 14-month-old Alex and 3-year-old Michael. Susan Smith, the young mother, and her ex-husband David stood before television cameras in Union, South Carolina, crying and begging the abductor to return the children. Then, on November 3, Susan Smith confessed to the children's disappearance. She explained that she had released the emergency brake on her 1990 Mazda and watched the car roll into the John D. Long Lake while her sons were sleeping in car seats in the backseat.

Defense attorneys and prosecutors presented different images of Smith's crime to the jury. The prosecutor called her a cold-blooded killer who drowned her children to win the affection of a man she was dating who did not like the boys. Her lawyers, on the other hand, described her as a deeply disturbed and depressed woman who was sexually molested by her stepfather and who twice had attempted suicide.

The jury found Susan Smith guilty on two counts of murder. Instead of sentencing her to the death penalty, however, the jury gave her life in prison. Smith is serving her sentence at the Leath Correctional Institution in Greenwood, South Carolina. Under South Carolina law, Smith will be eligible for parole in 2025, although the infamous nature of her crime makes it unlikely that she will ever be released.

Today, Susan Smith is one of 97,491 women in prison in the United States and one of almost 1,700 women in prison in South Carolina. While women represent only 6.8 percent of the nation's prison population, they are the fastest growing

In 1994, Susan Smith, a young South Carolina mother claimed that a black car-jacker abducted her two sons. A month later she confessed that she released the emergency brake and watched the car roll into the John D. Long Lake while her sons were sleeping in the backseat. If you were Smith's prison counselor, what kind of treatment would you recommend?

population in prison today. The annual growth rate of the female inmate population has averaged 5.2 percent since 1995, a rate higher than the 3.5 percent average increase of male inmates. Thirty-seven percent of all women prisoners are incarcerated in Texas (13,051), the Federal Bureau of Prisons (BOP) (11,234), and California (10,050). Later in this chapter, we will learn more about female inmates. We begin the chapter with a look at the history of American prisons. Then we will discuss the composition of the prison population, programs for prisoners, and the way America's prisons are organized and administered. We will conclude with the question "Does incarceration work?"

History of Prisons in America

Prisons are relatively modern social institutions, and their development is distinctly American. Until the mid-18th century, fines, banishment from the community, corporal punishment, and execution were the primary forms of punishing offenders. By the latter part of the century, incarceration was championed as a more humane form of punishment. It reflected and fueled a shift from the assumption that offenders were inherently criminal to a belief that they were simply not properly trained to resist temptation and corruption. The two prison systems that emerged in the United States—the Pennsylvania system and the Auburn system—were copied throughout the world.

The Pennsylvania and Auburn prison systems developed in the United States at the turn of the 19th century. Pennsylvania Quakers advocated a method of punishment more humane than the public corporal punishment used at the time. The Quakers shifted the emphasis from punishing the body to reforming the mind and soul. Together with an elite group of 18th-century Philadelphians, they ushered in the first **penitentiary,** a place for reform of offenders through repentance and rehabilitation. They believed prisoners needed to be isolated from each other in silence to repent, to accept God's guidance, and to avoid having a harmful influence on each other. Known as the **Pennsylvania system** or the separate system, this method was first used at the Walnut Street Jail, which the Quakers reorganized in 1790 as the country's first institution for punishment. The Eastern State Penitentiary, constructed in 1829, was also based on these principles. The prison was designed for solitary confinement at labor, with instruction in labor, morals, and religion. To make the isolation less severe and to help inmates prepare for employment after release, prison officials permitted inmates to work by themselves in their cells at various occupations, such as shoemaking, weaving, tailoring, and polishing marble. For the first time in American history, rehabilitation and deterrence emerged as goals of corrections.

The solitary confinement of the Pennsylvania system was expensive, and it reportedly drove prisoners insane and further hardened criminal tendencies. Reformers responded with what has been termed the **Auburn system:** regimentation, military-style drill, silence unless conversation was required

penitentiary

The earliest form of large-scale incarceration, it punished criminals by isolating them so that they could reflect on their misdeeds, repent, and reform.

Pennsylvania system

The first historical phase of prison discipline, involving solitary confinement in silence instead of corporal punishment. Conceived by the American Quakers in 1790 and implemented at the Walnut Street Jail.

Auburn system

The second historical phase of prison discipline. It followed the Pennsylvania system and allowed inmates to work silently together during the day but were isolated at night. Implemented at New York's Auburn prison in 1815, eventually sleeping cells became congregate and restrictions against talking were removed.

The Eastern State Penitentiary, completed in 1829, was designed on the Quakers' principles of solitary confinement in silence, with instruction in labor, morals, and religion. What name was given to this separate system of prisoner management?

in workshops, congregate working and eating, separation of prisoners into small individual cells at night, harsh discipline, shaved heads, black-and-white striped uniforms, and industrial workshops that contracted with private businesses to help pay for the institution. Prison factories in the 19th century produced shoes, barrels, carpets, engines, boilers, harnesses, clothing, and furniture—goods that could not be produced under the "solitary" system of Pennsylvania or not in quantities sufficient to make a profit. This merchandise was sold on the open market to American consumers or exported to Canada and Latin America, and the proceeds helped support prison operations. The first prison to use this system opened in Auburn, New York, in 1819. The Auburn system, congregate by day and separate by night, eventually gave way to congregate cells at night and removal of the restrictions against talking.

Prison reform in the United States caught the attention of prison officials around the world. The Pennsylvania system of isolation and silence became popular in Europe. In the United States, the two competing philosophies of prison life clashed, and the debate over which system was superior raged on for decades. Supporters of the Pennsylvania system argued that it made it easier to control prisoners and prevented prisoners from learning bad habits from each other. Supporters of the Auburn system claimed that prisoners' spirits needed to be broken before true reform could begin and that their system of harsh discipline and congregate but silent labor accomplished that. Auburn supporters also argued that their prison system was cheaper to build and that the use of contract labor would keep down costs.

A system that was congregate by day (and eventually by night as well) seemed more compatible with the political and economic tone of the time. The Pennsylvania system represented a traditional approach to production: handcrafted labor in solitary cells. In contrast, the Auburn system reflected the emerging developments of the Industrial Revolution: using power machinery, factory production, and division of labor. The attractiveness of the Auburn system's perceived economic benefits as well as a belief in the rehabilitative value of hard work settled the debate. Thus, the congregate system became the preferred model of incarceration in the United States. In 1913, Eastern State Penitentiary, the epitome of the Pennsylvania system, converted to the Auburn system, ending the great debate. Congregate prisons have been the mode ever since. Today, however, new voices are calling for a return to long-term solitary confinement in supermax prisons (one of several topics discussed in Chapter 13).

STAGES OF DEVELOPMENT

Prisons in America have progressed through nine stages of development (see Figure 7–1). Many of these changes were influenced by cultural movements in society. As you review the historical stages, think about how the goals of imprisonment changed in each era as society changed. Remember too that old ways did not disappear when new ways emerged. Rather, new thinking challenged the thinking of previous eras and facilitated the development of new correctional policy. Most often, new ideas simply developed alongside existing ones.

Penitentiary Era (1790–1825)   The first era in prison history was the penitentiary era. It included the emergence of the Pennsylvania and Auburn prisons, the demise of the Pennsylvania system of separate and silent, and the building of 30 state prisons on the Auburn pattern of congregate by day and separate by night. This pattern eventually changed to congregate both day and night.

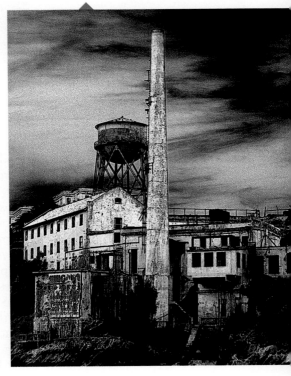

The Industrial Revolution ushered in the era of the industrial prison. The era had good intentions. What were they and what happened?

Mass Prison Era (1825–1876)   The second era was the mass prison era. During that period, the idea of prison as a place for punishment flourished across the United States. As a result, 35 more Auburn-system prisons were built, including Sing Sing in New York State in 1825 and San Quentin in California in 1852.

Reformatory Era (1876–1890)   The third era was the reformatory era. Influenced by progressive beliefs that education and science were vehicles for controlling crime, the first reformatory for young men opened at Elmira, New York, in 1876. The reformatory, whose prisoners had indeterminate sentences (a sentence for which a judge specifies a maximum length and a minimum length and for which an administrative agency, generally a parole board, determines the actual time of release), used a grading system that led to early release on parole and offered academic education, vocational training, individual rehabilitation, and military instruction and discipline. During this era, 20 reformatories opened for men, as well as the first prison for women, Mount Pleasant in Ossining, New York, and the first reformatory for women, the Indiana Reformatory for Women and Girls in Indianapolis.

Industrial Era (1890–1935)   Fourth was the industrial era. During this time, inmates worked in prison industries. The first

Stage	Penitentiary era	Mass prison era	Reformatory era	Industrial era
Years	1790–1825	1825–1876	1876–1890	1890–1935
Goal	Rehabilitation and deterrence	Incapacitation and deterrence	Rehabilitation	Incapacitation
Characteristics	Separate and silent Congregate and silent silent	Congregate labor and living spaces without silence Contract prison labor	Indeterminate sentencing Parole	Public-accounts industries Contract labor State-use labor Convict lease Public-works labor
Examples of institutions	Walnut Street Penitentiary, Philadelphia, PA Eastern State Penitentiary, Cherry Hill, PA Auburn Prison, Auburn, NY	Sing Sing Prison, Ossining, NY San Quentin State Prison, San Quentin, CA	Elmira, NY Indiana Reformatory for Women and Girls, Indianapolis, IN	Most major prisons

FIGURE 7-1
Stages of Prison History in the United States

public accounts system

The earliest form of prison industry, in which the warden was responsible for purchasing materials and equipment and for overseeing the manufacture, marketing, and sale of prison-made items.

contract system

A system of prison industry in which the prison advertised for bids for the employment of prisoners, whose labor was sold to the highest bidder.

prisons had used the **public accounts system** for work. The warden at the Walnut Street Jail had determined the product, purchased materials and equipment, and overseen the manufacture, marketing, and sale of prison-made items. At Auburn, prison industries expanded to include copper, weaving, tailor, blacksmith, and shoemaking shops. However, as more states adopted the Auburn model, the **contract system** replaced the public accounts system. Under the contract system, the prison advertised for bids for the employment of prisoners, whose labor was sold to the highest bidder. The desire to increase profits for the prison and the private contractor often led to exploitation of the prisoners under this system.

During the industrial era, prisons progressed from the public accounts and contract systems of the Pennsylvania and Auburn prisons to *convict lease, state use,* and *public works* systems. Which system was used in a state depended on the region the state was in and the period in which the transition was made.

Punitive era	Treatment era	Community-based era	Warehousing era	Just-deserts era
1935–1945	1945–1967	1967–1980	1980–1995	1985–Present
Retribution	Rehabilitation	Reintegration	Incapacitation	Retribution
Strict punishment and custody	Medical model Emerging prisoner unrest	Intermediate sanction: halfway houses, work release centers, group homes, fines, restitution, community service	Sentencing guidelines End of discretionary parole release Serious crowding More prison riots	Just deserts Determinate sentencing Truth in sentencing Three-strikes law Serious crowding
U.S. Penitentiary, Alcatraz, CA	Patuxent Institution, Jessup, MD	Major prison riots (Attica, NY; Santa Fe, NM	Most major prisons	Spreading through the United States

The **convict lease system** was prevalent in the post–Civil War South and functioned as a replacement for the institution of slavery. Many Southern prisons had been destroyed during the war. Southern states found it easier to relinquish supervision of their prisoners to a lessee. The lessee either employed prisoners as slave labor for private businesses within a state institution or transported them to work elsewhere in the state. Railway, lumber, and coal mining companies leased the greatest numbers of inmates. Lessees housed, fed, clothed, and disciplined inmates. The convict lease system generated income for the prison and reduced overhead because the contractors were responsible for feeding and sheltering the convicts they leased. Left to the mercy of the contractors, however, leased convicts were subjected to terrible abuses of nearly unimaginable brutality.

From attempts to deal with this problem emerged the state use system. Under the **state use system,** prisoners manufactured products for use by state governments and their agencies, departments, and institutions. By

convict lease system

A system of prison industry in which a prison temporarily relinquished supervision of its prisoners to a lessee. The lessee either employed the prisoners within the institution or transported them to work elsewhere in the state.

state use system

A system of prison industry that employs prisoners to manufacture products consumed by state governments and their agencies, departments, and institutions.

public works system

A system of prison industry in which prisoners were employed in the construction of public buildings, roads, and parks.

putting inmates to work manufacturing products for sale exclusively to government agencies, prisons were better able to keep inmates occupied while at the same time reducing direct competition with the private sector and avoiding the exploitative character of inmate leasing. As the Western states developed, a **public works system** emerged. This system used inmates to build public buildings, roads, and parks.

In time, national labor organizations saw prison industries as unfair competition and lobbied Congress to regulate prison industry. In 1929, the Hawes-Cooper Act banned the interstate shipment of prison-made goods. The Ashurst-Sumners Act of 1935 prohibited carriers from accepting prison-made goods for transportation. Ashurst-Sumners also mandated the labeling of prison-made goods. In 1940, Congress passed the Sumners-Ashurst Act, forbidding the interstate transportation of prison-made goods for private use, regardless of whether a state banned importation of prison goods (products manufactured for the federal government or other state governments were exempt). Thus, much of the private market was closed to goods made by inmates. Today, it is a violation of federal law for state prisons to sell their products in interstate commerce unless they are certified by a federal program known as Prison Industry Enhancement (PIE). Under provisions of the PIE program, inmates must be paid the same wages as free workers engaged in similar work. They must also be allowed to keep 20 percent of what they earn. The rest of their wages can be withheld to pay income taxes, child support obligations, room and board charges, and restitution to victims and to victim assistance funds.

Punitive Era (1935–1945)   The closing of prison industries ushered in the punitive era, with its emphasis on strict punishment and custody. The holding of prisoners in the Big House, in complete idleness, monotony, and frustration, characterized this era. The "escape proof" federal prison on the island of Alcatraz in San Francisco Bay opened on the eve of this era. It became the prototype of the latter-day supermax prisons that we will discuss in Chapter 13. It was retrofitted with the latest security hardware then available and staffed with an elite corps of officers. It opened in 1934 to receive the toughest prisoners in the federal BOP.

Treatment Era (1945–1967)   The sixth era, treatment, emerged in response to prison riots across the United States. After World War II, the prison population exploded. Overcrowding, idleness, poor food, and other deprivations led prisoners to take matters into their own hands. Prison riots erupted in California, Colorado, Georgia, Illinois, Louisiana, Massachusetts, Michigan, Minnesota, New Jersey, New Mexico, Ohio, Oregon, Pennsylvania, Utah, and Washington. The riots aroused public support for prisoner rehabilitation.

medical model

A philosophy of prisoner reform in which criminal behavior is regarded as a disease to be treated with appropriate therapy.

Reform through classification, therapy, and increased use of the indeterminate sentence was the focus of the **medical model,** in which criminal behavior was regarded as a disease to be treated. If the diagnosis showed poor socialization and inadequate work skills as the factors that caused a person to turn to crime, the prescription could involve a combination of social skills counseling and vocational training. Maryland's Patuxent Institution, with legions of mental health experts, promised to predict dangerousness accurately and to release only those prisoners who were no longer a threat to the community. However, Patuxent failed to keep that promise. Scholars and advocacy groups also began finding fault with the medical model. They argued that it did not have as favorable an effect on recidivism as supporters argued it would have. They also argued that the medical model encouraged inmates to give the false impression that they were rehabilitated and suitable for early release. Above all was the view that the medical model was a form of coercion and that genuine changes in human behavior could not be coerced. In addition, the social and political unrest of the 1960s had found its way into the nation's prisons. A race riot broke out at San Quentin in 1967, and protests, riots, and killings occurred in other prisons. Corrections experts believed that a new approach was needed—one in which offenders were supervised in the community rather than imprisoned in fortresslike institutions.

Community-Based Era (1967–1980)   Community-based corrections mostly developed after the 1960s, although some community-based programs had begun a century earlier. New York City Quakers opened the Isaac T. Hopper Home in 1845 as a shelter for released inmates; Zebulon Brockway opened the Detroit House of Corrections in 1861 as a shelter for released women; the Philadelphia House of Industry opened in 1889; and Maude Ballington Booth opened Hope Hall, a refuge for ex-inmates in New York, in the 1890s. After that, the community-based concept lay dormant until the 1950s when church groups founded more halfway houses (St. Leonard's House in Chicago and Crenshaw House in Los Angeles) and then until 1967 when President Lyndon Johnson's crime commission came to the conclusion that the community was a source of offenders' problems. The commission recommended that offenders be rehabilitated by using community resources. More halfway houses, community corrections centers, intensive supervision probation programs, work release centers, and the like quickly spread across the United States. By the end of the 20th century, halfway houses—which were practically unknown a century earlier—were an indispensable part of corrections.

Observers soon discovered that the community-based approach did not lower the crime rate, reduce the prison population, or make the community safer. In addition, more prison riots erupted. In 1969, there were 39 riots in the nation's prisons. In 1970, there were 59 more. Four days of rioting in September 1971 left 43 people dead at Attica prison in New York, the largest number ever killed in a U.S. prison riot. With the goals of community corrections unmet, the community-based era gave way.

Warehousing Era (1980–1995)   During the warehousing era, indeterminate sentencing was replaced by determinate sentencing in all states. Discretionary parole board release was abolished in a number of states and the federal government, and the pendulum swung from rehabilitation to incapacitation. Within 15 years, the number of people under correctional supervision jumped from 1.8 million to almost 6 million. Prisons were operating over capacity, and controlling prisoners in such an environment was difficult. For staff and inmates alike, the nation's prisons were dangerous places to be. Extreme crowding resulted in violent outbreaks, which further hardened the attitudes of correctional policymakers and caused them to crack down even more.

Just-Deserts Era (1985–present)   Along with the get-tough policies of the warehousing era emerged a distinct but parallel vision of corrections. The just-deserts philosophy focuses on punishment and provides a philosophy that supports the practice of warehousing. Chain gangs, striped uniforms, and boot camps have been resuscitated, parole has been cut back to 19th-century levels, and corrections has become as much of a political football as at any time in its history. Under the philosophy of just deserts, offenders are punished because they deserve it, the sanction used depending on the seriousness of the offense. Just deserts is not concerned with inmate rehabilitation, treatment, or reform. It separates treatment from punishment. Prisons today provide opportunities for inmates to improve themselves, but participation is not mandatory, nor is it a condition of release as it was for most of 20th century. Change is facilitated, not coerced. Determinate sentencing, capital punishment, truth in sentencing, and three-strikes laws have grown in popularity. As we move into the 21st century, supermax and "no-frills" prisons are becoming the trend.

Who Is in Prison Today?

On January 1, 2003, 1,440,655 adults were under the jurisdiction of state and federal prison authorities—163,528 under federal jurisdiction, and 1,277,127 under state authority.[1] Almost five percent (71,256) of state and federal prisoners were held in local jails, a topic we return to later in this chapter. In absolute numbers, there was a total increase of 36,623 prison inmates between January 1, 2002, and January 1, 2003. Overall, the nation's prison population grew 2.6 percent during that year, which was less than the average annual growth of 3.6 percent since the end of 1995. If these growth patterns continue, researchers at the Bureau of Justice Statistics estimate that the population of prisoners in state and federal custody will reach 1.5 million by 2005.[2] And by 2010, the number of adults having ever served time in prison is projected to increase from 5.6 million U.S. adult residents (about 1 in every 37 U.S. adults) to 7.7 million (1 in every 29 U.S. adults.[3] Nearly 1 in 15 persons born in 2001 (6.6 percent) will go to state or federal prison during their lifetime, up from 5.2 percent in 1991, and 1.9 percent in 1974. Other estimates include:

- The lifetime chances for men going to prison (1 in 9) are six times greater than those for women (1 in 56).
- About 1 in 3 black males, 1 in 6 Hispanic males, and 1 in 17 white males are expected to go to prison during their lifetime.

On January 1, 2003, 476 people per 100,000 U.S. residents were incarcerated in a state or federal prison. The rate of incarceration ranged from 141 people per 100,000 in Maine and Minnesota (the lowest) to 794 people per 100,000 in Louisiana (the highest). The Federal system led the country with the most inmates (163,528); North Dakota had the fewest (1,112; see Table 7–1). Since 1995, the number of sentenced inmates per 100,000 residents has risen from 411 to 476. Prison incarceration rates

TABLE 7-1	Prison Statistics Among the States and the Federal Government, January 1, 2003				
Number of inmates		**Incarceration rate per 100,000 population**		**Number of female prisoners**	
5 highest:					
Federal	163,528	Louisiana	794	Texas	13,051
California	162,317	Mississippi	743	Federal	11,234
Texas	162,003	Texas	692	California	10,050
Florida	75,210	Oklahoma	667	Florida	4,595
New York	67,065	Alabama	612	Georgia	3,129
5 lowest:					
North Dakota	1,112	Maine	141	Maine	90
Wyoming	1,737	Minnesota	141	North Dakota	103
Vermont	1,863	North Dakota	161	Vermont	132
Maine	1,900	Rhode Island	191	New Hampshire	144
New Hampshire	2,451	New Hampshire	192	Wyoming	167

Adapted from Paige M. Harrison and Allen J. Beck, *Prisoners in 2002* (Washington, DC: U.S. Department of Justice, Bureau of Justice Statistics, July 2003).

rose most in the South (from 526 to 536) and West (from 408 to 415). The rate in the Midwest rose from 370 to 373, and the rate in the Northeast remained the same at 304. When prison and jail incarceration rates are combined, the United States imprisons 701 people per 100,000 population, up from 601 in 1995. That's more than any other country in the world. Russia is second with 656 prisoners per 100,000.

States with almost identical populations and crime rates have widely different rates of incarceration. For example, in 2002, Wisconsin had a population of 5.4 million residents, a crime rate of 3,252 offenses per 100,000 population, and an incarceration rate of 391 per 100,000.[4] Minnesota had 5 million residents, a crime rate of 3,535 offenses per 100,000 population, and an incarceration rate of only 141 per 100,000 population. With similar population and crime rates, Wisconsin's incarceration rate was almost three times Minnesota's. The difference in rates reflects differences in the way the states use prison. It shows that a state's prison population is not related to the size of its total population or to its crime rate. Rather, a large prison population is a result of a conscious choice to use prison to punish offenders.

STATE AND FEDERAL INMATES HELD IN PRIVATELY OPERATED FACILITIES

The issue of correctional privatization, including the pros and cons of building and operating private prisons, is discussed in depth in Chapter 13. The focus here is on the current use of privately operated correctional facilities.

In 2003, researchers reported that 31 states and the federal system held 93,771 prisoners in 264 privately-operated prisons, up from 16,663 inmates in 110 private prisons in 1995.[5] (Nineteen states have no private prisons.) Although private prisons held a relatively small proportion of all inmates (almost 7 percent), they reported the largest percentage growth—up 459 percent since 1995, compared to the prisoner increase in the federal system (37 percent), and the state systems (19 percent).

Private facilities held 5.8 percent (73,497) of all state prisoners and 12.4 percent (20,274) of all federal inmates. Among the states, Texas and Oklahoma housed the most inmates in private prisons (16,773 and 6,470, respectively). Five states—Alaska, Montana, New Mexico, Oklahoma and Wyoming—held almost 25 percent of their prisoner population in private facilities.

The use of private prisons is concentrated in Southern and Western states. Overall, 8 percent of state inmates in the South and 6.2 percent of inmates in the West were in privately operated correctional facilities, compared to 1.8 percent in the Northeast and 2.7 percent in the Midwest.

STATE AND FEDERAL INMATES HELD IN LOCAL JAILS

On January 1, 2003, 32 states and the federal system housed almost 5 percent (71,256) of their prisoner populations in local jails. For many jurisdictions, housing state and federal inmates contributes to the problem of jail crowding discussed in Chapter 6. By region, most state and federal inmates are housed in jails in the South (10.2 percent), followed by the West (1.8 percent), the Northeast (1.3 percent), and the Midwest (0.7 percent).

GENDER

Women represent the fastest growing population in correctional facilities. Over the past decade, the number of women in prison has grown from 68,468 (in 1995) to 97,491 (in 2003), an increase of 42 percent. On January 1, 2003, women prisoners constituted 6.8 percent of the U.S. prison population (see Figure 7–2). The rate of incarceration for women was 60 per 100,000 female residents, compared with 906 men per 100,000 male residents. On January 1, 2003, more than a third of the women in prison in the United States were housed in three jurisdictions: Texas (13,051), the federal system (11,234), and California (10,050). The sharpest one-year increases in female incarceration rates occurred in Maine (52.5 percent), Vermont (38.9 percent), Wyoming (23.7 percent), and Oregon (22.8 percent). See Table 7–1 for the jurisdictions with the highest and lowest female prison populations.

According to Beth Richie, a professor of criminal justice and women's studies at the University of Illinois at

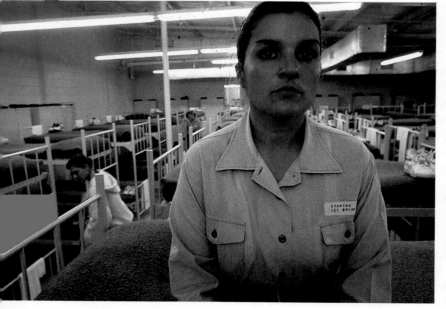

On January 1, 2003, 97,491 adult women were in prison, one-third in Texas, California and federal prisons. Women represent the fastest growing correctional population. Why do you think that's so?

How many persons are under the jurisdiction of state and federal correctional authorities?

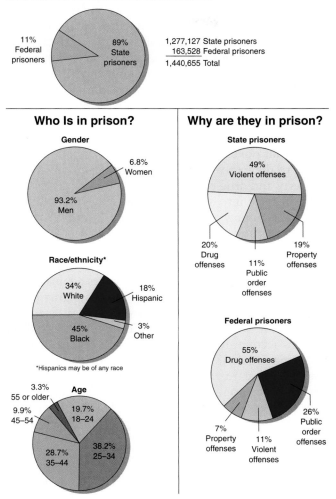

FIGURE 7-2
Persons Under the Jurisdiction of State or Federal Prisons

Source: Paige M. Harrison and Allen J. Beck, *Prisoners in 2002* (Washington, DC: U.S. Department of Justice, Bureau of Justice Statistics, July 2003).

Chicago, the racial/ethnic profile of women in prison represents one of the most vivid examples of racial disparity in the United States.[6] The majority of women in prison are women of color. Two-thirds are black, Hispanic, or of other nonwhite ethnic groups. They are also young and poor. Only one-third graduated from high school or earned a GED. Two-thirds have a history of physical or sexual abuse, and 3.5 percent are HIV positive. The most recent BJS estimate of the lifetime chance of being sent to prison at least once shows that about 5 of 1,000 white women, 36 of 1,000 black women and 15 of 1,000 Hispanic women will be incarcerated during their lifetime.[7] And sadly, the corrections literature suggests that, despite the fact that some women do quite well putting their lives back together when they are released from prison, most are likely to return to the same disenfranchised neighborhoods and difficult situations without having received any services to address their underlying problems. If it is true, as the corrections literature suggests, that prior arrest history predicts postprison recidivism, then the outlook for women prisoners is bleak: 65 percent of women in prison have a history of prior convictions. One-half have three or more convictions.

Scholars debate the reasons for the increase in women's incarceration over men's. Some suggest that, as women moved into jobs from which they were formerly excluded, they gained the opportunities and skills to commit criminal acts for which incarceration was appropriate punishment. Others disagree, saying that poverty of young, female, single heads of households has contributed to the increase in women's crime and incarceration, particularly for property and drug offenses. One scholar put it this way: "the war on drugs has translated into a war on women."[8] Others think the criminal justice system is becoming more "gender blind" due to the emergence of "get tough" attitudes and sentencing policies. Instead of seeing women offenders as weaker and giving them differential, if not preferential, treatment, judges and juries now sentence women more harshly whether they are first-time drug offenders or they have committed crimes against persons or property. The combined effects of harsh drug laws, changing patterns of drug use, and mandatory sentencing policies have lead to a significant increase in women's incarceration. Nonviolent, drug-related offenses account for the largest growth of female inmates (38 percent nationally). Quite likely, the reason for the increase in women's incarceration is a product of all these theories. Whatever the reason, 1.3 million children younger than 18 have mothers under correctional supervision.[9] In Chapter 10 we will discuss the characteristics of female prisoners and the issues they face.

> Nonviolent, drug-related offenses account for the largest growth of female inmates.

RACE

The primary observation to be made about the prison population in the United States is that African Americans are strikingly overrepresented. Although they comprise less than 12 percent of the U.S. population, they make up 45 percent of all incarcerated offenders. Conversely, whites are underrepresented: over 80 percent of the general population but only one-third of the prison population. More black males and females are in prison than white or Hispanic males and females.

When incarceration rates are estimated separately by age groups, black males in their 20s and 30s have high rates relative to other groups. Almost 10 percent of black non-Hispanic males age 25 to 29 were in prison on January 1, 2003, compared to almost 3 percent of Hispanic males and about 1 percent of white males in the same age group. For black male high school dropouts, the numbers are still worse: 41 percent between the ages of 22 and 30 are locked up.

Female incarceration rates reveal similar racial and ethnic disparities. Black non-Hispanic females were more than two times more likely than Hispanic females and five times more likely than white non-Hispanic females to be incarcerated as of January 1, 2003.

As is the case with so many other criminological controversies, there is a debate over the relationship between race and crime. Official crime data indicate that minority group members are involved in a disproportionate share of criminal activity, which results in their greater rates of punishment. According to the FBI's *Crime in the United States 2002*, blacks account for about 12 percent of the U.S. population, yet they account for 38 percent of violent crime arrests (murder, rape, robbery, and assault) and 30 percent of property crime arrests (burglary, arson, theft, and motor vehicle theft).[10] Others argue that the higher arrest rates, convictions, and sentences to prison of blacks are a function of racial profiling and racism in the criminal justice system. Still others blame faulty data collection. Some argue that although discriminatory practices exist, it is improbable that criminal justice bias alone could account for the disproportionate arrest rates of blacks. They suggest the social problems of unemployment, economic deprivation, social disorganization, and social isolation of the nation's inner cities as additional causes. The inner city, the residence of most of the nation's poor, experiences by far the highest violence rates. Middle class communities have more resources to deal with offenders, especially drug offenders, and get them into treatment. In low-income communities, those resources are not available so a drug problem is more likely to develop into a criminal justice problem. In 1998, the Department of Health and Human Services showed that black drug users are more likely to be arrested and incarcerated than white drug users: Blacks represent about 35 percent of people arrested for drug offenses and 50 percent of drug convictions.[11] These high rates may be a function of the fact that, on any given day, one of every three black males ages 20 to 29 is under the supervision of the criminal justice system—either in prison or jail or on probation or parole—making it likely that their drug use will be discovered by authorities.

The number of state, federal, and private prisons in the United States is 1,208. Minorities make up almost two-thirds of the prison population. Why is that so?

AGE

The nation's population is aging, and this is reflected in the prison population. Middle-aged inmates make up a growing portion of the prison population. In 1991, 65.2 percent of the nation's prisoners were between 18 and 34 years old, and 23 percent were between 35 and 44. In 2003, the representation of 18 to 34 year olds had decreased to almost 57 percent while the presence of 35 to 44 year olds had increased to almost 30 percent. The presence of inmates 55 and older remained at about 3 percent (see Figure 7–2). In Chapter 12, we'll discuss older prisoners in more detail.

MOST SERIOUS OFFENSE

Another characteristic to compare is the most serious offense of which a prisoner was convicted. On January 1, 2003, 49 percent of state prisoners were held for violent offenses, up from 46 percent in 1995. The percent of state prisoners held for property offenses dropped from 23 percent in 1995 to 19 percent in 2003, and the percent held for drug offenses dropped from 22 to 20 percent across the same time period. Still, the number of inmates doing time for drug violations in state and federal prison is triple what it was a decade ago. Convictions for public order offenses rose from 9 to almost 11 percent across the same period.

Among federal inmates, persons sentenced for drug offenses constituted the largest group (55 percent) on January 1, 2003, down from 60 percent in 1995. Immigration, weapon, and other public-order offenders made up approximately 26 percent of the federal prison population at the beginning of 2003, compared to 18 percent in 1995, most of which was accounted for by the increases in immigration offenses. The percentage of violent offenders in federal prison in 2003 was 11 percent, down from almost 13 percent in 1995, while property offenders constituted 7 percent in 2003, compared to almost 9 percent in 1995 (see Figure 7–2).

Programs for Prisoners

Among the most important elements of an inmate's institutional experience, whether in federal or state prison, are the programs and services available. The American Correctional Association's policy on conditions of confinement advocates strong programs that meet offenders' needs (see Exhibit 7–1). In this section, we'll consider some such programs: classification, orientation, unit management, a daily routine, work assignments, education and recreation, and health care.

CLASSIFICATION

classification

The process of subdividing the inmate population into meaningful categories to match offender needs with correctional resources.

Classification is the principal management tool for allocating scarce prison resources efficiently and minimizing the potential for escape or violence. Prisoner **classification** is the process of subdividing the inmate population into meaningful categories to match offender needs with correctional resources. As prisons become more crowded, classification decisions play a significant role. Because classification lies at the heart of inmate programming, we emphasize it here.

Classification is based on the premise that there are wide differences among prisoners. Its purpose is to assign inmates to appropriate prison

---

EXHIBIT 7–1   American Correctional Association

Conditions of Confinement Policy Statement

Maintaining acceptable conditions of confinement requires adequate resources and effective management of the physical plant, operational procedures, programs, and staff. To provide acceptable conditions agencies should do the following:

A. Establish and maintain a safe and humane population limit for each institution based upon recognized professional standards.

B. Provide an environment that will support the health and safety of staff, confined persons, and citizens participating in programs. Such an environment results from appropriate design, construction, and maintenance of the physical plant as well as the effective operation of the facility and programming of offenders.

C. Maintain a professional and accountable work environment for staff that includes necessary training and supervision as well as sufficient staffing to carry out the mission of the facility.

D. Maintain a fair and disciplined environment that provides a range of programs and services appropriate to the needs and requirements of offenders, in a climate that encourages responsible behavior.

---

housing and to help staff understand, treat, predict, and manage prisoner behavior. More than 100 years ago, the Elmira Reformatory in Elmira, New York, classified offenders as "specimens" and labeled them either "Mathematical Dullards," "Those Deficient in Self-Control," or "Stupid."[12] Today, the classifications are more sophisticated. The belief is that "somewhere between the extremes of 'all offenders are alike' and 'each offender is unique' lies a system (or systems) of categorization along pertinent dimensions that will prove to be of value in reaching correctional goals."[13] That is why, for example, not all people who have killed are in high-security prisons or on death row. People convicted of manslaughter generally are not placed under high security and are not sentenced to die.

Types of Classification   There are two types of prisoner classification: external and internal. **External classification** determines an inmate's security level (maximum, close, medium, minimum, or community) for *interinstitutional* placement. For example, maximum-security inmates are placed in a maximum-security facility. External classification answers the question "Where should I put this inmate?" Most states employ a system similar to South Carolina's Reception and Diagnostic Center (R&D; see Exhibit 7–2). R&D staff evaluate offenders sentenced to the state department of corrections to make the external classification decision.

    Internal classification is *intrainstitutional* placement. Once an inmate arrives at the institution, she or he undergoes a classification review. Classification staff review an inmate's behavior, personality, educational, chemical dependency, medical, and mental health needs. Staff then assign inmates to housing units or cellblocks, work, and programming based on their risk, needs, and time to serve. A survey by the National Council on Crime and

external classification
Interinstitutional placement of an inmate that determines an inmate's security level.

internal classification
Intrainstitutional placement that determines, through review of an inmate's background, assignment to housing units or cellblocks, work, and programming based on the inmate's risk, needs, and time to serve.

EXHIBIT 7–2   Reception and Evaluation Center Processes Inmates Entering Prison

The South Carolina Department of Corrections is required by law to provide care and custody for all offenders ordered by the courts to serve a prison sentence that exceeds 90 days. Approximately 1,000 inmates are received in the Department of Corrections each month. Every inmate must be evaluated and processed to assess both the needs of the inmate and the resources of the Department of Corrections. This is the responsibility of the staff of the Reception and Evaluation (R&E) Center located inside Kirkland Correctional Institution. The Kirkland R&E Center processes all male inmates entering the Department of Corrections. Female inmates are processed at the Women's Correctional Institution.

Initial processing begins immediately upon the inmate's arrival at the R&E. Court orders are reviewed to determine that the inmate has in fact been ordered to the Department of Corrections. The inmate is searched for possible weapons or contraband, and all personal belongings are removed from the inmate. Personal clothing is replaced by state issued clothing. While in the R&E Center every inmate wears a white jumpsuit that indicates he is in the evaluation process. Inmates are allowed to keep certain personal items: a wedding ring, a watch, a Bible, 10 photographs, 10 letters, and any legal paperwork. All other items are mailed home, or donated, at the choice of the inmate. An initial medical screening is performed to determine any immediate medical or mental health care needs that must be addressed.

Security status is determined for each individual based on type of sentencing, age, behavior while in the custody of the local law enforcement, escape risk, signs of self-destructive behavior, and the safety of the staff and other inmates. Once these issues have been evaluated, an initial housing assignment is made. Every inmate is fingerprinted, photographed, and provided with an inmate identification card that must be in his possession at all times.

When the initial identification processing is completed, the routine testing and interviewing process begins. Education assessment coordinators test for basic IQ and education level. Inmates who test below the eighth-grade level are required to attend basic education classes. Inmates are interviewed by classification personnel who gather personal data, self reported information on employment and education, juvenile histories, marks, scars and tattoos, information on alcohol and drug use, the inmate's account of his crime, and emergency contact information. All of these data are compiled into the inmate record and the automated inmate record system. This inmate record (file) will accompany the inmate throughout the system as he serves his sentence. Background checks are conducted through the National Crime Information Center (NCIC), and any prior criminal history is recorded. If the inmate has served a prior sentence in the S.C. Department of Corrections, the old inmate record is pulled and included as part of the current one. Clinical counselors determine the mental health status of each individual and identify inmates who require mental health counseling. Inmates determined to be alcohol and drug dependent are referred for treatment. A general orientation is conducted and basic rules and regulations of the Department of Corrections are explained. Everything from telephone calls, visitation, and correspondence policies to the disciplinary policy and grievance procedures are covered. Court orders are again reviewed for any special orders of the court that must be taken into consideration during initial institutional assignment.

Inmates sentenced under the Youthful Offender Act are segregated from other inmates by law. A complete physical examination is performed, which includes screening for TB, sexually transmitted diseases, and chest X rays when indicated. Inmates aged 17 to 25 are given Hepatitis B vaccinations. If required by law, DNA samples are drawn and forwarded to the State Law Enforcement Division. Necessary sick call visits are scheduled.

There are 918 beds allocated to the intake process. This means that each day as inmates are received, other inmates must be moved out of the R&E to their initial institution assignment. This is no small task. Tim Riley, R&E manager, states that it is only through the dedication and teamwork of the R&E staff that this is accomplished. "I have a great staff who are very supportive of each other and the Department of Corrections. They are always willing to go the extra mile to get the job done. The R&E is operational five days per week, 16 hours per day. This means staggering work hours to get the job done. Some officers enter the institution at 4:00 A.M. to get inmates ready for the 6:00 A.M. sick call. This is dedication. It is important that we do things right; after all, this is where the mission of the SCDC begins."

Riley goes on to say, "When DNA testing was first required by State law, members of the R&E staff formed the core team with medical that traveled to every institution in the state to meet the requirements. When the situation dictates it, I find my staff willing to do whatever it takes to get the job done. They have come together as a great team, especially now when vacant positions cannot be filled and everyone is doing more than what is required by their job."

Source: South Carolina Department of Corrections, *Agency News,* http://www.state.sc.us/scdc/News/RandE.htm.

THE STAFF SPEAKS

Delinquency (NCCD) found that only nine states had a formal internal classification system that used structured scoring instruments, staff specialists who were formally trained to use them, and a reclassification process to update previously classified prisoners.[14] NCCD found that some kind of internal classification process exists in all prison systems to assign newly arrived inmates to housing units, work assignments, and programs, but these processes are usually informal and rely on subjective criteria.

Three of the best-known systems of internal classification are the Adult Internal Management System (AIMS), the Prisoner (or Client) Management Classification system (PMC), and behavior-based systems (BBSs). AIMS is used by several facilities in the federal BOP and a number of state departments of corrections including Missouri, Ohio, South Dakota, and Washington. Its purpose is to reduce institutional predatory behavior by identifying inmates who are likely to be incompatible in terms of housing and inmates who are most likely to pose a risk to the safe and secure operation of a facility. AIMS uses personality checklists that are designed to determine an inmate's ability to be housed successfully with other inmates. Based on these scores, inmates are classified into one of five groups. Alpha I and Alpha II inmates are characterized as offenders most likely to be a threat to the safety and security of the facility. They are characterized as predators. Sigma I and Sigma II inmates are unlikely to be assaultive, but they pose other management problems, such as disregarding direct orders and disrupting the orderly operation of the institution. They are characterized as inmates at risk of being victimized. Kappa inmates are least likely to present management problems. They are neither predators nor prey.

PMC uses a semistructured attitudinal interview to assist staff in identifying potential predators and victims and those inmates who require special programs or supervision. The attitudinal items tap the inmate's attitude regarding the current offense; criminal history; family relationships; relationships with staff, inmates, and peers; and plans after release. In addition,

THE OFFENDER SPEAKS

other items assess the inmate's social status and demeanor during the interview. Based on these scores, inmates are classified into one of four groups: Limited Setting (LS) and Casework Control (CC) inmates are expected to be more aggressive and harder to control. Selective Intervention (SI) and Environmental Structure (ES) inmates are characterized as needing minimal supervision and requiring separation from LS and CC inmates. Once inmates are classified, detailed guidelines provide staff with management techniques for handling prisoners and programming approaches for inmates assigned to their designated housing units.

BBSs assess inmates according to behavioral measures as reflected by disciplinary records and work performance, in contrast to personality and attitude scales. Florida, Illinois, New Jersey, and Oregon use BBSs. Inmates are scored according to their level of aggression, which is determined by the severity and frequency of institutional misconduct and gang-related activities. Staff who use a BBS conduct a historical assessment of the inmate to achieve an understanding of an inmate's potential behavior. Staff review a host of factors such as type of disciplinary incidents, days spent in segregation, time remaining to serve, external custody level, and needs assessment. The factors are scored and placed into grids that identify the inmate's housing type, potential cellmates, and treatment and program needs.

Florida's BBS uses a system of five risk scores. Score 5 characterizes the most hostile, violent, and aggressive inmates with the potential for a high rate of disciplinary problems, fights, assaults, threats of bodily harm, and destruction of property. Score 1 means inmates are least likely to be involved with fights or assaults within prison. They have a low rate of disciplinary reports. New Jersey uses three behavioral classification systems. Highly aggressive inmates are those with a recent institutional history of aggressive, violent, or confrontational behavior. They are characterized as predators and visible agitators. Moderately aggressive inmates have less severe recent histories of violent or aggressive institutional conduct and behavior that would not threaten their potential return to society. Inmates classified as having low aggression have very limited or nonexistent histories of aggressive institutional misconduct. Often they are older and serve their sentences quietly.

Advantages of Classification   Good internal classification systems offer a number of advantages. First, separating inmates by risk level and program needs puts extremely aggressive inmates in high security, while those who require less or are at risk of being victimized are kept in low security. Within those levels of security, prisoners' needs may also be considered. Does the facility offer drug and alcohol treatment? Sex offender treatment? Anger management training? GED preparation? Such classification offers prisoners a chance for counseling, education, or vocational training, and it may keep aggressive inmates from assaulting passive inmates.

Second, a good classification system minimizes misclassification, thus promoting a safe environment for inmates and staff. When prisons are over capacity, as they are today, staff feel pressure to classify inmates quickly, which often results in misclassification. A good classification system will include safeguards against misclassification. For example, when there is not enough space in maximum-security facilities, a good system will direct staff to house only the lowest-risk high-security inmates in medium-security facilities.

Third, a good classification system more accurately places inmates and more effectively deploys staff. Without good classification, the tendency is to place inmates in more secure, more expensive prisons than necessary. Good classification controls the inmate population, assigns inmates to appropriate security levels, and better deploys staff.

Fourth, a good classification system enhances prison security by reducing tension in prison. Misclassification can jeopardize a prison's security and increase violence and escapes. A review of the major developments and trends in prisoner classification over a recent 20-year period found significant improvement in classification technology (e.g., computer software to help collect, store, and manage the data) and more sophisticated assessment of risk and of medical, mental health treatment, and education needs.[15]

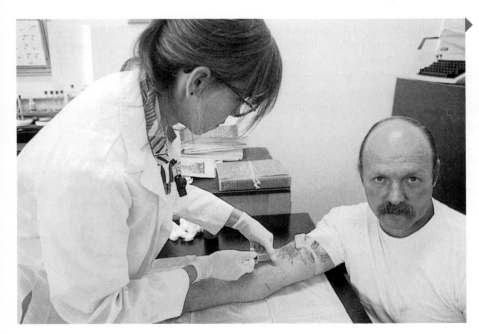

Classification of incoming inmates is based on many factors, including medical and health-care needs, custody needs, institutional risk, work skills, and educational needs. Classification serves the custody goals of a prison but tends to label prisoners. Is such labeling appropriate?

ORIENTATION TO THE INSTITUTION

While the process of internal classification is being conducted, state and federal prison systems provide inmates an orientation to the institution. For the first week or two, inmates participate in an admission and orientation program. It provides an introduction to all aspects of the institution and includes screening by staff from the case management, medical, and mental health units. Inmates receive copies of the institution's rules and regulations, including the inmate discipline policy, and they are introduced to the programs, services, policies, and procedures of the facility. Increasingly prison systems such as the Louisiana State Penitentiary at Angola use inmates to orient new arrivals to prison life.

UNIT MANAGEMENT

Unit management is based on the idea that cooperation is most likely in small groups that have lengthy interactions.[16] A unit is a self-contained living area for 50 to 100 inmates that is managed semiautonomously within the larger institution. In the federal system and in a number of states, prisons use a **unit management system.** The purpose of dividing prisons into functional units, each with its own permanently assigned staff and a unit manager who serves as a "mini warden," was largely to improve program delivery. Many units—drug treatment units, in particular—were established to focus on specific program needs. The unit team—typically composed of the unit manager, one or more case managers, two or more correctional counselors, and a unit secretary—is directly responsible for the inmates living in that unit. Unit staff receive input from other employees involved in an inmate's progress (such as work supervisors, teachers, and psychologists) and meet with the inmate on a regular basis to develop, review, and discuss the work assignments and programs the inmate should be involved in as well as any other needs or concerns.

unit management system

A method of controlling prisoners in self-contained living areas and making inmates and staff (unit manager, correctional counselor, and unit secretary) accessible to each other.

Traditional correctional institutions make decisions through a centralized and hierarchical management structure, whereas unit management strives to decentralize decision making. When decisions are made at the unit level, they are made with better information and by staff who know the inmates better. Unit management gives inmates direct daily contact with the staff who make most of the decisions about their daily lives. It results in improved inmate access to staff and greater staff access to inmates, providing staff with an awareness of significant inmate concerns and potential problems. Unit management also means that not all units will be managed in the same way. Having different management methods is a strength because different inmates require different management approaches. Unit management even had an impact on prison architecture, encouraging the movement to direct-supervision architecture discussed in Chapter 6.

The success of unit management is affected by internal classification. Inmates who are assigned to a given institution are then assigned to a specific unit based on their risks and needs. After the processes of internal classification and initial orientation, each inmate

Ethical Dilemma

Correctional Industry programs have had a controversial past, but they have been found to contribute to an offender's job training, rehabilitation, and financial responsibility. In tight budget times, should Industries also bear the burden of contributing to the correctional department's financial stability? Should the primary mission be inmate job preparation or be viewed as a source of revenue? For more information go to Ethical Dilemma 7-1 at http://www.mhhe.com/schmalleger2.

meets with the unit team to formulate a program plan, which may include drug treatment, education, and vocational training as well as institution maintenance jobs or other work assignments. The unit team reviews the inmate's progress and makes changes in the program plan as needed. Unit management emphasizes candid, open communication between staff and inmates. Direct and frequent communication helps staff know inmates, understand their needs, and respond appropriately to those needs.

DAILY ROUTINE

A typical prison day begins with breakfast at 6:30 A.M. For inmates with prison jobs, work begins about 7:30 A.M. By this time, inmates are expected to have cleaned their personal living areas and made their beds. After work and the evening meal, inmates may participate in organized or individual recreation, watch television, or engage in personal hobbies. In most prisons, inmates must remain in their quarters after the 10 P.M. count. The weekend and holiday routines are somewhat more relaxed for all inmates.

Prisons regularly count inmates to ensure that all are where they are supposed to be. How often inmates are counted varies considerably. In some prisons, formal inmate counts are taken five times a day, including a morning count at 6, an afternoon count at 4, and three counts between 10 P.M. and morning. Informal counts may be conducted in program areas at various times during the day, to ensure that inmates are in the proper place. Emergency counts may be held at any time. On weekends and holidays, when routines are more relaxed, counts are still made.

WORK ASSIGNMENTS

Work is a very important part of institutional management and offender programs. Meaningful work programs are the most powerful tool prison administrators have in managing crowding and idleness, which can lead to disorder and violence. Former BOP Director James V. Bennett attributed the rash of prison disturbances in the early 1930s to the lack of meaningful work programs.[17]

> Meaningful work programs are the most powerful tool prison administrators have in managing crowding and idleness.

Prison work is generally of one of three types: operational assignments within the institution, community projects, or prison industry. In operational assignments within the institution, inmates perform tasks necessary to the functioning of the facility or larger corrections system. Institutional maintenance assignments including farm and other agricultural activities are the largest single option for inmate work. Forty-five of the 50 states, the District of Columbia, and the BOP pay inmates a wage for services rendered to the institution. The average wage range for institutional maintenance work is $0.99 to $3.98 per day. Inmates working in institutional maintenance perform the following types of work: laundry, heating and air conditioning repair, building maintenance and custodial service, landscaping and grounds maintenance, and food preparation and service.

Community Service   Many correctional institutions allow inmates to gain work experience through community service. Through community service, offenders contribute their labor to benefit the community while developing job skills in a practical, nonprison setting. Community service work usually takes the form of construction, landscaping, horticulture, and agriculture activities. Construction/repair of public property and parks development and maintenance are by far the most common types of community service activities. Examples of other community service work include building houses for low-income persons, painting municipal swimming pools, providing snow removal services, providing backup fire-fighting services, and delivering antidrug programs in schools. In South Carolina, inmates who meet the criteria for community work build playground equipment, pick up trash on state highways, maintain and clean up state parks, aid flood victims, clean up debris after storm damage, and provide skilled labor for Habitat for Humanity. Inmate service organizations also raise money for the Special Olympics and other charities.

Prison Industries   Many states operate prison industries to employ and train inmates. Approximately 46 percent of the nation's 1,208 state, federal and private prisons operate prison industries. Historically, however, prison industry work programs for prisoners have generated considerable controversy, and for that reason they are discussed at length here.

In the past, organized labor and small businesses expressed fears that prison-made merchandise constituted unfair competition. With time, though, prison work programs were justified on four grounds, and they eventually won the support of labor unions and small businesses.

The first justification for prison work is that it generates safer prison management and better prison discipline through the reduction of idleness. Idleness in prison is dangerous. It can give rise to boredom and frustrations that can explode in disputes among inmates and in attacks on staff. Prison industry, then, is a management tool. It can enhance discipline within prison by keeping inmates occupied and raising their morale.

The second justification is that prison industry is cost-efficient. It is more expensive to operate a prison where inmates are idle, tense, and disruptive than it is to operate a prison where the inmates are busy and well disciplined. Investment in prison industry can lower expenditures on day-to-day prison operations and decrease the likelihood of having to expend resources to quell prison riots. Moreover, prison industries enable inmates to produce items of value for the government, such as furniture, electronics, signs, and military gear. Sale of these items, in turn, generates revenue that can be used to offset expenses that would otherwise have to be met through appropriated taxes. As of January 2000, prison industries produced overall sales in excess of $1.1 billion.[18] The type of prison industries vary by state. The most profitable in Maryland are meat processing, upholstery, and modular office systems. In Virginia, clothing manufacturing and assembling barbecue grills are the most profitable.

The third justification is that prison industry contributes to job training and rehabilitation. The primary tasks of prisons are to confine offenders and provide them with ways to improve themselves during confinement. Prisons cannot magically rehabilitate offenders, but they can provide opportunities for inmates to reform their behavior and rehabilitate themselves. Former BOP Director Michael Quinlan commented, "We can't 'cure' criminal behavior, but we know that *some* programs work for *some* inmates some of the time."[19] Prison industry programs are among those that can help. The work experience and vocational training they provide can increase ex-offenders' prospects for employment and reduce the likelihood of recidivism.

The fourth justification for prison industry is that it increases an inmate's financial responsibility. Inmate pay ranges from as little as 20 cents an hour in Florida to $8 an hour in Utah.[20] The wages that inmates earn through employment in prison labor programs can help support families, pay court-imposed fines, and compensate victims. In the federal system, inmates employed in federal prison industries must use 50 percent of their wages to pay their debts.

Prison-based industries today employ more than 57,000 inmates in agriculture, manufacturing, public works, prison construction, and prison maintenance.[21] Private companies generally take one of three approaches when partnering with prisons. The first is the **manpower model,** in which the prison's role is similar to that of a temporary personnel service. For example, prisoners at the North Central Correctional Facility in Rockwell City, Iowa, used to earn $6.50 an hour sorting, cleaning, and packaging 1.3 million eggs a day at the Boomsma chicken farm in Clarion, Iowa, until they were offered $8 an hour working for a boat factory in Fort Dodge. Other prisoners at the North Central facility work on the prison's second floor as telemarketers for the Heartland Communications Group, a publisher in Fort Dodge. There, some inmates sell magazine subscriptions, others make sales appointments for people who sell shock collars for dogs, and others try to get farmers to advertise their used farm equipment in *Farmers Hot Line Iowa.* Across the state in Bondurant, Iowa, women prisoners work for Diamond Crystal, the packager of dry blended food products. Twelve of the 130 employees at Diamond Crystal are women prisoners. The company has hired half a dozen women after their parole. Of Iowa's almost 8,000 inmates, only 225 work for prison industries.

The second approach is the **employer model.** In this approach, the prison provides the company space in which to operate and a labor pool of inmates to hire. The company supervises employees and makes all decisions related to personnel, products, wages, and market sales. This is the most common model. One of the best-known prison employer models operates at the Eastern Oregon Correctional Institution in Pendleton, Oregon, the famous mill town known for Pendleton fabrics. Here, prisoners make a line of T-shirts, jackets, and jeans known as Prison Blues®. Inside Oregon Enterprises owns the business. It operates a 47,000-square-foot factory on the prison grounds, a type of industrial park with bars. It pays its 100 inmate employees market wages. The Oregon Department of Corrections expects to make $10 million by 2006 on its prison industries. Similar programs operate across the United States.

The third approach is the **customer model,** in which a company hires a correctional institution to provide a finished product at an agreed-on price. In the customer model, the correctional institution owns and operates the business that employs the inmate workforce. For example, the Hennepin County Adult Correctional Facility in Minnesota operates a job shop employing 50 inmates. The shop provides a variety of light assembly,

manpower model
An approach to private business partnerships with prisons in which the prison's role is similar to that of a temporary personnel service.

employer model
The most common approach to private business partnerships with prisons. The prison provides a company space in which to operate and a labor pool to hire. The company supervises its inmate employees and makes all decisions.

customer model
In this model, a company hires a correctional institution to provide a finished product at an agreed-upon price. The correctional institution owns and operates the business that employs the inmate workforce.

Many state correctional systems channel prison labor into industrial and commercial programs. One such program is the Prison Blues® brand of jeans, T-shirts, work shirts, and yard coats manufactured by Inside Oregon Enterprises, a division of the Oregon Department of Corrections. What benefits to inmates do such work programs provide?

sorting, packaging, and warranty repair services for dozens of private firms in the Minneapolis–St. Paul area. In Arizona, the State Prison at Douglas repairs Braille machines and puts new materials into Braille, with equipment provided by the Foundation for Blind Children. (Read the "Eye on Corrections" feature.)

Federal Prison Industries and UNICOR In the federal system, legislation authorizing the establishment of paid inmate work programs was introduced into Congress in 1934. However, the American Federation of Labor (AFL) voiced its opposition, arguing that federal prison industries have an unfair competitive advantage over the public sector because they pay their inmates less than a private company worker would be paid for carrying out similar assignments. President Franklin Roosevelt took a personal interest in the matter and called AFL President William Green and BOP Director Sanford Bates to the Oval Office. Together, the three men were able to draw out Green's objections to the proposed legislation and his suggestions for improvement, and ultimately the AFL withdrew its opposition. On June 23, 1934, President Roosevelt signed the law that authorized the establishment of **Federal Prison Industries (FPI)**, and on December 11, 1934, he issued Executive Order 6917, which formally created FPI. FPI is a federal work program in which inmates are paid. Better known by its trade name, **UNICOR**, FPI is a self-supporting corporation owned by the federal government and overseen by a governing board appointed by the president.

Since 1934, FPI has operated factories and employed inmates in America's federal prisons. When the United States entered World War II in

Federal Prison Industries (FPI)

A federal, paid inmate work program and self-supporting corporation.

UNICOR

The trade name of Federal Prison Industries. UNICOR provides such products as U.S. military uniforms, electronic cable assemblies, and modular furniture.

December 1941, FPI manufactured bomb fins and casings, TNT cases, parachutes, cargo nets, and wooden pallets for the military. It also handled the military's laundry and built, remodeled, and repaired military patrol boats, tugboats, and barges. FPI also contributed in another way to the war effort. It trained inmates to move directly into jobs in defense industries after release from prison. During the 1990–1991 Persian Gulf War, FPI provided Kevlar helmets, camouflage battle uniforms, lighting systems, sandbags, blankets, cables for the Patriot missile system, and night-vision eyewear for military use during Operation Desert Shield and Operation Desert Storm. Today, FPI in Tennessee sews the military vests worn by U.S. soldiers and Marines fighting in Afghanistan and Iraq. Other products manufactured by UNICOR are electronic cable assemblies, executive and modular furniture (FPI ranks ninth in such manufacture in the United States), metal pallet racks, stainless steel food service equipment, mattresses, towels, utility bags, brooms, thermoplastics, military helmets, and government forms. UNICOR also provides services, such as data entry, sign making, and printing.

The mission of FPI is to employ and provide job skills training to the greatest practical number of inmates confined within the Federal Bureau of Prisons; contribute to the safety and security of federal correctional facilities by keeping inmates constructively occupied; produce market-priced quality goods for sale to the Federal Government; operate in a self-sustaining manner; and minimize FPI's impact on private business and labor. In 2002, UNICOR employed 22 percent (21,778 of medically-eligible federal inmates in 111 factories across the U.S.), grossed $678.7 million (up from $583.5 million in 2001), and made a profit of $9 million, up from $4.9 million in 2001.[22] UNICOR demonstrates its contribution to the private sector in a number of ways: It purchases its products from private sector suppliers, it does business with private sector subcontractors, and it is a major employer of noninmate members in the communities where it operates factories. To ensure that UNICOR does not compete unfairly with the private sector, product guidelines require a public announcement and a hearing process for any new product it proposes. UNICOR is one of the most successful and cost-effective enterprises of the federal government.

Inmates employed by UNICOR start out earning 23 cents per hour. To advance to the maximum wage of $1.15 per hour, inmates must have a high school diploma or GED. Although wages are low in most prison industry programs, most inmates who work in them are more interested in doing something meaningful that keeps them busy and makes serving time seem to go faster. In many cases, such prisoners also learn job skills and have a better chance of staying crime free after release.

In 1990, Congress mandated an independent market study of UNICOR. The accounting firm of Deloitte and Touche conducted the study. One of the principal findings was that UNICOR's impact on the private sector was negligible. UNICOR's sales amounted to only 2 percent of the federal market for the types of products and services that it provided. At about the same time, the federal BOP released a study that compared the postrelease activities of a group of inmates who had participated in UNICOR programs with those of another group of inmates who had not. The study found that inmates employed by UNICOR were 24 percent more likely, upon release, to

Eye On Corrections™

Program Allows Inmates to Become Unique Asset to the Blind

By Michelle Gaseau

It takes more than a year to become proficient enough in the Braille language to be a certified transcriber. It's not the type of vocation one would associate with the inmate population. But the long-term status of some Arizona inmates has allowed them to fulfill an important need in the community by helping the Foundation for Blind Children. Inmates at the Arizona State Prison in Douglas have played a part in a multifaceted project that provides Braille transcription services and repairs costly Braille machines for the foundation for free.

According to Tom Paplawsky, Correction Officer 4 and program supervisor at the prison's Mohave Unit, the program is small but helps inmates improve their language skills and help others in need. "I've had inmates tell me they feel like they are able to give something back to society. There is definitely a positive response to the opportunity. Those who are involved don't tend to have disciplinary problems and it gives them a skill," he said.

Inge Durre, director of the Arizona Instructional Resource Center of the Foundation for Blind Children, said the program has been a tremendous benefit for those who need these services. "It has been a wonderful mutual operation between the Douglas facility and the Foundation for Blind Children. It is also very gratifying for me in that I am supporting those programs [for inmates,]" she said.

Both Paplawsky and Durre recently spoke with *The Corrections Connection* about the program and its benefits:

Q: What does this program involve for inmates?
Paplawsky: There are two components: a Braille transcribing program where inmates are certified through the Library of Congress and will take a book or article and transcribe it and the other component is the Arizona Brailler Repair program, where we receive Braille machines and repair them for The Foundation for Blind Children in Phoenix. They come from all over the United States. As far as I know we are the only ones that are doing Brailler repair [in prisons].

Q: How are inmates trained and how do they participate?
Paplawsky: We have four inmates involved in the repair program and after the machines are

become employed and remain crime free for as long as 12 years after release than those who were not involved in UNICOR programs. Another study showed that inmates employed in federal prison industries had survival times (measured by the number of days before recommitment) that were 20 percent longer than those of the comparison group.[23]

EDUCATION AND RECREATION PROGRAMS

According to a 1994 study of 1,100 federal and state prisoners, the majority of prisoners cannot read or write well enough to function in society. In fact, the illiteracy rate among prisoners is three and one-half times that of the U.S. adult population.[24] Only 38 percent of the 1.4 million state and fixed in Mohave, they have to be tested. An inmate at the Gila Unit tests them to see if they are working properly. In the repair program inmates are paid through the work incentive pay program and can earn a maximum of 50 cents an hour.

Inmates basically express interest in it. To be involved, they have to have at least a high school equivalency plus they have to meet a literacy standard.

For the transcribing, it takes nine months to a year and a half to be certified and, like a lot of things in corrections, we get people interested up front but they might not hang in there. It's a tremendous amount of work; then once you are certified, it takes months to do a manuscript.

The Braille transcribing program went to a computerized version in 1996. The software allows for the keyboard to be used as a Brailler machine. We train inmates to become Braillers and work to get them certified. It is kind of a mentoring program where they tutor other in-mates. The student transcribing program is interesting because once they learn it they have to produce a manuscript and have it graded by the Library of Congress.

For the transcribing program, we pay our students a small stipend while they are learning and we have both inmates who would be assigned as clerks in the Braille lab and inmates who volunteer their time to transcribe books.

Q: How does the program benefit the Foundation?

Durre: We used other Braillewriter services and we were not pleased. We tried to find a solution for the issue. They were gone for so long and often times 50 percent of them either were in need of repair again or something else wouldn't work. We tried several facilities and it was a problem everywhere.

The inmates donate their time to us, but the parts have to be paid for by the owner [of the machine]. The majority of the Braillewriters are our own. We have 250 Braillewriters that belong to the foundation. Initially, we tried to set [the inmates] up with training from the manufacturer of the machines outside of Boston. [But] the machine's manual has pictures and numbers so if they have a technical mind, they can teach themselves. The transcribing program is a great benefit, and some of the inmates are excellent transcribers, with hardly any errors.

federal prisoners have completed high school, a GED, or further educa-tion.[25] That is a prisoner illiteracy rate of 62 percent. In comparison, 82 percent of the U.S. adult population has completed high school, a GED, or more, and only 18 percent cannot read or write at the high school level.[26] "The study's findings highlight the need to focus special preventive interventions not only in public schools, but also among juveniles who are incarcer-ated," said Laurie Robinson, assistant attorney general for the Department of Justice's Office of Justice Programs. "While lit-eracy alone will never be a vaccine against criminality, it is one of many skills needed to function—and function well—as a re-sponsible and law-abiding adult in our society."[27]

> While literacy alone will never be a vaccine against criminality, it is one of many skills needed to function—and function well—as a responsible and law-abiding adult in our society.

Prisons vary considerably in the education and recreation programs they provide for prisoners. Ninety-two percent of federal prisons, 90 percent of state prisons, and 80 percent of private prisons offered some type of educational program in 2000 but only 35 percent of prisoners participate in educational programs. For inmates without a high school diploma, some states provide adult basic education or GED classes. Some states offer academic and life skills programs. In December 2000, University of Kentucky sociologist Karen Lahm published the results of a study on educational and vocational prison programming in 30 states.[28] She found that general education programs are readily available across the United States, but postsecondary programming has been on the decline since President Bill Clinton's 1994 crime bill, which denied Pell grants to inmates. According to the American Correctional Association, only 4.3 percent of a state's prison budget is spent on treatment, including education and recreation.[29] Some jurisdictions are forming creative alliances with colleges to provide college-level educational opportunities for inmates. The Miami–Dade County Corrections Department uses the educational services of the Corrections Learning Network. The network offers college-level courses to inmates over a satellite network. The network gives the satellite equipment free to correctional facilities. There is no charge for the programming or the curriculum. All the network asks is that the facilities use it.

Lahm also found that, although prisons are offering a greater variety of educational opportunities than ever before, women's prisons are still more likely to offer gender-stereotyped vocational training in technical, sales, or administrative occupations and service occupations. Some jurisdictions, however, offer unique vocational programming for women. For example, Ohio offers a program called ONOW (Orientation to Nontraditional Occupations for Women) that prepares women inmates for jobs in trade industries such as plumbing, carpentry, and electricity that require math skills, physical fitness, and blueprint reading skills. (An exercise at the end of this chapter directs you to the U.S. Department of Education's Office of Correctional Education for summaries and critiques of 19 studies on the relationship between correctional education and recidivism.)

Generally, minimum-security federal institutions offer only literacy programs. Higher-security facilities usually provide a broader range of programs. Literacy is the only mandatory education program in the federal prison system. It is required by statute for all federal prisoners who are functionally illiterate. Non–English-speaking inmates are required to participate in English-as-a-second-language programs until they are able to function at the eighth-grade level. Inmates who do not have a GED or a high school diploma are required by BOP policy to enroll in an adult literacy program for 120 days.

Occupational training is also provided in a wide variety of areas but only 27 percent of inmates participate in vocational programs. In addition to receiving occupational training by working in prison industries, some inmates receive training in building construction, heating and air conditioning, auto mechanics, computer-assisted drafting, electronics, food preparation, and business education. The Nevada Correctional Center offers a three-year apprenticeship program for dental laboratory technicians at Northern Correctional Center in Carson City, Nevada. Inmates in the program receive

e Future of American rrections

by James W. Marquart,
Sam Houston State University

Reflections on the Future

If the past is any predictor of the future, then we will see continued expansion of the American prisoner population and continued refinement in the management of prisoners. First and foremost, there will be continued growth of the prison population, particularly among women and juveniles. The crime rate will go up, it will go down, and this cycle will repeat itself, but these crime cycles will not have a dampening effect. The reason, I believe, for this increase in the prisoner population is rooted in punitiveness, in punishment. In our society, public policy is governed by incapacitation, and we will continue to see prisoners obtaining long punitive sentences—lengthy minimum sentences. Prisoner population growth coupled with incapacitation and a continued emphasis on punishment will dominate the correctional scene for decades to come.

Another issue that will continue to develop is the decline of the American welfare state. We are seeing fewer and fewer people on welfare and a restriction on the number of social programs for the poor. This shrinkage of social programs will influence prison programming. I predict that there will be a decline in state-subsidized programming for prisoners. Until the late 1980s and early 1990s, most prison systems offered a variety of programs at state expense for prisoners. Recreation, health care, college, and school programs were provided to the inmate at state expense. We have seen lately a restriction in this, and I think this is going to be a major movement within prison organizations over the next several decades. If offenders want advanced college courses, technical school, or trade school, I predict that offenders are going to have to pay for it themselves.

Coupled with the decline in programming, I think we will see continued refinement in classification procedures. As classification procedures are refined to cull out the high-risk and dangerous inmates within the inmate population, we are going to set aside special settings for their incarceration. We will see continued growth in administrative segregation and in super maximum settings for high-risk, dangerous inmates within the prison community. No longer will there be emphasis on rehabilitation and treatment. A major emphasis is being placed on public safety, and the way to enhance public safety is through increased improvement in classification procedures to identify the most dangerous inmates. We will see little pockets of inmates within prison organizations: the young doing long sentences, the mentally ill, inmates with infectious diseases, women prisoners, sex offenders, high-risk, dangerous inmates within the prisoner population. There will be continuous segmentation of the inmate population into smaller and smaller groups for risk management purposes.

Another area where we will see growth and change will be in the staff. Staff will parallel the inmate population in terms of race and ethnicity—there will be greater minority participation within the correctional employment sector. Another issue that will continue to develop is the problem of staff having inappropriate relationships with prisoners. One of the biggest changes in terms of staff has been the desexualization of the workplace—female employees can work within male prisoner institutions.

The use of technology to manage offender populations is another expanding area. We will see greater use of architecture to help prison administrators manage inmates—pod type designs coupled with a greater use of such technologies as cameras and electronics and computers to help manage the inmate population. This kind of heavy technology will be used to manage the high-risk inmates to such an extent that the social distance between or any kind of human contact between keeper and keep will be minimized. Advancements in using technology will help to manage and control inmates, to keep staff away from dangerous inmates on the inside. I think we will definitely be using chips and other electronic devices to track and follow inmates and track their movement and behavior on the outside. This will become critical and will become a civil rights issue, but I think that public safety will win out over the use of such intrusive devices. This issue will become a major civil rights issue and it will be tested in the Supreme Court, but we are going to see great advancements in technology that monitor the movement of criminal offenders in the free society. The test cases are going to be with sex offenders and how these offenders are to be monitored in the free community.

ABOUT THE AUTHOR

James W. Marquart is a professor of criminal justice at Sam Houston State University in Huntsville, Texas. In 1991, his book, *Appeal to Justice: Litigated Reform of Texas Prisons* (University of Texas Press, 1989) received the Outstanding Book Award from the Academy of Criminal Justice Sciences. In 1995, his book, *The Rope, the Chair, and the Needle: Capital Punishment in Texas: 1923–1990*, (University of Texas Press, 1994), received the Outstanding Book award from the American Library Association.

30 college credits, a certificate of achievement after completing the first year, and assistance in finding a job after release from prison.

Although the number of inmates who can participate in occupational training is limited, all inmates are entitled to some form of recreation. However, the specifics about the nature and extent of recreation programming in prison and inmates' participation in such programs are not known.

Recreation and organized sports can make doing time more bearable and, as a result, make the jobs of correctional officers easier. They can also be used as an incentive for good behavior, and by reducing tension, they can cut the number of prison assaults. Physical and mental health experts tell us that recreation programs can be a vehicle for teaching ways to promote health and prevent disease. Inmates who play hard are more likely to stay fit, possibly reducing health costs. Nutrition experts know that eating healthful food, participating in a regular exercise program, and stopping smoking are central to maintaining good health in prison. They also reduce the cost of prison health care.

HEALTH CARE

Good health care is also an integral part of institutional security. Investments in prisoner health care mean fewer correctional disturbances, disciplinary actions, and inmate injuries and less negative publicity for the institution. The public health suffers when good health care is not provided, as it did in 1989 in New York City when 80 percent of tuberculosis cases were traced to people released from jail and prison. In Los Angeles, a meningitis outbreak in the county jail spread to surrounding neighborhoods. Thus, our policies toward prisoners have a direct impact on the public health of everyone.

It is also a fact that 40 state mental hospitals have closed in the past 10 years because of deinstitutionalization (the transfer of former mental hospital patients to community residential care settings), reductions in state spending for treatment of the mentally ill (one-third less today than in 1950), and changes in mental health law that have made involuntary commitment more difficult. At the same time, more than 400 new prisons have opened.[30] As a result, jails and prisons have become the institutions most likely to house the mentally ill. On the positive side, however, correctional facilities have an opportunity to provide prevention and treatment interventions to a seriously underserved and needy population. Our policies and programs for prisoners mean they can return to our communities as better citizens, in better health, under treatment for their medical and mental health conditions, and better equipped and motivated to protect themselves and others, possibly reducing the cost to taxpayers of future health care and reincarceration. Overall, more prisons provide counseling programs (96 percent), than either educational (89 percent) or work programs (91 percent). Drug and alcohol dependency counseling programs are the most common.

Providing inmates adequate health care is of concern to the courts and professional associations. In 1976, the U.S. Supreme Court ruled in *Estelle* v. *Gamble* that inmates have a constitutional right to reasonable, adequate health services for serious medical needs. However, the Court also made clear that such a right did not mean that prisoners have unqualified access to health care. Lower courts have held that the Constitution does not require the medical care provided prisoners to be perfect, the best obtainable, or even very good.[31] According to an excellent review of legal health care standards and the legal remedies available to prisoners, the courts support the **principle of least eligibility:** that prison conditions—including the delivery of health care—must be a step below those of the working class and people on welfare. As a result, prisoners are denied access to medical specialists, second opinions, prompt delivery of medical services, technologically advanced diagnostic techniques, the latest medications, and up-to-date medical procedures. In addition, prisoners do not have the right to sue physicians for malpractice, or if they do, the damages are lower than those awarded to people outside prison. Still, health care professionals and inmate advocates— such as the American Medical Association and the National Commission on Correctional Health Care—insist on alleviating the pain and suffering of all people, regardless of their status. They believe that no distinction should be made between inmates and free citizens. We will return to the mental health issues of special needs inmates in Chapter 12.

principle of least eligibility

The requirement that prison conditions—including the delivery of health care—must be a step below those of the working class and people on welfare.

> Mentally ill inmates often lack proper care in jail and prison systems. What can we do to address the plight of the mentally ill in our institutions? Should a person's mental illness have any bearing on their sentencing? Incarceration? For more information go to Ethical Dilemma 7-2 at http://www.mhhe.com/schmalleger2.

Ethical Dilemma

Prison Organization and Administration

All 50 states and the BOP operate prisons. In addition, four local jurisdictions in the United States operate prison systems: Cook County (Chicago), Illinois; Philadelphia; New York City; and Washington, D.C. It is estimated that there are 1,208 state, federal, and private prisons: 84 federal, 1,023 state, and 101 private prisons.[32] More than 8 of every 10 prisons house men only; facilities housing women only and facilities holding both, men and women, each accounted for fewer than 1 out of every 10 confinement facilities.

Jurisdictions use a variety of capacity measures to reflect both the space available to house inmates and the ability to staff and operate an institution. Some use rated capacity, the number of beds or inmates a rating official assigns to an institution. Some use **operational capacity,** the number of inmates that a facility's staff, existing programs, and services can accommodate. Others use **design capacity,** the number of inmates that planners or architects intend for the facility. For instance, an architect might design a prison for 1,100 inmates. Administrators might add more staff, programs, and services to be able to confine 1,300 in the same space. The design capacity was 1,100, but the operational and rated capacities are 1,300. The institution is operating 18 percent above design capacity.

operational capacity

The number of inmates that a facility's staff, existing programs, and services can accommodate.

design capacity

The number of inmates that planners or architects intend for the facility.

At yearend 2002, the federal prison system was operating at 33 percent over capacity. Overall, state prisons were operating between 1 percent and 16 percent over capacity. We return to the issue of prison capacity and overcrowding in Chapter 13.

STATE PRISON SYSTEMS

Organization The administration of state prisons is a function of the executive branch of government. The governor appoints the director of corrections, who in turn appoints the wardens of the state prisons. A change in governors often means a change in state prison leadership and administration. The organizational structure of the California Department of Corrections, which is similar to the structure of corrections departments in other states, is shown in Figure 7–3.

The organization of most state prison systems, like California's, involves a central authority, based in the state capital. Local communities, private contractors, or the state itself may provide prison services (from treatment and education to maintenance and repair). This method of organizational structure and delivery of services across wide geographic areas is often criticized for its fragmentation; duplication of structure, effort, and services; lack of coordination; and ambiguous goals. Still, for legal control and for maintaining an equitable distribution of resources, a centralized model has been maintained, while in other areas of corrections (e.g., community corrections and probation), services are often decentralized.

There is no correct way to organize corrections. Any arrangement that helps corrections reach its goals is appropriate. The organizational styles found across the United States developed over time and are the result of political interaction and accommodation among government agencies and interest groups. Today, prisons borrow consumer-oriented management techniques from private business. They periodically survey staff and inmates to identify problems and avoid confrontations. Technological improvements give prison administrators access to more information for decision making, and management training is more popular.

Size and Costs   State prison organizations vary in size. One of the smallest is North Dakota's, with 717 employees and an annual operating budget of $41 million. The largest is California's, with almost 50,000 employees and an annual operating budget of $5.3 billion.[33] More than 390,000 people work in adult correctional facilities; 260,943 are correctional officers, 50,627 are clerical, maintenance and food service workers, 53,988 are professional/technical staff, 13,322 are educators, and 11,158 are administrators.[34] Most correctional facility staff are male (67 percent) and white (64 percent). Nineteen percent of all correctional facility staff are black, and 7 percent are Hispanic.

In 2000, state operating budgets for corrections totaled $31.4 billion. The capital costs of building one prison cell can be as much as $80,000.[35] Some ask if the money spent on state corrections encroaches on funds for higher education because the money has to come from somewhere. Is there discussion about this kind of trade-off? Jennifer Gonnerman, a reporter for the *Village Voice* writes, "When parents get a tuition bill for their kids' college education, I always think they should get a little note that says tuition went up $200 last year because we decided to build two new prisons. Then we can all decide whether we think that's a good use of our money or not."[36] From 1993–2002, average annual prison costs in most states increased by one-fourth. For example, in South Carolina, the annual cost per inmate increased from $12,296 to $14,975.[37]

Prisons are expensive. Besides the cost of building a prison, there are also annual operating costs. In the same way it took money to build the classroom you are in, it takes money each year to operate it (pay for electricity, heat, air conditioning, supplies, building maintenance and upgrading,

CALIFORNIA DEPARTMENT OF CORRECTIONS
DEPARTMENTAL ORGANIZATION CHART

FIGURE 7-3
California Department of Corrections Departmental Organization Chart

teachers' salaries, etc.). As of January 1, 2000, states spent $31.4 billion for adult prisons—to build, staff, and maintain the facilities and to house the prisoners. Approximately $28.5 billion, or 91 percent of state prison expenditures, went for salaries, wages, benefits, and other operating expenses. On average, states spend approximately $25,000 a year to incarcerate one offender.[38]

maximum- or close/high-security prison

A prison designed, organized, and staffed to confine the most dangerous offenders for long periods. It has a highly secure perimeter, barred cells, and a high staff-to-inmate ratio. It imposes strict controls on the movement of inmates and visitors, and it offers few programs, amenities, or privileges.

Security Level   Prisons are classified by the level of security they provide. A **maximum- or close/high-security prison** is designed, organized, and staffed to confine the most violent and dangerous offenders for long periods. It imposes strict controls on the movement of inmates and their visitors, and custody and security are constant concerns. The prison has a highly secure perimeter with watchtowers and high walls. Inmates live in single- or multiple-occupancy barred cells. The staff-to-inmate ratio is high, routines are highly regimented, and prisoner counts are frequent. Programs, amenities, and privileges are few. There are 332 maximum- and close/high-security prisons in the United States confining 36 percent of the prisoner population.[39]

medium-security prison

A prison that confines offenders considered less dangerous than those in maximum security, for both short and long periods. It places fewer controls on inmates' and visitors' freedom of movement than does a maximum-security facility. It, too, has barred cells and a fortified perimeter. The staff-to-inmate ratio is generally lower than in a maximum-security facility, and the level of amenities and privileges is slightly higher.

Inmates in a **medium-security prison** are considered less dangerous than those in maximum-security prisons and may serve short or long sentences. Medium-security prisons impose fewer controls on inmates' and visitors' freedom of movement than do maximum-security facilities. Outwardly, medium-security prisons often resemble maximum-security institutions, and they, too, have barred cells. The staff-to-inmate ratio is generally lower than in a maximum-security facility. Medium-security prisons place more emphasis on treatment and work programs than do maximum-security prisons, and the level of amenities and privileges is slightly higher. Forty-eight percent of the prisoner population is serving time in 506 medium-security prisons.[40]

minimum-security prison

A prison that confines the least dangerous offenders for both short and long periods. It allows as much freedom of movement and as many privileges and amenities as are consistent with the goals of the facility. It may have dormitory housing, and the staff-to-inmate ratio is relatively low.

A **minimum-security prison** confines the least dangerous offenders for both short and long periods. It allows as much freedom of movement and as many privileges and amenities as are consistent with the goals of the facility while still following procedures to avoid escape, violence, and disturbance. The staff-to-inmate ratio is low, and inmates live in dormitory housing or private rooms. Some leave the institution for programming in the community. There are 370 minimum-security prisons in the United States confining 17 percent of the prisoner population.[41] They are sometimes referred to as **open institutions** because they have no fences or walls surrounding them.

Approximately 27 percent of men's prisons are maximum security. The rest are split between medium (42 percent) and minimum security (31 percent). The security level of women's prisons is approximately one-third each, minimum, medium and maximum.[42]

open institution

A minimum-security facility that has no fences or walls surrounding it.

FEDERAL BUREAU OF PRISONS

The BOP is an entirely separate system from state and local prison systems. Before the 1890s, the federal government did not operate its own prisons. Instead, the Department of Justice paid state prisons and county jails to house people convicted of committing federal crimes. The public outcry over the convict lease system, however, motivated the passage of a federal law prohibiting the leasing of federal offenders. Many state prisons and county jails subsequently became reluctant to house federal offenders because it was not economically advantageous to incarcerate inmates they could not lease. Moreover, the expansion of federal law enforcement activities and the enactment of new federal laws in the late 19th century led to an increase in the prosecution of federal lawbreakers and to overcrowding in the prisons where they were held. With a growing population of federal prisoners, and the growing reluctance of nonfederal prisons to house them, the federal government had no choice but to build prisons of its own. Congress authorized the establishment of three federal prisons in 1891: U.S. penitentiaries at Atlanta (Georgia), Leavenworth (Kansas), and McNeil Island (Washington).

Bureau of Prisons   In 1930, the BOP was established to provide more progressive and humane care for 13,000 federal inmates, to professionalize the prison service, and to ensure consistent and centralized administration of the 11 federal prisons in operation at that time. Between 1940 and 1980, the BOP held steady with approximately 25 institutions and some 25,000 inmates. Most of the BOP's growth in institutions and inmates occurred in the 1980s as a result of federal law enforcement efforts and new legislation that altered sentencing in the federal criminal justice system. From 1980 to 1989, the federal inmate population doubled, from 25,000 to more than 58,000. During the 1990s, the population doubled again as efforts to combat illegal drugs and illegal immigration contributed to increasing conviction rates. Former BOP director, Dr. Kathleen Hawk Sawyer, told the U.S. Senate Judiciary Subcommittee on Criminal Justice that, if current growth trends continue, there will be 205,000 federal prisoners in 2007, a 50 percent increase over current levels.

Exhibit 7–3 shows the mission statement of the BOP. The central office in Washington, D.C., six regional offices, two staff training centers, and 103 confinement and community-based correctional institutions carry out this mission. The BOP also houses the National Institute of Corrections (NIC), which advises and assists state and local correctional agencies throughout the country, primarily through technical assistance, training, and information services. The attorney general appoints the director of the BOP. Harley G. Lappin was sworn in as Director of the BOP on April 4, 2003. He is the seventh director of the Bureau since its establishment in 1930. The BOP organizational chart is shown in Figure 7–4.

The BOP employs more than 34,000 people nationwide. Almost 30 percent of the BOP workforce is female and one-third is minority. Thirty percent of BOP personnel have completed some college. Another 30 percent have a bachelor's degree or further education.

The BOP budget for 2003 was $4.4 billion.[43] The largest portion, $1.9 billion, was for institution security and administration, including the costs of facility maintenance, motor pool operations, and other administrative functions for all BOP facilities. The second highest cost was $1.5 billion for inmate care and programs. This included the costs of all food, medical supplies, clothing, welfare services, transportation, staff salaries, academic courses, social and occupational education courses,

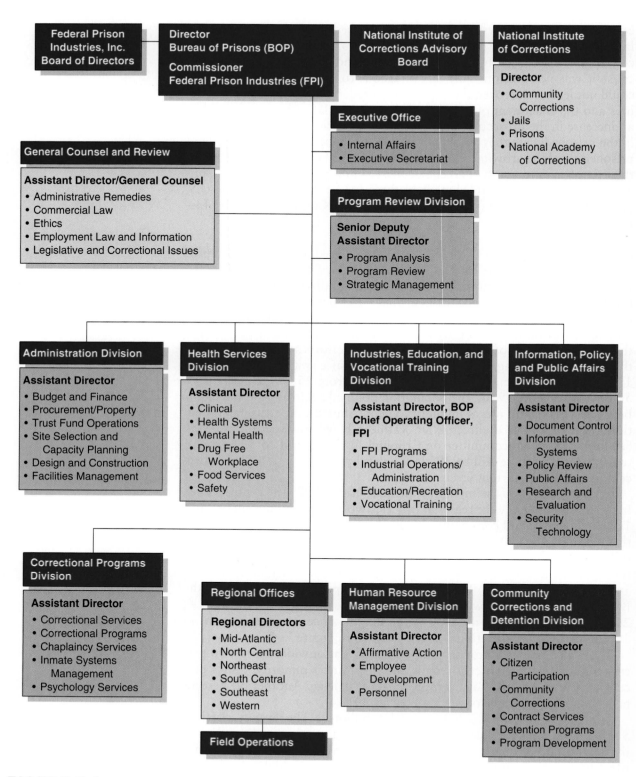

FIGURE 7-4
Organization of Federal Bureau of Prisons

CAREER PROFILE

Rachel Anita Jung
Training Officer   Arizona Department of Corrections

Rachel Anita Jung is staff training officer for the Arizona Department of Corrections. She plans the statewide corrections staff training curriculum and coordinates staff training at the Arizona State Prison in Yuma. She joined the department in 1996. Previously, she worked as an adult probation officer and a jail case manager.

Rachel received her bachelor's degree in criminal justice from California State University at San Bernardino, and her masters of science degree in criminal justice from the University of Alabama. She feels that a number of undergraduate courses helped her succeed in the corrections field. Constitutional law gave her an appreciation for the ethical issues in corrections. Procedural law gave her an understanding of offenders' due process safeguards. And criminological theory led her to understand that the causes of criminal behavior are complex. She says that criminological theory was "a real challenge."

Rachel believes that careers in corrections can really make a difference in offenders' lives. As a corrections training officer, she believes that her work has additional influences, because she has the opportunity to develop a curriculum that influences the way staff throughout the state interact with inmates.

In the future, Rachel hopes to move forward in corrections administration, possibly doing corrections research and influencing correctional policy.

> You have to be very inquisitive. You have to know a lot about people. You have to be a good communicator. You especially have to be a good listener and develop training programs that adapt to the evolving challenges in the field.

religious programs, psychological services, and drug abuse treatment. The average annual cost to incarcerate an inmate was $22,517 in 2002.

Institutions and Security Level   On January 1, 2003, 163,528 inmates were under the jurisdiction of the Federal prison system (of whom 12.4 percent or 20,274 prisoners were held in private facilities and local jails). The BOP operates 103 confinement and community-based correctional institutions of several different security levels to confine appropriately a broad range of federal offenders. The classification of facilities by security level is based on such factors as the presence of gun towers, security barriers, or detection devices; the types of housing within the institution; internal security features; and the staff-to-inmate ratio. Each facility is placed in one of five groups—minimum-security, low-security, medium-security, high-security, and administrative:

- Minimum-security institutions, also known as *federal prison camps* (FPCs), have dormitory housing, a relatively low staff-to-inmate ratio, and limited or no perimeter fencing. These institutions are work and program oriented. Many are adjacent to larger institutions or on military bases, where inmates help serve the labor needs of the institution, military base, or other federal entities such as the National Park Service and U.S. Forest Service. Approximately 20 percent of BOP inmates are in minimum-security facilities.

- Low-security federal correctional institutions (FCIs) have double-fenced perimeters, mostly dormitory housing, and strong work and program components. The staff-to-inmate ratio in these institutions is higher than in minimum-security facilities. Approximately 39 percent of BOP inmates are in low-security facilities.

EXHIBIT 7–3   **Federal Bureau of Prisons**

Mission Statement

It is the mission of the Federal Bureau of Prisons to protect society by confining offenders in the controlled environments of prison and community-based facilities that are safe, humane, and appropriately secure and that provide work and other self-improvement opportunities to assist offenders in becoming law-abiding citizens.

Source: Federal Bureau of Prisons, July 1998.

- Medium-security FCIs have fortified perimeters (often double fences with electronic detection systems), cell housing, and a wide variety of work and treatment programs. They have an even higher staff-to-inmate ratio than do low-security FCIs, providing even greater internal controls. Approximately 25 percent of BOP inmates are in medium-security facilities.

- High-security institutions, known as *U.S. penitentiaries* (USPs), have highly secure perimeters (featuring walls or reinforced fences), multiple- and single-occupancy cell housing, close staff supervision, and strict movement controls. Approximately 11 percent of BOP inmates are in high-security facilities.

- Administrative institutions have special missions, such as detention of noncitizens or pretrial offenders, treatment of inmates with serious or chronic medical problems, or containment of extremely dangerous or escape-prone inmates. Approximately 6 percent of BOP inmates are in administrative facilities. Figure 7–5 shows the locations of all BOP facilities.

By 2007, the BOP budget is estimated to be $6.5 billion, and an additional 29 facilities are expected to open—13 high-security penitentiaries, 15 medium-security FCIs, and one federal detention center.

Does Incarceration Work?

After reading this chapter, you might wonder if incarceration works. Whether incarceration works depends on whom you ask and how he or she interprets the question. What does "work" mean? Does it refer to the prevention of rearrest, reconviction, or reincarceration? Should a new offense be related to previous ones? What if a new offense occurs 5 or 10 years after release from prison? Should the prison experience deter potential *and* actual offenders? Should it lower the crime rate? If so, by how much, how fast, and at what cost? What about criminological theories that link crime to forces outside the individual and over which the offender has little or no control such as his or her biology or psychological makeup, social structures, and even the more radical explanations that link crime to economic development, race, class, and gender? Politicians and researchers see the question differently. Governors and directors of corrections see the question straightforwardly: Were it not for prison, there would be more crime. Removing convicted offenders from the community ensures public safety, and the cost of incarceration is the price tag for ensuring that safety.

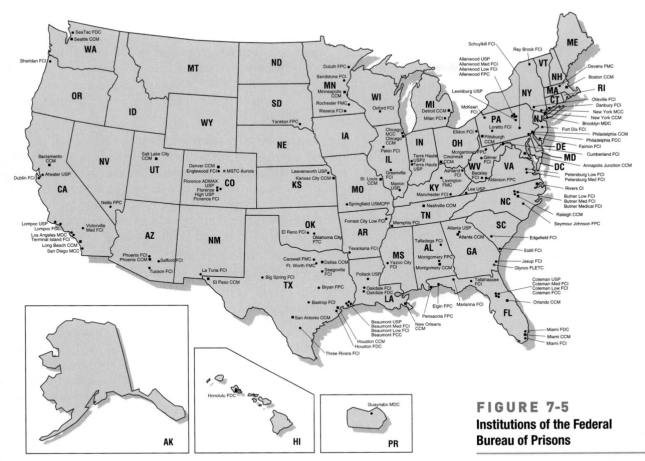

FIGURE 7-5

Institutions of the Federal Bureau of Prisons

Source: U.S. Department of Justice, Federal Bureau of Prisons, 2003. Some locations have more than one institution.

Researchers feel the effectiveness question can only be answered with randomly designed experiments, in which identically matched offenders are randomly assigned to prison or to other punishments. Even if such experiments were possible, there are differences between prisoners and people not sent to prison, and these differences will influence future offending.

If you look at the relationship between the crime index and the prison population over the past eight years, you might reach the conclusion that, as the nation's prison population grew, crime fell and, therefore, the experiment in locking up more people lowered the nation's volume of crime. For example, David Muhlhausen, a policy analyst at the Heritage Foundation, argues that increasing incarceration decreases crime. "Considering that there are still about 12 million crimes a year," Muhlhausen concludes, then "maybe we're not incarcerating enough people."[44] Unfortunately, if you look at the seven years before that, you find that, as the prison population increased, so too did crime. Furthermore, if you look at the past quarter century of prison buildup, you find periods during which crime increased, decreased, increased, and decreased. There is simply no strong or consistent relationship between incarceration rate and crime rate. Alfred Blumstein, a criminologist at Carnegie-Mellon University in Pittsburgh, believes that only about 25 percent of the drop in crime in recent years resulted from locking up more offenders. The rest resulted from other factors, including the ebbing of the crack cocaine epidemic, changes in policing strategies, and the strong economy of the 1990s.[45]

In June 2002, the Bureau of Justice Statistics reported on four measures of recidivism of 272,111 prisoners discharged from 15 states and tracked for three years after their release in 1994.[46] Overall, 68 percent were rearrested within three years. Specifically, the study found that, within three years from their release in 1994,

- 68 percent of the prisoners were rearrested for a new offense (almost exclusively a felony or a serious misdemeanor). Released prisoners with the highest rearrest rates were robbers, burglars, larcenists, motor vehicle thieves, those in prison for possessing or selling stolen property, and those in prison for possessing, using, or selling illegal weapons. Released prisoners with the lowest rearrest rates were those in prison for homicide, rape, other sexual assault, and DWI.
- 47 percent were reconvicted for a new crime.
- 25 percent were resentenced to prison for a new crime.
- 52 percent were back in prison, serving time for a new prison sentence or for a technical violation of their release.

BJS also found no evidence that spending more time in prison raises the recidivism rate. BJS evidence was mixed, however, regarding the question of whether spending more time in prison reduces recidivism. Specifically, BJS found that recidivism rates did not differ significantly among those released after serving 6 months or less (66 percent), those released after 7 to 12 months (65 percent), those released after 13 to 18 months (64 percent), those released after 19 to 24 months (65 percent), and those released after 25 to 30 months (68 percent). The increase in time served in prison, however, has implications for reentry (the subject of Chapter 8) in that longer prison stays may impact subsequent employment and earnings and are associated with less family contact, which, in turn, can have adverse effects on community reintegration upon release.[47] Thus, there is no indication that we have come any closer in reaching consensus on the question of whether incarceration works.

SUMMARY

1 ▶ The Pennsylvania and Auburn prison systems emerged in the United States at the turn of the 19th century. The Pennsylvania system isolated prisoners from each other to avoid harmful influences and to give prisoners reflection time so they might repent. The Auburn system allowed inmates to work together during the day under strict silence. At night, however, prisoners were isolated in small sleeping cells. With time, sleeping cells became congregate and restrictions against talking were removed.

2 ▶ There have been nine eras in U.S. prison history:

- Penitentiary Era (1790–1825);
- Mass Prison Era (1825–1876);
- Reformatory Era (1876–1890);
- Industrial Era (1890–1935);
- Punitive Era (1935–1945);
- Treatment Era (1945–1967);
- Community-Based Era (1967–1980);
- Warehousing Era (1980–1995);
- Just-Deserts Era (1985–present).

3 ▶ On January 1, 2003, 1,277,127 people were under the jurisdiction of state correctional authorities, and 163,528 people were under the jurisdiction of the federal prison system. Of these state and federal inmates, 93 percent were male, 34 percent were white, 45 percent were black, and 18 percent were Hispanic. Reasons for the increase in women prisoners include women's presence in the U.S. labor market, which has brought about increased opportunities for crime; the increased poverty of young, female, single heads of households, which means that more women are turning to crime to support themselves and their families; changes in the criminal justice system, which no longer affords women differential treatment; and the combined effects of harsh drug laws, changing patterns of drug use, and mandatory sentencing policies. Reasons for the increase in minority prisoners include an increase in serious criminal activity that results in incarceration; racial profiling and racism by the criminal justice system; and the prevalence of social conditions that exist in the nation's inner cities which is where most minorities in the United States regardless of race live, and the fact that large urban areas have the highest violence rates.

4 ▶ Classification is the principal management tool for allocating scarce prison resources efficiently and minimizing the potential for escape or violence. The purpose is to assign inmates to appropriate prison housing and to help staff understand, treat, predict, and manage prisoner behavior. There are two types of classification, external and internal. External classification determines an inmate's security level (maximum, close, medium, minimum, or community). Internal classification determines an inmate's assignment to housing units or cellblocks, work, and programming based on the inmate's risk, needs, and time to serve.

5 ▶ Prison work is generally of three types: operational assignments within the institution (including prison farms and other agricultural activities), community projects, or prison industry. In operational assignments within the institution, inmates perform tasks necessary to the functioning of the facility or larger corrections system. Through community service, offenders contribute their labor to benefit the community while developing job skills in a practical, nonprison setting. In prison industry, states partner with private sector industries to operate prison industries to employ and train inmates.

REVIEW & APPLICATIONS

REVIEW & APPLICATIONS

6 ▶ General education programs are readily available across the United States, but postsecondary programming has been on the decline since President Clinton's 1994 crime bill, which denied Pell grants to inmates. Occupational training is also provided in a wide variety of areas but is often limited to a few inmates. The exact nature and extent of recreation programming in prison and inmates' participation in them is not known. In 1976, the U.S. Supreme Court ruled in *Estelle v. Gamble* that inmates have a constitutional right to reasonable, adequate health care for serious medical needs. However, the Court also made clear that such a right did not mean that prisoners have unqualified access to health care.

7 ▶ All 50 states, the federal Bureau of Prisons (BOP), and four local jurisdictions operate correctional institutions. State prison administration, a function of the executive branch of government, is most often organized around a central authority, operating from the state capital. There are three levels of prison security: maximum, for the most dangerous offenders serving long sentences; medium, for less dangerous offenders serving long or short sentences; and minimum, for the least dangerous offenders. Most prisons are either medium or minimum security. The BOP operates 103 federal confinement and community-based correctional facilities. The BOP operates minimum-security prisons known as *federal prison camps,* low- and medium-security facilities known as *federal correctional institutions,* high-security institutions known as *U.S. penitentiaries,* and administrative institutions with special missions, such as detention of illegal immigrants, treatment of people with chronic medical problems, and containment of extremely dangerous or escape-prone inmates. The majority of federal prisoners are confined in low- and medium-security facilities.

8 ▶ Whether incarceration works depends on whom you ask and how he or she interprets the question. Politicians and researchers see the question differently. Governors and directors of corrections see the question straightforwardly: Were it not for prison, there would be more crime. Researchers feel the question can be answered only with randomly designed experiments. There is no indication that we have come any closer to reaching consensus on the question of whether incarceration works.

KEY TERMS

penitentiary, *p. 241*
Pennsylvania system, *p. 241*
Auburn system, *p. 241*
public accounts system, *p. 244*
contract system, *p. 244*
convict lease system, *p. 245*
state use system, *p. 245*
public works system, *p. 246*
medical model, *p. 246*
classification, *p. 254*
external classification, *p. 255*

internal classification, *p. 255*
unit management
  system, *p. 260*
manpower model, *p. 263*
employer model, *p. 263*
customer model, *p. 263*
Federal Prison Industries
  (FPI), *p. 264*
UNICOR, *p. 264*
principle of least
  eligibility, *p. 271*

operational capacity, *p. 271*
design capacity, *p. 271*
maximum- or close/high-
  security prison, *p. 274*
medium-security
  prison, *p. 274*
minimum-security
  prison, *p. 274*
open institution, *p. 274*

QUESTIONS FOR REVIEW

1. What were the differences between the Pennsylvania and Auburn prison systems? Which prison system became the preferred model of incarceration in the United States, and why?
2. What were the characteristics of the first reformatories?
3. How is the prison industry regulated today?
4. What was the reasoning behind the community-based approach?
5. What is meant by *just deserts?*
6. Approximately how many people are in prison today, and what are their characteristics by gender, race, age, and offense?
7. Distinguish between the two types of prisoner classification.

8. Distinguish between the three types of prison work programs.
9. What is UNICOR?
10. Describe the literacy problem among prisoners.
11. What are the benefits of recreation and organized sports in prison?
12. Why are jails and prisons more likely to house the mentally ill than are mental hospitals?
13. Describe state and federal prison organization and administration.
14. Distinguish among maximum-, medium-, and minimum-security prisons. How many state and federal prisoners are confined in each?

THINKING CRITICALLY ABOUT CORRECTIONS

▶ ▶ ▶ Stages of Prison Development

Charles Dickens, the English novelist, visited Eastern State Penitentiary in 1842. After witnessing solitary confinement, he wrote in *American Notes and Pictures from Italy* that "very few men are capable of estimating the immense amount of torture and agony which this dreadful punishment, prolonged for years, inflicts upon the sufferers." He added, "I hold this slow and daily tampering with the mysteries of the brain to be immeasurably worse than any torture of the body; and because its ghastly signs and tokens are not so palpable to the eye and sense of touch as scars upon the flesh, . . . I denounce it as secret punishment." How might Dickens's writing have influenced the stages of prison development and urged reformers to seek other systems of punishment?

▶ ▶ ▶ Goals for Prison

For 200 years, prisons have tried to change inmates' negative behaviors. Recently, the Bureau of Prisons has said that prison is not the ideal setting to do that, nor is such change realistic in prison, considering prisoners' resistance and the failure of previous attempts. What realistic goals for prison would you devise and what outcome measures would you propose to assess whether prisons are meeting those goals?

ON-THE-JOB DECISION MAKING

▶ ▶ ▶ Advantages of UNICOR

Imagine that you are chairperson of the five-member Federal Prison Industries Board of Directors appointed by the president. In 2002, FPI employed 21,778 federal prisoners, paid them between $0.23 and $1.15 an hour, generated sales in excess of $678 million, and made a profit of $9 million. (You can learn more about FPI at its Website at www.unicor.gov). Imagine further that it is an election year and the U.S. economy is stagnant. Organized labor and small businesses are complaining that FPI is too big and constitutes unfair competition. Prepare a 30-second "sound-bite" on the advantages of FPI's success that the president will give when addressing a national meeting of the AFL-CIO.

▶ ▶ ▶ Is There Value in Keeping R&E?

In 2002, the South Carolina Department of Corrections closed two prisons because of significant budget reductions. Inmates were transferred to other facilities. Now some critics argue that South Carolina's R&E Center (see Exhibit 7–2) is a luxury that is no longer affordable. They argue that prisoners should be distributed evenly across the state's 29 prisons. The Governor is asking you, as R&E manager, to compose a list of reasons for keeping and closing the Center.

CORRECTIONS ON THE WEB

▶ ▶ ▶ Office of Correctional Education

The Office of Correctional Education of the U.S. Department of Education published a list of 19 abstracts on the relationship between correctional education and recidivism. Access the abstracts by going to the Office of Correctional Education at http://www.ed.gov/offices/OVAE/AdultEd/OCE. Click on *Correctional Education Library,* or search for *recidivism*. Review the archived articles and write a summary of the literature on the relationship between correctional education and recidivism.

▶ ▶ ▶ State of Washington

According to the Website of the Department of Corrections for the state of Washington (www.wa.gov/doc/), the operational capacity of the state's prisons is 14,977 prisoners. (Recall that *operational capacity* means the number of inmates a facility's staff, programs, and services can accommodate.) As of December 22, 2003, Washington had incarcerated 16,242 prisoners. What percentage of operational capacity is the inmate population?

" I am no sentimentalist. I most fully subscribe to the right claimed by society to make examples of those who break laws, that others may feel constrained to respect and obey them . . . We have no right to cast them away altogether. Even their physical suffering should be in moderation, and the moral pain we must and ought to inflict with it should be carefully framed so as if posssible to reform, and not necessarily to pervert, them. "

—Captain Alexander Maconochie, British Royal Navy and
Superintendent of Norfolk Island Penal Colony, Australia, father of parole, 1840–1844

Parole:
Early Release
and Reintegration

▶ CHAPTER OBJECTIVES

After completing this chapter you should be able to do the following:

1. Present a brief history of American parole development.

2. Understand the function of parole in the criminal justice system.

3. Define *parole* and explain the parole decision-making process.

4. Describe the characteristics of the parole population.

5. Explain the circumstances under which parole may be revoked.

6. Summarize current issues in parole.

Some call "Iron" Mike Tyson the best heavyweight fighter who ever lived. In Indiana, however, he's a convicted felon and parole violator. On February 10, 1992, Mike Tyson was convicted of raping a Miss Black America contestant, Desiree Washington. He served 3 years of a 10-year prison sentence at the Indiana Youth Center in Plainfield, Indiana, and was allowed to serve the remainder of his sentence on parole. While on parole, Tyson assaulted two motorists in Maryland with whom he had a minor car accident. On December 1, 1998, he plead no contest and was sentenced to two concurrent two-year sentences and fined $5,000. For violating his parole, the State of Indiana ordered Tyson to serve an additional 60 days in a Maryland jail.

Former heavyweight champion Mike Tyson. Tyson spent three years in prison for rape and ordered to serve the remainder of his 10-year sentence on parole. While on parole he assaulted two motorists with whom he had a car accident. For that violation, he spent another 60 days in jail. Do you think persons who violate the conditions of their parole should be reincarcerated?

Stories like Tyson's are far too familiar in the parole field. As you will learn in this chapter, the majority of persons on parole either violate the technical conditions of their parole or commit a new crime. The half a million inmates set to be released from prison each year, in addition to those on parole, threaten to overwhelm the parole system and will pose a threat to public safety unless changes are made.

For more than a century, parole has been used for early release from prison—inmates are released from some type of institutional custody but remain in the legal custody of the government. Although the release of individuals from prison to the community is not new, a focus on the phenomenon of reentry is reshaping the debate on parole.

Parole as Part of the Criminal Justice System

People often confuse *parole*, *probation*, and *pardon*. All three place offenders in the community, but they are very different.

Parole is the conditional release of a prison inmate, prior to sentence expiration, with supervision in the community. A parole usually comes from authorities in the correctional system—responsibility for offenders passes from the judicial system to the correctional system upon imprisonment.

parole

The conditional release of a prisoner, prior to completion of the imposed sentence, under the supervision of a parole officer.

Release on parole may be mandatory or discretionary. **Discretionary release** is at the paroling authority's discretion, within boundaries established by the sentence and by law. **Mandatory release** is early release after a specific period of time, as specified by law. In those states that permit discretionary release, state laws give correctional officials the authority to change, within certain limits, the *length* of a sentence. Correctional officials may also change the *conditions* under which convicted offenders are supervised— they may release offenders from prison to supervision in the community or to an outside facility.

As we saw in Chapter 4, *probation* is a judge's sentence that allows a convicted offender to continue to live in the community, with restrictions on activities and with supervision for the duration of the sentence.

A **pardon** is an executive act that legally excuses a convicted offender from penalty. It is granted by a governor or the President. Those who are pardoned are excused from any further supervision.

discretionary release

Early release based on the paroling authority's assessment of eligibility.

mandatory release

Early release after a time period specified by law.

pardon

An executive act that legally excuses a convicted offender from a criminal penalty.

HISTORICAL OVERVIEW

The parole concept has its roots in an 18th-century English penal practice —indentured servitude. Judges transferred custody of physically fit condemned felons to independent contractors, paying those contractors a fee to transport the prisoners to the American colonies and sell their services, for the duration of their sentences, to the highest bidder. This practice was similar to today's parole in that the indentured servant had to comply with certain conditions to remain in supervised "freedom." This practice was discontinued with the beginning of the American Revolutionary War in 1775 because English offenders were joining colonial forces against England.

From 1775 through 1856, English offenders were sent to Australia as punishment. Those who committed further felonies in Australia were transported to England's most punitive prison on Norfolk Island, 1,000 miles off the east coast of Australia. In 1840, British Navy Captain Alexander Maconochie was appointed superintendent of the penal colony. Maconochie favored indeterminate sentences rather than fixed sentences. He recommended, and in part implemented, a marks system to measure the prisoner's progress toward release from prison, and he urged a system of graduated release and aftercare of prisoners to resettle them in the community. He developed a "ticket of leave" system, which moved inmates through stages: imprisonment, conditional release, and complete restoration of liberty. Inmates moved from one stage to the next by earning "marks" for improved conduct, frugality, and good work habits. Although Maconochie had control over island tickets-of-leave, he could not control a graduated return to society in England. Maconochie's ideas did not blend well with the official English position on punishment, which was rooted in deterrence and relied on the infliction of suffering. He was removed in 1844 and the penal colony at Norfolk Island lapsed into a period of extraordinary brutality before it closed in 1856. Maconochie is referred to as the father of parole.

In 1854, Sir Walter Crofton, director of the Irish prison system, implemented a system that was based on Maconochie's "ticket of leave" system.

Crofton's version required that, upon conditional release, a former inmate do the following:

1. Report immediately to the constabulary on arrival and once a week thereafter.
2. Abstain from any violation of the law.
3. Refrain from habitually associating with notoriously bad characters.
4. Refrain from leading an idle and dissolute life, without means of obtaining an honest living.
5. Produce the "ticket of leave" when asked to do so by a magistrate or police officer.
6. Not change locality without reporting to the constabulary.[1]

The former inmate who did not comply with the conditions of release was re-imprisoned. Crofton's system of conditional release is considered the forerunner of modern American parole.

Use of the term *parole* for early release from prison began with a letter from Dr. S. G. Howe of Boston to the Prison Association of New York in 1846. Howe wrote, "I believe there are many (prisoners) who might be so trained as to be left upon their parole (a promise made with or confirmed by a pledge of one's honor) during the last period of their imprisonment with safety."[2]

Early American Parole Development   The first legislation authorizing parole in the United States was enacted in Massachusetts in 1837, and the Elmira Reformatory in New York, which opened in 1876, was the first U.S. correctional institution to implement an extensive parole program. Zebulon Brockway, the institution's first superintendent, implemented a system of upward classification. The first grade was Brockway's personal interview with the new inmate. The second grade was the prison regime that

Captain Alexander Maconochie, who became superintendent of the British penal colony on Norfolk Island, Australia, in 1840, implemented a "ticket of leave" system to ease inmate transition from custody to freedom. Later, Sir Walter Crofton, director of the Irish prison system, implemented a system based on Maconochie's ideas. How did their systems influence current parole procedures?

Brockway established for the prisoner: a mix of labor (in the iron foundry or factories, on the farm, or on the maintenance crew), formal schooling, mandatory religious service, and military drill. An inmate who earned three marks each for labor, education, and behavior each month for six months in the second grade was promoted to the third grade. Six months after achieving the third-grade promotion, the inmate was granted a parole hearing before Brockway and five other Elmira staff members. Paroled inmates made their own living and work arrangements. Elmira employees and community volunteers provided parole supervision. Failure to comply with conditions of parole meant parole revocation and return to Elmira's second grade.[3]

By 1889, 12 states had implemented parole programs; by 1944, all 48 states had enacted parole legislation.

Parole Development in the Early 20th Century

The 1920s and early 1930s were a turbulent period in the United States. During Prohibition, organized crime increased, street gang warfare escalated, and the media provided obsessive coverage of criminals and their activities. Prison riots erupted in response to prisoner idleness and arbitrary rules and punishment. Prisons and the parole system failed to rehabilitate offenders.

> Offenders often leave prison without job skills, money, or personal coping skills. Should they be released on parole? Is parole working? What can agencies do to assist parolees? For more information go to Ethical Dilemma 8-1 at http://www.mhhe.com/schmalleger2.
>
> Ethical Dilemma

The Wickersham Commission, a commission on law enforcement and observance appointed by President Herbert Hoover, issued a report in 1931 that advocated uniformity in state parole practices by recommending that states establish centralized policymaking boards to write standards and guidelines for parole practices.[4] This report included a list of the "essential elements" of a good parole system:

1. indeterminate sentence law permitting the offender to be released (conditionally) at the time when he or she is most likely to make a successful transition back to society;

2. provision of quality release preparation—in the institution—for the offender who is reentering the community;

3. familiarity by the parole officer with the home and environmental conditions of the offender before he or she leaves the institution; and

4. sufficient staffing levels to ensure an adequate number of parole officers to supervise parolees.[5]

The Wickersham Commission reported that parole was logical because it was an inexpensive way to supervise offenders. Moreover, the commission reported, the parolee earns money, whereas the prisoner cannot support him- or herself and cannot contribute financially to his or her family. By 1944, all of the states had passed parole legislation.[6]

Despite the fact that all the states had enacted parole legislation by the mid-1940s, opposition was strong. The attitude that parole boards were turning hardened criminals loose on society sparked a series of angry attacks through national and state commissions, investigatory hearings, editorials and cartoons, press releases, and books.[7] Opponents claimed that parole had a dismal performance record, its goals were never realized, parole board members and parole officers were poorly trained, and parole hearings were little more than hastily conducted, almost unthinking interviews.

> In spite of the gap between its goals and reality, parole fulfilled important functions for officials in the criminal justice system.

In spite of the gap between its goals and reality, parole fulfilled important functions for officials in the criminal justice system. Wardens supported parole because the possibility of earning parole served as an incentive for offenders, making it easier to keep peace. Wardens also used parole to control prison overcrowding by keeping the number of people being released on parole about equal to the number of new prisoner admissions. Legislators supported parole because it cost less than incarceration. District attorneys supported parole because they felt it helped with plea bargaining. Without parole, district attorneys argued, there was little motivation for defendants, particularly those facing long prison sentences, to plead guilty to lesser crimes. District attorneys also supported parole because parolees could be returned to prison without new trial proceedings.

Together, these groups made a claim to the public that parole actually extended state control over offenders because parolees were supervised. Eventually, the public accepted the claim that parole was tough on criminals and that abolishing parole would end state control over dangerous persons.

Parole Development in the Late 20th Century   Opposition to parole resurfaced in the 1960s and 1970s, this time as part of a larger political debate about crime, the purposes of sanctioning, and the appropriateness of the unlimited discretion afforded various sectors of the criminal justice system (paroling authorities in particular). During this period, the debate on correctional policy addressed both the assumptions of the rehabilitative ideal and the results of indeterminate sentencing and parole.

In the 1970s, research indicated that prison rehabilitation programs had few positive benefits. Parolees were not rehabilitated, as parole advocates had claimed.[8] This position was supported on all sides of the political spectrum, including by those who believed that prisons "coddled" dangerous criminals and by those who questioned the ethics of coercing offenders into submitting to unwanted treatment as a condition of release.[9] These research findings led to many of the sentencing reforms of the 1970s and 1980s and helped usher in the warehousing and just-deserts eras discussed in Chapter 7. During a time when supporting *parole* represented a "soft" stance on crime and when crime rates and recidivism were up, the public did not want prisoners released on parole.

In 1987, the American Probation and Parole Association (APPA), the nation's largest association of probation and parole professionals, voiced its support of parole and objected to efforts to abolish it. Nevertheless, in that same year, six states abolished discretionary parole-board release. By the year 2000, 15 states and the federal government had abolished it, and another five states had abolished discretionary parole release for certain violent offenses or other crimes against a person. The APPA position statement on parole is presented in Exhibit 8–1.

EXHIBIT 8-1 American Probation and Parole Association

Position Statement on Parole

The mission of parole is to prepare, select, and assist offenders who, after a reasonable period of incarceration, could benefit from an early release while, at the same time, ensuring an appropriate level of public protection through conditions of parole and provision of supervision services. This is accomplished by:

- assisting the parole authority in decision making and the enforcement of parole conditions;

- providing prerelease and postrelease services and programs that will support offenders in successfully reintegrating into the community; and

- working cooperatively with all sectors of the criminal justice system to ensure the development and attainment of mutual objectives.

THE PAROLE PROCESS

Eligibility An inmate's eligibility for parole is determined by the sentence received from the court, as set by law. The **parole eligibility date** is the earliest date on which an inmate might be released. State statutes usually dictate parole eligibility dates and specify what portion of a sentence an offender must serve before being considered for release. Generally, state statutes apply formulas to deduct amounts of time from sentences to determine when an inmate might be eligible for release. The state statutes vary but, in general, reduce the sentence based on the number of days the inmate serves without disciplinary problems. The parole eligibility date, then, is determined by subtracting the maximum number of good-time days that could be earned from the length of the sentence. For example, a state statute might allow one day of good-time credit for every five days of good behavior. In this instance, an inmate could be eligible for parole after serving 292 days of a one-year sentence.

parole eligibility date
The earliest date on which an inmate might be paroled.

Reentry Preparation All states have some type of prisoner reentry programming, but they differ on a number of important dimensions. In most states, inmate participation is voluntary. For example, in Georgia and Pennsylvania, such participation is, in addition to being voluntary, only open to inmates who are placed in community correctional centers. In 2000, only 1,100 Pennsylvania and 700 Georgia inmates were transferred to community centers where reentry programming was available.[10] Most offenders leave prison with little or no meaningful reentry preparation.

Across the nation, the content of reentry preparation includes exposure to education, job readiness programs, and substance abuse counseling. Few states provide ex-offenders any assistance on securing housing upon release, and most programs begin just a few weeks before discharge. On the day of their release, inmates receive $25 to $200 plus clothing and bus fare to some location within the state. Most states require inmates to return to the county where they were originally sentenced or to where the parole board requires that they reside. In all states, sex offenders are required to register with local law enforcement.

Prisoner reentry problems are magnified for women leaving prison, especially minority women. Nearly two-thirds of the women confined in jails and state and federal prisons are black, Hispanic, or of other nonwhite ethnic groups. As reported in Chapter 7, women in prison have a high rate of prior sexual or physical abuse, high rates of positive HIV status and other sexually transmitted diseases, and high alcohol, and drug use, and addiction rates at the time of arrest. "In most of their communities," writes Beth Richie of the University of Illinois at Chicago, "there are few services and very limited resources available to assist women in the process of reentry."[11] Based on a series of interviews with women three times released from prison, Richie identifies seven challenges and barriers to successful reentry for women prisoners:

1. Many women require long-term prison-based treatment for substance abuse problems and continuation of treatment after release, with attention paid to gender-specific needs such as child care and protection from sexual harassment. Such treatment and protection are related to successful reentry.

2. Most women who enter correctional facilities receive emergency medical care while they are incarcerated, but most are released with their long-term health care needs unmet. Richie learned that women on parole need help to manage the ongoing complications of HIV, asthma, diabetes, and reproductive health problems. Unless women on parole receive ongoing medical care, health problems follow women back into the community after release.

3. More than one-half of the women Richie interviewed had chronic mental health issues for which they received no treatment during and after incarceration. Mental health treatment during and after incarceration facilitates successful reintegration.

4. Community social services must remove the barriers that keep women with arrest records from receiving their services. Women on parole return to abusive relationships and high-risk communities and need support to deal with violence.

5. Without educational and employment services, women on parole experience an increased pull to return to illegal activity as they exhaust their public aid options. Most women on parole do not have academic or job-related skills or experiences to support themselves or their children. Their life histories establish an immediate need for communities to do more (not less as argued for by politicians in favor of the no-frills movement discussed in Chapter 13) and to develop comprehensive educational and occupational programs during and after incarceration.

6. Housing that is safe, secure, and affordable is probably the most immediate need of a woman parolee. Where will she spend the night? Many have severed ties with their families because of their illegal activities. All of the women in Richie's sample had been homeless at least once for three months or more. Finding housing is related to the educational and employment opportunities already mentioned and complicated by the fact that women with criminal records are often barred from publicly funded low-income housing.

THE STAFF SPEAKS

7. It is easy to believe that women on parole are not caring parents. However, Richie found that ". . . even in those instances where the nature of the illegal activity and the situations that women found themselves in created a less than optimal environment for child rearing, most women report worrying about their children before and after they are arrested."[12] The challenge is to offer mothers in prison parental support. Even learning how to have a noncustodial relationship with their children, Richie argues, can help stabilize women as they make difficult transitions back into the community.

Women on parole face many problems. Communities can acknowledge the unique needs of such women and work to make reentry successful for them, or they can ignore them and watch as their problems follow them back into the community after release.

Most reentry programming begins just a few weeks before discharge; reentry advocates argue that release preparation should begin at incarceration and continue through release. A team of researchers in Florida interviewed ex-offenders and residents living in high-incarceration neighborhoods about the impact of incarceration on the participants and their families and communities. These interviews generated 16 recommendations to improve prisoner reentry[13]:

1. Target families of incarcerated offenders for services. For example, offer them short-term financial assistance for food, clothing and housing, and mental health care (to help them deal with anger, depression and low self-esteem). This is especially important for the children of prisoners.

2. Facilitate contact between families and incarcerated family members to promote the family bonds that are essential for successful reintegration. For example, provide families low-cost telephone service and assistance with transportation to prison.

3. Provide to children of prisoners services such as counseling, intervention for acting-out, and assistance in maintaining relationships with incarcerated parents to help stabilize their living situation.

4. Implement comprehensive prerelease transition plans that address family concerns (such as whether incarcerated people should return to their families or move to new neighborhoods), identify employment, and identify ways to cope with the strains of reintroducing the ex-offender into the family.

5. Provide transitional housing for ex-offenders to prevent them from heading to the streets or shelters and act as a service center to help ex-offenders obtain identification papers, clothing, employment, and so on.

6. Modify rules that prevent ex-offenders with felony records from acquiring a lease. Taking on responsibilities such as a lease will increase an offender's sense of responsibility.

7. Assist ex-offenders in obtaining and retaining employment to alleviate the financial strain they experience and the financial burden absorbed by their families. Identify programs to help ex-offenders become self-employed and develop employer-education programs to promote the hiring of ex-offenders.

8. Make training, education, and legal assistance available to ex-offenders. Training and education are fundamental to obtaining quality employment, and ex-offenders also need help in solving legal problems and restoring their civil rights. Students from local law schools could participate in internships to assist with the legal needs of ex-offenders and their families.

9. Reduce the financial pressures faced by ex-offenders immediately upon their release. Reducing the burdens imposed by the criminal justice system, such as supervision fees, and providing short-term financial assistance to pay for security deposits, first month's rent, and toiletries and other basic needs will reduce the incentive to participate in illegal activities to generate quick money.

10. Increase the availability of low-cost drug treatment for ex-offenders and their families.

11. Form self-help support groups so ex-offenders can talk to each other about the pressures and temptations they face, the frustrations of trying to make it, and the discouragements of everyday life.

12. Match ex-offenders with community mentors who might serve as advisors, contacts, and a support system. The mentor system can also apply to families, with families "adopting" other families.

13. Involve ex-offenders in neighborhood projects, from organized sports to reclamation, in order to increase positive contacts with other residents and reduce the stigma of incarceration and ensuing social isolation.

14. Develop awareness programs to reduce the stigma of incarceration. Target police, supervision officers, employers, educators, and the community at large for efforts to encourage tolerance for returning felons.

15. Develop neighborhood-based centers where ex-offenders can go to access services.

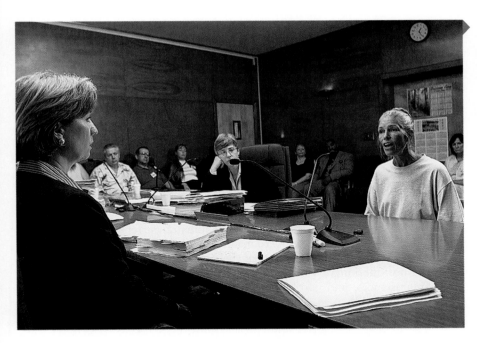

A parole board meets to consider a release candidate. While discretionary release by parole boards was at one time very common, it has been eliminated in many jurisdictions. Does parole provide offenders with an effective opportunity to reintegrate into society?

16. Provide services through coalitions and partnerships of public and private sources such as police partnerships that engage the residents in problem-solving strategies, social service partnerships that coordinate local service delivery, public-private partnerships that create new jobs for residents, and expert-citizen group partnerships that help residents develop grant proposals and new projects.

Granting Parole—The Paroling Authority   Every jurisdiction in the United States has a paroling authority. A **paroling authority** is a correctional agency (often called a *parole board* or *parole commission*) that has the authority to grant parole, set conditions of parole, supervise parolees, revoke parole, and discharge from parole.

Parole boards vary in size from 3 members (Alabama, Hawaii, Montana, North Dakota, Washington, and West Virginia) to 10 or more (Michigan, 10; Connecticut, 11; Ohio, 11; Illinois, 12; Texas, 18; and New York, 19). Of the 52 jurisdictions—the 50 states, the District of Columbia, and the federal government—only 34 have full-time salaried parole board members. Minnesota's paroling authority is its Commissioner of Corrections.[14]

The paroling authority's decision to grant or deny parole is partially based on its assessment of potential risk to the community. Risk-assessment factors may include the nature and circumstance of the crime; the offender's criminal record and prison record; and input from court officials, victims, and other interested parties.

Not all parole authorities use the same release criteria. Observations of federal parole hearings, for example, suggest that an inmate's institutional behavior and program participation are given little importance in release decisions.[15] "Noncompliance with required treatment programs or poor institutional behavior may be reasons to deny parole, but completion of

paroling authority

A person or correctional agency (often called a *parole board* or *parole commission*) that has the authority to grant parole, revoke parole, and discharge from parole.

treatment programs and good institutional behavior are not sufficient reasons to grant parole."[16]

A national survey of parole board members said that the most important factors in the decision to grant or deny parole were the nature of the inmate's offense and the inmate's prior criminal record, attitude toward the victim, institutional adjustment (as measured by the inmate's participation in prison programs), and insight into the causes of past criminal conduct.[17] Least important are the inmate's physical health and age, prison conditions, and the public awareness of the case. Studies of parole in Colorado found that, in order to process the large volume of cases, parole boards find it necessary to develop a routine and to look for a few factors that will decide their cases for them:

> ". . . the parole board first considers the inmate's current and prior offenses and incarcerations. Parole board members also determine if the inmate's time served is commensurate with what they perceive as adequate punishment. If it is not, the inmate's institutional behavior, progress in treatment, family circumstances, and parole plan will not outweigh the perceived need for punishment."[18]

salient factor score (SFS)

Scale, developed from a risk-screening instrument, used to predict parole outcome.

Some states use scoring instruments for risk assessment—the most commonly used are based on the U.S. Parole Commission's **salient factor score (SFS)**.[19] The salient factors are (1) number of prior convictions/adjudications, (2) number of prior commitments of more than 30 days, (3) age at current offense, (4) recent commitment-free period (three years), (5) probation/parole/confinement/escape violation at time of current offense or during present confinement, (6) heroin/opiate dependence, and (7) older age. The SFS places the offender in one of four risk categories: very good, good, fair, or poor. Parole officials consider this score in deciding whether parole is to be granted and, if so, what level of supervision will be required.

Policymakers disagree about which criteria are the most important, and each parole board member brings to the release decision a variety of assumptions, values, and views on the purpose of imprisonment (rehabilitation, incapacitation, or deterrence). The information used to make the parole decision varies significantly, depending on the goal or goals of the decision maker.[20]

State statutes also specify factors that paroling authorities must consider when making their decisions. These considerations generally include the likelihood of recidivism, the welfare of the community into which the inmate will be released, the inmate's prison conduct, and any treatment or rehabilitation plans developed for the inmate.

Parole plays a key role in criminal justice administration, and that puts a parole board in a powerful position. The majority of state parole boards determine the actual duration of incarceration and exercise discretionary release and revocation powers, specifying conditions of release and terms of supervision. The parole board's release policies can have a direct impact on institutional management. For example, parole boards can help reduce prison population by increasing the number of parolees. Lawsuits against the Alabama Department of Corrections, widespread crowding problems (with 27,000 people in prison, Alabama's prisons are about double design capacity), and voters' rejection of a tax referendum, forced Governor Bob

CAREER PROFILE

Kenneth Wong
State Parole Agent   California Department of Corrections

Kenneth Wong is a state parole agent with the California Department of Corrections. Before joining the San Francisco parole office in 1990, Ken worked three and one-half years as a correctional officer at the California State Prison at San Quentin and one and one-half years as an auto mechanic. Ken completed the automotive program of the College of Alameda and later enrolled in courses in human behavior at the University of California at Hayward.

As a parole officer, Ken works closely with police and social service agencies. He conducts antinarcotic testing, refers parole violators to the State Board of Prison Terms, and helps parolees make a smooth transition from prison to the community. His paramount concern is community protection.

Ken's advice to people interested in corrections is simple: "If you like working with people who've been in prison and if you have the patience to listen to their problems and make positive referrals and provide advice, then you should apply. The job is challenging, and there is always something new."

In 1996, the California Probation, Parole, and Correctional Association recognized Ken Wong as Parole Agent of the Year. The Association said Wong's job performance was exemplary and that he made a significant contribution to the field of corrections.

Ken plans to spend his career with the California Department of Corrections. He would like to pursue management positions, beginning with parole unit supervisor.

> " "I like being a parole agent because the job allows me to help people who got caught up in the criminal justice system and assist them with a smooth transition from prison back into society by providing a range of services. The most exciting thing about my job is I get to help parolees perform acceptably in the community and remove those who cannot." "

Riley to relieve the prison crisis by granting early parole to 5,000 persons sentenced for petty theft, DUI, and drug offenses. The state legislature created a special four-member panel to hear early release cases, in addition to the State's three-member parole board. Each panel hears 40 to 50 cases a day, four days a week. At its first hearing on December 3, 2003, the parole board approved early release for 15 prisoners, but denied it for 24 others.

Granting Parole—The Hearing   In general, parole hearings are attended by the applicant, the institutional representative, and hearing examiners or parole board members. A two-year study of 5,000 parole hearings in Colorado found that the parole board heard too many cases to allow for individualized treatment.[21] The time for a typical parole hearing was 10 to 15 minutes. A typical cases took longer.

In today's high-tech environment, a number of states such as West Virginia are experimenting with video conferencing equipment that links that state's seven regional jails and three prisons. Instead of requiring the five parole board members to travel around the state to conduct parole hearings at each institution, the new system is expected to save on travel costs and also permit crime victims to testify without having to be in the same room as the offender.

parolee

A person who is conditionally released from prison to community supervision.

The final decision to grant or deny parole is based on both eligibility guidelines and the interview. If parole is granted, a contract that defines the release plan is executed and the inmate is given a release date. The inmate who is conditionally released to community supervision is called a **parolee**.

If parole is denied, the common reason is "not enough time served." In that case, the inmate remains in prison, and a date is set for the next review. The waiting period between hearings depends on the jurisdiction and the inmate's offense.

Conditions of Parole   Paroling authorities set specific conditions for parole, on a case-by-case basis (see Figure 8–1). Parolees must comply with these conditions, which may include restitution, substance abuse aftercare, remote-electronic monitoring, and/or house arrest, among others.

Parolees are technically in state custody; they have merely been granted the privilege of living in the community instead of prison. Parole officers, who work closely with the parolee and the paroling authority, carry out the supervision of parolees, and they can return parolees to prison if they threaten community safety or otherwise violate the conditions of release. Depending on the severity of the crime and the risk presented by the offender, parole supervision can incorporate several types of contact with and "examination" of the parolee, including drug testing, setting of a curfew, remote-location monitoring, and employment verification. The paroling authority has at least three responsibilities:

1. to help a parolee with employment, residence, finances, or other personal issues that often present difficulties for a person trying to readjust to life in the community;
2. to protect the community by helping parolees avoid situations that might encourage recidivism; and
3. to expedite parole for those who meet the criteria established by the paroling authority and are unlikely to commit another crime.

The conditions under which parolees must live are very similar in form and structure to those for probationers. Sometimes the rules are established by law, but more often they are established by the paroling authority. The paroling authority can require any of the following forms of release: standard parole supervision, parole with enhanced treatment and programming conditions, halfway house placement, intensive supervision, parole with remote-electronic monitoring and/or voice and location tracking, or release with follow-up drug testing and payment of supervision fees and restitution.

Types of Parole   Release on parole may be mandatory or discretionary. Discretionary release is at the paroling authority's discretion, within boundaries established by the sentence and by law. Mandatory release generally occurs in jurisdictions using determinate sentencing statutes, and it requires the correctional authority to grant parole after a specific period of time, as specified by law, when the inmate has served the time that is mandated by the sentence minus good-time credits.

Historically, most state inmates were released to parole supervision after serving a portion of an indeterminate sentence based on a parole board decision (discretionary release). In 1977, 69 percent of offenders released

MARYLAND PAROLE COMMISSION   N⁰ 028239

ORDER FOR RELEASE ON PAROLE

The Parole Commission, by virtue of the authority conferred upon it by the laws of the State of Maryland, does hereby grant parole to:

(True Name) _____ Travis Glen Hardin, #273843, DOB November 24, 1950 _____
(Commitment Name/s)

who was convicted of: _____ Distribution of cocaine; Violation of probation _____

Court: Talbot County Circuit Court #6903

Sentenced: May 18, 1999

Term: 6 years;   2 years, 6 months

From: March 10, 1999;   consecutive

Therefore, the said Commission does hereby order the release on parole of the said prisoner from

_____ Eastern Correctional Institution _____
(Correctional Institution or Jail)

The Parolee, upon release, shall be deemed to remain in legal custody until the expiration of the full, undiminished term and upon violation of any condition of his parole shall be remanded to the authority from which paroled, where a hearing shall be conducted by the Parole Commission. If parole is revoked, the Commission shall determine the amount of time spent on parole, if any, which shall be credited to the parolee.

This order is subject to the rules, regulation, and conditions of this parole as set forth below and on page 2 of this agreement, and such further conditions as the Commission may impose at any time during the period of parole.

Upon being released, report to the Division of Parole and Probation office located at

_____ 301 Bay Street, Suite 302, Easton, MD 21601   (410-555-1212) _____
                                                            MARYLAND PAROLE COMMISSION

Parole Expiration Date: September 2007   By: _____ Patricia K. Cushwa _____
                                                                   Commissioner

Special Condition(s): substance abuse therapy,
     subject to curfew as directed by parole agent,   _____ March 20, 2003 _____
     community service if agent directs, employment within 30 days   Date

Home/Employment Plan: _____ live with mother – Lynn Fortney, 2055 Sokol Drive, _____
     Tilghman, MD 21671   (410-822-5555)

Anyone serving a sentence for a crime committed on or after May 1, 1991, must pay supervision and/or drug testing fees as prescribed in Article 41, Section 4.519 of the Annotated Code of Maryland.

Date(s) of Offense(s): _____ January 6, 2002 _____

MPC - 14 - (Revised 8/15/96)

WHITE – Parolee • PINK – Parole Commission Copy • YELLOW – Institution Copy • BLUE – Certified Copy • GREEN – Court Copy

FIGURE 8-1
Sample Order for Release on Parole

from state prison were released by a parole board. States began moving away from discretionary release policies in the 1980s in favor of determinate sentences and mandatory supervised release. (We will return to a discussion of this trend later in this chapter.) Consistent with the adoption of truth in sentencing and other mandatory release statutes, mandatory parole release increased from 45 percent in 1995 to 52 percent in 2002, while discretionary parole release decreased from 50 percent to 39 percent.[22]

Mandatory release is the most common method of release from prison today. Some argue that abandonment of discretionary release in favor of mandatory release has detrimental effects.[23] Without the prospect of discretionary release, inmates have fewer incentives for engaging in good behavior or participating in rehabilitative programs, and prison administrators have fewer mechanisms for relieving institutional crowding.

Characteristics of Parolees

The tremendous increase in the prison population discussed in Chapter 7 has given many people a sense of safety and security. However, the majority of the population is also unconcerned—or unaware—that at least 95 percent of those who enter prisons eventually return to the community, and most do so in about two and one-half years. Some have put it this way: More prisoners in results in more prisoners out!

> More prisoners in results in more prisoners out!

Almost 1,400 prisoners each day leave prison. About one in five leaves prison with no postrelease supervision (about 100,000 in 1998) because of changes in sentencing legislation that allow some prisoners to "max out" (serve their full sentences) and leave prison with no postcustody supervision. On January 1, 2003, 753,141 American adults were on parole—an increase of 2.8 percent (20,808 parolees) over January 1, 2002.[24] Eighty-nine percent of those adults were state parolees; the rest were federal.

The basic demographics of parolees have not changed much over the past 20 years. The typical adult parolee is a black, non-Hispanic male on mandatory parole and under active parole supervision for more than one year. The median age is 34, with an 11th grade education. Women make up 14 percent of the parole population (see Figure 8–2). The region with the highest number of parolees is the South, followed by the Northeast, West, and Midwest.

Not all who are sent to prison are released on parole. Those who are the most serious offenders (those who have life sentences or who face the death penalty) or who have disciplinary problems while incarcerated generally are not paroled. Instead, they live out their lives in prison or are released when they have served their entire sentences.

TRENDS IN THE PAROLE POPULATION

The estimated number of adults under community supervision and incarceration from 1995 through 2002 is shown in Table 8–1. The parole population has continually increased, averaging a growth of 1.5 percent per year. The low rate of growth in the parole population reflects changes in sentencing and parole release policies that have resulted in increasing

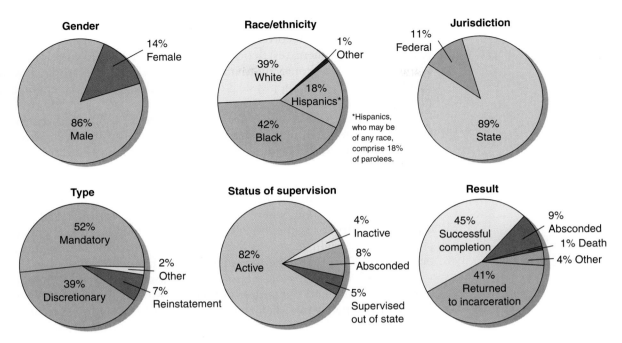

FIGURE 8-2
Selected Characteristics of Adults on Parole

Source: Lauren E. Glaze, *Probation and Parole in the United States, 2002* (Washington, DC: U.S. Department of Justice, Bureau of Justice Statistics, August 2003).

lengths of stay in prisons and declining prison release rates. Still, according to one criminologist, "The numbers of returning offenders dwarf anything known before, the needs of released inmates are greater, and corrections has retained few rehabilitation programs."[25] Many parolees have long histories of criminal or gang involvement and few marketable skills. Most employers are also reluctant to hire ex-offenders. A survey in five major cities revealed that two of three employers would not knowingly hire an

TABLE 8-1	Adults on Probation, in Jail or Prison, and on Parole, 1995–2002			
	Total estimated correctional population	**Probation**	**Jail**	**Prison**	**Parole**
---	---	---	---	---	---
1995	5,342,900	3,077,861	507,044	1,078,542	679,421
1996	5,490,700	3,164,900	518,492	1,127,528	679,733
1997	5,734,900	3,296,513	567,079	1,176,564	694,787
1998	6,134,200	3,670,441	592,462	1,124,469	696,385
1999	6,340,800	3,779,922	605,943	1,287,172	714,457
2000	6,445,600	3,826,209	621,149	1,316,333	724,486
2001	6,594,000	3,932,751	631,240	1,330,980	732,351
2002	6,732,400	3,995,165	665,475	1,361,258	753,141

Source: Lauren E. Glaze, *Probation and Parole in the United States, 2002* (Washington, DC: U.S. Department of Justice, Bureau of Justice Statistics, August 2003), p. 1.

ex-offender (regardless of the offense), and one of three said they had checked the criminal records of their most recent hires.[26] Further, there are increased employment restrictions on parolees convicted of felonies who want to practice a profession that requires licensing (for example, law, real estate, medicine, nursing, physical therapy, teaching, dentistry, engineering, pharmacy, and barbering).

Here's the contradiction: States spend at least $1.2 billion a year on parole, convincing offenders that they need to find legitimate employment, but then they frustrate them by barring them from many kinds of jobs that could improve the level of their existence.[27] And it's not only in the employment arena that parolees have problems. As of 1998, almost 4 million were permanently unable to vote because they had been convicted of a felony. Although some believe that disenfranchisement of felons is an acceptable penalty for crime, others argue that denying large segments of the population the right to vote is likely to cause further alienation and make people less willing to participate in legitimate free-world activities.

Table 8–2 defines parole populations among the states on January 1, 2003. California had the largest number of adults on parole, followed by Texas and Pennsylvania. Pennsylvania also had the highest rate of parole supervision (1,037 parolees supervised per 100,000 adult residents), which means it used parole more than any other state; Washington used parole the least (2 per 100,000 adult residents).

TRENDS IN PAROLE SUCCESS

Researchers at the U.S. Department of Justice's Bureau of Justice Statistics found that, of the 448,000 parolees discharged from supervision in 2002, 45 percent successfully completed the conditions of their supervision,

TABLE 8–2		Selected Parole Populations Among the States, January 1, 2003			
10 states with the largest parole populations	Number supervised	10 states with the highest rates of supervision	People supervised per 100,000 adult U.S. residents	10 states with the lowest rates of supervision	People supervised per 100,000 adult U.S. residents
California	113,185	Pennsylvania	1,037	Washington	2
Texas	103,068	Oregon	727	Maine	3
Pennsylvania	97,712	Louisiana	715	North Dakota	31
New York	55,990	Texas	654	Florida	40
Illinois	35,458	Arkansas	577	North Carolina	44
Louisiana	23,417	California	439	Nebraska	45
Georgia	20,912	New York	384	Rhode Island	52
Oregon	19,307	Illinois	377	West Virginia	71
Ohio	17,853	Maryland	325	Virginia	82
Michigan	17,648	Missouri	320	Connecticut	86

Source: Adapted from Lauren E. Glaze, *Probation and Parole in the United States, 2002* (Washington, DC: U.S. Department of Justice, Bureau of Justice Statistics, August 2003), p. 2.

41 percent were returned to prison or jail, and 9 percent absconded, 2 percent were "other unsuccessful," 1 percent was transferred, 1 percent died, and 1 percent was "other".[28] The success rate among those discharged from parole has remained fairly stable since 1995. States with the highest rates of success are Massachusetts and Mississippi (at 83 percent each). Utah (18 percent) and California (21 percent) had the lowest rates of success in 1999.

Researchers in Tennessee found that first-time releases to state parole do better than re-releases.[29] In every year during the 1990s, first-time releases to state parole were more successful than re-releases. In 1990, 56 percent of first-time releases were successful compared with 15 percent of re-releases. In 1999, of those exiting parole, 63 percent of first-time releases were successful, compared to 21 percent of re-releases.

Department of Justice researchers also found that success on parole depends on the method of release—whether it is discretionary or mandatory. In every year between 1990 and 1999, state prisoners released by a parole board had higher success rates than those released through mandatory parole. Between 1990 and 1999, the percent of successful discretionary releases varied between 50 percent and 56 percent, while the percent of successful mandatory releases ranged between 24 percent and 33 percent. When the researchers combined method of release and status of parolee (first time versus re-release), first-time mandatory parole releases had a higher success rate (79 percent) than did discretionary first-time parole releases (61 percent). However, when researchers looked at the success of parolees re-released from state prison, they found just the opposite: Discretionary parolees in 1999 who had been re-released from prison were more successful (37 percent) than were mandatory parolees (17 percent). Other characteristics of successfully discharged state paroles in 1999 included gender (female, 48 percent; male, 39 percent), race/Hispanic origin (Hispanic, 51 percent; white non-Hispanic, 41 percent; black non-Hispanic, 39 percent), age (older parolees had higher rates of success than did younger paroles), and time served in prison (the highest success rate, 74 percent, was found among parolees who served fewer than 12 months in prison; releases who served five years or more had the lowest success rate, 62 percent).

What these data show is the difficulty of predicting who will be successful on parole. Deciding who to release is a complicated issue. If discretionary release is used, then parole boards have to consider first-time release versus re-release, gender, race, age, and time served. With mandatory release, first-time release appears more successful but is also impacted by other factors.

Parole Revocation

Rates of relapse and recidivism are high, especially in the vulnerable period immediately following release. In fact, two-thirds of all parolees are re-arrested within three years, typically within the first six months of release. The number of parole violators returned to prison continues to rise. Of the nearly 448,000 parolees discharged from supervision in 2002, 183,680 (41 percent) were returned to prison either because of a rule violation or new offense, up from 27,177 in 1980 and 131,502 in 1990. The numbers are so high that parole failures account for a growing proportion of all new prison admissions. Currently, rearrests comprise 35 percent of all prison admissions, as compared with 17 percent in 1980.[30]

Why are they returning? Parole may be revoked for two reasons. A technical violation occurs when any of the technical conditions of parole (e.g., find and keep a job, live at home, sign no contracts, pay restitution and fees, perform community service, attend drug and alcohol abuse counseling) are violated. According to the U.S. Department of Justice, almost 30 percent of parole violators are re-incarcerated for technical violations. The Justice Department adds that a significant number of these are attributable to incomplete and/or inadequate release planning, imposition of unrealistic rules, and ineffective case management.[31] Other scholars tell us that technical violations are sometimes a function of clients' symptoms or their difficulties in following directions. Parolees with serious mental illness might violate the technical conditions of supervision because of cognitive impairment, delusions, confusion, or side effects of psychotropic medications.[32] And parolees with HIV/AIDS require collaborative assistance from correction departments, departments of public health, and community-based organizations that few communities can provide. Alaska's standard conditions of parole are presented in Figure 8–3.

The second type of violation is a new offense violation. This involves arrest for the commission of a new crime. A new offense violation might involve a technical violation. For example, an arrest for selling drugs and a positive test for drug use would be a violation for a new offense and a technical violation. Seventy percent of parole violators are re-incarcerated because of an arrest or conviction for a new offense. In Texas, the number is 79 percent. In New York, it is 87 percent. In California, it is 60 percent.

A parole officer questions one of his parolees about a suspected new offense violation. One reason for revoking parole is the parolee's arrest for a criminal offense. What are other reasons parole may be revoked?

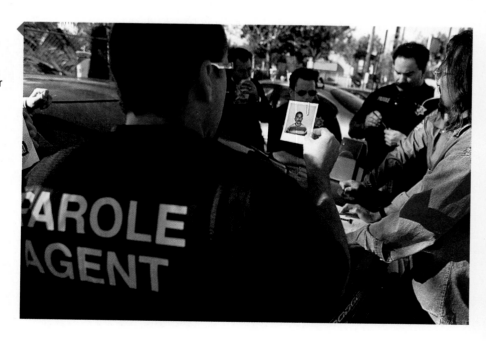

STATE OF ALASKA
STANDARD CONDITIONS OF PAROLE

The following standard conditions of parole apply to all prisoners released on mandatory or discretionary parole, in accordance with AS 33.16.150(a).

1. REPORT UPON RELEASE: I will report in person no later than the next working day after my release to the parole officer located at the PAROLE OFFICE and receive further reporting instructions. I will reside at

    _____.

2. MAINTAIN EMPLOYMENT/TRAINING/TREATMENT: I will make a diligent effort to maintain steady employment and support my legal dependents. I will not voluntarily change or terminate employment without receiving permission from my parole officer to do so. If discharged or if employment is terminated (temporarily or permanently) for any reason, I will notify my parole officer the next working day. If I am involved in an education, training, or treatment program, I will continue active participation in the program unless I receive permission from my parole officer to quit. If I am released, removed, or terminated from the program for any reason, I will notify my parole officer the next working day.

3. REPORT MONTHLY: I will report to my parole officer at least monthly in the manner prescribed by my parole officer. I will follow any other reporting instructions established by my parole officer.

4. OBEY LAWS/ORDERS: I will obey all state, federal, and local laws, ordinances, orders, and court orders.

5. PERMISSION BEFORE CHANGING RESIDENCE: I will obtain permission from my parole officer before changing my residence. Remaining away from my approved residence for 24 hours or more constitutes a change in residence for the purpose of this condition.

6. TRAVEL PERMIT BEFORE TRAVEL OUTSIDE ALASKA: I will obtain the prior written permission of my parole officer in the form of an interstate travel agreement before leaving the state of Alaska. Failure to abide by the conditions of the travel agreement is a violation of my order of parole.

7. NO FIREARMS/WEAPONS: I will not own, possess, have in my custody, handle, purchase, or transport any firearm, ammunition, or explosives. I may not carry any deadly weapon on my person except a pocket knife with a 3″ or shorter blade. Carrying any other weapon on my person such as a hunting knife, axe, club, etc. is a violation of my order of parole. I will contact the Alaska Board of Parole if I have any questions about the use of firearms, ammunition, or weapons.

8. NO DRUGS: I will not use, possess, handle, purchase, give, or administer any narcotic, hallucinogenic, (including marijuana/THC), stimulant, depressant, amphetamine, barbiturate, or prescription drug not specifically prescribed by a licensed medical person.

9. REPORT POLICE CONTACT: I will report to my parole officer, no later than the next working day, any contact with a law enforcement officer.

10. DO NOT WORK AS AN INFORMANT: I will not enter into any agreement or other arrangement with any law enforcement agency which will place me in the position of violating any law or any condition of my parole. I understand the Department of Corrections and Parole Board policy prohibits me from working as an informant.

11. NO CONTACT WITH PRISONERS OR FELONS: I may not telephone, correspond with, or visit any person confined in a prison, penitentiary, correctional institution or camp, jail, halfway house, work release center, community residential center, restitution center, juvenile correctional center, etc. Contact with a felon during the course of employment or during corrections-related treatment is not prohibited if approved by my parole officer. Any other knowing contact with a felon is prohibited unless approved by my parole officer. I will notify my parole officer the next working day if I have contact with a prisoner or felon.

12. CANNOT LEAVE AREA: I will receive permission from my parole officer before leaving the area of the state to which my case is assigned. My parole officer will advise me in writing of limits of the area to which I have been assigned.

13. OBEY ALL ORDERS/SPECIAL CONDITIONS: I will obey any special instructions, rules, or order given to me by the Alaska Board of Parole or by my parole officer. I will follow any special conditions imposed by the Alaska Board of Parole or my parole officer.

FIGURE 8-3
Sample State Conditions of Parole

Source: State of Alaska Board of Parole, *Parole Handbook, Appendix II; Conditions of Parole,* June 1998.

When a violation occurs, a revocation hearing date is set. The purpose of a revocation hearing is to determine whether the violation warrants the parolee's removal from the community. During a revocation hearing, the parolee has certain rights of due process because he or she could lose conditional freedom; but the parolee is not entitled to a full adversary hearing, as would be the case in a new criminal proceeding. If the parolee violates the conditions of parole, a revocation hearing could return the offender to prison to serve the remainder of the original sentence plus any new sentence that might be given because of new violations.[33] Returning parole violators to prison has consequences for prison crowding. Some argue that only parole violators who commit new offense violations should be returned to prison. Those who violate the technical conditions of their parole should be punished through community sanctions such as community service, remote-electronic monitoring, drug treatment, intensive parole supervision, or jail. The entire continuum of intermediate sanctions (the topic of Chapter 5), they argue, should be used before sending chronic technical violators to prison.

Some jurisdictions are experimenting with incentives that encourage positive actions on the part of the offender. The belief is that sometimes we focus too much on trying to control behavior through punishment and ignore the other side of the equation—encouraging compliance with incentives and rewards. These incentives include reduced reporting requirements, allowing reports to be made through phone calls or other methods that do not involve office visits, early termination of supervision, and extensions of time to accomplish specific activities. Although using rewards to recognize positive offender accomplishments can be an important component of a violation system, to date this aspect of supervision has received much less attention than the alternative, responding to failures with disciplinary sanctions.

> Using rewards to recognize positive offender accomplishments can be an important component of a violation system.

The primary difference between a criminal trial and a revocation hearing is the threshold of evidence that the hearing body needs in order to convict. In a criminal trial, a conviction may be obtained only if the government proves its facts *beyond a reasonable doubt*. In a revocation hearing, the panel need only find that a violation is shown *by a preponderance of the evidence*.[34] In addition, there is a more relaxed rule of what constitutes evidence—a rule that permits letters, affidavits, and reports to be presented in lieu of direct testimony.

Issues in Parole

Over the past few decades, the face of parole has changed. This chapter concludes with a discussion of several innovative programs in parole, including reentry courts and community partnership councils, successful reintegration programs (including those that involve victims), court rulings that have changed the parole revocation process, and the abolition of discretionary parole board release.

REENTRY COURTS AND COMMUNITY PARTNERSHIP COUNCILS

It is incumbent on criminal justice policymakers who are interested in greater public safety and more efficient use of public tax dollars to consider how we might better handle the challenges of the more than 500,000 offenders who leave prison each year. Because of the potential threats that parolees pose to victims, families, children, and communities, investing in effective parole programs may be one of the best investments we make.

One of the latest innovations in helping offenders released from prison make a successful adjustment to the community is the reentry court. A **reentry court** manages the return to the community of individuals released from prison, using the authority of the court to apply graduated sanctions and positive reinforcement and to marshal resources to support the prisoner's reintegration. The U.S. Attorney General has proposed that reentry courts operate like drug courts or other problem-solving courts (domestic violence court, community court, family court, gun court, and DWI court).[35] In drug court, for example, a judge is limited to managing a caseload of drug-involved offenders. The judge requires an offender to make regular court appearances and participate in drug treatment and testing. If the drug offender violates the conditions of release, the judge administers a predetermined range of graduated sanctions that do not automatically require return to prison (except for new crimes or egregious violations). Frequent appearances before the court, offers of assistance, and the knowledge of a predetermined range of sanctions for violations of the conditions of release assist the offender in getting back on track.

The U.S. Department of Justice proposes that a reentry court have six core elements:

- **Assessment and planning:** Correctional administrators and the reentry judge meet with inmates who are near release to explain the reentry process, assess inmates' needs, and begin building links to a range of social services, family counseling, health and mental health services, housing, job training, and work opportunities that support reintegration.

- **Active judicial oversight:** The reentry court sees all prisoners released into the community with a high degree of frequency, maybe once or twice a month. Also involved are the parole officer and others responsible for assessing the parolee's progress. In court, offender progress is praised, and offender setbacks are discussed.

- **Case management of support services:** The reentry court acts as a service broker and advocates on behalf of parolees for substance abuse treatment, job training, private employment, faith instruction, family member support, housing, and community services.

- **Accountability to the community:** Reentry courts appoint broad-based community advisory boards to develop and maintain accountability to the community. Advisory boards also help courts negotiate the sometimes difficult task of brokering services for parolees and advocate on their behalf.

- **Graduated sanctions:** Reentry courts establish a predetermined range of graduated sanctions for violations of the conditions of release that do not automatically require return to prison.

- **Rewarding success:** Reentry courts incorporate positive judicial reinforcement actions after goals are achieved. Examples include negotiating early release from parole or conducting graduation ceremonies similar to those used in drug courts.

reentry court
A court that manages the return to the community of individuals released from prison.

According to the U.S. Department of Justice, "The successful completion of parole should be seen as an important life event for an offender, and the court can help acknowledge that accomplishment. Courts provide powerful public forums for encouraging positive behavior and for acknowledging the individual effort in achieving reentry goals."[36] The U.S. Department of Justice is promoting the idea and asking communities to experiment with it, depending upon statutory framework, caseload considerations, administrative flexibility, and levels of collaboration among the judiciary, corrections officers, parole officers, police, business community, religious institutions, community organizations, and the like. Whichever form a reentry court takes, developing new ways that communities can manage and support offenders after release from prison with assistance in securing employment, housing, substance abuse treatment, family counseling, and other services is essential to our ability to reduce crime and keep communities safe.

Research on drug courts is still new, but already studies show that recidivism among all drug court participants has ranged between 5 and 28 percent and is less than 4 percent for program graduates.[37] The largest reentry court in operation today is in Richland County, Ohio.[38] The court accepted its first parolees in 2000. Reentry court supervision lasts a minimum of one year. During this time, parolees appear in court each month to discuss their progress. They receive an average of 12 monthly intensive supervision contacts, random drug and alcohol testing, and are required to participate in remote-location monitoring. Of the initial 160 reentry clients, 34 had successfully completed the program, 22 did not, and 104 were still active in the program as of August 31, 2002. Jeffrey Spelman, professor of criminal justice at Ashland University, compared the two groups and found that being female, completing high school, holding a job and over age 29 distinguished those who successfully completed reentry court from those who did not.

Professor Spelman also found evidence that reentry court benefited the terminated group. Of the 22 parolees terminated, only four were rearrested for a new criminal offense. The others were terminated as a result of multiple technical violations or one serious technical violation. The contrast between the 7 percent rearrest rate in Richland County's reentry court and BJS data from a 15-state recidivism study that found a one-year rearrest rate of 44 percent, suggests that reentry court is capable of making a difference in the lives of individuals even if they are terminated from the program. However, only time and further research will test the accuracy of these early results.

Another innovation in parole is Texas's Community Partnership Councils (CPC). Begun in 1995 as a way to facilitate community input into parole operations and also to assist with service provision and public education, CPCs have attracted national attention by uniting community leaders, local agencies and state parole administrators. Representatives of local agencies and civic groups such as law enforcement departments, prosecutors offices, school districts, clergy groups, chambers of commerce, victim groups, colleges and universities, charitable groups, and homeowners' associations meet with parole staff, learn about parole operations and issues, and then share what they've learned with their communities. CPCs can facilitate an early response to issues, preventing them from becoming crises, and help educate the public about community corrections. They can generate positive publicity and provide services for parole officers and parolees. For example, some CPCs develop projects such as job fairs for parolees, develop mentoring programs, and sponsor art fairs. CPCs have no legal power. They only influence parole through their advisory and support activities.

Recently a survey of Texas parole officers asked their opinion on CPC and the type of resources they need to help their clients avoid committing new crimes.[39] The results show that Texas parole officers see treatment resources and job assistance as what they need most for their parolees and that any help CPCs can give parole officers in meeting their clients' needs is a step in the right direction. The respondents also feel that CPCs can help elicit greater public understanding of parole, and they stress the need for educating the public about crime and parole.

REINTEGRATION OF OFFENDERS

The challenges facing most parolees are employment readiness, substance abuse treatment, housing, and health care.[40] Seven of 10 parolees are unable to fill out a Social Security or job application, write a business letter, calculate a price discount, read a bus schedule, or perform other text- and number-based tasks common to daily life. Many face roadblocks in securing legitimate housing due to public housing restrictions, shelter policies, and burned family bridges, and they become homeless. In Boston, a survey found that 22 percent of the homeless had recently lived in correctional settings. And medically, one-fourth of the U.S. population infected with HIV/AIDS and one-third of those with tuberculosis have been in prison. Most of them return to their families, communities, and partners after release, when the medical treatment begun in prison is often discontinued. Parolees with medical, mental health, and/or substance abuse problems are in particular need of reintegration programs. The reintegrative process for women is particularly in need of reform. Interviews with women on parole find that women parolees need comprehensive postrelease programs, empowerment and self-sufficiency programming, peer group support, and mother-child programs.[41]

> **Ethical Dilemma**
>
> ▶ A woman with young children is a repeat offender who has again violated her parole. Should she remain in the community or should she return to prison? What are the issues? Should a parolee's gender make a difference in treatment? For more information go to Ethical Dilemma 8-2 at http://www.mhhe.com/schmalleger2.

The problems of reintegration may appear insurmountable, but across the nation caring communities are developing sound reintegration processes that have a much better chance of reducing recidivism than previous efforts of the 1960s and 1970s, which emphasized job placement more than job readiness and did not address underlying problems common to many offenders such as substance abuse, housing, and medical care. Here we will consider four such programs: the Safer Foundation in Chicago, the Center for Employment Opportunities (CEO) in New York City, Project Re-Integration of Offenders (RIO) in Texas, and the Corrections Clearinghouse (CC) in Washington.[42] Although each program is unique, all share features that can be replicated—basic services involving life skills training and job preparation that begin *before* inmates are released and job placement, social support, and follow-up assistance *after* release. The programs stand to benefit not only the parolees and their families but also the greater public.

Chicago's Safer Foundation   Safer Foundation was founded in 1972. Its mission is to provide ex-offenders avenues for letting go of their criminal lives and entering the mainstream. Getting and keeping a job is an important means to that end. Safer operates an educational center in the Cook County (Chicago) jail, and it administers the largest work release center in Chicago. Offenders begin learning money management, job interviewing skills, stress management, and remedial education while they are in jail, and they continue those programs as residents of the work release center. Safer uses an elaborate network of volunteers to provide services and secure the expertise it could not otherwise afford. Case managers, called "lifeguards," are assigned to remain in touch with placed clients for a year after they have found a job to offer help with any problems that arise.

The data suggest that Safer has been effective in improving clients' basic skills and in helping offenders find work and stay on a job for more than 30 days (an important benchmark in order for Safer to claim government reimbursement). Nine of 10 offenders who completed Safer's programs had not been convicted of a new crime after six months. The cost per participant who stayed on the job for 30 days was $1,956.

Center for Employment Opportunities (CEO)   CEO was established in the late 1970s by the Vera Institute of Justice, a nonprofit organization in New York City. CEO provides ex-offenders day-labor employment in neighborhoods where they live, with the goal of providing them with permanent employment. Day-labor jobs include performing custodial services in court buildings, painting school dormitories and classrooms, maintaining nature trails, and cleaning state highways. Offenders are paid daily. Permanent jobs are often found in small to midsize companies. Job developers at CEO monitor participants' performance for six months and offer job development and support services indefinitely to former participants who run into problems. In the 1990s, CEO placed approximately 700 offenders a year in permanent jobs, and 75 percent of them were on the job after one month, and 60 percent were still employed after three months. The average cost per participant per year is $3,025.

Reintegration of Offenders (RIO)   Project RIO started in 1985 in Texas. According to the U.S. Department of Justice, RIO is the most ambitious state government program in the nation devoted to job placement for ex-offenders. Like Safer Foundation, RIO begins serving offenders while they are in prison with remedial education, life skills classes, and job readiness counseling. RIO has employers spend a day in prison talking with inmates about job opportunities. RIO continues working with offenders after release on job assessment, placement, and follow-up. RIO has a high placement rate (almost 75 percent), and RIO participants are much more likely to get jobs than are ex-offenders who do not participate in the program. Participation in RIO while in prison is a statistically significant predictor of postrelease employment. Minority offenders do especially well in RIO: 66 percent of black and Hispanic participants found employment, compared with only 30 percent of blacks and 36 percent of Hispanics who were not enrolled in the program.

I was on parole for 30 months after doing 16 years straight on a very lengthy sentence. When I got out, I paroled to a place where I had never been before—everything was new to me and the only person I knew in my whole town was my wife. Starting over again was great, I made new friends, got a good job, joined the church, and integrated back into society just like I was supposed to.

Then it happened. I began to fall apart for a very simple reason—I stopped doing what my parole officer told me to do and started doing what I wanted to do. Subsequently, I was violated and returned to prison to do more time on my sentence, and that is where I sit at this writing.

There are good people and bad people in the world, and parole officers are the same. I was lucky and got a good one. From day one she told me that whether or not I succeeded was entirely up to me. She laid out a simple plan for me to follow, which I did for a while. Even when I started breaking the rules, instead of punishing me she put me in places that offered help for the issues I had. Finally, I left her no choice but to violate me, and she did just that.

Parole is a good idea because the inmate will have some of the awesome powers of the state at his disposal to help with the reintegration process. Done alone, the process can be terrifying. If the inmate does not define and address

his own situation while he is in prison, the chance of that person making it on parole is slim to none. On the other hand, if the inmate has truly applied himself and has identified and addressed the "thing" that makes him able to break the law, parole is an excellent idea.

For myself, I know this: If I would have done what I needed to do while doing 16 years in prison, I would not be sitting here now praying for the chance to be free again and live a normal life.

Anonymous

THE OFFENDER SPEAKS

Does RIO prevent recidivism? According to a Texas A&M study, the answer is yes. Ex-offenders who found jobs through RIO had lower recidivism rates than unemployed ex-offenders who did not enroll in RIO, with demographic factors and reoffending risk taken into account. Perhaps the most interesting finding was that high-risk participants performed best. Within the one year follow-up period, 48 percent of high-risk Project RIO participants were rearrested, and 23 percent were reincarcerated, compared to 57 percent and 38 percent, respectively, of general prisoners who had not participated. In 1995, Texas spent $361 for each of the 11,371 prisoners who were placed on jobs.

Corrections Clearinghouse (CC)   Washington State's Corrections Clearinghouse was established in 1976 to coordinate job search activities for adult offenders during imprisonment and to follow their release from prison. CC staff offer prerelease employment-related courses and vocational assessments to inmates. Program staff teach inmates how to access and use the state's computerized job data bank so they can discover jobs while in prison. After release, CC staff continue job search assistance and postplacement support to help ex-offenders earn promotions that provide higher wages. The program also offers services to help ex-offenders address alcohol and drug abuse issues and find clothing after release. Of the 1,312 ex-offenders who received postrelease job search assistance in 1997 and 1998, 68 percent were still employed after 45 days at a cost of $276 per offender.

Overall, the evidence suggest that programs such as Safer Foundation, CEO, RIO, and CC are effective in placing ex-offenders in jobs.

Eye On Corrections™

DC Agency Leads Effort to Involve Mentors in Offender Re-entry

By Michelle Gaseau

One of the most important types of training that inmates can receive is actually not in a classroom. It involves preparing inmates for living and functioning in the community after release.

In Washington D.C., corrections officials have to manage a new element in the re-entry equation: The district's inmates are now placed in federal facilities that are sometimes hundreds of miles away. This can make reintegration and reconnection difficult for returning offenders.

"They are more estranged from the community than they were before. Long distance phone calls are harder to make for families. A lot of offenders come home estranged because of the confinement and the distance. A mentor can help with that," said Cedric Hendricks, Acting Associate Director of the Office of Legislative, Intergovernmental and Public Affairs for the Court Services and Offender Supervision Agency for the District of Columbia.

Since January, the agency, local churches, and religious institutions have been developing a mentoring program that involves the faith-based community in the district. "The hope is this faith-based network can be another part of the array of resources and services we try to tap into to facilitate successful reintegration [for offenders]," said Hendricks.

The first matches between offenders who have transitioned to halfway houses and mentors from faith-based institutions took place earlier this month. Getting the program to the mentor-offender matching point took coordination by many parties.

BRINGING THE MENTOR IDEA TO FAITH-BASED INSTITUTIONS

The Court Services and Offender Supervision Agency's (CSOSA) Faith-Based Mentoring Initiative began last year with a meeting involving more than 40 representatives from faith-based organizations, members of community groups, and others who have played a part in offender reentry. The meeting was called to bring those reentry efforts together with the programs of CSOSA.

"We met to undertake how to work together to address the needs of offenders. Out of that emerged the idea of mentoring," Hendricks said. He added that those organizations that attended understood that the needs were many and that mentors would have to be able to assist offenders in obtaining those services.

Housing, vocational training, job placement, clothing, family counseling, and substance abuse counseling are among the needs of offenders when they return to the community. "All of those things, churches can offer. The dialogue focuses on how to access those services in an organized manner and how we could continue to build a partnership and bring in more faith-based institutions from this town," Hendricks said.

The mentoring takes place as the offender begins his or her stay in the halfway house. Mentors will also now play a role in early meetings the offender has with case management and the CSOSA staff to coordinate a case management plan.

The mentoring project, which involves many faiths including Muslim and Jewish institutions, has rolled out slowly to ensure that participation and training are in place first. The project was announced to the public on the weekend of January 13 by city and correctional officials and through the faith community, which discussed it in worship services as a component of reentry for offenders.

"We encouraged faith-based institutions to dedicate some portion of their worship to the issue of reentry. Some included people from our agency and some included offenders," Hendricks said.

The next step for the project was encouraging mentors from these institutions to participate and then training them.

TRAINING MENTORS AND BEGINNING THE MATCH

The CSOSA created guidelines for the churches and other organizations involved in the mentoring process so that the project could ensure it had buy-in that would give it staying power.

The guidelines required that each interested faith-based group have a mentoring program in place prior to application to the CSOSA program. In addition, each individual mentoring program had to identify a mentoring coordinator so that the CSOSA had a regular point of contact. Then the mentors had to be trained. The CSOSA created an 8- to 10-hour training session for the mentors that touched upon communications skills, information pertinent to the offender population, and the goals of easing reentry for the offenders.

With 25 different faith-based institutions submitting applications and 120 mentors going through the training, the CSOSA was ready to move ahead. The CSOSA made its first matches of eight offenders to eight faith-based institutions earlier this month. Of this group of eight, the first is due for parole on the 8th of August. Through the month of July, the CSOSA will be making additional faith-based institution/offender matches. "We had contemplated one-on-one matches but decided to do group mentoring as the basis for engagement [with the community]," said Hendricks.

Hendricks said the project organizers decided to divide the city into clusters and chose a lead faith-based institution to serve as facilitator for the mentoring project for those areas. "As offenders come into the halfway house and we determine that a person can benefit from a mentor, they will be referred to the cluster coordinators and, based on where the person will live, they will see if a church is in the neighborhood. The idea of localism underlies this effort," he said.

At the case management meetings where the offender, officers, and case management staff hammer out the plan for reentry, the mentor will be brought in to lend a hand in finding needed resources. The idea is that the mentor will be another contact in the community to help the offender succeed.

"This becomes another resource. The idea of mentoring is to complement the work of the supervision officer," Hendricks said.

Source: "DC Agency Leads Effort to Involve Mentors in Offender Re-entry," Michelle Gaseau, The Corrections Connection Network News (CCNN). Eye on Corrections. www.corrections.com. July 1, 2002. Copyright © 2002, all rights reserved, The Corrections Connection Network News (CCNN), a division of J.S. Noonan, LLC. Reprinted with permission.

REINTEGRATION INVOLVING VICTIMS

Successful reintegration programs also involve victims.[43] Victims and victim organizations can assist in the reintegration of parolees by providing parole board members and parole officers with relevant information, offering their experience and expertise, and encouraging offender accountability.

Each year, about 30 million people in America become victims of crime. Most states give victims the right to (1) be notified about parole proceedings, (2) be heard on matters relating to the offender's parole, (3) be present at parole proceedings, and (4) receive restitution as a condition of parole. These rights are designed to ensure that the views of victims are taken into account before decisions about parole are made and to help victims prepare themselves for the offender's release. Victim input can highlight the need for strict supervision or special conditions such as restitution orders, order of protection, or mandated treatment in order to discourage reoffending and encourage reintegration.

Programs involving victims operate in a number of ways. Some encourage victims to volunteer relevant information to parole officers. For example, in stalking cases, victims can tell parole officers whether offenders are in areas where they are not supposed to be. Other programs encourage victim-offender communication. In these programs, victims educate offenders about the impact of the crime and generate remorse in the hope that they can change offender behavior in the future. Whether the program features one-on-one conversation or a victim talking to an audience of imprisoned or paroled offenders, the aim is to convey to offenders the consequences of their actions in terms of the victims' pain and suffering.

LEGAL DECISIONS AFFECTING PAROLE

As we will see in Chapter 11, numerous challenges to the correctional system have brought about changes in prisoners' rights. You may recall that due process guarantees that a person has a right to be heard fairly before being deprived of liberty. Three of the most widely cited cases affecting parolees' and probationers' rights are *Morrissey* v. *Brewer* (1972), *Gagnon* v. *Scarpelli* (1973), and *Greenholtz* v. *Inmates of the Nebraska Penal and Correctional Complex* (1979).

In *Morrissey* v. *Brewer*, John Morrissey pled guilty to writing bad checks in 1967. He was sentenced to not more than seven years of confinement in the Iowa State Prison and paroled in June 1968. Seven months later he was arrested for parole violation and incarcerated in the county jail. One week later, at the direction of the parole officer's written report, the Iowa Board of Parole revoked his parole, and he was returned to the penitentiary.

Morrissey's complaint stated that he had received no counsel and no hearing prior to parole revocation. The Supreme Court agreed and overturned the Iowa parole board's decision. The Court ruled that due process establishes a parolee's right to a preliminary and a final hearing before parole can be revoked. According to the Court, a preliminary hearing must be held at the time of arrest and detention to determine whether there is probable cause to believe that the parolee has violated the conditions of supervision. If probable cause is established, "a more comprehensive hearing prior to making of the final revocation decision" determines guilt or innocence and extends to the parolee certain minimum due process rights: written notification of the alleged violation, disclosure of evidence, opportunity for a hearing to present witnesses and evidence, the right to confront and cross-examine adverse witnesses, a neutral hearing body, and a written statement by the hearing authority as to the evidence relied upon and the reasons for revocation.[44]

Morrissey did not extend to parolees the right to legal representation in parole revocation hearings. This issue was addressed one year later, in *Gagnon* v. *Scarpelli*. In a Wisconsin court in July 1965, Gerald Scarpelli pled guilty to a robbery charge. He was sentenced to 15 years; the judge suspended the sentence and placed him on probation for seven years. One month later, Scarpelli was arrested and charged with burglary. His probation was revoked. He was sent to the Wisconsin state reformatory to serve a 15-year prison term and was paroled after three years. Before he was paroled, however, Scarpelli filed a *habeas corpus* petition. He alleged that his right to due process had been denied—he had no access to counsel and no hearing prior to probation revocation. The Court ruled in favor of Scarpelli. It applied the fundamental due process and two-stage hearing requirements that it had laid out one year earlier in *Morrissey*, thus equating probation with parole. In *Gagnon*, the Court ruled that state officials may be required to assign counsel at the hearing under "special circumstances" and that decisions should be made on a case-by-case basis, depending on the offender's competence, case complexity, and mitigating evidence.

In *Greenholtz* v. *Inmates of the Nebraska Penal and Correctional Complex* (1979), a case involving a routine parole board hearing, the U.S. Supreme Court ruled that parole is a privilege, rather than a right, and the full complement of due process rights need not be afforded at parole hearings. The Court also said that the parole board is not required to specify the evidence used in deciding to deny parole. As a result of this case, states are deciding what inmate privileges are appropriate at parole hearings.

ABOLITION OF DISCRETIONARY PAROLE BOARD RELEASE

Earlier in this chapter we discussed that there was strong opposition to parole in the 1930s and that opponents wanted to abolish it. They argued that parole boards were turning hardened criminals loose on society, parole had a dismal performance record, its goals were never realized, parole board members and parole officers were poorly trained, and parole hearings were little more than hastily conducted, almost unthinking interviews. In spite of the gap between goals and this 1930s reality, parole fulfilled important functions for wardens, legislators, and district attorneys.

The movement to abolish discretionary parole boards resurfaced in the 1970s, when the concept of "just deserts"—the idea that offenders deserve punishment for what they do to society—was being discussed.[45] However, states did not do away

Daniel Savasta, a U.S. probation officer, demonstrates an alcohol breath analyzer. The technology uses voice verification and allows probation/parole officers to monitor an offender's alcohol use while in his or her home. Testing can be scheduled at regular intervals, randomly, or on demand. Voice verification technology reduces the likelihood of an imposter taking the test. What are the advantages of such technology in supervising parolees?

Parole: Rehabilitation and Restoration Justice

by Jeremy Travis, Urban Institute

Reflections on the Future

Parole today looks quite different from its original formulation. Parole boards are on the wane. Parole supervision has been increased. We have decoupled the release decision from the supervision decision. Parole revocations now contribute significantly to the prison populations of the states. We have created a system of backend sentencing, sending tens of thousands of people back to prison. We seem far removed from the goal of rehabilitation and confidence in official exercise of discretion.

Yet even this national picture tells only part of the story because it masks enormous state variation. Some states have retained parole boards, some have abolished them; some states place all released prisoners on supervision, some only half; some states aggressively revoke parole, others are more lenient. So, we have replaced a single, unifying American approach, indeterminate sentencing, with a patchwork quilt of state-level experiments in sentencing reforms.

What is the future of parole, given this history? It is hard to imagine a political scenario that will restore the practice of parole release to its former position of dominance. The public and the politicians they elect are too distrustful of governmental discretion, particularly when criminal sentences are involved. Yet that same political mood is likely to call for increases in the reach of parole supervision—more people on parole, for longer periods of time, with more stringent conditions; more high-tech surveillance; and consequently more parolees violated and returned to prison.

Yet there are important cross currents that may carry the day. Sentencing reformers are challenging the practice of "backend" sentencing, calling for guidelines for parole revocations. Parole administrators are promoting the principles of restorative justice, embracing the goals of community service and victim-offender reconciliation, hoping to provide a higher purpose to community supervision. Drug policy analysts, noting that a larger portion of illegal drugs is consumed by offenders under community supervision, have urged adoption of new regimes of drug testing, sanctions and treatment to break the cycle of drug use and crime. Community justice advocates, tracking the success of community policing, have called upon parole departments to create new partnerships with community institutions, essentially sharing responsibility for prisoner reintegration. The renewed interest in prisoner reentry at the turn of the 21st century has focused the attention of housing providers, health care agencies, employment developers, and others on ways to improve the chances of successful reentry, thereby forging new definitions of the parole process itself.

In the middle of this ferment, one must note the absence of a strong research base that might guide these critical policy discussions. Given the centrality of the institution of parole to the system of indeterminate sentencing, the high public safety risks posed by this population, and the enormous costs of incarceration and community supervision, one would think that these policy options would be well evaluated. Unfortunately, that is not the case. Hopefully, the next century will produce the base of knowledge that will guide parole practice, under whatever name, to a more effective future.

ABOUT THE AUTHOR

Jeremy Travis is Senior Fellow at the Urban Institute. He is former director of United States Department of Justice's National Institute of Justice, Deputy Commissioner for Legal Matters of the New York City Police Department, and Chief Counsel to the Subcommittee on Criminal Justice of the House of Representative Committee on the Judiciary. Mr. Travis holds the J.D. and M.P.A. from New York University.

with parole altogether; they restructured it. As the data in Table 8–3 show, by the end of 2000, 16 states and the federal government had abolished discretionary release from prison by a parole board for all offenders. Another four states had abolished discretionary parole release for certain violent offenses or other crimes against a person. In these states, postrelease supervision still exists and is referred to as "mandatory supervised release," "controlled release," or "community control." Parole boards still have discretion over inmates who were sentenced for crimes committed prior to the effective date of the law that eliminated parole board release and the responsibility to place offenders under either conditional or supervised release, the authority to return an offender to prison for violating the conditions of parole or supervised release, and the power to grant parole for medical reasons. But how well is this working? Petersilia offers a sober thought: ". . . [I]n California, where more than 125,000 prisoners are released yearly, there is no parole board to ask whether the inmate is ready for release, since he or she *must* be released once his or her term has been served. Generally, a parolee must be released to the county where he or she lived before entering prison. Since the vast majority of offenders come from economically disadvantaged, culturally isolated, inner-city neighborhoods, they return there upon release."[46]

TABLE 8–3	States That Have Abolished Discretionary Release, 2000	
For all offenders	**For certain violent offenders**	
Arizona	Alaska	
California[a]	Louisiana	
Delaware	New York	
Florida[b]	Tennessee	
Illinois		
Indiana		
Kansas[c]		
Maine		
Minnesota		
Mississippi		
North Carolina		
Ohio[d]		
Oregon		
Virginia		
Washington		
Wisconsin		

a In 1976 the Uniform Determinate Sentencing Act abolished discretionary parole for all offenses except some violent crimes with a long sentence or a sentence to life.

b In 1995 parole eligibility was abolished for offenses with a life sentence and a 25-year mandatory term.

c Excludes a few offenses, primarily first-degree murder and intentional second-degree murder.

d Excludes murder and aggravated murder.

Source: Timothy A. Hughes, Doris James Wilson and Allen J. Beck, *Trends in State Parole, 1999–2000* (Washington, DC: U.S. Department of Justice, Bureau of Justice Statistics), October 2001.

The backdrop for the debate on just deserts was an extraordinary increase in the nation's crime rate that began in the mid-1960s and continued through the 1970s. Legislatures were growing anxious about crime and were willing to try new options in correctional approaches to the crime problem. They felt that rehabilitation and indeterminate sentencing were not working. Their answer was determinate sentencing and abolition of discretionary parole board release.

Why did some states abolish discretionary release from prison by a parole board? There are at least four reasons.

First, scholars concluded that indeterminate sentencing and discretionary parole did not achieve offender rehabilitation, which was unfair since it was based solely on parole board judgment, without explicit standards of fairness and equity in sentencing. Studies showed that wide disparities resulted when the characteristics of the crime and the offender were taken into account, and decisions were influenced by the offender's race, socioeconomic status, and place of conviction. Second, eliminating discretionary parole appeared to be tough on crime. Third, parole boards' lack of openness in the decision-making process, in which boards made their parole decisions on a case-by-case basis without benefit of a written set of policies and procedures, prompted criticism. Fourth, state politicians were able to convince the public that parole was the cause of the rising crime problem and that abolition was the solution.

REVIEW & APPLICATIONS

SUMMARY

1▶ Early English judges spared the lives of condemned felons by exiling them to America as indentured servants. Captain Alexander Maconochie, superintendent of the British penal colony on Norfolk Island, devised a "ticket of leave" system that moved inmates through stages. Sir Walter Crofton used some of Maconochie's ideas for his early release system in Ireland. In the United States, Zebulon Brockway implemented a system of upward classification.

2▶ Paroling authorities play powerful roles in the criminal justice system. They determine the length of incarceration for many offenders and can revoke parole. The paroling authority's policies have a direct impact on an institution's population. Paroling authorities use state laws and information from courts and other criminal justice agencies to make release decisions.

3▶ Parole is the conditional release of a prison inmate, prior to sentence expiration, with supervision in the community. The parole process of release begins in the courtroom when the judge sentences an offender to either a determinate or an indeterminate sentence. After serving a certain portion of his or her sentence, an offender is eligible for parole release. That portion varies from state to state. If an inmate maintains good conduct for a certain amount of time preceding the parole hearing and is granted parole, he or she must live in accordance with specified rules and regulations in the community. If a parolee violates either the technical conditions of parole or commits a new crime, he or she may have parole revoked.

4▶ On January 1, 2003, 753,141 American adults were on parole, representing an increase of 2.8 percent (20,808 parolees) over January 1, 2002. Eighty-nine percent are state parolees. The typical adult parolee is a black, non-Hispanic male, on mandatory parole, and under active parole supervision for more than one year. His median age is 34 and he has an 11th-grade education. Women make up 14 percent of the parole population. The region with the highest number of parolees is the South, followed by the Northeast, West, and Midwest.

5▶ Parole may be revoked for a technical violation (failure to comply with one of the conditions of parole) or for a new offense violation (commission of a crime). Two-thirds of all parolees are re-arrested within three years, typically within the first six months of release. Of the nearly 448,000 parolees discharged from supervision in 2002, 183,680 (41 percent) were returned to prison either because of a rule violation or new offense, up from 27,177 in 1980 and 131,502 in 1990. Currently, rearrests comprise 35 percent of all prison admissions as compared with 17 percent in 1980.

6▶ The reentry court concept, designed to manage parolee return to the community, requires that the parolee make regular court appearances for progress assessment. Community Partnership Councils unite community leaders and local agencies with parole officers and administrators to study parole operations and issues and assist with service provisions and public education. Reintegration of offenders today emphasizes job readiness and programs to address needs common to offenders such as substance abuse counseling, housing, and medical care before inmates are released and continues after release. Reintegration involving victims encourages victims to volunteer relevant information to parole officers and supports victim-offender communication. In these programs, victims educate offenders about the impact of the crime and generate remorse in the hope that they can change offender behavior in the future.

Three important U.S. Supreme Court decisions significantly affected parole. In *Morrissey* v. *Brewer* (1972), the U.S. Supreme Court said that parole, once granted, becomes a right and that parolees are to have certain due process rights in any revocation hearing. In *Gagnon* v. *Scarpelli* (1973), the U.S. Supreme Court held that a probationer has a limited right to counsel in a revocation hearing and that the hearing body must decide whether counsel should be provided on a case-by-case basis. In *Greenholtz* v. *Inmates of the Nebraska Penal and Correctional Complex* (1979), the U.S. Supreme Court ruled that parole is a privilege; therefore, the full complement of due process rights need not be afforded at parole hearings. As a result, states are deciding what inmate privileges are appropriate at parole hearings.

Today, 16 states and the federal government have abolished discretionary release from prison by a parole board for all offenders. Another 4 states have abolished discretionary parole release for certain violent offenses or other crimes against a person. In these states, post-release supervision still exists and is referred to as "mandatory supervised release," "controlled release," or "community control."

KEY TERMS

parole, *p. 288*
discretionary release, *p. 289*
mandatory release, *p. 289*
pardon, *p. 289*

parole eligibility date, *p. 293*
paroling authority, *p. 297*
salient factor score
  (SFS), *p. 298*

parolee, *p. 300*
reentry court, *p. 309*

QUESTIONS FOR REVIEW

1. What is *parole*?
2. Explain the difference between *mandatory release* and *discretionary release*.
3. What is the difference between *parole* and *probation*? Between *parole* and *pardon*?
4. What are the similarities among indenture and parole?
5. Who were Captain Alexander Maconochie and Sir Walter Crofton, and what were their contributions to parole development?
6. What did the Elmira Reformatory contribute to the history of American parole?
7. In spite of the opposition toward parole in the mid-20th century, why did parole continue?
8. What is parole eligibility?
9. Comment on the recommendations to improve prisoner reentry.
10. What is the paroling authority's role in the parole decision-making process?
11. What release criteria do parole boards use? Not use?
12. How does parole affect the criminal justice system?
13. What are conditions of parole?
14. How many American adults are on parole? What are the typical parolee's characteristics?
15. What's the contradiction between the money spent on preparing inmates for parole and employment restrictions?
16. On what does parole success depend?
17. Why do offenders return to prison? How many return?
18. What is a *revocation hearing* and when is it used?

REVIEW & APPLICATIONS

19. What are *reentry courts?*

20. What are *Community Partnership Councils?*

21. What do successful reintegration programs have in common?

22. Why are victims involved in offender reintegration?

23. What are three U.S. Supreme Court decisions that affected parole?

24. Why did some states and the federal government abolish or limit discretionary parole board release?

THINKING CRITICALLY ABOUT CORRECTIONS

▶ ▶ ▶ Policy-Driven Decision Making

Paroling authorities generally maintain a low profile, and their work is often known only to the offenders seeking release and the victims of their crimes. This is changing as the public demands to know more about paroling authorities' actions. In some states, legislatures and sentencing commissions have replaced the case-by-case parole decision-making process with a policy-driven decision-making process. A policy-driven decision-making process implements a written set of policies and procedures. Such a process standardizes the procedures and the information

used to make a paroling decision. What are the advantages and disadvantages of a policy-driven decision-making process?

▶ ▶ ▶ The Carceral Problem

In *The Prison Reform Movement* (1990), Larry Sullivan suggests that prison reforms have always failed because they never addressed the "carceral problem." That is, is it possible to instill free-society values in a caged population? What do you think about Sullivan's premise in terms of preparing prisoners for early release?

ON-THE-JOB DECISION MAKING

▶ ▶ ▶ Reponding to Technical Violations

You have just learned that one of your parolees tested positive for drugs. In your state a positive drug test is a technical violation of parole and requires a revocation hearing. You have long wished that your state had a set of guidelines for responding to such technical violations so that you could handle the violation without waiting for a hearing. In this case, you could immediately place the parolee in a substance abuse program rather than waiting for a decision that might yield the same result. Draft a proposal for such a technical violation response policy. First, formulate the basic expectations of the policy

(for example, "The least restrictive response to the behavior should be used."). Then determine what components the policy should include (for example, "Define clear goals and clarify the agency's concept of supervision.").

▶ ▶ ▶ Mentors and Offender Reentry

As chief parole officer in your area, write a two-page proposal recommending the involvement of mentors in offender reentry. Include what you believe are the advantages of mentoring for offender reentry and strategies for recruiting, training, and matching mentors with parolees.

CORRECTIONS ON THE WEB

▶ ▶ ▶ **U.S. Parole Commission**

The United States Parole Commission maintains a website at http://www.usdoj.gov/uspc. The site describes the Commission's mission, jurisdiction, members, history, and programs. Click the link *Answering Your Questions.* Compare federal parole with parole in your state by asking a member of your state's paroling authority similar questions.

▶ ▶ ▶ *Public Interest*

Almost 500,000 inmates a year leave prison to rejoin society. They get $20, clothing, and a bus ticket. On November 19, 2001, Kojo Nnamdi, host of the radio show *Public Interest,* discusses prisoner reentry with Jeremy Travis, senior fellow at the Urban Institute; Reginald Wilkinson, director of the Ohio Department of Rehabilitation and Correction; Errol Sull, president of the Correctional Education Company; and Elizabeth Gaynes, executive director of the Osborne Association. Open the audio link for American University Radio WAMU 88.5 FM at http://www.wamu.org. Search the archives for November 19, 2001 and click on "Local Prisoner Re-entry." After listening to the broadcast, generate a list of issues and questions similar to the ones presented in this 50-minute program and raise them with parole officials in your state.

The Prison World

Part Four explores life inside prison for inmates and staff, the legal challenges surrounding their roles and responsibilities, and the special needs created by inmates who are elderly, infected with HIV or AIDS, or mentally or physically challenged.

Custodial staff are most directly involved in the daily work of managing the inmate population. The extent to which correctional officers share beliefs, values, and behaviors is largely a function of the correctional officer subculture and each individual's personality.

Prisoners, too, develop a subculture that helps them adjust to the self-doubt, reduced self-esteem, and deprivations they experience as a result of confinement. Inmate subculture is also based on the life experiences that prisoners bring with them when they enter confinement. One question that we try to answer is, why does men's prisoner subculture encourage isolation while women's prisoner subculture encourages relationships.

For a century, prisoners were considered civilly dead, and prisons operated entirely without court intervention. However, in 1970, the U.S. Supreme Court declared that, if states were going to operate prisons, they would have to do so according to the dictates of the Constitution. Since then, prisoners have reclaimed many of their conditional rights under the U.S. Constitution. But today, changes in state and federal statues have slowed the pace of prisoners' rights cases, and the U.S. Supreme Court seems to have become less sympathetic to prisoners' civil rights claims.

Special needs inmates—those who are elderly, suffer from HIV, AIDS, or other chronic diseases, or are mentally or physically challenged—present significant problems for correctional managers. Special needs inmates may be more prone toward violence and disruption. They frequently require close monitoring to reduce risk of suicide, and they may tax scarce medical resources and become targets of abuse by other inmates.

The preprison drug use and sexual activity of many prisoners has brought HIV, AIDS, and tuberculosis into jails and prisons. Managing these problems requires training in early detection, treatment, classification, staff education, and adequate funding. These problems are compounded by the fact that many prisoners have co-occurring physical and mental health problems.

9

10

11

12

"Corrections is not a business where only one sex, race, religion, or type of person can succeed. It takes men and women of all races, religions, and color to create a dynamic and effective workforce to manage diverse inmates and solve the problems we face.

—Dora Schriro, former Missouri Director of Corrections

The Staff World: Managing the Prison Population

CHAPTER OBJECTIVES

After completing this chapter you should be able to do the following:

1. List the staff roles within the organizational hierarchy of correctional institutions.

2. Define *custodial staff.*

3. Identify the types of power available to correctional officers.

4. Explain what structured conflict is and how it applies to correctional institutions.

5. Define the word *subculture* and identify some of the essential features of correctional officer subculture.

6. Summarize correctional officer demographics.

7. List and describe the most common correctional officer personality types.

8. List and describe the seven correctional officer job assignments.

9. Describe how female correctional officers differ from males in their approach to the workplace.

10. Explain why stress is a problem in corrections work, and list some techniques for reducing stress.

11. List the elements that correctional administrators must consider when planning for staff safety.

On a calm Saturday afternoon in April 1998 at the Everglades Correctional Institute, a maximum-security prison in Florida, correctional officers staffing guard towers were shocked to see a big-rig truck heading toward prison fences and beginning to accelerate.[1] The truck rammed through four security fences and stopped in the middle of the prison yard. The driver, later identified as 31-year-old John Beaston, pulled out a shotgun and started firing at officers in the towers and the yard. Two officers were injured. Other officers returned fire.

A car, allegedly driven by 58-year-old Sandra Sigler, then drove through the hole the truck had ripped in the prison fences, picked up Beaston and inmate Jay Junior

The maximum-security Everglades Correctional Institute in Miami, Florida. The facility was the site of a daring 1998 escape involving a big-rig truck that rammed through four security fences. Can incidents like this be prevented?

Sigler, 31, and sped away. Jay Sigler, son of Sandra Sigler, had served 8 years of a 20-year sentence for armed robbery.

Prison superintendent Joe T. Butler spoke to reporters shortly after the prison break. "I guess we were blessed [that no one was killed], but my officers did respond appropriately and got the inmates to their respective dormitories," he said. "This happened in the daytime and there are a lot of activities in the prison at that time, both recreation and visitation."

The Everglades Correctional Institute is a state-of-the art facility, incorporating a number of high-technology security systems. The institution houses more than 1,500 prisoners. Butler said the breakout did not raise new security concerns. "I think anyone would think this was a very unusual situation," he noted. "How often do you hear about a semi truck . . . crashing through your security system?"

Although planned escapes with outside help are rare, correctional personnel must be constantly alert for possible threats to institutional security. Ever since prisons began, one observer after another has noted that security should be the number-one concern of correctional staff. Barnes and Teeters, for example, wrote more than half a century ago, "Above all else, the main purpose of the prison is to keep the prisoners from escaping."[2]

---

roles
The normal patterns of behavior expected of those holding particular social positions.

staff roles
The patterns of behavior expected of correctional staff members in particular jobs.

The Staff Hierarchy

Practically speaking, a prison of any size has a number of different staff roles—each with its own unique set of tasks. **Roles** are the normal patterns of behavior expected of those holding particular social positions. **Staff roles** are the patterns of behavior expected of correctional staff members in particular jobs. Eventually, many people internalize the expectations others have of them, and such expectations can play an important part in their self-perceptions.

Ideally, today's correctional staff members have four main goals:

1. to provide for the security of the community by incarcerating those who break the law;

2. to promote the smooth and effective functioning of the institution;

3. to ensure that incarceration is secure but humane; and

4. to give inmates the opportunity to develop a positive lifestyle while incarcerated and to gain the personal and employment skills they need for a positive lifestyle after release.[3]

Prison staff are organized into a hierarchy, or multilevel categorization, according to responsibilities. An institution's hierarchy generally has a warden or superintendent at the top and correctional officers at a lower level. A typical correctional staff hierarchy includes the following:

- administrative staff (wardens, superintendents, assistant superintendents, and others charged with running the institution and its programs and with setting policy);

- clerical personnel (record keepers and administrative assistants);

- program staff (psychologists, psychiatrists, medical doctors, nurses, medical aides, teachers, counselors, caseworkers, and ministers—many of whom contract with the institution to provide services);

- custodial staff (majors, captains, lieutenants, sergeants, and correctional officers charged primarily with maintaining order and security);

- service and maintenance staff (kitchen supervisors, physical plant personnel, and many outside contractors); and

- volunteers (prison ministry, speakers, and other volunteers in corrections).

Organizational charts graphically represent the staff structure and the chain of command within an institution. An organizational chart for a typical medium-to-large correctional institution is shown in Figure 9–1. **Custodial staff** are most directly involved in managing the inmate population, through daily contact with inmates. Their role is to control prisoners within the institution. **Program staff,** on the other hand, are concerned with encouraging prisoners to participate in educational, vocational, and treatment programs. Custodial staff, who make up over 60 percent of prison personnel, are generally organized in a military-style hierarchy, from assistant or deputy warden down to correctional officer. Program staff generally operate through a separate organizational structure and have little in common with custodial staff.

To a great extent, prison management involves managing relationships—among employees, between employees and inmates, and among inmates. Prisons are unique in that most of the people in them (the inmates) are forced to live there according to the terms of their sentence; they really do not want to be there. Such a situation presents tremendous challenges. The people on the front lines dealing around the clock with such challenges are the correctional officers.

custodial staff
Those staff members most directly involved in managing the inmate population.

program staff
Those staff members concerned with encouraging prisoners to participate in educational, vocational, and treatment programs.

> To a great extent, prison management involves managing relationships—among employees, between employees and inmates, and among inmates.

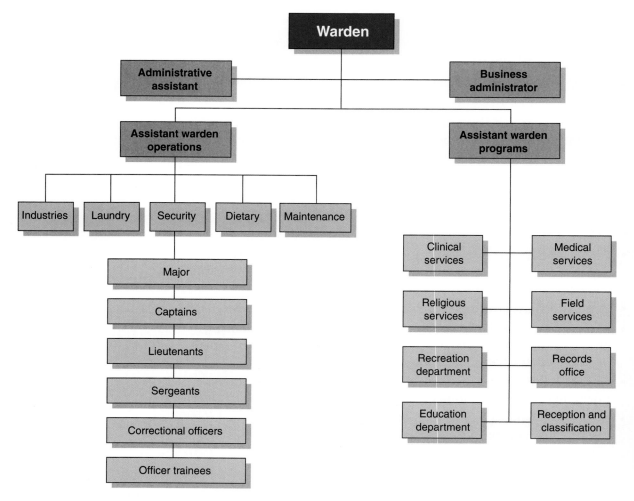

FIGURE 9-1
Organizational Chart of a Typical Midsize or Large Correctional Institution

The Correctional Officer– The Crucial Professional

Although security is still the major concern, correctional officers today are expected to perform a variety of other tasks. As one commentator has said,

> Correctional officers have more responsibilities [now] than in the past and their duty is no longer to merely watch over the prisoners. They now have to play several roles in keeping prisoners in line. They have to be "psychiatrists" when prisoners come to them with their problems, and they have to be "arbitrators and protectors" when inmates have complaints or problems with each other, while still watching out for their own safety. In these situations, the wrong decision could offend someone and start a riot. This makes correctional officers "prisoners" of the daily emotional and physical moods of the inmates.[4]

Don Josi and Dale Sechrest explain it this way: "Correctional officers today must find a balance between their security role and their responsibility to use relationships with inmates to change their behavior constructively. They routinely assume numerous essential yet sometimes contradictory roles (e.g., counselor, diplomat, caretaker, disciplinarian, supervisor, crisis manager), often under stressful and dangerous conditions."[5]

Josi and Sechrest then go on to say, "These divergent and often incompatible goals can prove problematic; role conflict, role diffusion, and role ambiguity may be difficult if not impossible to avoid."[6]

> Correctional officers today must find a balance between their security role and their responsibility to use relationships with inmates to change their behavior constructively.

BASES OF POWER

Correctional officers rely on a variety of strategies to manage inmate behavior. After surveying correctional officers in five prisons, John Hepburn identified five types of officers' power, according to the bases which they rest: legitimate power, coercive power, reward power, expert power, and referent power.

Legitimate Power   Correctional officers have power by virtue of their positions within the organization. That is, they have formal authority to command. As Hepburn says, "the prison guard has the right to exercise control over prisoners by virtue of the structural relationship between the position of the guard and the position of the prisoner."[7]

Coercive Power   Inmates' beliefs that a correctional officer can and will punish disobedience give the officer coercive power. Many correctional officers use coercive power as a primary method of control.

Reward Power   Correctional officers dispense both formal and informal rewards to induce cooperation among inmates. Formal rewards include assignment of desirable jobs, housing, and other inmate privileges. Correctional officers are also in a position to influence parole decisions and to assign good-time credit and **gain time** to inmates. Informal rewards correctional officers use include granting special favors and overlooking minor infractions of rules.

gain time
Time taken off an inmate's sentence for participating in certain activities such as going to school, learning a trade, and working in prison.

Expert Power   Expert power results from inmates' perceptions that certain correctional officers have valuable skills. For example, inmates seeking treatment may value treatment-oriented officers. Inmates who need help with ongoing interpersonal conflicts may value officers who have conflict-resolution skills. Such officers may be able to exert influence on inmates who want their help.

Referent Power   Referent power flows from "persuasive diplomacy." Officers who win the respect and admiration of prisoners—officers who are fair and not abusive—may achieve a kind of natural leadership position over inmates.

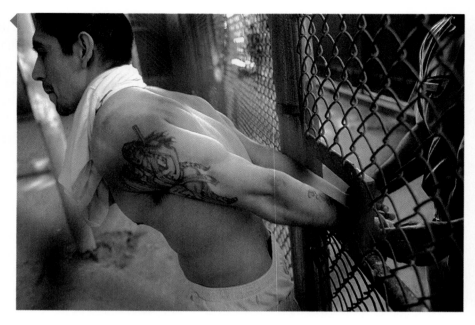

Securing an inmate in preparation for a trip back to his cell. Correctional officers need to elicit inmates' cooperation to effectively carry out their custodial duties. What are some techniques officers might use?

Some years before Hepburn's study, Gresham Sykes wrote that correctional officers' power can be corrupted through inappropriate relationships with inmates.[8] Friendships with prisoners, as well as indebtedness to them, can corrupt. According to Sykes, staff members who get too close to inmates and establish friendships are likely to find their "friends" asking for special favors. Similarly, officers who accept help from inmates may one day find that it is "payback time." In difficult or dangerous situations, help may be difficult to decline. In such cases, staff members must be careful not to let any perceived indebtedness to inmates influence their future behavior.

THE STAFF SUBCULTURE

> Prison life is characterized by duality. An enormous gap separates those who work in prisons from those who live in them.

Prison life is characterized by duality. An enormous gap separates those who work in prisons from those who live in them. This gap has a number of dimensions. One is that staff members officially control the institution and enforce the rules by which inmates live. Other formal and informal differences exist, including differences in background, values, and culture. Primarily, however, the relationship between correctional officers and inmates can be described as one of structured conflict.[9]

structured conflict

The tensions between prison staff members and inmates that arise out of the correctional setting.

Structured conflict is a term that highlights the tensions between prison staff members and inmates that arise out of the correctional setting. In one sense, the prison is one large society in which the worlds of inmates and staff bump up against one another. In another sense, however, the two groups keep their distance from each other—a distance imposed by both formal and informal rules. Conflict arises because staff members have control over the lives of inmates, and inmates often have little say over important aspects of their own lives. The conflict is structured because it occurs within the confines of an organized institution and because, to some extent, it follows the rules—formal and informal—that govern institutional life.

Both worlds—inmate and staff—have their own cultures. Those cultures are generally called *subcultures* to indicate that both are contained within and surrounded by a larger culture. One writer has defined **subculture** as the beliefs, values, behavior, and material objects shared by a particular group of people within a larger society.[10] That is the definition we will use. The subcultures of inmates and correctional officers exist simultaneously in any prison institution. The beliefs, values, and behavior that make up the **staff subculture** differ greatly from those of the inmate subculture. Additionally, staff members possess material objects of control, such as keys, vehicles, weapons, and security systems.

Kauffman has identified a distinct correctional officer subculture within prisons.[11] Those beliefs, values, and behaviors set correctional officers apart from other prison staff and from inmates. Their beliefs and values form an "officer code," which includes the following:

- Always go to the aid of an officer in distress.
- Do not "lug" drugs (bring them in for inmate use).
- Do not rat on other officers.
- Never make a fellow officer look bad in front of inmates.
- Always support an officer in a dispute with an inmate.
- Always support officer sanctions against inmates.
- Do not be a "white hat" or a "Goody Two-Shoes."
- Maintain officer solidarity in dealings with all outside groups.
- Show positive concern for fellow officers.

subculture

The beliefs, values, behavior, and material objects shared by a particular group of people within a larger society.

staff subculture

The beliefs, values, and behavior of staff. They differ greatly from those of the inmate subculture.

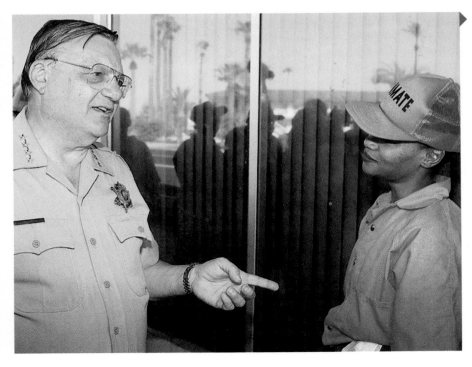

A prison superintendent talks with an inmate. Effective communication is one way of overcoming the differences in beliefs, values, and behaviors between inmates and prison staff. What barriers to communication might such differences create?

Eye On Corrections™

On-the-Job Training: The Real Experience

By Michelle Gaseau

Training staff properly can make a huge difference in keeping staff happy and keeping them on the job. On-the-job training can be a major part of ensuring that new officers are trained right. The get-your-hands-dirty experience of the sights and smells of the cell block is, according to many, when the real training begins.

One of the main elements of making this training work is having the right officer—a field training officer—work with the new recruits for a significant period of time. "When you start trying to train adults, repetition is an [important part of it.] The field training officer process is skills based. Where [the new officer] is required to go from reading to putting [his] hands on things, tasting, touching, smelling and hearing it," said Randy McCloud, Assistant Director for Security Systems and Training for the Texas Department of Criminal Justice (TDCJ).

Texas began a new on-the-job (OJT) training program earlier this year that involves specialized field training officers in each facility. The model is based on a program supported by the National Institute of Corrections (NIC) that emphasizes on-the-job testing and evaluation of new recruits.

FIELD OFFICER TRAINING FORMALIZES ON-THE-JOB PROCESS

According to Tom Reid, Program Manager for NIC, the field officer training was created to help improve on-the-job training programs nationwide.

"We wanted to develop a formal training program for new employees to bridge the gap between the academy and the [prison.] A lot of [the programs] are too informal. [In some places] it [the training] is not well documented; it is more like partnering," said Reid.

Reid said training with an experienced officer can help new recruits transfer the information they have learned that is in their heads into actual practice.

Usually the field training officer in an institution trains new recruits in addition to performing his or her regular duties. Agencies should choose FTOs who will be good teachers, who have good writing skills, and who have good job skills. The FTO position is a good testing ground for future supervisors.

"More and more [on the job training] is very critical as people recognize what they want out of training. If you want performance on the job, you need a good translator to take the conceptual information and translate it to behavior,'" said Reid. That is where NIC's training comes in.

NIC strives to improve on-the-job training by teaching the field training officers in an agency how to work with a new recruit, model for them, and fairly evaluate them.

"Informal [programs] are more show and tell. Our model is very specific, and each task has a performance evaluation attached to it [as well as] an instruction period, a practice period, and testing," Reid said.

Under NIC's model, which is competency based, it could take a new recruit between 4 and 12 weeks, depending on how long he or she practices certain skills. "You want someone who is competent and confident. If it takes them 12 weeks, it develops successful employees," he said.

TEXAS REVAMPS CO TRAINING

In 2001, the TDCJ made changes to its training program for new correctional officers (COs) and modified its two-phase training process. Phase one of the training consists of 200 hours of cognitive study in the classroom. Upon graduation, COs are assigned to their unit and they begin the OJT process. OJT is phase two and involves 84 hours working with a FTO.

Each institution has an FTO. Resource trainers in firearms, chemical agents, and other specialized areas are also used to train new COs.

"The whole process is a mentoring, coaching, and a support function," said McCloud. "I want them to learn the right way the first day."

The FTO has to certify that the officer has demonstrated competency in seven skill areas, including offender escorts, cell and housing searches, and strip searches.

McCloud said the TDCJ is looking at instituting an extension of the OJT process in which the CO can call on a seasoned employee for guidance when he or she has problems on the job. "The next natural progression that relates to this process is like a lifeline. In many institutions officers are assigned to a shift mentor. "We take the employee from the safety of the academy to the FTO process and further," said McCloud.

MICHIGAN COS LEARN THE ROPES

Following academy instruction, new recruits in Michigan are assigned to two months of on-the-job training in the facility where they will be working. The department is also using the concept to help seasoned employees understand the multitude of jobs being performed inside a facility.

For new recruits, the OJT process involves additional instruction in firearms and other areas, and then they are assigned to a status officer with whom they work on morning and day shifts. The new recruits go through training in the housing unit, gun tower, visiting room, yard, and food service with the status officer.

"It is critical. We structure it so they come to the academy first and they get the basics in the classroom. After six weeks, now we are going to put [officers] in the environment and let [them] apply what [they] have learned," said Carol Frederick, Academy Operations Manager for the Michigan Department of Corrections.

During OJT the status officer fills out a weekly evaluation sheet outlining the recruit's performance in various tasks. After OJT, the new officers return to the academy for a final training and debriefing.

According to Matt Davis, spokesman for the department, the process also gives the officers a chance to see if the job is what they want to do and demonstrates how they are going to react to comments and situations.

In an adaptation of OJT, some institutions also have created job shadowing or cross-training programs for employees of all areas. "What it is trying to do is expose various staff to other types of jobs that they may not have anticipated when they first became employed and see if they might be interested or have a knack for it. It is a constantly moving group of people. To maintain the quality [of employees] it is important to get the people in the right kind of jobs," said Davis.

Staff, under the warden's direction, are able to spend up to eight hours with another staff member to see what other jobs are like. For example, COs might want to see what the records supervisor does, or a CO might work with the hearings investigator, said Davis. Frederick said the cross training helps bridge the custody and noncustody rift that seems to occur naturally in corrections. "They come with a new appreciation of the other person's job," she said.

Both this and the OJT program, which has been in place since 1983, have helped the Michigan DOC consistently fill officer positions and retain them. "[High] quality recruits will be enticed by a wide variety of options available to them. It could mean more jobs available to them [in the future,]" said Frederick. *This article has been reprinted in part from CCNN. To read the article in its entirety, go to www.corrections.com.*

Source: "On the Job Training: The Real Experience," Michelle Gaseau, The Corrections Connection Network News (CCNN). Eye on Corrections. www.corrections.com. March 6, 2000. Copyright © 2000, all rights reserved, The Corrections Connection Network News (CCNN), a division of J.S. Noonan, LLC. Reprinted with permission.

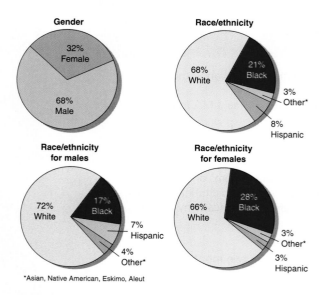

*Asian, Native American, Eskimo, Aleut

FIGURE 9-2

Profile of Custodial and Administrative Correctional Personnel in Adult State and Local Correctional Facilities

Source: American Correctional Association, *Vital Statistics in Corrections* (Lanham, MD: ACA, 2000), p. 143.

Ethical Dilemma

There are reports that find sexual misconduct is a problem in prisons for women. These reports state that male staff victimize women inmates. Should only female staff work in prisons for women? What are the issues? For more information go to Ethical Dilemma 9-1 at http://www.mhhe.com/schmalleger2.

GENDER AND ETHNICITY OF CORRECTIONAL OFFICERS

According to a year 2000 report, state and local adult and juvenile correctional facilities employ 414,000 custodial and administrative staff members.[12] The American Correctional Association (ACA) says that most correctional personnel at state and local levels are white males. Of 106,544 female custodial and administrative staff members, two-thirds are white (see Figure 9–2). Thirty-two percent of corrections personnel are members of minority groups. Of these, most are black.

Ideally, the ethnic breakdown of correctional staff should closely approximate the ethnic breakdown of the population of the United States. According to the U.S. Census Bureau,[13] out of a 2000 population of about 282 million people, 34.7 million (12.3 percent) were black, 35.3 million (12.5 percent) were Hispanic, and 13.1 million (4.7 percent) were members of other minority groups. Figure 9–3 compares ethnic groups as a proportion of prison personnel and as a proportion of the U.S. population.

From Figure 9–3, it is easy to see that blacks are overrepresented among correctional personnel. Although only 12 percent of the U.S. population, they account for 21 percent of the correctional workforce. Hispanics are underrepresented (accounting for 13 percent of the country's population and just 8 percent of the correctional workforce), as are other minorities (5 percent of the population, 3 percent of correctional staff). Whites, on the other hand, are slightly underrepresented.

In addition, the federal Bureau of Prisons employs another 30,432 administrative and custodial personnel, of which 8,097 (27 percent) are female.[14] About 20 percent of correctional staff members in federal institutions are black. In juvenile facilities, females make up slightly more than 42 percent of a correctional workforce of 21,012.[15]

The American Correctional Association also says that approximately 13 percent of all correctional staff positions are supervisory (i.e., above the level of sergeant). Females hold 16 percent of all supervisory positions but fewer positions at the level of warden or superintendent.[16]

CORRECTIONAL OFFICER PERSONALITIES

correctional officer personalities

The distinctive personal characteristics of correctional officers including behavioral, emotional, and social traits.

The staff subculture contributes to the development of **correctional officer personalities.** Those personalities reflect the personal characteristics of the officers as well as their modes of adaptation to their jobs, institutional conditions, the requirements of staff subculture, and institutional expectations.[17] We will next explore the common personality types that have been identified.[18]

The Dictator   The dictator likes to give orders and seems to enjoy the feeling of power that comes from ordering inmates around. Correctional officers with dictator personalities are often strongly disliked by prisoners and may face special difficulties if taken hostage during a prison uprising.

The Friend   The correctional officer who tries to befriend inmates is often a quiet, retiring, but kind individual who believes that close friendships with inmates will make it easier to control the inmates and the work environment. Inmates, however, usually try to capitalize on friendships by asking for special treatment, contraband, and the like.

The Merchant   Merchant-personality correctional officers set themselves up as commodity providers to the inmate population. If an inmate needs something not easily obtained in prison, the merchant will usually procure it—at a cost. Often, such behavior is a violation of institutional rules, and it can lead to serious violations of the law as the merchant–correctional officer smuggles contraband into the institution for the "right price."

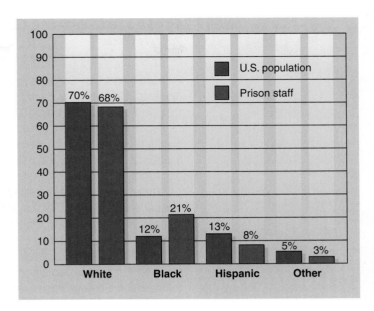

FIGURE 9-3

Ethnic Groups as a Proportion of the U.S. Population and as a Proportion of Prison Staff

Sources: American Correctional Association, *Vital Statistics in Corrections* (Lanham, MD: ACA, 2000). Population statistics derived from U.S. Bureau of the Census, *National Population Estimates of the United States: July 1, 2001* (Washington, DC: U.S. Government Printing Office, 2001), retrieved June 20, 2003, from http://eire.census.gov/popest/data/national/tables/ asro/ US-EST2001-ASRO-04.pht.

The Turnkey   Turnkey officers do little beyond the basic requirements of their position. A turnkey usually interacts little with other officers and does the minimum necessary to get through the workday. Unmotivated and bored, the turnkey may be seeking other employment. Some turnkey officers have become disillusioned with their jobs. Others are close to retirement.

The Climber   The correctional officer who is a climber is set on advancement. He or she may want to be warden or superintendent one day and is probably seeking rapid promotion. Climbers are often diligent officers who perform their jobs well and respect the corrections profession. Climbers who look down on other officers, however, or attempt to look good by making coworkers look bad, can cause many problems within the institution.

The Reformer   The reformer constantly finds problems with the way the institution is run or with existing policies and rules. He or she always seems to know better than anyone else and frequently complains about working conditions or supervisors.

The Do-Gooder   The do-gooder is another type of reformer—one with a personal agenda. A devoutly religious do-gooder may try to convert other

CAREER PROFILE

First Lieutenant Gary F. Cornelius
Programs Director
Fairfax County Adult Detention Center   *Fairfax County Office of the Sheriff*   *Fairfax, Virginia*

"Having staff work together on an idea and watching operations improve is one of the best parts of this job."

First Lieutenant Gary Cornelius is programs director with the Fairfax County Adult Detention Center in Fairfax, Virginia. He has held this position since October of 1995 but has been with the Sheriffs department since 1978.

He earned his Bachelor of Arts and Social Sciences with a focus in criminal justice from Edinboro State College in Pennsylvania in 1974. He later completed specialized police courses at the Northern Virginia Criminal Justice Academy Basic Police School as well as the U.S. Secret Service. He is a former officer of the Uniformed Division of the Secret Service.

Lieutenant Cornelius is also the author of five books, including *The Twenty Minute Trainer, The Correctional Officer: A Practical Guide,* and *The Art of the Con: Avoiding Offender Manipulation.* "Writing gives me a chance to share what I have learned and to learn new concepts through research," he says.

His duties include the development and oversight of inmate programs, ranging from recreation to rehabilitation and substance abuse. He oversees inmate education, manages volunteers and college interns, and supervises other staff members in charge of inmate recreation.

Cornelius says he enjoys watching his efforts—and the efforts of his teammates—result in positive changes. "Probably the best thing about my job is working with good people who care about both jail security and making programs work for the betterment of inmates," he says. "The most difficult aspect is convincing staff of the need for programs, rehabilitative efforts, and volunteers. And trying to get through the old-fashioned 'jailhouse mentality.'"

What are the skills that serve him best in his day-to-day affairs? "Tolerance for others' points of view, patience, not giving up, and diplomatic people skills when dealing with both civilians and sworn staff," he says.

correctional officers and inmates to his or her faith. Other do-gooders actively seek to counsel inmates, using personal techniques and philosophies that are not integrated into the prison's official treatment program.

Although the personalities described here may be exaggerated, their variety suggests that correctional officer personalities result from many influences, including the following:

- general life experiences;
- biological propensities;
- upbringing;
- staff subculture;
- working conditions; and
- institutional expectations and rules.

CORRECTIONAL OFFICER JOB ASSIGNMENTS

Seven different correctional officer roles or job assignments have been identified.[19] They are classified by their location within the institution, the duties required, and the nature of the contact with inmates.

Block Officers Block officers are responsible for supervising inmates in housing areas. Housing areas include dormitories, cell blocks, modular living units, and even tents in some overcrowded prisons. Safety and security are the primary concerns of block officers. Conducting counts, ensuring the orderly movement of prisoners, inspecting personal property, overseeing inmate activity, and searching prisoners are all part of the block officer's job. Block officers also lock and unlock cells and handle problems that arise within the living area. Block officers are greatly outnumbered by the inmates they supervise. Hence, if disturbances occur, block officers usually withdraw quickly to defensible positions within the institution.

block officers
Those responsible for supervising inmates in housing areas.

Work Detail Supervisors Work detail supervisors oversee the work of individual inmates and inmate work crews assigned to jobs within the institution or outside it. Jobs assigned to inmates may include laundry, kitchen, and farm duties, as well as yard work and building maintenance. Work detail supervisors must also keep track of supplies and tools and maintain inventories of materials. Prison buildings are sometimes constructed almost exclusively with the use of inmate labor—creating the need for large inmate work details. On such large projects, supervising officers usually work in conjunction with outside contractors.

work detail supervisors
Those who oversee the work of individual inmates and inmate work crews.

Industrial Shop and School Officers Industrial shop and school officers work to ensure efficient use of training and educational resources within the prison. Such resources include workshops, schools, classroom facilities, and associated equipment and tools. These officers oversee inmates who are learning trades, such as welding, woodworking, or automobile mechanics, or who are attending academic classes. Ensuring that students are present and on time for classes to begin, protecting the school and vocational instructors, and securing the tools and facilities used in instruction are all part of the job of these officers. The officers work with civilian instructors, teachers, and counselors.

industrial shop and school officers
Those who ensure efficient use of training and educational resources within the prison.

Yard Officers Yard officers supervise inmates in the prison yard. They also take charge of inmates who are (1) moving from place to place, (2) eating, or (3) involved in recreational activities. Like other officers, yard officers are primarily concerned with security and order maintenance.

yard officers
Those who supervise inmates in the prison yard.

Administrative Officers Administrative officers are assigned to staff activities within the institution's management center. They control keys and weapons. Some administrative officers oversee visitation. As a result, they have more contact with the public than other officers do. Many administrative officers have little, if any, contact with inmates.

administrative officers
Those who control keys and weapons and sometimes oversee visitation.

Perimeter Security Officers Perimeter security officers (also called *wall post officers*) are assigned to security (or gun) towers, wall posts, and perimeter patrols. They are charged with preventing escapes and detecting and preventing intrusions (such as packages of drugs or weapons thrown over fences or walls from outside). Perimeter security can become a routine job because it involves little interaction with other officers or inmates and

perimeter security officers
Those assigned to security (or gun) towers, wall posts, and perimeter patrols. These officers are charged with preventing escapes and detecting and preventing intrusions.

Ms. Eagle, a teacher in the Delaware Prison Life Skills Program, invited family members twice to come to the prison. On one occasion, she had the family members and students break into small groups—I wasn't in the same group with my mom—to discuss what various family members should do when someone comes home very late at night. Then each group reported its solutions to the whole class. In my group, a mom actually had a son who was going through this problem. The groups help each family to see how other families would solve the problem, and they also help everyone to see that everyone has the same problems.

An inmate in the Delaware Prison Life Skills Program

THE OFFENDER SPEAKS

because relatively few escape attempts occur. Newer institutions depend more heavily on technological innovations to maintain secure perimeters, requiring fewer officers for day-long perimeter observation.

Relief Officers **Relief officers** are experienced correctional officers who know and can perform almost any custody role in the institution. They are used to temporarily replace officers who are sick or on vacation or to meet staffing shortages.

relief officers

Experienced correctional officers who know and can perform almost any custody role within the institution, used to temporarily replace officers who are sick or on vacation or to meet staffing shortages.

Correctional Staff Issues

FEMALE OFFICERS

On a pleasant Sunday morning a few years ago, a high-custody female inmate at the Chillicothe (Missouri) Correctional Center was sitting in a dormitory, drinking her morning coffee. Having a good time, surrounded by friends, the inmate began laughing. Soon, however, the laughter turned to choking. Unable to breathe, she turned blue. Correctional officer Lisa Albin rushed to her side and found her hanging onto her bed, unable to speak. Albin remained calm as she applied the Heimlich maneuver to the inmate. After three attempts, the trapped coffee cleared the inmate's windpipe and she began breathing again. After the incident, the inmate wrote a letter of thanks to the superintendent, saying, "If it had not been for Mrs. Albin I could have very well died in that room. She literally saved my life and I will be forever grateful to her and for the training she received."[20]

Literature and films almost invariably portray correctional officers as "tobacco-chewin', reflective-sunglasses-wearin', chain-gang-runnin', good ol' boys."[21] Today's officer generally defies this stereotype, and women working in corrections have helped erode this otherwise persistent myth.

Like most women working in male-dominated professions, female correctional officers face special problems and barriers—many of which are rooted in sexism. Prisons are nontraditional workplaces for women. As a consequence, female correctional officers—especially those working in men's prisons—often find themselves in a confusing situation. As one author explains it, "On the one hand, to be female is to be different, an

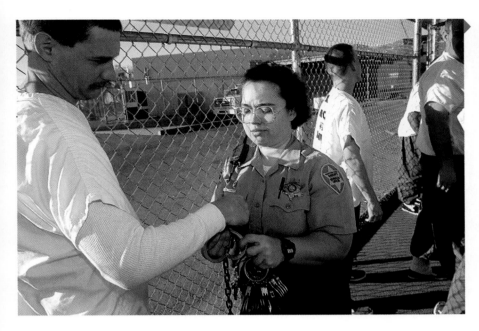

As the number of women who work in corrections increases, more men must confront the unfamiliar persona of a female authority figure. What kinds of skills do female correctional officers tend to rely on to resolve problems?

outsider. On the other hand, female guards have much in common with and are sympathetic to their male peers as a result of their shared job experience."[22]

According to studies, female correctional officers typically say that they perform their job with a less aggressive style than men.[23] This difference in style seems due mostly to differences in life experiences and to physical limitations associated with women's size and strength. Life experiences prepare most women for helping roles rather than aggressive ones. As a consequence, women are more likely to rely heavily on verbal skills and intuition. Female correctional officers use communication rather than threats or force to gain inmate cooperation. They tend to talk out problems. Studies have also found that female correctional officers rely more heavily than male correctional officers on established disciplinary rules when problems arise. Male staff members, on the other hand, are more likely to bully or threaten inmates to resolve problems.

According to research, 55 percent of female officers indicate that their primary reason for taking a job in corrections is an interest in human service work or in inmate rehabilitation.[24] In striking contrast, only 20 percent of male officers give this as their primary reason for working in corrections.

Perhaps as a result of such attitudes, gender makes a dramatic difference in the number of assaults on correctional officers. One national survey of maximum-security prisons in 48 states, the District of Columbia, and the federal Bureau of Prisons showed that female officers were assaulted only 27.6 percent as often as male officers.[25]

Though female correctional officers may take a different approach to their work, the skills they use complement those of male staff members. As one expert writes, "Women may humanize the workplace in small ways by establishing less aggressive relationships with inmates."[26]

Female correctional officers competently perform day-to-day custodial tasks. Are there any areas of a male prison that female correctional officers should be barred from supervising?

Studies also show that male officers, by and large, believe that female officers competently perform day-to-day custodial tasks. Most male staff members are "pro-woman," meaning that they applaud the entry of women into the corrections profession.[27] Many male correctional officers do express concerns about women's ability to provide adequate backup in a crisis, however. It is important to note that the need to use force in prison is relatively rare and that officers generally do not respond to dangerous situations alone. Nonetheless, some female correctional officers report that in emergencies some male officers adopt a protective, chivalrous attitude toward them. Women generally report that they resent such "special treatment," because it makes them feel more like a liability than an asset in an emergency.

Another issue concerning women in today's workplace is personal and sexual harassment. Studies show that few female correctional officers personally experience unwanted touching or other forms of sexual harassment. The forms of harassment women most commonly experience are physical (nonsexual) assaults, threats, unfounded graphic sexual rumors about them, and demeaning remarks from peers, inmates, and supervisors.[28]

A fair amount of harassment is tolerated in the correctional officer subculture. It is viewed as customary and is often accorded little significance. The response to any form of harassment, however, is determined by the officer experiencing it. He or she can tolerate it, resist it, or report it. Female correctional officers, however, express fear of being ostracized if they complain.

One writer has made the following recommendations for improving the acceptance of women as correctional officers:[29]

1. Require managers and guards to undergo training to sensitize them to the concerns of women working in prisons.
2. Establish a strong policy prohibiting sexual and personal harassment, with significant consequences for harassers.
3. Screen male job candidates for their ability and willingness to develop relationships of mutual respect with female colleagues.

STRESS

stress

Tension in a person's body or mind, resulting from physical, chemical, or emotional factors.

In all occupational categories, employers estimate that more than 25 percent of all reported sick time is due to stress.[30] **Stress**—tension in a person's body or mind, resulting from physical, chemical, or emotional factors—appears to be more commonplace in prison work than in many other jobs. Nonetheless, it is often denied. As one early writer on correctional officers' stress observed, "Most officers . . . try to disguise the toll taken by the job

One of the most interesting aspects of my job as a corrections officer is the fact that it allows me to interact with people from different socioeconomic backgrounds. Some are at the top of their careers and others at the bottom, not sure who they are, or where they're going. The job has taught me respect for the law and has given me the opportunity to progress as an individual.

As a corrections officer I consider myself to be a professional. I don't think of myself as guard but as someone who has been given the responsibility of rebuilding, retraining, and restoring. Being a corrections officer takes enthusiasm, dedication, and a desire to help people overcome difficult situations. We have good listening skills and the ability to interpret and respond to changes in inmates' behavior. As a corrections officer, I work to rehabilitate inmates who have behavior problems, and to manage them by talking calmly, rather than threatening them with violence or punishment.

I'm also a field-training officer (FTO) and I teach new officers how to do the job right; be fair but firm, show compassionate but not weakness, be able to react and respond quickly, treat people with respect, give the inmates someone to look up to, and finally, conduct yourself in a manner that creates and maintains respect for you and your department.

Marquis L. Westry
Corrections Corporal,
Mobile County Metro Jail
Mobile, Alabama

THE STAFF SPEAKS

and make the best of what is often a frustrating situation. Though not immune to the pressures of the workplace these officers project a tough, steady image which precludes sharing frustrations with other coworkers or family members. Some of these officers may be particularly vulnerable to stress."[31]

Correctional officers frequently deny that they are under stress, fearing that admitting to feelings of stress might be interpreted unfavorably. One correctional lieutenant, an 11-year veteran, reported repeatedly observing new correctional employees succumbing to the effects of stress by becoming depressed or turning to alcohol for relief. Although she wanted to intervene, she said she "couldn't" because "No one in law enforcement is allowed to show any emotion or signs of weakness."[32]

In misguided attempts to deal with the effects of stress, many COs resort to self-medication or other tactics to deal with feelings that they may not readily admit to, even to themselves. Unfortunately, such ineffective methods do not alleviate the pressure and may instead make it worse.

Stress among correctional officers has a number of sources. Feelings of powerlessness, meaninglessness, social isolation, and self-estrangement all contribute to stress. Some authors have identified job alienation as the major source of stress among correctional officers.[33] Correctional officers rarely participate in setting the rules they work under and the policies they enforce; as a result, they may feel alienated from those policies and rules and from those who create them.

Other factors that create stress follow:

- work overload;
- family conflict[34];
- lack of autonomy or control over one's life;
- threat of job loss;
- role conflict or role ambiguity;
- conflicts with coworkers;

Ethical Dilemma

Stress among correctional staff is widespread, and your facility has a stress-reduction program. You are feeling very stressed, but you are afraid to take advantage of the program, thinking it may reflect poorly on you at promotion time. Do you participate in the program anyway? For more information go to Ethical Dilemma 9-2 at http://www.mhhe.com/schmalleger2.

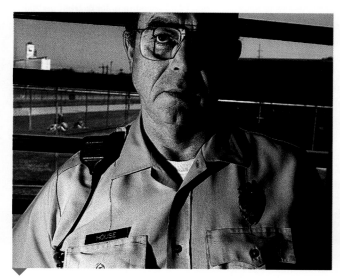

Stress is an unhappy outcome of the correctional officer's job. How does on-the-job stress arise in the correctional officer's role? How might it be reduced?

- conflicts with supervisors;
- problematic organizational culture;
- difficult working environment;
- insufficient resources to reach one's goals;
- inadequate job training;
- overqualification for one's current position;
- supervisors' problematic attitudes; and
- changes in the work environment.

Symptoms of stress can be psychological, behavioral, or physical. Psychological symptoms of stress include anxiety, irritability, mood swings, sadness or depression, low self-esteem, emotional withdrawal, and hypersensitivity (to others and to what others say). Behavioral symptoms of stress include an inability to make decisions, increased interpersonal conflict, blocked creativity and judgment, poor memory, lowered productivity, and difficulty concentrating. The physical symptoms of stress include insomnia, headaches, backaches, gastrointestinal disturbances, fatigue, high blood pressure, and frequent illnesses.

Poorer job performance and exhaustion are the results of stress. When stress reaches an unbearable level, burnout can occur. Burnout, a severe reaction to stress, is "a state of physical and emotional depletion that results from the conditions of one's occupation."[35]

Studies have shown that a person's ability to tolerate stress depends on the frequency, severity, and types of stressors confronted.[36] Stress tolerance also depends on a number of personal aspects, including past experiences, personal values and attitudes, sense of control, personality, residual stress level, and general state of health.

Authorities suggest a number of techniques for avoiding or reducing job stress. Among them are the following:[37]

1. Communicate openly. Tell people how you feel.
2. Learn not to harbor resentment, not to gossip, and to complain less often.
3. Learn to feel confident in your skills, your values and beliefs, and yourself.
4. Develop a support system. Close friends, pets, social activities, and a happy extended family can all help alleviate stress.
5. Be a good and conscientious worker, but don't become a workaholic.
6. Learn to manage your time and do not procrastinate.
7. Make it a habit to get a good night's sleep.
8. Exercise regularly.
9. Watch your diet. Avoid excessive fat, sugars, salt, red meat, and caffeine.
10. Learn some relaxation exercises such as self-affirmation, mental imaging, deep breathing, stretching, massage, or yoga.

11. Try to have fun. Laughter can combat stress quite effectively.
12. Spend time cultivating self-understanding. Analyze your feelings and your problems—and recognize your accomplishments.
13. Set goals and make plans. Both bring order and direction to your life.

One especially effective strategy for coping with job stress is to develop clear and favorable role definitions. According to J. T. Dignam and colleagues, "officers who have more opportunities for receiving assistance and goal clarification from supervisors and coworkers [are] less likely to experience role ambiguity than those for whom such support is not available or sought. Further, the risk of burnout or other deleterious consequences of occupational stress may be reduced for those who are 'insulated' by social support."[38]

Similarly, another group of researchers found that "support from colleagues or supervisors may be one of the most important factors ameliorating stress in the workplace."[39] The same researchers also found that when correctional officers felt "rewarding companionship" with fellow correctional officers, they reported fewer stressful events (even when objective measures showed an actual rise in such events). Most researchers agree that candidates need more extensive and thorough training to prepare them for the psychological and sociological consequences of becoming correctional officers.

STAFF SAFETY

Staff safety is a major stressor for individual correctional officers and a primary management concern for correctional administrators. Safety planning must include consideration of the following elements (adapted, in part, from studies of staff safety needs in both juvenile[40] and adult[41] institutions):

- a functionally designed physical plant that limits inmate movement and incorporates technologically advanced security systems, perimeter barriers, and rooms, doors, and locks;

- a behavior management system that establishes clear guidelines for acceptable behavior, reward systems to reinforce expected behavior, and disciplinary systems to discourage unacceptable behavior;

- appropriate staff and inmate relationships (in particular, staff must be aware of, and prepared to respond to, the dangers posed by prison gangs);

- policies and procedures, published in a manual and distributed to staff and supervisors, that support consistent implementation of rules and regulations and prevent the risk of staff letdowns resulting from excessive routine;

- shift scheduling that ensures a mutually supportive balance of senior and junior staff because a sound mix of age and experience facilitates the achievement of inmate control while providing opportunities for on-the-job development of junior officers by senior officers;

- effective supervision at every level;

- comprehensive staff training that ensures all correctional officers and their supervisors know every rule, regulation, policy, and procedure that affects their particular job (if, as the saying goes, knowledge is power, such training is key to empowering the staff to maintain a controlled, safe environment); and

- development of, and training for, a sound action plan that addresses all contingencies.

In addition to advocating thorough planning as just outlined, Stewart and Brown[42] urge continuing research to identify what works, what doesn't work, and emerging trends in staff safety. In particular, they recommend development of a safety program tailored to the needs of correctional officers nationwide. It should be modeled, they suggest, on safety programs designed for police officers, probation officers, and other officers in law enforcement.

JOB SATISFACTION

High levels of stress reduce the satisfaction correctional officers get from their jobs. In a sad indictment of the corrections field, a 1996 study found that correctional officers were significantly different from most other groups of correctional employees. "They showed the lowest levels of organizational commitment, possessed the highest levels of skepticism about organizational change, were the least positive about careers in corrections and the rehabilitation of offenders, possessed the lowest levels of job satisfaction, were the least involved in their jobs, and were described as having the poorest work habits and overall job performance."[43] In a separate study, correctional supervisors and managers were found to have much higher levels of job satisfaction and professionalism.[44]

One reason for the difference in job satisfaction between supervisory personnel and those on the front lines of corrections work is that correctional officers often feel alienated from policymaking.[45] As one writer puts it, "when looking at the atmosphere and environment of a state or federal prison, it would seem obvious what correction personnel like least about working there: surveys of personnel who resign or quit show that their biggest problems are with supervisory personnel rather than inmates."[46]

Correctional officers' job satisfaction appears to be tied to the amount of influence they feel they have over administrative decisions and policies. Officers who feel they have some control over the institution and over their jobs seem much more satisfied than officers who believe they have no control. Hence, it appears that correctional officers' job satisfaction can be greatly enhanced by caring administrators who involve the officers in policymaking.

For some correctional officers, the perception that their profession suffers a generally poor public image[47] further reduces their job satisfaction. Compared to local and state police officers and agents of the various federal law enforcement organizations, correctional officers may be viewed as the "poor relations" of the law enforcement family. As one researcher wrote, "Most people do not know of a child who says, 'I want to be a correctional officer when I grow up.'"[48]

Media portrayals of correctional officers exacerbate the situation. Movies and television often depict COs as lowly qualified "guards" (considered a derogatory title; "guards work at Macy's and banks")[49] whose primary function seems to be abusing prisoners. Correctional officers "believe they are seen as brutes, only a shade better than the people behind bars."[50] Consequently, COs have a difficult time overcoming these images as they attempt to convey the significance and professional demands of their positions to civic leaders and the public.[51]

There is evidence, however, that job satisfaction among correctional officers is rising. The rise may be partly due to increasing awareness of what correctional officers find most important in the work environment. Recent studies have identified the most important determinants of job satisfaction among correctional officers as (1) working conditions, (2) the level of work-related stress, (3) the quality of working relationships with fellow officers, and (4) length of service.[52]

In one of the most significant studies to date, treatment-oriented correctional staff reported far higher levels of job satisfaction than did custody-oriented staff.[53] The study was of survey data collected from 428 Arizona correctional service officers (CSOs) and 118 correctional program officers (CPOs). Job satisfaction was significantly greater among the human-services–oriented CPOs than among the traditional-custody–oriented CSOs. The findings suggest that additional attention should be given to enhancing and enriching the duties of correctional officers, extending their control over and involvement in prisoners' activities, and redefining their roles more as service workers than as control agents.

Determinants of job satisfaction appear to differ for male and female correctional officers. One study found that the quality of working relationships with other officers, the amount of stress experienced at work, the length of service as a correctional officer, and educational level were all positively related to job satisfaction for males.[54] Women officers, on the other hand, appeared to place more emphasis on the quality of working relationships with all other correctional officers (not just the ones with whom they worked) and tended to be happier in prisons at lower security levels. Other studies have related higher job satisfaction among white female officers to the officers' positive evaluation of the quality of supervision. In other words, white female correctional officers tend to be happier in prisons that they believe are well run.[55]

PROFESSIONALISM

On October 29, 1994, correctional officer Ken Davis was instantly catapulted to the forefront of national attention when he tackled a man shooting at the White House. Without warning, Francisco Martin Duran had leveled a Chinese-made AK-47 assault rifle at the White House from outside the iron gates and had begun firing. While most other bystanders either fled or stood stunned, Davis ran toward Duran and wrestled him to the ground, holding him until police and White House security officers arrived. Duran was later sentenced to 40 years in prison with no chance of parole on charges of attempting to assassinate President Clinton.

Davis, a correctional officer at the Victor Cullins Academy[56] in Maryland, was honored for his quick actions. During the ceremony honoring him, he noted a few lifestyle principles that could benefit all correctional officers. "Correctional officers serve and survive better," said Davis, "if they adopt the capacity for balance as a personal philosophy."[57] Balance

Correctional Leadership in the 21st Century

by Richard Kiekbusch,
University of Texas–Permian Basin

As we proceed into the 21st century, American corrections is in need of *leadership*—not just sound management, but *strong, purposeful leadership.*

We are a nation that makes generous use of its correctional resources. We have over six million adults under some form of correctional supervision, roughly 6.3 percent of America's adult population. There is certainly nothing inherently wrong with this heavy use of our broad array of institutional and community-based correctional programs. In employing these programs, however, we need to be reasonably sure that we are actually making our communities safer and not simply pandering to emotionally laced public demands and furthering the careers of "tough-on-crime" politicians. And this requires *leadership.*

"Leadership," though, is an overused term, a term that is liberally employed by speakers and writers who really don't know what it means. Exactly what *does* "leadership" mean in the context of 21st century American corrections? Further, who must provide it and what should they advocate? Here are my personal thoughts.

Management and *leadership* are not synonymous. Competent correctional managers run their agencies and institutions in compliance with public policy. Forceful leaders help shape public policy. Many managers are not capable of exercising genuine leadership or even desirous of doing so. Conversely, not all leaders are effective agency or institutional managers. American corrections needs both effective managers

and persuasive leaders—*but especially the latter.*

A person does not become a leader simply because he or she becomes a commissioner, director, or sheriff. There are scores of correctional executives in this country who are skillful managers but who do not exercise authentic leadership. Unfortunately, some of these executives actually confound corrections' need for informed, consistent, and durable public policy by accepting, or even seizing, the acclamation of "leader" and then failing to satisfy the requirements of genuine leadership.

What are those requirements? What traits characterize real correctional leaders? First and foremost, leaders stand for something. They have firm positions on the major issues confronting the corrections profession (e.g., sentencing policies, the role of community-based sanctions, inmate rights, capital punishment). Those positions, furthermore, are the products of a careful consideration of varied points of view on each issue. They are not simply a thoughtless reaffirmation of politically correct and popularly fashionable public opinions. Additionally, the true leader remains open to have his or her positions altered by new information or the persuasive arguments of others.

Real correctional leaders in this country understand their serious obligation to implement public policy emanating from our partisan political arena, but they also understand their corresponding obligation, equally as serious, to inform that arena. They acknowledge their nonpartisan

responsibility to ensure that political representatives who are debating and formulating corrections-related public policy clearly comprehend the implications and consequences of the laws and initiatives they are proposing. They understand that a critical component of leadership is public education.

Finally, as the leader advocates his or her positions on critical policy issues and attempts to inform the politicians and the public, he or she may tell them things they don't want to hear. The persistent correctional leader, then, runs the risk of annoying some powerful and influential people. Risk takers often pay a price for their risk taking. True correctional leaders must be willing to "pay the price"— even if that price involves the loss of an appointment or an election. Leadership, in other words, requires courage and sacrifice.

Who must provide the brand of correctional leadership that I have just described? Who must continuously educate the general public and its political policymakers on key correctional issues and demonstrate the requisite courage in doing so? Without question, the commissioners and directors of our federal and state correctional agencies must step up and meet this challenge. Another group, usually overlooked but critically important, upon whom we must be able to rely for correctional leadership are the elected sheriffs who operate the 3,000 plus jails across the country. Sheriffs, in particular, need to understand that, at this point in time, their corrections/detention responsibilities are at least as prominent as their law enforcement responsibilities.

Purposeful correctional leadership must also be supplied by the staff executives and elected officers of our principal professional associations—the American Correctional Association, the American Jail Association, and the National Sheriffs' Association at the very least.

Substantively, what policy positions should contemporary American correctional leaders take? What should they stand for? I prefer not to suggest specific policies and programs as these should be the result of informed discourse and should be tailored to meet the unique needs of particular locales and circumstances. I do suggest, however, three assumptions that should be embraced by our correctional leadership and undergird specific policy and program initiatives.

First, our correctional leaders must understand that the proper goal of the American criminal justice system is not to incarcerate as many people as possible. Rather, it is to keep our communities safe and to do so as inexpensively as possible. Incarceration is one means to that end, not an end in itself. Jail and prison beds are expensive commodities and should be used very selectively for those offenders whose supervision in noninstitutional programs would unduly compromise the safety of the communities in which those programs are located. Our correctional leadership should insist that any proposed legislation involving sentencing, good time, parole eligibility, or other mechanisms that affect institutional populations be carefully reviewed for their capital implications. Expansion or construction deemed excessive or unnecessary should be vigorously opposed. At the same time, our correctional leaders should encourage and support practicably designed and reasonably priced research projects that are intended to provide usable insights as to what types of offenders can be safely supervised in community-based programs and what types require secure incarceration. Our leaders must then press for the inclusion of the research findings in subsequent legislative discussions and debates.

Second, our correctional leaders must understand that society's principal efforts to prevent and control crime need to occur outside of the criminal justice system, not within it. We need strong families in which children receive a value-laden upbringing and a firmly entrenched sense of right and wrong. We need well-staffed and properly equipped schools that educate and not just baby-sit. And, the political incorrectness of this observation notwithstanding, we need assertive churches, synagogues, and mosques that infuse our young people with a sense of a higher moral authority. Our correctional leadership must help our legislators and other public officials to understand that correctional programs cannot serve as the primary vehicles of education and value formation. Before the institutional counselor, teacher, or chaplain arrives in a young person's life, the family, school, and church must have already been there. Our correctional leaders must understand that public policies pertaining to our families, our schools, and our churches are, in fact, crime control policies, and those leaders must establish a presence in policymaking in those areas.

And third, our correctional leaders must understand that "tough on crime" fiscal conservatism and offender rehabilitation programs are not mutually exclusive. Public policymakers must come to appreciate that to have an offender under supervision for an extended period of time and not offer the offender opportunities for self-improvement during that time constitutes relative inattention to public safety and markedly poor stewardship of the public dollar. Our correctional leaders must persuade our political representatives that, if they are truly "get-tough-on-crime" fiscal conservatives, they will endorse well-run inmate rehabilitation programs.

In conclusion, as we forge ahead into the 21st century, American corrections is in need of decisive leaders who understand the proper goals of American criminal justice, who acknowledge that society's principal crime prevention and crime control efforts must occur outside of the criminal justice system, and who support well-run offender rehabilitation programs.

ABOUT THE AUTHOR
Dr. Richard Kiekbusch is associate professor of Criminology at the University of Texas—Permian Basin. Dr. Kiekbusch earned his degrees from the University of Notre Dame. He has over 20 years' experience in correctional administration—including work in juvenile corrections, jail administration, and private corrections.

Training can enhance professionalism. As more and more prison staff develop a professional perspective, the structural organization of prisons and interactions among staff and inmates may significantly change. What kinds of training may help correctional officers adjust to a changing environment?

means understanding themselves, knowing when they can handle a situation and when they cannot, and admitting when they need help. It also means having a clear sense of their roles and keeping a clear view of their purpose and their career goals. A good sense of balance, said Davis, reduces job stress and "improves officer-officer relations" by leading to good teamwork. Correctional officers need to understand the importance of positive peer relationships in maintaining high morale. Officer Davis observed that inmates look for correctional officers without a personal sense of balance and "systematically and continuously work to manipulate the human frailties of correctional officers."

"There is danger in ignorance," Davis said. "Learning is a lifelong process. True knowledge is knowing what you do not know! Don't worry about sounding stupid. Know when to call for help. Don't be afraid to say, 'I need help,' 'I don't understand this duty post,' or 'This approach seems wrong.'"

Davis also noted that "listening is the heart of communication. Good listening practices shape a successful officer. Effective officers strive to perfect both active and passive listening skills, by exploring innovative ways to improve communication with peers and supervisors, inmates, visitors, and the public."

"One way for officers to accomplish the achievement of their personal career goals," noted Davis, "is to constantly groom themselves early in their career for higher rank and responsibility by learning from their experienced supervisors and by keeping a journal of lessons learned. This process will provide dividends for years to come. It will give you a bank of positive experiences to draw on in future times of career decisions and in times of crisis."

The International Association of Correctional Officers has published a Correctional Officer's Creed (see Exhibit 9–1), which summarizes the duties and responsibilities of a correctional officer.

EXHIBIT 9-1   **International Association of Correctional Officers**

The Correctional Officer's Creed

To speak sparingly . . . to act, not argue . . . to be in authority through personal presence . . . to correct without nagging . . . to speak with the calm voice of certainty . . . to see everything and to know what is significant and what not to notice . . . to be neither insensitive to distress nor so distracted by pity as to miss what must elsewhere be seen . . .

To do neither that which is unkind nor self-indulgent in its misplaced charity . . . never to obey the impulse to tongue slash that silent insolence which in time past could receive the lash . . . to be both firm and fair . . . to know I cannot be fair simply by being firm, nor firm simply by being fair . . .

To support the reputations of associates and confront them without anger should they stand short of professional conduct . . . to reach for knowledge of the continuing mysteries of human motivation . . . to think; always to think . . . to be dependable . . . to be dependable first to my charges and associates and thereafter to my duty as employee and citizen . . . to keep fit . . . to keep forever alert . . . to listen to what is meant as well as what is said with words and with silences.

To expect respect from my charges and my superiors yet never to abuse the one for abuses from the other . . . for eight hours each working day to be an example of the person I could be at all times . . . to acquiesce in no dishonest act . . . to cultivate patience under boredom and calm during confusion . . . to understand the why of every order I take or give . . .

To hold freedom among the highest values though I deny it to those I guard . . . to deny it with dignity that in my example they find no reason to lose their dignity . . . to be prompt . . . to be honest with all who practice deceit that they not find in me excuse for themselves. . .to privately face down my fear that I not signal it . . . to privately cool my anger that I not displace it on others . . . to hold in confidence what I see and hear, which by telling could harm or humiliate to no good purpose . . . to keep my outside problems outside . . . to leave inside that which should stay inside . . . to do my duty.

Source: Copyright © 2000 Bob Barrington. Used by permission of the International Association of Correctional Officers.

THE EFFECTS OF TERRORISM

The events of September 11, 2001, have created an awareness of potential crises that could arise in correctional institutions as a result of terroristic actions. Today's prison administrators must be concerned about the impact of a terrorism event within the community in which their facility is located, as well as the threat of a terrorist act being undertaken by an inmate or inmates within their facility. Of particular concern is the possibility of bioterrorism. A concentrated population such as exists within a prison or jail would be highly susceptible to rapid transmission of the ill effects of such an attack.[58]

In addition, incarcerating those convicted of terrorism presents new challenges for correctional administrators. Sheik Omar Abdel-Rahman, spiritual leader for many terrorists, including Osama bin Laden, is now serving a life sentence in a U.S. federal penitentiary for conspiring to assassinate Egyptian President Hosni Mubarak and blow up five New York City landmarks in the 1990s. Speculation that the sheik continues to motivate terrorist acts against the United States gained credibility when his attorney and three others were indicted in April 2002 for allegedly passing illegal

Elmardoudi   **Koubriti**

Convicted sleeper-cell terrorists Karim Koubriti, 24 (right), and Abdel-Ilah Elmardoudi, 37 (left). The men, illegal immigrants from North Africa, were found guilty in 2003 of two counts of conspiracy to provide material support or resources to terrorists and to engage in fraud and misuse of visas, permits, and other documents. They are awaiting sentencing as this book goes to press. How has America's fight against terrorism affected our nation's prisons and jails? What future impact might we anticipate?

communications between Abdel-Rahman and an Egyptian-based terrorist organization known as the Islamic Group.[59]

Jess Maghan, former training director for the New York City Department of Corrections, and now the director of the Forum for Comparative Corrections and professor of criminal justice at the University of Illinois at Chicago, points out that intelligence and analysis by justice agencies, including correctional agencies, can provide critical information needed to prevent terrorist attacks. According to Maghan "the interaction of all people in a prison (staff, officers, and inmates) can become important intelligence sources."[60]

Moreover, says Maghan, the flow of information between inmates and the outside world needs to be monitored in order to detect attack plans—especially when prisons house known terrorist leaders or group members. Information, according to Maghan, can be passed through legal visits (where people conveying information may have no idea of its significance); sub-rosa communications networks in prisons that can support communications between inmates and the outside world; and prison transportation systems.

The security problems presented by potential information leaks were demonstrated in 2003 at the U.S. Navy's Guantanamo Bay Naval Station prison in Cuba when a translator working with Arab internees was accused of having unlawful possession of classified information, including diagrams of the prison layout and names of the prisoners. Military leaders charged with responsibility for the incarceration of suspect al-Qaeda and Taliban members, like those at Guantanamo, face especially delicate situations as opponents of the Bush Administration's policies challenge the propriety of using military assets in what they argue is a "law enforcement" role.

As the United States faces more and more threats of terrorism it is likely that the issues identified here will take on greater significance for correctional facilities throughout the nation and around the world.

SUMMARY

1▶ There is a hierarchy of staff positions, from warden (or superintendent) at the top, down to correctional officer and correctional officer trainee. A typical correctional staff includes (1) administrative staff, (2) clerical personnel, (3) program staff, (4) custodial staff, (5) service and maintenance staff, and (6) volunteers.

2 ▶ The custodial staff consists of correctional officers only—not correctional administrators, treatment or educational staff, or other staff members.

3 ▶ The types of power available to correctional officers are legitimate power, coercive power, reward power, expert power, and referent power.

4 ▶ In correctional institutions, *structured conflict* refers to the tensions between prison staff members and inmates that arise out of institutional arrangements.

5 ▶ A *subculture* is a particular group of people within a larger society who share beliefs, values, behavior, and material objects. The subculture of correctional officers reinforces group solidarity and cohesion among correctional personnel.

6 ▶ According to a year-2000 report, state prisons and local jails employ 414,000 corrections personnel (including administrative staff). One-third are women. About 32 percent are minorities.

7 ▶ Common correctional officer personality types include (1) the dictator, (2) the friend, (3) the merchant, (4) the turnkey, (5) the climber, (6) the reformer, and (7) the do-gooder.

8 ▶ The seven correctional officer assignments are (1) block officers, (2) work detail supervisors, (3) industrial shop and school officers, (4) yard officers, (5) administrative officers, (6) perimeter security officers (also called *wall post officers*), and (7) relief officers.

9 ▶ Female correctional officers tend to be less aggressive in their approach to workplace problem solving than are male officers. They are more likely to resolve disputes through nonconfrontational means and tend to rely more heavily on verbal skills and interpersonal communication. Studies have also found that female correctional officers depend more on established disciplinary rules when problems arise.

10 ▶ Feelings of powerlessness, meaninglessness, social isolation, self-estrangement, and alienation are all sources of correctional officer stress. Techniques for reducing stress include open communication, self-confidence building, a support system, conscientious work performance, effective time management, adequate sleep, exercise, a wholesome diet, relaxation techniques, laughter, self-understanding, setting of realistic goals and plans, and avoidance of resentment.

11 ▶ Staff safety planners must consider the physical plant, behavior management processes, staff/inmate relationships, policies and procedures, age and experience in shift scheduling, supervision, staff training, and development of a sound action plan.

KEY TERMS

roles, *p. 328*
staff roles, *p. 328*
custodial staff, *p. 329*
program staff, *p. 329*
gain time, *p. 331*
structured conflict, *p. 332*
subculture, *p. 333*

staff subculture, *p. 333*
correctional officer personalities, *p. 336*
block officers, *p. 339*
work detail supervisors, *p. 339*
industrial shop and school officers, *p. 339*

yard officers, *p. 339*
administrative officers, *p. 339*
perimeter security officers, *p. 339*
relief officers, *p. 340*
stress, *p. 341*

REVIEW & APPLICATIONS

QUESTIONS FOR REVIEW

1. What staff roles does the hierarchy of a typical correctional institution include?

2. What is the role of a prison's custodial staff?

3. According to John Hepburn, what are five bases of the power that correctional officers use to gain inmate compliance?

4. What is meant by *structured conflict*?

5. What elements make up the staff subculture?

6. What percentage of corrections personnel are members of minority groups?

7. List common personality types found among correctional officers.

8. What are the seven correctional officer job assignments?

9. List and explain some challenges facing women who work as correctional officers.

10. What are some sources of stress for correctional officers?

11. Briefly explain the impact that terrorism is having on prisons and prison administration.

THINKING CRITICALLY ABOUT CORRECTIONS

▶ ▶ ▶ **Prison Rape**

James Gilligan, M.D., contends that rape in prisons is "an intrinsic and universal part of the punishments that our government metes out to those whom it labels as 'criminal.'"[61] In essence, Gilligan suggests, prison administrators passively employ inmate-on-inmate rape as a management tool to control the prisoner population.

Dr. Gilligan bases his charge on three contentions:

First, the relevant legal authorities, from judges to prosecutors who send people to prison, to the prison officials who administer them, are all aware of the existence, the reality, and the near-universality of rape in the prisons. Indeed, this is one reason why many conscientious judges are extremely reluctant to send anyone to prison except when they feel compelled to, either by the violence of the crime or, as is increasingly true, by laws mandating prison sentences even for nonviolent crimes, such as drug offenses.

Second, the conditions that stimulate such rapes (the enforced deprivation of other sources of self-esteem, respect, power, and sexual gratification) are consciously and deliberately imposed upon the prison population by the legal authorities.

Third, all these authorities tacitly and knowingly tolerate this form of sexual violence, passively delegating to the dominant and most violent inmates the

power and authority to deliver this form of punishment to the more submissive and nonviolent ones, so that the rapists in this situation are acting as the vicarious enforcers of a form of punishment that the legal system does not itself enforce formally or directly.

Given that rape is universally acknowledged as a crime, Dr. Gilligan's charge is tantamount to an accusation of criminal conspiracy of monumental proportions.

1. Do you believe there is merit to Gilligan's claims?

2. If so, how would you propose addressing this issue?

▶ ▶ ▶ **The Staff Subculture**

The staff culture is generally instilled in correctional officer trainees by more experienced officers and by work experiences. Socialization into the staff subculture begins on the first day of academy training or the first day of work (whichever comes first). One of the most important beliefs of the staff subculture is that officers should support one another.

Some people argue that the staff subculture is dangerous because it can sustain improper and even illegal behavior, while forcing correctional officers to keep to themselves what they know about such behavior. Others, however, suggest that the staff subculture is a positive element in the correctional world. It is important to correctional officer morale, they claim. They also suggest that it "fills the gaps" in formal training by establishing informal rules to guide staff behavior and decision making in difficult situations. The staff subculture can provide informal "workarounds" when the formal requirements of a correctional officer's position seem unrealistic.

1. Do you think the staff subculture contributes to or detracts from meeting the goals of institutional corrections? Why?

2. Do you think the staff subculture benefits or harms the lives and working environment of correctional officers? Explain.

3. What functions of the staff subculture can you identify? Rate each of those functions as positive or negative for its role in meeting the goals of institutional corrections.

ON-THE-JOB DECISION MAKING

▶ ▶ ▶ Use of Force

You are an experienced correctional officer, assigned to yard duty. As you patrol the prison yard, watching inmates milling around and talking, a fellow officer named Renée approaches you. Renée was hired only a week ago, and she has gained a reputation for being inquisitive—asking experienced correctional officers about prison work. Renée walks up and says, "You know, I'm wondering what I should do. Yesterday I saw an officer push an inmate around because the guy didn't do what he asked. I don't know if the inmate didn't hear what was being said, or if he was just ignoring the officer." Renée looks at the ground. "What am I supposed to do in a situation like that? Should I have said something right then? Should I talk to the officer privately? Should I suggest to the officer that maybe the inmate didn't hear him? He knows we aren't supposed to use force on inmates unless it's really necessary. If I see him do this kind of thing again, should I report him?" Looking up, Renèe says, "I know we're supposed to support each other in here. But what would you do?" How would you respond to Renèe's questions?

▶ ▶ ▶ Former CO Inmate

For about four years, Alex Kaminsky was one of your fellow correctional officers at the McClellan Correctional Facility. During your service together, you developed a friendship close enough to include social occasions outside the job, and your wives became good friends.

Two years ago, Kaminsky was convicted of dealing controlled substances to inmates and received a 12- to 20-year sentence. Upon your recent transfer to the Brownley Correctional Facility, you discover that Kaminsky is one of the inmates incarcerated there. He resides in one of the cell blocks that falls in your area of responsibility and works on the maintenance crew that you supervise.

1. Should you seek assignment to another area of the prison or seek to have Kaminsky transferred out, so as to prevent the necessity of having contact with him? Why or why not?

2. If Kaminsky approaches you, should you permit the reestablishment of a relationship that might (or might not) prove beneficial to his rehabilitation?

REVIEW & APPLICATIONS

REVIEW & APPLICATIONS

CORRECTIONS ON THE WEB

▷ ▷ ▷ **Arizona Peace Officer Standards and Training Board**

Access the Arizona Peace Officer Standards and Training Board Website at http://www.azpost. state.az.us. Click on *Correctional Officer Rules* and then read all eight sections of the state code relating to correctional officers. After reading the state code sections, write a short paragraph summarizing the expectations the state of Arizona has of its correctional officers.

▷ ▷ ▷ **Correctional Officer Stress**

Access the National Institute of Justice (NIJ) document *Addressing Correctional Officer Stress: Programs and Strategies* at http://www. schmalleger.com/pubs/costress.pdf. (Note: this is a 134-page document in PDF format. A high-speed connection is recommended for quick access.) Write a short paragraph or two summarizing why the NIJ authors feel that a stress-control program for correctional officers is necessary. What does the document say are some of the sources of such stress?

The Inmate World: Living Behind Bars

▶ **CHAPTER OBJECTIVES**

After completing this chapter you should be able to do the following:

1. Profile state inmate populations.

2. Explain what *inmate subculture* is.

3. Distinguish among *deprivation theory, importation theory,* and the *integration model* as they explain the development of inmate subculture.

4. Know what is meant by the *prison code,* and be able to list some elements of the prison code.

5. Explain what is meant by *prison argot.*

6. List some common roles that male inmates assume.

7. Describe some major differences between women's and men's prisons.

8. Compare some of the characteristics of female inmates with those of male inmates.

9. Explain how the social structure in women's prisons differs from that in men's prisons.

On March 8, 2002, the Tennessee Department of Correction announced the dedication of a new child visitation unit at the Tennessee Prison for Women. The 16-bed unit, part of a $24 million expansion at the prison, provides separate quarters for visiting children of incarcerated mothers. Under a special program, children aged three months to six years may spend weekends with their mothers in the new unit, away from the prison's inmate population. Mother and child eat meals in the unit and stay together overnight in one of the unit's single cells. Space is provided for child development activities, and plans are in the works for construction of an outdoor recreational area.[1]

As this story shows, prison inmates are not as isolated as they may sometimes seem. Not only do inmates routinely interact with one another; they also have relationships that extend beyond prison walls. This chapter will examine prison life, the inmate subculture, and the prison experience in general by looking first at men in prison and then at women in prison.

An inmate mother enjoys a visit with her young child. How much time should children be allowed to spend with imprisoned parents in correctional settings?

Men in Prison

As we have already seen, most state inmates are male, belong to racial or ethnic minority groups, are relatively young, and have been incarcerated for a violent offense. A recent Bureau of Justice Statistics study examined social, economic, and other characteristics of state inmates nationwide.[2] Highlights of that study are shown in Figure 10–1.

Prisons and other total institutions are small, self-contained societies with their own social structures, norms, and rules. While not entirely isolated, prison inmates are physically, emotionally, and socially restricted from anything more than minor participation in the surrounding society. As a consequence, they develop their own distinctive lifestyles, roles, and behavioral norms.

In his classic work *Asylums*, Erving Goffman used the phrase **total institution** to describe a place where the same people work, eat, sleep, and engage in recreation together day after day.[3] Life within total institutions is closely planned by those in control, and activities are strictly scheduled. Prisons, concentration camps, mental hospitals, and seminaries are all total institutions, said Goffman. They share many of the same characteristics— even though they exist for different purposes and house different kinds of populations. His words were echoed years later by Hans Toch, who noted that "prisons are 24-hour-a-day, year-in-and-year-out environments in which people are sequestered with little outside contact."[4]

Goffman also identified a number of modes of adaptation to prison life whereby inmates attempt to adjust to the conditions around them. Some

total institution

A place where the same people work, play, eat, sleep, and recreate together on a continuous basis. The term was developed by the sociologist Erving Goffman to describe prisons and other similar facilities.

inmates, said Goffman, *convert* to life within institutions, taking on the staff's view of themselves and of institutional society. Others *withdraw*. Still others make attempts at *colonization*—meaning that they strike a balance between values and habits brought from home and those dictated by the social environment of the prison. Finally, some inmates *rebel*, rejecting the demands of their surroundings and often ending up in trouble with authorities. As Victoria R. Derosia, of Castleton State College, points out in her book *Living Inside Prison Walls*, some people "will make it through incarceration relatively unscathed and move on to a better life as a rehabilitated (or habilitated) citizen, while others will repeatedly fail at life outside prison. Offenders will successfully or poorly adjust to prison because of, or in spite of, who they were before incarceration, who they were while in prison, what they chose to do or not to do in prison, and who they want to become once released."[5]

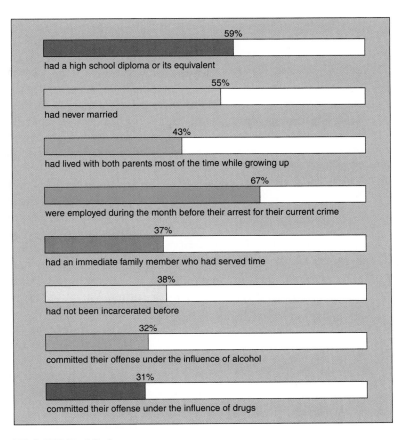

FIGURE 10-1
National Profile of State Prison Inmates

Sources: Bureau of Justice Statistics, *Characteristics of State Prison Inmates,* retrieved January 5, 2003 from http://www.ojp. usdoj.gov/bjs/crimoff.htm#inmates; and Allen Beck et al., *Survey of State Prison Inmates, 1991* (Washington, DC: U.S. Department of Justice, March 1993).

WHAT IS THE INMATE SUBCULTURE?

Although any prison has its own unique way of life or culture, it is possible to describe a general inmate subculture that characterizes the lives of inmates in correctional institutions nationwide. The **inmate subculture** (also called the *prisoner subculture*) can be defined as "the habits, customs, mores, values, beliefs, or superstitions of the body of inmates incarcerated in correctional institutions."[6]

Prisoners are socialized into the inmate subculture through a process known as *prisonization*. The concept of **prisonization** was identified by Donald Clemmer in his book *The Prison Community.*[7] Clemmer defined *prisonization* as the process by which inmates adapt to prison society, and he described it as "the taking on of the ways, mores, customs, and general culture of the penitentiary." When the process of prisonization is complete, Clemmer noted, prisoners have become "cons."

In a further study of prisonization, Stanton Wheeler examined how prisoners adapted to life at the Washington State Reformatory.[8] Wheeler found that prisonization has greater impact with the passage of time. The prisonization of inmates, said Wheeler, can be described by a *U*-shaped curve. When an inmate first enters prison, the conventional values of the outside

inmate subculture

(also *prisoner subculture*) The habits, customs, mores, values, beliefs, or superstitions of the body of inmates incarcerated in correctional institutions; also, the inmate social world.

prisonization

The process by which inmates adapt to prison society; the taking on of the ways, mores, customs, and general culture of the penitentiary.

society still hold sway in his life. As time passes, however, he increasingly adopts the prison lifestyle. Wheeler also found that within the half-year before release, most inmates begin to demonstrate a renewed appreciation for conventional values.

In *The Society of Captives*,[9] Gresham Sykes described what he called the **pains of imprisonment.** According to Sykes, new inmates face major problems, including the loss of liberty, a lack of material possessions, deprivation of goods and services, the loss of heterosexual relationships, the loss of personal autonomy, and a reduction in personal security. These deficits, Sykes noted, lead to self-doubts and reduced self-esteem. Prison society compensates for such feelings and reduces the pains of imprisonment for the prison population as a whole. It also meets the personal and social needs induced in inmates by the pains of imprisonment. In short, said Sykes, inmate society compensates for the losses caused by imprisonment, and it offers varying degrees of comfort to those who successfully adjust to it.

The inmate subculture can vary from one institution to another. Variations are due to differences in the organizational structure of prisons. Maximum-security institutions, for example, are decidedly more painful for inmates because security considerations require greater restriction of inmate freedoms and access to material items. As a result, the subcultures in maximum-security institutions may be much more rigid in their demands on prisoners than those in less secure institutions.

pains of imprisonment
Major problems that inmates face, such as loss of liberty and personal autonomy, lack of material possessions, loss of heterosexual relationships, and reduced personal security.

> Inmate society compensates for the losses caused by imprisonment, and it offers varying degrees of comfort to those who successfully adjust to it.

HOW DOES AN INMATE SUBCULTURE FORM?

Early students of inmate subcultures, particularly Clemmer and Sykes, believed that such subcultures developed in response to the deprivations in

In some prisons, inmate subculture is fragmented as inmates form competing gangs and other groups along ethnic, racial, and geographic lines. How could the differences among such groups affect the order and stability of a prison?

prison life. This perspective is called **deprivation theory.** Shared deprivation gives inmates a basis for solidarity.[10]

A more recent perspective is that an inmate subculture does not develop in prison, but is brought into prison from the outside world. Known as **importation theory,** this point of view was popularized by John Irwin and Donald R. Cressey.[11] It was further supported by the work of James Jacobs.[12] Importation theory holds that inmate society is shaped by factors outside prison—specifically, preprison life experiences and socialization patterns. Inmates who lived violent lives outside tend to associate with other violent inmates and often engage in similar behavior in prison.[13]

More realistic is the **integration model,** which acknowledges that both theories have some validity. According to the integration model, people undergo early socialization experiences. In childhood, some people develop leanings toward delinquent and criminal activity, acquiring—from peer groups, parents and other significant adults, television, movies, other mass media, and even computer and video games—values that support law-violating behavior. Those who become inmates are also likely to have experienced juvenile court proceedings and may have been institutionalized as juveniles. As a consequence, such people are likely to have acquired many of the values, much of the language, and the general behavioral patterns of deviant or criminal subcultures before entering adult prison.

The integration model also recognizes, however, the effects that the norms and behavioral standards of inmates in a particular prison have on those who are imprisoned. If a new inmate has already been socialized into a criminal lifestyle, the transition into the inmate subculture is likely to be easy. For some people, however—especially white-collar offenders with little previous exposure to criminal subcultures—the transition can be very difficult. The language, social expectations, and norms of prison society are likely to be foreign to them.

NORMS AND VALUES OF PRISON SOCIETY

Central to prison society is a code of behavior for all inmates. The **prison code** is a set of inmate rules antagonistic to the official administration and rehabilitation programs.[14] Violations of the code result in inmate-imposed sanctions, ranging from ostracism to homicide. Sykes and Messinger have identified five main elements of the prison code[15]:

1. Don't interfere with the interests of other inmates. Never rat on a con. Don't have loose lips.

2. Don't lose your head. Don't quarrel with other inmates. Play it cool. Do your own time.

3. Don't exploit other inmates. Don't steal. Don't break your word. Pay your debts.

4. Don't whine. Be tough. Be a man.

5. Don't be a sucker. Don't trust the guards or staff. Remember that prison officials are wrong and inmates are right.

deprivation theory
The belief that inmate subcultures develop in response to the deprivations in prison life.

importation theory
The belief that inmate subcultures are brought into prisons from the outside world.

> Inmates who lived violent lives outside tend to associate with other violent inmates and often engage in similar behavior in prison.

integration model
A combination of importation theory and deprivation theory. The belief that, in childhood, some inmates acquired, usually from peers, values that support law-violating behavior but that the norms and standards in prison also affect inmates.

prison code
A set of norms and values among prison inmates. It is generally antagonistic to the official administration and rehabilitation programs of the prison.

Prison life is living in an insane world with insane rules. There's strength in numbers, and even the weak seem to "click up" in here. Everyone knows their own kind, it seems. Predators know one another immediately, as well as the bull queers, fags, and dudes just walking it down, keeping their nose clean. . . .

Here, these groups can set themselves apart quickly. Staff keeps track of high profile inmates, and makes sure not to give them too much rope.

You definitely are classified by those you hang around with—labels are hard to shake in this environment. And the most important thing I've learned here

is, there's plenty of dudes here who just love to hate on you and keep you here doing their digits with them. Misery loves company.

It's best to hook up with those that have the same objectives out of doing time as yourself. For me it's simply walking this time down to go home, and that's the type of dude I choose to hang with. Granted, he has to be solid, but first and foremost he has to be smart enough to choose which battles are worth dying over.

At any given time one group can have drama with another or trouble within its own ranks. So be sure that what you are

willing to knuckle up over is well worth the repercussions, because you can be absolutely positive that staff will know what's happening almost as it's happening. This is a very small community—there are no secrets! Not even for staff.

You will hook up with dudes in here, and you feel some sort of bond grow between you and your bros. So you are there for them when they need you, and you can expect the same from them. Because even though this is prison, it's also where you live, and where they live.

—Anonymous

THE OFFENDER SPEAKS

PRISON ARGOT—THE LANGUAGE OF CONFINEMENT

prison argot

The special language of the inmate subculture.

Prison argot is the special language of the inmate subculture. *Argot* is a French word meaning "slang." Prison society has always had its own unique language, illustrated by the following argot-laden paragraph:

> The new con, considered fresh meat by the screws and other prisoners, was sent to the cross-bar hotel to do his bit. He soon picked up the reputation through the yard grapevine as a canary-bird. While he was at the big house, the goon squad put him in the freezer for his protection. Eventually, he was released from the ice-box and ordered to make little ones out of big ones until he was released to the free world. Upon release he received $100 in gate money, vowing never to be thrown in the hole or be thought of as a stool-pigeon again.[16]

Prison argot originated partly as a form of secret communication. Gresham Sykes, however, believed that it serves primarily as "an illustrative symbol of the prison community"—or as a way for inmates to mark themselves as outlaws and social outcasts.[17] Sykes's work brought prison argot to the attention of sociologists and criminologists. Since Sykes's time other authors have identified a number of words, terms, and acronyms in prison argot. Some of these terms are presented in Table 10–1.

SOCIAL STRUCTURE IN MEN'S PRISONS

Inmate societies, like other societies, have a hierarchy of positions. Inmates assume or are forced into specific social roles, and some inmates—by virtue of the roles they assume—have more status and power than others.

Early writers often classified prisoners by the crimes they had committed or their criminal histories. Irwin, for example, divided prisoners into such categories as thieves (those with a culture of criminal values), convicts (time doers), square johns (inmates unfamiliar with criminal subcultures), and dope fiends (drug-involved inmates).[18]

TABLE 10–1	**Prison Argot: The Language of Confinement**

ARGOT IN MEN'S PRISONS

ace duce: best friend

badge (or bull, hack, "the man," or screw): a correctional officer

ball busters: violent inmates

banger (or burner, shank, sticker): a knife

billys: white men

boneyard: conjugal visiting area

cat-J (or J-cat): a prisoner in need of psychological or psychiatric therapy or medication

cellie: cell mate

center men: inmates who are close to the staff

chester: child molester

dog: homeboy or friend

fag: a male inmate believed to be a natural (preprison) homosexual

featherwood: a peckerwood's "woman"

fish: a newly arrived inmate

gorilla: an inmate who uses force to take what he wants from others

hipsters: young, drug-involved inmates

homeboy: a prisoner from one's hometown or neighborhood

ink: tattoos

lemon squeezer: an inmate who has an unattractive "girlfriend"

man walking: phrase used to signal that a guard is coming

merchant (or peddler): one who sells when he should give; or one who sells goods and services to other inmates illegally

nimby: not in my back yard

peckerwood (or wood): a white prisoner

punk: a male inmate who is forced into a submissive role during homosexual relations

rat (or snitch): an inmate who squeals (provides information about other inmates to the prison administration)

real men: inmates respected by other inmates

schooled: knowledgeable in the ways of prison life

shakedown: search of a cell or a work area

shu (pronounced *shoe*): special housing unit

toughs: those with a preprison history of violent crimes

tree jumper: rapist

turn out: to rape or make into a punk

wolf: a male inmate who assumes an aggressive role during homosexual relations

ARGOT IN WOMEN'S PRISONS

cherry (or cherrie): an inmate not yet introduced to lesbian activities

fay broad: a white inmate

femme (or mommy): an inmate who plays a female role during a lesbian relationship

safe: the vagina, especially when used for hiding contraband

stud broad (or daddy): an inmate who assumes a male role in a lesbian relationship

Sources: Gresham Sykes, *The Society of Captives* (Princeton, NJ: Princeton University Press, 1958); Rose Giallombardo, *Society of Women: A Study of Women's Prison* (New York: John Wiley, 1966); Richard A. Cloward et al., *Theoretical Studies in Social Organization of the Prison* (New York: Social Science Research Council, 1960). For a more contemporary listing of prison slang terms, see Reinhold Aman, *Hillary Clinton's Pen Pal: A Guide to Life and Lingo in Federal Prison* (Santa Rosa, CA: Maledicta Press, 1996); Jerome Washington, *Iron House: Stories from the Yard* (Ann Arbor, MI: QED Press, 1994); Morrie Camhi, *The Prison Experience* (Boston: Charles Tuttle Co., 1989); Harold Long, *Survival in Prison* (Port Townsend, WA: Loompanics Unlimited, 1990).

Other writers have identified **inmate roles,** defining them as prison lifestyles or as forms of ongoing social accommodation to prison life. Each role has a position in the pecking order, indicating its status in the prison society.

About a decade ago, Frank Schmalleger developed a contemporary typology of male inmate roles.[19] It is based on actual social roles found among inmates in prison, and it uses the prison argot in existence when it was created to name or describe each type. Each type can be viewed as a prison lifestyle either chosen by inmates or forced on them. Some of the types were previously identified by other writers. Although the terminology used in the typology sounds dated, the types of inmates it identifies are still characteristic of prison populations today. The twelve inmate types are discussed in the following paragraphs.

inmate roles

Prison lifestyles; also, forms of ongoing social accommodation to prison life.

The Real Man Real men do their own time, do not complain, and do not cause problems for other inmates. They see confinement as a natural consequence of criminal activity and view time spent in prison as an unfortunate cost of doing business. Real men know the inmate code and abide by it. They are well regarded within the institution and rarely run into problems with other inmates. If they do, they solve their problems on their own. They never seek the help of correctional officers or the prison administration. Although they generally avoid trouble within the institution, they usually continue a life of crime once released.

The Mean Dude Some inmates are notorious for resorting quickly to physical power. They are quick to fight and, when fighting, give no quarter. They are callous, cold, and uncaring. Mean dudes control those around them through force or the threat of force. The fear they inspire usually gives them a great deal of power in inmate society. At the very least, other inmates are likely to leave the mean dude alone.

The Bully A variation of the mean dude is the bully. Bullies use intimidation to get what they want. Unlike mean dudes, they are far more likely to use threats than to use actual physical force. A bully may make his threats in public so that others see the victim's compliance.

The Agitator The agitator, sometimes called a "wise guy," is constantly trying to stir things up. He responds to the boredom of prison life by causing problems for others. An agitator may point out, for example, how a powerful inmate has been wronged by another inmate or that an inmate seen talking to a "rat" must be a snitch himself.

The Hedonist The hedonist adapts to prison by exploiting the minimal pleasures it offers. Hedonists always seek the easy path, and they plot to win the "cushiest" jobs. They may also stockpile goods to barter for services of various kinds. Hedonists live only in the now, with little concern for the future. Their lives revolve around such activities as gambling, drug running, smuggling contraband, and exploiting homosexual opportunities.

The Opportunist The opportunist sees prison as an opportunity for personal advancement. He takes advantage of the formal self-improvement opportunities of the prison, such as schooling, trade training, and counseling. Other inmates generally dislike opportunists, seeing them as selfish "do-gooders." Staff members, however, often see opportunists as model prisoners.

The Retreatist Some inmates, unable to cope with the realities of prison life, withdraw psychologically from the world around them. Depression, neurosis, and even psychosis may result. Some retreatists attempt to lose themselves in drugs or alcohol. Others attempt suicide. Isolation from the general prison population, combined with counseling or psychiatric treatment, may offer the best hope for retreatists to survive the prison experience.

The Legalist Legalists are known as "jailhouse lawyers," or simply "lawyers," in prison argot. They are usually among the better-educated prisoners, although some legalists have little formal education. Legalists fight confinement through the system of laws, rules, and court precedent. Legalists file writs with the courts, seeking hearings on a wide variety of issues. Although many legalists work to better the conditions of their own confinement or to achieve early release, most also file pleas on behalf of other prisoners.

The Radical   Radicals see themselves as political prisoners of an unfair society. They believe that a discriminatory world has denied them the education and skills needed to succeed in a socially acceptable way. Most of the beliefs held by radical inmates are rationalizations that shift the blame for personal failure onto society. The radical inmate is likely to be familiar with contemporary countercultural figures.

The Colonist   Colonists, also referred to as "convicts," turn prison into home. Colonists know the ropes of prison, have many "friends" on the inside, and often feel more comfortable in prison than outside it. They may not look forward to leaving prison. Some may even commit additional offenses to extend their stay. Colonists are generally well regarded by other prisoners. Many are old-timers. Colonists have learned to take advantage of the informal opportunity structure in prisons, and they are well versed in the inmate code.

The Religious Inmate   Religious inmates profess a strong religious faith and may attempt to convert both inmates and staff. Religious inmates frequently form prayer groups, request special meeting facilities and special diets, and may ask for frequent visits from religious leaders. Religious inmates are often under a great deal of suspicion from inmates and staff, who tend to think they are faking religious commitment to gain special treatment. Those judged sincere in their faith may win early release, removal from death row, or any number of other special considerations.

The Punk   The punk is a young inmate, often small, who has been forced into a sexual relationship with an aggressive, well-respected prisoner. Punks are generally "turned out" through homosexual rape. A punk usually finds a protector among the more powerful inmates. Punks keep their protectors happy by providing them with sexual services.

SEXUALITY IN MEN'S PRISONS

Violence and victimization occur in men's prisons, and a good deal of prison violence has sexual overtones. The top of the sexual hierarchy in male prisons is occupied by inmates engaged in situational homosexuality who are called, quite simply, "men." *Men* are heterosexual inmates who feel compelled to engage in homosexual behavior by the conditions of confinement.[20] Men with the power to own and control their own "punk" rise to the top of the inmate sexual hierarchy.

> Violence and victimization occur in men's prisons, and a good deal of prison violence has sexual overtones.

Punks are "owned" by powerful inmates, who provide them protection from sexual violence and from other inmates. Many punks are forced to fill the traditional role of a wife and can often be found doing their Man's laundry, ironing, and making up the Man's bed. Although punks are usually seen as totally powerless and dependent upon their Man, punks can influence their "owners" in various ways. As one inmate observer[21] describes it, "There are punk wiles just as there are feminine wiles. A contented punk is much more desirable than a sullen and reluctant one, so there is a definite incentive for the Men to back off from a confrontation with their punks on an issue which they don't consider essential, though no Man will tolerate a rebellious punk." He adds, "A Man has a social obligation to share his wealth with his punk, much as a rich man on the outside is expected to keep his wife in furs and take her out to eat. As one Man put it: 'You punks have got it made; you don't have to fight, and you get all the dope and commissary from the men with the most money.'"[22]

The most powerful Men in prison society, cell block leaders, gang leaders, and so on, will "own" the most desirable punks. Punks, however, can be sold or given away. Once a person has become a punk, he can never again become a Man—at least not while still in prison. Not all punks, however, are outcasts. Punks belonging to Men who have high-social status within the institution are treated with deference by other inmates. One rule of inmate society demands that a Man share what he has with his punk. Hence, Men will generally bestow what comforts they have accumulated in prison with their punks.

It is not uncommon for affectionate relationships to develop between Men and their punks. Some couples even "marry" in imitation ceremonies—many of which are followed by "parties" and attended by inmate "guests." As one writer explains it, "Imprisoned long enough, men can transfer any emotion they feel for women to their punks."[23]

One person who has contributed significantly to the study of sexual violence in men's prisons is Daniel Lockwood.[24] Using interviews and background data from prison files, Lockwood identified and studied 107 "targets" of aggressive sexual threats and 45 inmate "aggressors" in New York state male prisons. He also conducted a general survey that revealed that 28 percent of all male prisoners had been targets of sexual aggressors in prison at least once. Lockwood found that only one of the inmates he interviewed had actually been raped—an indication that the incidence of prison rape is quite low relative to other types of harm that may accompany sexual incidents, such as physical abuse, verbal abuse, threatening gestures, and threatening propositions.

Targets, when compared with nontargets, were found to be physically slight, young, white, nonviolent offenders from nonurban areas. They generally had a higher rate of psychological disturbance than other inmates and were more apt to attempt suicide while in prison. Figure 10–2 shows a note found by a new inmate in his cell at a New York state prison unit. The new inmate was young and not prison-wise. After discovering the note, the inmate asked to be moved to the prison's isolation area. His request was granted.[25]

The typical incident of sexual aggression, Lockwood found, is carried out by a group. About half the

Yo S
Check this out if you don't give me a peace of your ass I am going to take you off the count and that is my word.
I be down a very long time So I need it Very Bad I will give you 5 Pack's of Smokes if you do it OK That is my word So if you Want to live you Better do it and get it over with there are Three of us who need it.
OK. . .

FIGURE 10-2
Inmate Note

incidents Lockwood identified included physical violence, and another third involved threats. The incidents studied showed patterns of escalation from verbal abuse to physical violence.

Lockwood also found that prison rapes generally occur when gangs of aggressors circumvent security arrangements to physically control their victims. Fear, anxiety, suicidal thoughts, social disruption, and attitude changes develop in many victims of homosexual rape.

Women in Prison

In America today, there are far fewer women's prisons than men's prisons, and men in prison outnumber women in prison 12 to 1.[26] A state usually has one women's prison, housing a few hundred women. The size of a women's prison generally depends on the population of the state. Some small states house women prisoners in special areas of what are otherwise institutions for men.

> *In America today, there are far fewer women's prisons than men's prisons, and men in prison outnumber women in prison 12 to 1.*

Women's prisons are generally quite different from men's. Here's how one writer describes them:

> Often, there are no gun towers, no armed guards, and no stone walls or fences strung on top with concertina wire. Neatly pruned hedges, well-kept flower gardens, attractive brick buildings, and wide paved walkways greet the visitor's eye at women's prisons in many states. Often these institutions are located in rural, pastoral settings that may suggest tranquility and well-being to the casual observer.[27]

Such rural settings, however, make it hard for female inmates to maintain contact with their families, who may live far from the correctional facility.

Many prisons for women are built on a cottage plan. Cottages dot the grounds of such institutions, often arranged in pods. A group of six or so cottages constitutes a pod. Each cottage is much like a traditional house, with individual bedrooms; a day room with a television, chairs, couches, and tables; and small personal or shared bathrooms.

Security in women's prisons is generally more relaxed than in men's, and female inmates may have more freedom within the institution than their male counterparts. Practically speaking, women—even those in prison—are seen as less dangerous than men and less prone to violence or escape.

Treatment, education, recreation, and other programs in women's prisons have often been criticized as inferior to those in men's prisons. Recent research has uncovered continuing disparities in many areas.[28] For example, men's institutions often have a much wider range of vocational and educational training programs and services and larger and better-equipped law libraries. Similarly, exercise facilities—including weight

Although there are far fewer women in prison than men, the number of women behind bars is growing steadily. What might account for the rising number of imprisoned women?

CAREER PROFILE

Jack Osborn

Custody Utility Officer   Jefferson City Correctional Center   Jefferson City, MO

Jack Osborn is a custody utility officer at the Jefferson City Correctional Center in Missouri. As a utility officer, he may be assigned to any area or department that needs an additional staff member. Before becoming a correctional officer, Jack was a deputy sheriff for 10 years. He has completed two years of community college coursework.

Jack advises knowing the inmates and being able to interpret behavioral changes. "Know what silence means. Communicate—listen," says Jack. "Learn who runs drugs and gambling, who the punks are. That's where your trouble will come from." Jack believes that if you follow this advice and know the mechanics of the job, you should have a great career in corrections.

rooms, jogging areas, and basketball courts—are often better equipped and larger in men's institutions today than in women's.

Prison administrators have often found it impractical to develop and fund programs at the same level in women's and men's prisons, because of differences in interest, participation, and space and the fact that relatively low numbers of women prisoners don't allow for the same economies of scale found in men's institutions. Nonetheless, it is important to strive for parity of opportunity as an ideal. The American Correctional Association, for example, through its Guidelines for Women's Prison Construction and Programming,[29] insists that the same level of services and opportunities be available in women's prisons as in men's prisons in the same jurisdiction.

Ethical Dilemma

What is equal treatment when it comes to the operation of male and female prisons? Do you support a policy of equal treatment for male and female inmates? What are the current issues in the operation of a women's prison? For more information go to Ethical Dilemma 10-1 at http://www.mhhe.com/schmalleger2.

In some instances, women may be placed in an institution housing inmates with a range of security levels. Consequently, women who are low security risks may have less personal freedom than their male counterparts. Women may also not have the opportunity to transfer to a less secure institution as their risk level drops.

CHARACTERISTICS OF WOMEN INMATES

Many of our conceptions of female inmates derive more from myth than reality.

Many of our conceptions of female inmates derive more from myth than reality. Recent BJS surveys provide a more realistic picture of female inmates.[30] At the start of 2003, women comprised 6.8 percent of the prisoners in the nation. Since 1995, the female prison population has grown 42 percent,[31] a significantly higher rate of growth than experienced in the male prison population, which saw a 27 percent increase during the same period. These figures represent an average annual growth rate of 5.2 percent for females and 3.5 percent for males. As of January 1, 2003, there were 97,491 women under the jurisdiction of state and federal prison authorities.[32]

by Tara Gray, New Mexico State University

Police officers sometimes say their job is 99 percent boredom and 1 percent sheer terror. Inmates could easily say the same.

If there is one word that characterizes inmate life, it is probably the word, "boredom." To understand the extent of the boredom, lock yourself in your bathroom for one weekend. Before you lock yourself in, place a sleeping roll on the floor. Pack sack lunches sufficient to last you through two days and two nights. As you pack your lunches, imagine the food available to inmates in prison. Pack any reading materials you want with you, including homework, but know you won't have a telephone, television, computer, or any electronic device in your "cell." Tell your roommate that he or she is free to talk with you through the door.

Congratulations. By going through two days "behind the bars," you have just had a taste of giving up your freedom. It won't be quite like incarceration of course because you choose the date and the length of stay, which was considerably less than the average prison stay of 23 months. You also had more control over the food, the reading materials, and the roommate than most inmates have. But still, you couldn't help noticing you were living in a very small room—a toilet! You wanted to eat something besides the food that was issued! You wanted to call someone! You wanted to go somewhere!

Congratulations again. You tried to experience what it is like to leave everyone and everything you ever knew behind you and give up some important elements of freedom. You have had some important insights about what life is like behind bars. You have experienced the boredom but missed out on the other negative of inmate life: sheer terror.

What is the terror like for inmates? It depends greatly on the prison or jail. Some institutions resemble the violence of the ghetto or barrio. Others are relatively peaceful. In the most violent institutions, "watching your back" is a full time job. Everyone is to be feared, including every other inmate and some correctional officers. Assaults are frequent and deadly. Rapes are common for both women and men. Don't get too bored: Watch out.

ABOUT THE AUTHOR
Tara Gray teaches criminal justice at New Mexico State University. Prisons are her passion, and she remains convinced that prisons can be places of hope instead of places of terror and despair. Her latest book is *Exploring Corrections: A Book of Readings* (Allyn & Bacon, 2002). The book includes readings about living in prison and jail for men, women, and juveniles, as well as living with the threat of rape, with AIDS, in the "hole," on psychotropic drugs, or on death row. The book includes futuristic models of prison administration that show what is possible in a prison and how to keep hope alive.

Reflections on the Future

Female prisoners largely resemble male prisoners in race, ethnic background, and age. However, they are substantially more likely to be serving time for a drug offense and less likely to have been sentenced for a violent crime. Women are also more likely than men to be serving time for larceny or fraud.

Female inmates have shorter criminal records than male inmates. They generally have shorter maximum sentences than men. Half of all women receive a maximum sentence of 60 months or less, while half of all men are sentenced to 120 months or less.

Significantly, more than 4 in 10 of the women prisoners responding to BJS surveys reported prior physical or sexual abuse. One of the major factors distinguishing male inmates from female is that the women have experienced far more sexual and physical abuse than the men. A 2003 report by the National Institute of Corrections found that women enter correctional institutions through different "pathways" than men. According to the report, most women offenders are typically nonviolent and their crimes are less threatening to community safety than those committed by male offenders. "Women's most common pathways to crime," said the report, "result from abuse, poverty, and substance abuse"—all of which, according to the report, are interconnected.[33] Figure 10–3 is a comparison of selected characteristics of female and male state prisoners.

Women in prison

Criminal offense
31% are in prison for drug offenses
32% are in prison for violent offenses
26% are in prison for property offenses

Criminal history
46% are nonviolent recidivists
28% have no previous sentence
26% are violent recidivists

Family characteristics
78% have children
42% lived with both parents most of time growing up
33% had a parent/guardian who abused alcohol or drugs
17% were married at the time they committed the offense for which they were incarcerated
45% have never married
47% have a family member who had been incarcerated

Drug and alcohol use
41% used drugs daily in the month before the current offense
36% were under the influence of drugs at the time of the offense
12% were under the influence of alcohol at the time of the offense

Men in prison

Criminal offense
50% are in prison for violent offenses
19% are in prison for property offenses
20% are in prison for drug offenses

Criminal history
50% are violent recidivists
31% are nonviolent recidivists
19% have no previous sentence

Family characteristics
64% have children
43% lived with both parents most of time growing up
26% had a parent/guardian who abused alcohol or drugs
18% were married at the time they committed the offense for which they were incarcerated
56% have never married
37% have a family member who had been incarcerated

Drug and alcohol use
36% used drugs daily in the month before the current offense
31% were under the influence of drugs at the time of the offense
18% were under the influence of alcohol at the time of the offense

FIGURE 10-3
Characteristics of Women and Men in State Prisons

Source: Paige M. Harrison and Allen J. Beck, *Prisoners in 2002* (Washington, DC: Bureau of Justice Statistics, U.S. Department of Justice, July 2003); and Allen Beck et al., *Survey of State Prison Inmates, 1991* (Washington, DC: U.S. Department of Justice, March 1993).

OFFENSES OF INCARCERATED WOMEN

Drug offenses account for the incarceration of a large percentage of the women behind bars. Two-thirds of all women in federal prisons are serving time on drug charges.[34] Some sources estimate that drug crimes and other crimes indirectly related to drug activities together account for the imprisonment of around 95 percent of today's women inmates. In short, drug use and abuse, or crimes stimulated by the desire for drugs and drug money, are what send most women to prison (see Figure 10–4). This has been true for at least a decade. According to an American Correctional Association report, the primary reasons incarcerated women most frequently give for their arrest are (1) trying to pay for drugs, (2) attempts to relieve economic pressures, and (3) poor judgment.[35]

According to the BJS, before arrest, women in prison use more drugs than men and use those drugs more frequently.[36] About 54 percent of imprisoned women have used drugs in the month before the offense for which they were arrested, compared with 50 percent of the men. Female inmates are also more likely than male inmates to have used drugs regularly (65 percent versus 62 percent), to have used drugs daily in the month preceding their offense (41 percent versus 36 percent), and to have been under the influence at the time of the offense (36 percent versus 31 percent). Nearly one in four female inmates surveyed reported committing the offense to get money to buy drugs, compared with one in six males.

Female inmates who used drugs differed from those who did not in the types of crimes they committed. Regardless of the amount of drug use, users were less likely than nonusers to be serving a sentence for a violent offense.

FIGURE 10-4
Reasons for Incarceration

Source: Paige M. Harrison and Allen J. Beck, *Prisoners in 2002* (Washington, DC: Bureau of Justice Statistics, U.S. Department of Justice, July 2003).

SOCIAL STRUCTURE IN WOMEN'S PRISONS

As might be expected, the social structure and the subcultural norms and expectations in women's prisons are quite different from those in men's prisons. Unfortunately, however, relatively few studies of inmate life have been conducted in institutions for women.

One early study of women at the Federal Reformatory for Women in Alderson, West Virginia, was an effort to compare subcultural aspects of women's prisons with those of men's. Rose Giallombardo reached the conclusion that "many of the subcultural features of the institution are imported from the larger society."[37] Giallombardo believed that male and female inmate subcultures are actually quite similar, except that women's prisons develop "a substitute universe," a world "in which inmates may preserve an identity which is relevant to life outside the prison."

Giallombardo was unable to find in the women's prison some of the values inherent in a male inmate subculture, such as "Do your own time." The inmate subculture in a women's prison, she said, tends to encourage relationships rather than isolation. Hence, women are expected to share their problems with other inmates and to offer at least some support and encouragement to others. On the other hand, she observed, women prisoners tend to see each other as conniving, self-centered, and scheming. Hence, a basic tenet of the inmate subculture in a women's prison is "You can't trust other women." As Giallombardo put it, women prisoners tend to believe that "every woman is a sneaking, lying bitch."

Giallombardo concluded that the social structure of women's prisons and the social role assumed by each inmate are based on three elements:

1. the individual woman's level of personal dependence and her status needs (which are said to be based upon cultural expectations of the female role);
2. the individual's needs arising from incarceration, combined with the institution's inability to meet female inmates' emotional needs; and
3. needs related to the individual's personality.

A more recent study was of inmates in the District of Columbia Women's Reformatory at Occoquan, Virginia.[38] Esther Heffernan identified three roles that women commonly adopt when adjusting to prison. According to Heffernan, women's roles evolve partly from the characteristics the women bring with them to prison and depend partly on the ways the women choose to adapt to prison life. The roles she described are discussed in the following paragraphs.

The Cool Inmate   Cool women usually have previous records, are in the know, are streetwise, and do not cause trouble for other inmates while in prison. Cool women are seen as professional or semiprofessional criminals who work to win the maximum number of prison amenities without endangering their parole or release dates.

The Square Inmate   Square women are not familiar with criminal lifestyles and have few, if any, criminal experiences other than the one for which they were imprisoned. They tend to hold the values and roles of conventional society.

The Life Inmate   Life inmates are habitual or career offenders and are generally well socialized into lives of crime. They support inmate values and subculture. Life inmates typically have been in and out of prison from an early age and have developed criminal lifestyles dedicated to meeting their political, economic, familial, and social needs outside conventional society.

One writer, summarizing the results of studies such as those discussed here, found two features that distinguish women's prisons from men's prisons:[39]

1. The social roles in women's prisons place greater emphasis on homosexual relations as a mode of adaptation to prison life.

2. The mode of adaptation a female inmate selects is best assessed by studying the inmate's preinstitutional experiences.

PSEUDOFAMILIES AND SEXUAL LIAISONS

A unique feature of women's prisons is pseudofamilies. **Pseudofamilies** are familylike structures, common in women's prisons, in which inmates assume roles similar to those of family members in free society. Pseudofamilies appear to provide emotional and social support for the women who belong to them. Courtship, marriage, and kinship ties formed with other women inmates provide a means of coping with the rigors of imprisonment. One inmate has explained pseudofamilies this way: "It just happens. Just like on the outside, you get close to certain people. It's the same in here—but we probably get even closer than a lot of families because of how lonely it is otherwise."[40]

Some authors suggest that pseudofamilies are to women's prisons what gangs are to men's.[41] Men establish social relationships largely through power, and gang structure effectively expresses such relationships. Women relate to one another more expressively and emotionally. Hence, family structures are one of the most effective reflections of women's relationships in prison, just as they are in the wider society. At least one study of prison coping behavior found that new female inmates, especially those most in need of support, advice, and assistance in adjusting to the conditions of incarceration, are the women most likely to become members of prison pseudofamilies.[42]

To a large extent, the social and behavioral patterns of family relationships in prison mirror their traditional counterparts in the community.

pseudofamilies
Familylike structures, common in women's prisons, in which inmates assume roles similar to those of family members in free society.

The kinship of substitute families plays a major role in the lives of many female inmates, who take the relationships very seriously. How might these relationships supplant values such as "do your own time" commonly found in the subculture of men's prisons?

THE STAFF SPEAKS

Families in women's prisons come in all sizes and colors. They can be virtual melting pots of ethnicity and age. A member of a family may be young or old and may be black, white, or Hispanic. As in families in free society, there are roles for husbands and wives, sisters, brothers, grandmothers, and children. Roles for aunts and uncles do not exist, however.

"Stud broads," in prison argot, assume any male role, including that of husband and brother. Other inmates think of them as men. "Men" often assume traditional roles in women's prisons, ordering women around, demanding to be waited on, expecting to have their rooms cleaned and their laundry done, and so forth. Most women who assume masculine roles within prison are said to be "playing" and are sometimes called "players." Once they leave, they usually revert to female roles. A "femme" or "mommy" is a woman who assumes a female role in a family and during homosexual activity.

Most women in prison, including those playing masculine roles, were generally not lesbians before entering prison. They resort to lesbian relations within prison because relationships with men are unavailable.

Though gender roles and family relationships within women's prisons appear to have an enduring quality, women can and sometimes do change role genders. When a woman playing a male role, for example, reverts to a female one, she is said to have "dropped her belt." A stud broad who drops her belt may wreak havoc on relationships within her own family and in families related to it.

SPECIAL NEEDS OF FEMALE INMATES

Rarely are the special needs of imprisoned women fully recognized—and even less frequently are they addressed. Many of today's prison administrators and correctional officers still treat women as if they were men. Nicole Hahn Rafter, for example, says that many prisons have an attitude akin to "just add women and stir."[43]

A 2003 report by the National Institute of Corrections called for criminal justice agencies to acknowledge the "many differences between male and female offenders," and for the implementation of gender-responsive programming for treating the problems of imprisoned women.[44] Gender-responsive programming might, for example, strengthen policies against staff sexual misconduct in institutions that house women; provide more "safe and nurturing" drug treatment programs; and help inmate mothers to maintain strong relationships with their children.

Susan Cranford is division director of the Community Justice Assistance Division of the Texas Department of Criminal Justice. Rose Williams is warden of Pulaski State Prison in Hawkinsville, Georgia. Recently, Cranford and Williams suggested that "correctional staff should keep the unique needs of women offenders in mind."[45] They say that the effective running of a women's prison requires consideration of those needs.

A critical difference between male and female prisoners, say Cranford and Williams, is "the manner in which they communicate." Female offenders, they note, are usually much more open, more verbal, more emotional, and more willing to share the intimacies of their lives than men are. Male prisoners, like most men in free society, are guarded about the information they share and the manner in which they share it. "For men, information is power. For women, talking helps establish a common ground, a way to relate to others."

Gender-specific training is vital for COs who work in women's prisons, say Cranford and Williams. Proper training, they write, can head off the development of inappropriate relationships (especially initiated by male staff members), which could lead to sexual misconduct. Moreover, staff members who work with women should receive additional training in negotiating and listening skills.

An example of effective gender-specific training is the task-oriented curriculum entitled *Working with the Female Offender,* developed by Florida's Department of Corrections.[46] The program addresses unique aspects of managing female inmates and provides correctional staff training in the behaviors, actions, needs, and backgrounds presented by female offenders. A special segment examines how female offenders relate to supervision in various institutional or community corrections settings.

Finally, say Cranford and Williams, it is important to realize that a woman's children are usually very important to her and that many imprisoned women have children on the outside. Hence, parenting skills should be taught to imprisoned mothers, since most will rejoin and be with their children during critical stages in the children's development.

> ▶ Should women receive lighter sentences because they are more likely to be the sole caretakers of young dependent children? Should the children of incarcerated women have special visitation rights? For more information go to Ethical Dilemma 10-2 at http://www.mhhe.com/schmalleger2.
>
> **Ethical Dilemma**

MOTHERS IN PRISON

According to one BJS study,[47] an estimated 6.7 percent of black women, 5.9 percent of Hispanic women, and 5.2 percent of white women are pregnant at the time of incarceration.

An estimated 4,000 women prisoners give birth each year, even though most women's prisons have no special facilities for pregnant inmates.[48] Some experts recommend that women's prisons should routinely make counseling available to pregnant inmates, and that they should fully inform these women of the options available to them, including abortion and adoption.[49]

The ACA[50] recommends that institutions provide counseling for pregnant inmates, that "prenatal care" should be offered, and that deliveries should be made at community hospitals.[51] Similarly, the American Public Health Association's standards for health services in correctional institutions say that pregnant inmates should be provided with prenatal care, including medical exams and treatment, and that pregnant prisoners should be allowed a special program of housing, diet, vitamin supplements, and exercise.[52]

Once inmates give birth, other problems arise—including the critical issue of child placement. Some states still have partial civil death statutes, which mean that prisoners lose many of their civil rights upon incarceration. In such states, women may lose legal custody of their children. Children either become wards of the state or are placed for adoption.

Although there is some historical precedent for allowing women inmates to keep newborns with them in the institutional setting, very few women's prisons permit this practice. Overcrowded prisons lack space for children, and the prison environment is a decidedly undesirable environment for children. A few women's prisons allow women to keep newborns for a brief period. Most, however, arrange for foster care until the mother is able to find relatives to care for the child or is released. Others work with services that put prison-born infants up for adoption. Some facilities make a special effort to keep mother and child together. Even relatively progressive prisons that allow mother-child contact usually do so only for the first year.

Many women are already mothers when they come to prison. BJS statistics[53] show that more than three-quarters of all women in prison in the United States have young children (i.e., under the age of 18). Black (69 percent) and Hispanic (72 percent) female inmates are more likely than white (62 percent) female inmates to have young children. Also, black women are more likely than other women to have lived with their young children before being imprisoned.

The children of 25 percent of women inmates with children under age 18 live with the other parent. More than a third of white female inmates report that their children are living with the children's fathers, compared to a quarter of Hispanic women and less than a fifth of black women. Regardless of race, grandparents are the most common caregivers: 57 percent of imprisoned black mothers look to grandparents for child care, as do 55 percent of imprisoned Hispanic mothers and 41 percent of imprisoned white mothers. Nearly 10 percent of the inmate mothers reported that their children are in a foster home, agency, or institution.

Worry about children affects female inmates' physical and emotional well-being. Although 78 percent of mothers (and 62% of fathers) report having at least monthly contact with their children, only 24 percent of mothers (and 21% of fathers) report personal visits from their children at least monthly.[54] A majority of both mothers (54%) and fathers (57%) report never having had a personal visit with their children since their imprisonment began.

According to BJS, nearly 90 percent of women with children under age 18 have had contact with their children since entering prison. Half of all women inmates surveyed have been visited by their children, four-fifths have corresponded by mail, and three-quarters have talked with children on the telephone. Female inmates with children under age 18 are more likely than those with adult children to make daily telephone calls to their children.

Understandably, inmate mothers frequently express concern about possible alienation from their children due to the passage of time associated with incarceration. They often worry that their children will develop strong bonds with new caretakers and be unwilling to return to them upon release.[55]

Finally, it is important to note that a number of women's prisons operate programs designed to develop parenting skills among inmates. Included are the Program for Caring Parents at the Louisiana Correctional Institute for Women; Project HIP (Helping Incarcerated Parents) at the Maine Correctional Center; and Neil J. Houston House, a program for nonviolent female offenders in Massachusetts.[56]

In a BJS Special Report published in 2000,[57] Christopher Mumola estimated that 721,500 state and federal inmates were the parents of 1,498,800 children under age 18. Cranford and Williams reported that these children are about eight times as likely to become criminals as are the children of nonoffenders.

In the federal population, 63.4 percent of male prisoners and 58.8 percent of female prisoners have minor children. The state data reverse this distribution, with 65.3 percent of female inmates and 54.7 percent of male inmates having minor children.

It is noteworthy that male inmates are, for the most part, rarely provided with any special assistance for maintaining contact with their children during their incarceration. During the past decade, however, administrators in women's institutions across the country have implemented measures to foster stronger bonds between incarcerated mothers and their children. Ranging from the establishment of prison nurseries to the development of special visitation areas, these measures seek to facilitate the continued family contact that appears to be so important to female offenders.[58]

With 1 in 12 inmates pregnant at the time of admission[59] and 22 percent of all minor children with a parent in prison being under 5 years old,[60] correctional administrators need to address the unique problems presented by pregnant offenders and those with very young children. Some institutions have opted to create nurseries on site. At Nebraska's Correctional Center for Women, for example, inmates due for release before their children are 18 months old may keep the children with them in a specially designated floor of a standard prison building. The mothers are provided parenting and child-care classes, and they work only part time. While they work, other trained inmates provide child care.

Another example of programs designed to facilitate family bonding is the Ohio Reformatory for Women's annual three-day weekend camp, which brings children aged 6 to

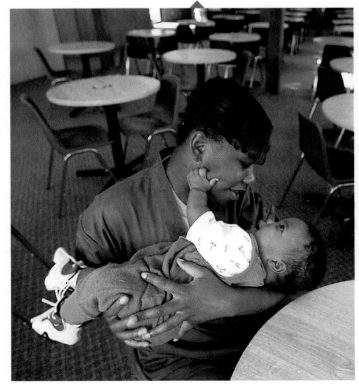

Mothers at the Colorado Women's Correctional Facility are allowed to hold their young children every Friday for a few hours. Most children of incarcerated mothers have little contact with their mothers. The lack of contact often upsets their emotional development. How might prisons contribute to the development of positive relationships between incarcerated mothers and their children?

Eye On Corrections™

Bureau of Prisons Requires Parenting Programs

By Michelle Gaseau

In many ways, the federal Bureau of Prisons is one of the leaders in providing parenting programs to offenders. Nationwide, each federal facility provides various programs for incarcerated mothers and fathers. At FCI–Allenwood in Pennsylvania, staff have found that its home-grown fatherhood program is so popular that a second session has been added.

"Inmates who are interested give us a brief memo stating they are interested in the program. We always have a waiting list. Just recently, we began offering two sessions per quarter," said Josette Zielinkski, Supervisor of Education at FCI–Allenwood.

The fatherhood program serves both English- and Spanish-speaking inmates and was developed by existing education staff at the facility. According to Zielinkski, the facility spends under $3,000 a year to fund the program, which uses in-house staff.

"The goal for the fathers is to promote constructive family values through mutual support and improve relationships during and after incarceration," said Zielinkski. "We've gotten lots of positive feedback from the inmates. The information is so good. The fear they have is thinking their kids will end up here too."

The fatherhood program utilizes 36 hours of classroom time in two different sessions. English-speaking and Spanish-speaking inmates each have their own classroom sessions with textbooks in both languages. "We've had one or two go through who have nieces and nephews and another guy who didn't have kids at all. He was a newlywed and wanted to have a head start because he was talking about having kids with his wife," said Zielinkski.

The program covers a wide range of material from fire safety in the home, presented by a representative from the local department of health, to childhood immunizations. According to Zielinkski, volunteers from an organization for women in transition speak to the fathers about child abuse and domestic violence, others talk to the fathers about family communication and reestablishing the family, and the facility's safety manager talks to the father groups about home safety, poisons, smoke, and carbon dioxide dangers in the home. The inmates also learn basic CPR.

Zielinkski said the interaction among the inmates is beneficial as well. "They realize they are not alone. They'll tell you what their kids are going through. Also they have really good questions. When they are in the class with the experts, they are more willing to ask the questions such as how to deal with their angry, bitter spouse. What level should their child be learning at, or how can I tutor my kids in the visiting room," she said. "They discuss the problems their kids are having. Also we hear about how the kids' moms are dealing with the fathers being here. They get on the phone with the kids' moms and they are angry. The inmates do a lot of conversing with each other."

The program also tries to help the fathers understand budgeting and finances so that they will be better prepared to meet their financial responsibilities to their children and family upon release. *This article has been reprinted in part from CCNN. To read the article in its entirety, go to www.corrections.com.*

12 from all over the state to spend days with their inmate mothers. Originally pioneered at Bedford Hills Correctional Facility, New York's maximum-security prison for women, such camping visits have become more common in other facilities as well. Some states even allow overnight camping trips, both on and off the prison grounds.

Inmates apply for the program in January each year. Local churches and other community service groups support the program.[61] Selection criteria include a review of inmates' disciplinary records during incarceration, and those whose crimes involved their children are prohibited from participating. During the weekend, activities such as storytelling, softball, crafts, and meals facilitate bonding between mother and child. The inmates return to the prison to sleep at night, but the children "camp out" in sleeping bags at a local church.

Another innovative effort is Florida's "Reading Family Ties: Face to Face" program.[62] Begun in February 2000, it uses high-speed videoconferencing technology to permit weekly family visits between incarcerated mothers in two rural institutions and their children in the Miami area. Inmate mothers may sit before an Internet-linked camera to read to their children. Logistical limitations, of course, are significant, but administrators plan to expand the program to other major cities in Florida.

Perhaps the most family-centered efforts are being tried in California. Oakland's Project Pride[63] permits mothers convicted of nonviolent offenses to serve the last portion of their sentences in residential community settings with their preschool-age children. Under the Family Foundations Program in Santa Fe Springs (CA),[64] sentencing of convicted mothers with substance abuse histories can include treatment in residential centers where they can live with their children.

Some hard-liners might decry such programs as unjustified coddling of convicted offenders. Few, however, can argue the benefits such programs provide to the children of incarcerated parents. Meanwhile, it remains to be seen whether the programs will serve to sustain family relationships, ease prisoners' return to the family environment after release, and, ultimately, reduce recidivism rates.

COCORRECTIONAL FACILITIES

In 1971, a disturbance at the federal women's prison at Alderson, West Virginia, led to calls for ways to expand incarceration options for women. The federal Bureau of Prisons responded by moving low-security female prisoners from the crowded Alderson institution to a federal minimum-security prison at Morgantown, West Virginia. The Morgantown facility had been built for young men but had not reached its design capacity. With this move, the modern era of coed prisons, or cocorrections, was born.

A **coed prison** is a facility housing both men and women, and **cocorrections** is the incarceration and interaction of female and male offenders under a single institutional administration.[65] It is estimated that as many as 52 adult correctional institutions in the United States are coed and that they confine almost 23,000 men and 7,000 women.[66]

Since its inception, cocorrections has been cited as a potential solution to a wide variety of corrections problems. The rationales in support of cocorrections are that it:

coed prison

A prison housing both female and male offenders.

cocorrections

The incarceration and interaction of female and male offenders under a single institutional administration.

1. reduces the dehumanizing and destructive aspects of incarceration by permitting heterosocial relationships:
2. reduces problems of institutional control;
3. creates a more "normal" atmosphere, reducing privation;
4. allows positive heterosocial skills to emerge;
5. cushions the shock of release;
6. increases the number of program offerings and improves program access for all prisoners; and
7. expands career opportunities for women.

An examination of the cocorrections literature from 1970 to 1990, however, found no evidence that cocorrections benefits female prisoners.[67] A former warden of a coed prison contends that "going coed" has often been done to appease male egos and smooth the running of men's prisons. Warden Jacqueline Crawford tells us that most women in prison have generally been exploited by the men in their lives. A coed prison, she says, furthers this experience because male prisoners continue the abuse women have come to expect from men.[68]

Others have found that many women's prisons have been turned into coed prisons, thus limiting correctional options for women. Overall, researchers have concluded, "Cocorrections offers women prisoners few, if any, economic, educational, vocational, and social advantages."[69] Whether prisoners released from coed prisons adjust better to the community or experience less recidivism has not been sufficiently studied.

Although literature related to single-sex prisons[70] has repeatedly shown poor overall performance in prisoner rehabilitation and public safety, correctional decision makers, policymakers, legislators, and the public are not calling for an end to one-sex imprisonment. If cocorrections is to become more than window dressing, however, it requires more attention to planning, implementation, and evaluation. Despite some early claims of success, coed prisons are not a quick fix for problems of prison administration.

SUMMARY

1▸ Most state inmates are male, belong to racial or ethnic minority groups, are relatively young, and have been incarcerated for a violent offense.

2▸ Prison inmates live their daily lives in accordance with the dictates of the inmate subculture. The inmate subculture consists of the customs and beliefs of those incarcerated in correctional institutions.

3▸ Deprivation theory holds that prisoner subcultures develop in response to the pains of imprisonment. Importation theory claims that inmate subcultures are brought into prisons from the outside world. A more realistic approach might be the integration model, which uses both theories to explain prisoner subcultures.

4 ▶ An important aspect of the male inmate subculture is the prison code. The prison code is a set of norms for the behavior of inmates. Central elements of the code include notions of loyalty (to prison society), control of anger, toughness, and distrust of prison officials. Because the prison code is a part of the inmate subculture, it is mostly opposed to official policies.

5 ▶ The inmate subculture also has its own language, called *prison argot.* Examples of prison argot are "fish" (a new inmate), "cellie" (cell mate), and "homeboy" (a prisoner from one's hometown).

6 ▶ Inmate roles are different prison lifestyle choices. They include the real man, the mean dude, the bully, the agitator, the opportunist, the retreatist, the legalist, and the punk.

7 ▶ There are far fewer women's prisons than men's in the United States. Women's prisons often have no gun towers or armed guards and no stone walls or fences topped by barbed wire. They tend to be more attractive and are often built on a cottage plan. Security in most women's prisons is more relaxed than in institutions for men, and female inmates may have more freedom within the institution than do their male counterparts in their institutions. Other gender-based disparities favoring male prisoners exist. A lack of funding and inadequate training have been cited to explain why programs available to women inmates are often not on a par with those available to male prisoners.

8 ▶ Female prisoners largely resemble male prisoners in race, ethnic background, and age. However, they are substantially more likely to be serving time for drug offenses and less likely to have been sentenced for violent crimes.

9 ▶ While there are many similarities between men's and women's prisons, the social structure and the subcultural norms and expectations of women's prisons differ from those of men's prisons in a number of important ways. One important difference is that the prisoner subculture in a women's prison tends to encourage relationships rather than isolation. As a consequence, pseudofamilies arise, with fully developed familial relationships and roles.

KEY TERMS

total institution, *p. 360*
inmate subculture, *p. 361*
prisonization, *p. 361*
pains of imprisonment, *p. 362*
deprivation theory, *p. 363*

importation theory, *p. 363*
integration model, *p. 363*
prison code, *p. 363*
prison argot, *p. 364*
inmate roles, *p. 365*

pseudofamilies, *p. 375*
coed prison, *p. 381*
cocorrections, *p. 381*

REVIEW & APPLICATIONS

REVIEW & APPLICATIONS

QUESTIONS FOR REVIEW

1. What did Erving Goffman mean when he wrote that prisons are *total institutions?*
2. What is the *inmate subculture,* and how is it central to understanding society in men's prisons?
3. What is *prisonization?*
4. According to Gresham Sykes, what are the pains of imprisonment?
5. Explain how inmate subcultures develop, according to deprivation theory, importation theory, and the integration model.
6. What is the *prison code?* How does it influence behavior in men's prisons?
7. Explain what is meant by *inmate roles,* and give some examples.

8. Compare female and male inmates by their criminal histories, their family characteristics, and the offenses for which they are incarcerated.
9. In what ways do women's prisons differ from men's prisons?
10. What are *pseudofamilies,* and why are they important to the society of women's prisons?
11. What is the most common type of offense for which women are imprisoned?
12. What are some issues relating to cocorrectional facilities?

THINKING CRITICALLY ABOUT CORRECTIONS

▶ ▶ ▶ **Prison Birth**

A woman who gives birth in prison may lose her child to state authorities or may have her parental rights severely restricted. In most cases, the child is removed from the inmate mother shortly after birth. Do you think this is fair? Why or why not?

▶ ▶ ▶ **Housing Assignments**

Not surprisingly, state policies differ significantly on the question of housing assignments for prisoners. Some permit inmates to choose their cell mates, while others enforce random cell assignments. What are the advantages and disadvantages of each policy style? Which style do you think is best?

ON-THE-JOB DECISION MAKING

▶ ▶ ▶ **Male Officers in Women's Prisons**

You are a correctional officer assigned to a women's prison. Six months ago, the superintendent of your institution ordered an investigation to determine the proper role of male officers within the facility. The investigation centered on charges by a handful of inmates that they had been sexually harassed by male COs. The alleged harassment included requests for sexual favors in return for special privileges, observation of female inmates in various states of undress while in their rooms and in shower facilities, and inappropriate touching during cell and facility searches (policy allows only female COs to conduct body searches).

Although the investigation was inconclusive, the activities of male COs have been restricted. They are no longer permitted to have any physical contact with inmates unless an emergency demands that they restrain or search inmates. They have been reassigned to areas of the facility where they cannot view shower and toilet facilities. They are expected to announce their presence in living areas, and they have been ordered to take special classes on staff-inmate interaction.

Unfortunately, however, there are not enough female COs for all of the reassignments required by the recent shift in policy. As a result, the routines of female officers are being significantly disrupted. Female officers are being asked to work shifts that are inconvenient for their personal lives (many are mothers or college students and had come to count on predictable shift work). Most female COs also feel that their work load has increased, since they have to cover areas of the institution and assume tasks that male officers would previously have handled.

A few female COs have already left for jobs elsewhere, citing difficulties created in the work environment by the new policies. The talk among the correctional staff is that many of the remaining female staff members might also soon leave. If more female COs leave the facility, it will be impossible for those who remain to keep the facility running under the new rules.

1. Did the superintendent make the right decision in limiting the activities of male COs? Why or why not?

2. Might there be other ways to resolve the issues raised by the investigation into sexual harassment? If so, what might they be?

▶ ▶ ▶ **Same-Sex Relationships**

You are a chaplain working in a large state-run correctional facility. You take pride in your reputation among the inmates as a fair and reasonable counselor who treats them with courtesy and respect and never judges them for past transgressions or present problems.

Ronald, an inmate whom you know well, comes to you with a special request. He wants to marry Lawrence, another inmate, and he wants you to perform the ceremony in private. He also tells you that he knows that the "marriage" will have no legitimacy on the outside but says that the ceremony will be deeply moving for him and for Lawrence. Ronald's incarceration record is sterling. His disciplinary record shows no infractions, and there are numerous positive annotations regarding the obvious sincerity of his efforts to rehabilitate himself in preparation for his return to free society.

You are concerned that Ronald may actually be straight, and that his relationship with Lawrence may arise more from the pains of imprisonment than from any innate sexual orientation. You are uncertain what prison regulations might say about such a ceremony, but you suspect that, were you to inquire, the ceremony would be officially disallowed. Additionally, church elders in your denomination have condemned same-sex marriages like the one you are being asked to perform. Still, you think that Ronald is well-meaning in his efforts to form a more stable relationship with Lawrence, and you believe that such a relationship can help him adjust to the stresses of prison life.

1. What do you do? Is this an issue that you need time to think about, or do you answer right away?

2. Would you consider counseling Ronald in order to better assess his "true" sexual orientation?

3. Is his "true" sexual orientation an important consideration?

4. Would you further consider counseling Ronald and Lawrence, individually and jointly, regarding their desire to formalize their relationship?

5. Would you take the issue to the prison superintendent?

CORRECTIONS ON THE WEB

▶ ▶ ▶ **Criminal Offenders**

Access the Bureau of Justice Statistics at http://www.ojp.usdoj.gov/bjs and click on *Criminal offenders*. Review the following topics: *Lifetime Likelihood of going to state or federal prison, Intimate victimizers,* and *Use of alcohol by convicted offenders*. Write a summary of the information you find under each topic.

▶ ▶ ▶ **Aid to Inmate Mothers**

Visit the Aid to Inmate Mothers (AIM) Website at http://www.inmatemoms.org. Click on the menu items *About, History,* and *Programs* in order to learn more about AIM. Write a paragraph or two describing what you have learned.

" **All persons under any form of detention or imprisonment shall be treated in a humane manner and with respect for the inherent dignity of the human person.** "

—United Nations General Assembly Resolution 43/173 December 9, 1988

The Legal World: Prisoners' Rights

▶ **CHAPTER OBJECTIVES**

After completing this chapter you should be able to do the following:

1. Explain what is meant by the hands-off doctrine.

2. Identify the sources of prisoners' rights.

3. List the five ways in which inmates can challenge their conditions of confinement.

4. Describe the major changes that took place during the prisoner rights era.

5. List and explain the four amendments to the U.S. Constitution on which most prisoners' claims are based.

6. Explain how the development of rights for female prisoners has differed from that of the rights of male prisoners.

▶ ▶ **In 1871, in the case of** *Ruffin* v. *Commonwealth*, a Virginia judge declared the following: A convicted felon . . . punished by confinement in the penitentiary instead of with death . . . is in a state of penal servitude to the State. He has, as a consequence of his crime, not only forfeited his liberty, but all his personal rights except those which the law in its humanity accords to him. He is for the time being the slave of the State. He is *civiliter mortuus*; and his estate, if he has any, is administered like that of a dead man. The Bill of Rights is a declaration of general principles to govern a society of freemen, and not of convicted felons and men civilly dead.

The judge in *Ruffin* was voicing what had long been believed: that prisoners had no rights. It was this kind of thinking that long supported a "hands-off" approach to prisoners' rights. If inmates were really civilly dead, the federal government and the federal courts certainly had no cause to tell the states how to run their prisons.

The Bill of Rights, which provides criminal defendants with a number of due process rights, and which also forms the basis of a number of inmate rights. What rights should inmates have?

The Hands-Off Doctrine

Under the **hands-off doctrine**, American courts for many decades avoided intervening in prison management. The doctrine was based on two rationales: (1) that under the *separation of powers* inherent in the U.S. Constitution, the judicial branch of government should not interfere with the running of correctional facilities by the executive branch and (2) that judges should leave correctional administration to correctional experts.[1]

San Quentin State Prison in Marin County, California. Opened in 1852, it is one of the state's oldest and best known correctional institutions. Under the hands-off doctrine, American courts long refused to intervene in prison management. When did the hands-off doctrine end?

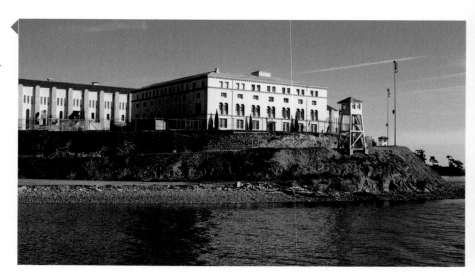

For a very long time in our nation's history, states ran their prisons as they saw fit. Prison inmates were thought of as "nonpersons," and rights pertained only to persons. Pleas from prisoners based on allegations of deprivations of their rights were ignored.

The hands-off doctrine and the philosophy of the prisoner as a slave of the state began to change in the mid-1900s. Public attitudes about punishment versus rehabilitation changed, and more and more people became aware that inmates had *no* rights. As a result, the courts began to scrutinize the correctional enterprise in America.

DECLINE OF THE HANDS-OFF DOCTRINE

The 1941 case of *Ex parte Hull* began a dismantling of the hands-off doctrine. Prior to *Hull*, it had been common for corrections personnel to screen inmate mail, including prisoner petitions for writs of *habeas corpus*. Corrections officials often confiscated the petitions, claiming they were improperly prepared and not fit to submit to court. In *Hull*, the Supreme Court ruled that no state or its officers may interfere with a prisoner's right to apply to a federal court for a writ of *habeas corpus*. Thus, court officials, not corrections officials, have the authority to decide whether such petitions are prepared correctly.

Though this seemed like a small step at the time, it would facilitate a major leap in prisoners' rights. Three years later, in *Coffin* v. *Reichard* (1944) the Sixth Circuit Court of Appeals extended *habeas corpus* hearings to consideration of the conditions of confinement. Even more important, the *Coffin* case was the first in which a federal appellate court ruled that prisoners do not automatically lose their civil rights when in prison.[2] In the words of the Court, a prisoner "retains all the rights of an ordinary citizen except those expressly, or by necessary implication, taken from him by law."

Another important development occurred in 1961, with the Supreme Court's ruling in *Monroe* v. *Pape*. Prior to *Pape*, it was believed that the phrase "under color of state law" in the Civil Rights Act of 1871 meant that a Section 1983 suit (explained in greater detail on page 391) could only involve actions authorized by state law. In *Pape*, however, the Court held that for activities to take place *under color* of state law, they did not have to be *authorized* by state law. The statute, said the Court, had been intended to protect against "misuse of power, possessed by virtue of state law and made possible only because the wrongdoer is clothed with the authority of state law."

Officials "clothed with the authority of state law" seemed to include state corrections officials. Thus, state corrections officials who violated an inmate's constitutional rights while performing their duties could be held liable for their actions in federal court, regardless of whether state law or policy supported those actions.[3]

A third important case establishing inmates' rights to access the courts was *Cooper* v. *Pate* (1964). In *Cooper*, a federal circuit court clarified the *Pape* decision, indicating that prisoners could sue a warden or another correctional official under Title 42 of the U.S. Code, Section 1983, based on the protections of the Civil Rights Act of 1871.

The case of *Holt* v. *Sarver* brought the hands-off era to a close, and opened a new era of prisoners' rights. What were the issues involved in that case?

Commenting on the importance of *Cooper*, one observer noted,

> Just by opening a forum in which prisoners' grievances could be heard, the federal courts destroyed the custodian's absolute power and the prisoners' isolation from the larger society. The litigation itself heightened prisoners' consciousness and politicized them.[4]

With prisoners' access to the courts now established, cases challenging nearly every aspect of corrections were soon filed. The courts, primarily the federal district courts, began to review prisoners' complaints and intervene on prisoners' behalf.

The hands-off era is said to have ended in 1970, when a federal district court, in *Holt* v. *Sarver*, declared the entire Arkansas prison system "so inhumane as to be a violation of the Eighth Amendment bar on cruel and unusual punishment." Robert Sarver, the Arkansas commissioner of corrections, admitted that "the physical facilities at both [prison units named in the suit] were inadequate and in a total state of disrepair that could only be described as deplorable." Additionally, he testified that inmates with trustee status, some of them serving life or long-term sentences, constituted 99 percent of the security force of the state's prison system.

Commissioner Sarver continued, testifying that "trustees sell desirable jobs to prisoners and also traffic in food, liquor, and drugs. Prisoners frequently become intoxicated and unruly. The prisoners sleep in dormitories. Prisoners are frequently attacked and raped in the dormitories, and injuries and deaths have resulted. Sleep and rest are seriously disrupted. No adequate means exist to protect the prisoners from assaults. There is no satisfactory means of keeping guns, knives, and other weapons away from the prison population."

The *Holt* court declared in 1970,

> The obligation . . . to eliminate existing unconstitutionalities does not depend upon what the Legislature may do or upon what the Governor may do. . . . If Arkansas is going to operate a Penitentiary System, it is going to have to be a system that is countenanced by the Constitution of the United States.

Prisoner litigation had brought sad conditions to light, and the court had intervened to institute reforms for the prisoners in Arkansas.

Prisoners' Rights

LEGAL FOUNDATIONS

prisoners' rights

Constitutional guarantees of free speech, religious practice, due process, and other private and personal rights as well as constitutional protections against cruel and unusual punishments made applicable to prison inmates by the federal courts.

Prisoners' rights have four legal foundations: the U.S. Constitution, federal statutes, state constitutions, and state statutes. Most court cases involving prisoners' rights have involved rights claimed under the U.S. Constitution, even though state constitutions generally parallel the U.S. Constitution and sometimes confer additional rights. State legislatures and Congress can also confer additional prisoners' rights.

The U.S. Constitution   The U.S. Constitution is the supreme law of our land. At the heart of any discussion of prisoners' rights lies one question:

What does the Constitution have to say? As scholars began to search the Constitution, they could find no requirement that prisoners give up all of their rights as American citizens (and human beings) after conviction.

It is important to remember, however, that **constitutional rights** are not absolute. Does freedom of speech mean that you have a protected right to stand up in a crowded theater and yell, "Fire"? It does not (at least not unless there *is* a fire). That is because the panic that would follow such an exclamation would probably cause injuries and would needlessly put members of the public at risk of harm. Hence, the courts have held that, although freedom of speech is guaranteed by the Constitution, it is not an absolute right; in other words, there are limits to it (*Schenck* v. *United States*, 1919).

So the question seems to be, which constitutional rights do you keep and which rights do you lose when you are convicted of a criminal offense and become a prisoner of the state? Answering that question has become a job of the courts. The answers are dependent upon the courts' interpretation of the U.S. Constitution, state constitutions, and federal and state laws. Generally speaking, the courts have recognized four legitimate **institutional needs** that justify some restrictions on the constitutional rights of prisoners:

1. maintenance of institutional *order;*
2. maintenance of institutional *security;*
3. *safety* of prison inmates and staff; and
4. *rehabilitation* of inmates.

According to the courts, *order* refers to calm and discipline within the institution, *security* is the control of individuals and objects entering or leaving the institution, *safety* means avoidance of physical harm, and *rehabilitation* refers to practices necessary for the health, well-being, and treatment of inmates.[5]

Federal Statutes   Laws passed by Congress can confer certain rights on inmates in federal prisons. In addition, Congress has passed a number of laws that affect the running of state prisons. The Civil Rights Act of 1871, for example, was enacted after the Civil War to discourage lawless activities by state officials. Section 1983 reads as follows:

> Every person who, under color of any statute, ordinance, regulation, custom, or usage, of any State or Territory, subjects, or causes to be subjected, any citizen of the United States or other person within the jurisdiction thereof to the deprivation of any rights, privileges, or immunities secured by the Constitution and laws, shall be liable to the party injured in an action at law, suit in equity, or other proper proceeding for redress.

This section imposes **civil liability** (but not criminal blame) on any person who deprives another of rights guaranteed by the U.S. Constitution. The Civil Rights Act of 1871 allows state prisoners to challenge conditions of their imprisonment in federal court. Most prisoner suits brought under this act allege deprivation of constitutional rights. Another important piece of legislation is the Civil Rights of Institutionalized Persons Act (CRIPA),[6] which is discussed in more detail in Chapter 12.

constitutional rights
The personal and due process rights guaranteed to individuals by the U.S. Constitution and its amendments, especially the first 10 amendments, known as the Bill of Rights. Constitutional rights are the basis of most inmate rights.

institutional needs
Prison administration interests recognized by the courts as justifying some restrictions on the constitutional rights of prisoners. Those interests are maintenance of institutional *order,* maintenance of institutional *security, safety* of prison inmates and staff, and *rehabilitation* of inmates.

civil liability
A legal obligation to another person to do, pay, or make good something.

A writ of *habeas corpus* is a court order requiring that a prisoner be brought before the court so that the court can determine whether the person is being legally detained. What is required of a state prisoner who wants to bring a *habeas corpus* action in federal court?

State Constitutions   Most state constitutions are patterned after the U.S. Constitution. However, state constitutions tend to be longer and more detailed than the U.S. Constitution and may contain specific provisions regarding corrections. State constitutions generally do not give prisoners more rights than are granted by the U.S. Constitution, except in a few states such as California and Oregon. Inmates in such states may challenge the conditions of their confinement in state court under the state's constitutional provision.

State Statutes   Unlike the federal government, state governments all have inherent police power, which allows them to pass laws to protect the health, safety, and welfare of their citizens. A state legislature can pass statutes to grant specific rights beyond those conferred by the state constitution. Often such legislation specifies duties of corrections officials or standards of treatment for prisoners. Prisoners who can show failure of officials to fulfill state statutory obligations may collect money damages or obtain a court order compelling officials to comply with the law.

MECHANISMS FOR SECURING PRISONERS' RIGHTS

Today, inmates have five ways to legally challenge prison conditions or the practices of corrections officials: (1) a state *habeas corpus* action, (2) a federal *habeas corpus* action after state remedies have been exhausted, (3) a state tort lawsuit, (4) a federal civil rights lawsuit, and (5) a petition for injunctive relief.[7]

writ of *habeas corpus*

An order that directs the person detaining a prisoner to bring him or her before a judge, who will determine the lawfulness of the imprisonment.

Writ of *Habeas Corpus*   A **writ of *habeas corpus*** is an order from a court to produce a prisoner in court so that the court can determine whether the prisoner is being legally detained. *Habeas corpus* is Latin for "you have the body." A prisoner, or someone acting for a prisoner, files a *habeas corpus* petition asking a court to determine the lawfulness of the imprisonment. The petition for the writ is merely a procedural tool. If a writ is issued, it has no bearing on any issues to be reviewed. It only guarantees a hearing on those issues.

Federal and state prisoners may file *habeas corpus* petitions in federal courts. State prisoners must first, however, exhaust available state *habeas corpus* remedies. In 2000, of 11,880 petitions that inmates filed in *federal* courts, 3,870 (33 percent) were *habeas corpus* actions; of 46,371 petitions that inmates filed in *state* courts, 21,345 (46 percent) were *habeas corpus* actions.[8]

tort

A civil wrong, a wrongful act, or a wrongful breach of duty, other than a breach of contract, whether intentional or accidental, from which injury to another occurs.

Tort Action in State Court   State inmates can file a tort action in state court. A **tort** is a civil wrong, a wrongful act, or a wrongful breach of duty, other than a breach of contract, whether intentional or accidental, from which injury to another occurs. In tort actions, inmates commonly claim that a correctional employee, such as the warden or a correctional officer, or the correctional facility itself failed to perform a duty required by law regarding the inmate. Compensation for damages is the most common objective. Tort suits often allege such deficiencies as negligence, gross or wanton negligence, or intentional wrong.

Federal Civil Rights Lawsuit   Federal and state inmates can file suit in federal court alleging civil rights violations by corrections officials. Most of these suits challenge the conditions of confinement, under Section 1983 of the Civil Rights Act of 1871, which is now part of Title 42 of the U.S. Code. Lawsuits may claim that officials have deprived inmates of their constitutional rights, such as adequate medical treatment, protection against excessive force by correctional officers or violence from other inmates, due process in disciplinary hearings, and access to law libraries. According to the Bureau of Justice Statistics, 1 of 10 civil cases filed in U.S. district courts is Section 1983 litigation, as it is commonly called.

When such suits seek monetary damages from federal agents for violation of constitutional rights, they are often referred to as *Bivens* actions, recalling the 1971 case in which the U.S. Supreme Court articulated inmates' entitlement to sue. In subsequent rulings (e.g., *FDIC v. Meyer*, 1994), the Court specified that "a *Bivens* action may only be maintained against an individual," not the federal agency by which he or she is employed, and it declined to extend the damage action authority of *Bivens* to permit suits against private entities operating correctional facilities under federal contract (*Correctional Services Corporation, Petitioner v. John E. Malesko*, 2001).

If inmates are successful in their civil suits, in state or federal courts, the courts can award three types of damages. **Nominal damages** are small amounts of money that may be awarded when inmates have sustained no actual damages, but there is clear evidence that their rights have been violated.

Compensatory damages are payments for actual losses, which may include out-of-pocket expenses the inmate incurred in filing the suit, other forms of monetary or material loss, and pain, suffering, and mental anguish. Some years ago, for example, a federal appeals court sustained an award of $9,300 against a warden and a correctional commissioner. The amount was calculated by awarding each inmate $25 for each day he had spent in solitary confinement (a total of 372 days for all the inmates) under conditions the court found cruel and unusual (*Sostre v. McGinnis*, 1971).

Punitive damages are awarded to punish the wrongdoer when the wrongful act was intentional and malicious or was done with reckless disregard for the rights of the inmate

Request for Injunctive Relief   An **injunction** is a judicial order to do or refrain from doing a particular act. A request for an injunction might claim adverse effects of a health, safety, or sanitation procedure and might involve the entire correctional facility. It is important for anyone working in corrections to realize that a lack of funds cannot justify failure to comply with an injunction (*Smith v. Sullivan*, 1977).

nominal damages

Small amounts of money a court may award when inmates have sustained no actual damages, but there is clear evidence that their rights have been violated.

compensatory damages

Money a court may award as payment for actual losses suffered by a plaintiff, including out-of-pocket expenses incurred in filing the suit, other forms of monetary or material loss, and pain, suffering, and mental anguish.

punitive damages

Money a court may award to punish a wrongdoer when a wrongful act was intentional and malicious or was done with reckless disregard for the rights of the victim.

injunction

A judicial order to do or refrain from doing a particular act.

FIGURE 11-1
Criminal Court Structure

The Criminal Court System   There is a dual court system in the United States; the federal and state court systems coexist (see Figure 11–1). The federal court system is nationwide, with one or more federal courts in each state. These courts coexist with state court systems. Whether a defendant is tried in a federal court or a state court depends on which court has jurisdiction over the particular case.

jurisdiction

The power, right, or authority of a court to interpret and apply the law.

The **jurisdiction** of a court is the power or authority of the court to act with respect to a case before it. The acts involved in the case must have taken place or had an effect in the geographic territory of the court, or a statute must give the court jurisdiction.

District courts are the trial courts of the federal system. They have original jurisdiction over cases charging defendants with violations of federal criminal laws. Each state has at least one United States district court, and some, like New York and California, have as many as four. There are also federal district courts in Puerto Rico, the District of Columbia, and the U.S. territories. There are currently 12 United States courts of appeals, arranged by circuit (11 numbered circuits, a District of Columbia circuit, and one federal circuit—see Table 11–1).

Each state has its own court system. Most state court structures are similar to the federal court structure—with trial courts, intermediate appellate courts, and a top appellate court. In most states, the trial courts are organized by county.

TABLE 11–1	United States Courts of Appeal
Court of appeals	**District courts included in circuit**
Federal Circuit	United States
District of Columbia Circuit	District of Columbia
First Circuit	Maine, Massachusetts, New Hampshire, Rhode Island, and Puerto Rico
Second Circuit	Connecticut, New York, and Vermont
Third Circuit	Delaware, New Jersey, Pennsylvania, and the Virgin Islands
Fourth Circuit	Maryland, North Carolina, South Carolina, Virginia, and West Virginia
Fifth Circuit	Louisiana, Mississippi, and Texas
Sixth Circuit	Kentucky, Michigan, Ohio, and Tennessee
Seventh Circuit	Illinois, Indiana, and Wisconsin
Eighth Circuit	Arkansas, Iowa, Minnesota, Missouri, Nebraska, North Dakota, and South Dakota
Ninth Circuit	Alaska, Arizona, California, Hawaii, Idaho, Montana, Nevada, Oregon, Washington, Guam, and the Northern Mariana Islands
Tenth Circuit	Colorado, Kansas, New Mexico, Oklahoma, Utah, and Wyoming
Eleventh Circuit	Alabama, Florida, and Georgia

Though federal offenses are prosecuted in federal court and state offenses are prosecuted in state courts, the federal courts have supervisory jurisdiction over the administration of criminal justice in the state courts. The U.S. Supreme Court has ruled that constitutional requirements for criminal procedure in federal courts also apply to the states. Violation of these constitutional requirements can be the subject of both state appeals and federal suits by prisoners.

INMATE GRIEVANCE PROCEDURES

Inmate grievance procedures are formal institutional processes for hearing inmate complaints. Grievance procedures, which typically employ internal hearing boards, are the method most frequently used by inmates to enforce the protections afforded to them by law.[9] Most inmate grievances concern discipline, program assignments, medical issues, personal property, and complaints against staff members. Only about 1 in 12 inmate grievances is approved or results in some action being taken by prison administrators to correct the problem.

The creation of formal mechanisms for the hearing of inmate grievances was encouraged by the comptroller general of the United States following the riot at New York's Attica Prison. The comptroller's report, published in 1977,[10] listed a number of reasons for establishing grievance mechanisms, including (1) promoting justice and fairness, (2) providing opportunities for inmates to voice complaints, (3) reducing the number of court cases

Corrections and Technology

by Thomas J. Cowper, New York State Police, Office for Technology

Reflections on the Future

The 21st century promises to be an era of rapid and dynamic change for society and for its public servants. New and amazing technologies are emerging almost daily, bringing with them capabilities for people and organizations that could hardly be imagined even as recently as the last decade of the 20th century. Computers and the Internet are only the tip of a technological iceberg that will emerge over the next few decades and advance at exponential rates. Radical new fields like nanotechnology, genetic engineering, and neurotechnology will give people new and expanded physical and cognitive powers, while fostering smaller, more powerful, and more pervasive computing devices that will be woven directly into the fabric of our lives, our human relationships, and our governmental processes. Wireless networks, wearable computers, and augmented reality systems will allow us to process, retrieve, and transmit information at unprecedented speeds, making it possible for one person to accomplish tomorrow what it takes three people to accomplish today. Biometric identification systems, radio frequency identification (RFID) chips (potentially implantable in people and most products), and data-mining technologies will improve homeland security and help reduce crime in our communities. Artificial intelligence, cybernetics, and robotics will dramatically improve the human-machine interface and accelerate the way people collectively exchange and utilize information.

The technological benefits from these advances, while immense, bring with them dangers and problems as well. The employment of new technologies by government agencies carries with it the tremendous responsibility to do so in a way that does not erode our fundamental constitutional guarantees even as we use it to protect the innocent from criminal predators. In the 21st century the public sector must employ new technologies in creative ways to deter, identify, capture, and incarcerate criminals and terrorists because those same social predators will undoubtedly exploit new technological capabilities to perpetrate age-old and innovative offenses against government institutions and civilians. This technological balancing act between effective use of technology to constrain criminals and restraint in the way public servants use it so as not to undermine civil liberties means that public sector professionals must fully understand the capabilities, implications, and political nuances of technology before they set about procuring it. The balancing act is further complicated as technology becomes more powerful and the complexities of procuring it increase. Missteps in implementing a new and powerful capability because of technological ignorance or naïveté may generate a public backlash that delays or prevents that capability from being used by the government no matter how effective or beneficial to society the technology may be.

Technology, along with becoming exponentially more powerful, is also getting smaller, more user friendly, less expensive, and, therefore, more available to everyone. Surveillance technologies, RFID, biometrics, and wireless communication are becoming commonplace and can be used both for beneficial and malicious purposes. As micro- and nano-technologies reduce the size and detectable signature of these devices, their use by criminals inside correctional institutions is inevitable. Corrections officers and administrators have to be capable not only of using technology to secure the institutions they serve, but they also have to be able to think creatively in order to anticipate how inmates might use new technologies to commit crimes inside their facilities.

At the same time it appears that the American prison population will continue to rise along with the expense of physical incarceration in "brick and mortar" facilities. Like most governmental processes, it is becoming increasingly evident that with the help of emerging technology new and innovative correctional philosophies and methodologies must be conceived and developed so as to maximize the use of taxpayer dollars in keeping dangerous criminals off our streets. Correctional institutions and their methods must become more efficient while remaining highly secure, and there are a number of emerging technologies, used correctly, that may greatly improve correctional efficiencies, reducing the overall number of incarcerated individuals and the number of correctional officers necessary for safe and effective operation.

For example, the Defense Advanced Research Projects Agency (DARPA) augmented cognition program is working to dramatically improve the way humans interact with computers in an effort to (1) enhance human cognitive abilities in stressful operational environments, (2) increase a person's situational and context awareness, and (3) empower one person to do the work of three or more individuals. The U.S. Navy intends to use this kind of advanced technology to reduce staffing levels on future combat ships, allowing today's 300-person vessels to be operated effectively in the future by a crew of 90. Robotics, telepresence, and cybernetic advances may decrease those numbers even further.

Similar efficiencies should be possible within correctional institutions of the future, providing increased facility security and officer safety while lowering the overall cost of correctional services. It cannot be done, however, by forcing Information Age technologies into Industrial Age business models. Emerging technologies bring with them unique and extraordinary capabilities, many of which cannot be realized or even conceived within current organizational mindsets, methodologies, and policies. It is not technology that is the central issue facing correctional services of the future; it is the way correctional professionals think about technology and accept the resulting changes. Over the next decade the exponential increases in technological advancement and the social, political, and cultural turmoil that will result demand that correctional officers and their institutions change, not just their business models and methodologies, but also the way they think about themselves, their inmates, and the public they serve.

Correctional services, a critical component in maintaining a free democracy, must actively participate in the development of technology necessary to create a peaceful and prosperous society. Creation of the right technology programs and systems within correctional facilities for the right reasons; training officers to employ technology correctly, ethically, and legally within the correctional environment; and envisioning and fostering the kind of future correctional system necessary to overcome tomorrow's Information Age criminal justice and social problems are complex and difficult challenges that require today's supervisors, managers, and administrators to be well versed in both progressive correctional methodology and emerging technology applications for the future. It requires knowledge and innovation; visionary leadership coupled with effective managerial insight. The way in which corrections professionals think about technology and how they implement it within correctional systems, structures, and organizations will be a major component of their success or failure in the coming years of the 21st century.

ABOUT THE AUTHOR
Captain Thomas J. Cowper is a 19-year veteran of the New York State Police, with nine years of patrol experience as a trooper and sergeant, including four years as a member of the State Police Mobile Response Team (SWAT). For the last 10 years he has been involved in the procurement, implementation, and management of law enforcement and public safety technologies, serving as the director of Communications for the State Police and currently as associate director for the Statewide Wireless Network project under the State's Office for Technology. Captain Cowper is the treasurer of the Society of Police Futurists International (PFI) and a member of the FBI Futures Working Group, a collaborative partnership between the FBI and PFI to study and strategize about the future of law enforcement. He is a graduate of the FBI National Academy, has a Bachelor of Science degree in Mechanical Engineering Technology from LeTourneau University, and has a master's degree in Public Administration from Marist College. He has been a firearms, defensive tactics, and leadership instructor at the State Police Academy and is a published author and a regular public speaker regarding emerging technologies and law enforcement issues.

Eye On Corrections™

The Future of Prisoner Rights

By Bill Collins

I think that over the last 30 years, litigation and the threat of litigation have probably had the greatest impact on corrections as any other force, and I would say it was a positive impact. There have been some cases where the court involvement has been extraordinarily painful, but the overall impact has been one that has forced positive change.

What I see happening now, and will probably continue to happen for the next few years, is that the threat of being held accountable by a court is diminishing because of a variety of factors. Supreme Court decisions going back 15 years or more have increasingly reduced inmate substantive rights but have discouraged courts from getting involved [as well.]

The passage of the Prison Litigation Reform Act has also cut down on the number of filings. It discourages involvement by the courts and reduces the attorney fees, which discourages private attorneys from getting involved.

There will be fewer cases being brought and fewer courts getting aggressively involved. The positive impact has been that corrections has made huge advances in its professionalism. Standards, policies, and procedures have been universally adopted. [Many feel] that corrections doesn't need court oversight any more and can make advances on its own.

The negative spin is that big organizations, like DOCs, and smaller ones, like jails, when you take away external oversight and accountability, tend not to continue to advance. They tend to slow down and relax their standards. I think we're more likely to see a gradual deterioration of the operation of institutions combined with the fact that legislators can trim corrections budgets and get rid of training for officers and frills for inmates and so on. In years past, if we didn't get that money for training, we could get sued. Now the legislature can say, "I don't think that's going to happen."

I'm a little concerned that we will see an eroding of some of the gains in recent years. Facilities will look better, but we may have some problems developing around operations.

In time we may hear about inmates getting the short end of the stick, and then the pendulum may swing the other way.

There will be some big cases from time to time. The thing I hope corrections agencies can continue to do is look at the human side of what they do. We have increasing amounts of technology, but I hope we don't lose sight of the human side we're dealing with.

filed by inmates, (4) assisting correctional administrators in the identification of institutional problems, and (5) reducing violence.

Formalized inmate grievance procedures are required under the 1977 U.S. Supreme Court ruling of *Jones* v. *North Carolina Prisoners' Labor Union* (discussed later in this chapter). Federal law allows a federal judge to refer a state inmate's lawsuit back to the state correctional system. For such a referral, court precedents require the state correctional agency to have an inmate grievance procedure certified by the U.S.

Inmate lawsuits are common. However, with the advent of more advanced grievance systems, the number of lawsuits drops, because through the grievance system some disputes can be resolved. But we still have lawsuits, and some of them are pretty outlandish. Just because someone files a lawsuit doesn't mean that it ever goes to trial.

We see quite a few filings or attempts at lawsuits on our grooming policy. It's pretty strict, because of our fears of inmates being able to change their appearance and being able to hide contraband in long hair. So male inmates have to have their hair above their collar and above their ears and no facial hair except if there are medical reasons. Males may have a neatly trimmed mustache. Females can have their hair shoulder length.

We get people saying that they have taken a vow of the Nazarite and that having a razor or scissors touch their hair would violate their beliefs. So far they have yet to prevail in court, because we have a genuine security interest. And inmates are always going to challenge issues of confinement, and some of those get pretty outlandish. We had one inmate file a lawsuit because he wanted to wear women's underwear. He did not win.

A couple of years ago we instituted a ban on all tobacco products, because of the fears of secondhand smoke and the cost of our health care. There have been some filings regarding that. They think it's their freedom—pursuit of happiness—and that it's cruel and unusual punishment not to have tobacco products. Those cases haven't gone anywhere yet either.

If a lawsuit is truly frivolous, it won't get to court—the judge will stop them before they get to that. Lawsuits I see without merit? Most of them.

Generally inmates have to exhaust the grievance process before they can file—which is good. It gives them a voice—last year we had more than 49,000 grievances filed by inmates in this system. Of those, about 1,300 were found to have merit, which is a small percentage—but it's still 1,300 cases where something wasn't quite right. And if that's the case, we need to know.

Dina Tyler
Assistant to the Director
Arkansas Department of Correction

Department of Justice. A referral can save the state correctional agency enormous amounts of time and money. Once the federal judge sends the case back to the state, correctional officials do not have to defend themselves in federal court, transport the inmate to and from federal court, or contend with the publicity that can go along with a court case. Hence, inmate grievance procedures are in the best interest of state correctional officials.

Certification of state grievance procedures by the U.S. Department of Justice requires that

1. both inmates and employees of the institution have advisory roles in the development of the procedures;
2. maximum time limits for responses to grievances be established;
3. provisions exist for rapid processing of emergency inmate grievances when undue delay could result in harm to an inmate; and
4. a mechanism exists for review of decisions by a person or committee not under the direct control of the prison in which the grievance originated.[11]

Today, most correctional systems use a three-step process for resolving grievances. First, a staff member or committee in each institution receives complaints, investigates them, and makes decisions. Second, if a prisoner is dissatisfied with that decision, the case may be appealed to the warden. Third, if the prisoner is still dissatisfied, the complaint may be given to the state's commissioner of corrections or the state's corrections board. This three-step procedure satisfies the requirements for U.S. Department of Justice certification.

> How much do you restrict an inmate's right to file a lawsuit when there is a legitimate problem, given the Prisoner Litigation Reform Act? For more information go to Ethical Dilemma 11-1 at http:// www.mhhe. com/schmalleger2.

Ethical Dilemma

CAREER PROFILE

Tammy Waldrop

Inspector   Correctional Facilities   Palm Beach County, Florida

Tammy Waldrop is an inspector with the Palm Beach County (Florida) Sheriff's Office, assigned to Corrections Administration. She has been in the position for almost one year. Quarterly, Tammy inspects all four correctional facilities in Palm Beach County to verify that each one complies with agency, local, state, and American Correctional Association standards. She investigates staff and inmate grievances and works with the Legal Advisors' office to resolve conflicts.

Tammy received her bachelor's degree in criminal justice from Florida Atlantic University in Boca Raton. She remembers that the undergraduate course that influenced her the most was a sociology course titled "Social Conflict." She says, "This course changed my perspective on life and my views on crime. It was the best preparation for my current job. It helped me understand the importance of changing conflict into occasions for problem solving."

In the future, Tammy would like to build on her present career, attend law school, concentrate on corrections law, and work in the Legal Advisors' office.

> " In corrections, the words *care*, *custody*, and *control* are repeatedly stated as your primary tasks. But remember three additional words in your interactions with inmates: *fair*, *firm*, and *consistent*. If you build your officer reputation on this foundation, you will not have any problems. Treat everyone with respect and the respect will come back to you. And never, never lie to an inmate. "

The Prisoner Rights Era (1970–1991)

> The prisoners' rights movement must be understood in the context of a 'fundamental democratization' that has transformed American society since World War II, and particularly since 1960.

Many refer to the era following *Holt* v. *Sarver* (1970) as the *prisoner rights era*. As some have observed, "The prisoners' rights movement must be understood in the context of a 'fundamental democratization' that has transformed American society since World War II, and particularly since 1960."[12] Over the past 40 years, an increasing number of once-marginal groups, including African Americans, Hispanics, gays, the economically disenfranchised, and the physically and mentally challenged, have acquired social recognition and legal rights that were previously unavailable to those outside of the American social mainstream. Seen in this context, the prisoner rights era was but a natural outgrowth of an encompassing social movement that recognized the existence and potential legitimacy of a wide number of group grievances.

Although the phrase *prisoner rights era* might give the impression that prisoners won virtually every case brought during that period, such is not the case. Although prisoners did win some significant court battles, it was the turnaround in legal attitudes toward prisoners that was most remarkable. As we shall see, courts went from practically ignoring prison systems to practically running those systems. It might be more appropriate to refer to the period as the "court involvement era." We will now review some of the most important cases won *and* lost by inmates, presented in order of the constitutional amendments on which they were based.

When we speak of prisoners' rights, we are generally speaking of the rights found in four of the amendments to the U.S. Constitution. Three of these—the First (free expression), Fourth (privacy), and Eighth Amendments (cruel and unusual punishment)—are part of the Bill of Rights (the first ten amendments to the Constitution). The fourth is the Fourteenth Amendment (deprivation of life, liberty, and property). Keep in mind that what we call inmate rights today is largely the result of federal court decisions that have interpreted constitutional guarantees and applied them to prisons and prison conditions. Often such a case sets a **precedent,** serving as an example or authority for future cases. Rulings in cases that find violations of inmate rights must be implemented by the administrators of affected correctional systems and institutions. (See Table 11–2 for more U.S. Supreme Court cases involving prisoner rights.)

precedent

A previous judicial decision that judges should consider in deciding future cases.

FIRST AMENDMENT

> Congress shall make no law respecting an establishment of religion, or prohibiting the free exercise thereof; or abridging the freedom of speech, or of the press; or the right of the people peaceably to assemble, and to petition the government for a redress of grievances.

First Amendment guarantees are important to members of free society. It is no surprise, then, that some of the early prisoners' rights cases concerned those rights. For example, in 1974, in *Pell* v. *Procunier,* four California prison inmates and three journalists challenged the constitutionality of regulation 415.071 of the California Department of Corrections. That regulation specified that "press and other media interviews with specific individual inmates will not be permitted." The rule had been imposed after a violent prison episode that corrections authorities attributed at least in part to a former policy of free face-to-face prisoner-press interviews. Such interviews had apparently resulted in a relatively small number of inmates gaining disproportionate notoriety and influence with other prisoners.

The U.S. Supreme Court held that "in light of the alternative channels of communication that are open to the inmate appellees, [regulation] 415.071 does not constitute a violation of their rights of free speech." Significantly, the Court went on to say, "A prison inmate retains those first amendment rights that are not inconsistent with his status as prisoner or with the *legitimate penological objectives* of the corrections system" (emphasis added). **Legitimate penological objectives** are the permissible aims of a correctional institution. They include the realistic concerns that correctional officers and administrators have for the integrity and security of the correctional institution and the safety of staff and inmates. The *Pell* ruling established a **balancing test** that the Supreme Court would continue to use, weighing the rights claimed by inmates against the legitimate needs of prisons.

legitimate penological objectives

The realistic concerns that correctional officers and administrators have for the integrity and security of the correctional institution and the safety of staff and inmates.

balancing test

A method the U.S. Supreme Court uses to decide prisoners' rights cases, weighing the rights claimed by inmates against the legitimate needs of prisons.

> A prison inmate retains those first amendment rights that are not inconsistent with his status as prisoner or with the legitimate penological objectives of the corrections system.

TABLE 11–2		Selected U.S. Supreme Court Cases Involving Prisoners' Rights
Case name	**Year**	**Decision**
Porter v. *Nussle* (Eighth Amendment)	2002	The "exhaustion requirement" of the Prison Litigation Reform Act of 1995 (PLRA) applies to all inmate suits about prison life, whether they involve general circumstances or particular episodes and whether they allege excessive force or some other wrong.
Booth v. *Churner* (Eighth Amendment)	2001	This case upheld a requirement under the PLRA that state inmates must "exhaust such administrative remedies as are available" before filing a suit over prison conditions.
Lewis v. *Casey*	1996	Earlier cases do not guarantee inmates the wherewithal to file any and every type of legal claim. All that is required is "that they be provided with the tools to attack their sentences."
Sandin v. *Conner* (Fourteenth Amendment)	1995	Perhaps signaling an end to the Prisoner Rights Era, this case rejected the argument that disciplining inmates is a deprivation of constitutional due process rights.
Wilson v. *Seiter* (Eighth Amendment)	1991	This case clarified the totality of conditions notion, saying that some conditions of confinement "in combination" may violate prisoners' rights when each would not do so alone.
Washington v. *Harper* (Eighth Amendment)	1990	An inmate who is a danger to self or others as a result of mental illness may be treated with psychoactive drugs against his or her will.
Turner v. *Safley* (First Amendment)	1987	A Missouri ban on correspondence between inmates was upheld as "reasonably related to legitimate penological interests."
O'Lone v. *Estate of Shabazz* (First Amendment)	1987	An inmate's right to practice religion was not violated by prison officials who refused to alter his work schedule so that he could attend Friday afternoon services.
Whitley v. *Albers* (Eighth Amendment)	1986	The shooting and wounding of an inmate was not a violation of that inmate's rights, since "the shooting was part and parcel of a good-faith effort to restore prison security."
Ponte v. *Real*	1985	Inmates have certain rights in disciplinary hearings.
Hudson v. *Palmer* (Fourth Amendment)	1984	A prisoner has no reasonable expectation of privacy in his prison cell that entitles him to protections against "unreasonable searches."
Block v. *Rutherford* (First Amendment)	1984	State regulations may prohibit inmate union meetings and use of mail to deliver union information within the prison. Prisoners do not have a right to be present during searches of cells.
Rhodes v. *Chapman* (Eighth Amendment)	1981	Double-celling of inmates is not cruel and unusual punishment unless it involves the wanton and unnecessary infliction of pain or conditions grossly disproportionate to the severity of the crime committed.
Cooper v. *Morin*	1980	Neither inconvenience nor cost is an acceptable excuse for treating female inmates differently from male inmates.
Jones v. *North Carolina Prisoners' Labor Union, Inc.* (First Amendment)	1977	Inmates have no inherent right to publish newspapers or newsletters for use by other inmates.
Bounds v. *Smith*	1977	This case resulted in the creation of law libraries in many prisons.
Estelle v. *Gamble* (Eighth Amendment)	1976	Prison officials have a duty to provide proper inmate medical care.
Wolff v. *McDonnell* (Fourteenth Amendment)	1974	Sanctions cannot be levied against inmates without appropriate due process.
Procunier v. *Martinez* (First Amendment)	1974	Censorship of inmate mail is acceptable only when necessary to protect legitimate governmental interests.

continued on next page

TABLE 11–2	Selected U.S. Supreme Court Cases Involving Prisoners' Rights—*concluded*		
Case name	**Year**	**Decision**	
Pell v. *Procunier* (First Amendment)	1974	Inmates retain First Amendment rights that are not inconsistent with their status as prisoners or with the legitimate penological objectives of the corrections system.	
Cruz v. *Beto* (First Amendment)	1972	Inmates have to be given a "reasonable opportunity" to pursue their religious faiths. Also, visits can be banned if such visits constitute threats to security.	
Johnson v. *Avery*	1968	Inmates have a right to consult "jailhouse lawyers" when trained legal assistance is not available.	
Monroe v. *Pape*	1961	Individuals deprived of their rights by state officers acting under color of state law have a right to bring action in federal court.	

Freedom of Speech and Expression   Visits to inmates by friends and loved ones are forms of expression. But prison visits are not an absolute right. In *Cruz* v. *Beto* (1972), the Supreme Court ruled that all visits can be banned if they threaten security. Although *Cruz* involved short-term confinement facilities, the ruling has also been applied to prisons.

Another form of expression is correspondence. As a result of various court cases, prison officials can (and generally do) impose restrictions on inmate mail. Inmates receive mail, not directly from the hands of postal carriers, but from correctional officers. They place their outgoing mail, not in U.S. Postal Service mailboxes, but in containers provided by the correctional institution.

Corrections officials often read inmate mail—both incoming and outgoing—in an effort to uncover escape plans. Reading inmate mail, however, is different from censoring it. In 1974, in *Procunier* v. *Martinez,* the U.S. Supreme Court held that the censoring of inmate mail is acceptable only when necessary to protect legitimate government interests. The case turned upon First Amendment guarantees of free speech.

Under a 1979 federal appeals court decision, in *McNamara* v. *Moody,* prison officials may not prohibit inmates from writing vulgar letters or those that make disparaging remarks about the prison staff. Similarly, while correctional administrators have a legitimate interest in curbing inmates' deviant sexual behavior, courts have held that viewing nudity is not deviant sexual behavior. Hence, prison officials may not ban mailed nude pictures of inmates' wives or girlfriends (*Peppering* v. *Crist,* 1981). Nor may they prevent inmates from receiving, by mail direct from publishers, publications depicting nudity unless those publications depict deviant sexual behavior (*Mallery* v. *Lewis,* 1983).

Inmate rights are not absolute, but are limited by legitimate penological objectives. What does the phrase "legitimate penological objectives" mean in this context?

In 1989, in the case of *Thornburgh* v. *Abbott*, in an effort to clear up questions raised by lower court rulings concerning mailed publications, the U.S. Supreme Court ruled as follows:

> Publications which may be rejected by a warden include but are not limited to publications which meet one of the following criteria: (1) it depicts or describes procedures for the construction or use of weapons, ammunition, bombs, or incendiary devices; (2) it depicts, encourages or describes methods of escape from correctional facilities or contains blueprints, drawings, or similar descriptions of Bureau of Prisons institutions; (3) it depicts or describes procedures for the brewing of alcoholic beverages or the manufacture of drugs; (4) it is written in code; (5) it depicts, describes, or encourages activities which may lead to the use of physical violence or group disruption; (6) it encourages or instructs in the commission of criminal activities; (7) it is sexually explicit material which by its nature or content poses a threat to the security, good order, or discipline of the institution or facilitates criminal activity.

Prison officials have not lost every mail case. In the case of *Turner* v. *Safley* (1987), for example, the Supreme Court upheld a Missouri ban on correspondence among inmates. Such a regulation is valid, the Court said, if it is "reasonably related to legitimate penological interests." *Turner* established that officials had to show only that a regulation was reasonably *related* to a legitimate penological interest. No clear-cut damage to legitimate penological interests had to be shown.

The U.S. Supreme Court sided with corrections officials in its 1977 decision in *Jones* v. *North Carolina Prisoners' Labor Union, Inc.* In *Jones*, the Court upheld regulations established by the North Carolina Department of Correction that prohibited prisoners from soliciting other inmates to join the union and barred union meetings and bulk mailings concerning the union from outside sources. Citing *Pell* v. *Procunier*, the Court went on to say, "The prohibition on inmate-to-inmate solicitation does not unduly abridge inmates' free speech rights. If the prison officials are otherwise entitled to control organized union activity within the confines of a prison, the solicitation ban is not impermissible under the First Amendment, for such a prohibition is both reasonable and necessary."

Freedom of Religion   Lawsuits involving religious practices in prison have been numerous for at least 40 years. In 1962, for example, in *Fulwood* v. *Clemmer,* the court of appeals for the District of Columbia ruled that the Black Muslim faith must be recognized as a religion and held that officials may not restrict members of that faith from holding services.

In 1970, the U.S. Supreme Court refused to hear an appeal from inmate Jack Gittlemacker, who wanted the state of Pennsylvania to provide him with a clergyman of his

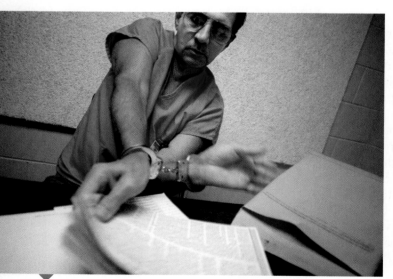

Inmates have limited rights to send and receive mail. Restrictions on inmates' mail focus on maintaining institutional security. Judicial interpretations of which amendment have led to inmates' rights to send and receive mail?

faith. The court held that although states must give inmates the opportunity to practice their religions, they are not required to provide clergy for that purpose.

In *Cruz* v. *Beto* (mentioned earlier), the Supreme Court also decided that inmates had to be given a "reasonable opportunity" to pursue their religious faiths. Later federal court decisions expanded this decision, requiring officials to provide such a "reasonable opportunity" even to inmates whose religious faiths were not traditional.

In 1975, the U.S. Court of Appeals for the Second Circuit ruled in *Kahane* v. *Carlson* that an Orthodox Jewish inmate has the right to a kosher diet unless the government can show good cause for not providing it. Similarly, the courts have held that "Muslims' request for one full-course pork-free meal once a day and coffee three times daily is essentially a plea for a modest degree of official deference to their religious obligations" (*Barnett* v. *Rodgers*, 1969).

On the other hand, courts have determined that some inmate religious demands need not be met. In the 1986 case *Udey* v. *Kastner*, for example, Muslim prisoners had requested raw milk, distilled water, and organic fruits, juices, vegetables, and meats. The special diet was so costly that a federal court allowed the prison to deny the inmates' request.

In 1986, a federal court of appeals considered the appeal of Herbert Dettmer, an inmate at Powhatan Correctional Center in Virginia. Beginning in 1982, Dettmer had studied witchcraft through a correspondence course provided by the Church of Wicca. Within a year, he was holding private ceremonies for meditation as described in the course. Dettmer decided that he needed certain items to aid him in these ceremonies. Those items included a white robe with a hood, sea salt or sulfur to draw a protective circle on the floor around him, and candles and incense to focus his thoughts. Late in 1983, Dettmer requested permission to order the items he felt he needed for meditating. The prison property officer refused permission because the prison rules did not list the items as "authorized personal property." The Supreme Court concluded that "the security officer's concern about inmates' unsupervised possession of candles, salt, and incense is reasonable."

In *O'Lone* v. *Estate of Shabazz* (1987), the U.S. Supreme Court found that a Muslim inmate's right to practice religion was *not* violated by prison officials who refused to alter his work schedule so that he could attend Friday afternoon services. The Court concluded that "even where claims are made under the First Amendment, this Court will not substitute its judgment on difficult and sensitive matters of institutional administration for the determinations of those charged with the formidable task of running a prison."

FOURTH AMENDMENT

The right of the people to be secure in their persons, houses, papers, and effects, against unreasonable searches and seizures, shall not be violated, and no Warrants shall issue, but upon probable cause, supported by Oath or affirmation, and particularly describing the place to be searched, and the persons or things to be seized.

Correctional officers preparing for a cell search at Rikers Island Jail in New York city. One of the officers is carrying an electric stun shield for protection from aggressive inmates. Prisoners do not retain the right to privacy in their cells or possessions because institutional interests of safety and security supersede constitutional guarantees of privacy. Under which amendment to the Constitution falls the right to be free from unreasonable searches and seizures?

The right to privacy is at the heart of the Fourth Amendment. Clearly, unreasonable searches without warrants are unconstitutional. Does this mean that an inmate has a right to privacy in his or her cell? When is it reasonable to search a cell without a warrant? Some suggest that the needs of institutional security prohibit privacy for inmates. Others argue that a prison cell is the equivalent of an inmate's house. Over the years, the courts have been fairly consistent in deciding that the privacy rights implied in this amendment must be greatly reduced in prisons to maintain institutional security.

In *United States* v. *Hitchcock* (1972), an inmate claimed that his Fourth Amendment rights had been violated by a warrantless search and seizure of documents in his prison cell. Previously, courts had generally held that "constitutionally protected" places—such as homes, motel rooms, safe-deposit boxes, and certain places of business—could not be searched without a warrant. In *Hitchcock*, however, the U.S. Court of Appeals for the Ninth Circuit created a new standard: "first, that a person have exhibited an actual (subjective) expectation of privacy and second, that the expectation be one that society is prepared to recognize as reasonable." The court concluded that, although Hitchcock plainly expected to keep his documents private, his expectation was not reasonable. In the words of the court,

> [It] is obvious that a jail shares none of the attributes of privacy of a home, an automobile, an office, or a hotel room. In prison, official surveillance has traditionally been the order of the day. . . . [Hence], we do not feel that it is reasonable for a prisoner to consider his cell private.

In *Hudson* v. *Palmer* (1984), a Virginia inmate claimed a correctional officer had unreasonably destroyed some of his permitted personal property during a search of his cell. The inmate also claimed that under the Fourth

My name is Brian Pierce. I'm an ex-con.

Let me tell you about myself. I grew up in a small southern Minnesota river town. In an effort to bring our family closer together, my parents purchased a small family-run tourist business they hoped we could eventually run as a family. My parents have always been hard workers and Christians. I am not sure what got me started really, but by the time I was 14 I was using drugs heavily and starting to spin the revolving door of Minnesota's illustrious correctional system.

First, I was court-ordered into a drug treatment center called the Cannon Valley Center in Cannon Falls, Minnesota. From there I went to a halfway house in Winona named the East House. When the county ran out of funding, they told me I could leave, despite the fact that the counselors did not think I was ready. Not long after getting home I was on the way to the Minnesota Correctional Facility at Red Wing, the end of the line for juveniles in Minnesota.

When I turned 18, I was moving too fast to slow down and was soon on my way to the Minnesota Correctional Facility at St. Cloud. I was sentenced to 38 months for third-degree burglary and received two shorter sentences that ran concurrently for theft charges. Under Minnesota's guidelines, I had to serve two-thirds of that sentence inside and the remaining one-third on parole.

St. Cloud is relatively old and made predominately out of dark gray granite. The wall is solid granite and somewhere around 20 feet high and several feet thick. It encompasses over 50 acres, including several cell houses, factories, maintenance facilities, and a yard for recreation. There are armed guard towers spaced evenly around the top of the wall.

Like most of my friends there, I got out and quickly got back into the same old routine. An Olmstead County judge gave me the option of pleading guilty to possession of a controlled substance but getting a stay of adjudication pursuant to Minnesota Statute Section 152.18 and being sentenced to treatment rather than a prison term. If I completed the recommended treatment, follow-up, and after-care, the charge would not appear on my record. Although it sounded good, I had already been in prison once and thought I would screw it up in the treatment program and end up doing the time anyway. I asked to have my sentence executed.

A few months after being released from St. Cloud for the second time in four years, I jumped my parole and began wandering around the country with a group of misfits selling Dunn-EZ, a homemade chemical cleaner, to small businesses. Eventually, we ended up in Atlanta, Georgia, where I met my wife. She was a single mother with two young boys and was as wild as I was. Together, my wife, the boys, and I traveled the country treading water for the next several months until we found ourselves in the Lowndes County, Georgia, jail for credit card fraud. It was the most miserable time I have ever had in jail—first, because the woman I loved was in with me and, second, because the conditions were unbelievable. I slept on the floor of a very small one-man cell with two other guys. At night the guards would come by and for a Little Debbie snack or two, they would sell you a full bottle of Nyquil. One of my cell mates would drink it and get high.

With the help of my parents, my new wife and I rode the Greyhound back to Minnesota. I had to finish up about 30 days' worth of my last Minnesota sentence so that my parole would expire. Because the time left on my sentence was so short, Minnesota refused to extradite me from Georgia for the parole violation (leaving the state) but was ready and willing to incarcerate me for every day I had coming if I returned to Minnesota.

Once released and working odd jobs, I enrolled in the University of Minnesota, Duluth. I received my B.A. *magna cum laude* in criminology, with a minor in psychology, almost four years later. Graduating from college felt so unbelievably good to me. I was energized and committed to going on to law school. I applied to the University of Minnesota's law school, where I received my Juris Doctorate *cum laude*, May 10, 1997. Midway through my first year I hooked up with a law professor interested in computers, as I was. Together we created the Human Rights Library on the World Wide Web.

I completed a one-year judicial clerkship with a judge on the Court of Appeals, and I am currently clerking for my second year with the Chief Judge of the Court of Appeals. In addition, I develop Websites for law firms and nonprofit human-rights organizations, and I am writing a book. I also do public speaking about drugs, crime, corrections, and rehabilitation.

—Brian Pierce

A prisoner has no reasonable expectation of privacy in his prison cell entitling him to the protection of the Fourth Amendment against unreasonable searches.

Amendment, the cell search was illegal. Echoing *Hitchcock*, the U.S. Supreme Court ruled that "a prisoner has no reasonable expectation of privacy in his prison cell entitling him to the protection of the Fourth Amendment against unreasonable searches." Similarly, in *Block* v. *Rutherford* (1984), the Court ruled that prisoners do not have the right to be present during searches of their cells.

In 1985, the Ninth Circuit Court of Appeals decided a case involving inmates at San Quentin State Prison (*Grummett* v. *Rushen*). The inmates had brought a class action lawsuit against prison administrators, objecting to the policy of allowing female correctional officers to view nude or partly clothed male inmates. Women officers, complained the inmates, could see male inmates while they were dressing, showering, being strip-searched, or using toilet facilities. Such viewing, said the inmates, violated privacy rights guaranteed by the U.S. Constitution.

At the time of the suit, approximately 113 of the 720 correctional officers at San Quentin were female. Both female and male correctional officers were assigned to patrol the cell block tiers and gun rails. Both were also assigned to supervise showering from the tiers and from the gun rails, but only male officers were permitted to accompany inmates to the shower cells and lock them inside to disrobe and shower. Female officers were allowed to conduct pat-down searches that included the groin area.

The court found that prison officials had "struck an acceptable balance among the inmates' privacy interests, the institution's security requirements, and the female guards' employment rights." According to the court,

> The female guards are restricted in their contact with the inmates, and the record clearly demonstrates that at all times they have conducted themselves in a professional manner, and have treated the inmates with respect and dignity. . . . Routine pat-down searches, which include the groin area, and which are otherwise justified by security needs, do not violate the Fourteenth Amendment because a correctional officer of the opposite gender conducts such a search.

EIGHTH AMENDMENT

> Excessive bail shall not be required, nor excessive fines imposed, nor cruel and unusual punishments inflicted.

Many prisoners' rights cases turn upon the issue of **cruel and unusual punishment**. Defining such punishment is not easy. A working definition, however, might be "punishments that are grossly disproportionate to the offense as well as those that transgress today's broad and idealistic concepts of dignity, civilized standards, humanity, and decency."[13] Cases concerning constitutional prohibition of cruel and unusual punishment have centered on prisoners' need for decent conditions of confinement. In one case, *Ruiz* v. *Estelle* (1980), the conditions of confinement in the Texas prison system were found unconstitutional, and a **consent decree** was imposed on the system. Inmate rights cases involving the Eighth Amendment cover areas as diverse as medical care, prison conditions, physical insecurity, psychological stress, and capital punishment.

cruel and unusual punishment
A penalty that is grossly disproportionate to the offense or that violates today's broad and idealistic concepts of dignity, civilized standards, humanity, and decency (*Estelle* v. *Gamble,* 1976, and *Hutto* v. *Finney,* 1978). In the area of capital punishment, cruel and unusual punishments are those that involve torture, a lingering death, or unnecessary pain.

consent decree
A written compact, sanctioned by a court, between parties in a civil case, specifying how disagreements between them are to be resolved.

A Newark, N.J., prison inmate takes tuberculosis medication as a nurse watches. A number of Eighth Amendment cases have established that prison officials have a duty to provide adequate medical care to inmates in their charge. How does the concept of "deliberate indifference" relate to that requirement?

Medical Care   The right to adequate medical care was one of the issues in *Holt* v. *Sarver* (1970), a case in which the Arkansas prison system was declared inhumane and in violation of the Eighth Amendment ban on cruel and unusual punishment.

In one case, medical personnel in state prisons had given inmates injections of apomorphine without their consent, in a program of "aversive stimuli." The drug caused vomiting, which lasted from 15 minutes to an hour. The state justified it as "Pavlovian conditioning." The federal courts, however, soon prohibited the practice (*Knecht* v. *Gillman*, 1973).

Another decision, that of *Estelle* v. *Gamble* (1976), spelled out the duty of prison officials to provide inmates with medical care. The Court held that prison officials could not lawfully demonstrate **deliberate indifference** to the medical needs of prisoners. In the words of the court, "Deliberate indifference to serious medical needs of prisoners constitutes the 'unnecessary and wanton infliction of pain' proscribed by the Eighth Amendment." A serious medical condition is one that "causes pain, discomfort, or threat to good health" (*Rufo* v. *Inmates of Suffolk County Jail*, 1992). The mental health needs of prisoners are governed by the same constitutional standard of deliberate indifference as those described in court opinions dealing with the physical health of inmates.[14]

deliberate indifference
Intentional and willful indifference. Within the field of correctional practice, the term refers to calculated inattention to unconstitutional conditions of confinement.

Prison Conditions   The 1976 federal court case of *Pugh* v. *Locke* introduced the **totality of conditions** standard. That standard, said the court, is to be used in evaluating whether prison conditions are cruel and unusual. The *Pugh* court held that "prison conditions [in Alabama] are so debilitating that they necessarily deprive inmates of any opportunity to rehabilitate themselves or even maintain skills already possessed." The totality-of-conditions approach was also applied in a 1977 federal case, *Battle* v. *Anderson*, in which officials in overcrowded Oklahoma prisons had forced inmates to sleep in garages, barbershops, libraries, and stairwells. Oklahoma prison administrators were found to be in violation of the cruel and unusual punishment clause of the U.S. Constitution.

totality of conditions
A standard to be used in evaluating whether prison conditions are cruel and unusual.

The Eighth Amendment's prohibition of cruel and unusual punishment has been tied to prisoners' need for decent conditions of confinement. In determining if conditions such as overcrowding and inadequate diet constitute a denial of such protection, courts have used the concept of totality of conditions. What is meant by the *totality of conditions?*

The U.S. Supreme Court ruled on the use of solitary confinement in *Hutto* v. *Finney* (1978). The Court held that confinement in Arkansas's segregation (solitary-confinement) cells for more than 30 days was cruel and unusual punishment. It then went on to exhort lower courts to consider the totality of the conditions of confinement in future Eighth Amendment cases. Where appropriate, it said, a court should specify the changes needed to remedy the constitutional violation.

In the 1991 case of *Wilson* v. *Seiter*, the U.S. Supreme Court clarified the totality-of-conditions standard. The Court noted,

Some conditions of confinement may establish an Eighth Amendment violation "in combination" when each would not do so alone, but only when they have a mutually enforcing effect that produces the deprivation of a single, identifiable human need such as food, warmth, or exercise—for example, a low cell temperature at night combined with a failure to issue blankets. . . . To say that some prison conditions may interact in this fashion is a far cry from saying that all prison conditions are a seamless web for Eighth Amendment purposes. Nothing so [shapeless] as "overall conditions" can rise to the level of cruel and unusual punishment when no specific deprivation of a single human need exists.

Several rulings have addressed inmate claims that overcrowding was cruel and unusual punishment. A U.S. Supreme Court case, *Rhodes* v. *Chapman* (1981), decided the issue of double-celling (housing two inmates in a cell designed for one) in long-term correctional facilities. In response to rising prison populations, Ohio authorities had begun double-celling. There was no evidence that Ohio authorities had wantonly inflicted pain through the practice, and double-celling had not resulted in food deprivation, a lower quality of medical care, or a decrease in sanitation standards. For those reasons, the Court denied the inmates' claims.

In *Rhodes*, the Court also emphasized that the Eighth Amendment prohibition of cruel and unusual punishment is a fluid concept that "must draw its meaning from the evolving standards of decency that mark the progress of a maturing society." In other words, what is considered cruel and unusual changes as society evolves.

In 1982, the U.S. Court of Appeals for the Seventh Circuit ruled, in *Smith* v. *Fairman*, that double-celling in a short-term facility (a jail) was not cruel and unusual punishment. The court said that government officials did not intend to punish inmates by double-celling. The double-celling was innocent overcrowding required by circumstances.

Many conditions of confinement that violate prisoners' Eighth Amendment rights can be remedied by changes in prison rules, by special training for correctional personnel, or by educational programs for prisoners. The remedies can be implemented through everyday administrative policies in the prison, once prisoners' court petitions have brought violations to light. Relief of overcrowding, however, is not always within the power of prison administrators. Prison officials have little control over the sizes of their prisons or the numbers of inmates the courts assign to them. New prison facilities are expensive and take time to build.

FOURTEENTH AMENDMENT

> . . . No State shall make or enforce any law which shall abridge the privileges or immunities of citizens of the United States; nor shall any State deprive any person of life, liberty, or property, without due process of law; nor deny to any person within its jurisdiction the equal protection of the laws.

When the Constitution and the Bill of Rights became law, the people of many states thought the document applied only to federal courts and to federal law. This attitude prevailed at least until the end of the Civil War. After the war, to clarify the status of the newly freed slaves and to apply the Bill of Rights to state actions, the Fourteenth Amendment was passed. The just-quoted portion of the Fourteenth Amendment is relevant to our discussion.

Most cases involving prisoners' rights and the Fourteenth Amendment deal with issues of **due process.** Due process requires that laws and legal procedures be reasonable and that they be applied fairly and equally. The right to due process is a right to be fairly heard before being deprived of life or liberty.

due process
A right guaranteed by the Fifth, Sixth, and Fourteenth Amendments to the U.S. Constitution and generally understood, in legal contexts, to mean the expected course of legal proceedings according to the rules and forms established for the protection of persons' rights.

By 1987, long after the hands-off doctrine had eroded, U.S. Supreme Court Justice Sandra Day O'Connor summarized the thrust of earlier opinions, holding that "prison walls do not form a barrier separating prison inmates from the protections of the Constitution" (*Turner* v. *Safley*). Without access to the courts, inmates have no due process opportunities.

> Prison walls do not form a barrier separating prison inmates from the protections of the Constitution.

To bring their cases to court, however, prisoners need access to legal materials, and many of them need legal assistance. What if one inmate understands how to file cases with the court, but a second inmate does not? Does the second inmate have a right to enlist the aid of the first? "Yes," said the U.S. Supreme Court in *Johnson* v. *Avery* (1968). Inmates have a right to consult "jailhouse lawyers" (other inmates knowledgeable in the law) when trained legal advisers are not available.

The case of *Wolff* v. *McDonnell* (1974) expanded the concept of due process by applying it to disciplinary actions within prisons. Prior to *Wolff*, prison administrators had the discretion to discipline inmates who broke prison rules. Disciplinary procedures were often tied to vague or nonexistent rules of conduct and were exercised without challenge. A prisoner might be assigned to solitary confinement or might have good-time credits reduced because of misconduct. Because the prisoner was physically confined and lacked outside communication, there was no opportunity for the prisoner to challenge the charge. The *Wolff* court concluded that sanctions (disciplinary actions) could not be levied against inmates without appropriate due process, saying,

> [The state of Nebraska] asserts that the procedure for disciplining prison inmates for serious misconduct is a matter of policy raising no constitutional issue. If the position implies that prisoners in state institutions are wholly without the protection of the Constitution and the Due Process Clause, it is plainly untenable. Lawful imprisonment necessarily makes unavailable many rights and privileges of the ordinary citizen, a retraction justified by the consideration underlying our penal system. . . . But though his rights may be diminished by the needs and exigencies of the institutional environment, a prisoner is not wholly stripped of constitutional protections when he is imprisoned for a crime.

The *Wolff* Court imposed minimal due process requirements on prison disciplinary proceedings that could lead to solitary confinement or reduction of good-time credits. The requirements included (1) advance notice by means of a written statement of the claimed violation, (2) a written statement by an impartial fact finder of the evidence relied on and the reasons for imposing punishment, and (3) an opportunity to testify and call witnesses unless the fact finder concluded such proceedings would undermine institutional security.

In 1976, inmates lost three due process appeals. First, in *Baxter* v. *Palmigiano*, the Supreme Court decided that due process for an inmate in a disciplinary hearing does not include a right to counsel, even when the consequences are potentially "serious." In a second opinion issued that year (*Meacham* v. *Fano*), the Court held that prisoners have no right to be in any particular prison and therefore have no due process protections before being transferred from one prison to another. A third case (*Stone* v. *Powell*) denied prisoners the right in most instances to seek federal review of state court Fourth Amendment search-and-seizure decisions.

Inmates' right to legal materials was formally recognized in 1977, in the U.S. Supreme Court decision in *Bounds* v. *Smith*. In *Bounds* the Court held that

> The fundamental constitutional right of access to the courts requires prison authorities to assist inmates in the preparation and filing of meaningful legal papers by providing prisoners with adequate law libraries or adequate assistance from persons trained in the law.

As a result of the *Bounds* decision, law libraries were created in prisons across the nation.

As we saw in Chapter 9, one challenge facing corrections personnel is to find safe, humane ways to manage inmate populations. Inmates often have grievances regarding conditions of confinement or disciplinary actions for infractions. Those grievances must be dealt with to maintain the safety and security of the institution. The Supreme Court's decision in *Jones* v. *North Carolina Prisoners' Labor Union, Inc.* (1977) required prisons to establish and maintain formal opportunities for the airing of inmate grievances. *Ponte* v. *Real* (1985) required prison officials to explain to inmates why their requests to have witnesses appear on their behalf at disciplinary hearings were denied.

The due process clause protects against unlawful deprivation of life or liberty. When a prisoner sued for damages for injuries (*Daniels* v. *Williams*, 1986), the Supreme Court ruled that prisoners could sue for damages in federal court only if officials had inflicted injury intentionally. According to the Court, "The due process clause is simply not implicated by a negligent act of an official causing unintended loss or injury to life, liberty, or property."

A 2001 ruling by a panel of federal judges in the case of *Gerber* v. *Hickman* addressed a unique claim of unlawful deprivation of life. Gerber wanted to impregnate his wife. He was, however, serving a life sentence in a California Department of Corrections (CDC) prison, and CDC regulations prohibit conjugal visits for life-term prisoners. Consequently, the Gerbers could not employ the usual method for creating the child they desire.

Undeterred, Gerber sought permission to artificially inseminate his wife. CDC officials denied his request, citing the facts that (1) impregnating his wife was not medically necessary for Gerber's physical well-being and (2) Gerber had failed to show that denial of the request would violate his constitutional rights.

In a civil suit, however, Gerber alleged that the CDC regulation violated the due process clause by denying him his constitutional right to procreate. On a defendant's motion, the suit was dismissed in federal district court. Gerber appealed to the U.S. Court of Appeals for the Ninth Circuit where a three-judge panel initially held "that the right to procreate survives incarceration." The panel reversed the district court's dismissal and

Inmates must be allowed access to the courts and assistance in preparing their cases. Most states stock law libraries in each correctional institution. Under which clause of the Fourteenth Amendment does inmates' access to the courts fall?

reinstated Gerber's claim, mandating further review of the case. Upon review, however, the full Ninth U.S. Circuit Court of Appeals ruled that prison inmates do not have a constitutional right to fatherhood. The appellate court's majority opinion cited the 1984 U.S. Supreme Court case of *Hudson* v. *Palmer* (mentioned earlier in this chapter), which held that "while persons imprisoned . . . enjoy many protections of the Constitution, it is also clear that imprisonment carries with it the . . . loss of many significant rights."

As we have seen, federal and state inmates can file suits in federal court alleging civil rights violations by corrections officials. In 1988, the U.S. Supreme Court (in *West* v. *Atkins*) decided that private citizens who contracted to do work for prisons could be sued for civil rights violations against inmates. The Court found that such contractors were acting "under color of state law," as required by Section 1983 of the Civil Rights Act of 1871.

As a result of Supreme Court decisions, most prisons now have rules that provide for necessary due process when prisoners appear before disciplinary committees. The makeup of disciplinary committees varies among institutions. The committees may include both inmates and free citizens.

END OF THE PRISONER RIGHTS ERA

By the late 1980s, the prisoner rights era was drawing to a close. Following a change in the composition of the Supreme Court, the justices sitting on the Court had become less sympathetic to prisoners' civil rights claims. As discussed earlier, the 1986 case of *Daniels* v. *Williams* helped establish the notion that due process requirements were intended to prevent abuses of power by correctional officials, not to protect against mere carelessness. Further, judicial and legislative officials began to realize that inmates frequently abused what had previously been seen as their right of access to the courts. As state costs of defending against **frivolous lawsuits** by inmates began to grow, federal courts began to take a new look at prisoners' rights.

frivolous lawsuits
Lawsuits with no foundation in fact. They are generally brought for publicity, political, or other reasons not related to law.

Examples of abuse of the court system by prison inmates abound. One inmate sued the state of Florida because he got only one bread roll with dinner. He sued two more times because he did not get a salad with lunch and because prison-provided TV dinners did not come with drinks. He sued yet again because his cell was not equipped with a television. Another inmate claimed prison officials were denying him freedom of religion. His religion, he said, required him to attend prison chapel services in the nude. Still another inmate, afraid that he could get pregnant through homosexual relations, sued because prison officials would not give him birth control pills.

As early as 1977, the U.S. Supreme Court refused to hear an appeal from Henry William Theriault, founder of the Church of the New Song (or CONS).[15] Theriault, an inmate at the federal penitentiary in Atlanta, had a mail-order divinity degree. Members of CONS celebrated communion every Friday night. They claimed that prison officials must supply them with steak and Harvey's Bristol Cream sherry for the practice. Although "Bishop Theriault" admitted that he had originally created CONS to mock other religions, he claimed that he became a serious believer as the religion developed and acquired more followers. The U.S. Supreme Court dismissed that argument and held that the First Amendment does not protect so-called religions that are obvious shams.

The Cases   In *Wilson* v. *Seiter* (1991), the U.S. Supreme Court again sided with prison officials in a way uncharacteristic of the previous two decades. In *Wilson*, the Court found that overcrowding, excessive noise, insufficient locker space, and similar conditions did not violate the Constitution if the intent of prison officials was not malicious. The Court ruled that the actions of officials did not meet the "deliberate indifference" standard defined in *Estelle* v. *Gamble* (1976).

After *Wilson*, inmates won very few new cases. The courts either reversed themselves or tightened the conditions under which inmates could win favorable decisions. Decisions supporting freedom of religion had been among the earliest and most complete victories during the prisoner rights era. Even in that area, however, things began to change. The courts held that crucifixes and rosaries could legally be denied to inmates because of their possible use as weapons (*Mark* v. *Nix*, 1993, and *Escobar* v. *Landwehr*, 1993). Although some jurisdictions had previously allowed certain Native American religious items within prisons (*Sample* v. *Borg*, 1987), the courts now ruled that prohibiting ceremonial pipes, medicine bags, and eagle claws did *not* violate the First Amendment rights of Native American inmates (*Bettis* v. *Delo*, 1994).

In the 1992 Supreme Court case of *Hudson* v. *McMillan*, the "deliberate indifference" standard was interpreted as requiring both actual knowledge *and* disregard of the risk of harm to inmates or others. This tighter definition allowed federal courts to side more easily with state prison officials in cases in which prisoners claimed there was deliberate indifference. In 1994, in the case of *Farmer* v. *Brennan*, the Supreme Court ruled that even when a prisoner is harmed and even when prison officials knew that the risk of harm existed, officials cannot be held liable if they took appropriate steps to mitigate that risk.

If there was any question that the prisoner rights era had ended, that question was settled in 1995 by the case of *Sandin* v. *Conner*. In *Sandin*, the Supreme Court rejected the argument that, by disciplining inmates, a state deprived prisoners of their constitutional right not to be deprived of liberty without due process. "The time has come to return to those due process principles that were correctly established and applied in earlier times," said the Court. A year later, the decision in *Lewis* v. *Casey* overturned portions of *Bounds* v. *Smith*. The *Bounds* case had been instrumental in establishing law libraries in prisons. The Court in *Lewis* held, however, that "*Bounds* does not guarantee inmates the wherewithal to file any and every type of legal claim but requires only that they be provided with the tools to attack their sentences."

In *Edwards* v. *Balisok* (1997), the Supreme Court made it even harder to successfully challenge prison disciplinary convictions. The Court held that prisoners cannot sue for monetary damages under Section 1983 of the U.S. Code for loss of good-time credits until they are able to sue successfully in state court to have their disciplinary conviction set aside.

The Legal Mechanisms   Changes in state and federal statutes have also slowed the pace of prisoners' rights cases. In 1980, Congress modified the Civil Rights of Institutionalized Persons Act.[16] It now requires a state inmate to exhaust all state remedies before filing a petition for a writ of *habeas corpus* in federal court. Inmates in federal prisons may still file *habeas corpus* petitions directly in federal court. In their petitions, federal inmates are now required to show (1) that they were deprived of some right to which they were entitled despite the confinement and (2) that the deprivation of this right made the imprisonment more burdensome.

The Prison Litigation Reform Act of 1996[17] (PLRA) was another legislative response to the ballooning number of civil rights lawsuits filed by prisoners. It restricts the filing of lawsuits in federal courts by:

1. requiring inmates to pay federal filing fees unless they can claim pauper status;[18]
2. limiting awards of attorneys' fees in successful lawsuits;
3. requiring judges to screen all inmate lawsuits and immediately dismiss those they find frivolous;
4. revoking good-time credit toward early release if inmates file malicious lawsuits;
5. barring prisoners from suing the federal government for mental or emotional injury unless there is an accompanying physical injury;
6. allowing court orders to go no further than necessary to correct the particular inmate's civil rights problem;
7. requiring some court orders to be renewed every two years or be lifted; and
8. ensuring that no single judge can order the release of federal inmates for overcrowding.

In May 2001, the U.S. Supreme Court further restricted inmate options under the PLRA. The ruling mandates that inmates must complete prison administrative processes that could provide some relief before suing over prison conditions, even if that relief would not include a monetary payment (*Booth* v. *Churner et al.*, 2001).

Female Inmates and the Courts

Female inmates frequently had to resort to the courts simply to gain rights that male inmates already had.

The prisoners' rights movement has been largely a male phenomenon. While male inmates were petitioning the courts for expansion of their rights, female inmates frequently had to resort to the courts simply to gain rights that male inmates already had.

EARLY CASES

One early state case, *Barefield* v. *Leach* (1974), demonstrated that the opportunities and programs for female inmates were clearly inferior to those for male inmates. In that case, a court in New Mexico spelled out one standard for equal treatment of male and female inmates. The court said that

Many claims of female inmates have focused on the failure of correctional institutions to provide them with educational opportunities and medical care comparable to those provided male inmates. The equal protection clause of which amendment guarantees female inmates conditions of confinement comparable to those of male inmates?

the equal-protection clause of the Constitution requires equal treatment of male and female inmates but not identical treatment. *Barefield*, however, was a state case—not binding on other states or the federal government.

In 1977, in *State, ex rel. Olson* v. *Maxwell*, the Supreme Court of North Dakota ruled that a lack of funds was not an acceptable justification for unequal treatment of male and female prisoners. Although this decision also came in a state court case, it would later be cited as a legal authority in a similar federal court case.

In *Glover* v. *Johnson* (1979), a U.S. district court case, a group of female prisoners in the Michigan system filed a class action lawsuit claiming that they were denied access to the courts and constitutional rights to equal protection. The prisoners demanded educational and vocational opportunities comparable to those for male inmates. At trial, a prison teacher testified that, although men were allowed to take shop courses, women were taught remedial courses at a junior–high school level because the attitude of those in charge was, "Keep it simple, these are only women." The court found that "the educational opportunities available to women prisoners in Michigan were substantially inferior to those available to male prisoners." Consequently, the court ordered a plan to provide higher education and vocational training for female prisoners in the Michigan prison system. *Glover* was a turning point in equal treatment for imprisoned women. Since 1979, female inmates have continued to win the majority of cases seeking equal treatment and the elimination of gender bias.

In the 1980 case of *Cooper* v. *Morin*, the U.S. Supreme Court accepted neither inconvenience nor cost as an excuse for treating female jail inmates differently from male inmates. Female inmates at a county jail in New York had alleged that inadequate medical attention in jail violated their civil rights. Later that same year, a federal district court rejected Virginia's claims that services for female prison inmates could not be provided at the same level as those for male inmates because of cost-effectiveness issues (*Bukhari* v. *Hutto*, 1980). Virginia authorities said that the much smaller number of women in prison raised the cost of providing each woman with services. The appellate court ordered the state of Virginia to provide equitable services for inmates, regardless of gender.

An action challenging the denial of equal protection and the conditions of confinement in the Kentucky Correctional Institution for Women was the basis of *Canterino* v. *Wilson*, decided in U.S. district court in 1982. The district court held that the "levels system" used to allocate privileges to female prisoners, a system not applied to male prisoners, violated both the equal-protection rights and the due process rights of female inmates. The court also held that female inmates in Kentucky's prisons must have the same opportunities as men for vocational education, training, recreation, and outdoor activity.

In 1982, in *McMurray* v. *Phelps*, a district court in Louisiana ordered an end to the unequal treatment of female inmates in that state's jails. (Recall that the federal courts have supervisory jurisdiction over state courts.) The next year, the Seventh Circuit Court of Appeals found that strip searches of female misdemeanor offenders awaiting bond in a Chicago lockup were unreasonable under the Fourth Amendment (*Mary Beth G.* v. *City of Chicago*, 1983). In addition, the court found that a policy of subjecting female arrestees to strip searches while subjecting similarly situated males only to hand searches violated the equal-protection clause of the Constitution.

RECENT CASES

Women inmates have continued to win significant court cases regarding conditions of confinement. In 1994, for example, in a class action suit by female inmates, a federal district court held the District of Columbia Department of Corrections liable under the Eighth Amendment for inadequate gynecological examinations and testing, inadequate testing for sexually transmitted diseases, inadequate health education, inadequate prenatal care, and an inadequate overall prenatal protocol (*Women Prisoners of the District of Columbia Department of Corrections* v. *District of Columbia*, 1994).

SUMMARY

1 ▶ The hands-off doctrine was a working philosophy of the courts in this country until 1970. It allowed corrections officials to run prisons without court intervention. The hands-off doctrine existed because courts were reluctant to interfere with activities of the executive branch and because judges realized that they were not experts in corrections.

2 ▶ The sources of prisoners' rights are the U.S. Constitution, federal statutes, state constitutions, and state statutes.

3 ▶ Inmates can challenge the conditions of their confinement through (1) a state *habeas corpus* action, (2) a federal *habeas corpus* action, (3) a state tort lawsuit, (4) a federal civil rights lawsuit, and (5) an injunction to obtain relief.

4 ▶ During the prisoner rights era (1970–1991), inmates won many court cases based on claims that conditions of their confinement violated their constitutional rights. Court decisions affected inmate rights to freedom of expression, including free speech; personal communications; access to the courts and legal services; religion; assembly and association; voice grievances about disciplinary procedures; protection from personal and cell searches; health care, including diet and exercise; protection from violence; adequate physical conditions of confinement; and rehabilitation.

5 ▶ Most prisoners' claims focus on denial of constitutional rights guaranteed by the First (freedom of expression and religion), Fourth (freedom from unlawful search and seizure), Eighth (freedom from cruel and unusual punishment), and Fourteenth (due process and equal protection of the law) Amendments.

6 ▶ The prisoners' rights movement has been largely a male phenomenon. Female inmates have had to petition the courts to gain rights that male inmates already had.

KEY TERMS

hands-off doctrine, *p. 388*

prisoners' rights, *p. 390*

constitutional rights, *p. 391*

institutional needs, *p. 391*

civil liability, *p. 391*

writ of *habeas corpus*, *p. 392*

tort, *p. 392*

nominal damages, *p. 393*

compensatory damages, *p. 393*

punitive damages, *p. 393*

injunction, *p. 393*

jurisdiction, *p. 394*

precedent, *p. 401*

legitimate penological objectives, *p. 401*

balancing test, *p. 401*

cruel and unusual punishment, *p. 408*

consent decree, *p. 408*

deliberate indifference, *p. 409*

totality of conditions, *p. 409*

due process, *p. 411*

frivolous lawsuits, *p. 414*

REVIEW & APPLICATIONS

REVIEW & APPLICATIONS

QUESTIONS FOR REVIEW

1. What constitutional rights were prisoners thought to have a hundred years ago?

2. Why was the hands-off doctrine so named? What was the basis for the doctrine?

3. Which statutes might have a bearing on the rights of prison inmates?

4. What are the legal mechanisms through which inmates have gained access to the courts?

5. To what degree are prison officials liable for their actions toward inmates?

6. What First Amendment rights have been gained by inmates? What First Amendment rights do inmates *not* have?

7. What Fourth Amendment rights have been gained by inmates? What Fourth Amendment rights do inmates *not* have?

8. What Eighth Amendment rights have been gained by inmates? What Eighth Amendment rights do inmates *not* have?

9. How does the Fourteenth Amendment relate to prisoners' rights? Are there Fourteenth Amendment rights enjoyed by the average citizen but not by inmates? If so, what are they?

10. What caused the relatively recent slowdown in the granting of rights to inmates by the courts?

11. Do the rights of male inmates correspond to the rights of female inmates? Why or why not?

12. Are there differences in legal status between HIV-negative inmates and HIV-positive inmates? If so, what are the differences?

THINKING CRITICALLY ABOUT CORRECTIONS

▶ ▶ ▶ **Freedom of Nonverbal Expression**

The right to freedom of nonverbal expression is said to be implied in the First Amendment. Hence, how people wear their hair and how they dress are expressions that some believe are protected by the First Amendment.

1. Might there be modes of dress that interfere with a correctional institution's legitimate goals?

2. If so, what might they be?

▶ ▶ ▶ **Checks and Balance**

On January 11, 2003, in a dramatic legal move shortly before leaving office, former Illinois Governor George Ryan commuted the sentences of every one of the state's 167 death-row inmates. Four of the sentences were reduced to 40-year terms; the remaining 163 sentences were commuted to life in prison. Governor Ryan based his action on his determination of inherent

arbitrariness and unfairness in the application of capital punishment and on the high risk of executing an innocent person.

While the scope of his action is unusual, the commutations typify the power placed in the hands of each state's chief executive. Essentially, this means that, within the respective states and based solely on personal opinion, a single individual is empowered to overturn sentencing decisions and attendant legal rulings on those decisions made at any level up to and including the nation's most powerful court, the U.S. Supreme Court.

1. Should this be the case?

2. Does the lack of a legal mechanism to counter a governor's decision regarding a pardon or a commutation violate the principle of checks and balances so intricately woven into America's state and federal governmental structures?

ON-THE-JOB DECISION MAKING

▶ ▶ ▶ Inmate Communications

You are a prison administrator. The prison where you work has a rule that inmates may write letters in English only. This rule seems sensible. After all, if inmates could write in languages not understood by correctional officers, they could discuss plans to escape, riot, or smuggle drugs or weapons into the prison. The courts allow the censoring of outgoing inmate mail; what good is that power if corrections personnel cannot read the mail?

It occurs to you, however, that inmates who cannot write in English will have difficulty communicating with the outside world and with their families. Inmates unable to write in English will not even be able to write to their attorneys. You also wonder what might happen if an inmate can write in English but his parents can read only a foreign language. If the inmate and his parents cannot afford long-distance phone calls, they will not be able to communicate with each other at all. You begin to consider how the English-only rule might be changed to facilitate wholesome communications while still preventing communications that might endanger the safety of the institution and the inmate population.

1. Can the English-only rule be amended to meet the inmate needs discussed here while still being consistent with legitimate institutional concerns? If so, how?

2. Does an inmate have a constitutionally protected right to communicate with his or her parents?

3. What if that right conflicts with prison policy?

▶ ▶ ▶ Law Libraries

The Supreme Court's ruling in *Bounds* v. *Smith* (1977) led to the establishment of law libraries for prisoner use in correctional facilities throughout the nation. Numerous subsequent prisoner civil suits resulted in follow-on rulings mandating the need to maintain these libraries with up-to-date reference materials in serviceable condition.

You are an advisor on correctional issues on the staff of your state's attorney general. In the past few weeks, she has repeatedly complained that these rulings impose excessive financial demands on the state's already nearly impoverished correctional system. In particular, she says, routine vandalism by inmates who tear pages from law books and take the pages back to their cells—or simply discard them—is especially costly. It also creates a circumstance wherein another inmate could threaten another civil suit upon finding a book to be "unserviceable" when attempting to use it, a threat to which the system can only respond by immediately purchasing a replacement book.

This, the attorney general says, typifies a cycle that causes an extraordinary drain on limited financial resources. She rants about the "ludicrous" fact that the reference material in her own office is so out-of-date as to be virtually unusable, but she cannot fix the problem because she spends that portion of her budget on repeatedly restoring the prisoners' law libraries in the various institutions throughout the state.

The attorney general has tasked you to resolve this issue.

1. What will you do?

2. Might advances in information technology be the key to a solution?

REVIEW & APPLICATIONS

CORRECTIONS ON THE WEB

▶ ▶ ▶ **Frivolous Lawsuits**

In 1996, the state of Ohio passed a law designed to limit frivolous lawsuits by state inmates. The law requires inmates to pay at least a portion of state court filing fees from their prison accounts, sets up a process by which a court may declare a lawsuit frivolous, institutes sanctions for inmates whose claims are dismissed as frivolous, and requires screening of new suits brought by inmates who file multiple cases in one year. Search the Internet for other ways in which states have attempted to limit frivolous inmate lawsuits. Write a report summarizing the techniques and laws that states employ to limit inmates to filing valid lawsuits.

▶ ▶ ▶ **Legal Search**

Visit the Corrections Connection online at http://www.corrections.com and use the site's search feature to find the word *legal*. Make a list of the five most interesting "hits" (or articles) that appear as the result of your search. View each article and write a brief description of each.

"The democratic principle that "all men are created equal" implies that persons with disabilities are entitled like everyone else to equal access and fair treatment appropriate to their context, whether the context is a prison, church, or place of employment."

—Marca Bristo, Chairperson, National Council on Disability, letter to the editor of the *Washington Times,* July 27, 1998.

12
CHAPTER

Special Prison Populations: The Elderly, HIV/AIDS, and the Mentally Challenged

▶ **CHAPTER OBJECTIVES**

After completing this chapter you should be able to do the following:

1. Define the term *special-needs inmate.*

2. Report on the management needs of special population inmates.

3. Report on the impact of substance abusers on the corrections system.

4. Discuss the five essential elements of cost-effective management of HIV/AIDS inmates.

5. Explain why there are so many inmates with mental illnesses in prison.

6. Describe the ways that prisons may provide medical and mental health services.

7. List the cost and health issues associated with older inmates.

8. Discuss the rationale for drug treatment programs in prisons and jails.

9. Discuss why the future of drug court is promising.

10. Discuss why treating HIV in prison is difficult.

11. Review the legal issues surrounding special population inmates.

▶ ▶ **California's correctional administrators** face a dilemma that typifies a national trend. As a result of tougher sentencing laws and more stringent parole policies, the prison population is aging dramatically. Since incarcerating an elderly inmate can cost as much as three times the per-inmate annual cost of incarcerating younger inmates, the growth of the older inmate population is a budget-buster.[1]

Proposals for resolving this problem include the early release of nonviolent offenders who have reached a level of frailty that reduces the degree of threat they represent to the community. Others suggest housing elderly prisoners in low-security facilities to reduce staff costs.

Two popular ideas would involve development of special housing arrangements for older inmates. First, because older inmates are often preyed upon by younger inmates, some recommend policy changes to permit grouping the older inmates together according to their degree of dangerousness. Doing so, they say, would significantly reduce the exposure of older inmates to abuse.

Second, some recommend relocating older inmates to institutions that are close to medical treatment facilities. This would reduce the extraordinary cost—as high as $233 per correctional officer trip for time and gasoline—of transporting ill prisoners to and from treatment. Since many older inmates suffer ailments that require frequent trips for medical care, placing them closer to treatment facilities would yield significant savings.

The elderly prisoner population in California increased 17 percent in one and a half years, from 12,216 on January 1, 2001, to 14,285 on June 30, 2003. The California Medical Facility at Vacaville and the Central California Women's Facility in Chowchilla provide acute medical care and hospice units for elderly male and female prisoners. Do elderly prisoners threaten public safety? Could they be paroled? Or, should they be held in nursing-home-like facilities away from the general population?

Special-Needs Inmates

special-needs inmates

Incarcerated individuals who require special treatment because they suffer from mental illness, chemical dependency (drug or alcohol), or communicable diseases (such as HIV/AIDS and tuberculosis), and general problems of the elderly.

Increasingly, prisons and jails are dealing with a growing population of special-needs inmates. **Special-needs inmates** require specific treatment or care because they suffer from mental illness, chemical dependency (drug or alcohol), or communicable diseases (especially HIV/AIDS and tuberculosis), and general problems of the elderly. Such inmates present operational and administrative problems for correctional staff—it is often difficult for the staff to know what they are observing or, once they recognize an inmate's special needs, how to address the situation.

A statewide research study on jail management in New Mexico indicated that special-needs inmates require extra attention from jail staff.[2] For example, they must be watched closely for possible suicide. Almost 9 of 10 such inmates disrupt normal jail activities. Seven of 10 require an excess of scarce medical resources. Four of 10 engage in acts of violence. Almost 3 of 10 are abused by other inmates. The characteristics of special-needs inmates, the treatment programs offered, and the policies for dealing with those inmates depend on the type of special need. This chapter reviews the management and treatment of special-needs inmates, beginning with substance-abusing inmates.

SUBSTANCE-ABUSING INMATES

Alcohol and other drug problems are the common denominator for most offenders in the criminal justice system. A **substance-abusing inmate** is an incarcerated person suffering from dependency on one or more substances including alcohol and a wide range of drugs.

Substance abuse takes a toll on users, the community, and the criminal justice system. In October 2002, the National Center on Addiction and Substance Abuse at Columbia University (CASA) released its findings on substance abuse and the prison population.[3] According to this study, 83 percent of America's jail and prison population—some 1.7 million prisoners at the end of 2000, up from 80 percent at the end of 1996—had seriously abused or were addicted to drugs and/or alcohol. Some had been arrested for offenses connected with drugs and alcohol (drug sales, DWI, etc.). Others had been under the influence of drugs or alcohol when they were arrested for other offenses. Many had used drugs or alcohol within the 24 hours preceding their arrests. The National Institute of Justice (NIJ) reports that 55 percent of convicted jail inmates used illegal drugs the month before their offense, with about one in four using a major drug such as cocaine, crack, or heroin. Thirty-six percent said they were using drugs at the time of their offense (with about one in four using a major drug), and 41 percent said they had been drinking alcohol. Almost 3 in 10 convicted men and 2 in 10 convicted women drank quantities that, combined with their weight and metabolism, amounted to blood alcohol

> Alcohol and other drug problems are the common denominator for most offenders in the criminal justice system.

substance-abusing inmate
An incarcerated individual suffering from dependency on one or more substances including alcohol and a wide range of drugs.

Over 80 percent of America's jail and prison population need some sort of substance-abuse treatment, but only 13 percent receive it while incarcerated. What should jails and prisons do to control the revolving door of drug and alcohol abusers and addicts in and out of prison?

concentrations of 10 grams per milliliter or higher, the definition of alco-
holic impairment in many states.[4]

Over the past 25 years, the number of drug offenders in federal prisons
has skyrocketed from 6,700 to over 78,500.[5] In state prisons during
this time, the number has grown from 20,000 to over 246,100.[6] These
dramatic increases can only add strain to an already overburdened system.
According to the June 2003 report by the National Institute of Justice's
Arrestee Drug Abuse Monitoring Program (ADAM), which tracks drug use
among arrestees in 35 cities, the percentage of men testing positive for
drugs when arrested ranges from 49 percent in Laredo, Texas, to 84 percent in Chicago. Among women, percentages range from 35 percent in
Laredo to 81 percent in New York City.[7]

One thing is for sure: We cannot arrest our way out of the problem. To
quote William Murphy, former president of the National District Attorney's Association and current elected district attorney for Richmond
County (Staten Island), New York, "Simply warehousing prisoners, without regard to addressing and dealing with the underlying problem of
substance abuse, produces unending taxpayer costs. Longer prison terms—
without treatment, training, and follow-up—make matters even worse.
Such practices breed the statistics that feed the system. They don't prevent
or put an end to crime."[8]

HIV-POSITIVE INMATES

HIV (human immunodeficiency virus)

A group of retroviruses that infect and destroy helper T cells of the immune system, causing the marked reduction in their numbers that is diagnostic of AIDS.

AIDS (acquired immunodeficiency syndrome)

A disease of the human immune system that is characterized cyto-logically, especially by reduction in the numbers of CD4-bearing helper T cells to 20 percent or less of nor-mal, rendering a person highly vul-nerable to life-threatening conditions. The disease is caused by infection with HIV commonly transmitted in infected blood and bodily secretions (as semen), espe-cially during sexual intercourse and intravenous drug use.

HIV-positive inmates

Incarcerated individuals infected with HIV.

HIV is the acronym for **human immunodeficiency virus,** which is any of a
group of retroviruses that infect and destroy helper T cells of the immune
system. When enough of a person's T cells have been destroyed by HIV, he or
she is diagnosed with **AIDS,** or **acquired immunodeficiency syndrome.** AIDS
is a disease of the human immune system characterized by the reduction in
the numbers of CD4-bearing helper T cells to 20 percent or less of normal.
In this state, a person is highly vulnerable to life-threatening conditions.

Reporting on HIV and AIDS in jail and prison is difficult because data
are published at different times and not the same questions are asked. For
example, Bureau of Justice Reports on HIV in jails were published in 1993,
1995, 1996 and 1999. Reports of HIV in prison were published in 1994,
1997 and 2000. Data on the number of AIDS related deaths is available for
state prison, but not always for jail or federal prison. In spite of these limitations, however, some things are known.[9] The prevalence of HIV and
AIDS is higher in correctional facilities than it is in the United States' population. Today there are more jail and prison HIV-positive inmates than
there were 10 or 12 years ago (see Table 12–1). However, due to advances
in medical science, fewer inmates are advancing to AIDS or dying of
AIDS.

In 2001, the U.S. Department of Justice reported that 8,615 (1.7 percent) jail inmates were known to be **HIV-positive inmates,** those infected
with the human immunodeficiency virus (HIV), an increase from 6,711 in
1993. Since 1993, the percent of total jail population with HIV has remained relatively stable (1.8 percent). While some were infected by sharing
needles with other drug abusers, others were infected through the exchange
of bodily fluids during hetero- or homosexual sex; among those some may
have become infected while incarcerated.

TABLE 12-1   HIV and AIDS in Correctional Institutions, 2000

HIV-positive prison inmates				Percent of population with confirmed AIDS		
Year end	Number	Percent of custody population		Year	U.S. general population	State and federal prisoners
1995	24,256	2.3%		1995	0.08%	0.51%
1996	23,881	2.2		1996	0.09	0.54
1997	23,886	2.1		1997	0.10	0.55
1998	25,680	2.2		1998	0.11	0.53
1999	25,801	2.1		1999	0.12	0.60
2000	25,088	2.0		2000	0.13	0.52

HIV-positive prison inmates				Number of confirmed AIDS cases		
Jurisdiction	Number	Percent of custody population		Year	Reported number	Estimated number
New York	6,000	8.5%		1995	5,099	5,157
Florida	2,640	3.7		1996	5,874	6,092
Texas	2,492	1.9		1997	6,184	6,326
California	1,638	1.0		1998	6,282	6,809
Federal system	1,014	0.8		1999	6,642	7,039
				2000	5,528	6,520

HIV-Positive Inmates		
Jails	8,615 (1999)	6,711 (1993)
State and Federal Prisons	25,088 (2000)	24,256 (1995)
Total	33,703	30,967

Number AIDS-related deaths among state and federal prisoners		
Year end	State	Federal
1995	1,010	—
1996	907	—
1997	538	—
1998	350	—
1999	242	16
2000	174	21

AIDS-Related Deaths		
Jails	78 (1999)	—
State and Federal Prison	195 (2000)	1,010 (1995)

Source: Excerpted from Laura M. Maruschak, *HIV in Prisons, 2000* (Washington, DC: U.S. Department of Justice, Bureau of Justice Statistics, October 2002).

Jails in the South and the Northeast hold 80 percent of all jail inmates known to be HIV positive (3,822 and 3,105, respectively). The HIV-positive jail population is 1,076 in the West, and 612 in the Midwest. The District of Columbia has the highest percentage of jail inmates known to be HIV positive (7.6 percent), followed by New York (4.3 percent) and Massachusetts (4.0 percent). Almost one-fifth (1,468) of the jail population with HIV is held in the four largest jails in the United States: Los Angeles County, New York City, Cook County (Chicago, Illinois), and Dade County (Miami, Florida).

The U.S. Department of Justice also reported that 78 jail inmates died from AIDS-related causes in 1999. AIDS-related deaths are the third leading cause of deaths in jails. Natural causes head the list (385 in 1999), followed by suicide (324).

In 2002, the U.S. Department of Justice reported that 25,088 (2 percent) prison inmates were known to be infected with HIV. The number of HIV-positive prison inmates in 2000 is larger than it was in 1995 (24,256), but the percentage of custody population in 2000 (2 percent) is smaller than it was in 1995 (2.3 percent) owing to an overall increase in the prison population.

THE OFFENDER SPEAKS

HIV-positive inmates were concentrated in a small number of states. New York (6,000), Florida (2,640), and Texas (2,492) housed nearly half of all HIV-positive prisoners in 2000. State prisons in the South held the most HIV-positive prisoners (10,767), followed by prisons in the Northeast (8,721), West (2,334), Midwest (2,252), and the Federal Bureau of Prisons (1,014).

Although the number of state and federal HIV-positive inmates is higher today than it was in 1999, the number of HIV cases that advance to AIDS is less, and the number that die from AIDS is significantly fewer. In 1999, there were 6,642 confirmed cases of AIDS in prison and 258 prisoners died from AIDS. In 2000, the number of confirmed AIDS cases declined to 5,528 and the number of state and federal inmates who died from AIDS was 195. Advances in medical treatment is arresting the advance of HIV into AIDS and death.

Cost-effective management of such inmates with HIV has at least five essential elements:

1. Early detection and diagnosis through medical and mental health screening of each new jail inmate upon admission.
2. Medical management and treatment by health specialists, including regular reevaluation and assessment.
3. Inmate classification and housing to discourage intravenous drug use and homosexual intercourse or to provide private rooms for terminally ill inmates.
4. Education and training of staff and inmates in the cause of AIDS, the stages of the disease, transmission methods, preventive measures, available treatment and therapies, testing issues and policies, confidentiality issues and policies, classification and program assignment policies, and supervision issues, including transportation and inmate movement.
5. Adequate funds to provide increasingly costly treatment to inmates with HIV or AIDS.

Dealing with HIV/AIDS Inmates   Today's jail professionals need a network of medical experts—university medical school faculty, state health department staff, federal health officials, and local health care providers—to consult about HIV and AIDS. Such consultation will give corrections professionals reliable information and familiarize the noncorrectional medical community with the problems facing jails.

A little bit of charm and persuasion also works. In August 2001, the Reverend Jesse Jackson visited the Cook County Jail in Chicago. He, along with 177 jail inmates and 25 ministers, took a two-minute HIV test.[10] "We're here to save your lives," Reverend Jackson told the inmates. He talked with them about the psychological barrier, the "taboo," that prevents at-risk people from testing themselves for HIV infection. He told the inmates that "Regardless of the results, people who take the test can't lose. Those who test negative should view themselves as lucky—they can get out of the way of AIDS through their knowledge, behavior, and commitment. HIV-positive detainees, on the other hand, can take solace in the fact that early detection leads to correction." Results were reported within two weeks, with only two tests coming back positive. Those persons received counseling and referrals.

HIV/AIDS is a serious problem for our nation's correctional facilities. To overcome the taboo that prevents at-risk people from testing themselves for HIV, the Reverend Jesse Jackson took an HIV test with Cook County (Chicago) jail inmates. Should HIV-positive inmates be treated any differently from other inmates? Should they be isolated?

MENTALLY ILL INMATES

Mental health is fundamental to a person's overall health, indispensable to personal well-being, and instrumental in leading a balanced and productive life. Every day, our nation's 3,365 local jails face the challenge of dealing with offenders who are not only mentally ill, but also suffering from co-occurring substance abuse and dependence disorders and require close monitoring, medication, and other services. The percentage of jail inmates with mental disorders significantly outweighs the percentage in the general population.[11] It is estimated that the lifetime prevalence of mental health disorders in the general population is 33 percent, but among the jail population it is as high as 60 percent. Jails are the largest provider of mental health services in the United States.

According to a survey conducted by researchers at the Bureau of Justice Statistics, almost one-third of state prisoners and a quarter of federal prisoners have a physical or mental problem such as schizophrenia, major depression, bipolar disorder, or post-traumatic stress disorder.[12] Eleven percent of prisoners have a learning disability, compared with only 3 percent of the general population.[13] Significant as these numbers are, many mental health experts believe that due to underreporting by people who do not want to disclose the information or are unaware of their illness, the numbers are actually higher.[14]

It is estimated that there are nearly five times more mentally ill people in the nation's jails and prisons (nearly 300,000) than there are in mental hospitals (60,000).[15] Six to 8 percent of the 10 to 12 million people who enter the nation's jails annually have severe mental illness. The three largest de facto psychiatric hospitals in the United States are now the Los Angeles

County Jail, Rikers Island Jail in New York City, and Cook County Jail in Chicago. Approximately 28 percent of the male inmates and 31 percent of the female inmates booked into the L.A. County Jail in 1998 had a mental disorder.[16] The L.A. County Jail spends $10 million a year on psychiatric medication!

Suggesting that these facilities replace mental hospitals altogether overstates their treatment capacity and the function of these facilities—the mental health care required is far beyond what most jails are equipped to offer. Correctional officers are not therapists and jails are not mental hospitals. All jails have a constitutional mandate to provide at least minimum mental health or psychiatric care to detainees, yet 2 of 10 jails have no access to mental health services, 8 of 10 jail officers receive little or no training in mental health issues, and record numbers of mentally ill jail inmates are released into the community without any discharge planning, increasing the probability they will relapse and return to incarceration. Still, citizens expect jails to provide mental health services.

Why So Many?   Why are there so many mentally ill people in the nation's jails? The reasons include failure to differentiate who should be in jail and who shouldn't, failure to treat people before they enter the criminal justice system, deinstitutionalization (moving the mentally ill from hospitals to nonsecure residential community settings), stricter commitment laws, less stringent discharge criteria, and reductions or curtailment of public funding. Former mental patients as well as people whose bizarre behavior might have landed them in a hospital bed a few years ago are now being arrested and are ending up in jail. While 40 state mental hospitals have closed in the last decade, more than 400 new prisons have opened,[17] state spending for treatment of the mentally ill is one-third less today than it was in 1950,[18] and changes in mental health laws have made involuntary commitment more difficult. As a result, jails and prisons have become the institutions most likely to house the mentally ill.

In addition, offenders often live as transients or in crowded conditions, increasing their levels of stress which can precipitate mental illness. Offenders also tend to be economically disadvantaged, meaning they are less likely to get mental health treatment. Finally, they have high rates of substance abuse, which is correlated with mental illness.

A family whose child stops taking medication calls county mental health professionals who tell the family they cannot do anything until the child becomes "dangerous." When the child deteriorates to the point at which she or he is dangerous, the mental health professionals are no longer the ones who respond; sheriffs' deputies and police take over, and encounters between such children and law enforcement often turns deadly. According to Thomas Faust, Executive Director of the National Sheriff's Association, justified killings by law enforcement involving people with mental illness are four times greater than such killings involving mentally healthy people.[19]

Correctional facilities have an opportunity to provide prevention and treatment interventions to a seriously underserved and needy population. Policies and programs for prisoners help them return to our communities as better citizens, in better health, under treatment for their medical and mental health conditions, and better equipped and motivated to protect

About 13 years ago, we began what's called the Maryland Community Criminal Justice Treatment Program. I developed this in partnership with the Maryland Correctional Administrators Association, because we were seeing numbers of people with mental illness coming into the local detention centers. So we developed comprehensive programs that provided each detention center—there are 23—with mental health services case management. The case managers' role is to try to connect people to community services upon release.

As we started understanding the population more, we started seeing that it wasn't just about mental health and corrections—it was about poverty and homelessness and substance abuse. So we had to try to develop community-based systems of support that brought together all of the different publicly based entities. We're very holistic—housing is crucial. You're not going to get someone to leave and "be compliant" while they're living under a bridge. We all start with "what would we want? What would we need?"

It's never just one thing. Our latest thing we're seeing is pregnant women—pregnant, incarcerated women. What started out as a program to meet the needs of mentally ill folks in the jail has branched into this program that addresses needs across the board.

Our project is an interesting blend of federal, state, and private money. With the leadership of both correctional administration and mental hygiene coming together, you realize these are all of our folks, and just because they rotate from system to system doesn't mean we drop them. We also believe these are the highest users of public services. You look at how many of them go into jails, how many of them are using the ER without insurance, using homeless shelters, using court time—it's a myriad of different public services that separately, at different times, provide for their needs. We believe if we can have one coordinated effort, we're not only serving the client better but reducing the need for them to be rotating from system to system.

Recidivism? Last year we only had 4.9 percent go back to jail.

Joan Gillece
Director of Special Needs Populations
Maryland Mental Hygiene Administration

themselves and others, while possibly reducing the cost to taxpayers of future health care and reincarceration. Good health care is also an integral part of institutional security. Investments in prisoner health care result in fewer correctional disturbances, disciplinary actions, and inmate injuries and in less negative publicity for the institution.[20] Without such health care, the public health will suffer as it did in 1989 in New York City when 80 percent of tuberculosis cases were traced to people released from jail and prison. In Los Angeles, a meningitis outbreak in the county jail spread to surrounding neighborhoods. Thus, our policies toward prisoners have a direct impact on the public health of everyone.

Provisions for Services   Prisons vary in the way they provide medical and mental health services. In Oregon, for example, prison medical and mental health professionals are state employees. Georgia, on the other hand, contracts for services with local medical and mental health care providers. According to the Bureau of Justice Statistics, 89 percent of the nation's prisons provide some type of mental health services to inmates. Nearly 70 percent screen inmates at intake; 65 percent conduct psychiatric assessments; 51 percent provide 24-hour mental health care; 71 percent provide therapy and/or counseling; 73 percent distribute psychotropic medication; and 68 percent help released inmates obtain community mental health services upon release. Only in eight states do inmates not receive mental health therapy.

The National Institute of Justice recently sponsored a survey and visits to selected sites to identify successful policies and practices for meeting the needs of jail inmates with mental disorders. Practices included screening, evaluation, and classification of booked detainees; case management

433

CAREER PROFILE

Jon Wood

Family Counselor   Kandiyohi County Community Corrections   Kandiyohi, Minnesota

Jon Wood is a family counselor with the Kandiyohi County Community Corrections office in Kandiyohi, Minnesota. He has held that position for the past five years, after working in a similar position as a contractor for two years. Prior to that he received a master's degree in community counseling and a bachelor's in applied psychology from St. Cloud State University in St. Cloud, Minnesota.

Jon says the bulk of his time is spent providing counseling to first-time offenders, either in a one-on-one capacity or in a family setting. He specializes in dealing with juveniles with mental health issues, many of which are just emerging or have not even been diagnosed yet. He also works with schools, collaborates with other mental health professionals who might be dealing with the same individuals, and deals with social service agencies and probation agents.

Most of his clients are very young—according to Jon, the problems start to show up around age 10. "They're showing some behaviors at school, and I try to coordinate treatment with psychologists and psychiatrists, so we can figure out what to do for them," he says. "And a big challenge is trying to talk parents into making it happen, given the stigma that is attached to mental health issues."

Jon says his goal is to help both parents and children understand the illnesses that they are facing and help them develop methods of dealing with them. This means developing new cognitive skills and learning problem solving and negotiation skills. "It's trying to help them find other ways to think," he says, "so they don't have to always be fighting each other or some authority figure.

"About once every two years I'll get a letter from a parent saying thanks. It doesn't happen very often but once in a while. And every now and then I'll run into an old client in a grocery store, and he tells me that he's going to college. So I know that something that we talked about made sense to him."

> " So often parents who are dealing with the juvenile justice system get to a point where they freak out, they don't want to have anything to do with it, and they throw their hands up in the air and give up. "

services at intake, consisting of crisis intervention services and short-term treatment programs; discharge planning with treatment referrals; development of specialized mental health courts and mechanisms for dealing with offenders with mental disorders; and promoting mental health services through linkages with the community mental health system and/or the expansion and development of programs (including telemedicine) to deliver mental health services to jail inmates.[21]

The American Association for Community Psychiatrists Committee on the Mentally Ill Behind Bars developed a list of recommendations to keep the mentally ill out of jail[22]:

1. Address the lack of access to community mental health and other diagnostic services in order to improve early diagnosis and treatment.

2. Create alternatives to incarceration for as many nonviolent mentally ill offenders as possible. For example, have a center to which police can take people who are experiencing a mental crisis.

3. Improve jail conditions that have negative effects on the mental health of inmates. For example, researchers are finding that serious bullying is a cause of suicide.[23] There were 324 suicides in the nation's jails in 1999.

There are five times more mentally ill people in jail and prison than there are in mental hospitals. What are some ways the needs of women correctional clients with mental disorders can be met?

4. Establish vigorous programs designed to reintegrate inmates with mental illness into the community, with specific attention paid to their housing needs.

5. Create oversight boards to prevent human rights abuses and to guarantee that adequate physical and mental health services are available upon release.

INMATES WITH TUBERCULOSIS

Jails are at great risk for the spread of **tuberculosis** (TB).[24] This is due to very close living quarters, overcrowding, poor sanitation, and the large number of inmates with a high risk of having TB, such as HIV-positive detainees, intravenous drug users, and immigrants. When a person who has TB coughs, sneezes, or laughs, tiny droplets of fluid containing TB bacteria are released into the air, which are then inhaled by others.

Experts concerned about TB in jails have indicated that the most important issues for jail professionals are to understand the causes and control of TB, to implement appropriate and cost-effective screening programs, and to develop close working relationships with local health authorities.

tuberculosis (TB)
A highly variable communicable disease that is characterized by toxic symptoms or allergic manifestations that in humans primarily affect the lungs.

OLDER INMATES

On January 1, 2003, the nation's prison and jail population exceeded 2 million inmates for the first time. Problems that were manageable two decades ago now threaten to overwhelm state and federal corrections systems. One issue that is being addressed by administrators across the nation is the aging of the prison population. Another is inmate deaths. Related to these issues are health issues, cost issues, and the construction of geriatric prison facilities.

The Aging of the Prison Population   Most of us imagine prisoners as young and aggressive. However, *elderly* and *passive* describe a significant portion of the prison population. The definition of *elderly* is subject to debate. Some define *elderly* as 65 years of age and older, some suggest 60 years, others suggest 55, and still others 50. There are some who do not consider chronological age at all. Rather, they believe that, because of the impact of prison lifestyle, including lower socioeconomic status and limited access to medical care, a prisoner's physiological age may be higher than his or her chronological age. In addition, some say that a lengthy prison stay can age an inmate 10 years beyond chronological age.

Despite the differences among definitions of *elderly*, it is possible to establish a common chronological starting point to define *older* inmates for purposes of comprehensive planning, programming, evaluation, and research within and among prison systems. After careful study of the issue, the NIC recommended in 1998 that correctional agencies nationwide adopt age 50 as the chronological starting point for defining *older inmates.*[25]

Aging inmates present a crisis for prison officials because of the costs of caring for them. Should states enact legislation that would allow prisons to release aging inmates prior to their sentence completion or parole eligibility? For more information go to Ethical Dilemma 12-1 at http://www.mhhe.com/schmalleger2.

Because researchers have not universally adopted this recommendation, a research focal point has not emerged, making trends in prison population aging difficult to identify and analyze, eliminating the possibility of generating point-by-point comparisons, and yielding confusing and potentially misleading results. For example, Neeley and colleagues project that, by the year 2010, inmates over the age of 50 will comprise 33 percent of the total prison population.[26] The most current age data gathered by federal agencies, however, is arrayed in age brackets 45–54 and 55 or older.[27] These data show that in mid-2002, the 234,500 inmates over the age of 45 comprised 12.6 percent of the prison and jail population; only 2.7 percent (51,400) were 55 or older. Are populations of older inmates increasing at a rate that makes Neeley's projections accurate? Do these current data indicate that the rate is accelerating or slowing? What percentage of the 234,500 inmates above the age of 45 are actually above the age of 50? How would that information affect interpretation of the data? Policymakers and researchers need clarity of information. The existing situation, however, renders such clarity impossible.

In an examination of the impact of California's three strikes law,[28] Ryan King and Marc Mauer of The Sentencing Project found that the law has significantly altered the demographics of that state's prison population in just the seven years since its inception. They estimate that, within 25 years, 30,000 prisoners will be incarcerated in California under sentences of 25 years to life. King and Mauer project this burgeoning population of older prisoners will place an extraordinary burden on the penal system's resources. Of particular concern is the increased cost of housing older inmates, who typically have greater need of costly medical care.

Pennsylvania, too, has recognized the special needs of aging inmates and has already taken measures to prepare for increased demands on state resources. In the late 1990s, the state invested $26 million to convert the State Correctional Institution of Laurel Highlands, a former mental hospital, into a facility capable of handling 260 long-term care, 60 personal care, and 532 general population inmates. While the average inmate age in other state institutions is 24 years, the average inmate at SCI–Laurel Highlands is 47 years—almost double the state average.[29]

"End-of-Life" Programs.   Before the onset of AIDS and the increased numbers of elderly prisoners, few prisoners died while incarcerated.[30] Inmate deaths occur more frequently now, and correctional administrators have taken measures to address the unique problems associated with helping terminally ill prisoners through their passing. As of March 2001, 19 states had formal **"end-of-life" programs,** and 14 states had such programs under development. These programs are designed to assist terminally ill inmates through their passing.

Health Issues   The physical, mental, and medical health care needs of older inmates have implications for prison policymakers, administrators, and staff. It is estimated that an elderly prisoner suffers from an average of three chronic illnesses.[31] Incarcerating older prisoners with impaired eyesight, physical handicaps, cancer, arthritis, diabetes, heart disease, hypertension, or Alzheimer's disease and treating these illnesses raise many concerns. For example, how ethical is it for prisons to provide surgery, physical therapy, and daily medication to elderly prisoners when people outside prison are unable to afford similar medical treatment?

Another issue that must be considered is the effect of health-related legislation. For example, the Americans with Disabilities Act (ADA) affects not only mainstream society, but also prisons and jails. Designing prison spaces that are accessible for elderly prisoners, with ramps, handrails, good lighting, and subtle grades, is now law under ADA.

Cost Issues   The economic consequences of incarcerating older prisoners are huge. The estimated national cost per year to confine an inmate over 55 years old is $70,000.[32] In North Carolina it costs $37,000 per year to keep elderly prisoners at the McCain Correctional Facility. The average annual cost for such an inmate in Maryland is $69,000. In California, it is $80,000.

Could elderly prisoners who are considered harmless be released early to go back to their families or to independent care living and thereby save prisons money? Systematic research on how elderly prisoners adapt after prison release is sketchy, although it is known that recidivism drops with age: According to the U.S. Parole Commission, older federal prisoners show lower recidivism rates. The U.S. Department of Justice reported that only 2 percent of inmates who are 55 or older when paroled return to prison.[33] It is doubtful that, when mandatory sentencing laws, three-strikes laws, and "truth-in-sentencing" laws were enacted, the economic impact of incarcerating elderly prisoners for long periods of time was actually considered. Unless legislatures give courts and prison administrators more leeway to interchange prison sentences with community sentences, states will find themselves in economic crises as they

"end-of-life" programs
Formalized measures to assist terminally ill inmates through their passing.

Get-tough-on-crime policies have led to an increased number of inmates serving longer periods of time behind bars. The Colorado Territorial Correctional Facility in Cañon City, includes a 32-bed infirmary for elderly prisoners with cancer, heart disease, diabetes and respiratory problems, and highlights the public health costs associated with elderly prisoners. What are some of the special needs of geriatric inmates?

attempt to provide for the 33 percent of the inmate population that is projected to be elderly by the year 2010.

Geriatric Prison Facilities   An increasing number of states are beginning to house their older prisoner population away from the general population, in nursing-home–like settings. Alabama, Arizona, Georgia, Illinois, Kansas, Kentucky, Maryland, Michigan, Minnesota, Mississippi, North Carolina, New Jersey, Ohio, Pennsylvania, South Carolina, Tennessee, Texas, Virginia, West Virginia, and Wisconsin have special prisons for the elderly, often called "aged/infirm," "medical/geriatric," "disabled," or simply "geriatric." The facility itself accommodates special needs of the elderly. Few stairs, reduced distances, more crafts and leisure activities, and staff trained in gerontological issues make these facilities unique. The majority confine only elderly male prisoners. Older female prisoners, who constitute only a small percentage of the total elderly prisoner population, are generally kept in a state's only women's prison.

A number of states are also opening prison hospices to offer a compassionate means of dealing with dying inmates.[34] A **hospice** is an interdisciplinary, comfort-oriented care facility that helps seriously ill patients to die with dignity and humanity in an environment that facilitates mental and spiritual preparation for the natural process of dying. Hospice programs provide a wide array of services, including pain management, spiritual support, and psychological counseling, as well as grief counseling for bereaved families.

In 1998, the National Institute of Corrections looked at prison care for terminally ill prisoners across the United States.[35] Of the slightly more than 1,000 inmates diagnosed as terminally ill, 800 were in regular prison hospitals, 150 in formal prison hospice settings, and 100 on parole or another form of compassionate release. The same survey found that 11 states and the BOP have started formal prison hospice programs, and 20 states are developing such programs.

Often, one of the challenges in starting a prison hospice is educating the prison staff in caring for the terminally ill and making a psychological adjustment to get over the resentment that prisoners are getting this level of care. According to Elizabeth Craig, executive director of the National Prison Hospice Association (NPHA) in Boulder, Colorado, "In my view, inmates are being punished by being incarcerated; we don't need to create more suffering for them."[36]

hospice
An interdisciplinary, comfort-oriented care facility that helps seriously ill patients to die with dignity and humanity in an environment that facilitates mental and spiritual preparation for the natural process of dying.

Drug Treatment Programs

The criminal justice system has become the largest source of mandated, or coerced, drug treatment in the United States.

The criminal justice system has become the largest source of mandated, or coerced, drug treatment in the United States.[37] Contrary to what some believe, research consistently indicates that offenders' motivations for entering drug treatment (voluntary or coerced) are not as important in treatment outcome as their ultimate length of stay in treatment. The longer inmates participate in treatment, the more likely they are to adopt prosocial attitudes and overcome their initial resistance. This point is important because treatment in a prison always involves an element of coercion.

With thousands of inmates returning to the general population each month, correctional health and public health are becoming increasingly intertwined. Health care and disease prevention in correctional facilities must become a top priority for correctional managers and all correctional personnel.

Officials estimate that 83 percent of prison and jail inmates need some sort of substance-abuse treatment, but only 13 percent receive it while incarcerated.[38] It is estimated that of the 60 percent of prisoners serving sentences for drug offenses, about one-third have moderate to severe substance-abuse problems that urgently need care. Most state institutions do not have the staff or the resources to provide treatment to every inmate who needs it.

The National Center on Addiction and Substance Abuse at Columbia University (CASA) is concerned about the low priority given to dealing with inmates' drug/alcohol addictions. From 1990 to 1999, the number of inmates who needed substance-abuse treatment climbed from 551,608 to 948,769.[39] In 1990, an estimated 13 percent of inmates needing treatment received it; by 1999, the figure remained 13 percent.

CASA estimates that states spend 5 percent of their prison budget on drug/alcohol treatment; the BOP spends less than 1 percent. Treatment need far outstrips treatment availability, and much treatment is either short-term or not intensive enough to address inmates' needs. "Considering the depth of the typical inmate's addiction," writes Dr. Lana Harrison, associate director of the Center for Drug and Alcohol Studies at the University of Delaware, "self-help or drug education programs are unlikely to effect long-lasting change. Nor is prison time, because 77 percent of state and 62 percent of federal inmates had served prior sentences."[40]

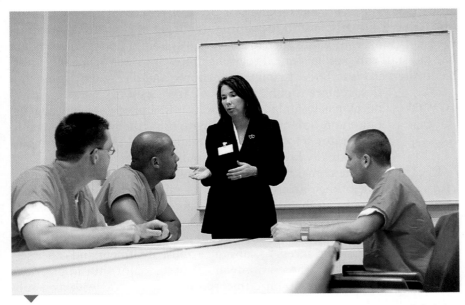

▼ Many inmates enter prison addicted to illegal drugs. Although there's evidence that drug and alcohol treatment in prison reduces recidivism, only 13 percent of inmates who need substance abuse treatment actually receive it. Should correctional facilities be required to provide substance abuse treatment? What are the benefits of substance abuse treatment?

Drug treatment programs provide evidence that rehabilitation is more likely to succeed for those offenders who complete drug treatment programs, and reducing drug-seeking behavior aids in management of jail facilities. A recent NIJ-sponsored research study found that the greatest benefit of drug treatment programs in jails was that they provided a "behavioral management tool" that controlled inmates' behavior and helped lower the incidence of inmate violence.[41]

The study evaluated five drug treatment programs in California and New York. At all five sites, substance abuse inmates in drug treatment programs had lower rates of serious physical violence and other behavioral problems (e.g., insubordination and possession of nondrug contraband) than those not in the programs. Since offenders seldom voluntarily seek substance-abuse treatment, jail is an opportunity to introduce treatment and encourage effective aftercare upon release. As for recidivism, 17 percent of the inmates in drug treatment and 23 percent of the control group were convicted again at least once during a one-year follow-up.

RECIDIVISM

It is generally accepted that drug and alcohol treatment in prison reduces recidivism. According to the Office of National Drug Control Policy, treatment while in prison and under postincarceration supervision can reduce recidivism by 50 percent.[42] Without treatment, three in four offenders are rearrested within three years, continuing the costly cycle of addiction and crime.

Unfortunately, only a small fraction of the jail inmates who need substance-abuse treatment actually receive it. When the last census of the nation's jails was published in 2001, only 61 percent of the nation's jails offered alcohol treatment and 54 percent offered drug treatment.[43] The absence of drug treatment programs is particularly common in small jails. Still, jail is a logical place to focus drug treatment efforts. To do so, however, jails must link with other local service systems. The problem is not one jail staff can handle alone. Programs that work, such as TASC (Treatment Alternatives to Street Crime), drug courts, and therapeutic communities, require a public policy of agencies working as teams to develop action plans, provide access, and offer technical assistance and training. These programs can help to reduce recidivism rates. However, the availability of treatment remains substantially lower than the need.

> The availability of treatment remains substantially lower than the need.

Regardless of the crimes they committed, offenders who test positive for drugs at the time of their arrest have longer criminal records and have been imprisoned more often than those who do not test positive. Over 40 percent of first-time offenders have a history of drug use. The proportion increases to over 80 percent for offenders with five or more prior convictions. Expanding access to substance abuse treatment and other services during and after incarceration will require a major shift in priorities and in the way we think about crime and punishment, as well as a substantial financial investment in expanded treatment and other services. However, the potential rewards are enormous in terms of reduced crime, incarceration, recidivism, and addiction.

PROGRAM EVALUATION

Recently the Bureau of Prisons evaluated its drug abuse treatment program. The inmates in the evaluation had been released into the community for 6 to 12 months after completing a three-stage treatment program. In the first stage, inmates participated in a residential drug abuse treatment program for 9 or 12 months. Inmates continued the treatment for up to 12 more months after they returned to the general prison population. Treatment continued with community drug treatment providers in a community residential center during a transition from prison to parole. The offenders who had completed the program were found less likely to have been rearrested, less likely to have had their supervision revoked (and be returned to prison), and less likely to have been detected for drug use than were similar offenders who had not participated in the drug abuse program.[44]

The study also found improved employment among women after release. Female inmates who had completed residential drug treatment were employed for more than 69 percent of the time they were in the community following release, while women who did not receive treatment were employed 59 percent of the time. In addition, an evaluation of inmate behavior found that institution misconduct among male inmates who had completed the residential drug abuse treatment program was reduced by 25 percent when compared to misconduct among similar male inmates who had not participated in the residential program, and institution misconduct among female inmates who had completed residential treatment was reduced by 70 percent. Because previous research had indicated that the first 6 to 12 months after release are often a critical period for an offender, the results of this evaluation suggest that drug treatment can improve the lives of offenders and reduce recidivism.

ALCOHOL: THE BIGGEST CULPRIT

According to CASA, alcohol is linked more closely with violent crimes than are drugs. More widely available than illegal drugs, alcohol is connected with rape, assault, child and spouse abuse, and most homicides arising from disputes or arguments. Twenty percent of state inmates convicted of a violent offense were under the influence of alcohol—and no other substance—when they committed their crimes; in contrast, only 4 percent of violent offenders were under the influence of drugs at the time of their crimes.

CASA also reports a link between alcohol abuse and addiction and property crime. Among state prisoners, 16 percent of property offenders were under the influence of alcohol (and no other substance) at the time of their crime; among federal prisoners, it was 5 percent.

Consequences of No Treatment   Untreated substance abusers are likely to return to substance abuse and crime upon release and thus maintain the market for illegal drugs and keep drug dealers in business. When substance-abusing prisoners do not receive treatment, the public is endangered. As CASA put it, "Release of untreated drug and alcohol addicted inmates is tantamount to visiting criminals on society."[45] Charles Hynes,

> Release of untreated drug and alcohol addicted inmates is tantamount to visiting criminals on society.

a district attorney in Brooklyn, New York, calls releasing untreated drug/alcohol-addicted inmates "lunacy."[46]

Results of Treatment   Why should prisoners receive drug treatment? According to Jeremy Travis, Senior Fellow at the Urban Institute and author of Chapter 8's Reflections on the Future, there are two powerful reasons.[47]

First, drug offenders consume a staggering volume of illegal drugs, and any reduction in their drug use represents a significant reduction in the nation's demand for illegal drugs. About 60 percent of the cocaine and heroin consumed by the entire nation in a year is consumed by individuals arrested in that year. Drug treatment has the potential for significantly reducing the nation's demand for illegal drugs.

Second, we now know that we can reduce drug use in the offender population. There is ample, consistent, and cumulative evidence that substance-abuse treatment for incarcerated populations leads to substantial reductions in substance abuse and future crimes. The National Treatment Improvement Evaluation Study found that prison-based treatment programs produced reductions in criminal behavior and in arrests.[48] Participation in correctional substance-abuse treatment is also associated with enhanced mental health and physical health. Treatment programs that start nine months to a year before prison release, provide community-based aftercare services (housing, education, employment, and health care), attract and retain staff who demonstrate concern for the offender's welfare, and give offenders a clear understanding of the program's rules and the penalties for breaking them provide the greatest chances for success.[49] Such programs have success rates as high as 80 to 90 percent. Community aftercare services are particularly important for substance abusers because they tend to have medical problems such as cirrhosis of the liver, diabetes, and HIV/AIDS.

Therapeutic Community   One successful prison-based substance treatment program is the therapeutic community. A **therapeutic community** (TC) is a residential treatment program in which inmates are housed in a separate unit within a prison or jail facility, characterized by highly structured treatment involving resocialization, intensive counseling, and an increasing level of responsibility as the inmate progresses through the program. TC relies on interactions within the peer group to help members confront their addictions and to commit to lifestyle changes that will enable them to remain drug free and crime free.

therapeutic community (TC)
A residential treatment program in which substance abuse inmates are housed in a separate unit within a prison or jail facility.

Post-release Outcomes   In September 2000, the Federal Bureau of Prisons published the results of a three-year evaluation of its residential drug abuse treatment programs that are designed for inmates with moderate to severe substance-abuse problems.[50] The study assessed the post-release outcomes of 1,842 men and 473 women released from 20 different federal prisons with residential drug treatment programs between August 1992 and December 1997. The evaluation revealed that male inmates who completed residential drug abuse treatment were 16 percent less likely to be rearrested or have their supervision revoked than were inmates who did not receive such treatment; the comparable figure for female inmates was 18 percent.

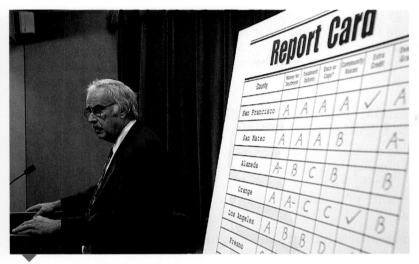

California Proposition 36 requires that first- and second-time nonviolent simple drug possession offenders be placed on probation instead of being sentenced to time behind bars. On Wednesday, June 27, 2001, California state Senate President Pro Tem John Burton held a news conference on the Lindesmith Center Drug Policy Foundation's grading of how 11 counties plan to implement Proposition 36. How do such new laws save taxpayers' money and rehabilitate drug offenders?

This reduction in recidivism was coupled with a 15 percent reduction in drug use by male participants and an 18 percent reduction in drug use by female participants. The study also found improved employment for women after release. The research strongly suggests that residential drug abuse treatment can make a significant difference in the lives of inmates following their release from prison and return to the community. Similar results have been reported in Delaware where researchers conducted a longitudinal study of inmates who completed in-prison and work-release TC treatment.[51] They were more drug free and arrest free than their control groups at 18-month and three-year follow-up periods. The Delaware research demonstrates the importance of treatment continuing during the transition stage to work and the free community.

Costs and Economic Benefits of Treatment   CASA estimates that the cost of proven treatment programs, accompanied by appropriate education, job training, and health care, averages $6,500 per year per offender. The annual economic benefit to society—in terms of avoided incarceration and health care costs, salary earned, taxes paid, and contribution to the economy—is $68,000 for every prisoner who successfully completes such treatment and becomes a taxpaying, law-abiding person. If we (1) combine the number of jail and prison inmates (2,178,567); (2) accept CASA's estimate that 83 percent of jail and prison inmates need substance abuse treatment (1,808,210) but only 13 percent receive it, leaving 1,573,142 inmates who do not; (3) assume, as CASA reports, that there's an estimated 200,000 drug dealers who do not use drugs and therefore do not need substance abuse treatment, reducing the number of inmates who need treatment to 1,373,142; and (4) if only 10 percent (137,314) of the inmates are successfully treated, the economic benefit in the first year of work after release would be $9.3 billion. That is $412 million more than what CASA says would be the $8.9 billion cost of providing training and treatment (at a cost of $6,500 each) for the entire 1.3 million inmates with drug and/or alcohol problems.

RECOMMENDATIONS FOR MANAGING SUBSTANCE-ABUSING OFFENDERS

Controlling the revolving door of drug and alcohol abusers and addicts in and out of prison is an important aspect of management for corrections officials. Donald Andrews and associates[52] identify "principles of effective treatment" that are associated with successful correctional treatment programs:

1. Treatment should be intensive (three to nine months), be behavioral in nature, and focus on high-risk offenders.
2. Behavioral strategies should be enforced in a firm but fair manner by qualified staff.
3. Treatment should target antisocial attitudes, values and beliefs supportive of criminal behavior, negative peer associations, and substance abuse.
4. Treatment providers should be responsive to offenders' learning styles and personalities.
5. Treatment providers should relate to offenders in interpersonally sensitive and constructive ways and should be trained and supervised appropriately.
6. Treatment should provide relapse prevention in the community.
7. Linkages and referrals to community services should be provided for institution-based programs.

Probation Programs   Drug offenders are prime candidates for tough probation programs. There is evidence that even coerced treatment programs can reduce both later drug use and later crimes.[53] The largest study of drug treatment outcomes found that criminal justice clients stayed in treatment longer than did clients without involvement in the justice system and had higher-than-average success rates.[54] Indeed, for offenders in outpatient drug treatment programs, rates of rearrest and relapse are significantly lower if they stay in treatment for more than three months than if they drop out earlier.[55]

Research has revealed the different risks and needs of traffickers, addicts, and low-level users.[56] Many Americans prefer prison sentences for drug traffickers but are willing to accept something other than prison for other drug offenders. Seventeen states have either reformed their drug laws or are considering doing so. In 1996, the people of Arizona led the way in drug reform by passing the Drug Medicalization, Prevention and Control Act. The centerpiece of the Act is the diversion of persons convicted of possession or use of a controlled substance. The Act requires drug users to be placed on probation and to participate in appropriate drug treatment. In the second year of operation, 62 percent of the probationers complied with

Correctional Health Care: An Integral Component of Public Health

by Edward A. Harrison, President, National Commission on Correctional Health Care

The cost of running correctional facilities is a tremendous and growing strain for many of our states and communities, and a principal cause is health care. Between 1985 and 1998 health care costs per prison inmate more than doubled (primarily because of more effective but more costly pharmaceuticals), while at the same time departments of corrections' medical budgets increased more than fivefold[1] (because of increased pharmacy costs and the growing inmate population). These rates of increase are far higher than those seen for other costs of incarceration.

Given that inmates have a constitutional right to necessary health care, provision of such care will become onerously expensive for taxpayers in the years ahead. For example, correctional facilities must contend with diseases, such as HIV and hepatitis C, that are both pervasive among inmates and costly to treat. Our urban jails have become the nation's largest mental health facilities and thus are burdened with the associated costs of treatment. As well, prisons must care for an aging inmate population (the result of longer sentences being served) and its greater need for health services. Clearly, the economics of correctional health care will help determine its future.

While the importance of inmate health care is something too many Americans still do not accept, that attitude—as well as public policy—is beginning to change. In 1998, Surgeon General designate David Satcher became the first Surgeon General to state publicly his desire to include inmates in the nation's public health strategy. Four years later Surgeon General Richard Carmona, himself once a jail physician, said that correctional health care would be a priority of his administration.

Melding public health and correctional health is an important step. According to NCCHC's seminal report "The Health Status of Soon-to-Be-Released Inmates: A Report to Congress,"[2] undiagnosed and underdiagnosed diseases in inmates, as well as untreated or undertreated illness, are threats to the nation's health and economy. Many inmates with undiagnosed and untreated diseases do not or cannot utilize community health services after they are released, and with nearly 11.5 million inmates released from all correctional facilities in the United States in 1998, the magnitude of the problem is potentially vast.

Fortunately, correctional health care presents a unique opportunity to reduce health risks and financial costs to the community. When treatment and prevention services are provided in the correctional setting, not only are they cost-effective or even cost-saving, but they also help protect the larger public health.

Closer collaboration between public health systems and correctional systems in our communities is what lies ahead. This will reduce wasteful duplication of services and improve patient care. Correctional systems and public health systems will share the costs associated with treating chronic health conditions. And by rectifying gaps in prevention, screening and treatment services in prisons and jails, communities can take advantage of a tremendous opportunity to improve public health by reducing the problems associated with untreated inmates returning to the community.

ABOUT THE AUTHOR

Edward A. Harrison is president of the National Commission on Correctional Health Care (NCCHC). NCCHC is the recognized national standards-setting body for correctional health care and for certifying correctional health professionals. Mr. Harrison received a Bachelor of Arts in communication from the University of Illinois and a Master of Business Administration from Northwestern University.

NOTES

1. Correctional Health Care: Guidelines for the Management of an Adequate Delivery System, Anno, B.J., 2001, National Commission on Correctional Health Care, Chicago, and National Institute of Corrections, Washington, DC.
2. The Health Status of Soon-to-Be-Released Inmates: A Report to Congress, 2002, National Commission on Correctional Health Care, Chicago.

Reflections on the Future

treatment. Probation supervision and community treatment cost approximately $1.1 million. Based on prison costs of almost $53 per day, Arizona saved an estimated $6.7 million in incarceration.[57] Four years later, 61 percent of California voters passed Proposition 36— the Substance Abuse and Crime Prevention Act. The Act requires that first- and second-time nonviolent drug offenders convicted of possession, use, or transportation of drugs be offered substance-abuse treatment instead of incarceration. As of February 2002, of the 4,329 defendants sentenced to drug treatment in Los Angeles County from July 1, 2001, to December 31, 2001, 69 percent were still receiving treatment.[58]

Judges and county officials say they are pleased with the program, and preliminary reports are that the program is working. Similar ballot initiatives are being considered across the country.

Drug Courts

You read in Chapter 5 that drug courts are a powerful tool in addressing the criminal behavior of people who commit a disproportionately large number of crimes. An individual who has a severe addiction commits 63 crimes a year.[59]

In 2001, Columbia University's National Center on Addiction and Substance Abuse (CASA) conducted an updated survey of its seminal drug court research discussed in Chapter 5. It found that drug courts continue to provide the most comprehensive and effective control of the drug-using offenders' criminality and drug usage while under the court's jurisdiction.

The revised study based on a review of 37 evaluations, finds that their results are consistent with the analysis presented in Chapter 5. "Drug courts provide closer, more comprehensive supervision and much more frequent drug testing and monitoring during the program than other forms of community supervision. More importantly, drug use and criminal behavior are substantially reduced while offenders are participating in drug court.[60] In fact, the average recidivism rate for those who complete drug court is between 4 and 29 percent, as compared to 48 percent for those who do not participate in drug court.

However, in spite of the successes reported in Chapter 5 by Goldkamp, the National Association of Drug Court Professionals, and CASA, others have reported no difference in arrest rates between drug court and comparison group members.[61] It is difficult to say exactly which of the ten components of effective drug court discussed in Chapter 5 or what combination of features of the drug court model are the most important for determining success.

Nevertheless, the future of drug court is promising. Over 300,000 adults and 12,500 juveniles have enrolled in drug courts. Over 73,000 adults and

Drug court is a special court with responsibility to handle substance-abusing offenders. Miami Drug Court Judge Jeffrey Rosinek oversees a coalition of prosecutors, defense attorneys, treatment and social service providers, probation officers, and police to treat, sanction and reward drug offenders with punishment more restrictive than regular probation but less severe than incarceration. Why is drug court better than traditional criminal court processing?

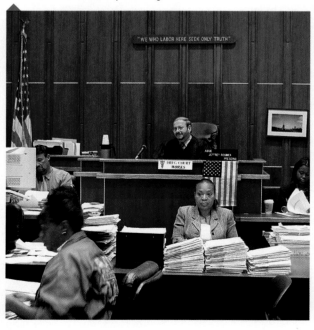

4,000 juveniles have graduated. The retention rate is 70 percent. Over three-fourths of drug court participants were previously incarcerated, a finding that lessens the problem of net-widening (see Chapter 5 for a definition of *net-widening*). Over 2,100 drug-free babies have been born. Over 3,500 drug-free parents have regained custody of their children. Over 4,550 drug-free parents are making child support payments. And, almost three-fourths of drug court graduates obtained employment. These results as well as federal funding for planning, implementing, and enhancing drug courts through the U.S. Department of Justice Drug Courts Program Office, and the support of national, state, and local leaders who recognize that traditional criminal justice policies have little impact on substance abuse, suggest that drug courts will play an increasingly visible role in the nation's future response to drug-related crime.

HIV and AIDS in Correctional Facilities

HIV and AIDS continue to be epidemic behind prison walls (see Table 12–1). Prisons and jails house a large concentration of people who are HIV positive or infected with AIDS and provide them treatment, education, and behavior modification therapies prior to release to the community.

Most correctional systems test their inmates for HIV, but testing policies vary widely:

- All states (except Iowa), the District of Columbia, and the Federal Bureau of Prisons test inmates if they have HIV-related symptoms or if the inmates request a test.
- Forty states and the Federal Bureau of Prisons test inmates after they are involved in an incident.
- 15 states test inmates who belong to specific "high-risk groups."
- 19 states test all inmates who enter their facilities.
- 3 states (Alabama, Nevada and Missouri) and the Federal Bureau of Prisons test inmates upon their release.
- 5 states (Arkansas, Georgia, Mississippi, Nevada and South Carolina) test all inmates currently in custody.
- 3 states (New York, Oregon and Virginia) and the Federal Bureau of Prisons test inmates selected at random.[62]

Treating HIV in prison is difficult for at least five reasons.[63] The first is the issue of privacy. People infected with HIV usually do not want to disclose their condition. The therapeutic regimen often involves taking multiple drugs several times a day, and going to the prison medication line often compromises a prisoner's privacy and increases the risk of stigmatization by other inmates and staff. Stigmatization can range from isolation and shunning to more overt forms of abuse. This is true even when high-quality health care is available. Anti-retroviral therapies (ART) can effectively treat HIV, but only if corrections officials help inmates overcome the obstacles to obtaining the treatment.

A second reason involves the frequency of taking medication and the prison routine. Some drugs must be taken with food and others in a fasting state. As the therapeutic regimen increases to five or six times a day, it strains the routine of most prisons to dispense medication frequently and to provide food as required.

The third reason is distrust of the medical and legal system. Not surprisingly, many inmates do not trust the legal and health care systems. This may be especially true for women and minorities who have a documented history of being experimented on without consent and being denied appropriate legal and medical care.

The fourth reason is fear of side effects. The HIV drug regimen is known to make patients feel worse than they already do. Consequently, inmates will be less likely to adhere to the strict dosages and timing.

The final reason is that the courts have rejected the idea that the level and quality of health care available to prisoners must be the same as is available to society at large.[64] This falls under the principle of least eligibility—the belief that prison conditions, including the delivery of health care, be a step below those of the working class and people on welfare. Thus, prisoners are denied access to medical specialists, timely delivery of medical services, technologically advanced diagnostic techniques, the latest medication and drug therapies, up-to-date surgical procedures, and second opinions.[65]

Overcoming these obstacles will not be easy. If an inmate undergoes complex drug therapy in prison but cannot obtain the same therapy upon release, his or her health is compromised. In addition, he or she may transmit the virus to others. The key is developing trust between HIV-infected prisoners and the prison health care team, extending the regimen when inmates are discharged, and building collaboration between correctional institutions and public health agencies.

EDUCATION AND PREVENTION

Education and prevention programs are becoming more common in correctional facilities, but only 10 percent of state or federal prison systems offer comprehensive education and prevention programs. Incarceration offers opportunities to provide high-risk inmates with HIV education and sexually transmitted disease education as well as prevention programs. Such programs benefit not only the inmate but also the health and well-being of the community to which the inmate returns. The types of education and prevention programs provided vary among correctional systems but may include instructor-led programs, peer-led programs, pretest/posttest counseling, multi-session prevention counseling, and audiovisual and written materials. Within programs, high-risk inmates may learn basic disease information, safer sex practices, tattooing risks, and triggers for behavior relapse, and they may develop more accurate risk self-perceptions.[66]

Some say that among the 50 states, HIV and AIDS care is most extensive in New York.[67] With the highest proportion (8.5 percent) of HIV-positive inmates—almost 6,000 of its 68,000 inmate population,[68] New York is one of the few states that has all 11 FDA-approved HIV drugs in all 69 state prisons as well as a statewide standard of care, established by the New York State AIDS Institute. Available programs include confidential testing, education, support services, one-on-one and group counseling, and transitional and prerelease counseling.

Sexually Transmitted Diseases in Jail

Most studies on infectious diseases in correctional facilities focus on prison. The problem of sexually transmitted diseases (STDs) in jail is addressed less frequently even though some believe that STDs are more common in jail than in prison.[69] However, rapid turnover and frequent movement of inmates makes jails difficult settings in which to study the prevalence of various diseases. But recently, the Society of Correctional Physicians published a report by Dr. Karl Brown, infectious disease supervisor at New York City's Rikers Island Jail, on the increase of STDs in jail and the difficulties diagnosing and treating four of the most common STDs found in jail today: syphilis, gonorrhea, chlamydia, and genital herpes. **Syphilis** is caused by the bacterium *Treponema pallidum.* Syphilis is passed from person to person through direct contact with a syphilis sore. Transmission of the bacterium occurs during sexual contact. **Gonorrhea** is caused by *Neisseria gonorrhea,* a bacterium that grows and multiplies in mucous membranes of the body. Gonorrhea bacteria grows in the warm, moist areas of the reproductive tract, including the cervix, uterus, and fallopian tubes in women, and in the urethra (urine canal) in women and men. The bacteria can also grow in the mouth, throat, and anus. Gonorrhea is spread through sexual contact. **Chlamydia** is the most frequently reported STD in the United States. It is caused by the bacterium *Chlamydia trachomatis.* Chlamydia is transmitted through sexual contact. **Genital herpes** is a lifelong infection caused by the herpes simplex viruses type 1 (HSV-1) and type 2 (HSV-2). A person can get HSV-1 by coming into contact with the saliva of an infected person. HSV-1 causes infections of the mouth and lips, so-called "fever blisters." A person almost always gets HSV-2 infection during sexual contact with someone who has a genital HSV-2 infection. According to Brown, after declining for many years, the rates of syphilis, gonorrhea and chlamydia began increasing in jails and juvenile detention centers in 2000, especially among female prisoners. The jail environment may be the key to controlling STDs but less than half of the nation's jails have a policy of routine screening, and even in those jails with routine screening, less than half of the inmates were tested for syphilis, gonorrhea or chlamydia. Brown also found another problem: approximately half of arrestees were released within 48 hours but most jails received the inmates' test results more than 48 hours after admission.

The type of screening for STDs in jail should be based on the prevalence of STDs as measured by the population served. For example, gonorrhea and chlamydia are four times higher in northern Florida than they are in northern California. The key to controlling STDs is to continuously collect, monitor, and analyze information, then to discuss the results with public health officials. Diagnosis also requires a thorough non-judgmental sexual history, and a careful genital exam.

syphilis

A sexually transmitted disease caused by the bacteria *Treponema pallidum.* If left untreated syphilis can cause serious heart abnormalities, mental disorders, blindness, other neurological problems, and death. Syphilis is transmitted when an infected lesion comes in contact with the soft skin of the mucous membrane.

gonorrhea

The second most common sexually transmitted disease. Often called *the clap,* gonorrhea is caused by the *Neisseria gonorrhea* bacteria found in moist areas of the body. Infection occurs with contact to any of these areas.

chlamydia

The most common sexually transmitted disease. Caused by the bacteria *Chlamydia trachomatis,* it can affect the eyes, lungs, or urogenital (urinary-genital) area, depending on the age of the person infected and how the infection is transmitted.

genital herpes

A sexually transmitted disease caused by the herpes simplex virus or HSV. It is one of the most common STDs in the United States.

Legal Issues

Providing inmates adequate health care is of concern to the courts and professional associations. In 1976, the U.S. Supreme Court ruled in *Estelle* v.

Gamble[70] that inmates have a constitutional right to reasonable, adequate health services for serious medical needs. However, the Court also made clear that such a right did not mean that prisoners have unqualified access to health care. Lower courts have held that the Constitution does not require that medical care provided to prisoners be perfect, the best obtainable, or even very good.[71] According to an excellent review of legal health care standards and the legal remedies available to prisoners, the courts support the principle of least eligibility (defined in Chapter 7). Prisoners do not have the right to sue physicians for malpractice, or if they do, the damages are lower than those awarded to people outside prison. Nevertheless, health care professionals and inmate advocates—such as the American Medical Association, the American Correctional Health Services Association and the National Commission on Correctional Health Care—insist on alleviating the pain and suffering of all persons, regardless of their status. They believe that no distinction should be made between inmates and free citizens.

Another important piece of legislation is the Civil Rights of Institutionalized Persons Act (CRIPA).[72] This law places prisoners in a class with others confined in government institutions, such as people with disabilities and elderly people in government-run nursing homes. Enacted in 1980, CRIPA evolved from the U.S. Department of Justice's Civil Rights Division's *amicus curiae* ("friend of the court") intervention in a 1972 lawsuit brought by parents, volunteer organizations, and individual residents at the Willowbrook State School for the Mentally Retarded. The suit alleged that the State of New York and school administrators were negligent in permitting abominable conditions to exist at the school. Ongoing problems at the site included severe crowding (65 percent above capacity), faulty plumbing, general filth, lack of adequate medical personnel, and failure to control residents, resulting in more than 1,300 incidents of injury, assaults, or fights within one eight-month period.

The Civil Rights Division helped the parents and others prove that the civil rights of the residents were being violated. Coupled with an admission by the deputy commissioner of the State of New York that conditions at Willowbrook were "a major tragedy," the Civil Rights Division's efforts forced a settlement and ultimate correction of the appalling conditions at the school.

The case became the impetus for CRIPA by publicizing conditions that were all too common in facilities run by government agencies at the time. The passage of CRIPA protects all institutionalized persons, including prisoners, by providing them an established avenue of relief.

INMATES WITH DISABILITIES

Inmates with special needs face numerous difficulties. Consider the case of Ronald Yeskey. Yeskey was sentenced to 18 to 36 months in a Pennsylvania correctional facility. He was recommended for a motivational boot camp, which would have shortened his sentence to six months. He was, however, refused admission to the boot camp because of a physical disability—hypertension. He sued, claiming that the **Americans with Disabilities Act (ADA)** of 1990 prohibits any "public entity" from discriminating against a "qualified individual with a disability" because of that disability.

Americans with Disabilities Act (ADA)

Public Law 101-336, enacted July 26, 1990, which prohibits discrimination and ensures equal opportunity for people with disabilities in employment, state and local government services, public accommodations, commercial facilities, and transportation. It also mandates the establishment of TDD/telephone relay services.

In a unanimous opinion, the U.S. Supreme Court held that state prisons fall squarely within the ADA's definition of a "public entity." Reacting to the decision, Yeskey's attorney noted, "The court's ruling means that prison officials cannot discriminate against prisoners with disabilities and must make reasonable modifications to prison operations so that these prisoners will have reasonable access to most prison programs."[73]

INMATES WITH HIV/AIDS

Most suits by prisoners with HIV/AIDS are claims that officials have violated a prisoner's rights by revealing the condition or by segregating the prisoner because of the condition. In 1988, officials in Erie County, New York, placed an HIV-positive female prisoner in a segregated prison wing reserved for mentally ill inmates. They also placed on her possessions red stickers revealing her HIV-positive status. The inmate sued, claiming denial of her rights to privacy and due process. The district court agreed (*Nolley* v. *County of Erie,* 1991). In the same year, however, the Eleventh Circuit Court of Appeals held that an Alabama policy of isolating all HIV-positive inmates did not violate the Fourth or Eighth Amendments (*Harris* v. *Thigpen* and *Austin* v. *Pennsylvania Dept. of Corr.*).

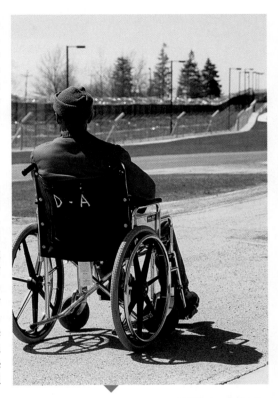

Prisoners in wheelchairs, and others with special needs, place an extraordinary strain on prison resources. Inmates with disabilities are protected under the federal Americans with Disabilities Act (ADA) of 1990. What does the Act require of correctional facilities? What are the alternatives to incarceration for inmates with disabilities?

Other legal issues relate to the work assignments of HIV/AIDS inmates. In 1994, in *Gates* v. *Rowland,* the Ninth Circuit Court of Appeals ruled that California correctional officials could continue to bar HIV-positive inmates from working in prison kitchens. The court made it clear that its decision was based more on the anticipated reactions of prisoners receiving the food than on any actual risk of infection. The court agreed that food service "has often been the source of violence or riots" because inmates "are not necessarily motivated by rational thought and frequently have irrational suspicions or phobias that education will not modify" and because prisoners "have no choice of where they eat." Correctional officials had based their policy, the court said, on "legitimate penological concerns."

INMATES WITH MENTAL ILLNESS

The federal courts have recognized the right of mentally ill inmates to treatment. According to a district court in Illinois, this right is triggered when it becomes reasonably certain that (1) the prisoner's symptoms demonstrate a serious mental disease or brain injury, (2) the disease or injury is curable or at least treatable, and (3) delaying or denying care would cause substantially more harm to the inmate (*Parte* v. *Lane,* 1981). In 1990, in *Washington* v. *Harper,* the U.S. Supreme Court ruled that inmates who are dangerous to themselves or others as a result of mental illness may be treated with psychoactive drugs against their will. Such involuntary drug treatment, however, has to be in the best interest of the inmate's mental health, not just for the convenience of the correctional institution.

Eye On Corrections™

Santa Clara County Learns from ADA Case

By Michelle Gaseau

The Americans with Disabilities Act and its application to corrections has been reinforced by Supreme Court rulings as well as state-level court decisions over and over. But complying with the law's regulations can be tricky. Consider, for example, the case of Santa Clara County in California.

Managers at the Santa Clara County Department of Correction believed they were in compliance with ADA because they had installed TDD machines, close-captioned televisions, and other services for hearing-impaired inmates. But a lawsuit filed by a former detainee in 1998 indicated the opposite, and the court's ruling cost the county hundreds of thousands of dollars. The issue raised in the 1998 lawsuit *Padilla v. Ryan* involved poor communication between the county jail and the county court about the special services needed for disabled detainees. The plaintiff was a hearing-impaired individual who was arrested on a Sunday night on a domestic violence–related charge. The individual's spouse was also hearing impaired. Usually it takes 48 hours for an individual to be processed and brought to court. In this case, the court had to send the plaintiff back to jail because it wasn't aware he was hearing impaired and the court was not prepared to provide translation services. As a result, the plaintiff spent an extra day in custody. Since the court could not be sued, the plaintiff went after the DOC and delved into other ADA issues as part of the lawsuit.

The local inmate-advocacy group did a facility walk-through with Santa Clara County's Chief of Corrections, Tim Ryan, to see what the facility offered to hearing-impaired inmates. The visit by the group did not move ADA compliance to the front burner, few changes were made, and the lawsuit followed. Ryan said that, as in other jails, other more pressing issues often take precedence over ADA compliance. Now he sees that this is a mistake many corrections officials could be in danger of making.

"The ADA is not a surprise issue, but you can be surprised by it," said Ryan, who took over the leadership of the department just before the lawsuit was filed. "We had proceeded down a path to do some things [related to the ADA]. Where we failed is we failed to manage it." Ryan explained that while some efforts were made to address ADA issues in the county jail, little follow-up was done to ensure they were working for disabled inmates. In addition, jail officials did not act quickly when a local inmate advocacy group raised the ADA issue with them.

CHANGES REQUIRED BY ADA SUIT

The suit required the Santa Clara County Jail to add a number of services for disabled inmates. Disability training for all staff was one requirement. The facility put in place specialized staff training for handling the hearing-impaired inmate. "We have changed some forms and procedures about how to assess those impairments and we are dealing with the person right from the beginning," said Ryan.

Changes include the following:

- a cell with a special TDD machine;
- forms for arresting officers to fill out that outline any disabilities noted;
- more personalized attention to disabled inmates during intake;
- public announcements, such as meals, relayed to hearing-impaired inmates individually; and
- an assessment interview completed by program staff with disabled inmates within 72 hours to ensure equal access to programs.

"Jail managers need to be assertive and responsive to the needs of the community and inmates. They need to be proactive in dealing with these issues," Ryan said. If they are not, Ryan warns, then the full expense of complying with the ADA can come crashing down on top of a jail.

Even now, after further changes have been made at the jail to comply with ADA and serve disabled inmates, Ryan said oversight practices are vital. "If we don't audit, then convenience takes over," Ryan said. If a facility is crowded, the jail's ADA-appropriate cell could be used to house anyone rather than holding it for a person of need. "It was easier to put the disabled person in another [non-ADA] cell, but we had to stop that. Get the officers to call a supervisor and make it a priority. It's a change in mentality," Ryan said.

COSTS CAN BE HIGH

Initially, Santa Clara County corrections officials believed that the changes requested for the facility would place an undue financial burden on the facility. Jail officials had determined that a $400,000 estimate to alter the jail's existing bell emergency alarms to include emergency lighting would support a claim of undue financial burden. "Our procedure was to have an officer go to the person and help them. Under the new concept we had to put in a light along with the bell. The court indicated we should not even raise that flag [financial burden] at all," Ryan said.

One of the reasons for this is that the court considered the county's entire budget rather than just the department's. According to Ryan, in the end, the cost to upgrade services far exceeded the initial $400,000 estimate. The costs also included training at $25 per hour for supervisors and $4 per officer for 400 officers, a new inmate orientation video to include communications for hearing-impaired inmates, and an upgrade of the fire alarm system.

Source: "Santa Clara County Learns from ADA Care," Michelle Gaseau, The Corrections Connection Network News (CCNN). Eye on Corrections. www.corrections.com. August 7, 2000. Copyright © 2000, all rights reserved, The Corrections Connection Network News (CCNN), a division of J.S. Noonan, LLC. Reprinted with permission.

REVIEW & APPLICATIONS

SUMMARY

1 ▶ Some inmates require special treatment or care because they suffer from mental illness, chemical dependency, a communicable disease, or typical problems associated with the elderly. These inmates present unique problems for correctional staff and administrators.

2 ▶ Special-needs inmates present significant management problems because they are typically more violent and prone to be disruptive, require close monitoring as suicide risks, tax scarce medical resources, and are often targets of abuse by other inmates.

3 ▶ A tenfold increase in prison populations over the past 25 years caused a commensurate increase in the number of inmates with substance-abuse problems. These inmates tremendously drain finite resources, are disruptive to daily life within the walls, and create unique management problems in all areas of prison life.

4 ▶ The five essential elements of cost-effective management of HIV/AIDS inmates are early detection and diagnosis, medical management and treatment, inmate classification and housing, education and training of staff and inmates, and funding.

5 ▶ The increase in the number of mentally ill inmates is attributable to several factors: the deinstitutionalization of the mentally ill to nonsecure residential environments; stricter commitment laws; failure to know who should and should not be in jail; failure to treat them before they enter the criminal justice system; less stringent discharge criteria; and reduction or elimination of public funding.

6 ▶ Some states provide medical and mental health services through contracted services, while others have professional service providers on staff. Services vary by state and may include intake screening, psychiatric assessment, therapy and/or counseling, psychotropic medication, and referral of released prisoners to community mental health services.

7 ▶ Estimates are that, on average, each older inmate is afflicted with three chronic illnesses that require ongoing and expensive medical treatment. Some question the equity of providing such free treatment to criminal offenders when the same free treatment is not provided to the public at large. The annual cost of incarcerating an elderly inmate is significantly higher than the average per-inmate cost of incarceration.

8 ▶ Drug treatment programs in prisons and jails serve as "behavior management" tools to control inmate behavior, expose a greater number of inmates to treatment than might otherwise seek help, and increase rehabilitative success.

9 ▶ The future of drug court is promising because many adults and juveniles have enrolled and graduated, the retention rate is high, net-widening is avoided, drug-free babies have been born, drug-free parents have regained custody of their children, drug court graduates have found employment, federal funding is available for planning and implementing drug courts, and policy makers recognize that traditional criminal justice policies have little impact on substance abuse.

10 ▶ Special difficulties related to HIV/AIDS among prison populations include privacy issues, disruption of the prison routine due to the frequency of taking medication, inmate distrust of the medical and legal systems, fear of side effects, and the legal dilemma embodied in the principle of least eligibility.

11 ▶ Inmates with disabilities, infectious diseases, and/or mental illness present unique legal and moral dilemmas for correctional administrators and the courts. The legal issues threaten to overwhelm the court systems with suits brought by prisoners. Meanwhile, the moral issues frequently mandate compassion, flexibility, and creativity among staff and administrators in navigating the daily routine of prison life.

KEY TERMS

special-needs inmates, *p. 426*

substance-abusing inmate, *p. 427*

HIV (human immunodeficiency virus), *p. 428*

AIDS (acquired immunodeficiency syndrome), *p. 428*

HIV-positive inmates, *p. 428*

tuberculosis (TB), *p. 435*

"end-of-life" programs, *p. 437*

hospice, p. *p. 438*

therapeutic community (TC), *p. 442*

syphillis, *p. 449*

gonorrhea, *p. 449*

chlamydia, *p. 449*

genital herpes, *p. 449*

Americans with Disabilities Act (ADA), *p. 450*

QUESTIONS FOR REVIEW

1. What is a *special-needs inmate,* and how does he or she impact the correctional system?

2. Explain the five essential elements of cost-effective management of inmates afflicted with HIV and/or AIDS.

3. Explain why so many mentally ill people are incarcerated, and list the measures for keeping the mentally ill out of jail that are proposed by the American Association for Community Psychiatrists Committee on the Mentally Ill Behind Bars.

4. Should elderly inmates whose debilitated physical and/or mental conditions clearly reduce their threat to the community be released from incarceration? Why or why not?

5. Should the use of drug courts be expanded as a measure to slow or reduce the explosive growth in prison populations? Why or why not?

6. Do you agree or disagree with the U.S. Supreme Court's ruling that prisons and jails must comply with the mandates of the Americans with Disabilities Act?

7. If you were empowered to do so, would you mandate application of the principle of least eligibility in making policy decisions regarding treatment of inmates? Why or why not?

REVIEW & APPLICATIONS

THINKING CRITICALLY ABOUT CORRECTIONS

▶ ▶ ▶ Aging Prison Population and Costs

As the prison population ages, the costs of incarcerating large numbers of older inmates will skyrocket. This, in turn, will strain correctional budgets and adversely impact correctional administrators' ability to provide essential services to the general prisoner population. Should elderly inmates be released from incarceration? Could services provided by other public agencies be tapped to meet the needs of elderly inmates? If so, which services might be invoked?

▶ ▶ ▶ The Principle of Least Eligibility

Discussions of the principle of least eligibility invariably fire emotions. Should inmates rate free medical care that is not available to law-abiding citizens? Why or why not? Would you support a ballot proposal to formalize the principle of least eligibility as law in your state? Why or why not? If such a law were adopted, do you think it would withstand challenge through the state and federal court systems? Why or why not?

ON-THE-JOB DECISION MAKING

▶ ▶ ▶ How to Use Personal Experience to Advance Correctional Training in HIV/AIDS

You are the warden of a state prison and on record as a supporter of the principle of least eligibility. Walter Edmunds is one of your most dependable correctional officers. Mature, calm, and unfailingly professional, Edmunds can be counted on in every crisis. You have come to rely on his leadership as a positive element among the correctional staff. Unfortunately, Edmunds has a young son dying of AIDS, which he contracted through a blood transfusion during an appendectomy.

Yesterday, your medical staff conducted training for your correctional officers on procedures for handling inmates suffering from HIV and AIDS. About 10 minutes into the training session, Edmunds apologized for interrupting and then asked why the prisoners received top-notch medical treatment for free, treatment that ordinary law-abiding citizens can't afford.

From that single question, things quickly deteriorated, and Edmunds became increasingly agitated. Before long, the training room was in a turmoil, as Edmunds' questions and angry comments whipped up the sympathy and anger of his fellow correctional officers.

Clearly out of his depth, the medical officer cancelled the remainder of the training session and then bolted to your office. By the time he finished relating the incident, one of your correctional lieutenants appeared to report that the unionized correctional staff was in an uproar and threatening to walk off the job. What would you do to defuse this situation? Once you contained the crisis, how would you handle Edmunds?

▶ ▶ ▶ Deciding Legitimate Penological Concerns

You are a correctional lieutenant at a state prison that has a conjugal visitation program. Carl Packard, one of your inmates, was recently diagnosed as HIV positive. During an interview with a member of the medical staff, Packard acknowledged recent illicit drug use during which he shared a needle with other inmates. He and the medic believe this needle sharing to be the source of Packard's HIV infection.

Yesterday, Packard applied for a conjugal visit with his wife. You summoned him to your office and asked if he had advised his wife of his infection. Packard stated he had not and that he had no intention of "tellin' that bitch nothin'." This morning, you sought guidance from the prison's legal advisor and the warden. They informed you that infection with HIV did not proscribe an inmate's participation in the conjugal visitation program, and that privacy policies prohibit you from informing Mrs. Packard of her husband's physical condition. You strongly believe that the threat to Mrs. Packard's health and safety outweighs what you consider to be ill-advised rules and policies.

1. What do you do?
2. What is your reasoning?

CORRECTIONS ON THE WEB

▶ ▶ ▶ **National Center for Victims of Crime**

Access the National Center for Victims of Crime at http://www. nvc.org. Click on the link to Resource Library and see what research resources the site offers on corrections-related topics. Review available publications listed in the *Featured NIC Publications* link.

▶ ▶ ▶ **South Carolina Department of Corrections Strategic Plan**

Review the reports on special-needs inmates at South Carolina's Department of Corrections website at http://www.state.sc.us/scdc. Click on the link to Statistical Reports, then Special Reports. Compare South Carolina's provisions for special-needs inmates with those you can locate at the websites for five other state correctional departments.

REVIEW & APPLICATIONS

Issues in Corrections

PART 5

Part Five focuses on some of the most controversial debates in contemporary corrections. Prison overcrowding became a problem shortly after a wing of the Walnut Street Jail was converted into the world's first prison in 1790, and it continues to be a problem today. When prisons are overcrowded, safety is compromised and conditions ripen for disturbances and riots.

One way to control prison overcrowding is to build more prisons. Today, the federal government and some states are building supermax prisons to deal with inmates whose violent behavior makes it impossible for them to live among the general prison population. Other options to control prison overcrowding are accreditation, which mandates acceptable staff-inmate ratios; privatization, the goal of which is to turn institutions into cost-effective private businesses; and technology, which can reduce the number of people required to supervise a given inmate population.

The increase in attention to victims' rights has also changed the corrections landscape. Today, all states and the federal government have laws that establish, protect, and enforce victims' rights. However, as you will learn, victims' rights laws are unevenly applied and sometimes partially ignored. Would a constitutional amendment, as recommended by Congress and the President, result in more even application and enforcement?

Possibly no other corrections issues has received more attention than capital punishment. The watershed U.S. Supreme Court case *Furman* v. *Georgia* (1972) changed the way judges and juries impose the death penalty. Since 1977, 885 people have been executed in the United States, and over 3,500 are on death row today. New research on defendant-victim racial characteristics, execution of the innocent, and social consensus is sharpening the debate over capital punishment.

Part Five concludes with an examination of juvenile corrections. The first juvenile court established in Cook County (Chicago, Illinois) in 1899 had high hopes for controlling and preventing delinquency. However, today society's response to rare yet high-profile juvenile offending, means that the needs of the vast majority of juveniles who are arrested for nonviolent offenses are virtually ignored. There is no magic bullet to prevent delinquency, but there are correctional strategies and "best practices" that work. Implementing them will be up to you, the next generation of correctional professionals.

13

14

15

16

❝A society should be judged not by how it treats its outstanding citizens but by how it treats its criminals.❞

—Fyodor Dostoyevsky, Russian writer 1821–1881

13 CHAPTER

Prison Issues and Concerns: Security, Privatization, Technology, and Accreditation

▶ CHAPTER OBJECTIVES

After completing this chapter you should be able to do the following:

1. List the four main reasons prisons are overcrowded.

2. Identify six methods of controlling prison overcrowding.

3. Identify five causes of prison riots.

4. Describe what can be done to prevent prison riots.

5. Outline the emergence of supermax housing and its impact on prisoners and staff.

6. Describe "no-frills" jails and prisons and their impact on corrections.

7. List the reasons correctional agencies and facilities should be accredited.

8. List the arguments for and against privatization.

9. Discuss the impact of technology on corrections.

▶ ▶ **A flip of the switch activated the** electromagnetic field between the inmates' metallic boots and the prison floor and stopped the prison disturbance in the film *Face/Off* starring John Travolta and Nicholas Cage. Sound far out? It may not be that unimaginable. Imagine reporting a crime to a "software agent" police officer at your local police department via the Internet. Imagine probation officers monitoring electronically transmitted smells to keep track of the lifestyles of convicted drug offenders. Imagine virtual courtrooms, digitally displayed evidence, and virtual tours of crime scenes. You do not even have to imagine. The technology is already here.

But what are the issues and concerns of the prison environment today? In this chapter, we shall consider seven aspects of the prison environment: overcrowding, riots and violence, supermax housing, "no-frills" prisons and jails, accreditation, privatization, and technocorrections.

Detection technology, like the magnetic field and the principles of geographical information systems that stopped the prison disturbance in *Face/Off*, starring Nicholas Cage and John Travolta, is changing corrections. How can technology address correctional health, safety and security issues?

Overcrowding

In the past, a prison was often referred to as "the big house." Today, however, a more appropriate description is "the full house." Over the past 25 years, prison population has increased sixfold—from 240,000 to 1.4 million. Some say that prisons are "capacity driven"; that is, if you cut the ribbon, they are full. Saying exactly how full, though, is difficult, because each state has its own method for measuring prison capacity. Twenty-five jurisdictions use rated capacity (the number of beds in a facility), 42 use operational capacity (the number of inmates that can be accommodated based on a facility's staff and existing programs and services), and 31 use design capacity (the number of inmates that planners intended the facility to house).[1] The problem is compounded because 32 jurisdictions use more than one definition, and some have their own definitions. In spite of the differences, by any measure today's prisons are overcrowded.

On January 1, 2003, state prisons taken as a whole, were operating between full capacity and 16 percent above capacity, while federal prisons were operating at 33 percent above capacity.[2] That would suggest that as many as 204,340 (16 percent) of the 1,277,127 state prisoners and 53,964

(33 percent) of the 163,528 federal prisoners were housed in overcrowded facilities. Eliminating the present overcrowding would require building 198 new prisons at a cost of $10.3 billion (assuming that each has a capacity of 1,300 and costs approximately $52 million to build) and then staffing and maintaining the new facilities at an average cost of $26 million each per year. Even if this were possible, the relief from overcrowding would be short-term because the prisoner population grows continually. Future prison growth is difficult to predict due to declining crime rates and changing federal, state, and local criminal justice policies. If the prisoner population continued the growth it experienced in 2002 (17,560 new inmates in 2002), keeping up with the increased number of inmates would require spending $728 million dollars a year to build 14 new prisons plus at least $26 million each per year for operating costs.

WHY ARE PRISONS OVERCROWDED?

There are four main reasons prisons are overcrowded. The first is a continuous increase in the number of people sent to prison. This number increased significantly between 1990 and 2000 and then slowed somewhat from 2000 to 2002. The overall increase was 89 percent. The annual average growth from 1990 to 2002 was 60,240 inmates. Nearly 1 of every 150 people in the United States is incarcerated. Probation and parole violators represent a significant percentage of the number of people admitted to prison each year. As we discussed in Chapter 7, technical violators accounted for 68 percent of all prison admissions in 1999.[3] This indicates that the concerns that emerged in the 1980s about admissions to prisons as a result of reduced tolerance for parole condition violations and their impact on the prison population are still well-founded.

The second reason is that offenders now serve a larger portion of their sentences. The amount of time served has increased from an average of 22 months for prisoners released in 1990 to 28 months for those released in 1998.[4] Sentencing laws changed, reducing the difference between the sentence imposed and the actual time served and restricting the possibility of early release from prison. Jurisdictions began to depart from the prevailing approach, known as *indeterminate sentencing* (broad authorized sentencing ranges, parole release, and case-by-case decision making), in the mid-1970s (see Chapter 3). Today, the trend in many jurisdictions is toward determinate sentencing—a fixed term of incarceration and no possibility of parole. In addition, most jurisdictions have adopted one or more of the following sentencing approaches: mandatory minimum sentences, three-strikes laws, or truth-in-sentencing laws requiring offenders to serve mandated percentages of imposed sentences (see Chapter 3). As a result, between 1990 and 2002, the number of offenders held in state and federal prisons grew annually by an average of almost 6 percent.

The third reason prisons are overcrowded is that many incoming prisoners are drug users, not the drug dealers the tougher drug laws were designed to capture. The goal of tougher drug laws was to arrest and convict drug dealers, thereby reducing drug use and the drug-related crime rate. This goal has not been achieved. At least 22 percent of the federal prison population consists of nonviolent drug offenders. Today, more than

Do you want to know why Louisiana has the highest incarceration rate in this country? Our sentences are too long, our sentences are too tough! You're doing more time for every crime than you do in most any other state. The problem with Louisiana? We don't ever let 'em go. Once you break the law, you don't get another chance. If it were up to me I'd say let's not keep dying old men in prison. They're too old to pull an armed robbery or be a ski-mask rapist. They ought to do about 20 years on most any serious crime and when they turn about 50 years old—when those two come together on a graph—they pretty well should have a good shot at going free.

Burl Cain
Warden
Louisiana State Penitentiary at Angola

THE STAFF SPEAKS

400,000 people are behind bars for drug crimes; nearly one-third of these are for simple possession. Arrest of people who use drugs is at an all-time high according to the FBI. At the same time, drug use is up among the young, especially for drugs like heroin and methamphetamines. According to an article in the *New York Times*, Americans do not use more drugs than people in other nations, but the United States is virtually alone among Western democracies in choosing the path of incarceration for drug offenders.[5]

The fourth reason prisons are overcrowded is a trend some people call the "prison industrial complex." Private corporations have a real estate investment in the prisons they build and operate. Correctional officers' unions are expanding in many states and securing the use of incarceration into the future. Rural communities such as Del Norte, California—a remote, impoverished county in the northwest corner of the state with an unemployment rate of more than 20 percent and all of its industries severely depressed since the 1980s—negotiated successfully with the California Department of Corrections to build Pelican Bay State Prison, one of the nation's largest state prisons (inmate population 4,000). States have an incentive to incarcerate, because the 1994 crime bill provides matching funds to states to keep violent offenders in prison longer by denying them parole and requiring they serve at least 85 percent of their sentence. There is no reason to believe that the nation's prison population will decrease even though crime has declined every year since 1991. To quote Dr. Allen Beck, the Department of Justice's lead statistician on criminal justice issues, "We've got crime going in one direction (down), and prison policy going in the other (up.)"

HOW CAN PRISON OVERCROWDING BE CONTROLLED?

In most jurisdictions across the United States today, we find at least six methods of controlling prison overcrowding:

1. Reduce the number of people going to prison.
2. Release the less dangerous to make room for the more dangerous.
3. Change prison or jail sentences to community-related sentences.
4. Increase the number of releases.
5. Expand existing prison capacity or build new prisons.
6. Implement an overall program of structured sentencing.

The first four methods are referred to as *front-end, trap-door, side-door,* and *back-door* strategies, respectively (see Chapter 5).

The fifth method of controlling prison overcrowding is the most commonly considered—build more prisons. For the past 25 years, political leaders have addressed public concerns about crime by devoting unprecedented financial resources to the construction of prisons. The number of prisons increased from 1,160 in 1995 to 1,208 in 2000. States added almost 303,000 new prison beds between 1995 and 2000. In 1990, the nation's prisons cost $12 billion.[6] In 2000, the cost was nearly $40 billion.[7] In spite of the new resources, however, prison overcrowding continues to worsen. Some experts believe that legislators will one day have to choose between new prison construction and funding for other areas, such as health care or education. From 1985 through 1996, spending for the nation's prisons increased an average of 7.3 percent per year, twice the annual increase for state education (3.6 percent).[8]

The sixth method of controlling prison overcrowding is the use of sentencing guidelines that are designed to save prison beds for more serious crimes and violent offenses. Structured sentencing is a compromise between indeterminate sentencing and mandatory determinate sentencing (see Chapter 3). Guidelines were conceived as a way to guide judicial discretion in sentencing. Under **structured sentencing,** a commission creates a set of guidelines that consider both the severity of a current offense and a few personal characteristics of the offender (notably, a prior criminal record). Guidelines for the type and duration of sentence are normally determined by deciding what type of punishment a particular crime deserves and calculating the probable cost of the sentence. Under a structured sentencing system, sentences are more uniform and less subject to the individual discretion of judges or parole board members. Sentencing guidelines have been a valuable tool for allocating state resources rationally and thoughtfully. They make it possible to anticipate and meet correctional resource needs on an ongoing basis rather than reacting after a crowding problem develops.

A jurisdiction establishing structured sentencing might consider implementing nonprison options such as interchangeability of punishments, also called **exchange rates.** A sentencing commission might, for example, decide that three days under house arrest or 40 community service hours is equivalent to one day of incarceration or that three years under intensive supervision is equivalent to one year in prison.

WHAT ARE THE CONSEQUENCES OF PRISON OVERCROWDING?

Researchers and prison administrators routinely observe the consequences of prison overcrowding. These include increases in idleness, drug trafficking, predatory sexual behavior, safety risks, gang confrontations, arguments, fights, assaults, murders, suicides, riots, medical and mental health problems, staff turnover, and stress. Other consequences include decreases in program

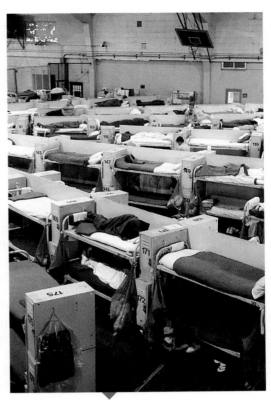

Although new prison facilities are being built, crowding continues to be an issue in many places. The auditorium of the Deuel Vocational Institution in Tracy, California, is converted into a dormitory to house prisoners. The prison has a design capacity of 1,725, but an operating capacity of 3,880. How can prison crowding be controlled?

structured sentencing

A set of guidelines for determining an offender's sentence.

exchange rates

An approach to sentencing that emphasizes interchangeability of punishments; for example, three days under house arrest might be considered equal to one day of incarceration.

opportunities, inappropriate housing assignments, judicial intervention to counteract illegal conditions, fines by state governments for operating over capacity, excessive wear and tear on prison facilities and equipment, and negative publicity about conditions in overcrowded facilities. Researchers have also linked overcrowding to higher rates of recidivism.[9] Two consequences described below are court intervention and inmate assaults.

Prisons Under Court Order   At midyear 2000, almost one-fourth (357) of all state, federal, and private prisons were under a court order to correct one or more conditions of confinement.[10] The total included 324 state prisons (down from 364 in 1995), and 33 private prisons (up from 15 in 1995). No federal prisons were under court order at midyear 2000.

Among the reasons prisons are under court order are to reduce crowding (105 prisons), improve inmate visiting, mail and telephone privileges (104 prisons), accommodate the physically challenged (95), permit religious expression (93), and offer mental health treatment (91). Fifty-nine prisons were under court order for improving the totality of prison conditions.

Inmate Assaults   Another serious consequence of prison overcrowding is prisoner violence. Approximately 34,400 inmate assaults on other inmates took place in the year preceding the 2000 census, 32 percent more than in 1995.[11] Fewer assaults, however, resulted in inmate deaths—51 in 2000 compared to 82 in 1995.

Overcrowding also affects staff. Inmate assaults on staff rose approximately 27 percent, from about 14,200 in 1995 to 18,000 in 2000, most occurring in maximum security prisons. The number of staff killed in such attacks was fewer in 2000 (5) than in 1995 (14).

Prison Security

For prisoners, staff, and their families on the outside, nothing is more frightening than a prison gang confrontation or a prison riot.

PRISON GANGS—SECURITY THREAT GROUPS

Prison gangs are one of the most significant developments in American prisons since the existence of the Gypsy Jokers Motorcycle Club was first recorded at the Walla Walla, Washington, penitentiary in 1950. To eliminate any publicity that gang members may draw about their gang or its activities and to describe accurately how these gangs negatively impact the security of prison operations, experts refer to them as **security threat groups (STGs)**. An STG is an inmate group, gang, organization, or association that has a name or identifying signs, colors, or symbols and whose members or associates engage in a pattern of gang activity or departmental rule violation so as to pose a threat to the staff, to public safety, to the secure and orderly operation of a correctional institution, or to other inmates. Most STGs were founded along racial and ethnic lines to offer inmates protection, but today many of them have joined alliances with other STGs to conduct organized criminal activity such as drug trafficking, prostitution, assault or extortion. Recently, Mark Pitcavage, a historian

security threat groups (STGs)
The current term for prison gangs.

and expert on race-based STGs, conducted a study of contemporary prison STGs. His interview with the Southern Poverty Law Center's *Intelligence Report* is presented in Exhibit 13-1.

In 2002, the National Major Gang Task Force (NMGTF) surveyed all adult prison systems in the United States, Guam, Puerto Rico, the U.S. Virgin Islands, and Canada. With almost 80 percent responding, NMGTF identified over 1,600 STGs with a total estimated membership of almost 114,000 inmates.[12]

There are six major STGs in the United States that are recognized nationally for their participation in organized crime and violence. They are:[13]

1. *Aryan Brotherhood:* Originated in 1967 in California's San Quentin Prison, its racial makeup is white.

2. *Black Guerilla Family:* Founded in 1966 at San Quentin Prison and considered the most politically oriented of the major state prison STGs, its racial makeup is black.

3. *Mexican Mafia:* Formed in the late 1950s in California's youth facility at Duel, its racial makeup is Mexican-American/Hispanic.

4. *La Nuestra Familia:* Originated in the California state prison at Soledad in the mid-1960s, its racial makeup is Mexican-American/ Hispanic.

5. *Neta:* Established in 1970 in the Rio Piedras Prison, Puerto Rico, its racial makeup is Puerto Rican–American/Hispanic.

6. *Texas Syndicate:* Originated in California's Folsom prison in the early 1970s in direct response to the other California prison gangs (notably the Aryan Brotherhood and the Mexican Mafia), which were attempting to prey on native Texas inmates, its racial makeup is Mexican-American/Hispanic.

New among the STGs is an influx of street gangs, such as Miami's "112 Avenue Boys" and Boston's "Franklin Field Pistons," that have less national organization than traditional STGs and do not easily fit into standard prison gang categories because of their smaller numbers, less cohesive ties, and less organized methods of operation.

STGs have a profound impact on prison security, and many prisons today have a Security Threat Group Unit that is responsible for the identification and overall coordination of all STG-related information at their facilities. STG members are five times more likely to incite or be involved in prison violence than are nonmembers.[14] In an attempt to control STG influence, some prison administrators transferred known STG members from one institution to another only to find that this practice actually increased STG organization and activity—it extended the STG's influence throughout a state's prison system. Other states enacted "gang enhancement" statutes that imposed severe sentences on STG activity. Today, many states are adopting a new strategy, segregating known STG members to highly restrictive supermax housing, correctional facilities that are designed to house the "worst of the worst" prisoners under complete lockdown and total isolation. Advocates of this approach contend that removing STG leaders from the general prison population reduces the amount of control that STG leaders exert. Critics of the approach argue that violence actually

EXHIBIT 13–1   **"Behind the Walls: An Expert Discusses the Role of Race-Based Gangs in America's Prisons"**

An interview with Mark Pitcavage

Intelligence Report (IR): Why do prisoners join gangs?

Mark Pitcavage (MP): Prison gangs offer protection—and money and drugs. Some offer ideology, racial or otherwise, but protection is the key.

IR: Is virtually every prisoner affiliated?

MP: No, no. A lot of prisoners never become affiliated. It all depends on the prison. If you're talking about a minimum-security prison, you're not going to see much of that. In maximum security prisons, you see much more gang activity.

In state prisons, where many inmates are serving long sentences, there is a great deal of gang activity. There are gangs in federal prisons, too. Some gangs even have federal and state prison chapters. But even in state prison, where there is generally more activity, a minority of prisoners will belong.

IR: What are the largest prison gangs?

MP: The most prominent white supremacist gangs are the Aryan Brotherhood, the Aryan Circle, the Nazi Low Riders, and the Peckerwoods. There are racist black groups, like the Black Guerilla Family, the Five Percenters, and the Moorish Science Temple. And major Hispanic gangs include the Mexican Mafia (known as "la eme," for its first letter) and La Nuestra Familia. And basically apolitical street gangs like the Crips and the Bloods are inside the prisons, too.

IR: Did something occur to help promote these gangs' growth?

MP: Many prison populations were desegregated during the 1960s, and one result was that many inmates felt they had to join a race-based gang for protection. If white prisoners and black prisoners were separated, then that would not be an issue. *[IR Editor's note: Some states have actually resegregated certain cell blocks as a security measure meant to weaken race-based gangs.]*

But the key to the Aryan Brotherhood—and the key to understanding virtually all prison gangs—is that ideology often takes a back seat to organized criminal activity. The Aryan Brotherhood is an organized crime group—that is the primary dynamic behind it. It's all about drugs, protection rackets, prostitution, extortion, witness intimidation, assaults, etc.

In many prisons, the Aryan Brotherhood actually makes alliances with gangs of other races. If they were ideological white supremacists, they wouldn't do that. That is why a lot of people who join race-based prison gangs while in prison don't stay with them once they're out or join other white supremacist groups. They just aren't primarily ideologically motivated.

IR: There was a major federal bust of 40 members of the Aryan Brotherhood, 30 in prison and 10 on the outside, in October 2002. A central allegation was that members killed or attempted to kill people inside and outside the prisons in order to control drug trafficking, gambling, and extortion. How do prisoners reach outside the walls to control or influence activity that involves the free world?

MP: There are a lot of ways you can pass on information from the prisons. Wives and girlfriends of prisoners often play an important role. The Aryan Circle, for example, uses its female supporters on the outside, who they call *sisters,* to conduct business operations and spread racist propaganda. And you can always meet privately with your attorney, who may be willing to carry messages to someone else on the outside. There are ways. If you are in a maximum-security prison or in administrative isolation, it obviously is more difficult.

IR: You note in your report that the men who murdered James Byrd Jr. in the Jasper, Texas, truck-dragging incident had developed their racial beliefs while behind bars. What is the link between incarceration and politicization?

MP: Exactly what dynamic occurs varies with each particular individual, but there are some universals. Prisoners have a lot of time on their hands, and as a result they are desperate for reading materials. They are desperate for stimulation. Some of them are just fine with pumping weights, but others aren't and seek out extremist publications as well as nonextremist publications. You see prisoners asking for free subscriptions, for correspondence, for people to send them materials, anything. They may not be ideological at that point, but they want *something*—and the material they get can lead to their politicization.

Another thing is that many prisoners want to justify or rationalize what they have done or what has happened to them. They don't want to say they did something wrong or deserved what they got. This is true whether you are black or white. By adopting a particular ideological slant, you can rationalize that you are not a simple criminal, that you are in jail for political reasons.

Left-wing extremists have rationalized bank robberies as expropriations from the state. A right-wing prisoner rationalizes his crime as fighting back against ZOG [or "Zionist Occupied Government," a term used by many neo-Nazis]—and he will be backed up morally by white supremacist publications.

continued

EXHIBIT 13-1 Concluded

The ideologies offer an excuse and a sense of empowerment that allows someone in jail to be transformed from a criminal into a "prisoner of war" or "political prisoner."

IR: Are there other benefits for prisoners?

MP: If you join a movement, you can receive all kinds of benefits from outside people in the movement. A lot of left-wing groups do serious prisoner support, sending you gifts or money, raising funds for your defense. They may write you letters, put up Web pages about you, and so on. Many right-wing groups do the same, setting up "prison ministries." Often young women are encouraged to write to male prisoners, something that is seen as a terrifically important benefit.

This can play out well for prisoners who get out. They enter a world where they are heroes. They are ex-"POWS," liberated "political prisoners" who can tell the youngsters outside what it's all about. As such, they have access to women, drugs, all kinds of things.

IR: How do outside groups recruit in the prisons?

MP: Sending materials and writing letters are the most common ways. Sometimes visits are used. Prisoners are lonely and have often been abandoned by their friends and family. Extremists capitalize on those feelings.

IR: Who decides what literature gets into prison?

MP: They're called *security threat group analysts.* The federal level has a whole bunch of them. On the state level, they may be substantial or sometimes just a few who monitor activities in all the prisons in a given state. They look at all the materials coming in and out of prison to see if they are allowable or if they are linked to extremism, street gangs, organized crime, violence and so on. If they identify a prisoner as a member of one of these groups, they may be able to take additional measures against him, such as placing him in administrative segregation. They have fairly wide latitude.

IR: Is there a relationship between getting recruited into these racist groups and then committing hate crimes or other violence after leaving prison?

MP: My suspicion is that there is probably not a huge link, because a lot of these people just join the gangs while they are in prison, and then leave them when they get out. But the fact is that some prisoners do get genuinely politicized, and on top of that, prison gives them an education in violence. It's a mess. I think that is what happened in Texas (with the murderers of James Byrd Jr.), and the result was one of the most inhumane acts ever perpetrated in modern America.

IR: Is there a significant distinction between those who come into prison without much racial awareness, like the men who killed James Byrd, and extremists who enter prison already highly politicized?

MP: People who are already ideologically extreme don't stop their activities in prison—some of them see prison as a great opportunity for recruiting. Take Leroy Schweitzer, the Montana Freeman (a form of "sovereign citizen") leader who's in federal prison in South Carolina serving a 22-year sentence for various financial scams. He's teaching prisoners how to engage in "paper terrorism," how to file bogus liens against public officials, attorneys, and others. He even showed one jewel dealer serving a 40-year sentence on money laundering charges how to file a (bogus) $1.5 billion lien against the judge in his case.

Other imprisoned ideologues try to influence followers outside of prison. Craig "Critter" Marshall, environmental extremist serving a five-year sentence for conspiracy to commit arson, told *Earth First!* readers last year that the only form of solidarity he wants is more arsons. He wrote something like, "When someone picks up a bomb, instead of a pen, is when my spirits really soar."

IR: How much of a threat do these gangs pose to prison staff?

MP: Prisons are dangerous. I don't know whether the violence from gang members is greater than that of nongang members, although obviously there is a greater potential for planned or organized violence. But there is a lot of training for this sort of thing now—prisons in general have better control mechanisms, whether it is cameras, doors that can automatically shut, or special training. But that doesn't stop prisoners from killing each other all the time—and it doesn't stop guards from being assaulted. Let's face it, prisons are nasty places.

may increase because conditions within supermax housing are so harsh that they emotionally damage inmates who may one day be returned to the general prison population or released or paroled into the community.

Two explanations for STG development are deprivation and importation. As we saw in Chapter 10, the basic premise of deprivation theory is that inmates develop a social system as a way to adapt to the pains of imprisonment. Because inmates are deprived of liberty, autonomy, goods and services, sexual relations, and security, they develop a culture that helps them get back what imprisonment has taken away. Importation theory, on the other hand, emphasizes that inmates' preprison attitudes and values guide their reactions and responses to the internal conditions of prison. Both theories are valid; most major STGs can be traced to preprison attitudes and values, but prison conditions influence when and to what extent STG activity and violence occur.

PRISON RIOTS AND DISTURBANCES

Each prison disturbance and riot is unique. The precipitating conditions, resolutions, and aftermath are shaped by the characteristics of the institution, its staff, its administration, and its inmate population, as well as the state or federal agency to which it belongs.

Each prison disturbance and riot is unique. The precipitating conditions, resolutions, and aftermath are shaped by the characteristics of the institution, its staff, its administration, and its inmate population, as well as the state or federal agency to which it belongs. No amount of comprehensive planning can prevent all disturbances and riots, because, as one expert contends, some have no root causes.[15] It is impossible to predict where and when they will occur. Still, understanding prison disturbances and riots can help correctional administrators avoid some problems, take steps to prevent certain events from launching into full-fledged riots, limit the extent of damage, and terminate disturbances and riots in the least costly way.

In May 2002, the ACA published the results of a survey of prison disturbances, riots, assaults, and escapes. ACA defined **disturbance** as an altercation involving three or more inmates, resulting in official action beyond summary sanctions, and for which there is an institutional record. Most prison disturbances were fights, stabbings, assaults, shouting obscenities at staff, refusal to follow orders (e.g., clean cell area and return to cell), hostage taking, and cell extraction. A **riot** is any action by a group of inmates that constitutes a forcible attempt to gain control of a facility or area within a facility. Comparing the data published in 2002 with data from a similar survey published four years earlier, the ACA concluded, "The pattern for violence in prison has decreased."[16] From 2000 to 2001, the number of states reporting a prison disturbance and the number of prison disturbances decreased. There were also decreases in the number of inmates killed by inmates and staff, staff and officers assaulted, inmate suicide attempts and deaths, inmates injured by staff, and escapes and walkaways.

Some states have alternate definitions of *disturbances* and *riots*, making comparisons difficult. Tennessee, for example, defines *disturbances* as events in which control of the inmate is temporarily lost or threatened to be lost or the peace of others is disturbed by violent, profane, indecent, offensive, or boisterous conduct or language. This definition of *disturbances*

disturbance
An altercation involving three or more inmates, resulting in official action beyond summary sanctions and for which there is an institutional record.

riot
Any action by a group of inmates that constitutes a forcible attempt to gain control of a facility or area within a facility.

in Tennessee accounted for 2,454 of the total disturbances in 2000 and 2,153 of them in 2001.

What some states call a *riot*, others downplay and call a *disturbance*. For example, in 1993 there were more than 186 disturbances in 21 corrections systems—but only 7 were classified as riots.[17] In Connecticut, a gang fight involving more than 300 inmates and causing over $100,000 in damage was called a *riot*. At Leavenworth, a racial fight involving 427 inmates that caused significant damage to the prison's auditorium, chapel, and industry buildings was called a *disturbance*. Correctional administrators label most incidents *disturbances* because the term is less sensational.

How many prison riots have there been in the United States? Nobody knows for sure. Not only do we have different opinions as to what constitutes a riot, but wardens and state officials are reluctant to publicize loss of control. Scholars estimate that almost 500 prison riots have taken place in the United States since 1855.[18]

Prison violence and riots are as old as prisons themselves. There were riots and mass escapes at the Walnut Street Jail in Philadelphia, at Newgate Prison in New York, and almost everywhere from the beginning of prisons in this country. One particularly eventful year was 1952, when riots erupted in 25 of the 152 U.S. prisons. Although no lives were lost, prison staff and inmates were in danger, and damage ran into the millions. Reasons for the riots included absence of inmate programs and work, idleness, unqualified staff who were poorly trained and poorly paid, old facilities (one-third were more than 70 years old), absence of procedures for hearing inmate grievances, overcrowding, insufficient prison budgets, absence of inmate classification, philosophical conflicts about the nature of prisoners (treat them as human beings who will one day rejoin society or "treat them rough"), and the presence of a new generation of prisoners.[19]

In 1954, reformers advocated overhauling and modernizing prison programs, replacing old prisons, hiring more and better staff, and developing an integrated state system. They advocated the creation of

- professionally staffed classification centers;
- prisons no larger than 500 beds;
- professionally trained, well-paid correctional officers;
- inmate self-governance;
- procedures that allow inmate grievances to be aired;
- prison work programs with fair wages paid to prisoners;
- periodic review of sentencing patterns and parole board decisions;
- dissemination of statistics on commitments and releases;
- prerelease orientation and job-finding assistance for discharged prisoners; and
- statewide prison leadership headed by nonpolitical, nationally recruited, and professionally trained individuals.[20]

> Reasons for the riots included absence of inmate programs and work, idleness, unqualified staff who were poorly trained and poorly paid, old facilities (one-third were more than 70 years old), absence of procedures for hearing inmate grievances, overcrowding, insufficient prison budgets, absence of inmate classification, philosophical conflicts about the nature of prisoners (treat them as human beings who will one day rejoin society or "treat them rough"), and the presence of a new generation of prisoners.

Corrections and law enforcement officers use their weapons to stop a riot. Prison riots can be costly in terms of human suffering, lost lives, and property destruction. What are some of the causes of prison riots and how can they be prevented?

Despite reformers' calls for overhauls of prison programs and management, violence-provoking conditions continue to exist in many prisons. One might wonder if anything has changed since the storm of prison riots in 1952. Three of the bloodiest and most violent prison riots in the United States occurred in severely overcrowded prisons in New York in 1971, in New Mexico in 1980, and in Ohio in 1993.

In the 1971 riot at the Attica Correctional Facility, New York, where 2,225 inmates were incarcerated in a prison designed for 1,200, 43 lives were lost: four inmates were killed during the riot as part of inmate "justice," and when police stormed in to retake the prison, they killed 10 civilian hostages and 29 prisoners. The New York State Special Commission that investigated the riot wrote, "With the exception of Indian massacres in the late 19th century, the State Police assault which ended the four-day prison uprising was the bloodiest one-day encounter between Americans since the Civil War."[21]

In the 1980 riot at the Penitentiary of New Mexico in Santa Fe, where 1,136 inmates were confined in space designed for 900 inmates, the taking of human life was brutal. Thirty-three inmates were tortured, dismembered, decapitated, burned alive, and killed by fellow inmates. Although staff were held hostage, none was killed.

The longest prison riot in U.S. history occurred at the Southern Ohio Correctional Facility in Lucasville in 1993, where 1,820 inmates were held in a prison built for 1,540. Inmates killed nine of their fellow inmates and one correctional officer in the 11-day siege.

The riot at Lucasville cost an estimated $15 million in property damage. At Santa Fe, the estimate was $28.5 million. At Attica, the cost was more than $3 million. A new chapter in the cost of prison riots was written on

August 28, 2000, when, after three decades of waiting, federal District Court Judge Michael A. Telesca accepted New York State's agreement to set aside $12 million (the largest amount ever in a prisoner rights case) to compensate more than 500 inmates and relatives for the abuse that the prisoners suffered. Four million dollars was set aside for lawyer fees, and $8 million was divided among 502 inmates and relatives of the inmates who died in the uprising. After the riot ended, inmates were stripped naked and threatened with castration, forced to crawl naked in the mud with an "X" on their backs as if to make them a target, severely beaten, and shot. After hearing the inmates' stories, Judge Telesca described the aftermath as littered with "brutal beatings and acts of torture" and unlimited racial epithets.

Causes of Prison Riots   According to sociology professor Burt Useem at the University of New Mexico, there are five theoretical explanations for the causes of prison riots.[22]

The first is random chance. Useem says that some prison riots have no root causes. It is impossible to predict where and when they will occur.

The second explanation is bad conditions. This explanation tells us that overcrowding, antiquated facilities, low staffing levels, insufficient staff training, lack of programs for inmates, lack of funding, and poor implementation of correctional policy account for prison riots. Overcrowding is the most important of these. It causes heightened prison tension and potential violent disruption. Overcrowding is responsible for curtailing or even eliminating opportunities for education, vocational training, and recreation. When the ratio of correctional officers to inmates becomes too low, something has to give. At Attica, Santa Fe, and Lucasville, overcrowding raised tensions, interfered with prisoner classification, reduced living space, and restricted access to programs. Restlessness and boredom grew.

The third explanation is rebellious inmates and racial antagonism. This includes gang members and violent or aggressive inmates. Riots tend to occur in higher-security facilities. Outside prison the ratio of racial minorities to whites is about one to five. In prison, however, whites are the minority. That different ratio, in addition to overcrowding, close living quarters, and lack of space, adds to racial antagonism. Antagonism is heightened when inmates separate themselves along racial or ethnic lines for self-protection. Researchers have discovered that as inmates' perception of overcrowding increases, their antagonism toward other racial and ethnic groups also increases. Prisoners at Attica, Santa Fe, and Lucasville were young, violence prone, and poorly classified. Most were undereducated, underemployed, and uncommitted to society's means for achieving social goals. The racial and ethnic minority imbalance, together with these individual factors, prompted many inmates to adopt tough attitudes and join STGs for self-protection.

> Antagonism is heightened when inmates separate themselves along racial or ethnic lines for self-protection. Researchers have discovered that as inmates' perception of overcrowding increases, their antagonism toward other racial and ethnic groups also increases.

The fourth explanation focuses on institutional structure and readiness. Riots occur when a prison's infrastructure wears thin and authorities fail to plan and prepare. Riot readiness serves as a deterrent and prevents a situation from turning into a riot. At Attica, a faulty weld joint in a metal gate gave way and allowed prisoners access to most areas of the institution. At Santa Fe, inmates pounded on "shatterproof" glass with a fire extinguisher until the glass fell out of the frame. At Lucasville, inmates collected master keys from staff hostages and opened cell doors.

The fifth explanation focuses on administrative factors. Poor prison management and administration are linked to prison riots. Poor management can result from frequent staff turnover, low correctional officer qualifications, inadequate training, poor staff-inmate communication, and low staff pay. At Attica, Santa Fe, and Lucasville, inmates' complaints about living conditions, lack of programs, and officers' excessive use of force and harassment went unheard by administration. Rumors of riots were not taken seriously.

Preventing Prison Riots   Prison violence provokes more violence. Measures to prevent prison riots must become a national priority, and change must occur. Three years before the Attica riot, the U.S. National Advisory Commission on Civil Disorders (the Kerner Commission) warned that the only effective way to prevent riots, whether in or out of prison, was to eliminate sources of tension by making good "the promises of American democracy to all citizens, urban and rural, white and black, Spanish surname, American Indian, and every minority group."[23] While that change is long-range, corrections officials can implement immediate measures to reduce the likelihood of inmate aggression, including the following:

- formal inmate grievance procedures;
- ombudsmen to mediate disputes;
- an improved classification system;
- smaller institutions;
- meaningful prison school and work programs;
- alternatives to incarceration;
- professional corrections staff who are trained and well paid;
- administrators who are visible and available to staff and inmates; and
- clearly written and understood policies on the use of force when necessary.

To ensure that the use of force is appropriate and justifiable, the ACA recommends establishing polices and procedures that govern its use (see Exhibit 13–2).

Supermax Housing and "No-Frills" Prisons and Jails

In an effort to control the behavior of violence-prone inmates, two new types of prisons are emerging—supermax housing and "no-frills" prisons and jails. Both alter the conditions of confinement for thousands of U.S. prisoners, raising important issues for the prisoners and staff who must live and work in them and the society that must accept the prisoners when they are released.

EXHIBIT 13–2   **American Correctional Association**

Policy on Use of Force

Use of force consists of physical contact with an offender in a confrontational situation to control behavior and enforce order. Use of force includes use of restraints (other than for routine transportation and movement), chemical agents, and weapons. Force is justified only when required to maintain or regain control or when there is imminent danger of personal injury or serious damage to property. To assure the use of force is appropriate and justifiable, correctional agencies should do the following:

A. Establish and maintain policies that require reasonable steps be taken to reduce or prevent the necessity for the use of force, that authorize force only when no reasonable alternative is possible, that permit only the minimum force necessary, and that prohibit the use of force as a retaliatory or disciplinary measure.

B. Establish and enforce procedures that define the range of methods for and alternatives to the use of force and that specify the conditions under which each is permitted. The procedures must assign responsibility for authorizing such force and assure appropriate documentation and supervision of the action.

C. Establish and maintain procedures that limit the use of deadly force to those instances in which it is legally authorized and where there is an imminent threat to human life or a threat to public safety that cannot reasonably be prevented by other means.

D. Maintain operating procedures and regular staff training designed to anticipate, stabilize, and defuse situations that might give rise to conflict, confrontation, and violence.

E. Provide specialized training to ensure competency in all methods of use of force, especially in methods and equipment requiring special knowledge and skills such as defensive tactics, weapons, restraints, and chemical agents.

F. Establish and maintain procedures that require that all incidents involving the use of force be fully documented and independently reviewed by a higher correctional authority. A report of the use of force, including appropriate investigation and any recommendations for preventive and remedial action, shall be submitted for administrative review and implementation of recommendations when appropriate.

SUPERMAX HOUSING

Prison systems have always needed a way to deal with inmates whose violent behavior makes it impossible for them to live with the general prison population. Generally such measures involve separating such inmates and are called *segregation* or *solitary confinement*. Prisoners who are dangerous or chronically violent, have escaped or attempted to escape from a high-security correctional facility, have incited or attempted to incite disruption in a correctional facility, or who have preyed on weaker inmates are removed from the general population. You may recall from Chapter 7 that, in 1829, the Eastern State Penitentiary in Cherry Hill, Pennsylvania, was built on the principle of solitary confinement. However, in 1913 the Pennsylvania legislature dropped "solitary" from sentencing statutes, and housing arrangements at Eastern State became congregate. From that point forward, specialized housing units were developed for management and control of troublesome inmates.

> **Ethical Dilemma**
> Supermax prisons are a relatively new and expensive trend whose overall constitutionality is unclear. Are these institutions a fad or a wise investment? For more information go to Ethical Dilemma 13-1 at http://www.mhhe.com/schmalleger2.

"Supermax" prisons are ultra–high-security correctional facilities such as this one—the Federal Administrative Maximum Security Prison in Florence, Colorado. What kinds of inmates should be held in such facilities?

supermax housing

A free-standing facility, or a distinct unit within a facility, that provides for management and secure control of inmates who have been officially designated as exhibiting violent or serious and disruptive behavior while incarcerated.

The federal Bureau of Prisons (BOP) returned to the idea of controlling the most violent and disruptive inmates in indefinite solitary confinement when it opened Alcatraz in 1934. Alcatraz, which had a capacity of 275, did not offer any treatment program; its sole purpose was to incarcerate and punish the federal prison system's most desperate criminals and worst troublemakers. Alcatraz was "America's Devil's Island, it was 'Hellcatraz'—a place where convicts slowly went insane from the tedium and hopelessness of endless years on 'the Rock.'"[24] By 1963, Alcatraz was judged an expensive failure; it symbolized a penal philosophy that was outdated in an era that espoused rehabilitation, not punishment, as the goal of incarceration. Alcatraz closed in the early 1960s under orders from U.S. Attorney General Robert Kennedy. During the era of rehabilitation that followed the Alcatraz closing, prison officials used the *dispersal model*—problem prisoners were distributed to a number of prisons. Prison officials hoped that dispersal among populations of generally law-abiding inmates would dilute the influence of problem prisoners. Inmates from Alcatraz were moved to federal prisons in Atlanta and Leavenworth.

By the 1970s, the goal of incarceration had shifted back to punishment. Disturbances, violence, and riots at state and federal prisons convinced the BOP to try again to control the most troublesome federal inmates in one location. The BOP reverted to the *concentration model*—all problem prisoners would be housed together in a separate facility. The federal prison at Marion, Illinois, was chosen for this purpose. The construction features at Marion, however, made it difficult for staff to maintain complete control over recalcitrant inmates. Open cell-fronts were a major limitation in Marion's design to control the toughest prisoners. Through their cell bars, inmates threw trash, urine, and feces at corrections officers; passed contraband; set fires; and verbally harassed and lunged at staff and other prisoners as they walked by. Tension, hostility, violence, and murder were all too common. On October 23, 1983, a state of emergency was declared, and the Marion facility was placed on lockdown status. Over the next few years, the BOP conceived plans to build a supermax facility that would implement construction features for controlling difficult inmates.

In 1994, the BOP opened its first **supermax housing** facility at Florence, Colorado, for the 400 most dangerous, violent, escape-prone, and STG federal inmate leaders. Construction cost totaled $60 million ($150,000 per cell). Annual operating cost per cell per year is another $40,000, or $19.2 million total annually. Supermax prisons are significantly more expensive to build than traditional prisons due in part to the enhanced and extensive high-security features on locks, doors, and perimeters; heavily reinforced walls, ceilings, and floors; and incorporation of advanced electronic systems and technology. Providing meals and other services at individual cell fronts, multiple officer escorts, and maintaining elaborate electronic systems contribute to the high cost. Cell design at the federal supermax prison in Florence, Colorado, resists vandalism. Each prisoner's bed, desk, stool, and bookcase are made of reinforced concrete and anchored in place. Each cell has a shower stall with flood-proof plumbing and a 12-inch black-and-white television set. Cell windows deny prisoners all views of the outside except the sky above. A simple hole-in-the-wall apparatus for lighting cigarettes has replaced matches and cigarette lighters. Meals are dispensed through cell slots in separate heated trays from airline-style carts pulled by small tractors. Cells are staggered so that inmates cannot make eye contact with other inmates. There are no congregate activities of any kind. Each cell has a double-entry door; an interior barred cage door backed up by a windowed steel door that prevents voice contact among prisoners.

The new prison has 1,400 electronically controlled gates, 168 television monitors, and three mirrored-glass gun towers. The 400 cells are subdivided among nine units—each unit is self-contained and includes a sick-call room, law library, and barber chair. After three years of good behavior, an inmate gradually regains social contact. "What puts a man in is his behavior, and what gets a man out is his behavior," said John M. Vanyur, the associate warden.[25]

This type of super-controlled environment is taking hold across the United States. Forty-one states, the District of Columbia, and the BOP now operate one or more supermax prisons.[26] Despite the considerable cost to build and operate a supermax prison, the facilities are politically and publicly attractive. "Supermax prisons have become political symbols of how "tough" a jurisdiction has become."[27]

California opened Pelican Bay State Prison in Crescent City in 1990 for 1,600 inmates in an X-shaped windowless bunker. Construction cost was $133,653 per cell. All inmates are denied access to prison work and group exercise yards. Pelican Bay, like the federal supermax housing facility in Florence, Colorado, is entirely automated. Inmates in the supermax housing unit have no face-to-face contact with staff or other inmates. Cell doors are solid stainless steel with slots for food trays. Cell doors open and close electronically. Officers can talk with or listen in on inmates through a speaker system. These inmates do not work. They have no recreational equipment. They do not mix with other inmates. They are not permitted to smoke. They eat all meals in their cells. They leave their cells only for showers and 90 minutes of daily exercise in small cement areas enclosed by 20-foot cement walls. Visits with family and friends are noncontact behind glass partitions. Prisoners are strip-searched and handcuffed whenever they are removed from their cells and placed in full shackles with waist and hobble chains.

The National Institute of Corrections (NIC) studied supermax prisons nationwide in 1997 and published a follow-up report in 1999. In 1999, it described the supermax prison as "a highly restrictive, high-custody housing unit within a secure facility, or an entire secure facility, that isolates inmates from the general population and from each other due to grievous crimes, repetitive assaultive or violent institutional behavior, the threat of escape or actual escape from high-custody facility(s), or inciting or threatening to incite disturbances in a correctional institution." Supermax housing does not include maximum or close custody facilities that are designated for routine housing of inmates with high-custody needs, inmates in

Eye On Corrections™

Overcrowding Forces States to Build: But Do They Match the Need? The Supermax Appeal

By Meghan Fay

States need to build new facilities due to overcrowding, but are states building facilities that meet their needs, and are they building facilities for the right reasons? Some have argued that states are building supermax prisons because they are an easy sell to legislators and the public, not because they are necessary.

"Being tough on crime is a very short-term solution. We can sell a supermax facility to the legislature because it makes good political rhetoric to the legislature, but [the question is] does our population really need it?" said Bob Brown, director of the National Institute of Corrections Academy.

Recently, Wisconsin has been the center of debate over the motivating factors that led to the construction of a $43 million, 509-bed supermax facility in Boscobel, a rural town in desperate need of economic rejuvenation.

"These 509 beds are not here to address our overcrowding problem," said Gerald Berge, warden of the supermax facility. "We are not going to use this as a population relief [method] in any way." However, in a 1996 weekly column, Governor Tommy G. Thompson implies that the facility was built to alleviate the state's overcrowding problem: "In addition to a supermax prison, my office has been working on a number of ways to alleviate overcrowding, including my proposal for a 500-bed detention facility in southeastern Wisconsin to hold convicts who violate parole or probation terms."

The controversy lies in the fact that a supermax is designed for the most violent offenders, but not all inmates belong in such a facility.

According to William Clausis, public information director for the Wisconsin Department of Corrections, the supermax facility "is not a capacity institution." Clausis insists that there is a need for one because the state's segregation units are overcrowded. There is a "need for a supermax to isolate the incorrigible inmates," he said. It is difficult to discipline inmates when there is no room in the facilities to segregate them.

According to Berge, there are 44 inmates in the facility. However, the supermax facility opened on November 10 [1999], and it is still too soon to tell what the average daily population will be. Filling all the beds is not the intention, said Berge. He recommends that at least 10 percent of capacity be kept free for potential problems within other institutions.

"There have been people who have suggested that supermax facilities have been built only for political reasons, Wisconsin's specifically, and that is vastly oversimplified," said Berge. "Clearly [there are] political aspects, but there are also serious corrections needs."

According to Clausis, of the total inmate population, 4,137 are sent out of state because the state capacity is 10,844. There are two medium security facilities under construction. The medium security level population is "where the bulk of our crowding is," said Clausis.

disciplinary segregation or protective custody, or other inmates requiring segregation or separation for other routine purposes. In fact, NIC opined that as comforting as it might be to prison staff to send nuisance inmates who continuously test the limits, frequently break minor rules, consume an inordinate amount of staff time, are situationally assaultive, or cannot control their behavior due to mental illness to supermax facilities, it is inappropriate to do so. Use of extended control housing for nuisance inmates is inefficient, consumes expensive high-security beds, has little overall operational impact, and is arguably overkill.

NIC found that a universal definition of supermax housing is problematic. The many states that provided information had different reasons and needs for supermax housing. Some supermax prisons house inmates who could not be controlled in traditional administrative segregation units, including prisoners who are uncontrollable due to mental illness. Others are an extension or expansion of segregation and house protective custody and/or disciplinary segregation inmates. Still others house inmates who would reside in close-custody among the general population in most other jurisdictions. As these prisons have increased in number, been reported on by the media, and gained popularity with the public, a variety of names have emerged to describe them. *Special housing unit, maxi-maxi, maximum control facility, secured housing unit, intensive housing unit, intensive management unit,* and *administrative maximum penitentiary* are but a few of the names used. The term *supermax* is the one heard most frequently in the media and in the field of corrections. Yet, as learned from the NIC survey, the term is applied to a wide variety of facilities and programs handling an equally wide variety of inmate populations. NIC's conclusion is, "Supermax as defined in the survey may exist in relatively few agencies."

To date, no studies have been done on the impact of supermax prisons on inmates after release. However, criminologists, psychiatrists, lawyers, and the courts who have studied the effects of long-term solitary confinement report evidence of acute sensory deprivation, paranoid delusion belief systems, irrational fears of violence, resentment, little ability to control rage, and mental breakdowns.[28] The vast majority of inmates in long-term solitary confinement remain anxious, angry, depressed, insecure, and confused. Some commit suicide. Some will have been so deprived of human contact that it will be hard for them to cope with social situations. If the correctional staff cannot confidently assess what the inmate will do when supermax restrictions are lifted, the risks that have been avoided by placing an inmate in a supermax facility are revisited when the inmate is released, either back into the general prison population or into society. Some say we must consider this concern and ask if we want these inmates back in our communities in the same, better, or worse condition than when they left.[29] In 1995, *60 Minutes* reporter Mike Wallace asked Lt. Al Dienes, Pelican Bay's Information Officer, "Does Pelican Bay make society safer?" Dienes replied, "I can't answer your question; it's beyond us."

The impact of supermax facilities on staff is also a subject of much discussion. Having to deal on a daily basis with inmates who have proven to be the most troublesome—in an environment that prioritizes human control and isolation—presents staff with extraordinary challenges.

> The vast majority of inmates in long-term solitary confinement remain anxious, angry, depressed, insecure, and confused.

Supermax Prisons

by Morris L. Thigpen, Sr., National Institute of Corrections, United States Department of Justice

In 1997, the National Institute of Corrections (NIC) conducted a national survey entitled "Supermax Housing." The definition used in that survey is generally accepted by most correctional administrators: "A freestanding facility, or a distinct unit within a freestanding facility, that provides for the management and secure control of inmates who have been officially designated as exhibiting violent or seriously disruptive behavior while incarcerated."

Our knowledge and use of supermax housing has become more sophisticated in the last five or six years, and I believe we will continue to see the use of supermax facilities until we invent a better method of managing the seriously disruptive and violent inmate. We do run the risk of the courts intervening, even with their reduced involvement in prison operations cases, if we are not cautious in several areas.

The process by which inmates are placed in supermax should be carefully examined. It can be easily abused. To avoid the abuse, the classification process should involve a team approach with staff from various disciplines such as medical, psychology, programs, as well as correctional officers. Final approval should come from the executive staff. If sufficient controls are not in place, inappropriate placements will take place such as nuisance inmates or those who have only infrequently been assertive.

The violent mentally ill inmate who can be controlled by other means is not a proper placement for supermax. It is imperative that all inmates placed in supermax be fully aware of how they can work their way out. There should be opportunities to demonstrate positive behavior patterns through program participation, not just through avoidance of negative acting-out behavior. This is obviously impossible if the policy for supermax is to deny any opportunity to demonstrate positive behavior.

The role of the supermax facility as defined in the overall correctional plan can significantly impact the type and operation of the facility. Staff who lead, manage, and operate the facility will have significant impact on the philosophy and culture developed in the facility. Staff assigned to supermax should be among the best, highly trained staff available. They should have demonstrated their ability to work in a hostile environment, maintain self control, and relate in a positive manner with difficult inmates. The nature of supermax is ripe for abuse by staff that are not prepared and trained for this assigned duty.

The supermax prison will continue to exist for a number of reasons. It is a status symbol of "tough on crime." It has political value. States without supermax facilities are seen as outside of current correctional practices. This type of facility is very expensive to build and exceedingly expensive to operate. Once it exists, it will continue to be used as a supermax unit whether it is needed or not. The majority of correctional staff will support the continued need as they view it now as a necessary component to insure the ability to control the serious and violent offender as well as to insure staff safety in managing the predatory inmates.

Several factors will continue to provide a stream of candidates for supermax. Sentencing changes leading to longer time to be served for violent offenders in an environment void of program and treatment interventions, along with increased idleness and gang activities will not have any tendency to decrease the number of those inmates likely to do time in supermax facilities.

Finally, it will be up to those of you who will be the future leaders in corrections to evaluate supermax facilities, define their purposes, shape their policies, and manage the populations that they serve, hopefully in a manner that will lead to positive, changed behavior.

ABOUT THE AUTHOR

Morris Thigpen is director of the National Institute of Corrections (NIC)—a position to which he was appointed in June 1994 by then–U.S. Attorney General Janet Reno. NIC is an agency within the U.S. Department of Justice, Federal Bureau of Prisons. Thigpen holds a B.S. degree from Millsaps College, Jackson, Mississippi, and an M.Ed. degree from Mississippi State University. He has served as Commissioner of Corrections in Alabama and as Mississippi's Deputy Administrator of the Department of Human Services.

Correctional administrators with experiences in operating supermax prisons talk about the potential for creating a "we/they syndrome" between staff and inmates. The nature and reputation of the inmate and frequently the inmate's behavior, combined with ultra-control and rigidity, magnify the tension between inmates and staff. When there is little interaction except in control situations, the adversarial nature of the relationships tends to be one of dominance and, in return, resistance on both sides. Stuart Grassian, a physician and expert on prison control units, believes that people who work in supermax facilities lose their capacity to be shocked by the kinds of things they see. "It may put money in your pocket," Dr. Grassian notes, "but over time it destroys you psychologically and brings out rage and sadism and violence and brutality."[30]

Some inmates in supermax housing facilities have challenged the conditions of their confinement. In 1995, inmates at Pelican Bay's supermax unit challenged the constitutionality of extreme isolation and environmental deprivation. They claimed that the degree of segregation was so extreme and the restrictions so severe, that the inmates confined there were psychologically traumatized and, in some cases, deprived of sanity. The federal court agreed. The court ruled in *Madrid* v. *Gomez* (1995) that "conditions in security housing unit did impose cruel and unusual punishment on mentally ill prisoners" and "those who were at particularly high risk for suffering very serious or severe injury to their mental health."[31] The court declared that the state of California could not continue to confine inmates who were already mentally ill or those who were at an unreasonably high risk of suffering serious mental illness in the supermax unit. The court also appointed a **special master** (a person appointed to act as the representative of the court) to work with the state of California to develop a satisfactory remedial plan and provide a progress report to the court.

special master
A person appointed by the court to act as its representative to oversee remedy of a violation and provide regular progress reports.

"NO-FRILLS" PRISONS AND JAILS

The image of prisons and jails as "country clubs" and "mini-resorts" is not new and it continues to make for great speeches, but it is erroneous. It ignores the harsh realities of imprisonment. Having only the information that appears on television and in newspapers and magazines, the public still believes that inmates are living the good life, lounging on recliners and channel surfing. In 1995, an NBC television poll found that 82 percent of Americans felt that prison life was too easy.[32] In March 1998, the *Atlanta Journal-Constitution* published a story on the elimination of sports from Georgia's prisons.[33] The article said the reason that sports programs in prison were cut back was public resentment toward criminals who have it too easy behind bars. However, there has been very little systematic empirical evidence to support this claim. Available research shows that public views on prison amenities are not as harsh as many assume. The public does not want luxurious prisons, but they want prisons to be productive, humane places that try to improve inmates during their incarceration. The public is willing to provide and retain amenities if these items are useful for inmate management and rehabilitation.[34]

Public perception has influenced reality, as corrections reform has focused on the conditions of confinement. **"No-frills" prisons and jails** that take away prisoner amenities and privileges are part of the corrections

"no-frills" prisons and jails
Correctional institutions that take away prisoner amenities and privileges.

landscape. New policies are designed to make jail and prison life as brutal as possible in the belief that such conditions deter even the most hardened criminals.

Proponents of "no-frills" jails and prisons argue that the only incentives offenders should have is the opportunity to straighten out their lives. They further argue that incentives such as smoking, use of weight equipment and electronic equipment, and wearing personal clothing only encourage offenders to fake their way through incarceration to get the privileges. Pleasures of any kind, they claim, contribute to the crime rate by making prison a tolerable way of life. Reducing or eliminating amenities and privileges is what inmates deserve. It is not vindictive revenge—the offender committed a serious crime that warrants incarceration, and incarceration is meant to be punitive.

From Alaska to Mississippi to Massachusetts, states are gearing up to pass no-frills legislation. Alaska passed the No-Frills Prison Act in 1997, which removed or prohibited premium cable television, cassette tape players, tobacco use, pornographic material, and weight-lifting equipment. Alaska Senator Dave Donley sponsored the bill and defended the legislation by observing that "this law will make people think twice before committing a crime in Alaska."[35] In Mississippi, Representative Mark McInnis said it clearly: "The people who run the prisons want happy prisoners. I want prisoners to be so miserable that they won't even think of coming back."[36] And in April 1998, former Massachusetts governor William Weld said that life in prison should be "akin to a walk through the fires of hell," where inmates should learn only the joys of busting rocks.[37] At the federal level, the No-Frills Prison Act was enacted in 1996. It prohibits in-cell television viewing (except for prisoners who are segregated from the general population for their own safety), coffee pot, hot plate, or heating element; R-, X-, or NC-17 rated movies; boxing, wrestling, judo, Karate, or any other martial art; or any bodybuilding or weight-lifting equipment; and use or possession of any electric or electronic musical instrument in all federal prisons.

Oftentimes the public favors taking away prison amenities because it assumes they are paid for by tax dollars. States that permit in-cell television and electric equipment do not pay for them. They are purchased by the inmates or their families. Political rhetoric contributes to the public misconception regarding who pays for prison amenities. Would the public be more supportive of prison amenities if it knew the inmates paid for them? According to a citizens survey in Tampa Bay, Florida, the answer is yes. "Respondents who were informed that prisoners pay for their privileges were more likely to support inmate access to all of the amenities except air-conditioning than were those who were told tax dollars are used to finance inmate privileges . . . It is only when citizens are informed that taxpayers absorb the cost that they become unsupportive . . . This finding suggests that educating people that inmates pay for the more "luxurious" items will result in higher levels of support for them."[38]

Arguably, proponents of "no-frills" jails and prisons have a point. Privileges, if not handled properly, can undermine rehabilitation. On the other hand, without privileges, offenders may not take advantage of the opportunity for rehabilitation in the first place. In a perfect world, prison would make offenders realize that their mistakes have caused them pain and deprived them of their freedom, and they would gratefully volunteer for rehabilitation programs to gain back their freedom. However, in a perfect world, these people would most likely not be incarcerated to start with because they would have realized that their behaviors were causing them unwanted consequences and would have taken corrective measure outside prison. Most offenders do not think this way. They do not think about the consequences beforehand. They think they will never get caught. The eventual consequences for their lack of responsibility are arrest and incarceration.

In August 2002, *Corrections Compendium,* the peer-reviewed journal of the American Correctional Association, published the results of a survey on inmate privileges in U.S. and Canadian prison systems.[39] Comparing the results of that survey with one taken four years earlier, the *Compendium* concluded that "The trend for decreased privileges has continued for a variety of reasons [to reduce the coddling of inmates, to control the problems of overcrowding and lack of resources, or for practical reasons such as elimination of secondhand smoke] . . . and will likely continue in the future."[40] Some of the results of the survey follow:

1. Smoking is prohibited in 53 percent of U.S. prisons. In Canada, only Saskatchewan is smoke free.

2. Free weights are prohibited in 38 percent of U.S. and 56 percent of Canadian prisons. Most systems that prohibit free weights have replaced them with weight machines or exercise courses.

3. Electronic equipment (for example, television, radio, CD or cassette players, calculators, electric shavers, typewriters, coffee/hot pots, clocks, musical instruments, fans, desk lamps, hair dryers/curlers, and video games) is prohibited in the District of Columbia in the United States and in New Brunswick, Nova Scotia, and Ontario, Canada. All other facilities attach restrictions to their use.

4. R-rated movies are prohibited in 58 percent of U.S. facilities and in 56 percent of Canadian prisons.

5. Books and magazines are restricted everywhere by content, quantity, space considerations, who sends them, and custody level. For example, prisoners in New Mexico may keep one book and one magazine at a time. Iowa prisoners may keep three publications at a time, but none may be older than three months.

To date, no court case has been heard on "no-frills" prisons and jails. Unless the eliminated or reduced amenity or privilege results in serious harm to the inmate, the "no-frills" movement will continue.

At present, there is no evidence that making prisons and jails more unpleasant has any effect on crime. Legislators claim that inmates will not want to be incarcerated or reincarcerated under such harsh conditions. However, more than 200 years of prison history has not proven that making a prison austere deters offenders. State wardens, corrections experts, and attorneys do not believe that eliminating privileges will reduce crime.[41] They cringe at the idea of trying to maintain civility without amenities and privileges. "What some outside the corrections profession perceive as privileges, we in the profession see as vital prison and jail management tools to insure the safety of the facility," said Bobbie Huskey, former president of the ACA.[42]

CAREER PROFILE

Mark A. Molesworth
Substance Abuse Unit Manager   Bismarck, North Dakota

Mark A. Molesworth is a unit manager for a long-term residential substance-abuse facility for male and female felons in North Dakota. He began his career as a temporary correctional officer during summer vacations. When he graduated from Minot State University with a B.S. degree in criminal justice, he was promoted to the rank of lieutenant and made director of the Adult Services Program at a minimum security unit. Mark is the single custodial father of two young children and is the past president of the board of directors of the Bismarck School of Hope (a nonprofit learning center for disabled preschool-age children). He is currently involved in the MPA program through the University of North Dakota.

Mark's philosophy is that all staff have two important roles regardless of their profession. First, 30 percent of our job is to make sure individuals who are incarcerated do not escape, hurt staff, hurt other inmates or themselves. Second, 70 percent of our role is directed toward rehabilitating inmates who will live in society after they leave our care. It is everyone's responsibility to provide appropriate role modeling and opportunities (treatment, education, employment, social, and cognitive) which permit residents to make the necessary changes which will enable them to live productively in society after their release. We cannot force people to change. But, if we do not provide the opportunity for change, we are a part of the problem.

Others have wondered what impact "no-frills" incarceration may have on institutional security. Eliminating "frills" might "increase disturbances, either in the short term if inmates react violently to the loss or in the long term if inmates have more idle time, resent the perceived vindictiveness of corrections managers, or conclude they have nothing more to lose by misbehaving."[43] A corrections official in Florida concluded, "From a correctional administrator's standpoint, there is a point at which further reductions create an undue risk to a safe and orderly operation." A 27-year veteran corrections administrator in the New Jersey Department of Corrections fears that the "take-back trend," as he calls it, might result in inmate retaliation on staff.[44] Sufficient time has not passed to study the long-term impact of "no-frills" incarceration. However, there is concern that eliminating privileges (such as weightlifting, television, and recreation) that keep inmates busy may encourage inmates to spend more time planning or causing trouble.

If privileges are eliminated, what positive incentives will correctional staff have with which to motivate appropriate inmate behavior? A survey of 823 wardens of state adult prisons indicates that programs and amenities serve a critical control function.[45] Correctional officers can grant access to privileges and amenities in exchange for adherence to rules and restrict access as punishment for rule violation. "The entire prison disciplinary structure is founded on punishments that amount to restriction of privileges," report the survey's authors. Chances are, prison administrators will not completely eliminate or abolish privileges or amenities; they will curtail availability and offer the privileges or amenities as reward for good behavior.

Accreditation

We introduced the issue of accreditation in Chapter 6. Here, we expand on that discussion. Accreditation is a process through which correctional facilities and agencies can measure themselves against nationally adopted standards and through which they can receive formal recognition and accredited status. ACA standards are the national benchmark for the effective operation of correctional systems throughout the United States and are necessary to ensure that correctional agencies and facilities operate professionally. The ACA administers the only national accreditation program for all components of adult and juvenile corrections. For that reason, the federal courts have increasingly relied on ACA's standards to decide if correctional agencies and facilities meet constitutional standards.

Founded in 1870 as the National Prison Association, the ACA is the oldest association specifically developed for practitioners in the corrections profession. Today, the ACA has more than 20,000 active members. The ACA initiated correctional accreditation in 1974 when it created the Commission on Accreditation for Corrections (CAC). CAC continually revises the standards based on changing practices, current case law, and agency experience. CAC is governed by 25 corrections professionals, architects, doctors, and legal experts who are elected/appointed from the following categories:

- National Association of Juvenile Correctional Agencies (1);
- Council of Juvenile Correctional Administrators (1);
- Association of State Correctional Administrators (2);
- National Sheriffs' Association (2);
- American Jail Association (1);
- North American Association of Wardens and Superintendents (1);
- International Community Corrections Association (1);
- American Probation and Parole Association (1);
- Association of Paroling Authorities International (1);
- National Juvenile Detention Association (1);
- American Bar Association (1);
- National Association of Counties (1);
- American Institute of Architects (1);
- Correctional Health (physician) (1);
- Juvenile Probation/Aftercare (1);
- Adult Probation/Parole (1);
- At-Large (6); and
- Citizen At-Large (not in corrections) (1).

Correctional accreditation is available for 21 different kinds of juvenile and adult correctional agencies and facilities, including institutions and community residential programs for adults and juveniles, jails and detention centers, probation and parole agencies, health care programs, and remote-location monitoring. The standards cover administrative and fiscal concerns, staff training and development, the physical plant, safety and emergency procedures, sanitation, food service, and rules and discipline. Standards are divided into two categories. To be accredited, an agency or facility must have 100 percent compliance with *mandatory* standards and 90 percent compliance with *nonmandatory* standards. Today, more than 500 of the 1,208 adult correctional institutions and 100 of the 3,365 local jails have been awarded ACA accreditation. The State of Illinois is a leader in the accreditation movement. Currently 42 of its 44 correctional facilities have been accredited by ACA, and two new facilities are under accreditation review.

WHY SHOULD CORRECTIONAL AGENCIES AND FACILITIES BE ACCREDITED?

There are at least eight reasons correctional agencies and facilities should be accredited:[46]

1. **Accreditation improves staff training and development.** Accreditation requires written policy and procedures to establish a training and staff development program for all categories of personnel. The training requirements address all preservice, in-service, and specialized training curricula with clear timelines and considers the institution's mission, physical characteristics, and inmate populations. The professional growth of employees is developed through training plans that annually identify current job-related training needs in relation to position requirements, current correctional issues, new theories, techniques, and technologies.

2. **Accreditation assesses program strengths and weaknesses.** Accreditation assesses correctional administration and management, the physical plant, institutional operations and services, and inmate programs. It also assesses issues and concerns that may affect the quality of life at a facility such as staff training, adequacy of medical services, sanitation, use of segregation and detention, incidents of violence, crowding, offender activity levels, programs, and provisions of basic services that may impact the life, safety, and health of inmates and staff.

3. **Accreditation is a defense against lawsuits.** Accredited agencies and facilities have a stronger defense against litigation through documentation and the demonstration of a "good faith" effort to improve conditions of confinement. For example, in *Grayson v. Peed* (1999), the Court said, "The appellant's own expert penologist conceded that [Sheriff] Peed's policies met the standards of both the Virginia Board of Corrections and the American Correctional Association . . . Appellant's claims that [Sheriff] Peed provided inadequate training for his employees must also fail. At the time of the incident, the jail had been accredited for more than ten years . . . by the American Correctional Association . . . whose training requirements often surpass minimal constitutional standards."

4. **Accreditation establishes measurable criteria for upgrading operations.** Through the standards and accreditation process agencies continuously review agency policy and procedure and have the ability to make necessary improvements when deficiencies are recognized.

5. **Accreditation improves staff morale and professionalism.** Accreditation is awarded to the "best of the best" in the corrections field. Staff have a better understanding of policies and procedures, and this contributes to improved working conditions for staff.

6. **Accreditation offers a safer environment for staff and offenders.** Staff and offenders benefit from increased accountability and attention to physical plant issues and security procedures. Whether for an agency or facility, the accreditation process ensures assessment of strengths and weaknesses.

7. **Accreditation reduces liability insurance costs.** As an incentive for agencies willing to participate in ACA's national accreditation program, insurance companies offer a reduction on liability insurance premiums to accredited agencies and facilities. Adherence to nationally recognized standards for fire, safety, health, and training reduces claim expenses, allowing up to a 10 percent credit on liability insurance premiums. In most cases, the resulting savings on insurance premiums more than offset the agency's or facility's cost of accreditation.

8. **Accreditation offers performance-based benefits.** Performance-based standards provide data that can be used to gauge the day-to-day management of the facility, thereby providing agencies with a cost-effective, proactive approach to offender care. They can also be used to justify requests for additional funding.

Traditionally, correctional agencies have sought accreditation for one of three reasons: first, to ensure that the organization is in compliance with national standards; second, to demonstrate to interested parties that the organization is operating at acceptable professional levels; and third, to comply with court orders.

Privatization

According to Malcolm Feeler, the involvement of the private sector in corrections began shortly after the first English colonists arrived in Virginia in 1607.[47] Convicted felons were transported by private entrepreneurs to America, as a condition of pardon, to be sold into servitude. During the 18th century, jails and prisons emerged in the American colonies as alternatives to servitude or the death penalty. Privately operated facilities copied from English custom became popular. Private contractors claimed they could both manage prisons and employ convicts in labor, arguing that the practice would be both rehabilitative and financially rewarding. San Quentin was the first U.S. prison constructed and operated by a private provider in the 1850s. However, after a number of major scandals surfaced surrounding the mismanagement of the facility by the private provider, California turned San Quentin prison over to the control of state government. By 1885, 13 states had contracts with private enterprises to lease out prison labor.

As discussed in Chapter 6, privatization is defined as a contract process that shifts public functions, responsibilities, and capital assets, in whole or

> **Ethical Dilemma**
> Should local, state, and federal institutions be privatized? Should crime pay? Do private prisons save locales money? What are the pros and cons? For more information go to Ethical Dilemma 13-2 at http://www.mhhe.com/schmalleger2.

in part, from the public sector to the private sector. In corrections, privatization is generally one of two types.

The first type is the "contracting out" of specific services that entails a competition among private bidders to perform governmental activities such as providing medical and mental health services, educational and vocational programming, food preparation, maintenance, work, and industry. This type of privatization emerged in the 17th century. Under these circumstances, the correctional agency remains the financier and continues to manage and maintain policy control over the type and quality of services provided. Contracts for specialized services generate little controversy.

The second type of privatization is full-scale private management of jails and prisons. Because it involves government transfer of assets, commercial enterprises, and management responsibilities to the private sector, it is controversial. In 1976, RCA Services assumed control of the Weaversville Intensive Treatment Unit in North Hampton, Pennsylvania, marking the modern beginning of privatization in corrections. The trend toward privately operated correctional institutions has continued with almost 78,000 adults now housed in 101 privately operated adult correctional institutions and 15,220 adults in 163 privately operated halfway houses and residential drug treatment centers in 30 states, Puerto Rico, and the District of Columbia.[48] Texas has the most facilities (43), followed by California (24), Florida (10), and Colorado (9). Most private correctional facilities are in the southern and western United States. At the federal level, in 2000, the Bureau of Prisons contracted with Corrections Corporation of America to maintain 3,300 beds with an estimated value of $760 million over 10 years; and in 2001, the INS (now called the Bureau of Immigration

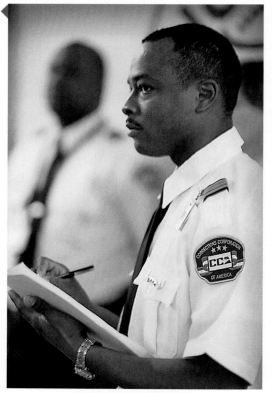

Almost 78,000 adults are held in 101 private prisons across the United States. Still the debate over privatization continues. Why do state governments contract with for-profit companies for such services?

and Customs Enforcement (ICE)) and the U.S. Marshal's Service renewed five private contracts worth approximately $50 million each.[49]

Outside the United States, 31 private facilities operate in Australia, Canada, England, Netherlands Antilles, New Zealand, Scotland, and South Africa. Total revenues allocated to private corrections in 2001 were estimated at more than $4 billion.

The catalyst for privatizing correctional institutions today is prison overcrowding. As noted earlier, adult prisons are operating between full and 15 percent over capacity. (No measure of capacity in juvenile corrections is available.) Other reasons for the growth in private corrections are the public's lack of confidence in the ability of correctional services provided by federal, state, and local governments to rehabilitate offenders and a reluctance to provide more funding for rising correctional costs. The enthusiasm for privatization is fueled by the prospect for more innovative, cost-effective prison management, including the involvement of the private sector in the financing of new prison construction. This enthusiasm is not shared by all, however.

THE DEBATE

Largely because there has been no conclusive research, arguments continue to rage over the merits of privately run correctional facilities. The overriding reason supporting privatization in corrections is the desire of state and local governments to rapidly increase bed space, save taxpayers money by providing correctional services traditionally supplied by government at less cost, improve the quality of correctional services, and reduce crime and recidivism. For example, one private provider built a 350-bed detention center in Houston, Texas, for the Immigration and Customs Enforcement (ICE), the first government agency to use private prisons. The project was completed within six months at a cost of $14,000 per bed. ICE calculated that government construction would have taken almost three years at a cost of $26,000 per bed. Estimates of rebuilding prisons in the District of Columbia say it would take the public sector five to six years, whereas it would take the private sector three to four years.

Most advocates of privatization also suggest that allowing facilities to be operated by the private sector could result in cost reductions of 20 percent. Most studies, however, report more modest savings. In fact, researchers at the University of Cincinnati looked at 33 cost-effectiveness evaluations of public and private prisons and concluded that prison size, age, and security level, not prison ownership (public vs. private), predict prison costs: "Relinquishing the responsibility of managing prisons to the private sphere is unlikely to alleviate much of the financial burden on state correctional budgets."[50] There are very few studies comparing the quality of inmate confinement between public and privately operated correctional institutions. Some report that private prisons outperform their public counterparts. Others do not.

In possibly the most carefully controlled comparative recidivism study of releasees from private and public prisons, Lonn Lanza-Kaduce and colleagues at the University of Florida matched 198 inmates from private prisons with 198 inmates from public prisons on the basis of offense, race, age, and prior record.[51] The researchers tracked the inmates for 12 months after each inmate's respective date of release and recorded any new rearrest, any technical violation, resentencing, and reincarceration. The researchers also measured the severity of recidivism (technical violation, misdemeanor offense, drug or weapon possession felony, property felony, or violent or personal felony). Releasees from private prisons had lower recidivism rates than did their public prison matches for all indicators of recidivism except technical violations. In the 12 months following release, 19 (10 percent) of the private facility releasees were rearrested, whereas 38 (19 percent) of the public releasees were rearrested. Only 11 (6 percent) of the private releasees were resentenced for a new offense compared with

20 (10 percent) of their public matches. Of the private prison releasees, 20 (10 percent) were reincarcerated within 12 months, but 28 (14 percent) of the public prison releasees were reincarcerated. Overall, 34 (17 percent) of the private facility releasees recidivated, whereas 47 (24 percent) of the public releasees recidivated. When the researchers analyzed seriousness of reoffending, they found that private prison releasees were more likely to return on technical violations. Public releasee recidivists were more likely to commit drug/weapon possession offenses, property offenses, or violent offenses in the year after release. In the aggregate, the recidivism of private releasees was less serious than that of public releasees. The researchers also found that, within the first three months of release, fewer private releasees recidivated than did public releasees. After 90 days, however, time to rearrest was similar for both groups.

Proponents also argue that public prisons are not without their problems, and unlike state and federal governments, private firms are free from politics, cumbersome bureaucracies, and costly union contracts. Proponents also suggest that privately run correctional facilities can be economic boons for the areas in which they are located, providing many jobs and feeding public coffers with increased tax revenues. Among groups supporting privatization are the ACA and the President's Commission on Privatization.

Opponents of privatization, on the other hand, build their arguments on mostly philosophical grounds. One writer says that the fundamental issue is a moral one: Should private parties make a profit from inflicting pain on others?[52] Will private prisons, in their pursuit for profits, find ways to keep cells filled, prison construction booming, and more offenders under private supervision? The notion that convicted offenders should be the responsibility of private entrepreneurs motivated by profit is contradictory to the public function of offender apprehension and conviction. Most opponents of privatization argue that the practice is inherently flawed by the profit motive of private corporations.[53] The corporate interest in maximizing profits, they claim, can have numerous negative consequences for inmates, correctional employees, and society. Some claim, for example, that the need to maintain healthy profit margins may preclude the cost of rehabilitation and recreational programs for inmates. Other opponents of privatization say that privately run companies save money by paying lower wages and benefits than states do.[54] Among the groups opposing privatization are the American Jail Association, the National Sheriffs' Association, and the American Federation of State, County, and Municipal Employees.

Recently, the National Council on Crime and Delinquency (NCCD) reviewed the literature on privatization and conducted a national survey of private correctional management firms. NCCD found that, rather than the projected 20 percent savings, the average saving from privatization was only about 1 percent, and most of that was achieved through lower labor costs.[55] "In summary," wrote NCCD, "the cost benefits of privatization have not materialized to the extent promised by the private sector. Although there are examples of cost savings, there are other examples in which such benefits have not been realized. Moreover, it is probably too early to determine if the initial cost savings can be sustained over a long time period."[56]

Some critics note that, although the administration of punishment may be delegated in part to the private sector, the government retains ultimate responsibility for it. Indeed, the courts have held government responsible for actions taken by a private provider that violate an inmate's constitutional rights or that put the prison staff, inmates, or surrounding community in harm's way. Today, private-public contracts include performance standards and monitoring procedures. Writing a good, clear contract that outlines the roles, responsibilities, and consequences for the private provider and government sector is key. Proponents note that governments almost always renew contracts with private operators—proving such contracts worthwhile. In spite of the arguments for and against privatization, "The core theme is that properly conceptualized, properly managed, and properly monitored privatization initiatives can serve the public interest."[57] Table 13–1 summarizes the reasons to accept or reject the privatization concept.

A number of private companies operate prisons and jails. Figure 13–1 shows the market shares held by the major providers of private prison and jail management. Some are well-known and even offer shares of their companies to the public.

> Some critics note that, although the administration of punishment may be delegated in part to the private sector, the government retains ultimate responsibility for it.

PRIVATIZING COMMUNITY SUPERVISION

There is also movement toward privatization in community corrections, including offender assessment, drug testing and treatment, electronic monitoring, halfway house management, and probation field services. Two states—Connecticut and Colorado—have successfully privatized community supervision. In both states, the impetus for privatizing community supervision was similar: Staffing and resources were not keeping pace with increasing caseloads. Community supervision officials felt they had exhausted the use of interns and volunteers, and funding for new staff was not possible. They used risk management principles to assign staff and resources in direct proportion to the risk level of a case. Both states partnered with the private sector to monitor the low-risk offender population, a group that generally has few needs, whose past records reflect little or no violence, and that successfully completes probation about 90 percent of the time.

In Connecticut, the privatization initiative to monitor low-risk offender populations by the private sector allowed scarce resources to be used to better monitor offenders with higher levels of risk. Private case management responsibilities in Connecticut included sending an introductory letter to the probationer, monitoring restitution payments and compliance with conditions of probation, responding to probationer's inquiries, preparing standardized reports for probation officers, providing verification of conditional compliance, and

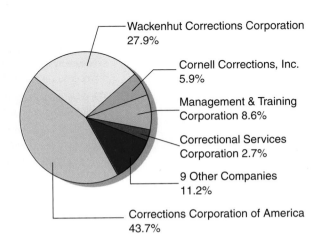

Wackenhut Corrections Corporation 27.9%

Cornell Corrections, Inc. 5.9%

Management & Training Corporation 8.6%

Correctional Services Corporation 2.7%

9 Other Companies 11.2%

Corrections Corporation of America 43.7%

FIGURE 13-1

Slicing up the Market

Percentage of market share based on U.S. contracts.

TABLE 13–1	Arguments For and Against Private Prisons
For private prisons	**Against private prisons**
1. Private operators can provide construction financing options that allow the government client to pay only for capacity as needed in lieu of accumulating long-term debt.	1. There are certain responsibilities that only the government should meet, such as safety and environmental protection. To provide incarceration, the government has legal, political, and moral obligations. Major constitutional competition among both public and private issues revolves around the deprivation of liberty, discipline, and preserving the constitutional rights of inmates. Related issues include the use of force, loss of time credit, and segregation.
2. Private companies offer modern state-of-the-art correctional facility designs that are efficient to operate and that are built according to value-engineering specifications.	2. Few private companies are available from which to choose.
3. Private operators typically design and construct a new correctional facility in half the time required for a comparable government construction project.	3. Private operators may be inexperienced with key correctional issues.
4. Private vendors provide government clients with the convenience and accountability of one entity for all compliance issues.	4. Operators may become monopolies through political ingratiation, favoritism, and so on.
5. Private corrections management companies are able to mobilize rapidly and to specialize in unique facility missions.	5. Government may lose the capability to perform the function over time.
6. Private corrections management companies provide economic development opportunities by hiring locally and, to the extent possible, purchasing locally.	6. The profit motive will inhibit the proper performance of duties. Private prisons have financial incentives to cut corners and offer lower wages, pensions, benefits, and staffing levels.
7. Government can reduce or share its liability exposure by contracting with private corrections companies.	7. The procurement process is slow, inefficient, and open to risks.
8. The government can retain flexibility by limiting the contract function and by specifying facility mission.	8. Creating a good, clear contract is a daunting task.
9. Adding other service providers injects competition among both public and private organizations.	9. Lack of enforcement remedies in contracts leaves only termination or lawsuits as recourse.

Source: James Austin and James Coventry, *Emerging Issues in Privatized Prisons* (Washington, DC: U.S. Department of Justice, Bureau of Justice Assistance, February 2001), p. 14.

providing statistical reports. Robert J. Bosco, director of Connecticut's Office of Adult Probation, says that the "success" of this privatization initiative "is in the agency's ability to use its resources to control recidivism of the highest-risk offender population."[58]

The situation in Colorado was similar. When Colorado officials adopted risk management and looked at how treatment and supervision were matched with levels of risk, they found more probation officers were needed than the Colorado General Assembly would fund. The result was a directive that allowed probation departments to contract with private agencies for the supervision of low-risk probationers. Thirteen of Colorado's 22 judicial districts have entered into such contracts. The private agencies directly bill the probationers for their supervision services, eliminating public expenditures for community supervision. According to Suzanne Pullen, management analyst with Colorado's Judicial Department, Office of Probation Services, "The diversion of these low-risk offenders allows local probation departments to focus more clearly on the supervision and case management of medium- and high-risk offenders that are burdening their caseloads."[59]

FUTURE TRENDS

According to Reginald A. Wilkinson, director of the Ohio Department of Rehabilitation and Correction,

> The next ten years will reveal whether the privatization of prisons will succeed. If so, the evolution from public to private management may prove to be painful to correctional traditionalists. Debate on the pros and cons, rights and wrongs, of "punishment for profit" will rage back and forth. In the end, the profit margin and public opinion may be the determining factors on how much of the corrections profession will be outsourced to for-profit providers.[60]

Other trends may include the following:

1. The number of private prisons is likely to increase but not at the pace exhibited during the past two decades.
2. The number of companies operating privatized prisons is likely to decrease as competition and the costs of doing business increase, thus forcing a consolidation of firms within the industry.
3. Important inroads can be expected for the geriatric inmate population.

Technocorrections

The technological forces that made the use of cell phones commonplace is converging with corrections to create "technocorrections." Technological changes have impacted communication, offender and officer tracking and recognition, and detection.

COMMUNICATION

Information is crucial to a well-run correctional system. Knowing what is happening gives correctional administrators the power not only to react to problems promptly, but also to anticipate and prevent them. In recent decades, communication technology has undergone significant changes. Correctional officers can now keep in touch by e-mail and can share

THE OFFENDER SPEAKS

information in electronic databases and on Web pages on the Internet. The majority of corrections departments now have online searchable prisoner registries, including photographs, and some post schedules of upcoming parole hearings on the Internet. Communication technology has also brought about videoconferencing and telemedicine

Videoconferencing   Videoconferencing is another way to share thoughts and ideas in the correctional community. Meetings and lectures that once required expensive travel can now be "attended" from the comfort of one's office or from a local teleconference site. In addition, satellite TV and video technology have enhanced distance learning for both officers and inmates. Correctional facilities in California, Florida, Georgia, Louisiana, New Mexico, Pennsylvania, West Virginia, and Wisconsin are also using video-conferencing for arraignments, interrogations, and visitation. Friends and family can now save on travel and avoid standing in line by scheduling videoconferences with inmates. The advantages to institutions include improved security, reduction in transportation costs, and decline in the spread of contraband and weapons.

Telemedicine   Telemedicine, one of the newest and most exciting advances in medicine, is providing prisoners with adequate, cost-effective health care. Taking a prisoner to a specialist outside the prison poses a danger to correctional officers and the community by giving the prisoner an opportunity to escape or to have contact with other people in a less-controlled environment. Telemedicine allows physicians to consult with on-site medical personnel through videoconferencing and compatible medical devices, such as medical microcameras. Health care in correctional settings is improved, and the substantial savings on in-prison consultations and on trips to local providers can offset the costs of introducing this technology. The Ohio State prison system's use of telemedicine consultations through television monitors and computer networking increased from 129 episodes in 1995 to more than 5,000 in 2000. According to Dr. Hagop Mekhjan, director of the Ohio State University Medical Center, the Ohio Department of Rehabilitation and Correction has probably saved millions of dollars in transportation costs and overtime labor.[61]

OFFENDER AND OFFICER TRACKING AND RECOGNITION

Automated kiosks, also discussed in Chapters 5, are on the way to replacing routine visits to probation and parole officers. Offenders are instructed to report to a kiosk at a specified location. There they are electronically interviewed and in some cases tested for alcohol by means of a breath analysis attachment. Using the kiosks, offenders can also e-mail their parole officers to schedule personal meetings. The system identifies the offender by reading a magnetic card and using a biometric fingerprint scanner. Besides fingerprint scanners, other biometric devices are making their way onto the market. One such device is called IriScan. The device scans the eye and identifies the person from the unique patterns in the iris. It is used to track inmates every time they enter or leave a facility.

Prison medical staff videoconference with an offsite physician about a prisoner's physical health. Advances in technology have helped make prisons and jails safer and more secure, while facilitating innovations like telemedicine. What promises might tomorrow's technologies hold for correctional institutions?

Remote-location monitoring, discussed in Chapter 5, is steadily improving and is likely to be used far more in the future. Fairly new in the field of corrections is the global positioning system (GPS). Already used in airplanes and automobiles, GPS is now also used for monitoring offenders under community supervision. The GPS tracking unit worn by an offender allows computers to pinpoint the offender's location at any time to the precise street address. In the field of inmate monitoring, there is also some discussion about implanting chips in offenders' bodies that would alert officials to unacceptable behavior. In some cases, when criminal activity was detected, the chip might give an electric shock that would temporarily shut down the offender's central nervous system.

Administrators are also relying on new telecommunications technology to help track inmates and former inmates. Speaker ID technology identifies a speaker even if he or she has a cold, just awoke from a deep sleep, or has a poor telephone connection. Systems using speaker ID can be used to keep track of who calls inmates in prison and to monitor criminal activity such as escape plans, gang activity, and smuggling of contraband. Speaker ID can also be used for low-risk offenders granted early parole as an alternative to incarceration. The system can make random calls and positively identify the speaker from his or her response. The offenders never know when or how they will receive calls. When no one answers the phone or the speaker is not identified, the system alerts authorities to a possible violation.

To increase the efficiency of inmate monitoring and cut administrative costs, a smart card, a plastic card embedded with a computer chip, can be used to store all types of information about the inmate, from medical care to meals eaten.

Remote-location monitoring is not just for inmates. Correctional officers can also wear personal alarm and location units that allow a computer to track their locations and respond to distress signals by sending the closest officers to the site of the emergency.

The use of facial recognition technology is also on the increase in corrections. All 300 employees of the Prince George County Correctional Center in Upper Marlboro, Maryland, swipe picture-image ID cards across a scanner. The swipe alerts the system that an employee is entering the facility. The system verifies the image from a database, and using the biometrics of the employee's face, compares it to the one captured by the camera.

Eventually, Prince George County will use biometric-based access control technology to screen visitors to determine if they are ex-inmates.

The principles of geographical information systems (GIS) are also changing corrections.[62] GIS links graphics with tabular information. Proponents foresee a time when corrections mapping can be used to do the following:

1. Track and display inmate location and movement via electronic monitoring devices.
2. Indicate whether a housing unit is balanced with regard to religion, group affiliation, age, race, and ethnicity.
3. Pinpoint the locations of gang members and link them to each inmate's behavioral and criminal history, as well as the inmate's rank in the hierarchy of the group.
4. Pinpoint areas in a prison that are potentially dangerous such as hallways or blind corners where a number of assaults may have occurred.
5. Incorporate aerial photos of a facility to check for possible security breaches and potential escape routes.
6. Provide a basis for proactive investigation and enforcement. For example, the flow of money in and out of prison might be mapped and then linked with data about visitation, telephone calls, and correspondence addresses to show a potential drug problem.
7. Link inmate data with the names, telephone numbers, and addresses of all the people the inmate had contact with during incarceration, in case of an escape.

DETECTION

To maintain prison security, researchers have developed new detection technologies. One is ground-penetrating radar (GPR), which can be used to locate underground escape tunnels. Another is heartbeat monitoring. Using the same technology employed by geologists to detect earthquakes, geophone machines can detect the heartbeat of an inmate trying to escape in a laundry or trash truck leaving the prison. In 1999, heartbeat monitoring prevented the escape of a prisoner in Tennessee. X-rays and magnetic resonance imaging scan the body for concealed weapons, eliminating the necessity for a physical search. Noninvasive drug detection technology places a swab or patch on the skin, which absorbs perspiration, and signals the presence of illegal drugs. Pupillometry (a binocularlike device that flashes a light to stimulate pupil contraction) can also measure drug or alcohol use. Another technological tool for drug testing has inmates look through a viewfinder. Ion scans can also detect drug particles on visitors to correctional facilities.

IMPLEMENTATION

Despite the growth of this technology, there are still obstacles to be overcome. Corrections personnel have been slow to embrace new technology, in part because new systems are unreliable, are difficult to maintain, and exhibit high life-cycle costs. Ethical concerns about the rights of offenders might be another barrier to implementing new technology. Through a program sponsored by the Department of Justice—Staff and Inmate Monitoring (SAINT)—the Navy's Space and Naval Warfare System Center in Charleston, South Carolina, is systematically addressing biometric and smart card technology through development, testing, and evaluation of a prototype system in the Navy Consolidated Brig in Charleston. There is no question, however, that new technologies are playing an increasingly important role in correctional institutions as a means to address critical health, safety, and security issues.

SUMMARY

▶ Prisons are overcrowded for four main reasons. First, over the past decade there has been an increase in imprisonment. Second, changes in federal and state sentencing laws require more offenders to serve longer periods. Third, there has been an increase in imprisonment for drug and violent offenses. Fourth, a prison industrial complex has emerged.

▶ This chapter examined six methods of controlling prison overcrowding. First, reduce the number of people who go to prison by making more use of *front-end strategies* such as diversion, community corrections, and intermediate sanctions. Second, put a cap or ceiling on the prison population, sometimes called a *trap-door strategy.* Third, use what are called *side-door strategies,* such as giving sentenced offenders the opportunity to apply to the sentencing court for release to intensive community corrections programs, usually six months after imprisonment. Fourth, use more parole and halfway houses, called *back-door strategies.* Fifth, build more prisons and/or expand existing facilities. Sixth, use structured sentencing guidelines that are designed to save prison space for serious crimes and violent offenses, while using community corrections and intermediate sanctions for lesser offenses.

▶ Prison riots occur for a number of reasons. Sometimes they are a result of spontaneous outburst. Most experts believe that the primary causes of prison riots are bad conditions (overcrowding, antiquated facilities, low staffing levels, insufficient staff training, lack of programs for inmates, lack of funding, and poor implementation of correctional policy), rebellious inmates and racial antagonism, institutional structure and readiness, and administrative factors (for example, frequent staff turnover, low correctional officer qualifications, inadequate training, poor staff-inmate communication, and low staff pay).

▶ Preventing prison riots requires changes both outside and inside the prison. Outside prison it is important for other social institutions to reduce sources of tension that contribute to crime. Inside prison experts recommend formal inmate grievance procedures, ombudsmen, improved classification systems, smaller institutions, meaningful educational and work programs, alternatives to incarceration, professional prison staff who are well trained and well paid, and clearly written and well-understood policies on the use of force.

▶ A supermax housing facility is a free-standing facility, or a distinct unit within a facility, that provides for management and secure control of inmates who have been officially designated as violent or who exhibit serious and disruptive behavior while incarcerated. It is not yet known

REVIEW & APPLICATIONS

what impact conditions of extreme isolation have on a prisoner or on the public when prisoners released from these facilities return to the community. However, criminologists, psychiatrists, lawyers, and the courts who have studied the effects of long-term solitary confinement report evidence of acute sensory deprivation, paranoid delusion belief systems, irrational fears of violence, resentment, little ability to control rage, and mental breakdowns. Supermax prisons also present extraordinary challenges for staff, possibly creating a "we/they syndrome" and magnifying tensions between inmates and staff.

6▶ "No-frills" prisons and jails eliminate prisoner privileges and amenities in the belief that this process will deter criminals from future criminal activity. It appears, however, that "no-frills" correctional facilities may actually produce the results they were designed to avert, thereby increasing the number of prison disturbances and making it difficult for corrections staff to motivate appropriate inmate behavior. Corrections professionals tell us that what outsiders perceive as privileges and amenities, they consider to be important management tools. Research from Florida shows that public views on prison amenities are not as harsh as many assume. The public is willing to provide and retain amenities if they are useful for inmate management and rehabilitation.

7▶ Correctional facilities and agencies should be accredited for eight reasons. Accreditation improves staff training and development, assesses program strengths and weaknesses, is a defense against lawsuits, establishes measurable criteria for upgrading operations, improves staff morale and professionalism, offers a safer environment for staff and offenders, reduces liability insurance costs, and offers performance-based benefits.

8▶ Arguments in favor of privatization include construction financing options that allow government clients to pay only for capacity as needed in lieu of accumulating long-term debt; modern state-of-the-art correctional facility designs that are efficient to operate; less time to build than comparable government construction projects; convenience and accountability of one entity for all compliance issues; rapid mobilization and specialization in unique facility missions; and economic development opportunities from hiring and purchasing locally. Reasons not to privatize include the moral issue of the government's responsibility for public safety; a lack of private companies from which to choose; private contractor inexperience with corrections issues; the potential for private vendors to become a monopoly through political ingratiation and favoritism; the potential for government to lose the capability to perform the function over time; the potential for the profit motive to inhibit proper performance of duties; slow procurement processes that are open to risks; the difficulty of creating a contract with a private vendor; and the potential for a lack of enforcement to result in termination or expensive lawsuits as the only recourse.

9▶ Technology has affected corrections in the areas of communication, offender and officer tracking and recognition, and detection.

KEY TERMS

structured sentencing, *p. 465*

exchange rates, *p. 465*

security threat groups (STGs), *p. 466*

disturbance, *p. 470*

riot, *p. 470*

supermax housing, *p. 476*

special master, *p. 481*

"no-frills" prisons and jails, *p. 481*

QUESTIONS FOR REVIEW

1. Explain the differences among rated capacity, operational capacity, and design capacity.
2. How has the increase in convicted offenders affected prisons?
3. What changes in federal and state sentencing laws have affected prison populations?
4. How have arrests for drug offenses affected prison populations?
5. What are the six methods of controlling prison overcrowding?
6. How does structured sentencing work?
7. What is meant by *exchange rates*?
8. Compare and contrast the causes of prison riots in the 1950s and the 1990s.
9. What are security threat groups?
10. What are some factors that can lead to a prison riot?
11. What are some ways to prevent prison riots?

12. Distinguish between a supermax housing facility and a prison built for maximum-security prisoners.
13. What are some of the psychological effects of long-term solitary confinement on prisoners and staff?
14. What is a "no-frills" prison or jail, and why are they emerging?
15. What impact can we expect "no-frills" prisons and jails to have on recidivism, institutional security, and inmate behavior control?
16. Explain the reasons correctional agencies and facilities should be accredited.
17. Discuss the arguments for and against privatization.
18. How has technology impacted corrections?

THINKING CRITICALLY ABOUT CORRECTIONS

▶ ▶ ▶ **Federal Requirements for Percentage of Sentence Served**

Under the Violent Offender Incarceration and Truth-in-Sentencing Incentive Grants Program passed by Congress in 1994, in order to qualify for federal funds to build new prisons and jails, states must require people convicted of a Part I violent offense to serve not less than 85 percent of the prison sentence. Do you think such a requirement is appropriate? Why or why not?

▶ ▶ ▶ **Supermax Consequences**

In the federal district court case *Madrid* v. *Gomez* (1995), the court said, "It is clear that confinement in the Pelican Bay SHU severely deprives inmates of normal human contact and substantially reduces their level of environmental stimulation." The court further said, "Based on studies undertaken in this case, and the entirety of the record bearing on this claim, the court finds that many, if not most, inmates in the SHU experience some degree of psychological trauma in reaction to their extreme social isolation and the severely restricted environmental stimulation in the SHU." What do you believe are the major consequences of supermax housing for inmates and staff, and if you were the warden of an SHU, how would you deal with them?

REVIEW & APPLICATIONS

ON-THE-JOB DECISION MAKING

▶ ▶ ▶ Overcoming Opposition to Privatization

It is 2012 and you are the director of your state's Department of Corrections and Rehabilitation. Your predecessors contracted with several private vendors to perform government activities such as food preparation and inmate programming. You signed contracts for full-scale private management of two state prisons. So far, your experience with privatization has been successful. Predictions from a decade ago that your state would not privatize the entire state department of corrections might be wrong. Your prisons continue to operate above capacity and you believe you spend more time in court than you do in your office. You need more bed space, but the public refuses to spend more on prisons. You are thinking seriously about a proposal that would turn over the management of all your state's adult prisons to the public sector. How will you overcome the opposition of your state's correctional officer association?

▶ ▶ ▶ What Inmates Need to Know In Order to Work Their Way Out of Supermax Prison

In this chapter's Reflections on the Future, Morris Thigpen, director of the National Institute of Corrections, tell us, "It is imperative that all inmates placed in supermax be fully aware of how they can work their way out." Assume your state is planning a supermax prison. You remember Thigpen's words. What will you propose as opportunities for inmates to demonstrate positive behavior to work their way out?

CORRECTIONS ON THE WEB

▶ ▶ ▶ Corrections Technology Program

The National Institute of Justice maintains a Corrections Technology Program. Visit the Program's Website directly at http://www.ojp.usdoj.gov/nij/sciencetech/text/tctp.htm or link to it through NIJ's homepage at http://www.ojp.usdoj.gov/nij/ by clicking *Programs, Technology Programs,* then search for *Corrections Technology.* Think about any of the technology issues discussed in this chapter and review a related article listed under *News and Highlights* or *Publications.*

▶ ▶ ▶ Measuring Prison Capacity

The Bureau of Justice Statistics (BJS), with the U.S. Census Bureau as its collection agent, obtains year-end and midyear counts of prisoners from departments of corrections in each of the 50 states and the federal Bureau of Prisons and reports on prison capacities. Review the three measures of prison capacity presented in this chapter. Then read the latest BJS publication of national prisoner statistics online at http://www.ojp.usdoj.gov/bjs/. Click on *Prisons* and then locate the latest report on the number of people in state and federal prisons. Scroll through the document and find the text and accompanying table on state and federal prison capacities. Note that some states use two or more definitions. What policy implications do you see if the measure of prison capacity varies as a function of the definition used?

> "As a victim you're amazed that no one will ask you about the crime, or the effect that it has on you and your family. You took the . . . defendant's blows, heard his threats, listened to him brag that he'd "beat the rap" or "con the judge." No one ever hears these things. They never give you a chance to tell them.
>
> —A victim

The Victim: Helping Those in Need

▶ **CHAPTER OBJECTIVES**

After completing this chapter you should be able to do the following:

1. Briefly summarize the history of America's victims' rights movement.

2. Identify and describe important federal victims' rights legislation.

3. Understand why a victims' rights amendment to the U.S. Constitution may be considered necessary.

4. List and describe crime victims' costs.

5. Understand how corrections agencies participate in meeting victims' needs, and list victim services provided by correctional agencies.

6. Explain how crime victim compensation programs work.

7. List the three avenues available to victims to recover financial losses due to crime.

8. Understand the nature of victim impact statements, and explain why they are useful.

More than a decade ago, 15-year-old Mary Vincent became the surviving victim of one of the most gruesome crimes of the twentieth century.[1] Vincent, who had been hitchhiking on a trip to her grandfather's house in Corona, California, was attacked and raped by Larry Singleton—an innocuous-looking 51-year-old man who offered her a ride. In an act of sadistic violation, Singleton hacked off Vincent's forearms with a hatchet and left her for dead on a hillside. She survived, and was found the next morning wandering near a road holding the stubs of her arms in the air to prevent blood loss.

Although victims' advocates argued for a lengthy prison term for Vincent's attacker, an apparently unrepentant Singleton was paroled after serving only eight years in prison. He took up residence in Florida, and Vincent lived in constant fear that he would attack her again. Vincent's concern finally abated in 1997 when Singleton was arrested and charged with the murder of 31-year-old Roxanne Hayes, a supposed prostitute. A year later he was convicted of first-degree murder. Singleton died of cancer in 2001 while on death row at Florida's Union Correctional Institution. Today, a recovered Vincent leads a full and active life in the Pacific northwest.

Violent crime survivor Mary Vincent throws the first pitch during the Giants "Resolve to Stop the Violence Project Day," in 1999 at 3Com Park, in San Francisco. Vincent was brutally raped by Larry Singleton—who cut off her forearms with a hatchet when she was 15-years-old. Singleton's release, after only eight years in prison, came to symbolize the lack of attention to the plight of crime victims that had once been characteristic of the American criminal justice system.

A Brief History of America's Victims' Rights Movement

victim

Someone who suffers direct or threatened physical, emotional, or financial harm as the result of the commission of a crime. The term *victim* also includes the immediate family of a minor or homicide victim.

According to the federal Bureau of Prisons (BOP), a **victim** is "someone who suffers direct or threatened physical, emotional, or financial harm as the result of the commission of a crime. The term 'victim' also includes the immediate family of a minor or homicide victim."[2]

Victims were rarely recognized in the laws and policies that govern our nation until the 1970s. From a legal perspective, crimes were considered offenses against the state (since the state made the law), not against the individual. Victims merely set the wheels of justice in motion (by filing charges) and, if necessary, helped carry out justice (by testifying in court). The victim had little or no status within the justice system, and victims' rights were virtually nonexistent.[3]

Tremendous strides have since been made in **victims' rights** legislation and victims' services. Few movements in American history have achieved as much success in prompting legislative response as did victims' rights activists' campaigns through the 1980s and 1990s.

The 1980 enactment of Wisconsin's Victims' Bill of Rights, the nation's first state bill of rights for crime victims, launched an era of dramatic progress in the victims' rights movement.[4] Passage of the federal Victim and Witness Protection Act of 1982[5] (VWPA) and release of the *Final Report* by the President's Task Force on Victims of Crime in the same year brought national visibility to crime victims' concerns.

The VWPA and the *Final Report* were catalysts for a decade of significant advances in victims' rights. By the date of release of the *Final Report*, four states had legislated victims' basic rights.[6] Today, all states have laws, modeled after the VWPA, that establish, protect, and enforce victims' rights. There are now more than 27,000 victim-related state statutes and 29 state victims' rights constitutional amendments.

Although no standard has been defined for victims' rights, most states' victims' bills of rights include basic provisions for treatment with dignity and compassion, ongoing access to information about the status of the case and the offender, notification of hearing and trial dates, permission to attend related judicial proceedings, input at sentencing and parole hearings (through victim impact statements), and restitution. (See Figure 14–1.)

Most states have legislated victims' rights to notification of events and proceedings at various stages of the judicial process; 39 have legislated victims' rights to attend criminal justice proceedings[7]; and 24 constitutionally protect these rights.[8] All states permit consideration of victim impact information at sentencing, with most permitting victim presentation of the information during the sentencing hearing. The majority of states require that victim impact information be included in the presentencing report, and at least half require that the court consider this information in its sentencing decision.

Despite the advances in victims' rights legislation, there remain serious deficiencies in those laws and in their implementation. Crime victims' rights, which vary significantly at both the federal and state levels, are often ignored, and many victims are still denied the right to participate in the justice process. Implementation of state-enacted constitutional victims' rights is often arbitrary and based on judicial preference. Many states make no provision for victims' rights in cases involving juvenile offenders.

victims' rights

The fundamental rights of victims to be represented equitably throughout the criminal justice process.

> Few movements in American history have achieved as much success in prompting legislative response as did victims' rights activists' campaigns through the 1980s and 1990s.

- THE RIGHT TO INFORMATION about the case as it progresses through the justice system;
- THE RIGHT TO NOTIFICATION of many different types of justice proceedings;
- THE RIGHT TO PARTICIPATE in court proceedings related to the offense;
- THE RIGHT TO BE REASONABLY PROTECTED from the accused offender;
- THE RIGHT TO INFORMATION about the conviction, sentencing, imprisonment, and release of the offender; and
- THE RIGHT TO RECEIVE RESTITUTION from the offender.

FIGURE 14-1
Victims' Rights

Source: Office for Victims of Crime.

LEGISLATION

Congressional concern for crime victims was evident in the VWPA; its stated purpose was "to enhance and protect the necessary role of crime victims and witnesses in the criminal justice process; to ensure that the federal government does all that is possible to assist victims and witnesses of crime, within the limits of available resources, without infringing on the constitutional rights of the defendant; and to provide model legislation for state and local governments."[9]

A subsection of the Crime Control Act of 1990,[10] known as the Victims' Rights and Restitution Act of 1990 (Victims' Rights Act), established a Bill of Rights for federal crime victims.[11] The Victims' Rights Act requires that federal law enforcement officials use their "best efforts" to ensure that victims receive basic rights and services. The **best efforts standard** made the federal law weaker than many state victims' rights laws in which provision for victims' rights and services is mandatory. The basic rights and services that officials must use their best efforts to provide include the following:

- fair and respectful treatment by authorities;
- reasonable protection from the accused;
- notification of court proceedings;
- presence at public court proceedings unless the court specifies otherwise;
- conference with the prosecutor;
- restitution; and
- updates to information about the offender, including conviction, sentencing, imprisonment, and release.

The Violent Crime Control and Law Enforcement Act,[12] passed in 1994, established new rights for victims of sexual assault, domestic violence, sex-

best efforts standard

A requirement of the federal Victims' Rights and Restitution Act of 1990 (also known as the Victims' Rights Act) which mandates that federal law enforcement officers, prosecutors, and corrections officials use their best efforts to ensure that victims receive basic rights and services during their encounter with the criminal justice system.

An assault victim arriving at the Macomb County, Michigan, Prosecutor's Office Crime Victims Rights Unit is greeted by victim advocate Kay McGuire. The unit's staff assists victims of violent crimes during the investigation, trial, presentencing, and post-sentencing phases of their victimization, and advises victims regarding compensation entitlements under Michigan's Crime Victim Compensation Act. What kinds of agencies have traditionally provided help to crime victims?

ual exploitation, child abuse, and telemarketing fraud. This legislation also designated significant funding for combating domestic violence and sexual assault, placed more than 100,000 community police officers on the street, and launched a number of other crime prevention initiatives.

In 1996, the federal Community Notification Act, known as Megan's Law, was enacted to ensure community notification of the locations of convicted sex offenders.[13]

In the Victims' Rights Clarification Act of 1997, Congress asserted victims' rights to attend proceedings and deliver victim impact statements within the federal system. This act was passed to ensure that victims and survivors of the Alfred P. Murrah Federal Building bombing in Oklahoma City, Oklahoma, could observe the trial and provide input at sentencing.

Table 14–1 summarizes the victims' rights defined by federal legislation.

THE PROPOSAL FOR A FEDERAL VICTIMS' RIGHTS CONSTITUTIONAL AMENDMENT

The 1982 President's Task Force on Victims of Crime made 68 recommendations for protection of victims' rights, including a recommendation that the Sixth Amendment to the U.S. Constitution be amended to guarantee

TABLE 14–1	Federal Victims' Rights Legislation
Legislation	**Provisions**
Victims' Rights Clarification Act, 1997	Ensured that victims of federal crimes had the right both to attend proceedings and to deliver or submit a victim impact statement.
Mandatory Victim Restitution Act, 1996	Made restitution mandatory on the federal level in all violent crime cases and in certain other cases.
Community Notification Act (also known as Megan's Law), 1996	Ensured that communities are notified of the release and location of convicted sex offenders.
Violent Crime Control and Law Enforcement Act, 1994	Created new rights for victims of sexual assault, domestic violence, sexual exploitation, child abuse, and telemarketing fraud.
Victims' Rights and Restitution Act (also called the Victims' Rights Act), 1990	Created the first federal bill of rights for victims of crime and required federal law enforcement officers, prosecutors, and corrections officials to use their *best efforts* to ensure that victims receive basic rights and services.
Victims of Crime Act (VOCA), 1984	Established the federal Office for Victims of Crime (OVC) to provide federal funds in support of victim assistance and compensation programs around the country and to advocate for the fair treatment of crime victims. Also established the federal Crime Victims' Fund to assist states in paying victim benefits.
Victim and Witness Protection Act (VWPA), 1982	Enacted a set of basic rights for crime victims and became a national model for state victims' rights laws.

Eye On Corrections™

Office for Victims of Crime Guides Services in Corrections

By Michelle Gaseau

Although ensuring public safety is typically part of a corrections agency's mission, many organizations are only beginning to make solid overtures to the victims of crime. Those agencies that have connected with the victims of crime have done so by notifying them of offender hearings and parole or release dates and by encouraging restitution and restorative justice initiatives.

Since 1988 the federal Office for Victims of Crime (OVC) has supported victim assistance and compensation programs but has also been interested in improving the relations that corrections agencies have with victims. To that end, the office seeks out and promotes promising practices in the field that bridge the gap for victims between the crime and the release of the offender.

"The victim is where everything begins. While [the offenders] are in the institution the victim does feel some relief, and it lessens the anxiety. At the time of release the anxiety goes up again, and victims begin to not have as much confidence in the system. That is where it is important for corrections probation and parole [agencies] to maintain that confidence," said John W. Gillis, Director of the Office for Victims of Crime.

Involving victims in a variety of areas in the field helps to engage the community, fosters a better understanding of the criminal justice system, and builds trust in the system. These services can take place at the community corrections level but also in the facility. The OVC has offered a number of recommendations to corrections agencies to help them focus on victims and include them in the system when they wish to be involved.

OVC RECOMMENDATIONS

As a first step, the OVC recommends that every state department of corrections and paroling authority establish a victim advisory committee that includes not only victims, but also service providers to guide and support victim-related policies, programs, and services. These committees review victim notification policies, victim-offender programming, and informational materials for victims.

Staff should also be designated for a variety of responsibilities related to victims' services. A specific staff liaison should be appointed to victims and service providers in the community.

"Direct service to the victim is something that we will try to [encourage]," said Gillis, who was recently confirmed to direct the OVC. "We're looking for programs that help in that area, and we're trying to make the victim as close to whole as possible."

According to the OVC, victim notification is important to support victim safety. Agencies should notify victims upon their request of any change in the status of offenders, including pardon or clemency, that would give them access to the community. Timely notice also gives victims the ability to exercise their rights to submit a victim impact statement or attend and/or testify at a parole hearing. Changes in an offender's status such as release for a funeral or a medical emergency, less restrictive classification, death, or pardon should also be communicated to victims.

Additional responsibilities associated with victim notification include providing the name, address, and phone number of the parole or probation officer assigned to an offender; the name of the offender if it has changed at all; the address, city, and county where the offender will be released or supervised; a recent picture and a general description of the offender upon release; assistance with a safety plan for the victim if authorities believe the release of the offender may threaten the victim or family; and notification of the offender's conditions of release. Agencies should also consider making information accessible to victims by toll-free number, in printed material, and in multiple languages.

Other recommendations by the OVC include collection and distribution of restitution payments as well as restorative justice mediation between victims and offenders when appropriate, such as with a property crime.

"In most organizations like corrections or criminal justice it has to come from the top down. That is important to the organization. When it does, it has a better chance of working. These are the people who can make it happen and, if not, it is left to the whim of those on the line as to whether or not to participate," said Gillis.

EFFORTS ON ALL SIDES

Organizations have developed a variety of victim-related programs and, according to Gillis, this programming should take place both in the community corrections setting and at the facility level.

"They are doing a lot of things in the area of victims. It does a lot of things. It cuts down on the amount of calls to the police departments, which increases the demand for services and the number of officers needed in the field. There are a lot of areas that are affected in parole and probation," he said.

Gillis, a victim of crime himself, said agencies should be cognizant of victims' rights to defer participation in these programs as well. "Victims don't want to come to the institution. There are some programs that want to encourage victims to come to the institution, and they [victims] are saying they don't want to do that," he added.

Gillis said that, in his own experience as a former commissioner on the California Board of Corrections, offenders sentenced to life in prison soon learn that showing remorse can benefit them at parole hearings later.

"After two or three parole hearings the lifers start to realize they should express remorse and accept responsibility. They want to send letters to victims and request that information be passed onto the victims. But victims don't want that contact," Gillis said.

Corrections agencies should be careful about the type of contact they champion but still support appropriate victim-offender programs. "There are a lot of dedicated people out there. At OVC we want to get in touch with those people and encourage them," Gillis said.

For more information about OVC, visit the Website at www.ojp.usdoj.gov/ovc. Additional information about OVC recommendations can be found in the OVC bulletin *New Directions in the Field*, August 1998. To order, visit the NCJRS Website at http://www.ncjrs.org/.

specific rights to crime victims. Although the recommendation has not yet been implemented, The National Organization for Victim Assistance (NOVA), Mothers Against Drunk Driving (MADD), the National Center for Victims of Crime (NVC—formerly the National Victim Center), and other national victims' organizations joined together in 1987 to create the National Victims' Constitutional Amendment Network (NVCAN). NVCAN provides leadership and coordinates ongoing efforts to amend the federal constitution in recognition of victims' rights.[14] NVCAN spent the next decade assisting state legislators in their efforts to pass amendments. Efforts to pass state constitutional amendments produced impressive results. Each of the 29 state victims' rights amendments passed by an overwhelming majority—80 to 90 percent in most states.[15]

> The proposal to adopt a federal constitutional amendment gained momentum in April 2002, when President George W. Bush announced his support of the bipartisan Crime Victims' Rights Amendment.

The proposal to adopt a federal constitutional amendment gained momentum in April 2002, when President George W. Bush announced his support of the bipartisan Crime Victims' Rights Amendment authored by U.S. Senators Feinstein and Kyl.[16] As proposed, the amendment would provide specific constitutionally protected rights to crime victims but could not be used as grounds for a new trial or in support of a claim for damages.

The Costs and Consequences of Victimization

According to a two-year National Institute of Justice (NIJ) study,[17] personal crimes result in costs of about $105 billion annually for medical expenses, lost earnings, and public victim assistance programs. For victims, crime costs may include (1) out-of-pocket expenses, such as for medical bills and property replacement; (2) reduced productivity at work, home, or school; and (3) nonmonetary losses, such as fear, pain, suffering, and reduced quality of life.

tangible losses

Costs such as medical expenses, lost wages, and property losses that accrue to crime victims as a result of their victimization.

Unlike **tangible losses** (such as medical expenses or lost wages), **intangible losses** (such as pain, suffering, and reduced quality of life) do not have a market price and cannot be bought or sold. Nevertheless, these losses are real and can be valued in dollars—victims would pay dearly to avoid them.

intangible losses

Costs such as fear, pain, suffering, and reduced quality of life that accrue to crime victims as a result of their victimization.

Tangible losses do not represent the true cost of victimization. Intangible losses, including pain, suffering, and reduced quality of life, place the annual cost of crime at an estimated $450 billion (see Figure 14–2). Violent crime (including drunk driving) accounts for $426 billion of this total; property crime, $24 billion. These estimates exclude several other types of crime such as white collar crime, personal fraud, and drug crime. Figure 14–2 shows the annual cost of crime in the United States.

The cost of crime victimization is far greater when its impact on society is considered. Such costs include (1) monies spent by the criminal justice system to find, prosecute, and confine offenders; (2) social costs associated with fear of crime (e.g., changed behavior, the fear of being outside at night, moving to a safer neighborhood; (3) mental health costs associated with healing "scars" from victimization; (4) private security

Ethical Dilemma

If you were the victim of an assault, would you be willing to take part in a restorative justice program with your perpetrator? What are the issues that would concern you? For more information go to Ethical Dilemma 14-1 at http://www.mhhe.com/schmalleger2.

President George W. Bush speaks at the 2002 National Crime Victim Service Awards Ceremony at the Department of Justice in Washington, DC. The president used the occasion to announce his support for a crime victims' rights amendment to the U.S. Constitution.

expenditures by the general population concerned about crime; (5) monies spent by employers to train temporary or new employees; (6) the costs of lost productivity borne by employers; (7) insurance claims processing costs (for example, life insurance claims for fatalities and workers' compensation claims); (8) workers' compensation and disability payments, especially those made to workers victimized while on the job; and (9) legal expenses incurred in recovering productivity losses from offenders and insurance companies (e.g., drunk drivers and their insurers). The National Crime Victimization Survey (NCVS) data include estimates of the number of hours of work and earnings lost due to medically related problems associated with victimization. Some specifics from the NIJ study show that

- Violent crime necessitates 3 percent of all U.S. medical spending and 14 percent of all injury-related medical spending.
- Violent crime results in wage losses equivalent to 1 percent of American earnings.
- Violent crime is a significant factor in mental health care usage. As much as 10 to 20 percent of mental health care expenditures in the United States may be attributable to crime, primarily for victims treated as a result of their victimization.
- Personal crime reduces the average American's quality of life by 1.8 percent. Violence alone causes a 1.7 percent loss. These estimates include only costs to victimized households, ignoring the broader impact of crime-induced fear on our society.

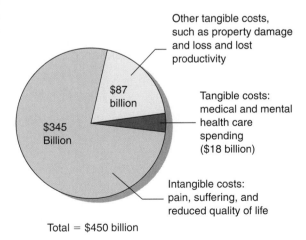

Other tangible costs, such as property damage and loss and lost productivity

Tangible costs: medical and mental health care spending ($18 billion)

Intangible costs: pain, suffering, and reduced quality of life

$87 billion

$345 Billion

Total = $450 billion

FIGURE 14-2

Annual Cost of Crime in the United States

Source: Ted R. Miller, Mark A. Cohen, and Brian Wiersema, *Victim Costs and Consequences: A New Look,* U.S. Department of Justice, National Institute of Justice Research Report (Washington, DC: GPO, February 1996), p. 17.

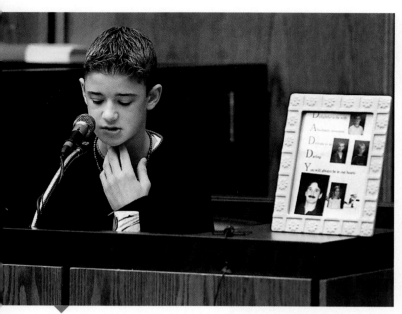

Crimes are costly both emotionally and financially. Brendan Costin, the 14-year-old son of murder victim Michael Costin, delivers a victim impact statement about his deceased father on the witness stand at the sentencing hearing of Thomas Junta on January 25, 2002, in Cambridge, Massachusetts. Junta was sentenced to 6 to 10 years in prison for beating Costin to death at their sons' hockey practice.

NIJ also reports the estimated total annual cost of crime to victims in the United States, including the value of intangible losses and victim losses due to crimes.

WHO PAYS THE BILL?

Victims and their families pay the bill for some crimes, while the public largely pays the bill for others. Insurers pay $45 billion in crime-related claims annually.[18] That is $265 per American adult. The government pays $8 billion annually for restorative and emergency services to victims, plus about one-fourth of the $11 billion in health insurance claim payments.

Taxpayers and insurance purchasers cover almost all the tangible victim costs of arson and drunk driving. They cover $9 billion of the $19 billion in tangible nonservice costs of larceny, burglary, and motor vehicle theft.

Victims pay about $44 billion of the $57 billion in tangible nonservice expenses for violent crimes—murder, rape, robbery, assault, and abuse and neglect. Employers pay almost $5 billion because of these crimes, primarily in health insurance bills. (This estimate excludes sick leave and disability insurance costs other than workers' compensation.) Government bears the remaining costs, through lost tax revenues and Medicare/Medicaid payments. Crime victim compensation accounts for 38 percent of homeowner insurance premium costs and 29 percent of automobile insurance premium costs.

Criminologists and public policy researchers are now using crime cost estimates to help assess the desirability of various policy options. Reported costs can be used to assess the wisdom of early offender release and diversion programs.

The Role of Corrections

In the past, correctional agencies were viewed only as facilities for punishing and rehabilitating offenders. Today, they also serve crime victims—protecting them from intimidation and harassment, notifying them of offender status, providing avenues for victim input into release decisions, and collecting restitution.[19] Public safety consultant Anne Seymour calls corrections-based victim services a "specialized discipline" within the field of victims' rights and services.[20]

Correctional agencies are also beginning to recognize the important role that victims can play in helping them develop policies, procedures, and programs that consider victims as well as correctional staff and offenders. Across the nation, crime victims are being asked to join advisory committees and agency boards, become official members of parole commissions, and serve as teachers in innovative classes that sensitize offenders to the impact of their offenses.

Correctional agencies are beginning to acknowledge victims' needs in their mission statements. In Oregon, for example, the state board of parole recently issued the following statement: "The Board's mission is to work in partnership with the Department of Corrections and local supervisory authorities to protect the public and reduce the risk of repeat criminal behavior through incarceration and community supervision decisions based on applicable laws, victims' interests, public safety, and recognized principles of offender behavioral change." Many state corrections departments have now issued similar mission statements.

Crime victims' involvement with correctional agencies helps ensure priority for victim safety and services within correctional agencies. Victim advisory committees now exist in a number of correctional agencies for that purpose.

VICTIM NOTIFICATION

Victim notification of the release or pending release of convicted offenders is an important service. Without notification, victims are denied an opportunity to take precautions to ensure their own safety.

The importance of providing offender release information to crime victims has long been recognized. In 1982, it was one of the primary recommendations of the President's Task Force on Victims of Crime. In the *Final Report*, the Task Force recommended that parole boards notify victims and their families in advance of parole hearings if victims provide the paroling authority with their names and addresses. In addition, the Task Force called on parole boards to allow victims of crime, their families, or their representatives to attend parole hearings and to provide information about the impact of the crime. According to the National Victim Services Survey, marked improvements have occurred in this area since 1985.[21]

There is, however, no consistent victim notification procedure. Some correctional agencies notify victims of only certain types of inmate releases (such as the release of sex offenders). Others notify victims of changes in offender classification. Some notify victims of an inmate's escape, while others notify victims of an inmate's clemency or death. At the federal level, the BOP has created one of the nation's first comprehensive victim notification programs, which has served as a model to the states for over a decade. The BOP notifies victims of any major change in an inmate's status.

Innovative technologies have emerged in recent years that augment victim access to notification and information. At least 10 state correctional agencies utilize automated voice notification systems that place telephone calls to victims, if requested, and inform them of offenders' pending release or release hearings. Victims can also contact a centralized call center, 24 hours a day, 7 days a week. Call center operators confirm offender status and provide referrals to community-based victim services. Many state correctional agencies are following the example of the Illinois Department of Corrections, which provides current updates on inmate status and location and relevant upcoming hearings to victims and the general public via the Internet.[22]

victim notification
Notification to victims of the release or pending release of convicted offenders who have harmed them.

There is no such thing as a victimless crime. In my particular situation, the victim of my crime is my brother. I literally stole his identity. I used that identity to obtain cash, credit cards, and debit cards to pay bills, pay for medication, and pay for things that were needed daily. My crimes destroyed my brother's credit and his credibility with lenders and investors.

I knew what I was doing was wrong when I did it. I knew and understood that there was a reasonable chance that I would get caught. I knew that what I was doing would most likely land me in prison. In my situation, prison was not a deterrent. At the time I committed my crime, I did not feel as though I had a choice. The crime itself seemed to me to be the lesser of two evils.

When I think of my brother, my victim, the first thing I think of is all of the pain that I have put him through. I put him and the family through a great deal of pain. I feel shame. I can only hope that, someday, my brother will find it in his heart to forgive me. I feel sorrow, because my crime has placed an enormous gulf between us.

THE OFFENDER SPEAKS

In most jurisdictions, victims must request certain types of notification. Many victims do not request notification simply because they have not been informed that they have a right to do so.

VICTIM AND WITNESS PROTECTION

> Every day in the United States, victims and witnesses are harassed, intimidated, and retaliated against by incarcerated offenders, through intimidating phone calls, mail, or threatened visits from friends and associates.

Every day in the United States, victims and witnesses are harassed, intimidated, and retaliated against by incarcerated offenders, through intimidating phone calls, mail, or threatened visits from friends and associates. Many correctional agencies have responded creatively to this problem. Today, when such problems occur, 37 states revoke an offending inmates' privileges, 36 transfer the inmate to a more restrictive level, 28 allow the filing of a new criminal charge, and 21 allow enhancement of the inmate's sentence. In addition, 40 state correctional agencies document such harassment and threats in the offender's case file, 35 recommend investigation for additional prosecution, and 31 recommend revocation of parole when a parolee harasses, intimidates, or attempts retaliation.[23] California authorities are using an innovative method to stop the increasing number of instances in which inmates use telephones or letters to threaten and harass victims. The California Department of Corrections has created a program to block victims' phone numbers from inmate access and check inmates' outgoing mail.

In managing offenders who are ordered by the court to community supervision or released early from prison with supervision, probation and parole officers need to ensure the safety of victims and the public. Officers will generally use surveillance to identify offenders who pose a continued threat and make monitoring efforts such as checking with contacts at the offender's home and place of employment and with neighbors to ensure that the offender is meeting the conditions of probation or parole.

Just as there are special units in law enforcement and prosecutors' offices, probation and parole departments have begun to establish special units, such as sex offender and domestic violence units, to provide intensive probation or parole to reduce the safety risks to victims and society as a whole. Agents in these units have smaller caseloads and have received specialized training in intensive supervision.

Correctional agencies also use intermediate sanctions to ensure victim safety. Such sanctions include electronic monitoring, house arrest, random

---

EXHIBIT 14-1   Department of Justice

Crime Victim Treatment Improvement Plan

Many people believe that much more needs to be done to involve victims and the community in the correctional process. A recent plan proposed by the Department of Justice to improve the treatment of crime victims recommended these specific steps:

- Every state department of corrections and every parole authority should establish an advisory committee of victims and service providers to guide and support victim-related policies, programs, and services.
- Correctional agencies should designate staff to provide information, assistance, and referrals to victims of crime.
- Mission statements of correctional agencies should recognize victims as an important constituency and should address victims' rights and services.
- A correctional agency should notify victims of any change in the offender's status that would allow the offender access to the community or to the victims.
- A correctional agency should place a high priority on ensuring victims' safety from intimidation, threats, or harm by offenders.
- Information about offender status and victims' rights should be accessible in several languages through toll-free numbers and printed materials.
- Correctional agencies should collect and distribute restitution payments as ordered by the court, and wage-earning opportunities should be increased for inmates, wards, and parolees who owe restitution.
- Victims' input should be sought for all decisions affecting the release of adult and juvenile offenders.
- Victim-impact awareness should be a basic component of the education and treatment programs of correctional agencies.
- Protected, supported, mediated dialogue between victim and offender should be available upon the victim's request.
- A crime victim should be notified of any violation of the conditions of the offender's probation or parole and should be allowed to comment before or during the violation hearing.
- Uniform practices should be developed and implemented for notification of a sex offender's release.

Source: Adapted from Office of Justice Programs, *New Directions from the Field: Victims' Rights and Services for the 21st Century* (Washington, DC: U.S. Department of Justice, 1998).

---

alcohol and drug testing, parole to a location other than the victim's community, mandatory restitution, and increased surveillance.

COMMUNITY NOTIFICATION

Most states have passed laws that either provide for community notification of sexual offender releases or authorize the general public or certain individuals or organizations to access sexual offender registries (see Figure 14-3). Often referred to as Megan's laws, in memory of seven-year-old Megan Kanka, who was murdered by a twice-convicted sex offender paroled to her New Jersey neighborhood, community notification laws recognize that a community has a compelling interest in being informed of

CAREER PROFILE

Mary Achilles
Victim Advocate   Commonwealth of Pennsylvania

> " Victims raise a variety of issues— 'I don't want him near my child's school or in my community.' I'm always engaging decision makers about what's best for the victim, the offender, and the community at large. "

Mary Achilles heads the Office of the Victim Advocate for the Commonwealth of Pennsylvania, where she supervises a staff of 16. The Office was formed in 1995 as an independent agency to provide services to both corrections and parole.

She began her career in 1979 as a prosecution assistant in the district attorney's office in Philadelphia, where she worked for 14 years. She moved to the department of corrections in 1993 and worked to establish the state's victim notification program. She holds a bachelor's degree in criminal justice and a master's in public administration.

On a daily basis, Mary deals with victims and allows them to provide input into the release process. Her office files petitions to the board of probation and parole on behalf of victims to deny release or set supervision conditions and also selects victims to view executions if they desire to do so.

Mary says she was drawn to her current role while working in the district attorney's office. "Helping prepare cases for trial, I started to see the inconvenience and the draw that they had on the victim," she says.

"Our philosophy is that we have to work with victims to prepare them for the fact that the offender will be released," she adds. "We'll petition the board to deny their release, but the reality is that 90 percent of all offenders will be released again.

"The challenge for us is that we work in agencies that are about the managing of offenders. Those agencies by design are about the movement of offenders through the process, and to get those agencies to be sensitive to the individual victim is always a battle."

Despite the challenges, Mary is enthusiastic about her job. "It is incredible to see the strength of the human spirit. Since we mostly deal with state-level offenders, we're talking murders and rapes and serial rapes, the horrible stuff people don't want to talk about. It's amazing to me how people can triumph over tragedy—how much stronger they can be as a result of it."

---

offenders' whereabouts. In 1996, a federal Megan's law was enacted that requires states to release relevant registration information when necessary to protect the public.[24]

Most state community notification laws impose a registration requirement on a sex offender at the time he or she is released on parole or probation, and the requirement typically remains in force for the duration of the parole or probation period.[25] A few states, including Alaska, California, Michigan, Montana, and South Carolina impose a lifetime registration requirement for sex offenders against children, while other states have established a fixed registration period of 15 or 25 years. Approximately 30 states have provisions for some type of DNA testing or registration for genetic identification purposes.

To be truly effective, **community notification** laws require coordination among law enforcement officials, courts, correctional agencies, victim service providers, the news media, and other key stakeholders. Correctional agencies play a major role in providing this service by determining when and to where sex offenders will be paroled and by conducting community outreach and public education projects.

community notification

Notification to the community of the release or pending release of convicted offenders.

A promising practice in planning and implementing community notification programs emerged in 1990 in the state of Washington.[26] The Washington approach considers the rights and interests of victims, the community, and offenders. The strategy incorporates the following elements: establishing requirements for registration, requiring registration information for offenders, implementing guidelines for failure to register, implementing guidelines for a preliminary offender risk assessment, compiling offender information packets for distribution to the prosecutor of the county where the offender plans to reside, distributing special bulletins to law enforcement agencies, developing notification policies, creating guidelines concerning who should have access to sex offender registry information, and conducting community outreach efforts that involve victims and address their rights and needs.

CRIME IMPACT CLASSES

Over the past decade, the number of educational programs in correctional institutions that involve both offenders and victims has greatly increased. The purpose of such programs is to help offenders understand the devastating impact their crimes have on victims and their families and friends, on their communities, and on themselves and their own families. For victims, participation in programs with offenders is useful because, although the harm they have suffered cannot be undone, they may prevent others from being victimized. Studies also show that participation in impact panels helps heal victims' emotional scars.[27]

FIGURE 14-3
Online Sex Offender Registry

The home page of sexoffender.com—a commercial site that combines sex offender information from many states. Community notification laws frequently result in the posting of online offender databases. How do such databases help victims?

Source: © Sexoffender.com. Used with permission.

Notable among victim-offender programs is the Impact of Crime on Victims (IOC) program, initiated by the California Youth Authority in 1986. The program has been replicated in more than 20 juvenile and adult correctional agencies and numerous diversion programs. IOC programs include a 40-hour curriculum that is designed to educate offenders about how different crimes affect victims and society.[28]

The U.S. Department of the Navy's Corrections and Programs Division took an important step in integrating victims into its corrections process when it issued guidelines in 1996 instructing U.S. Naval correctional facilities to implement impact-of-crime classes for prisoners before releasing them from custody. Information from inmates and correctional staff indicate that, after completing the classes, offenders have a greater understanding of the impact of their criminal conduct.

The passage of protective legislation represents a meaningful first step. But National Center for Victims of Crime surveys indicate that enforcement is generally lacking.[29] The NCVC reports that less than 40 percent of surveyed local criminal justice professionals knew their states had such legislation, and that rates of required victim notifications range as low as

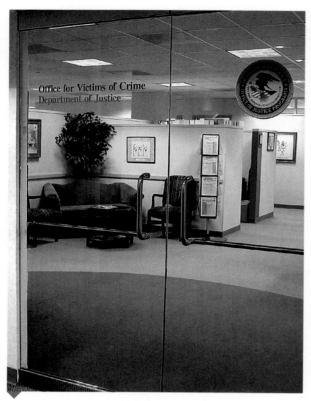

The entrance to the federal Office for Victims of Crime (OVC). OVC has developed model programs for assisting crime victims—including victimized correctional staff. What forms of criminal victimization might correctional staff experience?

30 percent. Criminal justice officials cite lack of funding as the most common reason for their inability to meet these responsibilities.[30]

VICTIM-OFFENDER DIALOGUE

During the past two decades, a number of victim-offender dialogue programs have been developed in juvenile and criminal justice agencies, predominantly in juvenile probation agencies. These programs, primarily used in property crime cases, give victims an opportunity to engage in a structured dialogue with their offenders, who have already admitted their guilt or been convicted/adjudicated. When conducted with sensitivity to the victim and with care to ensure that participation by both victim and offender is voluntary, the victim-offender dialogue process can be very effective in helping victims overcome feelings of trauma and loss.[31] The program gives victims greater satisfaction with the justice system, increases their likelihood of being compensated, and reduces fear of future victimization.

In recent years, correctional agencies have begun to experiment with victim-offender dialogue in violent crime cases. In 1995, for example, the Texas Department of Criminal Justice initiated a victim-offender mediation/dialogue program for victims of severe violence and their incarcerated offenders. Under this program, the victim initiates the contact.

THE VICTIMIZATION OF CORRECTIONAL STAFF

Correctional agencies have begun to recognize the impact of victimization on their employees. Correctional professionals are exposed to a wide range of victimization, including verbal harassment by inmates, sexual harassment by inmates or colleagues, physical or sexual assaults, hostage situations, and murder. To lessen the acute and chronic trauma this violence has on employees, many adult correctional agencies have developed written policies and procedures to respond to staff victimization and critical incidents.[32]

Most institutions have standard procedures for dealing with correctional staff victimization that focus on prevention. Many prison management departments, including California, South Carolina, and Texas have developed procedures for helping victimized staff. Guidelines for response to employee victimization have also been developed, under a national training and technical project funded by the Office for Victims of Crime (OVC).[33] The OVC project provides a comprehensive model for correctional agencies that is based on victims' rights laws, either state or federal.

Victim Compensation

Victims generally have three options for recovering crime-related financial losses: (1) state-sponsored compensation programs; (2) court-ordered resti-

As government has become increasingly centralized, a major source of citizen frustration is the inability to define what is being achieved by the justice system, both on an individual case basis and from the perspective of the community. As the media focus on the spectacular failures and the extremes of the normal spectrum, government is caught between overwhelming caseloads of minor criminals and the need to target resources to protect the public from the dangerous ones. In the rush to efficiency, the government bypasses the most effective agents, the community and the family, instead focusing on the individual cases that squeak the loudest.

In the Reparative Probation program, ordinary citizens of the State of Vermont make sentencing decisions about adult criminal offenders from their community. Board members meet with offenders and victims, resolving their disputes by providing the offenders with the opportunity to acknowledge their wrongdoing, apologize to their victims, and make amends to their community. The offenders are sentenced by the court, having pled guilty to a nonviolent crime. The sentence is then suspended, pending their completion of a reparative agreement.

Direct involvement in decision making about individual cases forces citizens to look at the offenders not as strangers, not as numbers, and not as monsters. The offenders are forced to confront the reality of their offense and its impact on the community and their victims. This confrontation, with a restorative outcome, shifts the paradigm from punishment to reintegration. The offender is held accountable, the victim is restored, and the community is repaired. Perhaps even more important, the dispute is resolved by the community, and the community is empowered.

John G. Perry
Director of Planning
Vermont Department of Corrections

THE STAFF SPEAKS

tution; and (3) civil remedies. **Victim compensation** programs, which exist in every state, may pay for medical care, mental health counseling, lost wages or loss of support, funeral and burial expenses, and/or crime scene cleanup.[34]

Restitution, the subject of the next section in this chapter, can be ordered in juvenile and criminal courts as a way to hold offenders financially accountable for their crimes.[35] The financial as well as preventative remedies that crime victims can seek through the civil justice system are not discussed in this text, but you should know that they represent one more avenue that victims can pursue in order to be compensated financially for their injuries. At the very least, correctional offices should consider implementing a policy of informing victims and victim service providers of the legal rights of crime victims to pursue reparations through the civil justice system.

The first victim compensation programs were established in New Zealand and Great Britain in 1964. These programs were based on a concept suggested by British Magistrate Margery Fry in the late 1950s. The first victim compensation program established in the United States was California's, created in 1965. By the time the President's Task Force on Victims of Crime released its *Final Report* in 1982, 36 states had victim compensation programs.[36] Today, all 50 states, the District of Columbia, the U.S. Virgin Islands, Guam, and Puerto Rico operate victim compensation programs.[37]

Victim compensation programs provide assistance to victims of almost all types of violent crime: rape, robbery, assault, sexual abuse, drunk driving, and domestic violence. These programs, as a rule, pay expenses but do not pay for lost, stolen, or damaged property. Eligibility and specific benefits vary from state to state.

victim compensation

A form of victim assistance in which state-funded payments are made to victims to help them recover financial losses due to crime.

Victim compensation programs provide assistance to victims of almost all types of violent crime: rape, robbery, assault, sexual abuse, drunk driving, and domestic violence.

In a typical year, state compensation programs pay approximately $240 million to more than 110,000 victims nationwide.[38] The amounts paid by each state vary considerably. Ten states pay less than $500,000 annually, and about 15 pay more than $3 million. The two states with the largest programs, California and Texas, pay nearly one-half of the total benefits paid in the United States.

Benefit maximums, which also vary from state to state, generally range from $10,000 to $25,000, although maximums are lower or higher for a few states. For example, California, Maryland, Minnesota, Ohio, Texas, and Wisconsin allow benefits of $40,000 to $50,000. Some states, such as New York, set no limit on payment of medical expenses; other states, such as Washington, pay medical expenses up to a predetermined maximum. Many states also set limits for other types of expense, such as funerals and mental health counseling. Nationally, the average amount paid to each victim applying for compensation is about $2,000.

PRESIDENT'S TASK FORCE ON VICTIMS OF CRIME

In 1982 the President's Task Force recommended federal funding to help support state victim compensation programs. It also documented problems in several state victim compensation programs: absence of a system for emergency compensation to cover immediate need for food, shelter, and/or medical assistance; insufficient maximum reimbursement levels; lack of coverage for domestic violence; and differences in residency requirements for eligible crime victims. Many of these problems have since been remedied through federal and state legislation and increased federal and state funding.

State-operated victim compensation programs have improved dramatically since 1982, in benefits provided and in recipients. However, some of the concerns raised by the President's Task Force, such as emergency compensation and insufficient maximums, have not been fully addressed by all states.

VICTIMS OF CRIME ACT

The Task Force's recommendation for federal support of state victim compensation programs was implemented through the Victims of Crime Act (VOCA),[39] passed in 1984. VOCA established the federal Office for Victims of Crime, which administers the federal Crime Victims' Fund, reimbursing states for up to 40 percent of victim compensation payments and providing technical assistance to state compensation programs.

All 50 states and the U.S. territories also receive annual VOCA victim assistance grants to support their victim assistance programs. A $500,000 base allocation is awarded to each state, the District of Columbia, the U.S. Virgin Islands, and Puerto Rico. The Northern Mariana Islands, Guam, and American Samoa each receive a $200,000 base allocation. Additional awards beyond the base allocation are distributed based on population. These awards support approximately 6,100 annual grants for crisis intervention, counseling, emergency shelter, criminal justice advocacy, and emergency

Ethical Dilemma

How do you ever adequately compensate crime victims for their pain and suffering? If you were a victim of a serious crime, what would be adequate compensation? For more information go to Ethical Dilemma 14-2 at http://www.mhhe.com/schmalleger2.

transportation programs.[40] More than $2.3 billion in VOCA victim assistance grants was awarded between FY 1986 and FY 2001.[41]

Victims must apply for compensation in the state where the crime occurs. Prior to VOCA, many states' programs provided compensation only to residents unless a reciprocal agreement had been made with a victim's state of residence. States are now required, by federal law, to cover residents, nonresidents, and victims of federal crimes. Two states still restrict eligibility to U.S. citizens.

RECENT TRENDS

Due to increases in publicity concerning victim compensation programs and new laws mandating that rights, services, and information be provided to victims, the number of victims applying for financial assistance has grown. As a result, many victim compensation program budgets were inadequate, and victims did not receive the compensation that they should have. Today, although a few states are still unable to pay all eligible claims, most do.

ELIGIBILITY REQUIREMENTS

Each state has victim eligibility requirements for compensation benefits. Although states' requirements vary, most programs require that the victim do the following:

- Report the crime promptly, usually within 72 hours. A few states allow more time or less, but most have "good cause exceptions" that apply to children, incapacitated victims, and others with special circumstances.
- Cooperate with law enforcement agencies in investigation and prosecution of the crime.
- Submit a timely application for compensation, generally within one year. Again, a few states allow more time or less, and most may waive the deadline under certain circumstances.
- Provide other information, as needed by the program.
- Not file claims for compensation of victimization that resulted from claimant criminal activity or misconduct.

The VOCA Victim Compensation Final Program Guidelines encourage state compensation program staff members to meet with victims and victim service providers; to review state statutes, program guidelines, and policies for responsiveness to crime victims' needs; and to identify potential barriers to victim cooperation with law enforcement agencies, such as apprehension about personal safety and fear of offender retaliation. Victims tend to be reluctant to cooperate if offenders threaten violence or death. Age and psychological, cultural, or linguistic barriers may also influence the amount of victim cooperation. For instance, a young child, senior citizen, or foreign national may have difficulty communicating. Embarrassment or shame may delay or prevent reporting of a sexual assault.

Compensation programs are the victim's last resort. All other potential sources, such as the offender's insurance or public benefits, must be exhausted before state victims' compensation may be paid. If, however, payment from another source is delayed, the program may provide funds to the victim, which must be repaid if and when the victim receives other payment.

The victim cannot have been engaged in criminal activity. Dependents' eligibility depends largely on the victim's eligibility. Dependents or relatives of a homicide victim, for example, who was committing a crime at the time of death are generally not eligible for benefits.

BENEFIT CRITERIA

All compensation programs cover the same major expenses, although limits vary. The primary costs covered by all states are medical expenses, mental health counseling, wages lost as a result of a crime-related injury, lost support (for dependents of homicide victims), and funeral expenses. Nationwide, medical fees represent well over half of all compensation awards, with lost wage and support payments comprising the next highest payment percentage. In a few states, 20 to 40 percent of awards are for counseling; compensation payment in this area is increasing rapidly throughout the country. Twenty-five to 30 percent of claim payment recipients are children age 17 and under.[42]

Many compensation programs also may pay for the following:

- moving or relocation expenses, when a victim may be in danger or relocation becomes medically necessary as a result of victimization;
- transportation for medical services when the provider is located far from the victim's residence or when other special circumstances exist;
- services, such as child care and/or housekeeping, that the victim cannot perform due to a crime-related injury;
- essential lost or damaged personal possessions (11 states pay for medically necessary equipment, such as eyeglasses or hearing aids, but only a few cover other such items);
- crime-scene cleanup—securing or restoring a home to its precrime condition; and
- rehabilitation—physical or job therapy, ramps, wheelchairs, and/or home or vehicle modification and/or driving instruction.

RESTITUTION

Restitution is repayment to the victim, by the offender, for losses, damages, or expenses that result from a crime. Restitution is a form of victim compensation that holds the offender liable for the victim's financial losses. Restitution is generally seen, not as a punishment or an alternative to fines or sanctions, but as a debt owed.[43]

Criminal courts often order restitution to compensate victims for expenses that are the direct result of a crime. It is most often ordered in cases of property crime, such as a burglary. It may also be ordered to reimburse victims for expenses related to physical and/or mental health recovery and, for survivors of homicide victims, to make up for loss of support. Restitution is also common for cases of theft of services (e.g., restaurant bills), fraud, forgery, and traffic or vehicle law violation. Judges have also begun to order community restitution in which convicted offenders pay back the community through service.

Restitution, as a significant remedy for crime victims, was first imposed on the federal level in 1982, when the VWPA required federal judges to order full restitution in criminal cases or state on the record their reasons for not doing so.[44] That same year, the *Final Report* of the President's Task Force on Victims of Crime reinforced the VWPA by recommending that judges order restitution in all cases in which the victim suffered financial loss or state compelling reasons for a contrary ruling in the case record.[45]

The importance of restitution was emphasized in 1994, with enactment of the federal Violent Crime Control and Law Enforcement Act, which made restitution mandatory in cases of sexual assault or domestic violence. In 1996, the Mandatory Victim Restitution Act made restitution mandatory in all violent crime cases and in certain other cases on the federal level.[46]

In the decade that followed VWPA, every state enacted statutes that addressed restitution, most following the lead of the federal model. However, states continue to amend their statutes, creating a patchwork of financial reparations for victims across the country. As of 1995, 29 states had mandated restitution in all cases. Today, some states mandate restitution only in cases involving violent crimes, while others mandate restitution only in cases involving property crimes. A number of states require that offenders be on probation or parole before victims may collect restitution, and many do not require restitution from juvenile offenders. Probationers who fail to make restitution payments may have their probation revoked.

Despite developments in legislation, restitution remains one of the most underenforced of victims' rights in terms of ordering and monitoring, collecting, and dispersing payments. A recent DOJ study of recidivism among probationers reported that, of 32 counties surveyed,[47] only half required restitution in at least one-third of all felony probation cases. Of felony probationers who had completed their sentences, only 54 percent had fully satisfied restitution orders.[48]

All in all, the NCVC reports a poor record nationwide for ordering and collecting restitution from convicted offenders.[49] Even so, national research studies indicate that restitution is one of the most significant factors affecting the satisfaction of victims with the criminal justice process.[50]

Collecting Restitution in Institutions   Many correctional agencies encourage inmates to fulfill restitution obligations. These agencies increase collections by offering incentives (such as increased visitation and prison commissary services or priority enrollment in education programs) for compliance and by denying privileges for failure or refusal to participate.

The California Department of Corrections (CDC) has implemented an Inmate Restitution Fine Collections System, supported by state law, that allows deduction of up to 50 percent of inmate wages for payment of court-ordered restitution. These funds are transferred to the State Board of Control Restitution Fund for disbursement. This system collected over $9 million from its inception in November 1992 through early 1998. CDC's Victim Services Program staff coordinate voluntary inmate and parolee restitution payments as well.

Community Restitution   Offenders who are truly indigent may be given the option to perform community service in lieu of monetary restitution. According to OVC, however, this option should be offered only with victim consent. Some victims prefer that the monetary restitution order stand until such time, if any, the offender is able to fulfill it. Other victims may feel somewhat compensated if they participate in the decision about the type and location of the service to be performed. Payment of victim restitution does not necessarily preclude an order for community restitution. In many instances the offender has done damage not only to the victim, but also to the community.

The Office for Victims of Crime

Established by VOCA, OVC's mission is to do the following:[51]

- help ensure that justice is done and that the victim achieves a sense of personal healing;
- administer the Crime Victims' Fund. Nearly 90 percent, or about $500 million, of the monies collected each year, all from fines and penalties paid by federal criminal offenders, is distributed to state victim assistance and compensation programs, helping to support more than 2,500 local victim services agencies, such as domestic violence shelters, children's advocacy centers, and rape treatment programs, and provide expense reimbursement to victims;
- advocate fair treatment of crime victims;
- develop and administer projects for enhancing victims' rights and services;
- provide training, on a number of victim issues, for many different professions—victim service providers, law enforcement personnel, prosecutors, clergy, and medical and mental health personnel;
- provide training on victim-witness issues for 70 federal law enforcement agencies, including the Federal Bureau of Investigation (FBI), the Department of Defense (DOD), and the National Park Service;
- provide services to people victimized on tribal or federal lands, such as military bases and national parks;
- maintain a fund to provide emergency services such as temporary shelter and travel to court for victims of federal crimes; and
- establish **victim assistance programs** on Indian reservations to recruit and train multidisciplinary teams to handle child sexual abuse cases and provide comprehensive victim services.

victim assistance program

An organized program that offers services to victims of crime in the areas of crisis intervention and follow-up counseling and that helps victims secure their rights under the law.

The Office for Victims of Crime has emerged as an invaluable support agency for state and territorial agencies, as well as for crime victims themselves. Its effective administration of victim compensation and assistance grant programs enables states and territories to provide greatly improved services to crime victims. Meanwhile, its *Fact Sheet* and *Help Series* publications provide crime victims with timely and comprehensive informational materials. A typical example[52] includes guidance to victims on their fundamental rights and an up-to-date listing of compensation and assistance program contact points within each state and U.S. territory. The

OVC makes these materials readily available through its well-designed and superbly maintained Website at http://www.ojp.usdoj.gov/ovc.

Victim Impact Statements

Victim impact statements are assertions—by a victim and/or friends or relatives of the victim—about the crime's impact on the victim and the victim's family. Victim impact statements, now permitted at all sentencing hearings,[53] may be verbal or written, depending on the jurisdiction. Many states and the federal government now require that victim impact statements be included in presentencing reports (see Figure 14–4). The Crime Control and Law Enforcement Act of 1994 gave federal victims of violent crime or sexual assault a federal **right of allocution**—the right to make a statement at sentencing. Another federal law, the Child Protection Act of 1990, provides that victim impact statements from young children be allowed to take the form of drawings or models.

right of allocution
A statutory provision permitting crime victims to speak at the sentencing of convicted offenders. A federal right of allocution was established for victims of federal violent and sex crimes under the Violent Crime Control and Law Enforcement Act of 1994.

VICTIM IMPACT STATEMENT

If you need more space to answer any of the following questions, please feel free to use as much paper as you need, and simply attach these sheets of paper to this impact statement. Thank you.

Your Name

Defendant's Name(s)

1. How has the crime affected you and those close to you? Please feel free to discuss your feelings about what has happened and how it has affected your general well-being. Has this crime affected your relationship with any family members, friends, co-workers, and other people? As a result of this crime, if you or others close to you have sought any type of victim services, such as counseling by either a licensed professional, member of the clergy, or a community-sponsored support group, you may wish to mention this.

2. What physical injuries or symptoms have you or others close to you suffered as result of this crime? You may want to write about how long the injuries lasted, or how long they are expected to last, and if you sought medical treatment for these injuries. You may also want to discuss what changes you have made in your life as a result of these injuries.

3. Has the crime affected your ability to perform your work, make a living, run a household, go to school, or enjoy any other activities you previously performed or enjoyed? If so, please explain how these activities have been affected by this crime.

FIGURE 14-4
Sample Victim Impact Statement

Victims in Context: Current and Future Perspectives

Reflections on the Future

As a consequence of increased concerns about the rights of victims, many changes have been introduced into the criminal justice system to improve the experience of victims and to better represent their needs. These initiatives include compensation programs, police-based victim services units, and victim impact statements in offender sentencing. Many of these innovations have emerged from pressure brought to bear on legislators by interest groups representing victims.

In support of their claims, victim advocates rely heavily on research that has documented the incidence and distribution of crimes, particularly violence, from the point of view of victims. Researchers have shown that multiple victimization is a problem far beyond what was originally imagined. Individuals who are victims once are much more likely to be victimized again than are those who have never before been victimized. This revictimization appears to concentrate among groups that are particularly vulnerable because of their age, gender, lifestyle, or where they live. Further, researchers report evidence that large numbers of

crimes have not been reported or have attracted little attention from the police. Crimes against women and children in domestic situations are of particular concern, as proponents in the victims' rights movement want not only to extend power to identifiable victims but also to give voice to those who find themselves unable or afraid to get help.

In addressing the needs of victims, major changes in police practice empower and protect victims, encouraging them to come forward to report crimes that previously have been kept from public scrutiny. Most noteworthy of these initiatives is mandatory arrest in domestic violence cases, where the onus for initiating an arrest is shifted from the victim (in cases where the police do not witness the assault) to the police (where they must arrest the assailant when there is physical evidence, upon arriving on the scene, that an assault has taken place). This change in police practice has been widely praised as a major improvement in the ways in which police respond to family violence cases. Previously, they may have ignored an assault or simply removed the offender for a

short period to allow a cooling-off period, only to have a recurrence of the offense shortly thereafter.

There are times when the complexity of social relationships makes even something as straightforward as mandatory arrest produce surprising and unintended results, however. For example, mandatory arrest rules in cases of domestic violence have meant that either or both parties in a dispute must be arrested if the police officer determines that an assault had taken place. So, if the police conclude that a husband and wife have been in a fight and she physically injures him, she must be arrested. This occurs even if she is the one who calls the police, defining herself as a victim of longstanding abuse. The most extreme example of this is provided by the cases in which women who have suffered longstanding domestic violence shoot their husbands. If it is determined by the courts that this homicide is not clearly a case of self-defense (the spouse is not in imminent danger at the time of the killing), she is guilty of murder. There have been cases in which this murder conviction has been overturned based on the "battered woman defense," which argues that women in abusive relationships perceive themselves to be constantly in danger and that striking out is an act of self-defense. This defense suggests that we need to look beyond the specific factors that operate in the incident that is defined as criminal to its precursors, understanding that crime occurs in context and is part of a larger social event.

It is also the case that changes in the law create the situation in which the victim of a physical assault cannot decide against the arrest if the attending officer determines, based on physical evidence, that an assault has taken place. Extending rights to victims, then, has not translated into giving them a free hand in determining the disposition of a case. Other principles pertain. The rights of the victim must be considered in light of the demands by society that victims are protected both from physical injury and from coercive attempts to shield the offender from punishment at the hands of the State.

How we view victims is influenced by public perceptions of crime, personal safety, and the willingness and effectiveness of the criminal justice system to respond to crime. A great deal of the momentum that built up in support for victim rights had been fueled by constantly rising crime rates. There has been a recent downturn in the number of crimes, however. Further, there is a renewed interest in offenders' rehabilitation and their return to the community. It is not yet clear what these trends will mean for victims and victims' rights. The drop in crime rates may translate into a decrease in resources for victim support, with an overall decline in money allocated to public safety. However, there is the new concern that the return of offenders to communities after release from prison may translate into increased levels of crime. Will these crimes be adequately addressed through victims' services where victims are protected from repeat offenders?

Serious efforts are under way to implement a victims' rights amendment to the Constitution to provide victims the same protection under the law afforded criminal defendants. Whatever comes of this and other legislative initiatives, it is clear that victims' rights are now an integral part of the adjudication process. Increasingly, victims recognize the importance of increasing their involvement in defining reasonable punishment for offenders. Victims as well play an important role in rehabilitation, as has been demonstrated in experiments with sentencing circles used in Native American communities and through victim offender reconciliation programs (VORPs). While these approaches are in their infancy, they acknowledge the role of victims in the context of crime. They address the need to help victims understand the reasons for their experience and to confront offenders with the harm done as a consequence of their actions.

ABOUT THE AUTHOR

Leslie W. Kennedy is dean and professor in the School of Criminal Justice at Rutgers University. He is a graduate of McGill University (B.A., 1971); University of Western Ontario (M.A., 1972); and University of Toronto (Ph.D., 1975). His research interests are in criminal victimization and community attitudes towards crime and safety. Kennedy is the author of numerous books and over 40 articles and chapters in books. He is currently working on research that involves mapping crime trends.

Victim impact statements typically include a tally of the physical, financial, psychological, and emotional impact of crime. As such, they provide information for courts to use in assessing the human and social cost of crime. Of equal significance, they also provide a way for victims to take part in the justice process. In most states, the right to make an impact statement is available to the direct victim, to family members of homicide victims, to the parents or guardians of a victimized minor, and to the guardian or legal representative of an incompetent or incapacitated victim.

According to OVC, the first victim impact statement was made in 1976 in Fresno County, California, by James Rowland,[54] who was then the county's chief probation officer. Rowland's contributions, which detailed the harm suffered by victims in that case, led Fresno County to make victim impact statements a part of all presentence reports.

In 1991, the U.S. Supreme Court case of *Payne* v. *Tennessee*[55] upheld the constitutionality of victim impact statements. Additionally, the *Payne* decision specifically permitted victim impact statements in cases involving potential application of the death penalty.

Victim impact statements are also frequently provided by victims or their survivors to parole hearing bodies. Statements are sometimes made in person; at other times they are submitted on audiotape or videotape, by teleconferencing, via computerized forms of communication, or in writing. Such statements give the paroling authority crucial information about the financial, physical, and emotional impact of crime upon the individuals most affected by it. In the past two decades, the passage of laws requiring victim input at parole has been seen as one of the greatest advances in victims' rights, with 43 states now providing this right.[56] This right loses its meaning, however, if paroling authorities do not notify victims of crime and their families of hearings in advance or do not schedule time during the hearing to allow them to describe the impact of crime on their lives.

The Future of Victims' Rights

The OVC report, *New Directions from the Field*,[57] summarizes hundreds of recommendations from the field and from listening to victims, their advocates, and allied professionals who work with crime victims throughout the nation. In the course of compiling those many recommendations, certain key ideas emerged. The following five global challenges for responding to victims of crime in the 21st century form the core of the ideas and recommendations presented in the report:

- enact and enforce consistent, fundamental rights for crime victims in federal, state, juvenile, military, and tribal justice systems and administrative proceedings;
- provide crime victims with access to comprehensive, quality services regardless of the nature of their victimization, age, race, religion, gender, ethnicity, sexual orientation, capability, or geographic location;
- integrate crime victims' issues into all levels of the nation's educational system to ensure that justice and allied professionals and other service providers receive comprehensive training on victims' issues as part of their academic education and continuing training in the field;

- support, improve, and replicate promising practices in victims' rights and services built upon sound research, advanced technology, and multidisciplinary partnerships; and
- ensure that the voices of crime victims play a central role in the nation's response to violence and those victimized by crime.

SUMMARY

1▸ Victims were rarely recognized in the laws and policies that govern our nation until the 1970s. Since then, tremendous strides have been made in victims' rights legislation and victim services.

2▸ The 1980 enactment of Wisconsin's Victims' Bill of Rights, the nation's first state bill of rights for crime victims, began an era of dramatic progress in the victims' rights movement. Passage of the federal Victim and Witness Protection Act (VWPA) of 1982 brought national visibility to crime victims' concerns. In 1990, the Victims' Rights and Restitution Act (Victims' Rights Act) established a bill of rights for federal crime victims. The Violent Crime Control and Law Enforcement Act of 1994 established new rights for victims of sexual assault, domestic violence, sexual exploitation, child abuse, and telemarketing fraud. In 1996, the Community Notification Act, know as Megan's Law, was enacted to ensure community notification of the locations of convicted sex offenders. In 1997, the Victims' Rights Clarification Act of 1997 asserted victims' rights to attend proceedings and deliver victim impact statements.

3▸ Many believe that a victims' rights amendment to the U.S. Constitution is needed to establish clear rights for crime victims and to protect those rights to the same degree that the rights of criminal suspects are already protected.

4▸ The costs that crime victims suffer can be divided into two major categories: (1) tangible losses, including medical bills, lost property, and lost wages; and (2) intangible losses, such as lost quality of life, fear, pain, and suffering.

5▸ Correctional agencies play an important role in meeting victims' needs. Services provided by correctional agencies include (1) victim and community notification of offender release or change in status; (2) victim and witness protection services; (3) classes for offenders on the impact of crime; and (4) opportunities for victim-offender dialogue.

6▸ Crime victim compensation programs pay for medical and mental health care, lost wages, funeral expenses, and crime-scene cleanup.

7▸ The three options available to victims for recovering crime-related financial losses are compensation, restitution, and civil remedies.

8▸ Victim impact statements are assertions by victims and/or friends or relatives of victims about the crime's impact on the victim and the victim's family. These statements are considered by judicial authorities in decisions regarding sentencing and parole.

REVIEW & APPLICATIONS

REVIEW & APPLICATIONS

KEY TERMS

victim, *p. 504*

victims' rights, *p. 505*

best efforts standard, *p. 506*

tangible losses, *p. 510*

intangible losses, *p. 510*

victim notification, *p. 513*

community
notification, *p. 516*

victim compensation, *p. 519*

victim assistance
program, *p. 524*

right of allocution, *p. 525*

QUESTIONS FOR REVIEW

1. Briefly outline the history of the American victims' rights movement.

2. Explain and date five federal laws that have significantly impacted victims' rights.

3. Why do some people consider a victims' rights amendment to the U.S. Constitution necessary?

4. What costs do crime victims suffer as a result of their victimization?

5. What can correctional agencies do to assist crime victims?

6. What are crime victim compensation programs and what do they do?

7. What three avenues are available to victims to recover financial losses due to crime?

8. Describe victim impact statements. In what ways are they useful?

THINKING CRITICALLY ABOUT CORRECTIONS

▶ ▶ ▶ Constitutional Amendment

In 1996, resolutions were introduced in the U.S. House and Senate to amend the Constitution to include crime victims' rights. A proposed federal constitutional amendment was reintroduced in modified form in 1999 with bipartisan support. In 2002, President George W. Bush announced his support for such an amendment. A federal constitutional amendment for victims' rights, say supporters, is needed for many different reasons, including to establish consistency in the rights of crime victims in every state and at the federal level; to ensure that courts engage in careful balancing of the rights of victims and defendants; to guarantee crime victims the opportunity to participate in criminal justice proceedings; and to further enhance the participation of victims in the criminal justice process. Do you agree or disagree that the U.S. Constitution should be amended to include victims' rights? Why?

▶ ▶ ▶ The Focus of Correctional Agencies

While correctional services for victims exist today in many correctional agencies and institutions across the country, some people believe that correctional agencies have enough to do without worrying about victims. Dealing with offenders is a full-time job, say such critics, and the time and expense required to meet the needs of victims are just not available. Besides, they say, corrections is about controlling and rehabilitating offenders, not about making victims "whole again."

1. Should correctional agencies and correctional personnel be involved in victims' support programs? Why or why not?

2. If you were a corrections professional, how would you feel about being called upon to assist crime victims?

ON-THE-JOB DECISION MAKING

▶ ▶ ▶ Restitution

You are director of a victim's advocacy program in your community. A criminal justice professor at a local university has asked you to participate in a public forum panel discussion addressing programs for restitution to crime victims. You decide to accept the invitation.

Upon arriving at the meeting the following week, you are surprised to find a significant turnout. The audience is larger than you expected, and the local news media are out in force. You did not anticipate this much interest.

As the meeting begins, it quickly becomes apparent that much of the audience is comprised of former offenders or offenders' family members. To your discomfort, you find yourself repeatedly faced with answering the same question over and over: How am I supposed to succeed in my efforts to live a noncriminal life when the bulk of my earnings get seized to repay my victim?

One particularly articulate offender conveys his dilemma: I am genuinely sorry, he says, for the suffering I caused. And while I know that nothing I do can erase my victim's painful memories of my crime, I truly want to repay her for the losses I caused, if only as a token of my genuine remorse.

But the reality, he says, is this: An unskilled ex-con's employment opportunities are limited. They are not going to get a "position" at the upper end of the pay scale. The work they find will be just "a job." It won't pay much, and it is unlikely that they will earn benefits. As a result, their weekly net pay will probably be insufficient to cover housing, feeding, and clothing themselves and their families.

When a significant percentage of that net pay is diverted to a restitution payment, he says, former offenders simply will not have enough left to meet their basic needs. It will not take long for the pressure to build. Under those circumstances, that pressure may generate a willingness to consider returning to the "easy money" available through crime. He says that makes the restitution program counterproductive because it contributes to defeating a primary aim of the rehabilitation effort: to encourage rejection of the criminal lifestyle.

1. How would you respond to the points this former offender has presented?

2. How do you answer the offender's question of "How am I supposed to succeed in my efforts to live a noncriminal life when the bulk of my earnings get seized to repay my victim?"

▶ ▶ ▶ Offenders Meet Victims

You work in a state correctional facility. A month ago you were promoted from yard supervisory work into a program position that tasks you with conducting classes for offenders and their victims. Classes are held within the institution, and usually about five or six victims show up at each session to confront inmates. Many of the victims come from a local victims' rights group and, although they have all been victims of violent crime, they are not the people who have been victimized by the inmates involved in the class. Classes usually involve victims telling inmates about the personal impact of their crimes and about the personal burdens crime places upon victims everywhere.

What strategies could you implement to ensure that inmates express true remorse for what they have done and that victims do not use the class as an opportunity to demean inmates?

REVIEW & APPLICATIONS

CORRECTIONS ON THE WEB

▶ ▶ ▶ National Center for Victims of Crime

Access the National Center for Victims of Crime at http://www. nvc.org. Click on the link to the *Victim Offender Reconciliation Program.* Go to *Mediating the Victim-Offender Conflict* and click on *Case Studies.* Read the case studies and decide whether or not the victims' needs and concerns were met through the reconciliation process.

▶ ▶ ▶ Victim Support Agencies

All 50 states operate victim compensation programs. Some states have crime victim support agencies attached to the office of the state's attorney general. Access the Texas crime victims' page at http://www.oag.state.tx.us/victims/victims.htm. Then search the Web to see if your state has a similar victim support organization and, if so, what information and services it provides.

> **"** Whatever you think about the death penalty, a system that will take life
> must first give justice. **"**
>
> —John J. Curtin Jr., President, American Bar Association, 1990–1991

Death:
The Ultimate
Sanction

▶ CHAPTER OBJECTIVES

After completing this chapter you should be able to do the following:

1. Discuss the history of capital punishment in the United States.

2. Describe the characteristics of people executed in the United States since 1977 and on death row today.

3. Discuss the politics influencing capital punishment.

4. List and summarize the major U.S. Supreme Court decisions that influenced capital punishment legislation.

5. Summarize the arguments for and against the death penalty.

6. Describe the five ways capital punishment jurisdictions weigh aggravating and mitigating circumstances to determine if a death sentence is appropriate.

7. Describe the death penalty appeals process.

8. Summarize Liebman's findings on the frequency of errors in capital punishment cases.

9. Summarize the issues surrounding juvenile executions.

10. Discuss the Supreme Court's reasoning for banning the execution of the mentally retarded.

▶ ▶ Do innocent people get sentenced to die? That is the fundamental question being asked in places like the Center for Wrongful Convictions at Northwestern University, the Innocence Project at Yeshiva University's Benjamin N. Cardozo School of Law, and the U.S. Congress. Northwestern's Center for Wrongful Convictions and Yeshiva's Innocence Project are dedicated to identifying and rectifying wrongful convictions and other serious miscarriages of justice. Congress is considering legislation that would acknowledge that inmates have a constitutional right to obtain biological evidence that might exonerate them. Texas is one of the few death penalty states with a law that requires the state to preserve biological evidence that can be used for genetic testing and that gives death row inmates access to state-paid DNA testing that could exonerate them.

DNA testing is now a major factor in changing the criminal justice system. It provides scientific proof that our system convicts and sentences innocent people—and that wrongful convictions are not isolated or rare events. According to the Death Penalty Information Center,[1] of the 112 people whose innocence was established after they were sent to death row since 1971, DNA testing played a substantial role in establishing the innocence and freedom of 13 of them.

Kirk Bloodsworth, the first person in the United States cleared by DNA testing, is typical.[2] He was 24, with neither a criminal history nor a deviant past, when a - Baltimore County judge ordered his execution following a conviction for the brutal rape, beating, and strangling death of 9-year-old Dawn Hamilton. Bloodsworth maintained his innocence and sounded so sincere that famed singer Willie Nelson and hundreds of other people wrote to him offering support.

After reading a book by crime novelist Joseph Wambaugh about genetic fingerprinting, Bloodsworth asked his attorney to have DNA experts analyze semen stains that had been found on the victim's underwear. The new analysis, undertaken independently by a private company and the FBI, conclusively cleared Bloodsworth of the crime. In 1993 he was released from prison. A few months later the governor of Maryland granted him a pardon.[3]

Bloodsworth, who had served almost nine years behind bars, thought that his nightmare had ended

Kirk Bloodsworth spent nine years on death row before he was pardoned by the governor of Maryland for a crime he did not commit. He was the first person in the United States cleared by DNA testing. How is it possible that innocent people can be convicted—and even sentenced to die—under our system of justice?

when he was released from prison. Far from it. His reentry into free society has been difficult and painful. His first night off death row, sleeping in his father's house, he relieved himself in the corner of the bedroom—thinking in the darkness that he was standing in front of his urinal in his death row cell. He suffers from recurring dreams of execution, and in 2004 that dream still haunts him—still grabs him in the night and drags him down the long hallway toward death. Right before the end, he says, he wakes up, drenched in sweat and choking to breathe.

History of Capital Punishment

Capital punishment was once common throughout the world and imposed for many crimes, including murder, rape, stealing, witchcraft, piracy, desertion, sodomy, adultery, concealing the birth or death of an infant, aiding runaway slaves, counterfeiting, and forgery. Death, however, was not the harshest punishment—torture was. Torture, so cruel that death came as a relief, sometimes lasted for days. Death was a form of leniency. Criminals were boiled, burned, roasted on spits, drawn and quartered, broken on wheels, disemboweled, torn apart by animals, gibbeted (hung from a post with a projecting arm and left to die), bludgeoned (beaten to death with sticks, clubs, or rocks), or pressed (crushed under a board and stones).

capital punishment
Lawful imposition of the death penalty.

Capital punishment began changing in the 18th century during the Enlightenment. This philosophical movement led to many new theories on crime and punishment. One of these theories proposed that punishment should fit the crime. Penalties involving torture began to disappear, and the use of the death penalty diminished.

At the turn of the 20th century, some states began to ban capital punishment and others began to limit its use. After World War I, as socialists challenged capitalism, a number of states reinstated the death penalty in order to deter threats of revolution. Around the same time, criminologists argued that capital punishment was a necessary social measure, and as the United States suffered through Prohibition and the Great Depression in the 1930s, there were more executions, an average of 167 per year, than in any other decade in American history.

By 1950, as prosperity followed World War II, public sentiment for capital punishment faded. The number of executions dropped. Support for capital punishment was at its lowest in 1966 (42 percent), and constitutional challenges were starting to surface. In the late 1960s, the Court began "fine-tuning" the way the death penalty was administered. In 1968 in *U.S. v. Jackson*[4] the Court held that the provision of the federal kidnapping statute requiring that the death penalty be imposed only upon the recommendation of a jury was unconstitutional because it encouraged defendants to waive their right to a jury trial to ensure they would not receive a death sentence. Later that year in *Witherspoon v. Illinois,*[5] the Court held that a potential juror's mere reservations about the death penalty were insufficient grounds to prevent that person from serving on the jury in a death penalty case. Jurors could only be disqualified if the prosecutors showed that the juror's attitude toward capital punishment would prevent him or her from making an impartial decision about punishment. The watershed case in capital punishment took place in 1972 when the Court decided *Furman* v. *Georgia*. In brief, the Court held that Georgia's death penalty statute, which gave the sentencing authority (judge or trial jury) complete sentencing discretion without any guidance as to how to exercise that discretion, could result in arbitrary sentencing and was therefore in violation of the Eighth Amendment's ban against cruel and unusual punishment. On June 29, 1972, the Court voided 40 death penalty statutes because they were no longer valid.

CAPITAL PUNISHMENT AROUND THE WORLD

As of August 2002, the majority of countries (111) had abolished the death penalty in law or in practice.[6] Eighty-four countries still retain it. The number of countries that abolished the death penalty increased from 90 in 1990 to 111 in 2002. Some recent international developments include the following:

- In 1999, Turkmenistan became the first of the five former Soviet Central Asian republics to abolish the death penalty.
- In 2000, Poland abolished the death penalty.
- Lebanese President Emile Lahoud imposed a moratorium on executions in 2001.
- Pakistani President Musharraf commuted the death sentences of approximately 100 young offenders to life imprisonment in 2001.
- Yugoslavia's Parliament abolished the death penalty in 2001 and replaced it with a 40-year prison term.
- A referendum to remove capital punishment from Ireland's Constitution was approved on June 8, 2001.
- In 2001, Chile's House of Congress passed a bill to abolish the death penalty and mandates that people convicted of major crimes serve at least 40 years in prison.
- In 2001, Philippine President Gloria Macapagal Arroyo declared a moratorium on executions by using her power to commute death sentences for everyone scheduled for execution.
- In 2002, Taiwan's legislature abolished a 1944 law that required the death penalty for certain violent crimes, including kidnapping and gang robbery.
- Serbia's parliament abolished the death penalty in 2002.
- In 2003, Armenia abolished the death penalty and commuted existing death sentences to life in prison.

In 2003, Supreme Court Justice Sandra Day O'Connor stressed the importance of international developments for U.S. courts and the need for the United States to create a more favorable impression abroad. "I suspect that over time we will rely increasingly, or take notice at least increasingly, on international and foreign courts in examining domestic issues." Justice O'Connor noted that doing so "may not only enrich our own country's decisions, I think it may create that all important good impression."

Capital Punishment in the United States

In the United States today, 38 states, the U.S. military, and the federal government allow capital punishment, and 12 states do not (see Figure 15–1).

Although research on executions in the United States has been hampered by a lack of official records, over 15,000 executions, beginning in the 1600s and continuing through 2003, have been confirmed.[7]

Executions were halted in 1968, pending a U.S. Supreme Court decision on the constitutionality of certain aspects of capital punishment. By 1977 the Court had ruled that capital punishment itself was not unconstitutional and did not violate the Eighth Amendment to the U.S. Constitution, thus paving the way for executions to resume. The first person to be executed after the moratorium ended was Gary Gilmore, who gave up his right to appeal and was executed by firing squad on January 17, 1977, by the State of Utah.

The number of executions from 1930 to 2003 is shown in Figure 15–2.

Today in the United States, what constitutes a **capital crime**—a crime that is punishable by death—is defined by law. This definition varies among jurisdictions. In Louisiana, for example, first-degree murder, aggravated rape of a victim under age 12, and treason are capital crimes; in Nevada, first-degree murder with at least 1 of 14 aggravating circumstances is a capital crime; and in New Jersey, purposeful or knowing

> In the United States today, 38 states, the U.S. military, and the federal government allow capital punishment, and 12 states do not.

capital crime

A crime for which the death penalty may but need not necessarily be imposed.

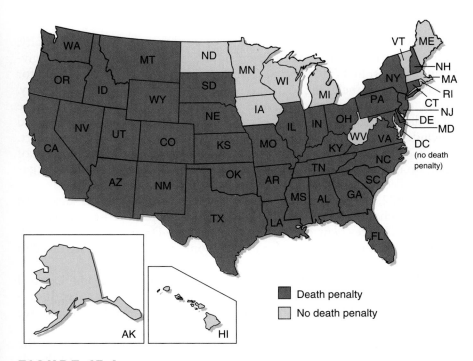

FIGURE 15-1
States with Death Penalty Statutes

Source: Adapted from *Death Row U.S.A., Fall 2003* (New York: NAACP Legal Defense and Education Fund, October 1, 2003).

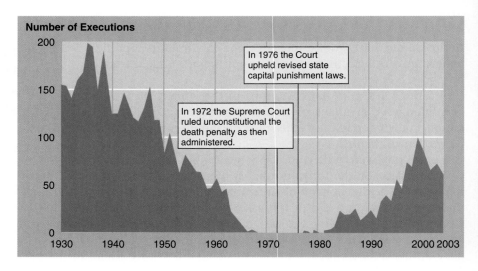

FIGURE 15-2
People Executed, 1930–2003

Sources: Thomas P. Bonczar and Tracy L. Snell, *Capital Punishment, 2002* (Washington, DC: U.S. Department of Justice, November, 2003); and Death Penalty Information Center, http://www.deathpenaltyinfo.org (retrieved January 1, 2004).

murder by one's own conduct, contract murder, and solicitation by command or threat in furtherance of a narcotics conspiracy are capital crimes.[8]

THE FEDERAL DEATH PENALTY

The Constitution of the United States does not mention the death penalty, but it does permit the federal government to deprive citizens of life after giving due process. In 1790, the first Congress mandated the death penalty for several offenses including treason, willful murder on federal property, forgery, piracy, counterfeiting, and several crimes on the high seas. By the end of the 19th century, the number of federal capital crimes had expanded to include kidnapping, spying, all murders, and arson of a dwelling or a fort.

Since 1927 the federal government has executed 37 people. Methods of execution in federal cases have included hanging, electrocution, and the gas chamber. Today the federal government uses lethal injection.

From 1972, the year of the Supreme Court's *Furman* decision (discussed later in this chapter), until the late 1980s, federal capital prosecutions were rare. In 1988, President Reagan signed the Anti–Drug Abuse Act, which authorized capital punishment for murder committed by people involved in certain drug trafficking activities.

In 1994, President Clinton signed into law the Violent Crime Control and Law Enforcement Act. Title VI is the Federal Death Penalty Act. It dramatically expanded the number of federal offenses punishable by death (see Table 15–1).

The Federal Death Penalty Act exempts a number of people from the death penalty including those less than 18 years of age at the time of the offense, the mentally retarded and insane, and women while they are pregnant. The new law permits federal employees who oppose the death

TABLE 15-1	Federal Laws Providing for the Death Penalty

HOMICIDE-RELATED CRIMES

- assassination or kidnapping resulting in the death of the President or Vice President
- bank robbery–related murder or kidnapping
- civil rights offenses resulting in death
- death resulting from aircraft hijacking
- death resulting from offenses involving transportation of explosives, destruction of government property, or destruction of property related to foreign or interstate commerce
- destruction of aircraft, motor vehicles, or related facilities resulting in death
- first-degree murder
- genocide
- mailing of injurious articles with intent to kill or injure resulting in death
- murder committed at an airport serving international civil aviation
- murder committed during a drug-related drive-by shooting
- murder of a member of Congress or a Supreme Court Justice
- murder related to the smuggling of aliens
- murder by a federal prisoner
- murder by an escaped federal prisoner already sentenced to life imprisonment
- murder by the use of a weapon of mass destruction
- murder committed by the use of a firearm during a crime of violence or a drug trafficking crime
- murder committed during an offense against a maritime fixed platform
- murder committed during an offense against maritime navigation
- murder committed in a federal government facility
- murder during a hostage taking

- murder during a kidnapping
- murder for hire
- murder involved in a racketeering offense
- murder involving torture
- murder of a court officer or juror
- murder of a federal judge or law enforcement official
- murder of a foreign official
- murder of a state correctional officer
- murder of a state or local law enforcement official or other person aiding in a federal investigation
- murder of a U.S. national in a foreign country
- murder related to a carjacking
- murder related to a continuing criminal enterprise or related murder of a federal, state, or local law enforcement officer
- murder related to rape or child molestation
- murder related to sexual exploitation of children
- murder with the intent of preventing testimony by a witness, victim, or informant
- retaliatory murder of a member of the immediate family of law enforcement officials
- retaliatory murder of a witness, victim, or informant
- terrorist murder of a U.S. national in another country
- willful wrecking of a train resulting in death

NONHOMICIDE CRIMES THAT MAY RESULT IN A FEDERAL DEATH SENTENCE

- attempting, authorizing, or advising the killing of any officer, juror, or witness in cases involving a continuing criminal enterprise, regardless of whether such killing actually occurs
- espionage
- trafficking in large quantities of drugs
- treason

Source: Thomas P. Bonczar and Tracy L. Snell, *Capital Punishment 2002* (Washington, DC: U.S. Department of Justice, November 2003), p. 13.

penalty to opt out of participating in executions, and it restricts the federal government's ability to seek the death penalty for Native Americans whose offense occurred within the boundaries of Indian country.

The last three federal executions were

- Timothy McVeigh, white, executed June 11, 2001;
- Juan Raul Garza, Hispanic, executed June 19, 2001; and
- Louis Jones Jr., black, executed March 18, 2003.

Procedures in Federal Capital Cases   Federal prosecutors who wish to file capital charges are required by the Department of Justice to first obtain authorization from the Attorney General. The request is reviewed by the Assistant Attorney General, by the Deputy Attorney General, and ultimately by the Attorney General.

For example, on Monday, November 17, 2003, lawyers for serial bomber Eric Rudolph met Attorney General John Ashcroft's death penalty committee. The committee's job was to listen, review evidence, and recommend to the Attorney General whether Rudolph should be added to the list of 124 people tried under the federal death law since it was reinstated in 1988. On Friday, December 13, 2003, Attorney General Ashcroft authorized prosecutors to seek the death penalty against Rudolph.

The new Federal Death Penalty Act changes an offender's right to counsel in three ways. First, it requires that a minimum of two lawyers be appointed to represent federal capital defendants. Second, at least one of the two lawyers must have experience in capital work. And third, the federal court must consider the Federal Public Defender's recommendation regarding which counsel are qualified for appointment in capital cases. Since 2000, federal juries have rejected the death penalty for 20 of the last 21 defendants who completed trial, and for 38 of the last 43.

Federal Death Row   Federal death row is at the United States Penitentiary, Terre Haute, Indiana. It is called the Special Confinement Unit (SCU). It opened in 1999 because of the increasing number of federal defendants sentenced to death. On January 1, 2004, 24 people were on federal death row in Terre Haute, Indiana.

SCU is a two-story renovated housing unit. It includes 50 single cells, upper tier and lower tier corridors, an industrial workshop, indoor and outdoor recreation areas, a property room, a food preparation area, attorney and family visiting areas, and a video-teleconferencing area that is used to facilitate inmate access to the courts and to their attorneys.

When Timothy McVeigh was executed in 2001 for the murder of 168 people in the Oklahoma City bombing, the United States Department of Justice instituted an elaborate process to handle any last-minute legal interruptions that might prevent or delay his execution. Two hours before McVeigh's execution, prison officials ended his visiting privileges to give him one final opportunity to seek a stay from the courts or President Bush. Forty-five minutes before the execution—and again at 10 minutes before the execution—the White House was contacted by telephone. In the event of a delay, a United States marshal was ready to instruct the executioner to step away from the execution equipment and to notify McVeigh and everyone present that the execution had been delayed or stayed. McVeigh received no stays.

Race and the Federal Death Penalty   According to a report by the U.S. Department of Justice, between 1988, when President Reagan signed the Anti–Drug Abuse Act into law, and October 1993, the Attorney General authorized federal prosecutors to seek the death penalty against 30 defendants. Over 70 percent were black, and one-half of the remaining defendants were Mexican American.[9]

   In another study of 682 potential federal capital cases forwarded to the Justice Department for review between 1995 and 2000, 80 percent of the defendants were minority.[10] The study found that minorities are overrepresented in the federal death penalty system, as both victims and defendants, relative to the general population. Then-Attorney General Janet Reno said, "This should be of concern to all of us." Later in this chapter we will examine the debate over such statistics.

Death Row Today

CHARACTERISTICS OF PEOPLE EXECUTED SINCE 1977

As of January 1, 2004, 885 people have been executed in the United States since Gary Gilmore's execution in January 1977. The peak year was 1999 when 98 people were executed. From 2002 to 2003, the number of executions dropped 8 percent, from 71 to 65. Executions are down 34 percent when compared to 98 executions in 1999. Thirty-five percent (313) of all executions have taken place in Texas. Has the death penalty affected the violent crime rate in Texas? You be the judge. From 1996 through 2002 (the last year for which complete *Uniform Crime Reports* data are available), the violent crime rate in the United States averaged 549 per year per 100,000 population. In Texas, the average was 581 per year per 100,000 population, 5.8 percent more than the national average.

Few issues generate more public controversy than the death penalty. In some states, there are movements to end the death penalty, while in others the move is to speed up death row appeals and complete the sentence of execution. Do demonstrations such as these influence the public policy implemented by state legislatures?

CAREER PROFILE

Rodge Wood

Prison Chaplain   Western Penitentiary   Pittsburgh, PA

Rodge Wood is the prison chaplain at Western Penitentiary in Pittsburgh, Pennsylvania. He holds a bachelor's degree in psychology from the University of Pittsburgh and a Master of Divinity from Virginia Theological Seminary at Alexandria. Before going to seminary school, Rodge spent a number of years in secular employment, in radio and television, always with a nagging desire to enter the ministry.

After beginning parish ministry, he discovered that his life had become integrated in ways that it never had been before. According to Rodge, he has a passion for the Gospel—the good news that Jesus Christ has for those who are sick, poor, in prison, outcast, or strangers—the marginalized of our society. He says, "There is a Gospel preference for these people. That is why I go into the prison."

In prison, Rodge's duties include giving sermons, counseling, and advising of high-custody inmates. He has come to believe in restorative justice—to move people beyond the crime and back into life. His group members are all lifers, have each killed somebody, and carry the burden of that daily. "I believe that God forgives and receives people back with eagerness. I talk about that a lot, with varying degrees of acceptance among group members," he says.

> " My work is difficult to describe. I meet weekly with a group of men sentenced to life in prison. The group has met with me since 1977 and I have come to understand the benefits of long-term work with people inside. We work toward building trust that allows their stories to be told. The object is to work toward forgiveness and finding life in a life sentence. I work alone, though, and I wonder what it is about prisons that keeps prison chaplains so isolated. "

The South leads the United States in executions with 728. In 2003, 89 percent of the executions took place in the South. Only 1.2 percent of all the people executed since 1977 have been female; 57 percent were white, 34 percent black, 7 percent Hispanic, 1.5 percent American Indian, and less than 1 percent Asian.[11] A total of 1,331 people had been killed by those who were executed. Males and females were victims in almost equal number. Eighty-one percent of the victims were white and 14 percent were black, despite the fact that nationally whites and blacks are murder victims in approximately equal numbers. The races of other victims were 4 percent Hispanic, 0.23 percent American Indian, and almost 2 percent Asian.

Defendant-victim racial combinations have been the subject of considerable debate.[12] Recognizing that whites and blacks are murder victims in approximately equal numbers, why is it that 81 percent of the victims in cases resulting in executions since 1977 have been white? This disparity is confirmed even in studies that control for similar crimes by comparing defendants with similar backgrounds. In 2003, no white person was executed exclusively for the murder of a black person. Does it imply that white victims are considered more important by the criminal justice system? U.S. Attorney General John Ashcroft argues that blacks and Hispanics are more likely than whites to be sentenced to death because they are more likely to be arrested on facts that can support a capital charge and because whites are more likely to negotiate plea bargains that spare their lives. Others disagree, citing consistent patterns of racial bias.[13] A study of all homicide cases in North Carolina from 1993 to 1997 in which a death sentence was possible found that those who killed white people were three and one-half times more likely to get the death penalty than those who killed nonwhites. Almost 12 percent of nonwhite defendants charged with murdering white victims were sentenced to die. In contrast, 6.1 percent of whites charged with murdering whites and 4.7 percent of nonwhites charged with murdering nonwhites received the death penalty. Similar studies have been conducted in Georgia, Kentucky, and other states.[14] The debate over what the numbers mean will continue.

CHARACTERISTICS OF PRISONERS UNDER SENTENCE OF DEATH

On October 1, 2003, 40 jurisdictions (38 states, the federal government, and the U.S. military) held a total of 3,504 prisoners under sentence of death. At the time of Gary Gilmore's execution on January 17, 1977, there were 423 people on death row. Ten years later the number was 1,984. In 1997, there were 3,335. After more than 20 years of continued growth in the number of people sentenced to die in the United States, the size of death row leveled off in 2000 (3,593) and decreased to 3,581 in 2001, 3,557 in 2002, and 3,504 in 2003.

Forty-one percent of the nation's death row population is in three states: California (632), Texas (451), and Florida (381). Figure 15–3 shows additional characteristics of inmates under sentence of death.

In 2002, prisoners spent an average of 10 years and 7 months on death row, 15 months less than that for inmates executed in 2001.[15] They may leave death row by means other than execution. Between 1973 and January 1, 2003, 268 people on death row died; 2,403 had their convictions or sentences overturned; and 176 were granted **clemency** and received a **commutation,** meaning that the severity of their punishment was lessened.[16] Table 15–2 shows the clemency process by state.

Are the frequency with which people are sentenced to die and the frequency with which states carry out executions related to murder rates and race? According to most scholars, murder rates have no effect on a state's willingness to execute. States with high and low murder rates have similar rates of execution. What about race? Does race influence whether a person is sentenced to die? James Liebman and his colleagues at Columbia University's School of Law found that states with larger nonwhite populations have lower death-sentencing rates but carry out more of the death sentences they impose. For example, death sentencing of nonwhites is higher in Idaho, where only 5 percent of the population is nonwhite, than it is in Mississippi, where 37 percent of the population is nonwhite, but Mississippi carries out more of the death sentences it imposes.

clemency

Kindness, mercy, forgiveness, or leniency, usually relating to criminal acts.

commutation

A change of a legal penalty to a lesser one; e.g., from death to life imprisonment.

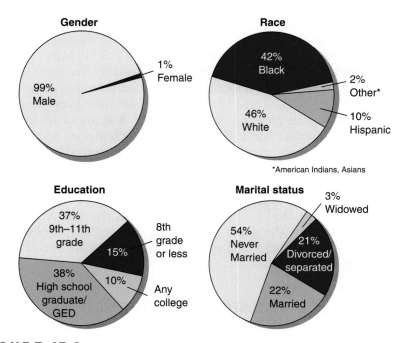

FIGURE 15-3
Characteristics of Prisoners Under Sentence of Death, 2003

Sources: *Death Row U.S.A., Fall 2003* (New York: NAACP Legal Defense and Education Fund, October 1, 2003), p. 1; and Thomas P. Bonczar and Tracy L. Snell, *Capital Punishment 2002* (Washington, DC: Bureau of Justice Statistics, 2003).

METHODS OF EXECUTION

Five methods of execution are used in the United States: (1) lethal injection, (2) electrocution, (3) lethal gas, (4) hanging, and (5) firing squad. As you can see in Table 15–3, lethal injection is the predominant method of execution, used in 37 states. In 1977, Oklahoma became the first state to adopt lethal injection as a means of execution. Five years later, Charles Brooks became the first person executed by that method, in Texas. Today nine states authorize electrocution; four states, lethal gas; three states, hanging; and three states, firing squad. Only one state—Nebraska—uses the electric chair as the sole method of execution. Seventeen states authorize more than one method—lethal injection and an alternative method, generally at the election of the condemned person. However, 5 of the 17 states stipulate which method must be used according to the date of sentencing. For example, Arizona uses lethal injection for people sentenced after November 15, 1992; those sentenced before that date may select lethal injection or lethal gas. Oklahoma authorizes electrocution if lethal injection is ever held unconstitutional and firing squad if both lethal injection and electrocution are held unconstitutional. The federal government authorizes a different method of execution under each of two different laws; the method of execution for federal prisoners prosecuted under the *Code of Federal Regulations*, Volume 28, Part 26, is lethal injection; for those offenses prosecuted under the Violent Crime Control and Law Enforcement Act of 1994, the method is that used in the state in which the person was convicted. If the state has no death penalty, the inmate is transferred to another state.

TABLE 15-2	Clemency Process by State[1]	
GOVERNOR HAS SOLE AUTHORITY (14)		
Alabama	New Jersey	South Carolina
California	New Mexico	Virginia
Colorado	New York	Washington
Kansas	North Carolina	Wyoming
Kentucky	Oregon	
GOVERNOR MUST HAVE RECOMMENDATION OF CLEMENCY FROM BOARD OR ADVISORY GROUP (9)		
Arizona	Indiana	Oklahoma
Delaware	Louisiana	Pennsylvania
Florida[2]	Montana	Texas
GOVERNOR MUST RECEIVE NONBINDING RECOMMENDATION OF CLEMENCY FROM BOARD OR ADVISORY GROUP (9)		
Arkansas	Mississippi	Ohio
Illinois	Missouri	South Dakota
Maryland	New Hampshire	Tennessee
BOARD OR ADVISORY GROUP MAKES DETERMINATION (3)		
Connecticut	Georgia	Idaho
GOVERNOR SITS ON CLEMENCY BOARD THAT MAKES THE DETERMINATION (3)		
Nebraska	Nevada	Utah

1   For federal death row inmates, the President alone has pardon power.
2   Florida's governor must have the recommendation of the Board, on which she or he sits.

Source: National Coalition to Abolish the Death Penalty, "Executive Clemency Process and Execution Warrant Procedure in Death Penalty Cases," 1993, with updates by Death Penalty Information Center (DPIC) through January 2000. Retrieved June 6, 2003, from http://www.deathpenaltyinfo.org.

When lethal injection is used, the condemned person is strapped to a gurney, and several heart monitors are positioned on his or her chest. Two needles (one is a backup) are inserted into arm veins. Long tubes connect the needle through a hole in a wall to several intravenous drips. The first is a saline solution that is started immediately. At the warden's signal, a curtain is raised, exposing the inmate to the witnesses in an adjoining room. The inmate is then injected with sodium thiopental, a general anesthetic that puts the inmate to sleep. Next flows pavulon or pancuronium bromide, which paralyzes the entire muscle system and stops the inmate's breathing. Finally, the flow of potassium chloride stops the heart. Death results from anesthetic overdose and respiratory and cardiac arrest while the condemned person is unconscious.[17]

The American Medical Association's Code of Ethics prohibits physicians from participating in a lethal injection, and some contend that leaves a lot of room for error. Fulton County (Atlanta, Georgia) public defender Michael Mears noted in his 2001 legal brief to the Fulton County Superior Court challenging lethal injection as "offensive to human dignity" that there have been 21 botched lethal injections nationwide. There have been

TABLE 15–3	Method of Execution, by State, 2002					
Lethal injection			**Electrocution**	**Lethal gas**	**Hanging**	**Firing squad**
Alabama[a]	Kentucky[a,d]	Ohio	Alabama[a]	Arizona[a,b]	Delaware[a,g]	Idaho[a]
Arizona[a,b]	Louisiana	Oklahoma[a]	Arkansas[a,c]	California[a]	New Hampshire[a,i]	Oklahoma[f]
Arkansas[a,c]	Maryland	Oregon	Florida[a]	Missouri[a]	Washington[a]	Utah[a]
California[a]	Mississippi	Pennsylvania	Kentucky[a,d]	Wyoming[a,e]		
Colorado	Missouri[a]	South Carolina[a]	Nebraska			
Connecticut	Montana	South Dakota	Oklahoma[f]			
Delaware[a,g]	Nevada	Tennessee[a,h]	South Carolina[a]			
Florida[a]	New Hampshire[a]	Texas	Tennessee[a,h]			
Georgia	New Jersey	Utah[a]	Virginia[a]			
Idaho[a]	New Mexico	Virginia[a]				
Illinois	New York	Washington[a]				
Indiana	North Carolina	Wyoming[a]				
Kansas						

Note:
  The method of execution of federal prisoners is lethal injection, pursuant to 28 CFR, Part 26. For offenses under the Violent Crime Control and Law Enforcement Act of 1994, the method is that of the state in which the conviction took place, pursuant to 18 U.S.C. 3596. If the state has no death penalty, the inmate is transferred to another state.
a   Authorizes two methods of execution.
b   Authorizes lethal injection for people whose capital sentence was received after 11/15/92; those sentenced before that date may select lethal injection or lethal gas.
c   Authorizes lethal injection for those whose capital offense occurred on or after 7/4/83; those whose offense occurred before that date may select lethal injection or electrocution.
d   Authorizes lethal injection for those sentenced on or after 3/31/98; those sentenced before that date may select lethal injection or electrocution.
e   Authorizes lethal gas if lethal injection is ever held to be unconstitutional.
f   Authorizes electrocution if lethal injection is ever held to be unconstitutional and firing squad if both lethal injection and electrocution are held unconstitutional.
g   Authorizes lethal injection for those whose capital offense occurred after 6/13/86; those whose offense occurred before that date may select lethal injection or hanging.
h   Authorizes lethal injection for those whose capital offense occurred after 12/31/98; those whose offense occurred before that date may select lethal injection or electrocution.
i   Authorizes hanging only if lethal injection cannot be given.

Source: Thomas P. Bonczar and Tracy L. Snell, *Capital Punishment 2002* (Washington, DC: U.S. Department of Justice, Bureau of Justice Statistics, November 2003).

"blowouts" in which the catheter popped out of the inmate's vein partway into the execution. In other instances, the condemned's veins were so poor from longtime drug use that personnel had to perform a "cut down," a surgical procedure to expose the veins.

WHAT IS DEATH ROW LIKE?

death row

A prison area housing inmates who have been sentenced to death.

Prisoners who are sentenced to death are held on **death row,** a prison within a prison. All states except Missouri and Tennessee segregate death row inmates from the general prison population. According to George Lombardi, director of the Missouri Department of Corrections, mainstreaming death row prisoners with the general population saves money; provides death row inmates more access to recreation, visitation, and prison programs and services; benefits non–death row inmates because, before mainstreaming, even non–death row prisoner movement was restricted due to security concerns over the segregated death row unit; and facilitates staff management of prisoners because recreation, visitation, and prison programs and services are seen as privileges that can be taken away. Mainstreaming in Missouri has also decreased inmate violence and disciplinary actions that surface when inmates feel they have nothing to lose.[18] Otherwise, according to Lombardi and others, the conditions among death rows in the majority of states are virtually indistinguishable. Inmates receive few, if any, rehabilitation, treatment, or work programs, and they leave their individual cells for an average of one hour a day. About one-half of the states allow contact visitation; the other half restrict it to inmates' attorneys. For that reason, death row existence has been called "living death" to convey a prisoner's loneliness, isolation, boredom, and loss of privacy.[19]

What many people forget is that a death row inmate's living environment is a correctional officer's workplace. The concrete and steel construction materials and furnishings that guarantee security and durability in death row amplify normal sounds within its hard walls. It takes little effort to imagine what effect shouting, flushing toilets, opening and closing steel doors, janitorial work, the blaring of televisions and radios, and voices wailing has not only on those who live there, but also on those who work there. In summer the oppressive heat and in winter the freezing cold are trapped by walls of steel and concrete. The quality of life experienced by inmates depends on the work environment created by the corrections officers who guard them, but even the corrections officers are affected by the surroundings.

Death row cells usually have steel bunks, toilets, and sinks. These are bolted to concrete floors and cinder-block walls. Small lockers or wall shelves hold prisoners' personal property, which may include toiletries, books, pictures, a clock, and usually a television. The television is the death row inmate's most valued possession, not only because of its entertainment value, but also because it makes available the world that the death row inmate has lost. Revoking television or telephone privileges is sometimes used by correctional officers as a threat to control behavior on death row. However, though, corrections officers say that death row inmates seldom exhibit disciplinary problems. One death row warden described death row inmates as "the group who causes the least trouble."[20] Researchers in Indiana examined the disciplinary records of 39 death row inmates who were transferred to the general prison population following modification of their sentences from death to capital life between 1972 and 1999. The researchers found that, despite the heinousness of their capital offenses, the majority of these former death row inmates did not commit acts of serious violence on death row or after their transfer to the general prison population. Most presented little persistent disciplinary management difficulty in the general prison population.[21] The reasons, researchers suggest, are aging, prior adjustment to institutionalization while on death row, restrictive death row conditions, and higher levels of supervision.

Most death row inmates spend 22 to 23 hours a day in five-by-eight- or six-by-nine-foot cells. They receive their meals through slots in the cell doors. Generally twice a week, they are handcuffed, escorted to, and locked in shower stalls for 5- or 10-minute showers. In some jurisdictions, death row inmates may visit the prison library; in others, books are taken to them.

Prisoners who are sentenced to death are held on death row. Do most death-sentenced prisoners need to be separated from the general prison population? Why or why not?

I am a 29-year-old death row inmate, and I want to talk to you about death row. I want to tell you that if you look, you will find people! We are small, tall, fat, skinny, and different races living together. I am very happy to say that there is a brotherhood here, but I call it my family, because they know when I am happy or sad.

I get help with schoolwork, law study, hobby crafts, and most of all my feelings. I will not hesitate to speak about my feelings because there are so many people here that are willing to talk about them with me. What I have learned in my years on the Row is the people here are not mean or crazy like everyone thinks. I see happiness and friendships here.

We do not fight against each other; nor do we disrespect each other. We share birthdays and holidays together. I myself had a birthday party this year. I believe that was the happiest time for me, because all these people sang happy birthday to me. It is the first time so many people did that for me.

I am not going to give an excuse for you to save my life. I am not going to say I am retarded or an ex–drug user or that I was beaten in my childhood. What I will say is I am a person! An American, of the United States of America. The world looks at America with respect. We go help other countries with food and medicine. We are against violence and aggression. However, having the death penalty does not set a very good example! Executing our people puts a deep scar that will not go away until we stop this madness.

I invite you to visit a state's death row and see for yourself. Meet a death row inmate, talk to him or her, and see what they are like. Society has put an X on our foreheads because they are made to believe that we do not care about the country. That is not true. We do care about this country of ours and this world, too.

I get really sad when I see news about people starving or dying with AIDS. It really hits home! I am not smart. I did not go to high school or college. But what I do know is street smarts. I know what it feels like to go hungry and not have anything. I know about goals and dreams because I have them too.

I do not want to die. And with your help I will not have to. Violence exists across the world because we want it to be there, just like executions! We can stop all the violence and suffering by pulling together and helping each other. Please come together and stop this madness. Restore the American Dream. Stop executions, help the poor, give medical care to people that need it, go into those cities and neighborhoods, help those families, give them jobs. Let them know you care.

Mark Allen Jenkins
#Z527, Holman Prison
Atmore, Alabama

THE OFFENDER SPEAKS

Most death row inmates slowly lose their ties with the outside world. Although some states permit contact visits, most allow only noncontact visits. Every time death row inmates leave death row for visits—whether contact or noncontact—they are strip-searched before and after. Over the years, visitors and mail come less frequently, and they sometimes cease altogether. Corrections officers assigned to death row are instructed not to establish relationships with inmates because it may make it more difficult to carry out their duties. Pennsylvania's policy manual for death row corrections officers reads, "Employees must not be too familiar or discuss personal items of interest with the inmates."[22]

Preparing for an execution is a correctional officer's toughest job. "We begin to dread electrocutions weeks before they take place," says former corrections officer Lynch Alford Sr. "We're almost glad when someone is commuted, regardless of what crime he committed. We just sit around and wait. We drink coffee. We don't talk about anything. We don't talk about the electrocution. We just get it over with as soon as possible and then go home immediately." A death row inmate who refuses to walk to the death chamber is carried by corrections officers, sometimes screaming and kicking. "Guards have been known to go all to pieces during episodes such as these. Their nerves just don't hold up. In my opinion it is something you never become accustomed to. It's the most gruesome job I've come in contact with during my 35 years with the department. The more you see, the more you hate it."[23]

POLITICS AND CAPITAL PUNISHMENT

According to the Gallup Poll,[24] public support for capital punishment in the United States was at its lowest in 1966 when only 42 percent of Americans supported it. It reached its highest level (80 percent) in 1994. However, as the number of innocent people released from death row increases, news of their innocence is making headlines and prompting a public debate. One-half of the 112 people removed from death row have been released since 1994. Since then, support for capital punishment dropped from 80 percent to 64 percent in July 2003. The last time support for the death penalty was lower was in 1978 when it measured 62 percent.

In May 2003, the Gallup Poll asked respondents to indicate which is the appropriate punishment for murder—the death penalty or life in prison without the possibility of parole (LWOP). A slim majority, 53 percent, chose death, while 44 percent chose LWOP. Since very little is known about death penalty proponents who support LWOP, researchers from California State University at Long Beach compared death penalty supporters who favor LWOP with death penalty supporters who oppose it.[25] Of all the characteristics they studied (sex, age, race/ethnicity, education, income, religious belief, religious activity, and political ideology), they found that people with higher incomes were more likely to oppose LWOP than people with lower incomes. This is consistent with earlier research on the death penalty: income is a leading predictor of punitiveness. People with higher incomes are more likely to support capital punishment than people with lower incomes. The researchers suggest that the explanation rests in the very reason(s) why someone believes in capital punishment in the first place. People with higher incomes view a life sentence as an "unjust" punishment for murder. On the other hand, people with lower incomes view life imprisonment as sufficient deterrence and incapacitation for certain types of murder. The explanation may also have something to do with the fact that people with higher incomes are better represented at trial, less likely to get the death penalty, and more likely to hold different views of punishment for the majority of people on death row who are poor. People with lower incomes, on the other hand, may view trial and punishment as operating against them, and hence, more likely to support LWOP.

Other polls find similar support for capital punishment and LWOP, but the level varies. In January 2003, an ABC News/Washington Post poll found that, although 64 percent of Americans supported the death penalty when no other alternative was offered, they were more closely divided on the appropriate punishment for those convicted of murder when given the option of LWOP than were respondents in the Gallup Poll. When given a choice, 49 percent chose the death penalty, and 45 percent chose LWOP. The poll also revealed that 39 percent of respondents would like to see their governor issue a blanket commutation of death row inmates similar to that issued by Governor Ryan recently in Illinois, and 58 percent would be opposed to such action.

> Americans are closely divided on the appropriate punishment for those convicted of murder. When given a choice, 49 percent chose the death penalty, and 45 percent chose life in prison.

Similar shifts are taking place in the political arena. Governors' use of executive clemency reached a 20-year high in 1999. Jurors and judges are

The men in the red jumpsuits—dead men walking! I don't judge them, I don't disrespect them, I just protect them from other inmates and themselves. I work on death row and have for a lot of years. Death row inmates sleep in cell blocks which consist of 16 individual cells with solid electronic steel doors. Some talk to everybody all the time, some don't talk to anyone, and others act as if they have multiple personalities. If they aren't talking, they're playing cards or checkers or doing push-ups. They get outside two times a day to exercise. Law says they can't work.

Some act like they are your buddies, and some act as if they can't stand you. For the most part, the ones that act like your buddy are usually trying to get you to do something for them. As a group, they are very manipulative in every exchange they have with everyone, including each other.

Most of the inmates say they are innocent. A few say they actually committed the crime, and others say they were framed. I know a lot about most of their cases and it seems to me that they belong here—on death row. But a few of the cases seem questionable. That's a private thought, and I don't let it change the way I deal with these offenders in red jumpsuits.

John Juehrs
Correctional Officer
Death Row
Central Prison
Raleigh, North Carolina

141

now imposing fewer death sentences. The number of persons sentenced to die dropped almost 57 percent in the past decade, from 327 in 1994 to 139 in 2003.

In January 2000, Illinois released its 13th person from death row after investigators found that he was innocent. Five of the 13 were released after post-conviction DNA testing proved their innocence. The fact that more people have been released from death row for mistaken convictions than have been executed in Illinois prompted former Republican Governor (and supporter of capital punishment) George Ryan to impose a moratorium on capital punishment due to mounting evidence that the death penalty was not being applied fairly. Ryan also granted clemency to more than 150 death row inmates by reducing their sentences to a maximum of life in prison. Ryan asked, "How many more cases of wrongful convictions have to occur before we can all agree that this system in Illinois is broken?"

On March 9, 2000, Ryan appointed a blue ribbon commission to determine what reforms, if any, would ensure that the Illinois capital punishment system was fair, just, and accurate. In April 2002, the commission presented its findings. Its recommendations include the creation of a statewide panel to review prosecutors' requests for the death penalty, banning death sentences for juveniles, significantly reducing the number of death eligibility factors, videotaping interrogations of homicide suspects, and controlling the use of testimony by jailhouse informants. See this chapter's Reflections on the Future for a listing of the commission's recommendations. Following Ryan's departure from office, the new governor, Rod Blagojevich, promised to continue the moratorium on executions, and the legislature overwhelmingly enacted significant death penalty reforms.

Professional organizations and the judiciary are also weighing in on the question of capital punishment. At its February 1997 midyear meeting, the American Bar Association's House of Delegates called for a death penalty moratorium until jurisdictions implement policies and procedures that ensure that death penalty cases are administered fairly and impartially, in accordance with due process, and with minimum risk of executing innocent people. In July 2000, ABA President Martha Barnett reiterated the call for a moratorium on executions, citing racial bias, racial profiling, execution of juveniles, inadequate counsel, and lack of due process.[26] On February 10, 2003, the ABA House of Delegates approved national standards of practice to ensure due process and minimize the risk of executing the innocent. In 2001, the Maryland Supreme Court imposed its own moratorium. And in the majority of states that authorize capital punishment, we find today legislative bills considering death penalty moratoriums, funding study of capital punishment, granting death row inmates access to DNA testing, affording extra assistance to lawyers handling capital cases, raising the amount of financial compensation that states provide innocent people found to have been convicted erroneously, allowing prosecutors to seek life without parole instead of the death penalty, and barring the execution of juveniles.

Voices from the bench are also speaking out. "If statistics are any indication," said U.S. Supreme Court Justice Sandra Day O'Connor, "the system may well be allowing some innocent defendants to be executed" and suggested that "perhaps it's time to look at minimum standards for appointed counsel in death cases and adequate compensation for appointed counsel when they are used." Justice Ruth Bader Ginsburg added that she has "yet to see a death penalty case among the dozens coming to the Supreme Court on eve-of-execution stay applications in which the defendant was well-represented at trial" and that "people who are well represented at trial do not get the death penalty." Others, such as recently retired Florida Supreme Court Chief Justice Gerald Kogan, have said, "There are several cases where I had grave doubts as to the guilt of a particular person. . . . If one innocent person is executed along the way, then we can no longer justify capital punishment."[27] And in 1994, when the U.S. Supreme Court denied review in the Texas death penalty case of Bruce Edwin Callins, Justice Harry A. Blackmun wrote in his dissent opinion that, "From this day forward, I no longer shall tinker with the machinery of death. For more than 20 years I have endeavored to develop rules that would lend more than the mere appearance of fairness to the death penalty endeavor. Rather than continue to coddle the court's delusions that the desired level of fairness has been achieved, I feel obligated simply to concede that the death penalty experiment has failed."[28]

The American Correctional Association (ACA), in its Policy Statement on Capital Punishment (see Exhibit 15–1), encourages corrections professionals to support and participate in the debate about capital punishment. There are many arguments favoring capital punishment and many arguments opposing it. Some of the arguments—pro and con—are summarized in Table 15–4. Where do you stand?

The Courts and the Death Penalty

"Death is different [from other punishments]," said U.S. Supreme Court Justice William Brennan. For that reason, every phase of a capital crime proceeding, from jury selection to sentencing instructions, has been influenced by court rulings. The legal history of today's death penalty can be traced through several landmark cases. In the June 29, 1972, decision in *Furman* v. *Georgia*,[29] the U.S. Supreme Court ruled by a vote of five to four that the death penalty, as imposed and carried out under the laws of

One State's Approach to Establishing a Fair System of Capital Punishment

Report of the Illinois Governor's Commission on Capital Punishment—State of Illinois

Reflections on the Future

On March 9, 2000, shortly after declaring a moratorium on executions in Illinois, Governor George Ryan appointed the Commission on Capital Punishment to determine what reforms, if any, would ensure that the Illinois capital punishment system was fair, just, and accurate. The Commission members are uniform in their belief that the body of recommendations as a whole would, if implemented, answer the Governor's call to enhance significantly the fairness, justice, and accuracy of capital punishment in Illinois.

The following is a summary of the Commission's recommendations, ordered according to the procedural stage to which they apply.

A. *Investigation:* We recommend videotaping all questioning of a capital suspect conducted in a police facility and repeating on tape, in the presence of the prospective defendant, any of his statements alleged to have been made elsewhere.

Recognizing an increasing body of scientific research relating to eyewitness identification, we propose a number of reforms regarding such testimony, including significant revisions in the procedures for conducting lineups.

B. *Eligibility for the death penalty:* The Commission unanimously concluded that the current list of 20 factual circumstances under which a defendant is eligible for a death sentence should be eliminated in favor of a simpler and narrower group of eligibility criteria. A majority of the Commission agree that the death penalty should be applied only in cases where the defendant has murdered two or more persons, or where the victim was either a police officer or a firefighter or an officer or inmate of a correctional institution, or was murdered to obstruct the justice system, or was tortured in the course of the murder.

We also have recommended that the death penalty be barred in certain instances because of the character of the evidence or the defendant. We recommend that capital punishment not be available when a conviction is based solely upon the testimony of a single eyewitness, or of an in-custody informant, or of an uncorroborated accomplice, or when the defendant is mentally retarded.

C. *Review of the prosecutorial decision to seek the death penalty:* In order to ensure uniform standards for the death penalty across the state, we recommend that a local state's attorney's decision to seek the death penalty be confirmed by a statewide commission, comprised of the Attorney General, three prosecutors, and a retired judge.

D. *Trial of capital cases:* We have proposed a number of additional measures to augment the reforms already adopted by the Illinois Supreme Court to enhance the training of trial lawyers and judges in capital cases. Included are our suggestions for increased funding.

We have offered several recommendations aimed at intensifying the scrutiny of the testimony of in-custody informants, including a pretrial hearing to determine the reliability of such testimony before it may be received in a capital trial.

To allow for future audits of the functioning of the capital punishment system, we also suggest that a designated array of information about the nature of the defendant and the crime be collected by the trial court.

E. *Review:* We recommend that, when a jury determines that death is the appropriate sentence in a case, the trial judge, who has also heard the evidence, must concur with that determination or else sentence the defendant to natural life.

We recommend that, as in several other states, the Illinois Supreme Court review each death sentence to ensure it is proportionate; that is, consider whether both the evidence and the offense warrant capital punishment in light of other death sentences imposed in the state.

ABOUT THE AUTHORS

The Members of the Commission on Capital Punishment are Judge Frank McGarr, Chair; Senator Paul Simon, Co-Chair; Thomas P. Sullivan, Co-Chair; Deputy Governor Matthew R. Bettenhausen; Kathryn Dobrinic; Rita Fry; Theodore Gottfried; Donald Hubert; William J. Martin; Thomas Needham; Roberto Ramirez; Scott Turow; Mike Waller; Andrea Zopp; Judge William H. Webster, Special Advisor to the Commission; and Jean M. Templeton, Research Director. This excerpt is from the *Report of the Governor's Commission on Capital Punishment* (Springfield, IL: State of Illinois, April 2002).

> **EXHIBIT 15-1** American Correctional Association
>
> ## Policy Statement on Capital Punishment
>
> Correctional professionals have a fundamental responsibility to support participation in the public dialogue concerning capital punishment and to make available to the public and their policymakers the unique perspectives of those working in the profession. Toward this end, correctional agencies should do the following:
>
> **A.** Support conducting research on capital punishment, to inform the public debate with accurate information about all aspects of capital punishment.
>
> **B.** Support full public discussion of capital punishment, focusing on the morality, purposes, and efficacy of this form of punishment.
>
> **C.** Accept and encourage a diversity of opinion within the field, assuring that employment, promotion, and retention are never affected by the expression of opinion either in support of or in opposition to capital punishment.
>
> **D.** Encourage correctional professionals to fully consider this issue and permit them to present their opinions within the profession and in appropriate public forums.
>
> **Source:** The material above is copyrighted by the American Correctional Association. All rights reserved. The reproduction, distribution, or inclusion in other publications of these materials is prohibited without prior written permission from the American Correctional Association.

Georgia, was cruel and unusual punishment in violation of the Eighth and Fourteenth Amendments. According to the Court, Georgia's death penalty statute gave the sentencing authority (judge or trial jury) complete freedom to impose a death or life imprisonment sentence without standards or guidelines; the death penalty had been imposed arbitrarily, discriminatorily, and selectively against minorities. The Supreme Court voided 40 death penalty statutes, thereby commuting the death sentences of all 629 death row inmates around the United States, and suspended the death penalty because existing statutes were no longer valid. It is important to note that the Court majority did not rule that the death penalty itself was unconstitutional, but only the way in which it was administered at that time.

States responded to the *Furman* decision by rewriting their capital punishment statutes to limit discretion and avoid arbitrary and inconsistent results. The new death penalty laws took two forms. Some states imposed a **mandatory death penalty** for certain crimes, and others permitted **guided discretion,** which sets standards for judges and juries to use when deciding whether to impose the death penalty.

In 1976, the U.S. Supreme Court rejected mandatory death penalty statutes in *Woodson* v. *North Carolina* and *Roberts* v. *Louisiana,* but it approved guided discretion statutes in *Gregg* v. *Georgia* and two companion cases.[30]

In *Gregg,* the Court also approved automatic appellate review, a proportionality review whereby state appellate courts compare a sentence with those of similar cases, and a **bifurcated trial,** or special two-part trial. The first part of a bifurcated trial, the *guilt phase,* decides the issue of guilt. If the defendant is found guilty, the second part of the trial, the *penalty phase,* takes place. The penalty phase includes presentation of facts that mitigate or aggravate the circumstances of the crime. **Mitigating circumstances** are

mandatory death penalty
A death sentence that the legislature has required to be imposed upon people convicted of certain offenses.

guided discretion
Decision making bounded by general guidelines, rules, or laws.

bifurcated trial
Two separate hearings for different issues in a trial, one for guilt and the other for punishment.

mitigating circumstances
Factors that, although not justifying or excusing an action, may reduce the culpability of the offender.

TABLE 15-4	**Arguments Favoring and Opposing the Death Penalty**

PRO

- It deters people from crime through fear of punishment; it exerts a positive moral influence by stigmatizing crimes of murder and manslaughter.

- It is a just punishment for murder; it fulfills the "just deserts" principle of a fitting punishment; life in prison is not a tough enough punishment for a capital crime.

- It is constitutionally appropriate; the Eighth Amendment prohibits cruel and unusual punishment, yet the Fifth Amendment implies that, with due process of law, one may be deprived of life, liberty, or property.

- It reduces time spent on death row to reduce costs of capital punishment and the attendant costs of postconviction appeals, investigations, and searches for new evidence and witnesses.

- It protects society from the most serious and feared offenders; it prevents the reoccurrence of violence.

- It is more humane than life imprisonment because it is quick; making the prisoner suffer by remaining in prison for the rest of his or her life is more torturous and inhumane than execution.

- It is almost impossible for an innocent person to be executed; the slow execution rate results from the process of appeals, from sentencing to execution.

CON

- It does not deter crime; no evidence exists that the death penalty is more effective than other punishments.

- It violates human rights; it is a barbaric remnant of an uncivilized society; it is immoral in principle; and it ensures the execution of some innocent people.

- It falls disproportionately on racial minorities; those who murdered whites are more likely to be sentenced to death than are those who murdered blacks.

- It costs too much; $2 million to $5 million are poured into each execution, while other criminal justice components such as police, courts, and community corrections lack funding.

- It boosts the murder rate; this is known as the *brutalizing effect;* the state is a role model, and when the state carries out an execution, it shows that killing is a way to solve problems.

- Not everyone wants vengeance; many people favor alternative sentences such as life without parole.

- It is arbitrary and unfair; offenders who commit similar crimes under similar circumstances receive widely differing sentences; race, social and economic status, location of crime, and pure chance influence sentencing.

aggravating circumstances

Factors that may increase the culpability of the offender.

factors that may reduce the culpability of the offender. **Aggravating circumstances** are factors that may increase the offender's culpability. Florida's death penalty statute, including its list of mitigating and aggravating circumstances (subsections 5 and 6), is shown in Exhibit 15–2.

Florida, along with 11 other states (Arizona, Colorado, Idaho, Illinois, Mississippi, Montana, Nebraska, Nevada, New Hampshire, North Carolina,

EXHIBIT 15-2   The Florida Death Penalty Statute

921.141 Sentence of death or life imprisonment for capital felonies; further proceedings to determine sentence.

(1) SEPARATE PROCEEDINGS ON ISSUE OF PENALTY. Upon conviction or adjudication of guilt of a defendant of a capital felony, the court shall conduct a separate sentencing proceeding to determine whether the defendant should be sentenced to death or life imprisonment as authorized by s. 775.082. The proceeding shall be conducted by the trial judge before the trial jury as soon as practicable. If, through impossibility or inability, the trial jury is unable to reconvene for a hearing on the issue of penalty, having determined the guilt of the accused, the trial judge may summon a special juror or jurors as provided in chapter 913 to determine the issue of the imposition of the penalty. If the trial jury has been waived or if the defendant pleaded guilty, the sentencing proceeding shall be conducted before a jury impaneled for that purpose, unless waived by the defendant. In the proceeding, evidence may be presented as to any matter that the court deems relevant to the nature of the crime and the character of the defendant and shall include matters relating to any of the aggravating or mitigating circumstances enumerated in subsections (5) and (6). Any such evidence that the court deems to have probative value may be received, regardless of its admissibility under the exclusionary rules of evidence, provided the defendant is accorded a fair opportunity to rebut any hearsay statements. However, this subsection shall not be construed to authorize the introduction of any evidence secured in violation of the Constitution of the United States or the Constitution of the State of Florida. The state and the defendant or his counsel shall be permitted to present argument for or against sentence of death.

(2) ADVISORY SENTENCE BY THE JURY. After hearing all the evidence, the jury shall deliberate and render an advisory sentence to the court, based upon the following matters:

(a)   whether sufficient aggravating circumstances exist as enumerated in subsection (5);

(b)   whether sufficient mitigating circumstances exist that outweigh the aggravating circumstances found to exist; and

(c)   based on these considerations, whether the defendant should be sentenced to life imprisonment or death.

(3) FINDINGS IN SUPPORT OF SENTENCE OF DEATH. Notwithstanding the recommendation of a majority of the jury, the court, after weighing the aggravating and mitigating circumstances, shall enter a sentence of life imprisonment or death, but if the court imposes a sentence of death, it shall set forth in writing its findings upon which the sentence of death is based as to the facts:

(a)   that sufficient aggravating circumstances exist as enumerated in subsection (5), and

(b)   that there are insufficient mitigating circumstances to outweigh the aggravating circumstances.

In each case in which the court imposes the death sentence, the determination of the court shall be supported by specific written findings of fact based upon the circumstances in subsections (5) and (6) and upon the records of the trial and the sentencing proceedings. If the court does not make the findings requiring the death sentence, the court shall impose sentence of life imprisonment in accordance with s. 775.082.

(4) REVIEW OF JUDGMENT AND SENTENCE. The judgment of conviction and sentence of death shall be subject to automatic review by the Supreme Court of Florida within 60 days after certification by the sentencing court of the entire record, unless the time is extended for an additional period not to exceed 30 days by the Supreme Court for good cause shown. Such review by the Supreme Court shall have priority over all other cases and shall be heard in accordance with rules promulgated by the Supreme Court.

(5) AGGRAVATING CIRCUMSTANCES. Aggravating circumstances shall be limited to the following:

(a)   The capital felony was committed by a person under sentence of imprisonment or placed on community control.

(b)   The defendant was previously convicted of another capital felony or of a felony involving the use or threat of violence to the person.

(c)   The defendant knowingly created a great risk of death to many people.

(d)   The capital felony was committed while the defendant was engaged, or was an accomplice, in the commission of, or an attempt to commit, or flight after committing or attempting to commit, any robbery, sexual battery, arson, burglary, kidnapping, or aircraft piracy or the unlawful throwing, placing, or discharging of a destructive device or bomb.

(e)   The capital felony was committed for the purpose of avoiding or preventing a lawful arrest or effecting an escape from custody.

(f)   The capital felony was committed for pecuniary gain.

continued on next page

EXHIBIT 15-2   The Florida Death Penalty Statute—*concluded*

(g) The capital felony was committed to disrupt or hinder the lawful exercise of any governmental function or the enforcement of laws.

(h) The capital felony was especially heinous, atrocious, or cruel.

(i) The capital felony was a homicide and was committed in a cold, calculated, and premeditated manner without any pretense of moral or legal justification.

(j) The victim of the capital felony was a law enforcement officer engaged in the performance of his official duties.

(k) The victim of the capital felony was an elected or appointed public official engaged in the performance of his official duties if the motive for the capital felony was related, in whole or in part, to the victim's official capacity.

(6) MITIGATING CIRCUMSTANCES. Mitigating circumstances shall be the following:

(a) The defendant has no significant history of prior criminal activity.

(b) The capital felony was committed while the defendant was under the influence of extreme mental or emotional disturbance.

(c) The victim was a participant in the defendant's conduct or consented to the act.

(d) The defendant was an accomplice in the capital felony committed by another person and his participation was relatively minor.

(e) The defendant acted under extreme duress or under the substantial domination of another person.

(f) The capacity of the defendant to appreciate the criminality of his conduct or to conform his conduct to the requirements of law was substantially impaired.

(g) The age of the defendant at the time of the crime.

(7) VICTIM IMPACT EVIDENCE. Once the prosecution has provided evidence of the existence of one or more aggravating circumstances as described in subsection (5), the prosecution may introduce, and subsequently argue, victim impact evidence. Such evidence shall be designed to demonstrate the victim's uniqueness as an individual human being and the resultant loss to the community's members by the victim's death. Characterizations and opinions about the crime, the defendant, and the appropriate sentence shall not be permitted as a part of victim impact evidence.

(8) APPLICABILITY. This section does not apply to a person convicted or adjudicated guilty of a capital drug trafficking felony under s. 893.135.

Source: Florida Statute 921.141.

---

and Washington) and the federal death penalty statutes use what's called a "sufficiency" standard by which the judge and jury weigh mitigating and aggravating circumstances to determine if a death sentence is appropriate. Under this standard, the aggravating circumstances must sufficiently outweigh mitigating circumstances. In Florida, the jury must determine (1) whether sufficient aggravating circumstances exist, (2) whether sufficient mitigating circumstances exist that outweigh aggravating ones, and (3) based on these considerations whether to impose death or life imprisonment.

The other "weighing" processes used by states can be divided into four categories:

1. *Aggravating outweighs mitigating by a preponderance of the evidence*: Two states (Delaware and Maryland) require the jury to find that aggravating circumstances outweigh mitigating ones by a preponderance of the evidence.

2. *Aggravating outweighs mitigating beyond a reasonable doubt*: Six states (Arkansas, New Jersey, New York, Ohio, Tennessee, and Utah)

require the jury to find that aggravating circumstances outweigh mitigating ones beyond a reasonable doubt. In New York, the aggravating circumstances must substantially outweigh mitigating ones beyond a reasonable doubt.

3. *At least one aggravating circumstance exists:* In six states (Georgia, Kentucky, Missouri, South Carolina, South Dakota, and Wyoming), the jury cannot impose the death penalty unless it finds at least one aggravating circumstance beyond a reasonable doubt. The jury must consider mitigating evidence, but the statute does not specify weighing.

In New Mexico, the jury must find at least one aggravating circumstance beyond a reasonable doubt to impose the death penalty. It must weigh aggravating and mitigating circumstances, weigh them against each other, consider both the defendant and the crime, and determine whether it should impose death. But on review to the state supreme court, the court must overturn a death sentence if mitigating circumstances outweigh aggravating ones.

In Louisiana, the jury must find at least one aggravating circumstance beyond a reasonable doubt and, after considering mitigating circumstances, determine that death should be imposed. The sentencing hearing focuses on the circumstances of the offense, the character and propensities of the offender and the victim, and the impact of the victim's death on family, friends, and associates.

4. *Different sentencing structures exist:* Three states structure their sentencing hearings and require consideration of mitigating evidence in a different way. In Oregon, the jury must consider (1) if the defendant acted deliberately and with reasonable expectation of causing death, (2) whether there is a probability that the defendant would commit violent criminal acts that would be a continuing threat to society, (3) whether the defendant acted unreasonably in response to provocation, and (4) whether to impose a death sentence. To decide whether to impose a death sentence, the jury must consider aggravating and mitigating evidence concerning any aspect of the defendant's character or background, circumstances of the offense, and any victim impact evidence. The state must prove each issue beyond a reasonable doubt, and the court cannot impose a death sentence if at least one juror believes that it should not be imposed.

In Texas, the jury must decide beyond a reasonable doubt whether there is a probability that the defendant would commit violent crimes and be a continuing threat to society. It must consider all of the evidence, including the defendant's character and background and the circumstances of the offense, that mitigates imposing the death penalty. If all jurors agree that the defendant is a continuing threat, they must then decide whether there are sufficient mitigating circumstances to warrant life imprisonment rather than a death sentence. All jurors must agree to impose a death sentence after considering all of the evidence including the circumstances of the offense and the defendant's character, background, and personal moral culpability. The Texas statute defines *mitigating evidence* as evidence that a juror might regard as reducing the defendant's moral blameworthiness.

In Virginia, the prosecution must prove beyond a reasonable doubt that (1) there is a probability based on evidence of the defendant's prior history or the circumstances surrounding the offense that the defendant would commit violent crimes that would be a continuing serious threat to society or (2) the defendant's conduct in committing the offense was outrageously or wantonly vile, horrible, or inhuman, in that it involved torture, depravity of mind, or aggravated battery to the victim. The jury must consider mitigation, but the statute does not specify weighing.

In 2002, the U.S. Supreme Court handed down another decision that shaped capital sentencing. In *Ring* v. *Arizona*,[31] the Court held that only juries, not judges, can determine the presence of "aggravating factors" to be weighed in the capital sentencing process. Although judges may still reduce sentences, the Court held that a defendant may not receive a penalty that exceeds the maximum penalty that he or she would have received if punished according to the facts in the jury verdict. The ruling will immediately apply to those sentenced to death in Arizona, Colorado, Idaho, and Nebraska. It is unclear at this time what effect it will have on Alabama, Delaware, Florida, Indiana, and Montana, where a jury makes a recommendation of life in prison or the death penalty, but the judge makes the final ruling. In the 29 other states that have the death penalty as well as in the federal system, juries determine whether aggravating circumstances exist and weigh them against mitigating circumstances.

APPEALING THE DEATH PENALTY

The time between the imposition of the death sentence and the execution of a death row inmate is an average of 10 years and 7 months. Death penalty cases may pass through as many as 10 courts, across three stages: trial and direct review, state postconviction appeals, and federal *habeas corpus* appeals (see Figure 15–4).

In stage one, trial and direct review, a death sentence is imposed. As a consequence of the *Furman* decision, the laws of all states require that legal issues about the trial and sentence automatically be appealed to the state appellate courts. Alabama and Ohio have two rounds of appeals in the direct review process; this means that the legal issues may be heard first in the state court of criminal appeals (court 1) before reaching the state supreme court (court 2). These courts evaluate the trial for legal or constitutional errors and determine if the death sentence is consistent with sentences imposed in similar cases. State appellate courts seldom overturn a conviction or change a death sentence. The defendant then petitions the U.S. Supreme Court (court 3) to grant a petition for a writ of *certiorari*—a written order to the lower court whose decision is being appealed to send the records of the case forward for review. About five years—half of the time required for the entire appeals process—is consumed by stage one, direct review. Nationally, the rate of **serious error** (error that substantially undermines the reliability of the guilt finding or death sentence imposed at trial) discovered on direct review is 41 percent. States with the highest rate of serious error found on direct review are Wyoming (67 percent), Mississippi (61 percent), North Carolina (61 percent), Alabama (55 percent), and South Carolina (54 percent).

serious error
Error that substantially undermines the reliability of the guilt finding or death sentence imposed at trial.

If the defendant's direct appeals are unsuccessful and the Supreme Court denies review, stage two—state postconviction appeals—begins. At this point, many death row inmates allege ineffective or incompetent trial counsel, and new counsel is engaged or appointed. The new counsel petitions the trial court (court 4) with newly discovered evidence; questions about the fairness of the trial; and allegations of jury bias, tainted evidence, incompetence of defense counsel, and prosecutorial or police misconduct. If the trial court denies the appeals, they may be filed with the state's appellate courts (either directly to the state supreme court or, if there exists a dual level of appellate review, through a petition first to the state court of criminal appeals (court 5) followed by a petition to the state supreme court (court 6). Most often, the state appellate courts deny the petition. Defendant's counsel then petitions the U.S. Supreme Court (court 7). If the U.S. Supreme Court denies the petition for a writ of *cer-*

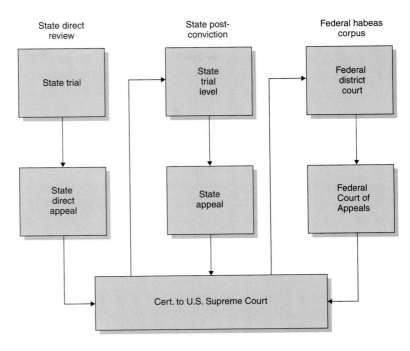

FIGURE 15-4

The Capital Criminal Process: Trial Through State and Federal Postconvictions

Source: James S. Liebman, Jeffrey Fagan, and Valerie West, *A Broken System: Error Rates in Capital Cases, 1973-1995* (New York: Columbia University School of Law, 2000), p. 23. Reprinted with permission.

tiorari, stage two ends and stage three begins. The rate of serious error found on state postconviction appeals is 10 percent. State postconviction reversals are highest in Maryland (52 percent), Wyoming (33 percent), Indiana (25 percent), Utah (23 percent), and Mississippi (20 percent).

In stage three, the federal *habeas corpus* stage, a defendant files a petition in U.S. District Court (court 8) in the state in which the defendant was convicted and is incarcerated and alleging violations of constitutional rights. Such rights include the right to due process (Fourteenth Amendment), prohibition against cruel and unusual punishment (Eighth Amendment), and effective assistance of counsel (Sixth Amendment). If the District Court denies the petition, defense counsel submits it to the U.S. Court of Appeals (court 9) for the circuit representing the jurisdiction. If the Court of Appeals denies the petition, defense counsel asks the U.S. Supreme Court (court 10) to grant a writ of *certiorari*. If the U.S. Supreme Court denies *certiorari*, the office of the state attorney general asks the state supreme court to set a date for execution. Federal courts find serious error in 40 percent of the capital cases they review. The highest rate of serious error is found in California (80 percent), Montana (75 percent), Mississippi (71 percent), Idaho (67 percent), and Georgia (65 percent). The Eleventh Circuit—the nation's most active capital appeals circuit with jurisdiction over Alabama, Georgia, and Florida—finds serious error in 50 percent of the death cases it reviews.

In 1996, in an effort to reduce the time people spend on death row and the number of federal appeals, the U.S. Congress passed the Anti-Terrorism and Effective Death Penalty Act (AEDPA). The AEDPA defines filing deadlines and limits reasons for second, or successive, federal appellate reviews to (1) new constitutional law, (2) new evidence that could not have been discovered at the time of the original trial, or (3) new facts that, if proven, would be sufficient to establish the applicant's innocence. Under the AEDPA, if the U.S. Supreme Court denies the petition for a writ of *certiorari* in the final federal *habeas corpus* appeal, defense counsel may once again petition the federal courts; however, before a second, or successive, application for a writ of *habeas corpus* may be filed in U.S. District Court, defense counsel must petition the appropriate U.S. Court of Appeals for an order authorizing the District Court to consider the application. The petition to the U.S. Court of Appeals is decided by a three-judge panel; the panel must grant or deny the authorization to file the second, or successive, application within 30 days after the petition is filed. If the panel approves the petition, the District Court must render a decision regarding the application within 180 days. If the motion is appealed to the Court of Appeals representing the jurisdiction, the court must render its decision within 120 days. If the petition is filed with the U.S. Supreme Court, the Court may grant the petition for *certiorari* or let the lower court's decision stand.

Why do people spend 10 years and 7 months on death row and why does judicial review of capital overturned cases take so long? In short, judicial review takes so long because capital sentences are "persistently and systematically fraught with error that seriously undermines their reliability."[32] The high rate of error found at each of the three stages of appeal confirms the need for more, not less, judicial review.

Death Penalty Issues in the 21st Century

Three issues spark the capital punishment debate: execution of the innocent, of juveniles, and of the mentally retarded. As of June 2002, people with mental retardation are constitutionally protected from receiving the death penalty. It is unclear how this change will impact the debate on executing the innocent and juveniles.

HOW RELIABLE ARE DEATH SENTENCES? THE LIEBMAN STUDY

According to some scholars, Americans seem to be of two minds about the death penalty. One is the fear that capital trials put people on death row who do not belong there. The other is that capital appeals take too long. The two sides are not as oppositional as it might appear, however. It may be that capital sentences spend too much time under appellate review and they are fraught with unacceptable levels of error. At least that is the conclusion of one of the most controversial studies of appellate reviews of capital sentences ever undertaken in the United States known as the Liebman study.

Possibly owing to the fact that four times as many people had their death sentences overturned or received clemency than were executed since 1977, the Judiciary Committee of the United States Senate asked Columbia law professor James Liebman to calculate the frequency of error in capital cases.[33] Liebman and his colleagues studied 4,578 appeals between 1973 and 1995. Their conclusion is that the overall rate of prejudicial error in the American capital punishment system is 68 percent. More than two of every three capital judgments reviewed by the courts during the 23-year study period were found to be seriously flawed. Ten states (Alabama, Arizona, California, Georgia, Indiana, Maryland, Mississippi, Montana, Oklahoma, and Wyoming) have overall error rates of 75 percent or higher. Almost 1,000 of the cases sent back for retrial ended in sentences less than death, and 87 ended in *not guilty* verdicts.

> ... the overall rate of prejudicial error in the American capital punishment system was 68 percent. More than two of every three capital judgments reviewed by the courts during the 23-year study period were found to be seriously flawed.

Liebman and his colleagues found two types of serious error. The first is incompetent defense lawyering (accounting for one-third of all state postconviction appeals). The second is prosecutorial suppression of evidence that the defendant is innocent or does not deserve the death penalty (accounting for almost 20 percent). When the errors were corrected through the stages already discussed, 8 of 10 people on retrial were found to deserve a sentence less than death, and 7 percent were found innocent of the capital crime. Figure 15–5 shows the flow of 100 death sentences imposed and reviewed between 1973 and 1995. It shows that for every 100 death sentences imposed, 41 were turned back at the trial and direct review phase because of serious error. Of the 59 that passed to the state postconviction stage, 10 percent—6 of the original 100— were turned back due to serious flaws. Of the 53 that passed to the next stage of federal *habeas corpus*, 40 percent—an additional 21 of the original 100—were turned back because of serious error. Together, 68 of the original 100 were thrown out after 9 to 10 years had passed because of serious flaws. Of the 68 individuals whose death sentences were overturned for serious error, 82 percent (56) were found on retrial not to deserve the death penalty, including 5 who were found innocent of the offense. According to the Death Penalty Information Center, since 1973, 112 people in 25 states have been released from death row with evidence of their innocence.[34] Each one spent an average of eight years and nine months on death row.

> **Ethical Dilemma**
> The death penalty brings up powerful emotions on both sides, and it is a source of conflict for those who are not sure how they feel. Should a person's age (under 18) or mental capacity be considered when considering the death penalty? For more information go to Ethical Dilemma 15-1 at http://www.mhhe.com/schmalleger2.

What if a death sentence is imposed today in the United States? What could the defendant, relative, lawyer, or judge expect? Liebman and his colleagues answer this way: "The capital conviction or sentence will probably be overturned due to serious error. It'll take 9 or 10 years to find out, given how many other capital cases being reviewed for likely error are lined up ahead of this one. If the judgment is overturned, a lesser conviction or sentence will probably be imposed."[35]

If death sentences are not reliable, the error has serious consequences for the wrongly convicted, for the family of the victim whose search for justice is incomplete, for the family of the person wrongly convicted in terms of the prolonged and distorted grief they suffer, for subsequent victims of the real offender still at large, and for the public in terms of lost confidence in the criminal justice system. A report in the *Chicago Tribune* on October 27, 2003, revealed that police and prosecutors rarely pursue new leads and

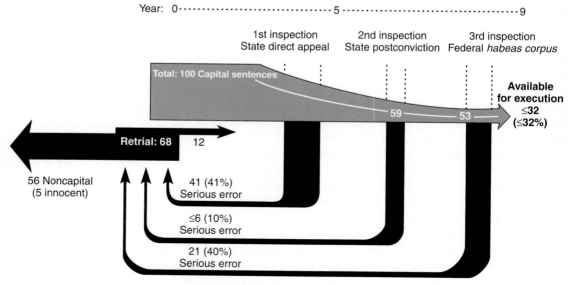

FIGURE 15-5

The Attrition of Capital Judgments

Source: James S. Liebman, Jeffrey Fagan, and Valerie West, *A Broken System: Error Rates in Capital Cases, 1973-1995* (New York: Columbia University School of Law, 2000), p. 23. Reprinted with permission.

suspects after a wrongly convicted defendant has been released from death row. The actual perpetrators remain in society to commit additional crimes, and many death row exonerees remain under a cloud of police suspicion because law enforcement failed to find the true offender.

Equally important is the cost of serious errors. A capital trial, incarceration, and execution average $2.5 to $5 million, compared to about $1 million for life in prison without parole. Florida reports $3.2 million and Tennessee $1 to $2 million, five capital trials in New York cost $68 million, and the cost per execution to California taxpayers is $4 to $5 million. The most comprehensive study in the United States found that the death penalty costs North Carolina $2.16 million per execution *over* the cost of a non–death penalty murder case with a life sentence.[36]

Wrongful convictions add still more costs in terms of multimillion dollar settlements. Illinois death row inmate Dennis Williams received $13 million from Cook County (Chicago) after he was exonerated. Most state legislatures have passed laws that compensate people wrongfully convicted. Nobody knows the exact amount that has been paid out, but it is reasonable to believe that prejudicial error is costly. It includes money lost on education, health and human services, community protection, and economic growth and development.

How can we reduce serious capital error? Liebman identifies two options. The first is to end the death penalty entirely. The second is to curb the scope of the death penalty to reach only the small number of offenses on which there is broad social consensus that only the death penalty will serve. The reforms he suggests follow:[37]

1. Require proof beyond any doubt that the defendant committed the capital crime.
2. Require that aggravating factors substantially outweigh mitigating ones before a death sentence may be imposed.
3. Bar the death penalty for people with extenuating circumstances such as juveniles.
4. Make life imprisonment without parole an alternative to the death penalty and clearly inform juries of the option.
5. Abolish judge overrides of jury verdicts imposing life sentences.
6. Use comparative review of murder sentences to identify what counts as the "worst of the worst."
7. Base charging decisions in potentially capital cases on full and informed deliberations.
8. Make all police and prosecution evidence bearing on guilt vs. evidence and on aggravation vs. mitigation available to the jury at trial.
9. Insulate capital-sentencing and appellate judges from political pressure.
10. Identify, appoint, and compensate capital defense counsel in ways that attract an adequate number of well-qualified lawyers to do the work.

EXECUTING JUVENILES

The first recognized juvenile execution in the United States occurred in 1642 when Thomas Graunger was executed in Plymouth, Massachusetts, for committing the crime of bestiality when he was 16 years old.[38] Since then, the United States has executed 365 people for offenses they committed when children. In the current era of capital punishment (1976 through January 1, 2004), 22 people were executed for offenses they committed as juveniles.[39] The last was Scott Allen Hain on April 3, 2003, by lethal injection in Oklahoma. Four months after his 17th birthday, Hain and an accomplice committed murder. He was sentenced to die in May 1988. Today there are 82 death row inmates (all male) sentenced as juveniles, constituting about 2 percent of the total death row population.

In spite of the overall public support for capital punishment noted earlier, almost 70 percent of Americans oppose the execution of juveniles, according to a Gallup Poll conducted in May 2002.[40] Professional organizations such as the American Academy of Child and Adolescent Psychiatry, the American Medical Association, and the American Psychological Association oppose the imposition of the death penalty for crimes committed by juveniles. Many now point to the latest medical research from Harvard University that found that the frontal and prefontal lobes of the brain that regulate impulse control and judgment change dramatically between the ages of 12 and 22. They are not fully operational by age 14 as previously held.[41] As a class, young people have a greater tendency toward impulsiveness, lesser reasoning skills, and less awareness of the consequences of their decisions and actions, regardless of how big they are or how tough they talk.

Today, 15 states and the federal government prohibit by statute the execution of offenders under the age of 18. Of the 22 states that permit the execution of juveniles, 15 have juveniles on death row, and 7 have executed people whose crimes were committed when they were under 18: Georgia, Louisiana, Missouri, Oklahoma, and South Carolina have used it once; Virginia has used it three times; and Texas has used it 14 times, more than all other states combined. The most recent states to ban the juvenile death penalty are Montana in 1999 and Indiana in 2002.

Ethical Dilemma

Should we hold children accountable for their actions to the same degree as we do adults when it comes to the death penalty? For more information go to Ethical Dilemma 15-2 at http://www.mhhe.com/schmalleger2.

The United States Supreme Court first addressed the constitutionality of applying the death penalty to juvenile offenders in 1988 in *Thompson* v. *Oklahoma*. The Court ruled in a five-to-four opinion that it was unconstitutional to sentence a 15-year-old to death. The following year, in *Stanford* v. *Kentucky* and *Wilkins* v. *Missouri,* the Court held that the Eighth Amendment's prohibition against cruel and unusual punishment did not forbid imposition of the death penalty for crimes committed by people at 16 and 17 years of age. Justice Scalia's majority opinion reasoned that, since a majority of the 37 states that had death penalty statutes at the time allowed capital punishment for juveniles, the practice did not violate evolving standards of decency.

Court observers note that, because of two dissenting opinions in 2002 and the Court's 2002 decision in *Atkins* v. *Virginia*[42] that banned executions for the mentally retarded, there is a strong possibility that the Court will revisit the constitutionality of executing juveniles. In denying *certiorari* in *Patterson* v. *Texas,*[43] three Justices wrote that, since the Court's 1989 decision in *Stanford,* application of the death penalty to juvenile offenders has been the subject of further debate and discussion in the United States and in other civilized countries. The Justices noted, "Given the apparent consensus that exists among the States and in the international community against the execution of a capital sentence imposed on a juvenile offender . . . it would be appropriate for the Court to revisit the issue at the earliest opportunity."[44] Also in 2002, *In re Stanford,*[45] four Justices wrote, "The practice of executing juvenile offenders is a relic of the past and is inconsistent with evolving standards of decency in a civilized society. We should put an end to this shameful practice."[46] And, as a result of the decision in *Atkins,* juvenile justice advocates hope for a reversal of *Stanford,* in which the Court held it was not unconstitutional to execute 17-year-old offenders.

In 2003, significant attention was directed to the trial of Lee Malvo in Virginia who was 17 at the time of a series of shootings in Maryland and Virginia. While a death sentence is certainly possible in Malvo's case, numerous articles in the media and journals have pointed to the latest medical research discussed above delineating the developmental differences between juveniles and adults.

Worldwide today, only the United States and Iran continue to cling to their rights to impose the death penalty on people who commit their crimes while still juveniles. The International Covenant on Civil and Political Rights, a binding treaty with 144 signatories, and the U.N. Convention on the Rights of the Child prohibit the death penalty for offenders under the age of 18. When the United States ratified the treaty in 1992, it filed a reservation and maintained its right to impose capital punishment on any person (other than a pregnant woman), including those under the age of 18. The United States maintained that the convention would encourage government interference in family matters and override a state's right to impose the death penalty for murders committed by minors. In response, nations around the world filed formal objections condemning the United States' reservation. The U.N. Human Rights Committee requested the United States to withdraw the reservation, but it declined.

BANNING THE EXECUTION OF PEOPLE WITH MENTAL RETARDATION

In 1986, the U.S. Supreme Court banned the execution of the mentally retarded. In 1989, the Court held that executing people with mental retardation was not a violation of the Eighth Amendment. But on June 19, 2002, the Court held in *Atkins* v. *Virginia* that execution of the mentally retarded is cruel and unusual punishment prohibited by the Eighth Amendment. The Court argued that a national consensus has developed against executing the mentally retarded. Aside from the 12 states that ban executions altogether, beginning in 1988 Arizona, Arkansas, Colorado, Connecticut, Florida, Georgia, Indiana, Kansas, Kentucky, Maryland, Missouri, Nebraska, New Mexico, New York, North Carolina, South Dakota, Tennessee, Washington, and the federal government passed statutes banning the execution of the mentally retarded. The Court argued that it was not so much the number of states that passed similar statutes, but the consistency of the direction of change. In the words of the Court, "Given the well-known fact that anticrime legislation is far more popular than legislation providing protections for persons guilty of violent crime, the large number of States prohibiting the execution of the mentally retarded people (and the complete absence of States passing legislation reinstating the power to conduct such executions) provides powerful evidence that today our society views mentally retarded offenders as categorically less culpable than the average criminal. The evidence carries even greater force when it is noted that the legislatures that have addressed the issue have voted overwhelmingly in favor of the prohibition."[47]

In spite of the Supreme Court's ruling, Daryl Renard Atkins, the Virginia inmate whose case persuaded the U.S. Supreme Court to exclude mentally retarded murderers from executions remains on death row as of January 1, 2004. Atkins, who has an IQ of 59 (a score of 70 or below is generally considered an indicator of mental retardation), still must prove he is mentally retarded in state court before he can leave death row and get a life sentence. In its 2002 ruling, the Supreme Court left it to the states to define mental retardation and returned Atkins' case to the Virginia Supreme Court, which then passed it down to the York County Circuit Court. According to the Virginia Attorney General's office, nobody in Virginia has successfully appealed a death sentence based on the Atkins decision.[48] Virginia's definition of mental retardation requires "significant subaverage intellectual functioning" at the onset of adulthood. Richard Bonnie, director of the University of Virginia's Institute of Law, Psychiatry and Public

Eye On Corrections™

"Death Penalty Review: Where Is It Going?

By Michelle Gaseau

In recent years the death penalty has come under increasing scrutiny as state and federal officials take a hard look at who is being executed and how offenders get to death row.

DEATH PENALTY FOR JUVENILES

The issue of the juvenile death penalty broke into the headlines recently when the Supreme Court opted not to hear a case (*Stanford* v. *Kentucky*) that challenged the use of the death sentence for juvenile offenders. While many criticized the Court for not taking the opportunity to weigh in officially, four Justices made it clear they opposed the use of capital punishment for this group of offenders.

Some death penalty experts predict, however, that the court will take a stand on the issue soon. According to Jim Coleman, a professor of Law for Duke University and chair of the American Bar Association's Death Penalty Moratorium Implementation Project, the Supreme Court will eventually take a case that debates the constitutionality of the juvenile death penalty.

In the interim, some states may pass their own laws prohibiting the use of the death penalty for juveniles under age 18 as Indiana did this year. In fact, 18 of the 40 death penalty jurisdictions in the United States have chosen age 18 as the minimum age for eligibility for the death penalty, 5 use age 17, and 17 use 16 as the minimum age.

Death penalty proponents, however, say that the debate over age is extraneous because some 16 and 17 year olds are as mature as 18 year olds.

Dudley Sharp, Resource Director for the criminal justice organization Justice for All, said that each case should be considered separately, and juries should be given the option to use the death penalty sentence if warranted.

"The specific crime does make a difference and the benefit is that the jury only considers an individual crime. [The argument against the juvenile death penalty] is stupid. There's no rational defense. If someone is 17 years and 364 days then no, but after midnight, it's yes?" Sharp said.

Coleman believes that public opinion does play a role in the eventual acceptance or rejection of the juvenile death penalty. He said that the recent sniper case in Maryland, for example, might slow the trend of raising execution eligibility ages.

"The fact that [accused sniper] John Malvo is 17 and not subject to the death penalty under federal and Maryland law but is in Virginia and Alabama will have an impact on public opinion," said Coleman. "These unfortunately are the kinds of cases that have disproportionate weight in the debate."

Like Sharp, he believes that these cases should be considered individually, just as states do when they determine whether a juvenile should be tried as an adult.

One area of the death penalty that has been addressed more definitively is the execution of the mentally impaired.

MENTAL IMPAIRMENTS

The Supreme Court ruled in June 2002 that executing offenders with mental retardation is unconstitutional, which many death penalty opponents are pleased about. But some say that the ruling has made the issue somewhat more complicated. The reason: the lack of a standard that states can use to apply the ruling in cases that go before state courts.

What the Supreme Court did say in its ruling was that offenders with an IQ of 70 or below fell into this category where executions are prohibited. But many other factors also play a role in determining mental retardation such as the ability to function in the community.

According to Coleman, "What we find in the different states is some have an absolute 70 cut-off for IQ, and others say more or less 70. It's not a bright line." Coleman said, "The Supreme

Court might have to step in. You could get different results depending on what state you're in because it is a constitutional decision, and it has to be applied consistently."

One concern Sharp has with the fallout of this ruling is that, if it is too broadly applied, then murderers will have a chance to walk off death row. "No one wants people executed or punished that are not aware of how wrong the crime is. We don't want people who can't participate in their own defense to be executed. [But] what we don't want is fully culpable, brutal murderers to escape a just sanction solely because of a broad or too severe interpretation," Sharp said.

More attention is also being paid to issues of innocence on death row.

DNA AND INNOCENCE ON DEATH ROW

One of the most high-profile events related to the death penalty in recent years was the call by Illinois Governor George Ryan for a moratorium on executions in 2000. One of the reasons for the ban was a string of exonerations of death row inmates in his state, which has caused many to question how the death penalty has been imposed.

According to Coleman, the idea that mistakes are being made in the prosecution of offenders has shaken many. "I think the real problem is that the officials who are administering [the death penalty] aren't willing to admit mistakes and take responsibility for them. These public officials won't even discuss it," he said. "What has happened is people talk about punishment and are glossing over the steps between capturing [a person] and punishment."

According to Sharp, who served on the Illinois commission that looked into the death penalty cases in question, some of the cases had legitimate problems, and many of those originated from Cook County, Illinois. Sharp said that, during the time period in which these cases were tried, false confessions were used by the prosecution, and there were other problems with the offenders' convictions.

The irony, he said, is that many of the recommendations ultimately made by the commission were already on the books, and the officials in Cook County that made these mistakes no longer were in the criminal justice system there. "There has been a two-year moratorium, and during that time they haven't discovered any other innocent people on death row," said Sharp. "My position is you learn from history, but does that history repeat itself today? No."

In the Illinois cases, innocence was determined for these death row inmates through a number of ways including DNA testing as well as independent investigations by a college journalism class. "Any case that is a biologically based murder or rape will be tested before trial from now on, and DNA will be one of the great forensic tools for convicting people," Sharp said.

There are other concerns with the death penalty, such as whether it is applied consistently from jurisdiction to jurisdiction. Maryland for example, is under a death penalty moratorium in order for state officials to investigate whether discrimination exists in the use of the death penalty. According to Coleman, officials were concerned that some counties were "overusing" the death sentence, while others were not using it at all.

Sharp, however, says inferences that the death penalty is discriminatory are false. According to statistics compiled by the Bureau of Justice Statistics in 2001, new death sentence convictions in 2000 included 115 white men (including 25 Hispanic men), 86 black men, 1 American Indian, 4 Asian men, 7 white women, and 1 American Indian woman. Although capital cases are six times more likely to involve white victims than black victims, Sharp said this is a reflection of the crimes committed, not racial bias.

Sharp also refutes the belief that the death penalty is being used less frequently. Although the trends in capital punishment show that fewer people are being executed in recent years, people are still landing on death row.

Sharp said the decrease in executions is actually related to the decrease in the murder rate nationwide. "I don't think you can find a decrease of executions that is outside the decrease in murders," he said. Death penalty opponents disagree and say that all indications are that the death penalty will die one piece at a time over the next several years.

Source: "Death Penalty Review: Where Is It Going," Michelle Gaseau, The Corrections Connection Network News (CCNN). Eye on Corrections. www.corrections.com. November 4, 2002. Copyright © 2002, all rights reserved, The Corrections Connection Network News (CCNN), a division of J.S. Noonan, LLC. Reprinted with permission.

Policy said borderline cases such as Atkins will eventually provide the guidance missing in the Court's decision. "What is going to have to emerge," said Bonnie, "are standards of forensic practice—the kinds of records people will have to obtain, the kinds of tests they have to employ" to prove that someone is mentally retarded.[49]

SUMMARY

1▶   Capital punishment has been imposed throughout history, for crimes ranging from horse stealing and witchcraft to crimes against humanity and murder. Before the 18th century, torture often preceded death. In the 18th century, use of the death penalty diminished as philosophers argued that punishment should fit the crime. After World War I, states reinstated use of the death penalty to deter threats to capitalism, and criminologists argued that capital punishment was a necessary social measure. After World War II, however, sentiment for capital punishment faded, and constitutional challenges surfaced, culminating in the Supreme Court decision of *Furman* v. *Georgia* in 1972.

2▶   As of January 1, 2004, 885 people have been executed in the United States since Gary Gilmore's execution in January 1977. The peak year was 1999 when 98 people were executed. Thirty-five percent (313) of all executions have taken place in Texas. The South leads the United States with 728 executions. Only 1.2 percent of all the people executed since 1977 have been female; 57 percent were white, 34 percent black, 7 percent Hispanic, 1.5 percent American Indian, and less than 1 percent Asian. Today, 3,504 prisoners are on death row. Forty-one percent of the nation's death row population is in three states: California (632), Texas (451), and Florida (381). Ninety-nine percent of all prisoners on death row are male, with whites predominating (46 percent). Prisoners spend an average of 10 years and 7 months on death row.

3▶   Among the influences on capital punishment are public opinion; executive, legislative, and judicial changes; and professional organizations. Public opinion continues to support capital punishment, with more people choosing life imprisonment as an option. More Governors are granting clemency, and fewer death sentences have been imposed. In the wake of the Illinois moratorium on capital punishment in 2000, professional organizations and legislatures across the country are calling for death penalty moratoriums, funding study of capital punishment, granting death row inmates access to DNA testing, affording extra assistance to lawyers handling capital cases, raising the amount of financial compensation that states provide innocent people found to have been erroneously convicted, allowing prosecutors to seek life without parole instead of the death penalty, and barring the execution of juveniles.

4▶   Three landmark cases that influenced capital punishment were *Furman* v. *Georgia* (1972), *Gregg* v. *Georgia* (1976), and *Ring* v. *Arizona* (2002). In *Furman* v. *Georgia*, the U.S. Supreme Court ruled that capital punishment, as imposed by Georgia, constituted cruel and unusual punishment—Georgia's death penalty statute gave the sentencing authority (judge or trial jury) complete freedom to impose a death sentence without standards or guidelines. As a result of the *Furman* ruling, state death penalty statutes took two forms—mandatory death penalty or sentencing based on guided discretion. In *Woodson* v. *North Carolina* and *Roberts* v. *Louisiana*, the Court rejected mandatory statutes. However, in *Gregg* v. *Georgia*, the Court ruled that Georgia's new guided discretion death penalty legislation was not unconstitutional. In *Ring* v. *Arizona,* the Court held that only juries, not judges, can determine the presence of aggravating factors to be weighed in the capital sentencing process. The Court held that a defendant may not receive a penalty that exceeds the maximum penalty that he or she would have received if punished according to the facts in the jury verdict.

5 ▶ Arguments in favor of the death penalty include the following: It deters rational people from becoming habitual killers; it is "just" punishment for taking someone's life; it is constitutional as long as it is achieved with due process of law; it reduces the amount of time a person spends on death row; it protects society from feared offenders; it is more humane than life imprisonment; and it is almost impossible for an innocent person to be executed. Arguments against the death penalty include the following: It violates human rights; it does not deter violent crime; it is implemented arbitrarily and unfairly; it falls disproportionately on racial minorities; it actually boosts the murder rate by promoting homicides in the months following an execution; not everyone wants vengeance; and it costs too much to support a capital trial, appeals, and execution.

6 ▶ There are five ways capital punishment jurisdictions weigh aggravating and mitigating circumstances to determine if a death sentence is appropriate: (1) the judge and jury may weigh mitigating and aggravating circumstances by what is known as the "sufficiency" standard; (2) aggravating circumstances may outweigh mitigating circumstances by a preponderance of the evidence; (3) aggravating circumstances may outweigh mitigating circumstances beyond a reasonable doubt; (4) at least one aggravating circumstance may be found to exist; and (5) different sentencing structures that exist in Oregon, Texas, and Virginia may be used.

7 ▶ Death penalty cases may pass through as many as 10 courts and across three stages: trial and direct review, state postconviction appeals, and federal *habeas corpus* appeals.

8 ▶ Liebman found that the frequency of errors in capital punishment cases is 68 percent. More than two of every three capital judgments reviewed by the courts during a 23-year study period were found to be seriously flawed. Ten states (Alabama, Arizona, California, Georgia, Indiana, Maryland, Mississippi, Montana, Oklahoma, and Wyoming) had overall error rates of 75 percent or higher. Almost 1,000 of the cases sent back for retrial ended in sentences less than death, and 87 ended in *not guilty* verdicts.

9 ▶ Almost 70 percent of Americans oppose the execution of juveniles. Professional organizations oppose the imposition of the death penalty for crimes committed by juveniles, pointing to the latest medical research from Harvard University that found that the frontal and prefontal lobes of the brain that regulate impulse control and judgment change dramatically between the ages of 12 and 22. Today, 15 states and the federal government prohibit by statute the execution of offenders under the age of 18. In the current era of capital punishment (1976 through January 1, 2004), 22 people were executed for offenses they committed as juveniles. Today, there are 82 death row inmates (all male) sentenced as juveniles. The United States Supreme Court first addressed the constitutionality of applying the death penalty to juvenile offenders in 1988 in *Thompson* v. *Oklahoma.* The Court ruled that it was unconstitutional to sentence a 15 year old to death. The following year, in *Stanford* v. *Kentucky* and *Wilkins* v. *Missouri,* the Court held that the Eighth Amendment's prohibition against cruel and unusual punishment did not forbid

imposition of the death penalty for crimes committed by people at 16 and 17 years of age. Worldwide today, only the United States and Iran continue to cling to their rights to impose the death penalty on people who commit their crimes while still juveniles.

10 ▶ In 2002, the Court held in *Atkins* v. *Virginia* that execution of the mentally retarded is cruel and unusual punishment prohibited by the Eighth Amendment because a national consensus has developed against executing the mentally retarded. The Court said that the large number of States prohibiting the execution of mentally retarded people provided powerful evidence that our society views mentally retarded offenders as categorically less culpable than the average criminal.

KEY TERMS

capital punishment, *p. 537*

capital crime, *p. 539*

clemency, *p. 545*

commutation, *p. 545*

death row, *p. 548*

mandatory death penalty, *p. 555*

guided discretion, *p. 555*

bifurcated trial, *p. 555*

mitigating circumstances, *p. 555*

aggravating circumstances, *p. 556*

serious error, *p. 560*

QUESTIONS FOR REVIEW

1. What is *capital punishment*?

2. How many jurisdictions in the United States permit capital punishment? How many do not?

3. What is a *capital crime*?

4. What are the characteristics of people executed since 1977? On death row today?

5. What execution methods are used in the United States today? Which is used most?

6. What politics influence capital punishment?

7. List and explain at least four arguments in favor of and against capital punishment.

8. What are the three landmark U.S. Supreme Court cases that most affected capital punishment legislation? What impact did they have?

9. What is a *bifurcated trial*?

10. What are *aggravating* and *mitigating circumstances*?

11. What are the five ways judges and juries weigh aggravating and mitigating circumstances to determine if a death sentence is appropriate?

12. What is the process for appealing a death sentence?

13. What is meant by *serious error*? What are the two types?

14. What is the Anti-Terrorism and Effective Death Penalty Act? What is its purpose?

15. According to Liebman, what is the overall rate of prejudicial error in capital punishment? What is the rate of error on direct review, on state postconviction appeals, and on federal *habeas corpus*?

16. According to Liebman, how can we reduce the rate of serious capital error?

17. What is the latest medical research from Harvard University that is influencing the debate on juvenile executions? How many jurisdictions permit juvenile executions?

18. How many juveniles have been executed since 1977? How many people who were under the age of 18 when they committed their crimes are on death row today?

19. What justification did the U.S. Supreme Court offer in banning the execution of the mentally retarded?

REVIEW & APPLICATIONS

THINKING CRITICALLY ABOUT CORRECTIONS

▶ ▶ ▶ Murder Rates and the Death Penalty

Death penalty states have higher murder rates than non–death penalty states. The average murder rate among death penalty states was 5.2 per 100,000 population in 2002; for non–death penalty states, the rate was 2.9. The South executes the largest percentage of offenders who are convicted of a capital crime (89 percent) and records the highest murder rate (6.8 murders per 100,000 people); the Northeast executes the fewest (less than 1 percent) and records the lowest murder rate of 4.1. What conclusions might you draw from these data?

▶ ▶ ▶ Costs of Execution

Research shows that execution costs more than life imprisonment. Do you think there is a point at which the economic consequence of execution outweighs its value to the public? Explain.

ON-THE-JOB DECISION MAKING

▶ ▶ ▶ Should the Cost of a Capital Trial Be a Factor in a Prosecutor's Decision to Seek the Death Penalty?

Capital murder trials are longer and more expensive at every step than other murder trials. The irreversibility of the death sentence requires courts to follow heightened due process in the preparation and course of the trial. Defendants are much more likely to insist on a trial when they are facing a possible death sentence. Crime investigations, pretrial preparations and motions, expert witness investigations, jury selection, and the necessity for two trials—one on guilt and one on sentencing—make capital cases extremely costly, even before the appeals process begins. After conviction, there are constitutionally mandated appeals that involve both prosecution and defense costs. Even if a jury recommends life over death or ends as a hung jury or if the condemned person's sentence is commuted after he or she has served time on death row, the state has already paid the cost of a capital trial. Assume that you are the prosecuting attorney in a rural county of 7,500 people in a southern state. A capital case is coming up for trial. Estimates of costs for the case begin at $500,000. How will you justify paying for the prosecution of the case?

▶ ▶ ▶ The Impact of Legislation on Professionalism in Corrections

According to a study at Kentucky's University of Louisville, blacks who killed whites in Kentucky were more likely to be charged with a capital offense and receive a death penalty than were others. As a result of this study, the Kentucky Senate passed the Kentucky Racial Justice Act, which states, in part, that "no person shall be subject to or given a death sentence that was sought on the basis of race." This legislation permits introduction of statistical evidence of racial bias in Kentucky's capital sentencing process in cases sentenced after July 15, 1998.[50] What impact do you think this law might have on your life as a corrections professional in Kentucky?

REVIEW & APPLICATIONS

CORRECTIONS ON THE WEB

▶ ▶ ▶ **Death Penalty Information Center**

The Death Penalty Information Center, a source of current information on the death penalty, maintains a Website at http://www.deathpenalty-info.org. Test your knowledge of capital punishment by taking the DPIC *Death Penalty Quiz.* Click on *Resources,* and then *Death Penalty Quiz.*

▶ ▶ ▶ **Aggravating and Mitigating Circumstances**

Compare the aggravating and mitigating circumstances different states consider in determining the sentence for a capital crime. See Figure 15–1 for the list of jurisdictions that currently permit the death penalty. Use a Web browser (e.g., Google or Yahoo). In the search box, type the name of any of the 38 states with death penalty statutes followed by the words "death penalty statutes." For example, if you want to find the aggravating and mitigating circumstances for the state of Florida type, "florida death penalty statute." Or, you can go to www.findlaw.com. Click on *States,* and then select one of the 38 death penalty states. For example, click Arizona, Arizona revised statues, Title 13 Criminal Code, scroll down to Chapter 7 Imprisonment, and click 13-703 Sentence of death or life imprisonment; aggravating and mitigating circumstances; definition.

“ **The vast majority of youth are good citizens who have never been arrested for any type of crime.**

—Shay Bilchik, Executive Director, Child Welfare League of America ”

16 CHAPTER

Juvenile Corrections: End of an Era?

CHAPTER OBJECTIVES

After completing this chapter you should be able to do the following:

1. Explain *parens patriae*.

2. Describe houses of refuge, reform schools, and industrial schools.

3. Discuss the history of the juvenile court.

4. Summarize five U.S. Supreme Court cases that changed modern day juvenile court proceedings.

5. Discuss the two types of juvenile crime.

6. List the characteristics of the typical juvenile delinquent.

7. List and explain the three stages of the juvenile justice process.

8. List disposition options for adjudicated juvenile offenders.

9. List and explain four teen court models.

10. Explain how youth gangs affect juvenile correctional institutions.

▶ ▶ **Here is a portion of a story** that recently appeared in a Midwestern city newspaper[1]:

A teenager accused of killing his father and stepmother disliked his stepmother and used disparaging terms to describe her to his buddies, one of the youth's friends testified yesterday.

"Brandon never really liked Becky," Trevor Howe said during a hearing in Hardin County Juvenile Court. "He also called her the 'B' word."

Howe, 16, testified at a hearing to determine whether Brandon Grigaliunas, 16, should be tried as an adult for the October slayings of his father, Scott, 39, and stepmother, Rebecca, 42, in their home in Kenton, about 50 miles northwest of Columbus.

Grigaliunas is charged with two delinquency counts each of aggravated murder and murder. In juvenile court, the most serious penalty he could face is juvenile detention until age 21. As an adult, he could face life in prison.

He was 15 at the time of the shootings, and county prosecutor Lora Manon made the request to have him tried as an adult.

Excerpt from Tom Sheehan, "Buddy Testifies Teen Didn't Like His Stepmother," *Columbus Dispatch*, 2/2/00, p.1b. Copyright © 2000 Columbus Dispatch. Used with permission.

Ultimately, prosecutor Manon's motion for an adult trial was granted. In a subsequent plea agreement that prevented the possibility of life imprisonment, Grigaliunas pleaded guilty to two counts of voluntary manslaughter and was sentenced to a 10-year prison term.[2]

A youthful offender is welcomed to boot camp by officers in a Montana facility. Can juveniles be more easily reformed than adults?

Although the majority of juvenile offenders are charged with property offenses rather than violent offenses, the majority of juvenile offenses reported by the media involve violent crime, which overstates the violence issue and unduly alarms the public. High-profile juvenile violence—such as the shootings at Columbine High School on April 20, 1999, and the National Zoo in Washington on April 24, 2000—is changing juvenile corrections from treatment to punishment. As a result, attention and scarce resources focus on a small portion of juvenile offenders, neglecting the vast majority.

Juvenile justice will face other challenges in its second century of existence. The United States Congress, the Department of Justice, the American Bar Association, the NAACP, think tanks, academic researchers, and others are revealing a juvenile justice system that disproportionately arrests, prosecutes, and sentences minority youth. Data from several sources show that minority youth are more likely than white youth who commit comparable crimes to be arrested, be referred to juvenile court, be detained, face trial as adults, be jailed with adults, and be sentenced to correctional institutions.

Some argue that minority youth are victims of racial bias built into the justice system. Others maintain that juvenile justice policies discriminate against low-income youth, who are overwhelmingly minority, those from single-parent homes, Or those in foster care. Still others claim that overrepresentation simply means that minority youth are committing more crimes or more serious crimes. Whatever the explanation, significant change is underway. In 1992, the U.S. Congress strengthened its commitment to end disproportionate juvenile minority confinement by elevating the issue as a core requirement in federal juvenile justice legislation. The Office of Juvenile Justice and Delinquency Prevention (OJJDP) has taken the lead in developing solutions in partnership with the states.

> . . . the U.S. Congress strengthened its commitment to end disproportionate juvenile minority confinement by elevating the issue as a core requirement in federal juvenile justice legislation.

History of the Juvenile Justice System

The historical origins of America's juvenile justice system can be traced to early England, where bridewells (the first houses of corrections) confined both children and adults until 1704, when John Howard brought to England a model of a Roman institution for juvenile offenders (see Chapter 2). Colonists took these ideas with them to America, and reformers tailored the ideas to their experiences, creating houses of refuge, reform schools, and industrial schools for juveniles. Both the English and American juvenile justice systems utilize the doctrine of *parens patriae,* or the state as parent. The first known application of *parens patriae* in America occurred in 1636 when Bridget Fuller was ordered by the governor of Plymouth Colony to take Benjamen Eaton, keep him in school for two years, and keep him employed.[3] By the end of the 19th century, every American state had affirmed its right to act as guardian of minors.

parens patriae
A Latin term that refers to the state as guardian of minors and incompetent people.

HOUSES OF REFUGE

The New York House of Refuge, the first legally chartered American custodial institution for juvenile offenders, was founded in 1825 by penal reformer Thomas Eddy, educational reformer John Griscom, and the Society for the Prevention of Pauperism. Its purpose was to provide poor, abused, and orphaned youths with food, clothing, and lodging in exchange for hard work, discipline, and study. The concept spread, and houses of refuge were established throughout America.

Living conditions in houses of refuge were not as generous as the term *refuge* might imply. Administrators of these institutions subjected juveniles to hard physical labor and were known to use corporal punishment. Residents were expected to earn their keep and comply with strict institutional rules. Guards and superintendents, substitutes for parents or guardians, exhibited little tolerance or understanding.

Despite the path-breaking role the house of refuge played in the development of the American juvenile justice system, such institutions were short-lived. The movement as a whole died out by the middle of the 19th century.

REFORM SCHOOLS

reform school

A penal institution to which especially young or first-time offenders are committed for training and reformation.

The nation's first state-sponsored **reform school** opened in Massachusetts in 1848. Named the Lyman School, for Theodore Lyman, a former mayor of Boston, the institution resembled a prison. The school was designed to house 300 boys. Because of liberal admissions policies and unregulated commitment procedures, the reformatory was filled within a few years. The Massachusetts legislature authorized an addition, doubling the structure's capacity.

In the late 1800s, with the school again becoming overcrowded, a ship in Boston Harbor was designated an annex to it. Any boy under age 14 could be committed to either Lyman School or its Nautical Branch. Boys who were housed at the Nautical Branch were trained in navigation and the duties of seamen and then transferred to passing vessels that needed cabin boys or young laborers.

Because the Lyman School housed only boys, the Massachusetts legislature voted to create a separate institution for girls. Belief that the physical and emotional makeup of girls was inherently more delicate than that of boys led reformers to focus on a new European model for the girls school.

European-style reform schools introduced a small residential arrangement, breaking down structural barriers so that staff and inmates could interact, providing a more intimate setting for treatment. Advocates of the European-style reform school believed that personal contact with youth was the cornerstone of the rehabilitative effort. Under the new design, as many as 30 inmates with similar personality traits were placed in separate small homes or cottages and supervised by paid "cottage parents." Residents of each house or cottage lived, worked, and attended school together, meeting with inmates in other living quarters only infrequently.

The first of the European-style reform schools was the Lancaster Industrial School for Girls in Massachusetts, established in 1854. The Lancaster cottages had features associated with both school and home and provided academic classes and domestic training programs. Lancaster's cottage plan gained national attention as prison reform advocates encouraged adoption of this system for youthful offenders throughout the United States.

INDUSTRIAL SCHOOLS

After the Civil War, state welfare services expanded and began to require that juvenile reform schools and adult penal institutions help pay operating costs by contracting inmate labor to local manufacturers. The use of juvenile contract labor hindered the growth of reform schools. Manufacturers controlled the children during working hours, and exploitation and brutality were common. Some reform schools were converted into housing units to better serve manufacturers' labor needs.

Concerned citizens and elected officials recognized the inadequacies of reform schools. Public efforts were made to improve institutional life and to reduce the number of children being incarcerated. Special state committees

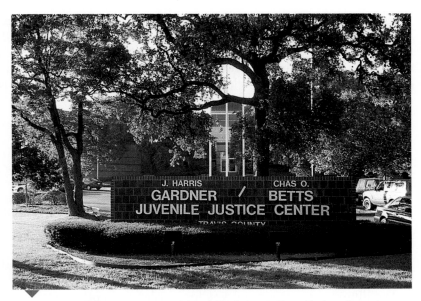

The Gardner/Betts Juvenile Justice Center in Travis County, Texas. The juvenile court movement of the late-1800s gave rise to the juvenile justice system that we know today. Why are juveniles held separately from adult prisoners?

investigated abuses in contract labor systems, and reform schools were added to the list of public institutions that were subject to annual inspection by regulatory agencies.

THE FIRST JUVENILE COURT

The movement toward establishing a separate juvenile court began in 1870, when the Illinois Supreme Court heard *People ex rel. O'Connell* v. *Turner.*[4] Daniel O'Connell was committed to the Chicago Reform School for vagrancy. His parents protested the confinement and petitioned the court for Daniel's release. In its decision, which ordered Daniel's release, the Illinois Supreme Court

- recognized that Daniel's parents genuinely wanted to care for their son;
- held that vagrancy was a matter of misfortune, not a criminal act;
- viewed Daniel's commitment to the Chicago Reform School as a punishment, not merely as a placement in a school for troubled children; and
- deemed Daniel's incarceration imprisonment, meaning that the doctrine of *parens patriae* did not apply and formal due process protections were required.

By the end of the 19th century, debate about juvenile facilities had established the need for differentiating between juveniles and adults in court procedures. Some states had even established children's aid societies to represent juveniles in court and to supervise them in the community.

The first completely separate juvenile court was established in Illinois in 1899. The Illinois legislature passed a law called "An Act to Regulate the

Treatment and Control of Dependent, Neglected and Delinquent Children," which established a juvenile court in Cook County that had jurisdiction over any youth who committed an act that would be a crime if committed by an adult. However, young criminal offenders were not the only juveniles who needed help or supervision—the legislation was revised also to give the juvenile court jurisdiction over

> . . . any child who for any reason is destitute or homeless or abandoned; or dependent on the public for support; or has not proper parental care or guardianship; or who habitually begs or receives alms; or who is found living in any house of ill fame or with any vicious or disreputable person; or whose home, by reason of neglect, cruelty or depravity on part of its parents, guardian or other person in whose care it may be, is an unfit place for such a child; and any child under the age of eight years who is found peddling or selling any article or singing or playing any musical instrument upon the street or giving any public entertainment.[5]

The intent of the new legislation was to give the juvenile court jurisdiction when the child's best interests would be served.

The Illinois act was a prototype for legislation in other states, and juvenile courts were quickly established in Wisconsin (1901), New York (1901), Ohio (1902), Maryland (1902), and Colorado (1903). By 1945, all states had established separate juvenile courts. New terminology accompanied the establishment of the juvenile court, to differentiate it from adult criminal court. Juvenile offenders are "delinquents" rather than "criminals," they are "taken into custody" rather than "arrested"; a "petition" rather than a "charge" is filed; juveniles are "held on petition" rather than "indicted"; there is an "adjudicatory hearing" rather than a "trial"; the court returns a "finding" rather than a "verdict" and imposes a "disposition" rather than a "sentence"; and the offender is "adjudicated" rather than "convicted," sent to a "training school" rather than a "prison," and put on "aftercare" rather than "parole."

The U.S. Supreme Court and the Juvenile Justice System

For most of the 20th century, all juvenile hearings were considered civil proceedings—rules of criminal procedure did not apply. Juveniles had no constitutional protections, and there were no challenges to the admissibility of evidence or the validity of testimony. Five landmark U.S. Supreme Court decisions dramatically changed the juvenile justice system, establishing due process rights for juvenile offenders.

Five landmark U.S. Supreme Court decisions dramatically changed the juvenile justice system, establishing due process rights for juvenile offenders.

KENT v. UNITED STATES (1966)

In 1959, Morris A. Kent Jr., age 14, was taken into custody in Washington, D.C., on a petition alleging burglary and attempted purse snatching. He was placed on juvenile probation and returned to his mother's custody. In September 1961, an intruder entered a woman's apartment, raped her, and stole her wallet. Police found Kent's fingerprints at the crime scene. Kent, now age 16 and still on probation, was taken into custody and charged with rape and robbery. He confessed to these offenses and several similar incidents. Kent's mother retained an attorney, who, anticipating that the case would be transferred to an adult criminal court, filed a motion to oppose the transfer.

The juvenile court judge did not rule on this motion; instead, he waived jurisdiction and remanded Kent to the jurisdiction of the adult criminal court system. Kent was tried in U.S. District Court, found guilty of six counts of housebreaking, and found "not guilty by reason of insanity" on the rape charge. He received indeterminate sentences of 5 to 15 years on each count of housebreaking.

Kent's lawyer appealed the conviction, citing that the juvenile court judge failed to hear motions filed on Kent's behalf before waiving the case to adult criminal court and that Kent's due process rights had been denied. The U.S. Supreme Court heard the case, and Kent's conviction was reversed.

In *Kent*,[6] the Court ruled that, in a case involving transfer of jurisdiction, the juvenile defendant is entitled to certain essential due process rights: (1) a hearing; (2) representation by an attorney; (3) access to records involved in the transfer; and (4) a written statement of reasons for the transfer.

IN RE GAULT (1967)

On June 8, 1964, Gerald F. Gault, age 15, was taken into custody for making a crank telephone call to an adult neighbor and taken to a detention home by the sheriff of Gila County, Arizona. At the time, Gault was on juvenile probation for involvement in the theft of a woman's wallet in February 1964.

The complainant was not present at the juvenile court hearing on the following day. No one was sworn at the hearing, no transcript or recording of the proceedings was made, and no decision was issued. Gault was returned to the detention home—where he remained for several days—and then released. At a second hearing, on June 15, the judge committed Gault to the Arizona State Industrial School "for the period of his minority." Gault's attorney filed a petition for a writ of *habeas corpus* that was heard by the U.S. Supreme Court in December 1966.

In its May 1967 *Gault*[7] decision, the U.S. Supreme Court ruled that, in proceedings that might result in commitment to an institution, juveniles have the right to (1) reasonable notice of charges; (2) counsel; (3) question witnesses; and (4) protection against self-incrimination.

IN RE WINSHIP (1970)

Samuel Winship, age 12, was charged with stealing $112 from a woman's purse. Winship's attorney argued that there was "reasonable doubt" of Winship's guilt. The court agreed, but, because New York juvenile courts operated under the civil court standard of "preponderance of the evidence," it adjudicated Winship delinquent and committed him to a training school for 18 months.

The U.S. Supreme Court in *Winship*[8] ruled that the reasonable doubt standard should be required in all delinquency adjudications.

MCKEIVER v. *PENNSYLVANIA* (1971)

Joseph McKeiver, age 16, was charged with robbery, larceny, and receiving stolen property in Philadelphia, when he and 20 or 30 other juveniles took 25 cents from three boys. McKeiver had no prior arrests, was doing well in school, and was employed. McKeiver's attorney requested a jury trial; his request was denied, and McKeiver was adjudicated and put on probation.

McKeiver's attorney appealed to the state supreme court on the grounds that the juvenile court violated the Sixth Amendment's guarantee of the right to an impartial jury and the Seventh Amendment's guarantee of the right to a trial by jury. The state supreme court affirmed the lower court, arguing that, of all due process rights, a trial by jury is the one most likely to destroy the traditional nonadversarial character of juvenile court proceedings.

The U.S. Supreme Court in *McKeiver*[9] held that the due process clause of the Fourteenth Amendment did not require jury trials in juvenile court (although a state could provide a jury trial if it wished), that juries are not necessarily more accurate than judges, and that juries could be disruptive and therefore adversarial to the informal atmosphere of the juvenile court.

BREED v. *JONES* (1975)

In February 1971, Gary S. Jones, age 17, was charged with armed robbery and adjudicated delinquent in a Los Angeles juvenile court. The judge deferred disposition, pending receipt of a predisposition report and a recommendation from the probation department. Jones was returned to detention. When the court reconvened for the disposition hearing, the judge waived jurisdiction to adult criminal court. Counsel for Jones filed a petition for a writ of *habeas corpus*, arguing that waiver to criminal court violated the double jeopardy clause of the Fifth Amendment. The U.S. District Court denied the petition, saying that Jones had not been tried twice because juvenile adjudication is not a trial. Jones was tried in adult criminal court, convicted of robbery, and committed to the California Youth Authority for an indeterminate period.

The U.S. Supreme Court in *Breed*[10] ruled that juvenile adjudication for violation of a criminal statute is equivalent to a

> **Ethical Dilemma**
>
> Our juvenile justice system has a disproportionate number of minority inmates in custody. What role does discrimination play or is it a result of real differences in conduct? What should be done? For more information go to Ethical Dilemma 16-1 at http://www.mhhe.com/schmalleger2.

TABLE 16–1	**Oldest Age for Original Juvenile Court Jurisdiction in Delinquency Matters**
Age	**State**
15	Connecticut, New York, North Carolina
16	Georgia, Illinois, Louisiana, Massachusetts, Michigan, Missouri, New Hampshire, South Carolina, Texas, Wisconsin
17	Alabama, Alaska, Arizona, Arkansas, California, Colorado, Delaware, District of Columbia, Florida, Hawaii, Idaho, Indiana, Iowa, Kansas, Kentucky, Maine, Maryland, Minnesota, Mississippi, Montana, Nebraska, Nevada, New Jersey, New Mexico, North Dakota, Ohio, Oklahoma, Oregon, Pennsylvania, Rhode Island, South Dakota, Tennessee, Utah, Vermont, Virginia, Washington, West Virginia, Wyoming

criminal court trial; therefore, the double jeopardy clause applied. The Court ordered that Jones be released or remanded to the original juvenile court for a disposition hearing. Jones, now over 18, was released.

IMPACT ON JUVENILE COURT

The U.S. Supreme Court's decisions in these cases affirmed juvenile due process rights. As a result, the "best interest of the child" is no longer the only concern for juvenile courts; they also are required to protect the juvenile's constitutional rights.

The Contemporary Juvenile Justice System

State statutes define age limits for juvenile court jurisdiction. In most states, the juvenile court has original jurisdiction over all youths under age 18 at the time of offense, that they are taken into custody, or of referral to court (see Table 16–1[11]).

JUVENILE CRIME

Annually, U.S. law enforcement agencies take approximately 1.6 million juveniles into custody.[12] According to the Federal Bureau of Investigation (FBI), juveniles accounted for 16.5 percent of all 2002 arrests and 14.9 percent of all 2002 violent crime arrests. Most juvenile arrests were for property crime offenses (see Figure 16–1).

More than 90 percent of the cases handled by juvenile courts are for **delinquent offenses**—acts committed by a juvenile that, if committed by an adult, could result in criminal prosecution. The remaining cases are for **status offenses**—acts that are considered offenses only when they are committed by juveniles (e.g., running away, truancy, ungovernability, and liquor law violations). Liquor law violations account for 28 percent of status offense cases; truancy, 24 percent; running away, 16 percent; ungovernability, 12 percent; and miscellaneous other status offenses, 20 percent.[13]

PROFILE OF THE JUVENILE DELINQUENT

Of the estimated 1.8 million delinquency cases handled by U.S. juvenile courts in 1998:[14]

• 36 percent involved a juvenile under age 15;

delinquent offenses

Acts committed by juveniles that, if committed by adults, could result in criminal prosecution.

status offenses

Acts that are law violations only for juveniles such as running away, truancy, or ungovernability (sometimes referred to as *incorrigibility* or *being beyond parental control*).

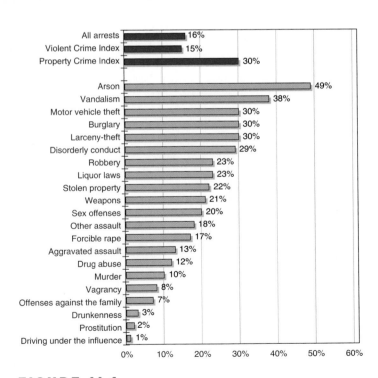

FIGURE 16-1

Percent of Arrests Involving Juveniles in 2002

Source: Adapted from Federal Bureau of Investigation, *Crime in the United States 2002* (Washington, DC: U.S. Government Printing Office, 2003).

- 76 percent involved boys;
- 67 percent involved white juveniles and 29 percent involved black juveniles; and
- 56 percent were drug and property offenses.

The Juvenile Justice Process

Juvenile offenders are processed through one or more of three phases of the juvenile justice process: intake, adjudication, and disposition. Juvenile courts throughout the United States process almost 1.8 million delinquency cases every year.[15] Figure 16–2 shows the flow of events in the U.S. juvenile justice system, and Figure 16–3 shows the number of juveniles who were adjudicated delinquent and their subsequent disposition. Juvenile courts also process approximately 162,000 status offense cases annually, none of which fall into the "delinquency" category.[16] Typically, 52 percent of status offense cases are adjudicated, and probation is ordered in almost 60 percent of the cases.[17]

INTAKE

intake

The first stage of the juvenile justice process. A court-appointed officer reviews the case and recommends a course of action—dismissal, informal disposition, formal disposition, or transfer to adult criminal court.

In the first phase of the juvenile justice process, **intake,** cases that are referred to juvenile court (by law enforcement agencies, social agencies, school personnel, parents or guardians, probation officers, or victims) are reviewed by a court-appointed officer (usually a prosecutor or probation officer), who recommends a course of action. The intake officer recommends that the case be (1) dismissed, (2) resolved informally (no petition is filed with the court), (3) resolved formally (a petition for an adjudication hearing is filed with the court), or (4) transferred to adult criminal court. The juvenile court establishes guidelines for the intake officer.

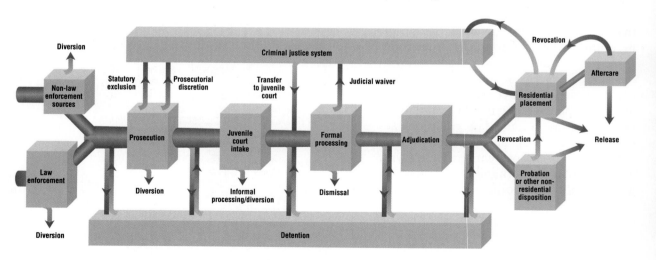

FIGURE 16-2
The Flow of Events in the U.S. Juvenile Justice System

Source: Office for Juvenile Justice and Delinquency Prevention.

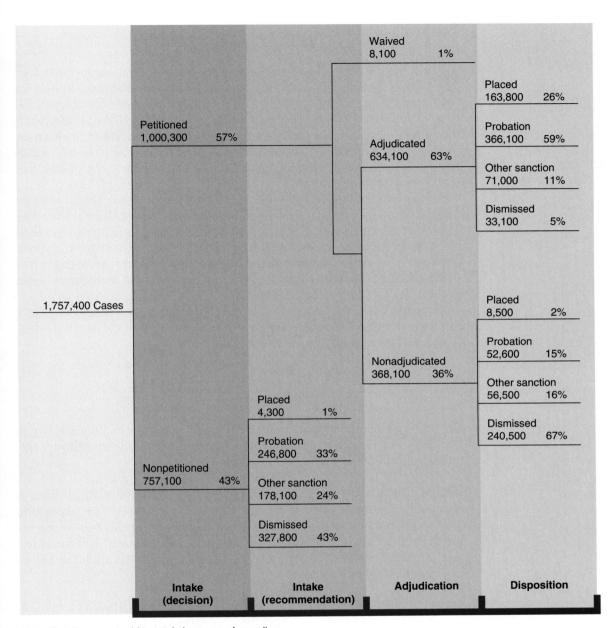

Note: Detail may not add to totals because of rounding

FIGURE 16-3
Juvenile Court Processing of Delinquency Cases, 1998

Source: Charles Puzzanchera, Anne L. Stahl, Terrence A. Finnegan, Nancy Tierney, and Howard N. Snyder, *Juvenile Court Statistics 1998* (Washington, DC: U.S. Department of Justice, Office of Juvenile Justice and Delinquency Prevention, June 2003), p. 47.

CAREER PROFILE

Sophia Nelson
Drug Counselor and Parent Educator   West Palm Beach, Florida

" Be ready for a roller-coaster ride of emotions. Every day your clients are up and down. Your personality has to be able to adjust to that for you to be successful. "

Sophia Nelson is a drug counselor and parent educator in West Palm Beach, Florida. She's been in her job for four years. As a drug counselor, she carries a caseload of 55 clients and conducts intake assessments and provides treatment. As a parent educator, she facilitates group counseling for children and single mothers. She assists the children in her groups in improving their communication and interaction skills and building confidence. She helps single mothers improve their life skills and develop and acquire the knowledge, skills, and attitudes they need to maintain strong family ties, find and keep good jobs, manage their finances, and lead productive lives.

Sophia graduated from Bethune-Cookman College in Daytona Beach, Florida, with a degree in criminal justice. The courses she recalls enjoying the most were those in which there was significant classroom discussion, especially courses in prisoners' rights, correctional counseling, and social policy. She says she knew from these courses that she wanted a career working with people. Now that she's a drug counselor and parent educator, she feels she contributes to her community by helping people avoid drugs and develop more healthy lifestyles. She says, "I see lives change each day."

For now, Sophia wants to keep working with drug offenders and teaching life skills to parents and children. But one day she hopes to be a prison warden and influence correctional policy on a large scale.

Criteria considered in the decision in many jurisdictions include severity of the alleged offense, any prior history of delinquent behavior, attitude, age, and emotional stability.

Informal Disposition   In cases that are resolved informally, disposition is decided by the intake officer, and the case goes no further. The disposition imposed is usually informal probation or some form of diversion—requiring the youth to make restitution or referring the youth to a local social service agency. Diversion is generally an option only for status offenders or low-risk delinquent offenders.

Formal Disposition   In cases that are to be resolved formally, the intake officer files a petition for an adjudicatory hearing and decides whether the youth should be confined while awaiting the hearing.

Detention Hearing   If the intake officer decides that secure placement is advisable, the youth is taken to a **juvenile detention facility**. In general terms, a juvenile detention facility serves to keep juvenile offenders in secure custody through various stages of the juvenile justice process, to protect the community and the juvenile, and to ensure appearance at scheduled hearings.

A juvenile who is placed in a detention facility by an intake officer must have a **detention hearing**, usually within 48 hours. During this hearing, the court reviews the intake officer's confinement decision and orders either release or continued detention pending adjudication and disposition.

juvenile detention facility

A facility for keeping juvenile offenders in secure custody, as necessary, through various stages of the juvenile justice process.

detention hearing

A judicial review of the intake officer's detention decision.

THE STAFF SPEAKS

Also during the detention hearing, the court determines whether the youth has legal representation and, if not, appoints defense counsel. The court may also appoint a **guardian *ad litem***, who serves as a special guardian for the youth throughout the court proceedings. In many jurisdictions, defense counsel also serves as guardian.

ADJUDICATION

In the second phase of the juvenile justice process, adjudication, a juvenile court hears the case. A **juvenile court** is any court that has original jurisdiction over matters involving juveniles.

Adjudicatory Hearing   During the adjudicatory hearing, attorneys typically present physical evidence, examine and cross-examine witnesses, and argue on behalf of their clients. If, after hearing arguments, the court rules that the evidence supports the allegations, a predisposition report is ordered and a disposition hearing scheduled.

DISPOSITION

In the third phase of the juvenile justice process, the juvenile court decides on a **disposition**.

Predisposition Report   The court's disposition decision is based on its review of the intake report (information regarding the current offense and any previous delinquent behavior; crime severity and prior adjudication greatly influence the decision) and the **predisposition report**, a document usually prepared by a probation officer, similar to the PSI discussed in Chapter 4. A predisposition report typically includes (1) medical and psychological background; (2) educational history; (3) information gathered from interviews with the juvenile, family members, and other people who know the youth; (4) availability of appropriate placement options; and (5) recommendations for suitable disposition. Any treatment "needs" of the youth are also considered.

Disposition Hearing   At the disposition hearing the court imposes the appropriate sanction. In some jurisdictions, the youth is remanded either to the state correctional system or to a social service agency. Many juvenile courts ensure that adjudicated juveniles receive an appropriate

guardian *ad litem*

A person appointed by the juvenile court, often defense counsel, to serve as a special guardian for the youth being processed through the juvenile justice system.

juvenile court

Any court that has jurisdiction over matters involving juveniles.

disposition

The third stage of the juvenile justice process in which the court decides the disposition (sentence) for a juvenile case.

predisposition report

A report that documents (1) the juvenile's background; (2) educational history; (3) information gathered from interviews with the juvenile, family members, and others; (4) available placement options; and (5) recommended dispositions.

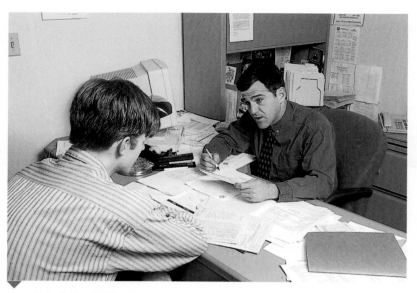

Juvenile probation officers play an important role in the juvenile justice process, beginning with intake and continuing through the period in which a juvenile is under court supervision. Why is writing the predisposition report such an important part of the probation officer's responsibilities?

disposition by establishing predefined sanctions based on type of offense, past delinquency, effectiveness of previous interventions, and assessment of special treatment, counseling, or training needs. Some of the more widely used sanctions are juvenile probation and commitment to group homes, residential treatment centers, boot camps, and juvenile correctional institutions.

If the sanction imposed is probation, the youth is permitted to remain in the community under the supervision of a court services officer. Figure 16–4 shows a supervision agreement used by the juvenile court of Topeka, Kansas.

If a youth poses a threat to public safety but incarceration is not warranted, the court may impose Intensive Supervised Probation (ISP). The major differences between regular probation and ISP are (1) more rigid conditions and (2) more frequent contact between the probation officer and the probationer—more face-to-face interaction, closer monitoring of the juvenile's activities, and more frequent evaluation of the juvenile's progress.

group home

A nonsecure residential facility for juveniles.

Another sanction that may be imposed is referral to a **group home**. Group homes are operated by private agencies, under contract with local or state government, or by the public corrections unit, under direction of the juvenile court. Typically, group homes accommodate 15 to 30 residents. They provide living quarters, recreational and leisure areas, kitchen and dining room, and meeting room space. Youths attend school in the community, participate in field trips, and may be granted special passes to visit family, attend religious services, or participate in activities. The range of services provided by the group home often depends on the type of offender usually referred. Some group homes are treatment oriented, providing individual and/or group counseling to youths with problems such as substance abuse or lack of self-control.

residential treatment center

A residential facility that provides intensive treatment services to juveniles.

Another community-based program is the **residential treatment center**. Residential treatment centers often provide long-term care and intensive treatment services.

Today, most states have juvenile boot camps. Boot camp programs vary in size, requirements, and structure. For the most part, juvenile corrections officials have been slow to accept the boot camp concept; they consider the amount of time devoted to military drill, ceremony, and exercise an encroachment on the time available for education or rehabilitation programs.

The most restrictive sanction that a juvenile court may impose is commitment to a juvenile correctional institution. Although the juvenile justice system is different from the adult criminal justice system, many juvenile

SUPERVISION AGREEMENT

Name _____ Andrea Johnson _____   Case Number _____ 00JV2751 _____

In accordance with authority conferred by the laws of the state of Kansas, you have been placed under the supervision of Court Services. It is the order of the Court that you comply with any special conditions, programs, or counseling as set forth by the supervision Court Services Officer.

The following conditions will apply:

__X__ 1.   You will attend all regularly scheduled appointments with the Court Services Officer and comply with their directions. If you are ill, it is your responsibility to make other arrangements.

__X__ 2.   You will obey all laws of the State and ordinances of the City. You are to immediately report any contacts with law enforcement to your Court Services Officer.

__X__ 3.   You are to obey the rules of your home. Persistent disobedience will be considered a violation of your supervision.

__X__ 4.   You are not to leave the state of Kansas nor change residence without permission of your Court Services Officer. You are to notify the officer of any change in address prior to moving. You will reside in the home of your parent(s) or approved guardian and will not be permitted to spend the night sway from home without prior permission of said parent(s) or guardian.

__X__ 5.   You will attend school every day and obey all school regulations. Suspension, truancies, and tardies could result in further court action. If you are home due to illness or school suspensions, you are to consider yourself on a form of house arrest. This means if you are ill, you are only permitted to leave to attend verifiable doctors appointments. If you are on suspension, you are not to leave your home unless you are with a parent or guardian.

_____ 6.   If you have been excused from attending school, you will obtain employment (get a job) and work faithfully at that job in order to maintain it. You will not quit any job without first discussing it with your Court Service Officer. If you are fired or laid off from a job, you are required to report that fact to your Court Service Officer by the end of the next business day.

__X__ 7.   You will neither possess nor carry firearms or other weapons.

__X__ 8.   You will neither use nor possess any alcohol, narcotics, or other controlled substances.

_____ 9.   You are to submit to chemical tests of blood, breath, or urine.

__X__ 10.   You have a curfew. If you are under the age of 15, your curfew is 9:00 p.m. Sunday through Thursday, and 10:30 p.m. Friday and Saturday. If you are 15 or older, your curfew is 10:00 p.m. Friday and Saturday. If you are 15 or older, your curfew is 10:00 Sunday through Thursday, and 12:00 midnight Friday and Saturday, Curfew means that you will be inside your own residence by the stated time, With parent or guardian's permission, you may attend a school or church sponsored function at the school or church you attend, but must be home not later than 30 minutes after the end of the event.

FIGURE 16-4
Sample Juvenile Court Supervision Agreement

___X__ 11.   It will be considered a violation of your supervision if you display clothing or insignia indicating membership in a gang, or carry a beeper, pager, or cellular telephone equipment.

___X__ 12.   You will not be discharged from supervision until all costs, fees, and restitution has been paid in full.

Traffic/City Ordinance Fines: _____	District Court Costs: $25.00	Guardian Ad Litem Fees: _____	Restitution: $299.95

___X__ Payment Plan _____ $54.16/month for 6 months _____

___X__ I will complete __20__ hours Community Service Work (X) in addition to, or (   ) in lieu of the above.

SPECIAL CONDITIONS:

___X__ a). Do not go into Electronics Plus for 6 months.

___X__ b). Within two weeks, write a letter of apology to Ms. Valerie Carte, owner of Electronics Plus.

___X__ c). Do not quit your weekend job at Bruno's grocery store until court costs and restitution are paid.

___X__ d). Write a three page paper on why shoplifting in wrong and hand deliver it to Judge Gray in three weeks.

I have read, understood, initialed and agreed to abide by all terms and special conditions of my supervision as explained by the assigned Court Services Officer. I understand fully that my failure to comply could result in the imposition of additional condition, revocation and/or out of home placement.

DATE: ___May 17, 2004___   SIGNED: ___Andrea Johnson___
                                               Respondent

                                        ___Rosalind Johnson___
                                            Parent or Guardian

                                        ___Gary Bayens___
                                          Court Services Officer

cc: Working File
      Respondent
      Parent or Guardian

FIGURE 16-4
Sample Juvenile Court Supervision Agreement—concluded

correctional institutions resemble adult correctional institutions. Access to the facilities is restricted, and perimeter fences are equipped with razor wire. Surveillance cameras, located throughout the complex, are monitored from a central security location. Housing units are austere physical structures that emphasize security.

Characteristics of the estimated 73,000 juvenile offenders confined in juvenile correctional facilities are similar to those of adult prisoners: 86 percent are male, 40 percent are black, 30 percent have committed property offenses (larceny, burglary, auto theft, or vandalism), and 25 percent have committed violent crimes (murder, rape, robbery, or assault).[18] The average age of confined youths is 15.[19] The average time served is eight months.[20]

A few states have responded to violent juvenile crime by enacting **blended sentencing** legislation in which the juvenile court may impose both a juvenile sentence and an adult criminal sentence. In 1996, the Kansas legislature passed a blended sentencing law that created a new category referred to as "extended jurisdiction juvenile prosecution," for serious and violent offenders.[21] Under this legislation, two sentences are imposed, but the adult criminal sentence is waived if the juvenile offender does not violate any of the provisions of the juvenile sentence.

blended sentencing

A two-part (juvenile and adult) sentence in which the adult sentence may be waived if the offender complies with all provisions of the juvenile sentence.

TRANSFER TO ADULT CRIMINAL COURT

All states and the District of Columbia allow adult criminal prosecution of juveniles under certain circumstances. Juveniles may be transferred to adult criminal court under one of three provisions: waiver, direct file, or statutory exclusion. Under **waiver provisions**, the juvenile court orders transfer of the case to adult criminal court. In all but four states (Massachusetts, Nebraska, New Mexico, and New York), a juvenile court judge is authorized to waive the juvenile court's original jurisdiction over cases that meet

waiver provisions

Provisions under which the juvenile court orders transfer of the case to adult criminal court.

An officer greets a new arrival at a boot camp for juveniles in Forsythe County, Georgia. Boot camp facilities for juveniles are meant to shock young offenders by reorienting them towards productive goals. What other kinds of programs might do the same thing?

direct file provisions

Provisions under which the prosecutor determines whether to initiate a case against a juvenile in juvenile court or in adult criminal court.

statutory exclusion provisions

Provisions under which adult criminal court jurisdiction for certain juvenile cases is established by state law.

teen courts

Courts in which youths adjudicate and impose disposition for a juvenile offense.

certain criteria and to refer them to criminal court for prosecution. Under **direct file provisions**, the prosecutor determines whether to initiate a case against a juvenile in juvenile court or in adult criminal court. Fifteen states have statutes that specify circumstances in which the prosecutor may make the transfer decision. Under **statutory exclusion provisions**, state law specifies adult criminal court jurisdiction for certain juvenile cases. An increasing number of states (28 in 1998) automatically exclude from juvenile court any cases that meet specific age and offense criteria. Fifteen states (in 1998) permit certain juvenile cases to be filed directly in criminal court. In 1998, 8,100 juvenile cases were transferred to adult criminal court. Of these, 36 percent involved a crime against a person, 40 percent involved property crime, 16 percent involved a drug law violation, and 8 percent involved a public order offense.[22]

Teen Courts

Teen courts, also called *peer* and *youth courts,* have become a popular alternative to the traditional juvenile court for relatively young or first-time offenders. The teen court was first used in Grand Prairie, Texas, in 1976.[23] Since then the number of teen courts has grown to an estimated 675 nationwide in 2000.[24] Teen courts handled approximately 65,000 cases in 1998.

Teen courts use one of four models: Adult Judge, Youth Judge, Tribunal, or Peer Jury. In the Adult Judge model, an adult serves as judge, ruling on legal terminology and courtroom procedure, and youth serve as attorneys, jurors, clerks, bailiffs, and so on. The Youth Judge model parallels the Adult Judge model, with the exception that a youth serves as judge. In the Tribunal model, youth attorneys present the case to a panel of three youth judges. The Peer Jury model uses no attorneys—the case is presented to a youth jury by a youth or adult, and the jury questions the defendant directly. Forty-seven percent of teen courts use the Adult Judge model, 12 percent the Peer Jury, 10 percent the Tribunal, and 9 percent the Youth Judge. The remaining 22 percent use more than one model.

Most teen courts require that the defendant plead guilty before participating in the program; only a small number determine guilt or innocence. In teen courts, offenders are sentenced by their peers.

Teen courts are particularly effective in jurisdictions in which disposition of misdemeanor offenses is given low priority because of heavy caseloads and focus on more serious offenders. Teen courts also teach young people valuable life skills and provide positive peer influence. Volunteers serve as jurors, attorneys, court clerks, bailiffs, and, in some cases, judges.

According to the Office of Juvenile Justice and Delinquency Prevention (OJJDP), community service was the most common disposition imposed in teen court cases in

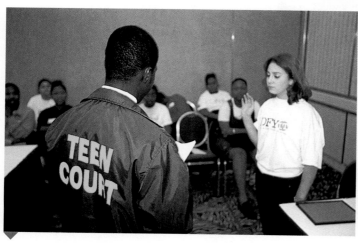

Teen courts allow youths to adjudicate peers accused of minor law violations and to impose a reasoned disposition on juveniles who come before them. Why might such courts be more effective than "traditional" juvenile courts?

I am a 33-year-old female who has been involved in both the juvenile and adult system. I was in the juvenile system for truancy and running away.

I feel that the juvenile justice system was effective due to the peer culture in the group home that I was ordered into. At first, I had a male probation officer that was too authoritative. I started responding to supervision better when I was transferred to a female probation officer. I felt she was more understanding.

My male juvenile P.O. had the attitude of "Do what I say, this is the way it is, no option or choices, just authority." When I was transferred to the female I started to make more progress. I think a female probation officer should have been assigned to me right away. However, the juvenile justice system was not effective in that I got too many chances.

I learned that even juveniles can't get away with too much. I learned the lesson to respect myself. I came from a very dysfunctional family, and the juvenile system taught me to not rely on family a lot and take care of myself.

The juvenile justice experience was not fun, but it was helpful.

—Anonymous

THE OFFENDER SPEAKS

the year 2000. Other dispositions included victim apology letters, apology essays, teen court jury duty, drug/alcohol classes, and monetary restitution.

Tammy Hawkins, Teen Court Coordinator for Odessa, Texas, says that teen court makes quite an impact when you give a teenaged jury sole discretion in handing down sentences. "The juvenile defendant receives this sentence from his peers and sees that they are saying, 'We as your peers do not agree with your actions and breaking the law is not acceptable.' A child is more likely to listen to one of their own, as opposed to an adult representative of the juvenile justice system. After all, as one defendant put it, 'Your peers are the ones that you want to accept you.'"[25]

▶ There has been a movement to waive violent juvenile offenders to the adult system. If convicted, such offenders serve their prison sentences in adult prisons. Should young offenders under the age of 18 be housed with sophisticated adult offenders? For more information go to Ethical Dilemma 16-2 at http://www.mhhe.com/schmalleger2.

Ethical Dilemma

Youth Gangs

In a 1999 OJJDP National Youth Gang Center (NYGC) survey, 3,024 law enforcement agencies reported that an estimated 30,818 gangs, with an estimated 846,428 members, were active across the United States.[26] About half of these agencies reported worsening gang problems. All states, and nearly all large cities, reported youth gang problems.[27]

The youth gang problem is one of the most important issues for juvenile corrections today. Many of the youths confined for serious crimes commit violent acts as gang members. For some correctional institutions, a primary housing consideration is a youth's gang affiliation—rival gang members must be housed separately. Juvenile correctional personnel regularly deal with problems that stem from gang-related activity within the institution: extortion, violence, and attempts to smuggle in contraband.

One of the more pressing gang-related issues facing today's juvenile corrections agencies is identification of youth gangs. According to the FBI, a **gang** is "a criminal enterprise having an organizational structure, acting as a continuing criminal conspiracy, which employs violence and any other criminal activity to sustain the enterprise."[28] Members of the group need not wear similar clothing ("colors") or tattoos or use hand signs (called "throwing") or initiation rituals, and the group might not even have

gang
A criminal enterprise having an organizational structure, acting as a continuing criminal conspiracy, that employs violence and any other criminal activity to sustain itself.

Eye On Corrections™

OJJDP to Shift Focus to Reentry and Faith-Based Initiatives

By Michelle Gaseau

The Office of Juvenile Justice and Delinquency Prevention will be taking a different path in coming years to work more quickly with violent youth upon their release and stop the cycle of violence as well as reach out to organizations in the community to help.

Former Administrator for the OJJDP Terrence S. Donahue discussed the shift in focus during an online videoconference broadcast earlier this month. The videoconference, which is archived on The Corrections Connection Juvenile Information network at www.juvenilenet.org, included examples of promising programs as well as a question and answer session with viewers across the country.

According to Donahue, the OJJDP will promote a major national initiative through the Office of Justice Programs to effect change with violent youth being released into the community. "Our primary goal is to create a process or system beyond probation and parole. To bring the most difficult youth back into the community and give them a chance to break a pattern that, if we don't change, will lead to becoming adult offenders," he said.

Donahue said the OJJDP would use a three-phase effort that will include a community-based reentry structure that encourages assistance from the community, transitional programming from facility to community, and the direct support of community programs. With community-based reentry, the OJJDP will encourage local communities to become involved in the transition of youth from facilities to help them stabilize there rather than return to their old habits of criminal activity. "We're hoping an assessment process [will take] a look at forensic needs, psychological needs, and substance abuse needs. A [transition] plan will link them while in the institution to services in the community," he said.

Donahue said transitional programs within institutions would also be refined and that community organizations that would provide the assistance for these youth would also receive funding. Mentoring programs and tutoring are examples Donahue gave as initiatives OJJDP would support as well as the involvement of the faith community.

He said the OJJDP in particular is looking to take action quicker with the 14- to 18-year-old population. "We really need to give more direction and intervention if we are going to stop the process of young juveniles entering the criminal life," he said. *This article has been reprinted in part from CCNN. To read this article in its entirety, go to www.corrections.com.*

a specific name (e.g., "Crips" or "Bloods"). Participation in criminal activity is what distinguishes community groups or social clubs from gangs. Other terms that have been used to distinguish among types of gangs are *street gang* and *youth gang*. The term **youth gang** tends to emphasize the age of a gang's members and is usually applied to gangs comprised of members between the ages of 12 and 24. According to the OJJDP, the phrase **street gang** refers to an organized group of people on the street, often engaged in significant illegitimate or criminal activity.[29] The membership age of street gangs varies, says OJJDP, while some street gangs are more street-based than others.[30]

Police departments tend to view gangs somewhat differently than our definitions might indicate. According to a recent survey of police agencies nationwide, the most important distinguishing characteristic of a youth gang is that its members commit crimes together.[31] The fact that the gang has a name and that its members "hang out together" is somewhat less important. See Table 16–2 for additional information on the criteria used by law enforcement agencies to distinguish youth gangs from other types of organizations.

Graffiti is a common method of communication for gangs.[32] It serves as the gang "newspaper" or "bulletin board," communicating many messages, including challenges, warnings, and pronouncements. Juvenile corrections professionals must become familiar with gang language, graffiti, and symbols to be able to deal with gang power and control. A partial listing of gang slang is shown in Table 16–3, and the names of some of the gangs currently operating in the United States are given in Table 16–4.

One reason that gangs successfully recruit members within the correctional setting is that the transition to a confined existence can be traumatic. Residents often challenge new arrivals, usually within the first few days, threatening physical harm to intimidate and exploit the youth. A youth who is the object of such an encounter may believe that joining a gang is the only way to survive.

youth gang

A gang whose membership is generally comprised of people between the ages of 12 and 24.

street gang

An organized group of people on the street often engaged in significant illegitimate or criminal activity.

TABLE 16–2	Criteria Used by Law Enforcement Agencies to Define a Youth Gang	
	Agencies selecting as most important criterion	
Gang Characteristic	**Number**	**Percent**
Commits crimes together	613	50%
Has a name	228	19
Hangs out together	119	10
Claims a turf or territory of some sort	104	9
Displays/wears common colors or other insignia	101	8
Has a leader or several leaders	89	7

Note: Number of observations was 1,221.

Source: Office of Juvenile Justice and Delinquency Prevention, *1998 National Youth Gang Survey* (Washington, DC: U.S. Department of Justice, November 2000), Table 45.

TABLE 16–3	Selected Terms Commonly Associated with Gangs
100-proof	The real thing
5-0	The police
13	Same as Sur
A-K	An assault rifle
All that	Something that possesses good qualities
Ay yo trip	To gain another's attention
Bag up	To be arrested by the police
Baller	A gang member who makes money
Bama	A person who can't dress
Bang	To fight to kill
Battle	To compete (i.e., as in freestyle rapping)
Blood	A member of a Los Angeles gang whose color is red
Blunt	A marijuana cigarette
Crab	A derogatory name for a Crip
Crip	A member of a Los Angeles gang whose color is blue
Cuz	A greeting, primarily used for Crip members
Down	To meet expectations
Five-O	The police
Fly girl	A very attractive female
Gangbanging	To participate in gang activity
Gat	A gun
Hay shen	A term for crack cocaine
Head up	To fight one-on-one
Hezee	A home or house
Highroller	A Crip term for someone in the gang who makes much money
Homeboy/homie	Someone from the neighborhood or gang
Hood	The neighborhood or turf
Jet	To go or leave
Jumped in	To be initiated into a gang, usually by getting beaten up
Kickin' it	To hang out with the gang
Knockin boots	To have sex
Loco	A crazy person
No diggity	To accept as the truth
OG	An original gangster; a designation awarded when someone has killed someone
Peel	To kill
Rifa	To rule
Salty (you)	To think you know everything
Set	An individual gang
Smoke	To kill
Snaps	A term for money
Sur	South or southside
Tecato	Heroin addict
Tray-eight	A .38-caliber handgun
Whadup dawg	A way of greeting friends
Yash	A greeting used on the telephone to attract attention

Source: Adapted from several online sources, including Gang Busters, Inc., *Gangs Terminology* (http://www.gang-busters.com/terms/html/terms.html); Mike Carlie, *Into the Abyss: A Personal Journey into the World of Street Gangs* (http://courses.smsu.edu/mkc096f/gangbook); Robert Walker, *Gangs OR Us* (http://www.gangsorus.com/slang.html); and http://www.velocity.net/~acekc/gangslang.htm.

TABLE 16-4	Names of Some Youth Gangs Operating in the United States	
3-D Kings	Insane Cobras	
10th Street Thugs	Insane Ganger Disciples	
Asian Boyz	Latin Counts	
Asian Family	Latin Disciples	
Asian Gangsters	Latin Eagles	
Baby Demons	Latin Force	
Bad Boys	Latin Kings	
Black Angels	Locos	
Black Gangster Disciples	Maniac Latin Disciples	
Bloods	Masters of Destruction	
Born to Kill	Mexican Mafia	
Brown Mexican Pride	Midnight Crypts	
Crips	Natoma	
Devil Boys	Nazi Low Riders	
Dogg Pound	Playboy Gangster Crips	
Fourth World Mafia	T-Dogs	
Gangster Disciples	Toy Soldiers	
Gaylords	Vice Lords	
Hmong Nation	Young Bloods	
Hollywood Criminals	West Side Crips	
Imperial Vice Lords	Wetback Power	

Note: Some of the groups listed here also contain adult members, although youth "branches" consist primarily of members aged 12 to 24.

Source: Adapted from Florida Department of Corrections, "Security Threat Groups in Florida," retrieved June 20, 2003, from http://www.dc.state.fl.us/pub/gangs/fl.html; Massachusetts Department of Corrections, "Gang Security Threat Group Information," retrieved June 20, 2003, from http://www.state.ma.us/doc/gang/Ganglist.htm; and Robert Walker, "Gangs in the United States," retrieved June 20, 2003, from http://www.gangsorus.com/usgangs.html.

Another reason that incarcerated juveniles join gangs is boredom. Their typical daily routine includes eating meals, exercise, and schoolwork. Leisure activities, family visitation, social programs, and other special services are intermittent and are permitted only if the juvenile complies with institution rules. Involvement in gang activity may represent excitement and adventure for confined juveniles.

The American Correctional Association and Juvenile Justice Reform

Since it was founded in 1870, the American Correctional Association (ACA) has advocated juvenile justice reform. In a 1997 campaign for juvenile justice reform, the ACA called for

- legislative and community action to fund and operate early-intervention strategies;

The Increasing Problem of Juvenile Crime: Resources and Knowledge to Reduce Delinquency

by Alan C. Young, Lakewood, Colorado Police Department

Juvenile victimization, violence, and crime are some of the most critical issues of the 21st century.

Instances of youth-violence have been widely publicized, such as the April 20, 1999, Columbine High School shootings. In the wake of recent and highly visible incidents of youth violence, many communities have begun youth service improvement initiatives. Schools, law enforcement agencies, and communities have started to form partnerships to curtail youth violence. Juvenile justice organizations are planning with victim services agencies, mental health organizations, parks and recreation departments, human and social services agencies, child welfare offices, and private industry to address youth problems. The improvement initiatives are often based on thorough assessments of the problems of troubled youth and work by inventorying the best practices in the nation for serving youth.

If funding of programs is a predictor, then the Office of Juvenile Justice and Delinquency Programs (OJJDPS) "Best Practices in Juvenile Accountability Overview"[1] provides a look into the future. It states that the following community goals should be funded:

- Develop and administer accountability-based sanctions for juvenile offenders.
- Hire additional juvenile judges, probation officers, and court-appointed defenders and fund pretrial services for juveniles.
- Hire additional prosecutors so cases can be prosecuted and backlogs reduced.

- Provide funding to enable prosecutors to effectively address problems related to drugs, gangs, and youth violence.
- Provide funding for technology, equipment, and training to assist prosecutors in identifying violent juvenile offenders and expediting their prosecution.
- Provide funding to enable juvenile courts and probation offices to be more effective in reducing recidivism.
- Establish court-based juvenile justice programs that target young firearms offenders through the creation of juvenile gun courts.
- Establish drug court programs to provide continuing judicial supervision over juvenile offenders with substance-abuse problems.
- Establish and maintain interagency information-sharing programs that enable the juvenile and criminal justice systems, schools, and social services agencies to make more informed decisions regarding the early identification, control, supervision, and treatment of juveniles who repeat serious delinquent or criminal acts.
- Establish and maintain accountability-based programs that work with juvenile offenders who are referred by law enforcement agencies or programs that are designed in cooperation with law enforcement officials.

A juvenile justice system given the resources and knowledge to match juveniles with appropriate treatment programs while holding them accountable for their behavior can have a positive and lasting impact on the reduction of delinquency.

According to OJJDP, the organizations with the best practices for the future will recognize each youth's developmental stage and build on each youth's individual strengths. They will combine restorative restitution and community service with victim input. They will teach juvenile offenders how to make positive choices and resolve disputes and help them understand how their actions affected their victims. They will use flexible, graduated sanctions and empower families to support positive activities for youth and success in school. Finally, they will connect youth with prosocial peers and conduct program activities in neighborhoods for all youth including those coming back to the community after confinement.[2]

ABOUT THE AUTHOR

Alan C. Youngs is division chief of the Community Resources Division of the Lakewood Colorado Police Department.

NOTES:
1. Juvenile Accountability Incentive Block Grants Program, *Best Practices in Juvenile Accountability: Overview* (Washington, DC: JAIBG, April 2003).
2. Adapted from J. Robert Flores, Administrator, "Best Practices in Juvenile Accountability: Overview," JAIBG Bulletin, April 2003.

Cambodian gang members in Long Beach, California. Juvenile gangs are a national problem, but they also permeate correctional settings. How can the influence of gangs be reduced inside of facilities such as detention centers?

- support of continued research and responsible action based on the results of research already available on prevention programs that work;
- support of system reforms that allow juvenile justice officials, family, social, educational, and other agencies and institutions to relate to a specific child and to work together for the best interests of the child, including accountability or shared use of confidential information about children at risk;
- support of programs that address the causes of violent and delinquent activity in communities;
- opposition to efforts to establish automatic certification of juvenile offenders to adult status for certain offenses;
- opposition to determinate sentencing for juvenile offenders; and
- support of the use of confidential systems for information sharing about juvenile offenders.[33]

Juvenile justice officials and the courts rely on the ACA for guidance. The ACA responds to more than 20,000 members, disseminating information, establishing advisory standards for juvenile corrections, providing technical assistance, and training juvenile corrections personnel.

SUMMARY

1▶ *Parens patriae* is a legal philosophy that is used to justify intervention in children's lives when their parents are unwilling or unable to care for them.

2▶ Houses of refuge, the first legally chartered custodial institutions for juvenile offenders, were established in the early 19th century. Reform schools, which were established in the middle of the 19th century, sought to reform rather than punish young offenders through vocational (especially trade and industrial), physical, and military education. Reform schools for girls used "cottagelike" residential units. Industrial schools emerged in the latter part of the 19th century and emphasized vocational training for youthful offenders.

3▶ The first completely separate juvenile court in the United States was established in Cook County (Chicago), Illinois, in 1899 and had jurisdiction over youth who committed acts that would be crimes if they had been committed by adults and over youth who were in danger of growing up to be paupers or in need of supervision. By 1945, separate juvenile courts had been established in all states.

4▶ Five U.S. Supreme Court decisions established due process rights for juvenile offenders:

- *Kent* v. *United States* (1966)—a juvenile who is to be transferred to adult criminal court is entitled to a hearing, representation by an attorney, access to records being considered by the juvenile court, and a statement of reasons for the transfer.

- *In re Gault* (1967)—in a proceeding that might result in commitment to an institution, a juvenile is entitled to reasonable notice of charges, counsel, question witnesses, and protection against self-incrimination.

- *In re Winship* (1970)—proof beyond a reasonable doubt, not simply a preponderance of the evidence, is required during the adjudicatory stage for a delinquent offense.

- *McKeiver* v. *Pennsylvania* (1971)—trial by jury is not a constitutional requirement for juvenile adjudication.

- *Breed* v. *Jones* (1975)—transfer to adult criminal court after juvenile court adjudication constitutes double jeopardy.

5▶ Most cases handled by the juvenile courts are for delinquent offenses—acts committed by a juvenile that if they had been committed by an adult could result in criminal prosecution. The remaining cases are for status offenses—acts that are offenses only when committed by juveniles. Such offenses include running away, truancy, ungovernability, and liquor law violations.

6▶ Juvenile delinquents are young people, usually under age 18, who commit acts that if they had been committed by an adult could result in criminal prosecution. The typical juvenile offender is a 16-year-old white male property offender.

7▶ The three stages of the juvenile justice process are intake, adjudication, and disposition. During the intake stage, a court-appointed officer recommends a course of action—dismissal, informal disposition, formal disposition, or, in some instances, transfer to adult criminal court—for a juvenile who has been referred to the juvenile court. Adjudication is judicial determination of guilt or innocence. Disposition is judicial imposition of the most appropriate sanction.

8 ▶ Disposition for the majority of juvenile offenders is probation. Other dispositions include placement in group homes, residential treatment centers, juvenile boot camps, or juvenile correctional institutions.

9 ▶ Teen court, an alternative to the traditional juvenile court, operates under one of four models: adult judge (an adult serves as judge); youth judge (a youth serves as judge); tribunal (youth attorneys present the case to youth judges); or peer jury (a youth or adult presents the case to a youth jury). Common teen court dispositions are apologies, educational and/or counseling programs, restitution, and community service.

10 ▶ A gang is a group of individuals involved in continuing criminal activity. Youth gangs are a serious problem for juvenile correctional professionals. For some juvenile institutions, gang affiliation is an important consideration in housing arrangements.

KEY TERMS

parens patriae, p. 579	guardian *ad litem, p. 589*	waiver provisions, *p. 593*
reform school, *p. 580*	juvenile court, *p. 589*	direct file provisions, *p. 594*
delinquent offenses, *p. 585*	disposition, *p. 589*	statutory exclusion
status offenses, *p. 585*	predisposition report, *p. 589*	provisions, *p. 594*
intake, *p. 586*	group home, *p. 590*	teen courts, *p. 594*
juvenile detention	residential treatment	gang, *p. 595*
facility, *p. 588*	center, *p. 590*	youth gang, *p. 597*
detention hearing, *p. 588*	blended sentencing, *p. 593*	street gang, *p. 597*

QUESTIONS FOR REVIEW

1. Explain the principle of *parens patriae.*
2. Distinguish among houses of refuge, reform schools, and industrial schools.
3. Where and when was the first completely separate juvenile court established?
4. What five U.S. Supreme Court rulings established due process rights for juveniles? What impact did each have on juvenile court proceedings?

5. What is a *delinquent offense?* A *status offense?*
6. What is the typical juvenile delinquent's age? Gender? Race?
7. Identify and explain the three stages of the juvenile justice process.
8. What are the three provisions for transferring juveniles to adult criminal court?
9. What is *blended sentencing?*

REVIEW & APPLICATIONS

REVIEW & APPLICATIONS

10. What is a guardian *ad litem*?

11. What is a predisposition report? To what does it compare in adult criminal court?

12. What is the most common sanction imposed by a juvenile court?

13. What is a group home? A residential treatment center?

14. What are the characteristics of the typical offender confined in a juvenile correctional institution?

15. What is teen court? How does it operate?

16. What is a gang? What impact do youth gangs have on juvenile correctional institutions?

17. Why is it important for juvenile corrections professionals to stay informed about gang affiliation, membership, and graffiti?

18. What is the American Correctional Association's position on juvenile justice reform?

THINKING CRITICALLY ABOUT CORRECTIONS

▶ ▶ ▶ **Sentencing Project**

The Sentencing Project reports that abuse (physical and sexual) and suicide rates are higher for children who serve time in adult correctional institutions than for those held in juvenile correctional institutions—youths held in adult institutions are 7.7 times more likely to commit suicide, 5 times more likely to be sexually assaulted, twice as likely to be beaten by staff, and 50 percent more likely to be attacked with a weapon.[34] What conclusions might you draw from this report?

▶ ▶ ▶ **Public Access to Juvenile Court Proceedings**

Juvenile court proceedings are becoming more accessible to the public. At least 21 states now permit open juvenile court proceedings for serious or violent crime charges or repeat offenses. In 1995, Georgia passed a law allowing the public admission to adjudicatory hearings for youths who have been charged with delinquent offenses.

1. Do you think juvenile court proceedings should be open to the public?

2. Why or why not?

ON-THE-JOB DECISION MAKING

▶ ▶ ▶ **Youth Violence**

In recent months, there has been a spate of violent crimes committed by youthful offenders in your community, including numerous murders, assaults, rapes, and armed robberies. Gang violence, in particular, seems to be escalating.

Josh McFadden, a crusading journalist in your town, has been whipping up public sentiment for the inclusion of a "get-tough" referendum on the upcoming ballot. In daily newspaper articles and during frequent guest appearances on local television programs, McFadden beats the same old drum: It's time to treat all criminals as criminals, no matter what their age, he says. His strident calls for abolition of delinquency laws and automatic waiver to adult court of all juveniles who commit violent felonies seem to be touching a nerve.

You are a juvenile probation officer. You and your coworkers truly believe juveniles need special handling that is different from what they would receive in the adult criminal justice system.

In recent weeks, you have been flooded with requests to appear on various discussion panels. Your supervisor has been reluctant to enter the fray, but authorizes you to participate in an upcoming panel discussion to be televised within the community. Josh McFadden will be on the panel.

1. What issues would you present to support retention of the current procedures for handling juvenile offenders?

2. How would you address the waiver of jurisdiction to adult court question?

▷ ▷ ▷ Teen Court

Read the following case:

IN THE MATTER OF: BETH LEONARD

CHARGES: Three (3) counts of retail theft.

Hoover police were summoned to the Hoover Mall branch store of Fancy This on March 17, 2000, at 11:20 A.M. regarding a shoplifter. Beth Leonard, a 16-year-old high school honor student, was arrested at 11:52 A.M. for three (3) counts of retail theft.

An employee noticed Beth entering the dressing room with a blue short outfit and a swimsuit. Beth exited the dressing room carrying only her purse. After a quick scan of the room, the attendant, unable to locate the clothes, called security. Beth was led to the manager's office, where she confessed to putting the items on under her clothing and attempting to leave.

When the police arrived, they asked for identification and discovered a bottle of Spring Musk Perfume bearing a new, undamaged sales sticker in Beth's purse. Upon prompting, Beth admitted that she had taken this item from the Perfumeria, a mall perfume store.

A further search of Beth's purse revealed two pairs of earrings with sales stickers from Carter's, a mall accessory shop. Beth admitted to taking these items without purchasing them.

While searching Beth's purse, the officer located her wallet and found $85 in cash. When asked why she didn't just pay for the items, Beth stated she was planning to purchase a gift for her parents' wedding anniversary.

A conference was later held between Beth, her parents, and the arresting officer. During this conference, Beth stated that all her girlfriends did this and they never got caught. She was dared by one to bring certain items to her with the sales tags still intact to prove that she had not paid for them. It was dumb, but she did it, and she was sorry.

1. If you were the intake officer handling this case, would you recommend that a teen court handle it?

2. Why or why not?

CORRECTIONS ON THE WEB

▷ ▷ ▷ FBI Website

Go to the FBI Web page at http://www.fbi.gov and in the search box type *"gang."* Then scroll to the document *Law Enforcement True Story, Gang Alert.* Read the scenarios and decide which the FBI would classify as a gang.

▷ ▷ ▷ National Youth Court Center

Access the National Youth Court Center at its website (http://www.appa-net.org). Determine the status of teen courts in your state.

▷ ▷ ▷ Street Gangs

Read Professor Mike Carlie's online book *Into the Abyss: A Personal Journey into the World of Street Gangs* (http://courses.smsu.edu/mkc096f/gangbook/default.htm).

REVIEW & APPLICATIONS

Appendix

Careers in Corrections

Career development experts tell us that career development is a lifelong process that involves continual and consistent maintenance. Your interests, skills, and preferences change throughout your life. Thus, it is important that you know the steps involved in career planning, developing employability and job readiness, and finding the right job.[1]

Career Planning

Successful career planning is a continual process of self-assessment, occupational research, decision making, contacting potential employers, working at a job, and reevaluating your situation (see Figure A–1).

SELF-ASSESSMENT

self-assessment

Learning who you are and what you can and want to do by evaluating your interests, skills, and values.

Career planning begins with **self-assessment**—learning who you are and what you can and want to do by evaluating your interests, skills, and values. Self-assessment tools, which pose a series of questions and identify potential career choices based on your answers, are available from most college and university career counselors as well as in bookstores and on the Internet. The questions involved pertain to (1) personal information—education, experience, achievements, personality factors, and interest in various activities; (2) skills—abilities in such areas as athletics, analysis, management, communication, and persuasion; and (3) values—ranking work-related issues (such as job location, pressure, security, responsibility, teamwork, and wages) in order of importance.

In addition, for a position in corrections, certain personal and physical attributes will be required by your employer. The California Department of Corrections (www.cdc.state.ca.us), for example, requires that a correctional officer candidate have a "history of law-abiding behavior" and "emotional maturity and stability, . . . leadership ability, tact, . . . alertness, integrity, dependability, good judgment, and the ability to work cooperatively with others." The Texas Department of Criminal Justice (www.tdcj.state.tx.us) requires, among other qualifications, that candidates in addition to not having any felony convictions not have had Class A or B misdemeanor convictions within the past five years.

Begin at the bottom and work up.
Periodically reevaluate your career/life plans by starting again at step 1.

				Planning	
				Re-evaluation	
			Work		
			Work offers/acceptance	Success at work	
		Employment Contacts			
		Job/work search	Resumes/letters	Job/work interviews	
	Decision Making				
	Career objectives	Personal objectives	Community service	Lifelong learning	
Occupational research					
Information search	Information interview	Job shadow	Hands-on-experience	Trends	
Self-assessment					
Personality/attitudes	Skills/achievements	Knowledge/learning style	Values	Interests	Entrepreneurism

You may need to move from an upper step to a lower one (e.g. from step 4 to step 2) should a lack of openings in a particular field require research into a different one.

FIGURE A–1
Steps to Career/Life Planning Success

Source: Career Services at University of Waterloo.

In general, correctional officer applicants must

- be at least 18 years old (in some states 21 years old);
- be a U.S. citizen;
- have a high school diploma or general equivalency certificate (GED); and
- have no felony convictions.

OCCUPATIONAL RESEARCH

The second step in career planning is research. Make a list of the potential career choices identified by your self-assessment, as well as any additional careers that you would like to know more about. Other jobs in corrections besides officer positions include health service and information science jobs. See Table A–1 for a list of typical jobs at a state department of corrections. Research job requirements, job characteristics, working conditions, duties, employment outlook, salary, and methods of entry for each of the career alternatives. Read everything you can find and talk to people.

Reading The best source for information on careers and job opportunities is the Internet. See Table A–2 for a list of sources on the Internet for criminal justice jobs. Information is also available in libraries (public, school, and special) and at the career development centers at your school. Among others, three U.S. Department of Labor publications—*Dictionary of Occupational Titles, Occupational Outlook Handbook,* and *Guide for Occupational Exploration*—provide information on more than 20,000 jobs and cross-reference each career field with others that are similar in nature. The U.S. Department of Labor also publishes two periodicals, *Occupational Outlook Quarterly* and *Monthly Labor Review,* that are excellent sources of information about occupational trends and salaries.

TABLE A-1	Virginia Department of Corrections Position Types

The following is a list of some types of positions that may be found in major institutions, field units, probation and parole offices, detention centers, work centers, day reporting centers, regional offices, or central offices.

Accountant	Office manager
Agriculture supervisor	Office services assistant
Assistant warden	Office services specialist
Boiler operator	Operations officer
Building grounds superintendent	Personnel analyst
Building/grounds supervisor	Physician
Business manager	Plumber steamfitter
Buyer	Postal assistant
Carpenter	Probation officer
Corrections lieutenant	Program support technician
Corrections major	Programmer/analyst
Corrections nurse technician	Psychologist
Corrections officer	Radiologic technologist
Corrections sergeant	Recreation supervisor
Dental assistant	Regional administrator
Dental hygienist	Regional director
Dentist	Regional program manager
Electrician	Registered nurse
Electronics technician	Safety specialist
Executive secretary	Secretary senior
Fiscal assistant	Store clerk
Fiscal technician	Store operations manager
Food service supervisor	Storekeeper
H_2O/treatment plant operator	Surveillance officer
Human resource officer	Treatment program supervisor
Human rights advocate	Warden
Inmate hearings officer	Warehouse supervisor
Nurse clinician	Welder
Nurse practitioner	

Source: http://www.vadoc.state.va.us/about/employment/opportunities.htm.

networking

Meeting new people who can give you information about careers, the job market, and specific positions. It is often done through people you know.

Talking to People   **Networking** is meeting new people (often through people that you know) who can give you information about careers, the job market, and specific positions. Broadening your acquaintance base to include solid professional contacts through networking builds long-term professional relationships that facilitate job hunting and professional development and enhance personal growth.

Developing a network is an integral part of job hunting; in some fields, networking is considered the most effective method of job searching and is

TABLE A-2	Job Information Websites of Criminal Justice Agencies and Other Groups

American Correctional Association Job Bank http://www.aca.org/career/home.asp

Bureau of Alcohol, Tobacco and Firearms (BATF) job information http://www.atf.gov/jobs/index.htm

Central Intelligence Agency (CIA) job information http://www.odci.gov/employment/index.html

Correctional Service of Canada job information http://www.csc-scc.gc.ca//text/employment_e.shtml

Drug Enforcement Administration (DEA) job information http://www.usdoj.gov/dea/job/agent/page-01.htm;
   http://www.usdoj.gov/06employment/index.html

Federal Bureau of Investigation (FBI) job information https://fbijobs.com; http://www.fbi.gov

Federal Bureau of Prisons (BOP) job information http://bop.gov/recruit.html; http://www.bop.gov

Federal Jobs Digest http://jobsfed.com/

U.S. Customs Service http://www.customs.ustreas.gov; http://www.customs.ustreas.gov/xp/cgov/careers/

U.S. Department of Justice Career Opportunities Search http://jobsearch.usajobs.opm.gov/a9dj.asp

U.S. Citizenship and Immigration Services http://uscis.gov

U.S. Marshals Service http://www.usdoj.gov/marshals

the number-one way people obtain jobs. It has no time limit, nor does it end when you secure a position. Start developing contacts before you begin your career planning, and keep in touch with those contacts—they might hear of a job opening for you. Continue to keep in touch after you get a job—you may need to use your network again.

How do you begin networking? How do you establish contacts if you do not have any? Anyone can be a contact: the student who sits next to you in class, your parents' next-door neighbor, your doctor, your professor, previous supervisors, people with whom you have something in common (attending the same school, working out at the same gym, belonging to the same professional association, etc.). Join organizations and participate in local programs that are related to your area of interest.

One of the key elements of networking is talking to people about your career interests and goals. Most people are more than willing to share information; in fact, the majority are flattered by the attention and truly want to help. Talk to the people you meet about what they do, their backgrounds, and their perspectives on the job market for their specialties, and ask if they know anyone else with whom you might speak. Take advantage of any and every opportunity to build your network—talk to people while you are waiting in line, riding the bus, attending a seminar or playing golf. The other key element is follow-up—keep your contacts apprised of your career status; let them know about your latest career move or your progress in a new job.

Informational interviewing, talking to people who are currently employed in a career field that you are interested in exploring, is an excellent means of researching a particular job or position. Introduce yourself to the person you wish to talk to, either by calling or writing, and ask if you might have 30 minutes of time to discuss the job or position. Explain that you are gathering career information and ask for an appointment. An informational interview can provide

informational interviewing
Talking to people who are currently employed in a career field of interest.

- an accurate portrayal of the career field you are investigating;
- specifics about necessary skills, entry-level positions, employment trends, and so on;
- information about related volunteer, part-time, or internship opportunities;
- additional professional contacts;
- increased confidence in interacting with professionals;
- information about possible job openings; and
- information about concerns that should not be discussed in a job interview (e.g., salaries, hours, and minority issues)

DECISION MAKING

The third step in career planning is making your career decision. Carefully review all of the information that you have gathered. For which of the corrections careers that you researched are you best qualified emotionally, physically, and academically? Which are most appealing? Which are most likely to enhance your career development? List career choices in order of preference. Then begin your job search (see Figure A–2).

Seeking Employment

Finding a job can be a tough process that requires an overwhelming amount of thought, time, and energy. Make the job search part of your everyday routine; decide how much time you will devote to the search and when, and stick with that decision.

Be creative in your job search; use all of the resources available to you—classified ads, Internet ads, professional associations, advisors, employment services (local and Internet), and so on—to identify available positions. One of the best sources of information on careers in corrections is the Internet. Your state's department of corrections will most likely list employment opportunities on its Website. Federal or private corrections positions can also be researched on the Internet.

According to the U.S. Department of Justice National Institute of Corrections (http://www.nicic.org), people interested in a career in corrections should contact the federal, state, or local agency in which they would like to work or contact a private correctional services provider.

- For the Federal Bureau of Prisons, go to http://www.bop.gov.
- For links to state corrections department Websites, go to http://www.corrections.com/state.html#state_DOC_online.
- For links to county sheriffs offices, go to http://www.corrections.com/county.html.

Once you have narrowed your search and found a position to which you would like to apply, the next step is to submit a resume or an application. Many civil service jobs (i.e., county, state, or federal government jobs in which hiring and promotion are determined by competitive examinations) do not require a resume; all applicants instead complete a detailed application.

JOB SEARCH CHECKLIST

✓ Establish specific goals. Determine two or three potential career areas that are compatible with your values, skills, and interests.

✓ Prepare your search tools. Write a resume and sharpen your interviewing skills. Are you ready for your interview?

✓ Identify and research potential employers by utilizing different resources, such as the following:

- Career development center
- Professional associations
- Newspaper classifieds
- Internet sites

- Deans/professors/other advisors
- Trade organizations
- Career library resources/texts
- State/county employment offices

✓ Conduct informational interviews, which differ from job interviews—they provide you with an excellent opportunity to meet with individuals in a specific career field and obtain up-to-date information on that field. This can help your career decision making and develop a network of contacts.

✓ Initiate contact with employers. Establish a mailing list of potential employers within the targeted fields you identified from your earlier research. Mail your resume with a focused cover letter and then follow up with telephone calls to request interview appointments.

✓ Follow up with each contact. Remember, follow-up is your responsibility.

✓ Get organized, and stay on schedule. Devote at least 20 hours a week to your job search. Develop a schedule and create a list of organizations, contact people, contact dates, and outcomes.

✓ Accept an offer—consider these factors when offered a position:

- size of the organization
- job security
- travel/relocation requirements
- hours
- formal training arrangements
- people you met with

- advancement potential
- entry level salary
- salary potential
- geographical factors
- education/fringe benefits
- name recognition of employer

FIGURE A–2
Job Search Checklist

SUBMITTING AN APPLICATION

The first step in applying for a correctional officer position and many other positions in corrections is to submit an application, either by mail, in person, or online. Check with the agency to see where these applications can be obtained. In some states, applications can be obtained at any state Employment Development Department office. Make a copy of the application for yourself before you submit it.

WRITING YOUR RESUME

The job to which you are applying may require that you submit a resume. The state of Minnesota, for instance, requires that an application and a resume be submitted for civil service positions.

resume
A list of your job and other related experiences and education.

A good **resume** or list of your job and other related experiences and education, may not necessarily get you the job, but a bad resume can ensure that you do not get the job. Your resume is not meant to convey your complete life history. Through your resume, you convey your capability for a particular position; it must be clear, directed, and persuasive—its objective is to secure an interview. Your resume should (1) support a career direction and (2) be selective. Career direction gives the resume focus; all of the information included in the resume should support the career direction that you are trying to convey. Career guidance experts tell us, "You should make yourself as attractive as possible on paper so that the employer feels as though she would be missing out by not interviewing you."[2] Your resume should project you as someone who produces, accomplishes, and is results oriented. Use active verbs and descriptive terms; that is, write, "researched and drafted reports" rather than "responsible for research and reports." What works best today is a conservative style and a focus on key achievements—particularly those that relate to the position for which you are applying; find out as much as you can about the prospective employer and then modify the resume to highlight those items that will most benefit the company or organization. The most effective resume is one that is tailored to a specific job; the results are well worth the extra effort. According to Tom Jackson, "The Perfect Resume is a written communication that clearly demonstrates your ability to produce results in an area of concern to selected employers, in a way that motivates them to meet you."[3]

When creating your resume, keep the following in mind:

- Follow the "one page rule"—one page is ideal; two are acceptable (however, do not add a second page simply to expand content); three are unacceptable.
- Your resume should be scanned easily: it must be organized effectively to carry the reader's eye from major point to major point (a prospective employer will look for words and phrases that convey the necessary qualifications).
- The eye should be drawn to eye-catching type; use **bold,** CAPITAL, or underscored text to emphasize a particular item, but do not overdo it.
- Use bullets to break job and skill descriptions into easy-to-read component parts that begin with eye-catching verbs.

- Highlight talents, skills, and experience to some extent, but do not overdo it.
- Word processing allows great flexibility in the selection of fonts, but choose something simple. Avoid ornateness and avoid combining several fonts.
- Employers want employees who can set goals and complete tasks; present yourself as someone who gets things done.
- Identify your strengths and convey them on paper, this is not arrogance or boasting. The person who is reading your resume wants to know that you are exceptional.
- Always honestly summarize your work experience and skills, including any technologies you are familiar with (spreadsheet or database software, computer hardware, telephone systems, word processing, etc.).
- Do not use personal pronouns; "I" is implied.
- Complete sentences are not necessary.
- Avoid abbreviations.

Your resume can be a primary tool in obtaining more attractive positions, thus, extra time spent on its preparation is a good investment. All resumes should be accurate and truthful, but each should highlight different strengths, as they relate to the potential job. The resume should go through several stages of drafting and editing until it is as perfect as it can be.

RESUME FORMAT

The selected resume format should establish a natural flow of information that simplifies the review process, and should incorporate a consistent pattern of information placement, allowing the reader to anticipate where certain information will be found. An employer usually reviews information on the left side first—names of employers, job titles, and so on should be placed on the left. Less important information (dates, locations, etc.) should be placed on the right. No resume format is universally preferred, although the chronological resume and the functional resume are the most widely used (See Figures A–3 and A–4).

Chronological Resume The **chronological resume** format is the most widely accepted and preferred resume style. It is most effectively used by people who have established or are establishing credentials within a particular field or whose credentials show career growth and direction within one particular employment environment. To be effective, the chronological resume should project a sense of quality by emphasizing skills and accomplishments, and it should be organized carefully (in terms of layout) to present most effectively a particular background. In this format, your education and work experience are presented in reverse time sequence, with the most recent degrees and jobs appearing first. In developing a chronological resume,

chronological resume
A resume that organizes information in reverse time sequence and emphasizes work history.

- de-emphasize history for the sake of content;
- devote more space to the most recent position;

Derrick A. Salyer
1555 Campus Lake Drive, Richmond, KY 40477
(606) 555-1212

OBJECTIVE

To secure a position as a juvenile court probation officer.

EDUCATION

Bachelor of Science, May 2004
Eastern Kentucky University, Richmond, KY
Major: Correctional Services
GPA: 3.20/4.00
Dean's List, Distinguished Undergraduate Award

Associate of Arts, December 1999
Houston Community College, Houston, TX
Major: General Studies

Self-financed 50% of education through work, loans, and scholarships

EXPERIENCE

Intern, January–May 2004
Kentucky Department of Juvenile Justice, Richmond, KY
—Assisted department staff with hosting of three live national satellite videoconferences
—Served as liaison to downlink sites
—Attended all planning sessions

Intern, August–December 2003
Richmond Juvenile Court Services, Richmond, KY
—Assisted intake officer with presentence report investigation and writing
—Attended detention and adjudication hearings
—Answered questions relating to the presentence report

Sales Associate, March 2000–July 2003
Just For Feet, University Mall, Richmond, KY
—Coordinated sales associates' schedules
—Managed evening cashier sales associates
—Achieved and maintained Best Shift/Least Checkout Errors monthly in 1998

ACTIVITIES

Criminal Justice Student Association, 2004 President, 2003 Vice President
Alpha Phi Sigma (Criminal Justice Honor Society) Spirit Award, 2002

REFERENCES

Available upon request.

FIGURE A–3
Chronological Resume Format

Tanisha Williams
1500 Maplewood Drive, Palmdale, CA 93510
(213) 555-1212

CAREER INTERESTS:
Correctional industry management

SKILLS:
PLANNING/ORGANIZATION
- Successfully established and operated a T-shirt design shop
- Developed market/trade survey programs to determine customer interest
- Initiated radio T-shirt give-away contests
- Established connection with local homeless shelter to employ the homeless

ADMINISTRATION/MANAGEMENT/SALES MARKETING
- Supervised team of 20 sales associates
- Hired and delegated supervision of 18-person T-shirt design shop to two associate managers
- Approved corporate sales contracts
- Increased corporate sales 32%
- Managed commercial sales advertisements—three radio, one television, and one newspaper—averaging $32,000 annually

EMPLOYMENT EXPERIENCE

OWNER AND OPERATOR   **2001–Present**
TANISHA'S SHIRTS AND DESIGNS
Lancaster, California

SALES ASSOCIATE AND MANAGER   **1995–2001**
HUTTON'S TEES
Lancaster, California

EDUCATION

BACHELOR OF SCIENCE, CRIMINAL JUSTICE ADMINISTRATION, 2003
California State University
Northridge, California

REFERENCES AVAILABLE UPON REQUEST

FIGURE A-4
Functional Resume Format

- fully describe the three or four positions most supportive of the career direction—summarize other work experience unless it is exceptionally meaningful;
- avoid excessive repetition in detail and substance; and
- emphasize career growth.

Functional Resume   The **functional resume** emphasizes abilities over work history by organizing information according to skills, results, contributions made, or functions successfully performed. It is best used by those who are changing careers or have been out of the work force for some time. In developing a functional resume,

- select functions that describe job-related abilities (versatile abilities, if possible);
- list functions in order of importance and relevance to your career direction, emphasizing accomplishment and achievement while illustrating specific abilities; and
- avoid including employment detail (employer names, dates of employment, job titles) within the functional descriptions; include a work history section that sets forth this information.

What to Include   Regardless of which resume format you use, your resume should include the following:

1. Identification—name (first, middle initial, last), address (permanent and/or present), telephone numbers (work and/or home, fax), and e-mail address (if applicable). Accurate information is critical; a prospective employer who is unable to reach you with the information provided is not likely to try to verify contact information. If the information changes, correct your resume and reprint it.
2. Objective/Career Interest—the type of work you want to do, the position you want, or the skills/attributes you anticipate using and the employment sector in which you wish to establish a career. A career interest statement is a broader, long-range career direction that simply lists the field or occupation in which you wish to be employed.
3. Education—schools attended, degrees received, dates of graduation, majors and other concentrations of study, and academic achievement (class rank and grade point average for an undergraduate or graduate program). The education section can also include extracurricular activities of particular significance and academic honors and awards.
4. Skills/Accomplishments/Qualifications—descriptions, grouped by major functional skill area. Choose three to five functional skill areas that correspond to your career objective.
5. Experience. For a chronological resume, list experience in reverse chronological order, beginning with your current or most recent position.
6. Optional—personal statements (relatively neutral comments about personal interests such as a foreign language, community activity, travel, sports, public speaking, unique hobbies, and military experience); honors and awards (academic honors, memberships in national honor societies, scholarships, etc.); curricular and cocurricular activities

(those that demonstrate leadership), community activities, or volunteer experiences (demonstrates personal work habits, leadership potential, and level of motivation/commitment); professional associations and licenses; and publications.

References should always be listed on a separate page, not on the resume. Do not approach the selection of references casually; your references are critical to the strength of your employment credentials.

The resume copy should be meticulously reviewed before it is forwarded to a potential employer (you might have a friend or a qualified professional critique it).

THE COVER LETTER

If your prospective employer requires a resume, a cover letter (see Figures A–5 and A–6) should always accompany it. Like the resume, the cover letter should be direct, persuasive, descriptive, and attractive. Remember, the cover letter is specific to the potential employer; it should emphasize credentials and experience that apply to the position. Your cover letter can differentiate you significantly from others competing for the same position. The following is the basic format for the cover letter:

1. First paragraph—serves to get the attention of the person receiving the letter and answers the question "Why are you writing?" This can be as simple as stating that you are "a graduating student seeking employment at [name of employer]" or that you are "responding to a job posting from [name of source]." If (in the ideal situation) you are referred by a professional or personal contact, use it to your advantage—begin your letter with "Karen Davis recommended that I contact you regarding employment."

2. Second paragraph—details your interest in and your fit with the company or organization. Keep in mind that employers are more interested in what you can do for them than in what they can give you. Answer implied questions, such as the following:

   a. "Why are you interested in working for this firm or organization?" This part need only be a sentence or two but should include reference to specifics about the organization—its mission, type of work, geographic location, size, reputation in the community, and/or types of positions available. Employers' hiring decisions are often based not only on qualifications, but also on level of interest in the firm or organization. Be genuine. This is an opportunity to show that you researched the employer.

   b. "Why are you the right person for the job?" In two or three sentences, tell the prospective employer what skills you will bring to the job without reiterating details included in your resume. Give specific examples of skills and accomplishments related to this position that you emphasized in your resume. You might consider a wrap-up sentence commenting on how the organization might benefit from your skills and experience.

3. Last paragraph—expresses appreciation for the prospective employer's time and consideration and provides details about what you plan to do next—how you will follow up (e.g., with a telephone call) and when

WRITING A COVER LETTER

Your Street Address
City, State Zip Code
Today's Date

Contact Person's Name
Contact Person's Title (if applicable)
Company/Organization Name
Street Address
City, State Zip Code

Dear (Contact Person's Name, or Contact Person's Title if name is unknown):

OPENING PARAGRAPH: Clearly state why you are writing, name the position or type of work for which you are applying, and mention how you heard of the opening. If you are writing without prior knowledge of an available opening, say that you are interested in openings that may currently be available.

MIDDLE PARAGRAPH: Explain why you are interested in working for this employer, and/or your reasons for desiring this type of work. Describe applicable experience, achievements, or other qualifications in this environment or type of employment.

MIDDLE PARAGRAPH: Refer the reader to your enclosed resume, which positively illustrates your training, skills, and experience. DO NOT DUPLICATE RESUME INFORMATION IN THE COVER LETTER—"highlight," and elaborate on how you can make a tangible contribution to this company/organization.

CLOSING PARAGRAPH: Use a closing appropriate to acquiring an interview. If you know the contact person's name and telephone number, use a pro-active strategy—say that you will call to request an appointment in the very near future. If you do not know the contact person's name, ending your letter with a question often encourages a response (e.g., May we meet soon to discuss this matter further?)

Sincerely,

Your signature

Your Full Name (typewritten)

Enclosure

FIGURE A–5
Tips on Writing Cover Letters

1500 Maplewood Drive
Palmdale, CA 93510
January 12, 2004

Ms. Caroline Butterworth
Human Resources
State of California
Department of Corrections
Sacramento, CA 94283-0001

Dear Ms. Butterworth:

I am applying for the position of Supervisor of Correctional Industries in your Southeast
Region. I am a graduate of California State University, Northridge, with a bachelor's
degree in criminal justice administration. I believe that my work experience and education
make me a strong candidate for this position.

My degree in criminal justice administration has given me an excellent understanding of
the criminal justice field, particularly institutional corrections and the corrections industry.
I completed a 15-week internship at the Chino, California Institution for Men, where I
gained considerable insight into prison industry operations—especially security—and the
importance of helping prisoners to develop and maintain job skills prior to release.

My work experience spans 10 years, which includes self-employment (in T-shirt
design and sales—I hired and supervised a staff of 20) and industry organization and
management.

I look forward to speaking with you about utilizing my business skills and criminal justice
qualifications in the position of Supervisor of Correctional Industries. I will contact you
next week to arrange an interview. Please call me if you have questions.

Sincerely,

Tanisha Williams

Tanisha Williams

Enclosure

FIGURE A-6
Sample Cover Letter

(either a specific date or within a certain number of weeks; wait at least one week). If you do not know whom to call to follow up, you might ask the employer to contact you at a particular telephone number or by e-mail. If a job listing says, "No phone calls, please," state in the cover letter that you look forward to hearing from the employer soon.

THE EXAMINATION PROCESS: TESTING AND BACKGROUND INVESTIGATION

If you have applied for a correctional officer position, once your application has been submitted, the next step will be a written examination. Most state and federal agencies will send you a letter after your application has been processed. The letter will give you a scheduled test date. In general, to be hired as a correctional officer, candidates must

- pass a written exam;
- pass a psychological exam;
- have good vision (with glasses or contact lenses), including no color-blindness, and good hearing (with or without a hearing aid);
- be able to perform the essential functions of a correctional officer, with or without reasonable accommodation (i.e., be in good physical health and of sound mental and emotional condition, demonstrated by passing a physical abilities test);
- pass a drug test;
- undergo a background investigation and be fingerprinted;
- pass a medical exam; and
- be eligible to carry a firearm.

Written Exam   The written exam most likely will test your skills in grammar, spelling, punctuation, reading comprehension, and basic mathematics (see Table A–3).

Physical Abilities Test and Vision Test   After successful completion of all written examinations, you will be scheduled for a physical abilities test and possibly a visual acuity test.

Background Check   A background investigation will be conducted by the agency. It may include fingerprinting, photos, and a background interview. This investigative phase includes a thorough check of police records, personal, military, and employment histories; and reference checks. The criteria for the background investigation are respect for the law, honesty, mature judgment, respect for others, employment and military record, financial record, driving record, and use of drugs and intoxicants. Background investigations may take a few months to complete.

THE JOB INTERVIEW

job interview

A meeting with a prospective employer in which a job applicant projects his or her most impressive qualities.

The **job interview** plays a very important role in your job search. To interview successfully, you must understand the interview process and prepare well. Do not assume that the interview is or should be one-sided. During an

TABLE A-3   State of Illinois Examination Information for Corrections Officers

Three examinations are required of all applicants: the Test of Adult Basic Education (TABE), the Inmate Disciplinary Report Written Exam (IDR), and the Physical Agility Test (PAT). Applicants must meet the minimum standards on each examination to be eligible for hire. Upon completion of these examinations, an oral interview is conducted with each applicant. Applicants have the opportunity to earn up to a total of 100 screening points and are placed on eligibility lists in rank order. Institutions hire applicants based on scores.

Weighted values are assigned to each of the following dimensions based on its relationship to successful job performance.

1. *Test of Adult Basic Education (TABE):* The Department of Corrections requires that all applicants for security positions successfully complete a written reading comprehension and vocabulary examination. Applicants must receive a minimum score equivalent to the 10th-grade reading level. Applicants meeting this criterion can move on to the next phase in the screening process. The TABE is used to establish a baseline for reading comprehension. No screening points are awarded for its successful completion.

2. *Written Examination:* This written examination consists of the viewing of a videotaped incident after which the applicant is required to answer 30 multiple choice questions regarding the video. This examination measures an individual's ability to observe and interpret information.

3. *Physical Agility Test:* Since being in good physical shape is a prime consideration for being a correctional officer/youth supervisor trainee, applicants are required to successfully complete a physical agility test to be eligible for hire. The test is comprised of four exercises designed to measure an applicant's ability to perform the job duties required of a correctional officer/youth supervisor trainee. Applicants must complete all four of the exercises to continue in the screening process. No screening points are awarded for successful completion of the Physical Agility Test.

4. *Oral Interview:* Applicants are interviewed by a team of two Department of Corrections officials using a standardized interview questionnaire. Upon conclusion of the interview, the officials independently rate the applicant based on the six categories. An applicant can receive from 0 to 5 points in each category for a total of 30 possible points. The average of the scores is calculated to determine each applicant's total interview score.

Source: http://www.idoc.state.il.us/subsections/jobopp/page2.shtml

interview, you must *project* your most impressive qualities. In other words, you must sell yourself to the prospective employer. As part of the evaluation process, the interviewer will be deciding how you will function as an employee. Therefore, it is essential to demonstrate how your skills, knowledge, and experience match the requirements of the position for which you are interviewing.

It is essential that you speak confidently (not arrogantly) about your skills, knowledge and experience. In preparing, take time to think about answers to potential interview questions (see Table A–4). When the interviewer asks a question for which you are unprepared, think before you speak; take a second or two and organize your thoughts. Then answer as best you can.

Reread your resume or the copy of your application before every interview—chances are the interviewer did just that, too. In addition, review

TABLE A-4 Fifty Questions Most Often Asked by Employers During an Interview

1. Tell me about yourself.
2. What personal goals, other than those related to your occupation, have you established for yourself for the next 10 years?
3. What do you see yourself doing five years from now?
4. What do you really want to do in life?
5. What are your short-range and long-range career objectives?
6. How do you plan to achieve your career goals?
7. What are the most important rewards you expect in your career?
8. What do you expect to be earning in five years?
9. Why did you choose the career for which you are preparing?
10. Which is more important to you, the money or the type of job?
11. What do you consider your greatest strengths and weaknesses?
12. How would you describe yourself?
13. How do you think a friend or professor who knows you well would describe you?
14. What motivates you to put forth your greatest effort?
15. How has your college experience prepared you for your career?
16. Why should I hire you?
17. What qualifications do you have that makes you think that you will be successful in this environment/setting?
18. How do you determine or evaluate success?
19. What do you think it takes to be successful in an organization like ours?
20. In what ways do you think you can make a contribution to this organization?
21. What qualities should a successful supervisor possess?
22. Describe the relationship that should exist between a supervisor and those reporting to him or her.
23. What two or three accomplishments have given you the most satisfaction? Why?
24. Describe your most rewarding college experience.
25. If you were hiring a graduate for this position, what qualities would you look for?
26. Why did you select your college or university?
27. What led you to choose your field or major?
28. What college subjects did you like best? Why?
29. What college subjects did you like least? Why?
30. If you could do so, how would you plan your academic study differently?
31. What changes would you make in your college or university? Why?
32. Do you have plans for continued study? An advanced degree?
33. Do you think that your grades are a good indication of your academic achievement/ability?
34. What have you learned from participation in extracurricular activities?
35. In what kinds of environments are you most comfortable?
36. How do you work under pressure?
37. In what part-time or summer job have you been most interested? Why?

continued on next page

TABLE A-4	Fifty Questions Most Often Asked by Employers During an Interview—*concluded*

38. How would you describe the ideal job for you following graduation?
39. Why did you decide to seek a position with this organization?
40. What do you know about this organization?
41. What three things are most important to you in your career/job?
42. Are you seeking employment in an organization of a certain size? Why?
43. What criteria are you using to evaluate the organization/employer for which you hope to work?
44. Do you have a geographical preference? Why?
45. Will you relocate? Do relocations bother you?
46. Are you willing to travel?
47. Are you willing to spend at least six months in training?
48. Why do you think you might like to live in the area in which our organization is located?
49. Describe a major problem you have encountered and how you dealt with it.
50. What have you learned from your mistakes?

your resume or application for possible questions you might be asked. Formulating answers ahead of time will allow you to be more relaxed and articulate during the interview. If you applied for a civil service job, review the examination bulletin and know the duties and responsibilities of the classification for the position. Job interview attire can be summed up in two words: *conservative* and *businesslike*. Proper dress will give you confidence and enhance your professional image. For most professional-level jobs, the standard dark suit is appropriate for both men and women; less formal clothing may be more appropriate for some jobs. Use common sense. College faculty and career planning counselors can help, as well as someone you may know who is employed in the same field as the position for which you are interviewing. Keep perfume or cologne and jewelry to a minimum. Do not chew gum or other food during the interview.

Take with you to the interview copies of your resume or application, your list of references (or reference letters), any other relevant documents such as your social security card and driver's license, and your transcripts. (A civil service interview panel, however, may not ask to see any of these documents.) It is also a good idea to bring a pen or pencil and notebook and a list of questions.

For some positions, two interviews are required. A typical first job interview usually lasts 30 to 60 minutes, although it may run longer. Often called a *screening interview*, the first interview is used to shorten a long list of candidates. You also may be asked to complete a job-related questionnaire that may serve to shorten the list of candidates (see Figure A–7).

An oral interview with a civil service panel for a position in corrections may be structured or unstructured. It may include questions regarding your personal history; problem-solving abilities; ability to work effectively with other people, including supervisors, peers, and a diverse public; ability to

SUPPLEMENTAL QUESTIONNAIRE
SELF-SCREENING
PROBATION AND PAROLE OFFICER I

The following requirements are needed by all candidates for this position. If you answer "yes" to all requirements listed, sign below and return this form with your completed application. If you answer "no" to any of the requirements, do not complete the rest of the form and do not submit an application. An answer "no" in any one area will result in a rating of "not qualified" for this position.

1.   Are you willing and able to cope with unmotivated and hostile individuals who have committed all types of crimes?

         Yes _____   No _____

2.   Are you willing to do field checks knowing that you will be going into areas where you may be subject to threats or physical danger?

         Yes _____   No _____

3.   Are you willing to testify before the court, parole board, and other judicial hearings to answer questions, present progress reports, and make recommendations?

         Yes _____   No _____

4.   Are you willing to be trained in the use of firearms and deadly force?

         Yes _____   No _____

5.   Are you willing to be trained in the use of defensive tactics which involve physical contact?

         Yes _____   No _____

6.   Are you willing to participate in the arrest of criminal offenders?

         Yes _____   No _____

The answers I have given are true and correct to the best of my knowledge, and I understand that I must be willing and able to perform tasks requiring physical strength and agility.

SIGNATURE _____ DATE _____

FIGURE A–7
Sample Job Screening Questionnaire

communicate effectively; and personal qualities including motivation, integrity, and self-discipline. If the interview is for a civil service position, note the names of the panel members who are conducting the interview. An interview for a civil service job may be tape recorded. The recording is in your best interest. It can be used to verify the discussion that took place on either the part of the interviewee or the panel if an appeal is filed.

Remain alert for indications that you are on track. If the interviewer seems relaxed, is following closely, and encouraging you with comments and nods, you are probably on target. If the interviewer appears puzzled, stop and restate your reply. If the interviewer has obviously lost interest, try getting back on track by asking if you covered the point adequately. Maintain eye contact when answering questions, but do not be afraid to avert your eyes when thinking about an answer. A firm handshake will end the interview on a positive note. Thank the interviewer or panel members.

A prospective employer may request a second interview, either because initial interviews indicated that more than one of the applicants might qualify for the position or because others are involved in the hiring decision. Keep in mind when preparing for the second interview that you may now be in direct competition with others whose qualifications are as appropriate as yours. Prepare carefully by doing the following:

- engage in a more extensive study of the organization to gain in-depth knowledge;
- evaluate your skills, knowledge, and experience and how they are applicable to the position for which you are applying;
- review general interview skills;
- gather appropriate documents, such as resumes, references, and transcripts;
- compare your personal agenda with the organization's agenda;
- make additional copies of pertinent records; and
- prepare a list of questions.

Remember, interviewing is a two-way street. Not only is it an opportunity for the organization to ask questions of you, it is also your opportunity to learn more about the organization. Get answers to your questions; this information will help you decide which of the job offers you receive you should accept, and asking the same question of different individuals will allow you to compare responses. Whatever the outcome of any job interview, bear in mind that the employer is thinking first of organizational needs, not of you. Do not let rejections weaken your self-confidence.

THE THANK YOU LETTER

A thank you letter should always immediately follow a job interview. In fact, you should start thinking about the thank you letter as soon as the interview is over and mail it within 24 hours of the interview. The thank you letter is not just "a nice thing to do"; it is also a sales opportunity—another opportunity for you to "sell" yourself. The thank you letter should be simple; the following is the basic format:

1. First paragraph—thank the reader for the interview and restate the position for which you are applying and your interest in it.

2. Second paragraph—restate your qualifications and reiterate what you have to offer to the company. Refer to specific points discussed during the interview.

3. Last paragraph—restate the first paragraph.

Reevaluation

Because your interests, skills, and preferences change, you should periodically reevaluate your career choice to determine if you could more effectively use your skills, abilities, and talents in a different occupation or at a different organization. Correspond with your contacts on a fairly regular basis and investigate available positions, but be careful not to take steps that may jeopardize your present position—you may find that it is still the best job for you.

KEY TERMS

self-assessment, *p. A-0*

networking, *p. A-2*

informational interviewing, *p. A-3*

resume, *p. A-6*

chronological resume, *p. A-7*

functional resume, *p. A-10*

job interview, *p. A-14*

Endnotes

Chapter 1

1. Susan Candiotti, "Walker Lindh Sentenced to 20 Years," CNN.com Law Center, October 4, 2002, http://www.cnn.com/2002/LAW/10/04/lindh.statement (accessed March 29, 2003).
2. Richard A. Serrano, "FBI Probing Prison Attack on John Lindh: American Taliban Was Accosted by Another Inmate," *San Francisco Chronicle*, March 7, 2003, http://www.sfgate.com/cgi-bin/article.cgi?file=/chronicle/archive/2003/03/07/MN50908.DTL (accessed March 28, 2003).
3. Fox Butterfield, "Crime Keeps on Falling, but Prisons Keep on Filling," *New York Times* News Service, September 28, 1997.
4. Quoted ibid.
5. John P. Conrad, "The Pessimistic Reflections of a Chronic Optimist," *Federal Probation*, vol. 55, no. 2, 1991, p. 4.
6. Ibid., p. 8.
7. See, for example, Jory Farr, "A Growth Enterprise," http://www.press-enterprise.com/focus/prison/html/agrowth industry.html (accessed March 28, 2002).
8. Timothy A. Hughes, et al., *Trends in State Parole, 1990–2000* (Washington, DC: U.S. Department of Justice, 2001).
9. Margaret Werner Cahalan, *Historical Corrections Statistics in the United States, 1850–1984* (Washington, DC: U.S. Department of Justice, 1986).
10. Paige M. Harrison and Allen J. Beck, *Prisoners in 2002* (Washington, DC: BJS, 2003).
11. Lauren E. Glaze, *Probation and Parole in the United States, 2001* (Washington, DC: BJS, 2002).
12. Sidra Lea Gifford, *Justice Expenditure and Employment in the United States, 1999* (Washington, DC: Bureau of Justice Statistics, 2002), p. 3. Corrections expenditures include the costs of operation and employment for jails, prisons, probation, parole, and correctional administration.
13. Ibid.
14. U.S. General Accounting Office, "Federal and State Prisons: Inmate Populations, Costs and Projection Models," Letter Report, November 25, 1996, GAO/GGD-97-15, http://www.fas.org/irp/gao/ggd97015.htm (accessed March 23, 2003).
15. Butterfield.
16. Cahalan.
17. American Correctional Association, *Vital Statistics in Corrections* (Lanham, MD: American Correctional Association, 2000).
18. Gifford, p. 6.
19. Uniform Crime Reporting statistics in this chapter come from FBI, *Uniform Crime Reports: Crime in the United States, 2002* (Washington, DC: U.S. Government Printing Office, 2003).
20. Some of the material in this section is adapted from Bureau of Justice Statistics, *The Nation's Two Crime Measures* (Washington, DC: U.S. Department of Justice, November 1995).
21. Callie Rennison and Michael R. Rand, *Criminal Victimization, 2002* (Washington, DC: BJS, August 2003).
22. The figure may be somewhat misleading, however, because an offender who commits a number of crimes may be prosecuted for only one.
23. Much of the following material is adapted from Bureau of Justice Statistics, *Report to the Nation on Crime and Justice*, 2d ed. (Washington, DC: BJS, 1988), pp. 56–58.
24. President's Commission on Law Enforcement and Administration of Justice, *The Challenge of Crime in a Free Society* (Washington, DC: U.S. Government Printing Office, 1967), p. 159.
25. National Advisory Commission on Criminal Justice Standards and Goals, *Corrections* (Washington, DC: U.S. Government Printing Office, 1975), p. 2.
26. Bureau of Justice Statistics, *Correctional Populations in the United States, 1995* (Washington, DC: U.S. Government Printing Office, 1997).
27. Bob Barrington, "Corrections: Defining the Profession and the Roles of Staff," *Corrections Today* (August 1987), pp. 116–120.
28. Arlin Adams, *The Legal Profession: A Critical Evaluation,* 93 Dick. L. Rev. 643 (1989).
29. Harold E. Williamson, *The Corrections Profession* (Newbury Park, CA: Sage, 1990), p. 79.
30. Adams.
31. Ibid., p. 20.
32. P. P. Lejins, "ACA Education Council Proposes Correctional Officer Entry Tests," *Corrections Today*, vol. 52, no. 1 (February 1990), pp. 56, 58, 60.
33. Mark S. Fleisher, "Teaching Correctional Management to Criminal Justice Majors," *Journal of Criminal Justice Education,* vol. 8, no. 1 (Spring 1997), pp. 59–73.
34. See Robert B. Levinson, Jeanne B. Stinchcomb, and John J. Greene III, "Corrections Certification: First Steps Toward Professionalism," http://www.aca.org/development/doc_certificationfirststeps.pdf (accessed March 23, 2003).
35. See the ACA's Professional Certification Program Web page at http://www.corrections.com/aca/development/certification.htm for more information.
36. The AJA defines a jail manager as "a person (sworn or civilian) who directs, administers, and/or is in charge of the operations of an adult jail facility, division, bureau, department, program, and/or shift; and/or a person (sworn or civilian) who supervises the work and performance of an employee or employees in an adult jail facility." See AJA, *CJM: Handbook for Candidates*, http://www.corrections.com/aja/cjm_handbook.pdf (accessed March 25, 2003).
37. Michale Omi and Howard Winant, *Racial Formation in the United States: From the 1960s to the 1980s* (New York: Routledge and Kegan Paul, 1986), p. 145.

38. National Center for Women and Policing, *Equality Denied: The Status of Women in Policing, 2001* (Beverly Hills, CA: NCWP, 2002), p. 11.
39. Dianne Carter, "The Status of Education and Training in Corrections," *Federal Probation,* vol. 55, no. 2 (June 1991), pp. 17–23.
40. Williamson.

Chapter 2

1. *Gazette d' Amsterdam,* April 1, 1757. Cited by Michel Foucault, *Discipline & Punish: The Birth of the Prison,* trans. Alan Sheridan (New York: Vintage Books, 1995).
2. Edward M. Peters, "Prison Before the Prison: The Ancient and Medieval Worlds," in Norval Morris and David J. Rothman (eds.), *The Oxford History of the Prison* (New York: Oxford University Press, 1995), p. 6.
3. James Hastings et al., *Dictionary of the Bible,* vol. 1 (New York: Charles Scribner and Sons, 1905), pp. 523 ff. Cited in Arthur Evans Wood and John Barker Waite, *Crime and Its Treatment: Social and Legal Aspects of Criminology* (New York: American Book Company, 1941), p. 462.
4. Foucault, p. 8.
5. See Peters, pp. 14–15.
6. Wood and Waite, p. 462.
7. Pieter Spierenburg, "The Body and the State: Early Modern Europe," in Norval Morris and David J. Rothman (eds.), *The Oxford History of the Prison* (New York: Oxford University Press, 1995), pp. 52–53.
8. Ibid., p. 53.
9. Harry Elmer Barnes and Negley K. Teeters, *New Horizons in Criminology,* 3d ed. (Englewood Cliffs, NJ: Prentice Hall, 1959), p. 290.
10. Some of the information in this section comes from Harry Elmer Barnes, *Story of Punishment* (Montclair, N.J.: Patterson Smith, 1930) and George Ives, *A History of Penal Methods* (London: Stanley Paul, 1914).
11. Barnes and Teeters, p. 349.
12. Ives, p. 53.
13. Henry Burns Jr., *Corrections: Organization and Administration* (St. Paul, MN: West, 1975), p. 86.
14. Barnes and Teeters, p. 292.
15. Ives, p. 56.
16. John Howard, *The State of the Prisons* (London: J. M. Dent, 1929).
17. Spierenburg, p. 53.
18. Burns, p. 87.
19. Spierenburg, p. 62.
20. See Abbott Emerson Smith, *Colonists in Bondage* (Chapel Hill, NC: University of North Carolina Press, 1947).
21. For a good account of the practice, see Robert Hughes, *The Fatal Shore: The Epic of Australia's Founding* (Vintage Books, 1988).
22. James Trager, *The People's Chronology* (Henry Holt and Company, 1994).
23. See Aleksandr Solzhenitzyn, *The Gulag Archipelago, 1918–1956* (1974) and *The Gulag Archipelago 2 and 3* (1975, 1978).
24. "Siberia," *Microsoft Encarta 96 Encyclopedia* (Redmond, WA: Microsoft Corporation, 1995).
25. Barnes and Teeters, p. 293.
26. Peters, p. 7.
27. Spierenburg, pp. 49–77.
28. Ibid., p. 67.
29. Spierenburg, p. 72.
30. Randall McGowen, "The Well-Ordered Prison," in Norval Morris and David J. Rothman (eds.), *The Oxford History of the Prison* (New York: Oxford University Press, 1995), p. 83.
31. Foucault, p. 11.
32. See Wood and Waite, p. 463.
33. Harry Elmer Barnes, *The Repression of Crime* (New York: Doran, 1926), p. 101.
34. John Howard, *The State of the Prisons* (London: J. M. Dent and Sons, Ltd., 1929).
35. Spierenburg, pp. 49–77.
36. McGowen, p. 86.
37. "Enlightenment, Age of," *Microsoft Encarta '96, CD-ROM* (Redmond, WA: Microsoft Corporation, 1995).
38. Ibid.
39. Some of the information in this section comes from The Nanaimo Region John Howard Society (of Canada) at http://www.island.net/~ccampbel/index.html (accessed May 30, 2003).
40. John Howard, *The State of the Prisons.*
41. Randall McGowen, "The Well-Ordered Prison: England 1780–1865," in Norval Morris and David J. Rothman (eds.), *The Oxford History of the Prison* (New York: Oxford University Press, 1995), p. 87.
42. Some of the information in this section comes from *The Internet Encyclopedia of Philosophy,* http://www.utm.edu/research/iep/ (accessed June 26, 1999).
43. Some of the information in this section comes from the Bentham Project at University College, London, http://www.ucl.ac.uk/Bentham-Project/jb.htm (accessed June 25, 1999).
44. For further information, see Frank E. Hagan, "Panopticon," in Marilyn D. McShane and Frank P. Williams III (eds.), *Encyclopedia of American Prisons* (New York: Garland, 1996), pp. 341–342.
45. Wood and Waite, p. 456.
46. From "The Secret of Great Workers," *The Penny Magazine,* vol. 1, no. 1 (March 31, 1832), citing M. Dumont, "Recollections of Mirabeau."
47. See Margaret Wilson, *The Crime of Punishment* (New York: Harcourt, Brace and Co., 1931), p. 165.
48. See the All Saints Project, http://www.drsoft.com/allsaints/pnotes.htm (accessed July 30, 2003). This site includes input from the Royal Canadian Mounted Police and the Nova Scotia Crime Prevention Association.
49. See Lucia Zedner, "Wayward Sisters: The Prison for Women," in Norval Morris and David J. Rothman (eds.), *The Oxford History of the Prison* (New York: Oxford University Press, 1995).
50. Zedner, p. 333.
51. Ibid., p. 336.
52. Ibid.

Chapter 3

1. Details for this story come from Fred Bayles, "Kennedy Kin Skakel Convicted of Murder," *USA Today,* June 7, 2002; and Fred Bayles, "Parts of Victim's Diary Read at Start of Skakel Trial," *USA Today,* May 7, 2002.

2. Connecticut Penal Code, Chapter 952, Section 53a–35a.

3. John P. Conrad, "The Pessimistic Reflections of a Chronic Optimist," *Federal Probation,* vol. 55, no. 2 (1991), p. 7.

4. Sigmund Freud, *Totem and Taboo,* trans. and ed. by James Strachey (New York: Norton, 1990).

5. Lisa Kennedy, "The Miseducation of Nushawn Williams," *POZ online,* August 2000, http://www.poz.com/archive/august2000/inside/nushawnwilliams.html (accessed June 20, 2002); Jackie Cooperman, "AIDS Scare Triples in Scope," ABCNEWS.com, October 28, 1997.

6. "'AIDS Monster' Denied Parole in New York," *Austin Chronicle,* August 31, 2001, http://www.austinchronicle.com/issues/dispatch/2001-08-31/cols_aboutaids.html (accessed June 20, 2002).

7. Andrew von Hirsch, *Doing Justice: The Choice of Punishments* (New York: Hill and Wang, 1976), pp. 48–49.

8. Morgan O. Reynolds, *The Reynolds Report: Crime and Punishment in the U.S.,* NCPA Policy Report No. 209 (Dallas, TX: National Center for Policy Analysis, 1997), http://www.public-policy.org/~ncpa/studies/s209/s209.html (accessed August 30, 2003).

9. Edwin Zedlewski, *Making Confinement Decisions,* Research in Brief (Washington, DC: National Institute of Justice, 1987).

10. John J. DiIulio, "Crime and Punishment in Wisconsin," *Wisconsin Policy Research Institute Report,* vol. 3, no. 7 (1990), pp. 1–56; see also William Barr, *The Case for More Incarceration* (Washington, DC: U.S. Department of Justice, Office of Policy Development, 1992).

11. Franklin Zimring and Gordon Hawkins, *Scale of Imprisonment* (Chicago, IL: University of Chicago Press, 1991).

12. David F. Greenberg, "The Cost-Benefit Analysis of Imprisonment," *Social Justice,* vol. 17, no. 4 (1991), p. 49.

13. Francis T. Cullen and Paul Gendreau, "Assessing Correctional Rehabilitation: Policy, Practice, and Prospects," in Julie Horney (ed.), *Criminal Justice 2000,* vol. 3 (Washington, DC: National Institute of Justice, 2000).

14. Robert Martinson, "What Works? Questions and Answers About Prison Reform," *Public Interest,* vol. 35 (Spring 1974), pp. 22–54.

15. Cullen and Gendreau, "Assessing Correctional Rehabilitation."

16. Edgardo Rotman, *Beyond Punishment: A New View on the Rehabilitation of Criminal Offenders* (Westport, CT: Greenwood, 1990), p. 11.

17. California Proposition 36 Steering Committee, *Impact Analysis,* February 28, 2001, http://www.dph.sf.ca.us/Prop36/Meetings/Minutes/2-28%20SteerComm.pdf (accessed June 18, 2002).

18. Marty Price, "Crime and Punishment: Can Mediation Produce Restorative Justice for Victims and Offenders?" http://www.vorp.com/articles/crime.html (accessed February 9, 1999).

19. United Nations, *Restorative Justice: Report of the Secretary-General* (Vienna, Austria: United Nations Commission on Crime Prevention and Criminal Justice, 2002).

20. Graeme Newman, *The Punishment Response* (Philadelphia: Lippincott, 1978), p. 104.

21. See, for example, Andrew R. Klein, *Alternative Sentencing: A Practitioner's Guide* (Cincinnati, OH: Anderson, 1988).

22. Much of what follows is derived from Bureau of Justice Assistance *National Assessment of Structured Sentencing* (Washington, DC: Bureau of Justice Assistance, 1996).

23. S. A. Shane-DuBow, A. P. Brown, and E. Olsen, *Sentencing Reform in the U.S.: History, Content and Effect* (Washington, DC: U.S. Department of Justice, 1985).

24. J. Cohen and M. H. Tonry, "Sentencing Reforms and Their Impacts," in A. Blumstein et al. (eds.), *Research on Sentencing: The Search for Reform* (Washington, DC: National Academy Press, 1983), pp. 305–459.

25. State of Washington, Sentencing Guidelines Commission, *Adult Sentencing Manual 2000,* http://www.sgc.wa.gov/adult_sentencing_manual_2000.htm (accessed June 20, 2002).

26. Governor's Commission on Certainty in Sentencing (Georgia), letter to Governor Roy E. Barnes, December 1, 1999, http://www.state.ga.us/certainty/letter.pdf (accessed June 20, 2002).

27. Code of Alabama, 12-25-2. The commission was established by executive order on August 30, 1999.

28. The materials in this section are derived from the Website of the Federal Sentencing Commission, http://www.ussc.gov.

29. Title II of the Comprehensive Crime Control Act of 1984; 18 U.S.C. § 3551–3626 and 28 U.S.C. § 991–998.

30. See, for example, Alexandra A. E. Shapiro and Jonathan P. Bach, "Applying 'Apprendi' to Federal Sentencing Rules," *New York Law Journal,* March 23, 2001, http://www.lw.com/pubs/articles/pdf/applyingApprendi.pdf (accessed June 30, 2002); and Freya Russell, "Limiting the Use of Acquitted and Uncharged Conduct at Sentencing: *Apprendi v. New Jersey* and Its Effect on the Relevant Conduct Provision of the United States Sentencing Guidelines," *California Law Review,* vol. 89 (July 2001), p. 1199.

31. M. Tonry, *Sentencing Matters* (Oxford, UK: Oxford University Press, 1995).

32. U.S. Department of Justice, *Mandatory Sentencing* (Washington, DC: Office of Justice Programs, 1997).

33. In mid-1996, the California Supreme Court ruled the state's three-strikes law an undue intrusion on judges' sentencing discretion and gave judges greater leeway in deciding when the law applies. In 1998, however, the same court held that cases falling "within the spirit of the law" must be sentenced as the law requires. In 1999, California's three-strikes law was upheld by the U.S. Supreme Court in the case of *Riggs v. California,* 525 U.S. 1114 (1999) cert. denied.

34. G. L. Pierce and W. J. Bowers, "The Bartley-Fox Gun Law's Short-Term Impact on Crime in Boston," *Annals of the American Academy of Political and Social Science,* vol. 455 (1981), pp. 120–132.

35. C. Loftin, M. Heumann, and D. McDowall, "Mandatory Sentencing and Firearms Violence: Evaluating an Alternative

to Gun Control," *Law and Society Review,* vol. 17 (1983), pp. 287–318.

36. C. Loftin and D. McDowall, "The Deterrent Effects of the Florida Felony Firearm Law," *Journal of Criminal Law and Criminology,* vol. 75 (1984), pp. 250–259.

37. D. McDowall, C. Loftin, and B. Wierseman, "A Comparative Study of the Preventive Effects of Mandatory Sentencing Laws for Gun Crimes," *Journal of Criminal Law and Criminology,* vol. 83, no. 2 (Summer 1992), pp. 378–394.

38. Joint Committee on New York Drug Law Evaluation, *The Nation's Toughest Drug Law: Evaluating the New York Experience,* a project of the Association of the Bar of the City of New York, the City of New York, and the Drug Abuse Council, Inc. (Washington, DC: Government Printing Office, 1978).

39. Michael Tonry, *Sentencing Reform Impacts* (Washington, DC: U.S. Department of Justice, National Institute of Justice, 1987).

40. Much of what follows is taken from John Clark, James Austin, and D. Alan Henry, *Three Strikes and You're Out: A Review of State Legislation* (Washington, DC: National Institute of Justice, 1997).

41. Bureau of Justice Assistance, *National Assessment of Structured Sentencing* (Washington, DC: U.S. Department of Justice, February 1996).

42. Elizabeth A. King, "Inter Alia," *Corrections Compendium,* April 2002, p. 22.

43. Several states have had such laws on the books for many years. For example, South Dakota has had three-strikes–type legislation since 1877.

44. James Austin, "'Three Strikes and You're Out': The Likely Consequences on the Courts, Prisons, and Crime in California and Washington State," *St. Louis University Public Law Review,* vol. 14, no. 1 (1994).

45. The Washington law does permit the governor to grant a pardon or clemency, but it also recommends that no person sentenced under this law to life in prison without parole be granted clemency until he or she has reached 60 years of age and is judged no longer a threat to society.

46. *Andrade* v. *Attorney General of the State of California,* 270 F.3d 743 (2001).

47. *Lockyer* v. *Andrade,* U.S. Supreme Court, No. 01-1127 (Decided March 5, 2003).

48. *Ewing* v. *California,* U.S. Supreme Court, No. 01-6978 (Decided March 5, 2003).

49. Austin, "'Three Strikes and You're Out,'"

50. Countywide Criminal Justice Coordination Committee, *Impact of the "Three Strikes Law" on the Criminal Justice System in Los Angeles County* (Los Angeles: CCJCC, November 15, 1995). The number of inmates the jail system can house is limited by a federal court order and the sheriff's budget. Therefore, the use of early-release mechanisms for lower-risk offenders has been accelerated to make room for the growing number of two- and three-strikes cases. This policy has not increased the size of the jail population, but it has changed its composition.

51. California Sheriff's Association, *Three Strikes Jail Population Report* (Sacramento, CA: California Sheriff's Association, 1995).

52. Center for Urban Analysis, Santa Clara County Office of the County Executive, *Comparing Administration of the "Three-Strikes Law" in the County of Los Angeles with Other Large California Counties* (Santa Clara, CA: Center for Urban Analysis, Santa Clara County Office of the County Executive, May 1996).

53. Los Angeles County Sheriff's Department, *"Three Strikes" Law—Impact on Jail: Summary Analysis* (Los Angeles: Los Angeles County Sheriff's Department, August 31, 1996).

54. John Clark et al., *Three Strikes and You're Out: A Review of State Legislation* (Washington, DC: National Institute of Justice, 1997).

55. Tamar Lewin, "3-Strikes Law Is Overrated in California, Study Finds," *New York Times,* August 23, 2001.

56. Ryan S. King and Marc Mauer, *Aging Behind Bars: "Three Strikes" Seven Years Later* (Washington, DC: Sentencing Project, 2001).

57. Ibid.

58. Fox Butterfield, "States Easing Stringent Laws on Prison Time," *New York Times,* September 2, 2001.

59. "Crime Spree Blamed on Early Release," The Associated Press, March 12, 2003.

60. See U.S. Sentencing Commission, *Report to Congress: Cocaine and Federal Sentencing Policy* (Washington, DC: U.S. Sentencing Commission, 2002), http://www.schmalleger.com/pubs/cocaine2002.pdf.

61. See "Justice Department Fights to Maintain Crack/Powder Cocaine Sentencing Disparities," DRCNet, March 22, 2002, http://www.drcnet.org/wol/230.html#sentencingcommission, (accessed June 26, 2002).

62. Edith E. Flynn et al., "Three-Strikes Legislation: Prevalence and Definitions," in National Institute of Justice, *Task Force Reports From the American Society of Criminology* (Washington, DC: National Institute of Justice, 1997).

63. Paula M. Ditton and Doris J. Wilson, *Truth in Sentencing in State Prisons* (Washington, DC: Bureau of Justice Statistics, 1999), p. 1.

64. Robin I. Lubitz and Thomas W. Ross, "Sentencing Guidelines: Reflections on the Future," *Sentencing and Corrections: Issues for the 21st Century,* no. 10 (Washington, DC: National Institute of Justice, 2001).

65. Edgardo Rotman, *Beyond Punishment: A New View on the Rehabilitation of Criminal Offenders* (Westport, CT: Greenwood Press, 1990), p. 3.

Chapter 4

1. Lauren E. Glaze, *Probation and Parole in the United States, 2002* (Washington, DC: U.S. Department of Justice, Bureau of Justice Statistics, August 2003).

2. B. J. George, "Screening, Diversion and Mediation in the United States," *New York Law School Law Review,* vol. 29 (1984), pp. 1–38.

3. M. Douglas Anglin, Douglas Longshore, and Susan Turner, "Treatment Alternatives to Street Crime: An Evaluation of Five Programs," *Criminal Justice and Behavior,* vol. 26, no. 2 (1999), pp. 168–195.

4. Thomas P. Bonczar, *Characteristics of Adults on Probation, 1995* (Washington, DC: U.S. Department of Justice, Bureau of Justice Statistics, 1997).

5. John Augustus, *A Report of the Labors of John Augustus, for the Last Ten Years, in Aid of the Unfortunate* (Boston: Wright and Hasty, 1852); reprinted as J*ohn Augustus, First Probation Officer* (New York: National Probation Association, 1939), p. 26.
6. Ibid., pp. 4–5, 78–79.
7. Sanford Bates, "The Establishment and Early Years of the Federal Probation System," *Federal Probation,* vol. 14 (1950), pp. 16–21; Joel R. Moore, "Early Reminiscences," *Federal Probation,* vol. 14 (1950), pp. 21–29; and Richard A. Chappell, "The Federal Probation System Today," *Federal Probation,* vol. 14 (1950), pp. 30–40.
8. Lauren E. Glaze, *Probation and Parole in the United States, 2002.*
9. Camille Graham Camp and George M. Camp, *The Corrections Yearbook, 2000: Adult Corrections* (Middletown, CT: Criminal Justice Institute, Inc., 2001), p. 178.
10. Caroline Wolf Harlow, *Prior Abuse Reported by Inmates and Probationers* (Washington, DC: Department of Justice, Bureau of Justice Statistics, April 1999).
11. Kathy L. Waters, "Probation, Parole and Community Corrections: A Difficult Topic to Understand?" *Corrections Today,* vol. 65, no. 1 (February 2003), p. 10.
12. Robert J. Bosco, "Connecticut Probation's Partnership with the Private Sector," *Topics in Community Corrections: Privatizing Community Supervision* (Longmont, CO: National Institute of Corrections, 1998), p. 12.
13. Ibid, p. 15.
14. Joan Petersilia, Susan Turner, James Kahan, and Joyce Peterson, *Granting Felons Probation: Public Risks and Alternatives* (Santa Monica, CA: RAND, 1985).
15. W. R. Benedict and L. Huff-Corzine, "Return to the Scene of the Punishment: Recidivism of Male Property Offenders on Felony Probation," *Journal of Research in Crime and Delinquency,* vol. 34 (1997), pp. 237–252.
16. James A. Gondles Jr., "The Probation and Parole System Needs Our Help to Succeed," *Corrections Today,* vol. 65, no. 1 (February 2003), p. 8.
17. Jenni Gainsborough and Marc Mauer, *Diminishing Returns: Crime and Incarceration in the 1990s* (Washington, DC: Sentencing Project, September 2000), p. 3.
18. William H. DiMascio, *Seeking Justice: Crime and Punishment in America* (New York: Edna McConnell Clark Foundation, 1997), p. 43.
19. Joan Petersilia, "Probation in the United States," in Michael Tonry, *Crime and Justice: A Review of Research,* vol. 22 (Chicago: University of Chicago Press, 1997), pp. 149–200.
20. Paul Gendreau, "The Principles of Effective Intervention with Offenders," in Alan Harland (ed.), *Choosing Correctional Options That Work: Defining the Demand and Evaluating the Supply* (Thousand Oaks, CA: Sage, 1996).
21. See, for example, Joan Petersilia and Susan Turner, *Evaluating Intensive Supervision Probation/Parole: Results of a Nationwide Experiment* (Washington, DC: National Institute of Justice, 1993); Ben Crouch, "Is Incarceration Really Worse? Analysis of Offenders' Preferences for Prison Over Probation," *Justice Quarterly,* vol. 10 (1993), pp. 67–88; and Joan Petersilia and Elizabeth Piper Deschenes, "Perceptions of Punishment: Inmates and Staff Rank the Severity of Prison Versus Intermediate Sanctions," *The Prison Journal,* vol. 74 (1994), pp. 304–328.
22. Stanley W. Hodge and Victor E. Kappler, "Can We Continue to Lock up the Nonviolent Drug Offender?" in Charles B. Fields (ed.), *Controversial Issues in Corrections* (Boston: Allyn & Bacon, 1999), pp. 137–151.
23. Institute of Medicine, Committee for the Substance Abuse Coverage Study, "A Study of the Evolution, Effectiveness, and Financing of Public and Private Drug Treatment Systems," in D. R. Gerstein and H. J. Harwood (eds.), *Treating Drug Problems,* vol. 1 (Washington, DC: National Academy Press, 1990).
24. R. Hubbard, J. Rachael, S. Craddock, and E. Cavanaugh, "Treatment Outcome Prospective Study (TOPS): Client Characteristics and Behaviors Before, During, and After Treatment," DHHS Publication No. (ADM) 84-1349, in F. Tims and J Ludford (eds.), *Drug Abuse Treatment Evaluation: Strategies, Progress and Prospects* (Rockville, MD: National Institute on Drug Abuse, 1984), pp. 29–41.
25. Mark Sanders, "Building Bridges Instead of Walls: Effective Cross-Cultural Counseling," *Corrections Today,* vol. 65, no. 1 (February 2003), pp. 58–59.
26. Camille Graham Camp and George M. Camp, *The Corrections Yearbook, 2000: Adult Corrections* (Middletown, CT: Criminal Justice Institute, 2001), pp. 199–200, 205–206.
27. Michael D. Norman and Robert C. Wadman, "Probation Department Sentencing: Recommendations in Two Utah Counties," *Federal Probation,* vol. 64, no. 2 (December 2000), pp. 47–51.
28. Michael D. Norman and Robert C. Wadman, "Utah Presentence Reports: User Group Perceptions of Quality and Effectiveness," *Federal Probation,* vol. 64, no. 1 (June 2000), pp. 8, 9.
29. American Bar Association, *Standards Relating to Sentencing Alternatives and Procedures* (Chicago: American Bar Association, n.d.).
30. Paul F. Cromwell, Rolando V. del Carmen, and Leanne F. Alarid, *Community-Based Corrections,* 5th ed. (Belmont, CA: Wadsworth, 2002).
31. Cecil E. Greek, "The Cutting Edge: A Survey of Technological Innovation," *Federal Probation,* vol. 65, no. 1 (June 2001), p. 51.
32. Michelle Gaseau, *Mapping to Improve Supervision and Community Corrections,* October 23, 2000, http://www.corrections.com (accessed November 10, 2003).
33. Peggy Burke, "Probation and Parole Violations: An Overview of Critical Issues," in Madeline M. Carter (ed.), *Responding to Probation and Parole Violators* (Washington, DC: National Institute of Corrections, April 2001), p. 6.
34. Joan Petersilia, "Probation in the United States," in Michael Tonry (ed.), *Crime and Justice: A Review of Research,* vol. 22 (Chicago: University of Chicago Press, 1997), p. 151.
35. "Leading Officials Issue Plan for 'Reinventing' Probation," *Criminal Justice Newsletter,* vol. 30, no. 7 (April 1, 1999), pp. 1–2.
36. Burke, "Probation and Parole Violations," pp. 5, 6.

37. Becki Ney and Donna Reback, "Developing Baseline Information: Understanding Current Policy and Practice," in Madeline M. Carter (ed.), *Responding to Probation and Parole Violators* (Washington, DC: National Institute of Corrections, April 2001), p. 33.

Chapter 5

1. Herbert A. Johnson, *History of Criminal Justice* (Cincinnati, OH: Anderson, 1988).
2. Paige M. Harrison and Jennifer C. Karberg, *Prison and Jail Inmates at Midyear 2000* (Washington, DC: National Institute of Justice, Bureau of Justice Statistics, April 2003).
3. "California Lawmakers Battle Over Prison Budget," *Corrections Today,* vol. 65, no. 3 (June 2003), p. 20.
4. Michael Tonry, "Intermediate Sanctions in Sentencing Guidelines," in Michael Tonry (ed.), *Crime and Justice: A Review of Research,* vol. 23 (Chicago: University of Chicago Press, 1998), pp. 199–253.
5. Michael Tonry and Mary Lynch, "Intermediate Sanctions," in Michael Tonry (ed.), *Crime and Justice: A Review of Research,* vol. 20 (Chicago: University of Chicago Press, 1996), pp. 102–103.
6. Camille Graham Camp and George M. Camp, *Adult Corrections Yearbook* (Middletown, CT: Criminal Justice Institute, 2001), p. 170.
7. Betsy A. Fulton, Susan Stone, and Paul Gendreau, *Restructuring Intensive Supervision Programs: Applying What Works* (Lexington, KY: American Probation and Parole Association, 1994).
8. Doris Layton MacKenzie, "Evidence-Based Corrections: Identifying What Works," *Crime & Delinquency,* vol. 46, no. 4 (October 2000), pp. 457–472.
9. Joan Petersilia, Arthur J. Lurigio, and James M. Byrne, "Introduction," in James M. Byrne, Arthur J. Lurigio, and Joan Petersilia (eds.), *Smart Sentencing: The Emergence of Intermediate Sanctions* (Newbury Park, CA: Sage, 1992), pp. ix–x; Elizabeth Deschenes, Susan Turner, and Joan Petersilia, *Intensive Community Supervision in Minnesota: A Dual Experiment in Prison Diversion and Enhanced Supervised Release* (Washington, DC: National Institute of Justice, 1995); and Joan Petersilia and Susan Turner, *Evaluating Intensive Supervision Probation/Parole: Results of a Nationwide Experiment* (Washington, DC: National Institute of Justice, May 1993).
10. Doris Layton MacKenzie and J. W. Shaw, "Inmate Adjustment and Change During Shock Incarceration: The Impact of Correctional Boot Camp Programs," *Justice Quarterly,* vol. 7 (1990), pp. 125–150; and Joan Petersilia and Susan Turner, "Intensive Probation and Parole," in Michael Tonry (ed.), *Crime and Justice: A Review of Research,* vol. 17 (Chicago: University of Chicago Press, 1993), pp. 281–335.
11. William M. DiMascio, *Seeking Justice: Crime and Punishment in America* (New York: Edna McConnell Clark Foundation, 1997), p. 36.
12. National Association of Drug Court Professionals, http://www.nadcp.org/whatis/ (accessed April 12, 2002).
13. John S. Goldcamp, "What We Know About the Impact of Drug Courts: Moving Research from "Do They Work?" to "When and How They Work," testimony before the Senate Judiciary Subcommittee on Youth Violence, October 3, 2000, p. 1.
14. National Association of Drug Court Professionals, http://www.nadcp.org/whatis/ (accessed April 16, 2002).
15. Goldcamp, "What We Know," p. 4.
16. Ibid., p. 7.
17. http://www.nadcp.org/whatis/ (accessed April 16, 2002).
18. Drug Courts Program Office, *About the Drug Courts Program Office* (Washington, DC: U.S. Department of Justice, Drug Courts Program Office, June 2000).
19. John Roman, Wendy Townsend, Avinash Singh Bhati, *Recidivism Rates for Drug Court Graduates: Nationally Based Estimates, Final Report* (Washington, DC: National Institute of Justice, July 2003).
20. Bureau of Justice Assistance, *How to Use Structured Fines (Day Fines) as an Intermediate Sanction* (Washington, DC: Department of Justice, November 1996).
21. Liisa Kyle, "Finn Fined US $103,600 for Speeding," *Toronto Star,* January 19, 2002, p. G27.
22. Bureau of Justice Assistance, *How to Use Structured Fines (Day Fines) as an Intermediate Sanction.*
23. Ibid.
24. Morris and Tonry, *Between Prison and Probation,* p. 152.
25. Julie C. Martin, "Community Service for Offenders," in Tara Gray (ed.), *Exploring Corrections* (Boston: Allyn & Bacon, 2002), pp. 311–318.
26. Michael Tonry, "Parochialism in U.S. Sentencing Policy," *Crime & Delinquency,* vol. 45, no. 1 (1999), p. 58.
27. DiMascio, *Seeking Justice,* pp. 43–45.
28. Warren Young, *Community Service Orders* (London: Heinemann, 1979); Gill McIvor, *Sentenced to Serve: The Operation and Impact of Community Service by Offenders* (Aldershot, UK: Avebury, 1992); and Peter J. O. Tak, "Netherlands Successfully Implements Community Service Orders," *Overcrowded Times,* vol. 6 (1995), pp. 16–17.
29. DiMascio, *Seeking Justice,* p. 37.
30. *FY 2001 Annual Report* (Atlanta: Georgia Department of Corrections, Probation Division, 2002).
31. Dale G. Parent, "Day Reporting Centers: An Evolving Intermediate Sanction," *Federal Probation,* vol. 60, no. 4 (December 1996), pp. 51–54; and George Mair, "Day Centres in England and Wales," *Overcrowded Times,* vol. 4 (1993), pp. 5–7.
32. Charles Bahn and James R. Davis, "Day Reporting Centers as an Alternative to Incarceration," *Journal of Offender Rehabilitation,* vol. 27, no. 3/4 (1998), pp. 139–150.
33. Dale G. Parent, Jim Byrne, Vered Tsarfaty, and Julie Esselman, *Day Reporting Centers* (Washington, DC: National Institute of Justice, 1995).
34. Dale Parent, "Day Reporting Centers: An Emerging Intermediate Sanction," *Overcrowded Times,* vol. 2 (1991), pp. 6, 8; and Jack McDevitt and Robyn Miliano, "Day Reporting Centers: An Innovative Concept in Intermediate Sanctions," in James M. Byrne, Arthur J. Lurigio, and Joan Petersilia (eds.), *Smart Sentencing: The Emergence of Intermediate Sanctions* (Newbury Park, CA: Sage, 1992).

35. Liz Marie Marciniak, "The Addition of Day Reporting to Intensive Supervision Probation: A Comparison of Recidivism Rates," *Federal Probation,* vol. 64, no. 1 (June 2000), pp. 34–39.

36. Ibid., p. 37.

37. Charles Bahn and James R. Davis, "Day Reporting Centers as an Alternative to Incarceration," p. 149.

38. Interview with Joe Russo, Program Manager at the National Law Enforcement and Corrections Technology Center, in Dana Razzano, "Strides Made in Electronic Monitoring: Improving Accuracy and Lowering Price," Corrections.com, http://www.corrections.com (accessed April 17, 2002).

39. Darren Gowen, "Remote Location Monitoring—A Supervision Strategy to Enhance Risk Control," *Federal Probation,* vol. 65, no. 2 (September 2001), pp. 38–41.

40. Darren Gowen, "Overview of the Federal Home Confinement Program, 1988–1996," *Federal Probation,* vol. 64, no. 2 (December 2000), pp. 11–18.

41. Dan M. Bowers, "Home Detention Systems," *Corrections Today,* July 2000, pp. 102–106.

42. James Bonta, Suzanne Wallace-Capretta, and Jennifer Rooney, "Can Electronic Monitoring Make a Difference? An Evaluation of Three Canadian Provinces," *Crime & Delinquency,* vol. 46, no. 1 (January 2000), pp. 61–75.

43. Camille Graham Camp and George M. Camp, *Adult Corrections Yearbook* (Middletown, CT: Criminal Justice Institute, 2001), p. 124.

44. Kay Knapp, Peggy Burke, and Mimi Carter, *Residential Community Corrections Facilities: Current Practice and Policy Issues* (Longmont, CO: National Institute of Corrections, August 1992).

45. Richard Lawrence, "Restitution Programs," in Tara Gray (ed.), *Exploring Corrections* (Boston: Allyn & Bacon, 2002), pp. 319–320.

46. Ibid., p. 320.

47. General Accounting Office, *Federal Guidance Needed If Halfway Houses Are to Be a Viable Alternative to Prison* (Washington, DC: U.S. Government Printing Office, 1975).

48. Division of Criminal Justice, Office of Research and Statistics, *Executive Summary: 2000 Community Corrections Study Results* (Denver: State of Colorado, Division of Criminal Justice, Office of Research and Statistics, March 22, 2001), http://www.cdpsweb.state.co.us/ors/docs.htm (accessed May 18, 2001).

49. U.S. General Accounting Office, *Federal Guidance,* p. 12.

50. Doris L. MacKenzie and Eugene E. Hebert (eds.), *Correctional Boot Camps: A Tough Intermediate Sanction* (Washington, DC: National Institute of Justice, 1996).

51. Camille Graham Camp and George M. Camp, *Adult Corrections Yearbook* (Middletown, CT: Criminal Justice Institute, 2001), pp. 120–122; and *Corrections Yearbook: Jails* (Middletown, CT: Criminal Justice Institute, 2001), p. 43.

52. Doris Layton MacKenzie et al., "Boot Camps as an Alternative for Women," in Doris L. Mackenzie and Eugene E. Hebert (eds.), *Correctional Boot Camps: A Tough Intermediate Sanction* (Washington, DC: National Institute of Justice, 1996).

53. Doris L. MacKenzie and A. Rosay, "Correctional Boot Camps for Juveniles," in *Juvenile and Adult Boot Camps* (Laurel, MD: American Correctional Association, 1996).

54. Sheldon X. Zhang, *Evaluation of the Los Angeles County Juvenile Drug Treatment Boot Camp, Executive Summary* (Washington, DC: U.S. Department of Justice, National Institute of Justice, 2000).

55. Merry Morash and Lila Rucker, "Critical Look at the Ideal of Boot Camp as Correctional Reform," *Crime & Delinquency,* vol. 36 (1990), pp. 204–222.

56. DiMascio, *Seeking Justice,* p. 41.

57. Doris L. MacKenzie and J. W. Shaw, "The Impact of Shock Incarceration on Technical Violations and New Criminal Activities," *Justice Quarterly,* vol. 10, no. 3 (1993), pp. 463–486.

58. Dionne T. Wright and G. Larry Mays, "Correctional Boot Camps, Attitudes, and Recidivism: The Oklahoma Experience," *Journal of Offender Rehabilitation,* vol. 28, no. 1/2 (1998), pp. 71–87.

59. Jeanne B. Stinchcomb and W. Clinton Terry III, "Predicting the Likelihood of Rearrest Among Shock Incarceration Graduates: Moving Beyond Another Nail in the Boot Camp Coffin," *Crime & Delinquency,* vol. 47, no. 2 (April 2001), pp. 221–242.

60. Dale Parent, "Boot Camps Failing to Achieve Goals," *Overcrowded Times,* vol. 5 (1994), pp. 8–11; Doris Layton MacKenzie, "Boot Camps: A National Assessment," *Overcrowded Times,* vol. 5 (1994), pp. 14–18; and Philip A. Ethridge and Jonathan R. Sorensen, "An Analysis of Attitudinal Change and Community Adjustment Among Probationers in a County Boot Camp," *Journal of Contemporary Criminal Justice,* vol. 13, no. 2 (May 1992), pp. 139–154.

61. W. J. Dickey, *Evaluating Boot Camp Prisons* (Washington, DC: National Institute of Justice, 1994); Peter Katel and Melinda Liu, "The Bust in Boot Camps," *Newsweek,* February 21, 1994, p. 26; and Dale Parent, "Boot Camps Failing to Achieve Goals."

62. Doris L. MacKenzie and Claire Souryal, *Multi-Site Evaluation of Shock Incarceration: Executive Summary* (Washington, DC: National Institute of Justice, 1994); see also Doris L. MacKenzie and A. Piquero, "The Impact of Shock Incarceration Programs on Prison Crowding," *Crime & Delinquency,* vol. 40 (1994), pp. 222–249.

63. Stinchcomb and Terry, "Predicting the Likelihood of Rearrest Among Shock Incarceration Graduates," pp. 239–240.

64. Velmer S. Burton, James W. Marquart, S. J. Cuvelier, L. F. Alarid, and R. J. Hunter, "A Study of Attitude Change Among Boot Camp Participants," *Federal Probation,* vol. 57, no. 3 (1993), pp. 46–52; see also Michael W. Osler, "Shock Incarceration: Hard Realities and Real Possibilities," *Federal Probation,* vol. 55, no. 1 (1991), pp. 34–42.

65. Judith Greene and John Dobble, *Attitudes Toward Crime and Punishment in Vermont: Public Opinion About an Experiment with Restorative Justice* (Washington, DC: U.S. Department of Justice, National Institute of Justice, 2000); see also David R. Karp, "Harm and Repair: Observing Restorative Justice in Vermont," *Justice Quarterly,* vol. 18, no. 4 (December 2001), pp. 727–757, for an analysis of the

decision-making process for negotiating "thin" versus "thick" reparative contracts with offenders.

66. George F. Cole, Barry Mahoney, Marlene Thornton, and Roger A. Hanson, *The Practice and Attitudes of Trial Court Judges Regarding Fines as a Criminal Sanction* (Washington, DC: National Institute of Justice, 1987).

Chapter 6

1. The information used in this introductory story was obtained from a Lexis/Nexis search of general news and major newspaper sources including the *Chicago Sun-Times,* May 27, 1999, April 30, 2002, and April 14, 2003; *Houston Chronicle,* May 1, 2002; *Newsday* (New York), April 9, 2003; *New York Daily News,* May 27, 1999, and November 22, 2000; *New York Times,* April 30, 2002, and May 9, 2002; *St. Petersburg Times,* April 14, 2003; *Tampa Tribune,* April 30, 2002; *The Daily Telegraph* (Sydney, Australia), April 30, 2002; *The Gazette* (Montreal, Quebec), April 9, 2003; and *The Independent* (London), April 30, 2002. See also "Darryl Strawberry Chronology," www.newsday.com/sports/baseball/ny-spstrawchrono.story (accessed May 8, 2003); and "Darryl Strawberry Mugshots," www.mugshots.net/darryl_strawberry (accessed May 8, 2003).
2. Michael O'Toole, "Jails and Prisons: The Numbers Say They Are More Different Than Generally Assumed," *American Jails Magazine,* www.corrections.com/aja/mags/articles/toole.html (accessed May 9, 2003).
3. Paige M. Harrison and Jennifer C. Karberg, *Prison and Jail Inmates at Midyear 2002* (Washington, DC: Bureau of Justice Statistics, April 2003).
4. National Advisory Commission on Criminal Justice Standards and Goals, *Corrections* (Washington, DC: U.S. Government Printing Office, 1973), p. 273.
5. Marilyn D. McShane and Frank P. Williams III (eds.), *Encyclopedia of American Prisons* (New York: Garland, 1996), p. 494.
6. Ibid., p. 496.
7. Ronald L. Goldfarb, *Jails: The Ultimate Ghetto* (Garden City, NY: Doubleday, 1975), p. 29.
8. John Irwin, *The Jail: Managing the Underclass in American Society* (Berkeley, CA: University of California Press, 1986).
9. David M. Parrish, "The Evolution of Direct Supervision in the Design and Operation of Jails," *Corrections Today,* www.corrections.com/aca/cortoday/october00/parrish.html (accessed October 26, 2000).
10. Linda Zupan, *Jails: Reform and the New Generation Philosophy* (Cincinnati, OH: Anderson, 1991).
11. Dennis McCave, "Testing the Seams: When the Limits Are Pushed in Direct Supervision," *American Jails,* vol. 16, no. 1 (2002), pp. 51–56.
12. Ibid., p. 56.
13. Ibid.
14. Peter Perroncello, "Direct Supervision: A 2001 Odyssey," *American Jails,* vol. 15, no. 6 (2001), p. 25. See also B. G. Harding, Larry Link, Marion Van Court, and Jeff White, *2001 Directory of Direct Supervision Jails* (Longmont, CO: National Institute of Corrections Information Center, December 2001).

15. Caroline Wolf Harlow, *Profile of Jail Inmates, 1996* (Washington, DC: U. S. Department of Justice, Bureau of Justice Statistics, April 1998).
16. James Austin, Luiza Chan, and Williams Elms, *Women Classification Study—Indiana Department of Corrections* (San Francisco, CA: National Council on Crime and Delinquency, 1993).
17. Gail L. Elias and Kenneth Ricci, *Women in Jail: Facility Planning Issues* (Washington, DC: U.S. Department of Justice, National Institute of Corrections, March 1997).
18. Tim Brennan and James Austin, *Women in Jail: Classification Issues* (Washington, DC: U.S. Department of Justice, National Institute of Corrections, March 1997).
19. Merry Morash, Timothy S. Bynum, and Barbara A. Koons, *Women Offenders: Programming Needs and Promising Approaches* (Washington, DC: U.S. Department of Justice, National Institute of Justice, August 1998).
20. William C. Collins and Andrew W. Collins, *Women in Jail: Legal Issues* (Washington, DC: U.S. Department of Justice, National Institute of Corrections, December 1996).
21. Linda Zupan, "The Persistent Problems Plaguing Modern Jails," in Tara Gray (ed.), *Exploring Corrections* (Boston: Allyn and Bacon, 2002), pp. 37–62.
22. Kenneth Kerle, "Women in the American World of Jails: Inmates and Staff," *Margins: Maryland's Law Journal on Race, Religion, Gender, and Class,* vol. 2, no. 1, (Spring 2002), pp. 41–61.
23. Todd D. Minton, *Jails in Indian Country, 2001* (Washington, DC: U.S. Department of Justice, Bureau of Justice Statistics, May 2002).
24. Samuel Walker, Cassia Spohn, and Miriam DeLone, "Corrections: A Picture in Black and White," in Tara Gray (ed.), *Exploring Corrections* (Boston: Allyn and Bacon, 2002), pp. 13–24.
25. Michael Tonry, *Malign Neglect* (New York: Oxford, 1995).
26. Samuel Walker, Cassia Spohn, and Miriam DeLone, "Corrections: A Picture in Black and White," in Tara Gray (ed.), *Exploring Corrections* (Boston: Allyn and Bacon, 2002), p. 16.
27. Paige M. Harrison and Jennifer C. Karberg, *Prison and Jail Inmates at Midyear 2002,* p. 10.
28. James J. Stephan, *Census of Jails, 1999* (Washington, DC: U.S. Department of Justice, Bureau of Justice Statistics, August 2001).
29. American Correctional Association, *Vital Statistics in Corrections* (Lanham, MD: American Correctional Association, 2000), p. 30.
30. Linda Zupan, "The Persistent Problems Plaguing Modern Jails," in Tara Gray (ed.), *Exploring Corrections* (Boston: Allyn and Bacon, 2002).
31. American Correctional Association, *Vital Statistics in Corrections,* p. 26.
32. National Sheriff's Association, *The State of Our Nation's Jails, 1982* (Washington, DC: National Sheriff's Association, 1982).
33. Kenneth Kerle, "Women in the American World of Jails: Inmates and Staff," *Margins: Maryland's Law Journal on Race, Religion, Gender, and Class.*
34. James J. Stephan, *Census of Jails, 1999.*
35. National Sheriff's Association, *The State of Our Nation's Jails, 1982.*

36. Ibid., p. 231.
37. Ibid., p. 151.
38. As cited in National Institute of Corrections, *Briefing Paper: Trends in Jail Privatization* (Boulder, CO: National Institute of Corrections Information Center, February 1992).
39. Semoon Chang and Jack S. Tillman, "Should County Jails Be Privatized?" *American Jails*, vol. 16, no. 4, (September/October 2002), p. 48.
40. Mark A. Cunniff, *Jail Crowding: Understanding Jail Population Dynamics* (Washington, DC: U.S. Department of Justice, National Institute of Corrections, January 2002).
41. Ibid., p. 21.
42. Caroline Wolf Harlow, *Profile of Jail Inmates, 1996*, p. 3.
43. National Institute of Justice, *The Orange County, Florida, Jail Educational and Vocational Programs* (Washington, DC: U.S. Department of Justice, 1997).
44. Ibid., p. 3.
45. Pat Nolan, "Prison Fellowship and Faith-Based Initiatives," *On the Line*, vol. 25, no. 5, (November 2002), p. 2.
46. Bryon R. Johnson, David B. Larson, and Timothy C. Pitts, "Religious Programs, Institutional Adjustment, and Recidivism Among Former Inmates in Prison Fellowship Programs," *Justice Quarterly*, vol. 14, no. 1, (March 1997), pp. 145–166.
47. T. David Evans, Francis T. Cullen, Roger D. Dunaway, and Velmer S. Burton Jr., "Religion and Crime Reexamined: The Impact of Religion, Secular Controls and Social Ecology on Adult Criminality," *Criminology*, vol. 33, no. 2 (May 1995), pp. 195–217.
48. Sheldon Crapo, "Breaking the Cycle of Crime . . . One Life at a Time," *American Jails*, vol. 11, no. 1 (March/April 1997), p. 24.
49. "Mecklenburg County Jails Achieve National Accreditation," http://www.charmeck.org/departments/mcso/community+connections/newrelease.asp#presentation (accessed May 16, 2003).

Chapter 7

1. Paige M. Harrison and Allen J. Beck, *Prisoners in 2002* (Washington, DC: Bureau of Justice Statistics, July 2003).
2. Allen J. Beck and Jennifer C. Karberg, *Prison and Jail Inmates at Midyear 2000* (Washington, DC: Bureau of Justice Statistics, March 2001), p. 2.
3. Thomas P. Bonczar, *Prevalence of Imprisonment in the U.S. Population, 1974–2001* (Washington, DC: U.S. Department of Justice, Bureau of Justice Statistics, August 2003), p. 7.
4. Federal Bureau of Investigation, *Crime in the United States 2002* (Washington, DC: Federal Bureau of Investigation, 2003), http://www.fbi.gov (accessed December 20, 2003).
5. James J. Stephen and Jennifer C. Karberg, *Census of State and Federal Correctional Facilities, 2000* (Washington, DC: U.S. Department of Justice, Bureau of Justice Statistics, August 2003).
6. Beth R. Richie, "Challenges Incarcerated Women Face as They Return to Their Communities: Findings from Life History Interviews," *Crime and Delinquency*, vol. 47, no. 3 (July 2001), pp. 368–389.
7. Bureau of Justice Statistics, *Special Report: Women Offenders* (Washington, DC: U.S. Department of Justice, 1999).
8. Meda Chesney-Lind, "Putting the Breaks on the Building Binge," *Corrections Today*, vol. 54, no. 6 (August 1992), p. 30.
9. Richie, "Challenges Incarcerated Women Face."
10. Federal Bureau of Investigation, *Crime in the United States 2002* (Washington, DC: U.S. Department of Justice, 2003), http://www.fbi.gov (accessed December 20, 2003).
11. Jennifer Gonnerman, "An Expert Analyzes the Prison Population Boom," *Village Voice*, February 22, 2000, p. 56.
12. Carl B. Clements, "The Future of Offender Classification: Some Cautions and Prospects," *Criminal Justice and Behavior*, vol. 8 (1981), pp. 15–16.
13. Carl B. Clements, "Offender Classification: Two Decades of Progress," *Criminal Justice and Behavior*, vol. 23 (1996), p. 123.
14. J. Alexander, J. Austin, S. Brown, L. Chan, S. He, and P. Stokes, *Internal Prison Classification Systems: A Field Test of Three Approaches* (San Francisco, CA: National Council on Crime and Delinquency, 1997).
15. Clements, "Offender Classification."
16. Robert B. Levinson, *Unit Management in Prisons and Jails* (Lanham, MD: American Correctional Association, 1999).
17. As cited in John W. Roberts, *Work, Education, and Public Safety: A Brief History of Federal Prison Industries* (Washington, DC: U.S. Department of Justice, Federal Bureau of Prisons, n.d.), p. 15.
18. American Correctional Association, *Vital Statistics in Corrections* (Lanham, MD: American Correctional Association, 2000), pp. 121–126.
19. As quoted in John W. Roberts, *Work, Education, and Public Safety: A Brief History of Federal Prison Industries*, p. 11.
20. American Correctional Association, *Vital Statistics in Corrections*, pp. 118–120.
21. Ibid., pp. 121–126.
22. Cited in *Hoover's Online*, http://www.hoovers.com (accessed September 1, 2003).
23. W. Saylor and G. Gaes, *PREF: A Study of "Rehabilitating" Inmates Through Industrial Work Participation, and Vocational and Apprenticeship Training* (Washington, DC: Federal Bureau of Prisons, 1996).
24. Karl O. Haigler, Caroline Harlow, Patricia O'Connor, and Anne Campbell, *Executive Summary of Literacy Behind Prison Walls: Profiles of the Prison Population from the National Adult Literacy Survey* (Washington, DC: U.S. Department of Education, National Center for Education Statistics, 1994).
25. Bureau of Justice Statistics, *National Corrections Reporting Programs* (Washington, DC: U.S. Department of Justice, 1994), p. 12. See also Haigler et al., *Executive Summary of Literacy*, and Christine Linquist, Jennifer Hardison, and Pamela K. Lattimore, *Reentry Courts Process Evaluation (Phase I), Final Report* (Research Triangle Park, NC: RTI International, April 2003), p. 2.
26. Bureau of the Census, *Statistical Abstract of the United States, 1997* (Washington, DC: U.S. Department of Commerce, 1997), p. 159.
27. Quoted in "Prisoners Less Educated, Less Literate, Study Finds," press release, U.S. Department of Education, Office of Public Affairs, December 2, 1994, http://ww.ed.gov/Press Releases/12-1994/pris.html.

28. Karen F. Lahm, "Equal or Equitable: An Exploration of Educational and Vocational Program Availability for Male and Female Offenders," *Federal Probation*, vol. 64, no. 2 (December 2000), pp. 39–46.

29. American Correctional Association, *Vital Statistics in Corrections*, pp. 6–9.

30. Bazelon Center for Mental Health Law, *Position Statement on Involuntary Commitment, 1999*. As cited in the Sentencing Project, *Mentally Ill Offenders in the Criminal Justice System: An Analysis and Prescription* (Washington, DC: Sentencing Project, January 2002), pp. 3, 4.

31. Michael S. Vaughn and Leo Carroll, "Separate and Unequal: Prison Versus Free-World Medical Care," *Justice Quarterly*, vol. 15 (1998), pp. 3–40.

32. Stephan and Karberg, *Census of State and Federal Correctional Facilities, 2000*.

33. Excerpted from California and North Dakota's departments of corrections websites, http://www.corr.ca.gov/communicationsoffice/facts_figures.asp, http://www.state.nd.us/lr/fiscal/03-05/agency/530eb.pdf (accessed December 20, 2003).

34. Stephan and Karberg, *Census of State and Federal Correctional Facilities, 2000*, p. 12.

35. "Drug Court Resources—Facts and Figures," http://www.ncjrs.org/drug_courts/facts.html (accessed May 15, 2002).

36. Gonnerman, "An Expert Analyzes," p. 56.

37. See "South Carolina Department of Corrections, Cost Per Inmate Fiscal Year, 1988–2002," http://www.state.sc.us/scdc/statistics/Statistics2000-2001/InmateCost.htm (accessed November 11, 2003).

38. Scott Shane, "U.S. Tops World in Prison Population," *Mobile Register*, June 1, 2003, 17A, 19A.

39. Stephan and Karberg, *Census of State and Federal Correctional Facilities, 2000*, p. 7.

40. Ibid.

41. Ibid.

42. Ibid.

43. Shawn Mansfield (personal communication, July 9, 2003).

44. Scott Shane, "U.S. Tops World in Prison Population."

45. Ibid.

46. Patrick A. Langan and David J. Levin, *Recidivism of Prisoners Released in 1994* (Washington, DC: Bureau of Justice Statistics, June 2002).

47. Christine Lindquist, Jennifer Hardison and Pamela K. Lattimore, *Reentry Courts Process Evaluation (Phase I), Final Report*.

Chapter 8

1. Charles L. Newman, *Sourcebook on Probation, Parole and Pardons*, 3d ed. (Springfield, IL: Charles C Thomas Publisher Ltd., 1970), pp. 30–31. See also Norval Morris, *Maconochie's Gentlemen: The Story of Norfolk Island and the Roots of Modern Prison Reform* (New York: Oxford University Press, 2002).

2. Philip Klein, *Prison Methods in New York State* (New York: Columbia University Press, 1920), p. 417. Cited in U.S. Department of Justice, *Attorney General's Survey of Release Procedures*, vol. 4 (Washington, DC: U.S. Government Printing Office, 1939–1940), p. 5.

3. M. W. Calahan, *Historical Corrections Statistics in the United States, 1850–1984* (Washington, DC: Bureau of Justice Statistics), 1986.

4. G. W. Wickersham, *Reports of the United States National Commission on Law Observance and Enforcement: Wickersham Commission, Report on Penal Institutions, Probation and Parole* (Washington, DC: U.S. Government Printing Office, 1930–1931), p. 324.

5. Ibid., p. 325.

6. Edwin H. Sutherland and Donald R. Cressey, *Principles of Criminology* (Chicago: J. B. Lippincott, 1955), p. 568.

7. David J. Rothman, *Conscience and Convenience: The Asylum and Its Alternatives in Progressive America* (Boston: Little, Brown, 1980), pp. 159–161.

8. Douglas R. Lipton, Robert Martinson, and Judith Wilks, *The Effectiveness of Correctional Treatment: A Survey of Treatment Evaluation Studies* (New York: Praeger, 1975).

9. Peggy McGarry, *Handbook for New Parole Board Members* (Philadelphia: Center for Effective Public Policy, 1989), p. 4.

10. James Austin, "Prisoner Reentry: Current Trends, Practices, and Issues," *Crime and Delinquency*, vol. 47, no. 3 (July 2001), pp. 314–334.

11. Beth E. Richie, "Challenges Incarcerated Women Face as They Return to Their Communities: Findings from Life History Interviews," *Crime and Delinquency*, vol. 47, no. 3 (July 2001), p. 370.

12. Ibid., p. 379.

13. Todd R. Clear, Dina R. Rose, and Judith A. Ryder, "Incarceration and the Community: The Problem of Removing and Returning Offenders," *Crime and Delinquency*, vol. 47, no. 3 (July 2001), pp. 335–351.

14. Camille Graham Camp and George M. Camp, *The Corrections Yearbook 1997* (Middletown, CT: Criminal Justice Institute, 1997), p. 181.

15. A. M. Heinz, J. P. Heinz, S. J. Senderwotz, and M. A. Vance, "Sentencing by Parole Boards: An Evaluation," *Journal of Criminal Law and Criminology*, vol. 67 (1976), pp. 1–31.

16. Mary West-Smith, Mark R. Pogrebin, and Eric D. Poole, "Denial of Parole: An Inmate Perspective," *Federal Probation*, vol. 64, no. 2 (December 2000), p. 5.

17. Ronald Burns, Patrick Kinkade, Matthew C. Leone, and Scott Phillips, "Perspectives on Parole: The Board Members' Viewpoint," *Federal Probation*, vol. 63, no. 1 (June 1999), pp. 16–22.

18. Mary West-Smith, Mark R. Pogrebin, and Eric D. Poole, "Denial of Parole: An Inmate Perspective."

19. Peter B. Hoffman and Lucille K. DeGostin, "Parole Decision-Making: Structuring Discretion," *Federal Probation*, vol. 38, Issue 4 (1974), pp. 24–28.

20. McGarry, *Handbook for New Parole Board Members*, p. 4.

21. Mary West-Smith, Mark R. Pogrebin and Eric D. Poole, "Denial of Parole: An Inmate Perspective."

22. Lauren E. Glaze, *Probation and Parole in the United States, 2002* (Washington, DC: U.S. Department of Justice, Bureau of Justice Statistics), August 2003.

23. Arthur J. Lurigio, "Effective Services for Parolees with Mental Illnesses," *Crime and Delinquency*, vol. 47, no. 3 (July 2001), pp. 446–461.

24. Glaze, *Probation and Parole in the United States, 2002.*
25. Joan Petersilia, *When Prisoners Return to the Community: Political, Economic, and Social Consequences* (Washington, DC: U.S. Department of Justice, National Institute of Justice, November 2000).
26. Harry J. Holzer, *What Employers Want: Job Prospects for Less Educated Workers* (New York: Russell Sage Foundation, 1996).
27. Estimated from American Correctional Association, *Vital Statistics in Corrections* (Lanham, MD: American Correctional Association, 2002), pp. 6–9.
28. Glaze, *Probation and Parole in the United States, 2002.*
29. Robert F. Kronick, Dorothy E. Lambert, and E. Warren Lambert, "Recidivism Among Adult Parolees: What Makes the Difference?" *Journal of Offender Rehabilitation,* vol. 28, no. 1–2 (1998), pp. 61–69.
30. Timothy A. Hughes, Doris James Wilson, and Allen J. Beck, *Trends in State Parole, 1990–2000,* p. 14.
31. "FY 2000 Cooperative Agreement: Transition from Prison to the Community," *Federal Register,* May 12, 2000.
32. Arthur J. Lurigio, "Effective Services for Parolees with Mental Illnesses," p. 457.
33. Peggy B. Burke, *Abolishing Parole: Why the Emperor Has No Clothes* (Lexington, KY: American Probation and Parole Association, 1995).
34. U.S. Parole Commission, *Notes and Procedures Manual* (Chevy Chase, MD: U.S. Government Printing Office, 1989), p. 143.
35. *Reentry Courts: Managing the Transition from Prison to Community* (Washington, DC: Office of Justice Programs, September, 1999).
36. Ibid., p. 9.
37. Ibid., p. 5.
38. Jeffrey Spelman, "An Initial Comparison of Graduates and Terminated Clients in America's Largest Re-Entry Court," *Corrections Today,* vol. 65, no. 2 (August 2003), pp. 74–83.
39. James F. Quinn, Larry Gould, and Linda Holloway, "Community Partnership Councils: Meeting the Needs of Texas' Parole Officers," *Corrections Compendium,* vol. 26, no. 7 (July 2001), pp. 1–19.
40. John J. Larivee, "Returning Inmates: Closing the Public Safety Gap," *Corrections Compendium,* vol. 26, no. 6 (June 2001), pp. 1–10.
41. Beth E. Richie, "Challenges Incarcerated Women Face as They Return to Their Communities: Findings from Life History Interviews," *Crime and Delinquency,* vol. 47, no. 3 (July 2001), pp. 368–389.
42. Peter Finn, "Job Placement for Offenders: A Promising Approach to Reducing Recidivism and Correctional Costs," *National Institute of Justice Journal,* July 1999, pp. 2–11.
43. Susan Herman and Cressida Wasserman, "A Role for Victims in Offender Reentry," *Crime and Delinquency,* vol. 47, no. 3 (July 2001), pp. 428–445.
44. Edward J. Latessa and Harry E. Allen, *Corrections in the Community,* 2d ed. (Cincinnati, OH: Anderson Publishing Co., 1999), p. 221.
45. Andrew von Hirsch, *Doing Justice: The Choice of Punishments, Report of the Committee for the Study of Incarceration* (New York: Hill and Wang, 1976).
46. Petersilia, *When Prisoners Return to the Community,* p. 2.

Chapter 9

1. CNN Online, "Truck Rams Prison Fence in Florida Breakout," April 11, 1998. Accessed November 11, 2000.
2. Harry Elmer Barnes and Negley K. Teeters, *New Horizons in Criminology,* 3d ed. (Englewood Cliffs, NJ: Prentice Hall, 1959), p. 463.
3. See Sylvia G. McCollum, "Excellence or Mediocrity: Training Correctional Officers and Administrators," *The Keeper's Voice,* vol. 17, no. 4 (Fall 1996).
4. Anthony R. Martinez, "Corrections Officer: The 'Other' Prisoner," *The Keeper's Voice,* vol. 18, no. 1 (Spring 1997).
5. Don A. Josi and Dale K. Sechrest, *The Changing Career of the Correctional Officer: Policy Implications for the 21st Century* (Boston: Butterworth-Heinemann, 1998), p. 11.
6. Ibid., p. 12.
7. John Hepburn, "The Exercise of Power in Coercive Organizations: A Study of Prison Guards," *Criminology,* vol. 23, no. 1 (1985), pp. 145–164.
8. Gresham Sykes, *The Society of Captives* (Princeton, NJ: Princeton University Press, 1958).
9. See, for example, James B. Jacobs and Lawrence J. Kraft, "Integrating the Keepers: A Comparison of Black and White Prison Guards in Illinois," *Social Problems,* vol. 25, no. 3 (1978), pp. 304–318.
10. Adapted from John J. Macionis, *Society: The Basics,* 2d ed (Englewood Cliffs, NJ: Prentice Hall, 1994), p. 405.
11. Kelsey Kauffman, *Prison Officers and Their World* (Cambridge, MA: Harvard University Press, 1988), pp. 85–86.
12. American Correctional Association, *Vital Statistics in Corrections* (Lanham, MD: ACA, 2000), p. 143; and James J. Stephan and Jennifer C. Karberg, *Census of State and Federal Correctional Facilities, 2000* (Washington, DC: BJS, 2003).
13. U.S. Bureau of the Census, *The Population Profile of the United States: 2000 (Internet Release),* http://www.census.gov/population/www/pop-profile/profile2000.html (accessed June 29, 2002).
14. ACA, *Vital Statistics in Corrections.*
15. Ibid.
16. Ibid.
17. See, for example, E. Poole and R. M. Regoli, "Work Relations and Cynicism Among Prison Guards," *Criminal Justice and Behavior,* vol. 7 (1980), pp. 303–314.
18. Adapted from Frank Schmalleger, *Criminal Justice Today: An Introductory Text for the 21st Century,* 6th ed. (Upper Saddle River, NJ: Prentice Hall, 2001).
19. Lucien X. Lombardo, *Guards Imprisoned: Correctional Officers at Work,* 2d ed. (Cincinnati, OH: Anderson, 1989).
20. Adapted from Dora B. Schriro, "Women in Prison: Keeping the Peace," *The Keeper's Voice,* vol. 16, no. 2 (Spring 1995).
21. Ibid.
22. M. I. Cadwaladr, "Women Working in a Men's Jail," *FORUM,* vol. 6, no. 1 (1994).
23. Ibid.
24. N. C. Jurik and J. Halemba, "Gender, Working Conditions, and the Job Satisfaction of Women in a Non-Traditional Occupation: Female Correctional Officers in Men's Prisons," *Sociological Quarterly,* vol. 25 (1984), pp. 551–566.

25. Joseph R. Rowan, "Who Is Safer in Male Maximum Security Prisons?" *The Keeper's Voice,* vol. 17, no. 3 (Summer 1996).

26. Ibid.

27. See, for example, Stephen Walters, "Changing the Guard: Male Correctional Officers' Attitudes Toward Women as Co-workers," *Journal of Offender Rehabilitation,* vol. 20, no. 1 (1993), pp. 47–60.

28. Cadwaladr.

29. Ibid.

30. Public Service Commission (of Canada), "Stress and Executive Burnout," *FORUM,* vol. 4, no. 1 (1992). Much of the material in this section is taken from this work.

31. B. M. Crouch, "The Guard in a Changing Prison World," in B. M. Crouch (ed.), *The Keepers: Prison Guards and Contemporary Corrections* (Springfield, IL: Charles C Thomas, 1980).

32. Shannon Black, Ph.D., "Correctional Employee Stress & Strain," *Corrections Today,* October 2001, p. 99.

33. Lombardo.

34. Eric G. Lambert, "Work-Family Conflict: An Unexplored Stressor for Correctional Staff," *Corrections Compendium,* vol. 26, no. 5 (May 2001).

35. Public Service Commission.

36. Ibid.

37. "Not Stressed Enough?" *FORUM,* vol. 4, no. 1 (1992). Adapted from C. C. W. Hines and W. C. Wilson, "A No-Nonsense Guide to Being Stressed," *Management Solutions,* October 1986, pp. 27–29.

38. J. T. Dignam, M. Barrera, and S. G. West, "Occupational Stress, Social Support, and Burnout Among Correctional Officers," *American Journal of Community Psychology,* vol. 14, no. 2 (1986), pp. 177–193.

39. M. C. W. Peeters, B. P. Buunk, and W. B. Schaufeli, "Social Interactions and Feelings of Inferiority Among Correctional Officers: A Daily Event-Recording Approach," *Journal of Applied Social Psychology,* vol. 25, no. 12 (1995), pp. 1073–1089.

40. Jessie W. Doyle, "6 Elements That Form a Context for Staff Safety," *Corrections Today,* October 2001, pp. 101-104.

41. Terry L. Stewart and Donald W. Brown, "Focusing on Correctional Staff Safety," *Corrections Today,* October 2001, pp. 90–93.

42. Ibid.

43. David Robinson, Frank Porporino, and Linda Simourd, "Do Different Occupational Groups Vary on Attitudes and Work Adjustment in Corrections?" *Federal Probation,* vol. 60, no. 3 (1996), pp. 45–53. See also Francis T. Cullen et al., "How Satisfying Is Prison Work? A Comparative Occupational Approach," *The Journal of Offender Counseling Services and Rehabilitation,* vol. 14, no. 2 (1989), pp. 89–108.

44. Timothy J. Flanagan, Wesley Johnson, and Katherine Bennett, "Job Satisfaction Among Correctional Executives: A Contemporary Portrait of Wardens of State Prisons for Adults," *Prison Journal,* vol. 76, no. 4 (1996), pp. 385–397.

45. Lombardo.

46. Martinez.

47. Thomas Gillan, "The Correctional Officer: One of Law Enforcement's Toughest Positions," *Corrections Today,* October 2001, p. 113.

48. Shannon Black, Ph.D., "Correctional Employee Stress & Strain," p. 99.

49. Andrew Metz, "Life on the Inside: The Jailers," in Tara Gray (ed.), *Exploring Corrections,* (Boston: Allyn & Bacon, 2002), p. 65.

50. Ibid, p. 64.

51. Shannon Black, Ph.D., "Correctional Employee Stress & Strain," p. 99.

52. Stephen Walters, "The Determinants of Job Satisfaction Among Canadian and American Correctional Officers," *Journal of Crime and Justice,* vol. 19, no. 2 (1996), pp. 145–158.

53. John R. Hepburn and Paul E. Knepper, "Correctional Officers as Human Services Workers: The Effect on Job Satisfaction," *Justice Quarterly,* vol. 10, no. 2 (1993), pp. 315–337.

54. Stephen Walters, "Gender, Job Satisfaction, and Correctional Officers: A Comparative Analysis," *The Justice Professional,* vol. 7, no. 2 (1993), pp. 23–33.

55. Dana M. Britton, "Perceptions of the Work Environment Among Correctional Officers: Do Race and Sex Matter?" *Criminology,* vol. 35, no. 1 (1997), pp. 85–105.

56. The Victor Cullins Academy is a facility operating under contract with the Youth Services Division of the state of Maryland.

57. The material in this section comes from Jess Maghan, "Ken Davis: The Complete Correctional Officer," *The Keeper's Voice,* vol. 16, no. 2 (Spring 1995).

58. Keith Martin, *Corrections Prepares for Terrorism* (Corrections Connection News Network, January 21, 2002), http://www.corrections.com (retrieved March 10, 2002).

59. Associated Press, "Attorney, Three Others Indicted for Alleged 'Support of Terrorism,'" *Dallas Morning News,* April 9, 2002, http://www.dallasnews.com/latestnews/ stories/ 040902dnnatterrorindictment.66910.html (accessed July 5, 2002).

60. Jess Maghan, "Intelligence-Led Penology: Management of Crime Information Obtained from Incarcerated Persons," paper presented at the Investigation of Crime World Conference, 2001, p. 6.

61. James Gilligan, M.D., "Sexual Violence as the Cornerstone of Prison Management," in *Violence: Reflections on a National Epidemic* (New York: Vintage Books, 1997), pp. 165–172, http://www.nospank.net/gilligan.htm (accessed June 24, 2003).

Chapter 10

1. News Release, *Women's Prison Dedicates New Child Visitation Unit* (Nashville, TN, March 8, 2002), http://www.state. tn.us/correction/newsreleases/tpfw-child.html (accessed July 3, 2003).

2. Allen Beck et al., *Survey of State Prison Inmates, 1991* (Washington, DC: U.S. Department of Justice, March 1993), http://www.ojp.usdoj.gov/bjs/pub/ascii/sospi91.txt.

3. Erving Goffman, *Asylums: Essays on the Social Situation of Mental Patients and Other Inmates* (Garden City, NY: Anchor Books, 1961).

4. Hans Toch, *Living in Prison: The Ecology of Survival,* reprint ed. (Washington, DC: American Psychological Association, 1996), p. xv.

5. Victoria R. DeRosia, *Living Inside Prison Walls: Adjustment Behavior* (Westport, CT: Praeger Publishers, 1998).

6. "Inmate Subculture," in Virgil L. Williams (ed.), *Dictionary of American Penology: An Introductory Guide* (Westport, CT: Greenwood, 1979).

7. Donald Clemmer, *The Prison Community* (Boston: Holt, Rinehart, Winston, 1940).

8. Stanton Wheeler, "Socialization in Correctional Communities," *American Sociological Review*, vol. 26 (October 1961), pp. 697–712.

9. Gresham M. Sykes, *The Society of Captives: A Study of a Maximum Security Prison* (Princeton, NJ: Princeton University Press, 1958).

10. Stephen C. Light, *Inmate Assaults on Staff: Challenges to Authority in a Large State Prison System*, dissertation, State University of New York at Albany (Ann Arbor, MI: University Microfilms International, 1987).

11. John Irwin and Donald R. Cressey, "Thieves, Convicts and the Inmate Culture," *Social Problems*, vol. 10 (Fall 1962), pp. 142–155.

12. James Jacobs, *Statesville: The Penitentiary in Mass Society* (Chicago: University of Chicago Press, 1977).

13. Miles D. Harer and Darrell J. Steffensmeier, "Race and Prison Violence," *Criminology*, vol. 34, no. 3 (1996), pp. 323–355.

14. John M. Wilson and Jon D. Snodgrass, "The Prison Code in a Therapeutic Community," *Journal of Criminal Law, Criminology, and Police Science*, vol. 60, no. 4 (1969), pp. 472–478.

15. Gresham M. Sykes and Sheldon L. Messinger, "The Inmate Social System," in Richard A. Cloward et al. (eds.), *Theoretical Studies in Social Organization of the Prison* (New York: Social Science Research Council, 1960), pp. 5–19.

16. Peter M. Wittenberg, "Language and Communication in Prison," *Federal Probation*, vol. 60, no. 4 (1996), pp. 45–50.

17. Sykes.

18. John Irwin, *The Felon* (Englewood Cliffs, NJ: Prentice Hall, 1970).

19. Adapted from Frank Schmalleger, *Criminal Justice Today*, 7th ed. (Upper Saddle River, NJ: Prentice Hall, 2003).

20. See, for example, Donald Tucker, *A Punk's Song: View from the Inside* (AMS Press, Inc., 1981), from which some of the information here is adapted.

21. Ibid.

22. Ibid.

23. Ibid.

24. Daniel Lockwood, *Sexual Aggression Among Male Prisoners*, dissertation, State University of New York at Albany (Ann Arbor, MI: University Microfilms International, 1978); and Daniel Lockwood, "Issues in Prison Sexual Violence," *The Prison Journal*, vol. 58, no. 1 (1983), pp. 73–79.

25. Adapted from Toch, p. 274.

26. Beck, Karberg, and Harrison, p. 1.

27. Phyllis J. Baunach, "Critical Problems of Women in Prison," in Imogene L. Moyer (ed.), *The Changing Roles of Women in the Criminal Justice System* (Prospect Heights, IL: Waveland Press, 1985), pp. 95–110.

28. See John W. Palmer and Stephen E. Palmer, *Constitutional Rights of Prisoners*, 6th ed. (Cincinnati, OH: Anderson, 1999).

29. American Corrections Association, *Standards for Adult Correctional Institutions* (Lanham, MD: ACA, 1990).

30. Lawrence A. Greenfeld and Tracy L. Snell, *Women Offenders*, Bureau of Justice Statistics Special Report (Washington, DC: Bureau of Justice Statistics, December 1999, revised October 3, 2000); and Paige M. Harrison and Allen J. Beck, *Prisoners in 2002*, Bureau of Justice Statistics Bulletin (Washington, DC: Bureau of Justice Statistics, 2003).

31. Harrison and Beck.

32. Ibid.

33. Barbara Bloom, et al., *Gender-Responsive Strategies: Research, Practice, and Guiding Principles for Women Offenders* (Washington, DC: National Institute of Corrections, 2003).

34. Bureau of Justice Statistics, "Comparing Federal and State Prisoners," press release, October 2, 1994.

35. American Correctional Association.

36. Bureau of Justice Statistics.

37. Rose Giallombardo, *Society of Women: A Study of a Women's Prison* (New York: John Wiley, 1966).

38. Esther Heffernan, *Making It in Prison: The Square, the Cool, and the Life* (New York: Wiley-Interscience, 1972).

39. Williams, p. 109.

40. Kathryn Watterson, *Women in Prison: Inside the Concrete Tomb*, 2d ed. (Boston: Northeastern University Press, 1996), p. 291.

41. For example, see John Gagnon and William Simon, "The Social Meaning of Prison Homosexuality," in David M. Petersen and Charles W. Thomas (eds.), *Corrections: Problems and Prospects* (Englewood Cliffs, NJ: Prentice Hall, 1980).

42. Doris Layton MacKenzie, James Robinson, and Carol Campbell, "Long-Term Incarceration of Female Offenders: Prison Adjustment and Coping," *Criminal Justice and Behavior*, vol. 16, no. 2 (1989), pp. 223–238.

43. Nicole Hahn Rafter, *Partial Justice: Women, Prisons and Social Control* (New Brunswick, NJ: Transaction, 1990).

44. Barbara Bloom, et al., *Gender Responsive Strategies*.

45. Susan Cranford and Rose Williams, "Critical Issues in Managing Female Offenders," *Corrections Today*, vol. 60, no. 7 (December 1998), pp. 130–135.

46. John DeBell, "The Female Offender: Different . . . Not Difficult," *Corrections Today*, vol. 63, no. 1 (February 2001), pp. 56–61.

47. Tracy L. Snell, "Women in Prison," *Bureau of Justice Statistics Bulletin* (Washington, DC: BJS, March 1994).

48. As estimated by Vesna Markovic, "Pregnant Women in Prison: A Correctional Dilemma?" *The Keepers' Voice* (Summer 1995).

49. Ibid.

50. American Correctional Association, *Standards for Adult Correctional Institutions*, 3d ed. (American Correctional Association, January 1990).

51. Gerald Austin McHugh, "Protection of the Rights of Pregnant Women in Prison and Detention Facilities," *New England Journal of Prison Law*, vol. 6, no. 2 (Summer 1980), pp. 231–263.

52. Ibid., p. 246.

53. Snell, op. cit.

54. National Institute of Corrections, *Services for Families of Prison Inmates* (Washington, DC: NIC, 2002), p. 3.

55. Phyllis Jo Baunach, "Critical Problems of Women in Prison," in Imogene L. Moyer (ed.), *The Changing Roles of Women in the Criminal Justice System* (Prospect Heights, IL: Waveland Press, 1985), p. 16.

56. John J. Sheridan, "Inmates May Be Parents, Too," *Corrections Today,* vol. 58, no. 5 (August 1996), p. 100.

57. Christopher J. Mumola, *Incarcerated Parents and Their Children,* Bureau of Justice Statistics Special Report (Washington, DC: Bureau of Justice Statistics, August 2000).

58. Kelsey Kauffman, "Mothers in Prison," *Corrections Today* (February 2001), pp. 62–65.

59. Harrison and Beck.

60. Mumola, p. 1.

61. Suzanne Hoholik, "Weekend Camp Lets Mother, Kids Bond," *The Columbus Dispatch,* vol. 130, no. 22 (July 22, 2000), pp. A1–A2.

62. Rini Bartlett, "Helping Inmate Moms Keep in Touch," *Correctional Compass* (Tallahassee, FL: Department of Corrections, February 2001), http://www.dc.state.fl.us/pub/compass/0102/page07.html (accessed June 2, 2003).

63. Kauffman, p. 62.

64. Kauffman, p. 63.

65. John Ortiz Smykla, "Coed Prison: Should We Try It (Again)?" in Charles B. Fields (ed.), *Controversial Issues in Corrections* (Boston: Allyn and Bacon, 1999), pp. 203–218.

66. John Ortiz Smykla and Jimmy J. Williams, "Co-Corrections in the United States of America, 1970–1990: Two Decades of Disadvantages for Women Prisoners," *Women & Criminal Justice,* vol. 8, no. 1 (1996), pp. 61–76.

67. Ibid.

68. Jacqueline K. Crawford, "Two Losers Don't Make a Winner: The Case Against the Co-correctional Institution," in John Ortiz Smykla (ed.), *Coed Prison* (New York: Human Sciences Press, 1980), pp. 263–268.

69. Smykla and Williams, p. 61.

70. Lawrence W. Sherman et al., *Preventing Crime: What Works, What Doesn't, What's Promising* (Washington, DC: NIJ, 1997).

Chapter 11

1. Frances Cole, "The Impact of *Bell* v. *Wolfish* Upon Prisoners' Rights," *Journal of Crime and Justice,* vol. 10 (1987), pp. 47–70.

2. Ibid.

3. D. J. Gottlieb, "The Legacy of *Wolfish* and *Chapman:* Some Thoughts About 'Big Prison Case' Litigation in the 1980s," in I. D. Robbins (ed.), *Prisoners and the Law* (New York: Clark Boardman, 1985).

4. James B. Jacobs, *New Perspectives on Prisons and Imprisonment* (Ithaca, NY: Cornell University Press, 1983).

5. Todd Clear and George F. Cole, *American Corrections,* 4th ed. (New York: Wadsworth, 1997).

6. Civil Rights of Institutionalized Persons Act, 42 U.S.C. § 1997 et seq. (1976 ed., Supp. IV), as modified 1980. (Current through P.L. 104–150, approved June 3, 1996.)

7. R. Hawkins and G. P. Alpert, *American Prison Systems: Punishment and Justice* (Englewood Cliffs, NJ: Prentice Hall, 1989).

8. John Scalia, *Prisoner Petitions Filed in U.S. District Courts, 2000, with Trends 1980–2000* (Washington, DC: U.S. Department of Justice, December 2001).

9. Florida Department of Corrections, Office of the Inspector General, *Annual Report* 1994–1995, http://www.dc.state.fl.us/pub/IGannual/19941995/page6.html (accessed May 30, 2002).

10. *Report of the Comptroller General of the United States: Grievance Mechanisms in State Correctional Institutions and Large-City Jails* (Washington, DC: U.S. Government Printing Office, June 17, 1977), Appendix I.

11. Hans Toch, "Democratizing Prisons," *Prison Journal,* vol. 74 (1995), pp. 62–72.

12. James B. Jacobs, "The Prisoners' Rights Movement and Its Impacts," in Edward J. Latessa, Alexander Holsinger, James W. Marquart, and Jonathan R. Sorensen, *Correctional Contexts: Contemporary and Classical Readings,* 2d ed. (Los Angeles: Roxbury, 2001), p. 211. Reprinted from James B. Jacobs, *Crime and Justice,* vol. II, University of Chicago Press, 1980.

13. See *Estelle* v. *Gamble,* 429 U.S. 97 (1976), and *Hutto* v. *Finney,* 437 U.S. 678 (1978).

14. American Civil Liberties Union, *ACLU Position Paper: Prisoners' Rights* (Fall 1999), http://www.aclu.org/library/PrisonerRights.pdf (accessed June 10, 2002).

15. In 1977, Theriault's appeal to the U.S. Supreme Court was denied (see 434 U.S. 953, November 14, 1977).

16. In Section 1997e, Congress created a specific, limited exhaustion requirement for adult prisoners bringing actions pursuant to section 1983.

17. Prison Litigation Reform Act, Pub. L. no. 104–134, 801–10, 110 Stat. 1321 (1996).

18. If a prisoner wishes to proceed as an indigent on appeal, the prisoner must file in the district court, with the notice of appeal, a motion for leave to proceed as an indigent, a certified copy of a prison trust account statement, and Form 4 from the Appendix of Forms found in the *Federal Rules of Appellate Procedure.*

Chapter 12

1. Details for this story come from Jennifer Warren, "The Graying of Prisons," *Los Angeles Times,* June 9, 2002.

2. G. Larry Mays and Daniel L. Judiscak, "Special Needs Inmates in New Mexico Jails," *American Jails,* vol. 10, no. 2 (1996), pp. 32–41.

3. National Center on Addiction and Substance Abuse, *Trends in Substance Abuse and Treatment Needs Among Inmates* (New York: National Center on Addiction and Substance Abuse, Columbia University, October 2002).

4. Caroline Wolf Harlow, *Profile of Jail Inmates 1996* (Washington, DC: Bureau of Justice Statistics, April 1998), pp. 8–9.

5. Federal Bureau of Prisons, "Quick Facts," http://www.bop.gov (accessed October 25, 2002).

6. Paige M. Harrison and Allen J. Beck, *Prisoners in 2002* (Washington, DC: U.S. Department of Justice, Bureau of Justice Statistics, July 2003), pp. 10–11.

7. National Institute of Justice, *Annualized Site Reports 2001* (Washington, DC: U.S. Department of Justice, National Institute of Justice, June 2003).

8. As quoted in Joseph C. Peters, "Breaking the Cycle," remarks to the Academy of Criminal Justice Sciences annual meeting, New Orleans, LA, March 22, 2000.

9. Laura M. Maruschak, *HIV in Prisons and Jails, 1999* (Washington, DC: U. S. Department of Justice, Bureau of Justice Statistics, July 2001); and Laura M. Maruschak, *HIV in Prisons, 2000* (Washington, DC: U.S. Department of Justice, Bureau of Justice Statistics, October 2002).

10. Jaime Shimkus, "Side by Side, Ministers and Detainees Test for HIV Infection," *CorrectCare* Fall 2001, p. 16.

11. L. A. Teplin, "Psychiatric and Substance Abuse Disorders Among Male Urban Jail Detainees," *American Journal of Public Health,* vol. 84, no. 2 (1994), pp. 290–293.

12. Reported in Theodore M. Hammett, Cheryl Roberts, and Sofia Kennedy, "Health-Related Issues in Prisoner Reentry," *Crime and Delinquency,* vol. 47, no. 3 (July 2001), pp. 390–409.

13. Karl O. Haigler, Caroline Harlow, Patricia O'Connor, and Anne Campbell, *Executive Summary of Literacy Behind Prison Walls: Profiles of the Prison Population from the National Adult Literacy Survey* (Washington, DC: U.S. Department of Education, National Center for Education Statistics, 1994).

14. Fox Butterfield, "Experts Say Study Confirms Prison's New Role as Mental Hospital," *New York Times,* July 12, 1999.

15. Thomas N. Faust, "Shift the Responsibility of Untreated Mental Illness out of the Criminal Justice System," *Corrections Today,* April 2003, pp. 6–7.

16. Michael P. Maloney, Michael P. Ward, and Charles M. Jackson, "Study Reveals That More Mentally Ill Offenders Are Entering Jail," *Corrections Today,* April 2003, pp. 100–103.

17. Ibid., p. 3.

18. The Bazelon Center for Mental Health Law, *Position Statement on Involuntary Commitment, 1999.* As cited in The Sentencing Project, *Mentally Ill Offenders in the Criminal Justice System: An Analysis and Prescription* (Washington, DC: The Sentencing Project, January 2002), p. 4.

19. Thomas N. Faust, "Shift the Responsibility of Untreated Mental Illness out of the Criminal Justice System."

20. John M. Greacen, "Then & Now: Reflections on 25 Years of Correctional Health Care," *CorrectCare,* vol. 16, issue 1 (Winter 2002), pp. 9, 22.

21. Henry J. Steadman and Bonita M. Veysey, *Providing Services for Jail Inmates with Mental Disorders* (Washington, DC: National Institute of Justice, Office of Justice Programs, January 1997).

22. American Association for Community Psychiatrists, *Position Statement on Persons with Mental Illness Behind Bars, 1999,* http://www.wpic.pitt.edu/aacp/finds/mibb.html (accessed May 16, 2003). See also Arthur J. Lurigio, "Effective Services for Parolees with Mental Illnesses," *Crime and Delinquency,* vol. 47, no. 3 (July 2001), pp. 446–461.

23. Eric Blaauw, Frans Willem Winkel, and Ad J. F. M. Kerkhof, "Bullying and Suicidal Behavior in Jails," *Criminal Justice and Behavior,* vol. 28, no. 3 (June 2001), pp. 279–299.

24. Mason R. Goodman, "An Overview of Tuberculosis in Jails in the United States for Health Care and Administrative Corrections Professionals," *American Jails,* vol. 10, no. 4 (1996), pp. 45–50.

25. Joann B. Morton, *An Administrative Overview of the Older Inmate,* (Washington, DC: National Institute of Corrections, August 1992), http://www.nicic.org.

26. Connie L. Neeley, Laura Addison, and Delores Craig-Moreland, "Addressing the Needs of Elderly Offenders," *Corrections Today,* vol. 59, no. 5 (August 1997), pp. 120–124.

27. Paige M. Harrison and Jennifer C. Karberg, *Prison and Jail Inmates at Midyear 2002* (Washington, DC: U.S. Department of Justice, Bureau of Justice Statistics, April 2003), p. 11.

28. Ryan S. King and Marc Mauer, *Aging Behind Bars: "Three Strikes" Seven Years Later* (Washington, DC: The Sentencing Project, August 2001).

29. Mardi Hunsberger, "A Prison with Compassion," *Corrections Today* (December 2000), pp. 90–92.

30. Margaret Ratliff and Felicia Cohn, "Hospice with GRACE," *Corrections Today* (February 2000), pp. 64-67; and "Prison Systems Establishing Inmate 'End-of-Life' Programs," *Criminal Justice Newsletter,* vol. 31, no. 9 (March 29, 2001), p. 6.

31. Ronald H. Aday, "Golden Years Behind Bars: Special Programs and Facilities for Elderly Inmates," *Federal Probation,* vol. 58, no. 2 (June 1994), pp. 47–54.

32. Jurgen Neffe, "The Old Folks' Slammer: Aging Prison Population in the United States," *World Press Review,* vol. 44, no. 6 (June 1997), pp. 30–32; and Irina R. Soderstrom and W. Michael Wheeler, "Is It Practical to Incarcerate the Elderly Offender? Yes and No," in Charles B. Fields (ed.), *Controversial Issues in Corrections* (Boston: Allyn and Bacon, 1999), pp. 72–89.

33. Alexandra Pelosi, "Age of Innocence: A Glut of Geriatric Jailbirds," *The New Republic,* vol. 216, no. 18 (May 5, 1997), pp. 15–18.

34. Anne Seidlitz, "National Prison Hospice Association Facilities Deal with Inmate Deaths," *CorrectCare,* vol. 12, no. 1 (Spring 1998), p. 10.

35. National Institute of Corrections, *Hospice and Palliative Care in Prisons* (Longmont, CO: National Institute of Corrections, September 1998).

36. Seidlitz, "National Prison Hospice Association Facilities Deal with Inmate Deaths," p. 10.

37. Lana D. Harrison, "The Revolving Prison Door for Drug-Involved Offenders: Challenges and Opportunities," *Crime and Delinquency,* vol. 47, no. 3 (July 2001), pp. 462–485.

38. National Center on Addiction and Substance Abuse, *Trends in Substance Abuse and Treatment Needs Among Inmates.* See also Candice Byrne, Jonathan Faley, Lesley Flaim, Francisco Pinol, and Jill Schmidtlein, *Drug Treatment in the Criminal Justice System* (Washington, DC: Executive Office of the President, Office of National Drug Control Policy, August 1998).

39. Ibid., pp. 24–25.

40. Lana D. Harrison, "The Revolving Prison Door for Drug-Involved Offenders: Challenges and Opportunities," pp. 465–466.

41. Sandra Tunis et al., *Evaluation of Drug Treatment in Local Corrections* (Washington, DC: U.S. Department of Justice, 1997).

42. *The National Drug Control Strategy, 1998* (Washington, DC: The White House, February 1998).

43. James J. Stephan, *Census of Jails, 1999,* p. 10.

44. Federal Bureau of Prisons, *Triad Drug Treatment Evaluation, Six-Month Report, Executive Summary* (Washington, DC: Federal Bureau of Prisons, no date), http://www.bop. gov/triad.html.

45. Joseph A. Califano Jr., "Foreword," *Behind Bars: Substance Abuse and America's Prison Population* (New York: Columbia University, National Center on Addiction and Substance Abuse, 1998), p. v.

46. As quoted in Califano, "Foreword."

47. Jeremy Travis, *Framing the National Agenda: A Research and Policy Perspective. Speech to National Corrections Conference on Substance Abuse,* April 23, 1997.

48. Center for Substance Abuse Treatment, *NTIES: The National Treatment Improvement Study—Final Report* (Rockville, MD: U.S. Department of Health and Human Services, Substance Abuse and Mental Health Services Administration, 1997).

49. Marcia R. Chaiken, *Prison Programs for Drug-Involved Offenders* (Washington, DC: National Institute of Justice, October 1989); D. A. Andrews, Ivan Zinger, Robert D. Hoge, James Bonta, Paul Gendreau, and Francis T. Cullen, "Does Correctional Treatment Work? A Clinically Relevant and Psychologically Informed Meta-Analysis," *Criminology,* vol. 28, no. 3 (1990), pp. 369–404; and Donald Lipton and Frank Pearson, "The CDATE Project: Reviewing Research on the Effectiveness of Treatment Programs for Adults and Juvenile Offenders," paper presented at the annual meeting of the American Society of Criminology, Chicago, IL, 1996.

50. Bernadette Pelissier, William Rhodes, William Saylor, Gerry Gaes, Scott D. Camp, Suzy D. Vanyur, and Sue Wallace, *TRIAD Drug Treatment Evaluation Project Final Report of Three-Year Outcomes: Part I* (Washington, DC: Federal Bureau of Prisons, Office of Research and Evaluation, September 2000).

51. James A. Inciardi, S. S. Martin, C. A. Butzin, R. M. Hooper, and Linda D. Harrison, "An effective model of prison-based treatment for drug-involved offenders," *Journal of Drug Issues,* vol. 27, no. 2 (Spring 1997), pp. 261–278.

52. Donald Andrews, I. Zinger, R. D. Hoge, James Bonta, Paul Gendreau, and Frank T. Cullen, "Does Correctional Treatment Work? A Clinically Relevant and Psychologically Informed Meta-analysis," *Criminology,* vol. 28 (1990), pp. 97–104; and Paul Gendreau, "The Principles of Effective Intervention with Offenders," in Alan Harlan (ed.), *Choosing Correctional Options That Work* (Thousand Oaks, CA: Sage, 1996), pp. 117–130.

53. Douglas Anglin and Yih-Ing Hser, "Treatment of Drug Abuse," in Michael Tonry and James Q. Wilson (eds.), *Crime and Justice: A Review of Research,* vol. 13 (Chicago: University of Chicago Press, 1990); and Michael Tonry and Mary Lynch, "Intermediate Sanctions," in Michael Tonry (ed.), *Criminal Justice: A Review of Research,* vol. 20 (Chicago: University of Chicago Press, 1996), p. 137.

54. Institute of Medicine, Committee for the Substance Abuse Coverage Study, "A Study of the Evolution, Effectiveness, and Financing of Public and Private Drug Treatment Systems," in D. R. Gerstein and H. J. Harwood (eds.), *Treating Drug Problems,* vol. 1 (Washington, DC: National Academy Press, 1990).

55. R. Hubbard, J. Rachael, S. Craddock, and E. Cavanaugh, "Treatment Outcome Prospective Study (TOPS): Client Characteristics and Behaviors Before, During, and After Treatment," in F. Tims and J Ludford (eds.), *Drug Abuse Treatment Evaluation: Strategies, Progress and Prospects* (Rockville, MD: National Institute on Drug Abuse, 1984), pp. 29–41.

56. Stanley W. Hodge and Victor E. Kappler, "Can We Continue to Lock up the Nonviolent Drug Offender?" in Charles B. Fields (ed.), *Controversial Issues in Corrections* (Boston: Allyn & Bacon, 1999), pp. 137–151.

57. Administrative Office of Courts, *Drug Treatment and Education Fund, Annual Report, Fiscal Year 1999,* Arizona Supreme Court, November 2001.

58. Anna Gorman, "Judges Say New Drug Law Is Working," *Los Angeles Times,* February 5, 2002, http://www.mapinc.org/ newsprop/v02/n193/a06.htm (accessed February 19, 2002).

59. Robert L. Hubbard, James J. Collins, J. Valley Rachal, and Elizabeth R. Cavanaugh, "The Criminal Justice Client in Drug Abuse Treatment," in Carl G. Laukefeld and Frank M. Jims (eds.), *Compulsory Treatment of Drug Abuse: Research and Clinical Practice* (Washington, DC: U.S. Department of Health and Human Services, National Institute of Health, 1988), pp. 57–80.

60. National Association of Drug Court Professionals, http://www.nadcp.org/whatis/ (accessed April 12, 2002).

61. For example, see Steven Belenko, J. A. Fagan, and T. Dumanovsky, "The Effects of Legal Sanctions on Recidivism in Special Drug Courts," *Justice System Journal,* vol. 17, no. 1 (1994), pp. 53–81.

62. Laura M. Maruschak, *HIV in Prisons, 2000.*

63. *Management of the HIV-Positive Prisoner* (New York: World Health CME, no date).

64. Michael S. Vaughn and Leo Carroll, "Separate and Unequal: Prison Versus Free-World Medical Care," *Justice Quarterly,* vol. 15, no. 1 (March 1998), pp. 3–40.

65. Ibid., pp. 31–32.

66. Hammett et al., "Health-Related Issues in Prisoner Reentry," pp. 25–44.

67. Nina Siegal, "Lethal Lottery," in Tara Gray (ed.), *Exploring Corrections* (Boston, MA: Allyn and Bacon, 2002), pp. 122–126.

68. Laura M. Maruschak, *HIV in Prisons, 2000.*

69. Karl Brown, "Managing Sexually Transmitted Diseases in Jails," *HEPP Report,* vol. 6, issue 9 (September 2003), pp. 1–3.

70. *Estelle* v. *Gamble* 429 U.S. 97 (1976).

71. Michael S. Vaughn and Leo Carroll, "Separate and Unequal: Prison Versus Free-World Medical Care," pp. 3–40.

72. Civil Rights of Institutionalized Persons Act, 42 U.S.C. § 1997 et seq. (1976 ed., Supp. IV), as modified 1980. (Current through P.L. 104–150, approved June 3, 1996.)

73. Associated Press, "Supreme Court Upholds Rights of Disabled Inmates," June 15, 1998.

Chapter 13

1. Paige M. Harrison and Allen J. Beck, *Prisoners in 2002* (Washington, DC: U.S. Department of Justice, Bureau of Justice Statistics, July 2003).

2. Ibid.

3. Peggy Burke, "Probation and Parole Violators: An Overview of Critical Issues," in Madeline M. Carter (ed.), *Responding to Probation and Parole Violators* (Washington, DC: National Institute of Corrections, April 2001); and Camille Graham Camp and George M. Camp, *The Corrections Yearbook, 2000: Adult Corrections* (Middletown, CT: Criminal Justice Institute, 2001).

4. Christine Lindquist, Jennifer Hardison, and Pamela K. Lattimore, *Reentry Courts Process Evaluation (Phase I) Final Report* (Research Triangle Park, NC: RTI International, April 2003), p. 2.

5. Timothy Egan, "Less Crime, More Criminals," *New York Times,* March 7, 1999.

6. James J. Stephan, *State Prison Expenditures, 1996* (Washington, DC: U.S. Department of Justice, Bureau of Justice Statistics, August 1999).

7. Jenni Gainsborough and Marc Mauer, *Diminishing Returns: Crime and Incarceration in the 1990s* (Washington, DC: Sentencing Project, September 2000).

8. James J. Stephan, *State Prison Expenditures, 1996.*

9. David P. Farrington and C. P. Nuttal, "Prison Size, Overcrowding, Prison Violence, and Recidivism," *Journal of Criminal Justice,* vol. 8, no. 4 (1980), pp. 221–231.

10. James J. Stephan and Jennifer C. Karberg, *Census of State and Federal Correctional Facilities, 2000* (Washington, DC: U.S. Department of Justice Statistics, August 2003), p. 9.

11. Ibid., p. 9.

12. Keith L. Martin, "Staying Ahead of Gangs/STGs in Corrections," *Corrections.com,* http://www.corrections.com/news/feature/index.html (accessed October 29, 2002).

13. Excerpted from Florida Department of Corrections, "Gang and Security Threat Group Awareness," http://www.dc.state.fl.us/pub/gangs/prison.html (accessed March 30, 2003).

14. Mary E. Pelz, "Gangs," in Marilyn D. McShane and Frank P. Williams III (eds.), *Encyclopedia of American Prisons* (New York: Garland, 1996), p. 213.

15. Burt Useem and Peter Kimball, *States of Siege: U.S. Prison Riots, 1971–1986* (New York: Oxford University Press, 1991).

16. American Correctional Association, "Riots, Disturbances, Violence, Assaults and Escapes," *Corrections Compendium,* vol. 27, no. 5 (May 2002), pp. 6–19.

17. J. Lillis, "Prison Escapes and Violence Remain Down," *Corrections Compendium,* vol. 19, no. 6 (1994), pp. 6–21.

18. Vernon B. Fox, *Violence Behind Bars: An Explosive Report on Prison Riots in the United States* (New York: Vantage, 1956); and Reid H. Montgomery Jr., "Bringing the Lessons of Prison Riots into Focus," *Corrections Today,* vol. 59, no. 1 (February 1997). pp. 28–33.

19. "Prison Riots . . . Why?" *The Prison Journal,* vol. 33, no. 1 (April 1953); and "Aftermath of Riot," *The Prison Journal,* vol. 34, no. 1 (April 1954).

20. Negley K. Teeters, "The Dilemma of Prison Riots," *The Prison Journal,* vol. 33, no. 1 (April 1953), pp. 19–20.

21. New York State Special Commission on Attica (McKay Commission), *Attica: The Official Report of the New York State Special Commission on Attica* (New York: Bantam, 1972), p. xi.

22. As cited in Susan L. Clayton and Gabriella M. Daley, "Mock Riot," *Corrections Today,* July 2000, pp. 128–131.

23. U.S. National Advisory Commission on Civil Disorders (Kerner Commission), *Report* (Washington, DC: Kerner Commission, 1968), p. 2.

24. David A. Ward and Allen F. Breed, *The U.S. Penitentiary, Marion, Illinois: Consultants' Report Submitted to the Committee on the Judiciary, U.S. House of Representatives, Ninety-Eighth Congress, Second Session* (Washington, DC: U.S. Government Printing Office, 1985), p. 1.

25. As quoted in Francis X. Clines, "A Futuristic Prison Awaits the Hard-Core 400," *New York Times,* October 17, 1994, p. A1.

26. Estimates of the number of supermax prisons vary. See David Lovell, Kristin Cloyes, David Allen, and Lorna Rhodes, "Who Lives in Supermaximum Custody? A Washington State Study," *Federal Probation,* vol. 64, no. 2 (December 2000), pp. 33–39; and Corey Weinstein, "Even Dogs Confined to Cages for Long Periods of Time Go Beserk," in John P. May and Khalid R. Pitts (eds.), *Building Violence* (Thousand Oaks, CA: Sage, 2000), pp. 118–124. And see Chase Riveland, *Supermax Housing: Overview and General Considerations* (Washington, DC: National Institute of Corrections, January 1999), p. 1.

27. Riveland, *Supermax Housing,* p. 5. See also Gerald Berge, Jeffrey Geiger, and Scot Whitney, "Technology Is the Key to Security," *Corrections Today,* July 2001, pp. 105–109.

28. See, for example, Richard H. McCleery, "Authoritarianism and the Belief System of Incorrigibles," in Donald R. Cressy (ed.), *The Prison: Studies in Institutional Organization and Change* (New York: Holt, Rinehart and Winston, 1961), pp. 260–306; *Wright v. Enomoto* (July 23, 1980), pp. 5, 15; *Madrid v. Gomez,* 889 F. Supp. 1146 (N.D. Cal. 1995); and Craig Haney, "Infamous Punishment: The Psychological Consequences of Isolation," *National Prison Project Journal* (Spring 1993).

29. Stephen J. Ingley, "Corrections Without Correction," in John P. May and Khalid R. Pitts (eds.), *Building Violence* (Thousand Oaks, CA: Sage, 2000), pp. 18–22.

30. As quoted in Corey Weinstein, "Even Dogs Confined to Cages for Long Periods of Time Go Beserk," in John P. May and Khalid R. Pitts (eds.), *Building Violence* (Thousand Oaks, CA: Sage, 2000), p. 122.

31. *Madrid v. Gomez,* 889 F. Supp. 1146 (N.D. Cal. 1995).

32. Mark Curriden, "Hard Time: Chain Gangs Are in and Exercise Rooms Are out in the Prisons of the 90s," *ABA Journal,* vol. 81 (July 1995), pp. 72–76.

33. "Sports in Prison," *Atlanta Journal-Constitution,* March 22, 1998, pp. E9–E12.

34. Brandon K. Applegate, "Penal Austerity: Perceived Utility, Desert, and Public Attitudes Toward Prison Amenities," *American Journal of Criminal Justice,* vol. 25, no. 2 (2001), pp. 253–268.

35. Nygel Lenz, ""Luxuries" in Prison: The Relationship Between Amenity Funding and Public Support," *Crime and Delinquency,* vol. 48, no. 4 (October 2002), p. 501.

36. As quoted in Garry Boulard, "What's Tough Enough," *State Legislatures,* vol. 21, no. 10 (December 1995), p. 26.

37. Keynote speech, U.S. Attorney General's Summit on Corrections, April 27, 1998.

38. Nygel Lenz, ""Luxuries" in Prison," p. 519.
39. "Inmate Privileges and Fees for Service," *Corrections Compendium,* vol. 27, no. 8 (August 2002), pp. 4–26.
40. Ibid., pp. 8–9.
41. "5 Florida County Jails Make It Real Hard Time: No Television," *New York Times,* August 14, 1994, p. L27.
42. As quoted in Brett Pulley, "Always a Good Sound Bite: The 'Good Life' Behind Bars," *New York Times,* September 22, 1996, Section 13, p. 2.
43. "5 Florida County Jails."
44. John J. Rafferty, "Prison Industry: The Next Step," *Corrections Today,* vol. 60, no. 4 (July 1998), p. 22.
45. W. Wesley Johnson, Katherine Bennett, and Timothy J. Flanagan, "Getting Tough on Prisoners: Results from the National Corrections Executive Survey, 1995," *Crime and Delinquency,* vol. 43, no. 1 (January 1997), pp. 24–41.
46. Adapted from the Website of the American Correctional Association, http://www.corrections.com/aca/standards/benefits.htm (accessed June 15, 2002).
47. Malcolm M. Feeler, "The Privatization of Prisons in Historical Perspective," *Criminal Justice Research Bulletin,* vol. 6, no. 2 (1991), pp. 1–10.
48. James J. Stephan and Jennifer C. Karberg, *Census of State and Federal Correctional Facilities, 2000* (Washington, DC: U.S. Department of Justice, Bureau of Justice Statistics, August 2003), p. 1.
49. Joel Caplan, "Policy for Profit: The Private-Prison Industry's Influence over Criminal Justice Legislation," *ACJS Today,* vol. 26, issue 1 (January/February 2003), pp. 15–20.
50. Travis C. Pratt and Jeff Maahs, "Are Private Prisons More Cost-Effective Than Public Prisons? A Meta-Analysis of Evaluation Research Studies," *Crime and Delinquency,* vol. 45, no. 3 (July 1999), pp. 358–371.
51. Lonn Lanza-Kaduce, Karen F. Parker, and Charles W. Thomas, "A Comparative Recidivism Analysis of Releasees from Private and Public Prisons," *Crime and Delinquency,* vol. 45, no. 1 (January 1999), pp. 28–47.
52. David Shichor, *Punishment for Profit: Private Prisons/Public Concerns* (Thousand Oaks, CA: Sage, 1995).
53. Joel Caplan, "Policy for Profit: The Private-Prison Industry's Influence over Criminal Justice Legislation."
54. Maeve McMahon, review of *Punishment for Profit: Private Prisons/Public Concerns,* by David Shichor, *Canadian Journal of Criminology,* vol. 39, no. 1 (January 1997), p. 115.
55. James Austin and Gary Coventry, *Emerging Issues on Privatized Prisons* (Washington, DC: U.S. Department of Justice, Bureau of Justice Statistics, February 2001).
56. Ibid., p. 29.
57. Charles W. Thomas, *Testimony Regarding Correctional Privatization,* presented before the Little Hoover Commission of the State of California, Sacramento, CA, 1997. As quoted in James Austin and Garry Coventry, *Emerging Issues on Privatized Prisons,* p. 21.
58. Robert J. Bosco, "Connecticut Probation's Partnership with the Private Sector," in National Institute of Corrections, *Topics in Community Corrections: Privatizing Community Supervision* (Washington, DC: National Institute of Corrections, 1998), p. 12.
59. Suzanne Pullen, "An Evaluation of Private Probation Supervision and Case Management in Colorado," in National Institute of Corrections, *Topics in Community Corrections: Privatizing Community Supervision,* p. 15.
60. Reginald A. Wilkinson, "The Future of Adult Corrections," *Corrections Management Quarterly,* vol. 1, no. 1 (Winter 1997).
61. "Telemedicine Expanding in Ohio Prison System," *TECHbeat,* Spring 2002, p. 10.
62. "CORMAP It," *TECHbeat,* Summer 2002, p. 5.

Chapter 14

1. Details for this story come from Glen Puit, "1978 Mutilation: Family Relieved by Singleton's Death," *Las Vegas Review-Journal,* January 6, 2002.
2. Federal Bureau of Prisons, Program Statement number 1490.03, December 14, 1994.
3. Much of the material in this chapter is adapted from Office for Victims of Crime, *New Directions from the Field: Victims Rights and Services for the 21st Century* (Washington, DC: U.S. Department of Justice, 1998).
4. National Organization for Victim Assistance, *1988 NOVA Legislative Directory* (Washington, DC: National Organization for Victim Assistance, 1988), p. 191.
5. Victim and Witness Protection Act of 1982, Pub. L. No. 97–291.
6. Office of Justice Programs, *President's Task Force on Victims of Crime: Four Years Later* (Washington, DC: U.S. Government Printing Office, May 1986), p. 4.
7. Office for Victims of Crime, *The Crime Victim's Right to Be Present* (Washington, DC: OVC Legal Series Bulletin no. 3, November 2001).
8. National Victim Center, *1996 Victims' Rights Sourcebook: A Compilation and Comparison of Victims' Rights Laws* (Arlington, VA: National Victim Center, 1997).
9. Victim and Witness Protection Act of 1982, Pub. L. No. 97-291, Section 2(b).
10. Crime Control Act of 1990, Pub. L. No. 101–647.
11. Op. cit., Title V, Section 502–503.
12. Violent Crime Control and Law Enforcement Act of 1994, Pub. L. No. 103–322.
13. Megan's Law amendment to the Jacob Wetterling Crimes Against Children and Sexual Violent Offender Act, 42 U.S.C. Section 14071.
14. NVCAN was created following a meeting sponsored by the National Organization for Victim Assistance (NOVA) and Mothers Against Drunk Driving (MADD) in 1985.
15. See the National Victims' Constitutional Amendment Network (NVCAN), *1996 Constitutional Amendment Action Kit.*
16. National Victims' Constitutional Amendment Network, *President Bush Announces Support for Bi-partisan Victims' Rights Amendment,* http://www.nvcan.org/home.htm (accessed June 24, 2002).
17. National Institute of Justice, *Victim Costs and Consequences: A New Look* (Washington, DC: NIJ, January 1996).
18. Ibid.

19. Much of the material in this section comes from Office for Victims of Crime, *New Directions*.

20. Anne Seymour, "Promoting Victim Justice Through Corrections-Based Victim Services," *Corrections Today*, July 2000, pp. 140–142.

21. A. Seymour, *National Victim Services Survey of Adult and Juvenile Correctional Agencies and Paroling Authorities, 1996* (Arlington, VA: National Victim Center, April 1997).

22. Office for Victims of Crime, *New Directions*.

23. A. Seymour, *National Victim Services Survey*, p. 5.

24. Megan's Law, Pub. L. No. 104–145, 110 Stat. 1345.

25. Information in this paragraph comes from the National Center for Victims of Crime Public Policy Issues page, http://www.ncvc.org/law/issues/community.htm (accessed November 25, 2002).

26. See Office for Victims of Crime, *New Directions*.

27. See Dorothy Mercer, R. Lord, and J. Lord, "Sharing Their Stories: What Are the Benefits? Who Is Helped?" paper presented at the Annual Meeting of the International Society for Traumatic Stress Studies, Chicago, IL, November 8, 1994.

28. Office for Victims of Crime, *New Directions*.

29. Dean G. Kilpatrick, David Beatty, and Susan Smith Howley, *The Rights of Crime Victims—Does Legal Protection Make a Difference?* (Washington, DC: NIJ, December 1998).

30. Ibid.

31. Office for Victims of Crime, *New Directions*.

32. A. Seymour, *National Victim Services Survey*.

33. A. Seymour, *Promising Practices and Strategies for Victim Services in Corrections* (Washington, DC: Office for Victims of Crime, 1999).

34. Office for Victims of Crime, *State Crime Victim Compensation and Assistance Grant Programs* (Washington, DC: OVC Fact Sheet, January 2002).

35. Office for Victims of Crime, *New Directions*.

36. President's Task Force on Victims of Crime, *Final Report* (Washington, DC: U.S. Government Printing Office, December 1982), p. 39.

37. National Association of Crime Victim Compensation Boards, *Crime Victim Compensation: An Overview* (Washington, DC: National Association of Crime Victim Compensation Boards, 1997), p. 1; and Office for Victims of Crime, *State Crime Victim Compensation and Assistance Grant Programs*.

38. Office for Victims of Crime, *Nationwide Analysis, Victims of Crime Act: 1996 Victims of Crime Act Performance Report, State Compensation Program* (Washington, DC: U.S. Department of Justice, Office of Justice Programs, Office for Victims of Crime, April 14, 1997).

39. Victims of Crime Act of 1984, Pub. L. No. 104–235.

40. Office for Victims of Crime, *Victims of Crime Act Crime Victims Fund* (Washington, DC: OVC Fact Sheet, January 2002).

41. Office for Victims of Crime, *State Crime Victim Compensation and Assistance Grant Programs*.

42. President's Task Force on Victims of Crime, *Final Report*.

43. Much of the material is this section is taken from the Office for Victims of Crime fact sheet, http://www.ncjrs.org/ovcfs.htm (accessed September 1, 1998).

44. Victim and Witness Protection Act of 1982, Pub. L. No. 97–291, Sec. 4.

45. President's Task Force on Victims of Crime, *Final Report* (Washington, DC: U.S. Government Printing Office, December 1982), p. 72.

46. The Mandatory Victim Restitution Act, Title II of the Antiterrorism and Effective Death Penalty Act of 1996, Pub. L. No. 104–132 (1996), 18 U.S.C. Section 3663A (1996).

47. P. A. Langan and M. A. Cunniff, *Recidivism of Felons on Probation, 1986–89* (Washington, DC: U.S. Department of Justice, Bureau of Justice Statistics, February 1992).

48. R. L. Cohen, *Probation and Parole Violators in State Prison, 1991* (Washington, DC: Bureau of Justice Statistics, 1995).

49. Kilpatrick, Beatty, and Howley, *The Rights of Crime Victims*, p. 5.

50. R. L. Cohen, *Probation and Parole Violators in State Prison, 1991*.

51. Much of the material in this section is taken from the office for victims of crime fact sheet, op. cit.

52. Office for Victims of Crime, *What You Can Do If You Are a Crime Victim* (Washington, DC: OVC Fact Sheet, April 2002).

53. The National Victim Center, "INFOLINK: Victim Impact Statements," http://www.nvc.org/infolink/info72.htm (accessed January 2, 1999).

54. See Ellen K. Alexander and Janice Harris Lord, *Impact Statements: A Victim's Right to Speak, A Nation's Responsibility to Listen* (Washington, DC: Office for Victims of Crime, 1994).

55. *Payne v. Tennessee*, 501 U.S. 808, 111 S.Ct. 2597, 115 L. Ed. 2d 720.

56. National Victim Center, *1996 Victims' Rights Sourcebook*.

57. Office for Victims of Crime, *New Directions*.

Chapter 15

1. http://www.deathpenaltyinfo.org (accessed January 10, 2004).

2. Excerpted from Susan Levine, "10 Years After Being Freed by DNA Evidence, His Life Is Still Trying," *Pittsburgh Post-Gazette*, March 2, 2003, p. A-12.

3. Details for this story come from Edward Connors et al., *Convicted by Juries, Exonerated by Science: Case Studies in the Use of DNA Evidence to Establish Innocence after Trial, Issues in Child Abuse Accusations*, vol. 10 (1998), http://www.ipt-forensics.com/journal/volume10/j10_3_6_2.htm (accessed August 19, 2003).

4. *U.S. v. Jackson*, 390 U.S. 570 (1968).

5. *Witherspoon v. Illinois*, 391 U.S. 510 (1968).

6. See the Death Penalty Information Center Website for *The Death Penalty in 2003: Year End Report* and for current international death information, http://www.deathpenaltyinfo.org (accessed January 10, 2004).

7. M. Watt Espy and John Ortiz Smykla, "Executions in the U.S. 1608–2003: The Espy File" (Inter-University Consortium for Political and Social Research, 1994).

8. Thomas P. Bonczar and Tracy L. Snell, *Capital Punishment, 2002* (Washington, DC: U.S. Department of Justice, Bureau of Justice Statistics, November 2003), p. 2.

9. http://www.deathpenaltyinfo.org (accessed July 28, 2003).

10. United States Department of Justice, *The Federal Death Penalty System: A Statistical Survey* (Washington, DC: U.S. Department of Justice, September 12, 2000).

11. Legal defense Fund, *Death Row U.S.A., Fall 2003* (New York: NAACP Defense and Education Fund, October 1, 2003), p. 9, http://www.deathpenaltyinfo.org.

12. Robert M. Bohm, *Deathquest: An Introduction to the Theory and Practice of Capital Punishment in the United States*, 2nd ed. (Cincinnati, OH: Anderson, 2003).

13. John Boger, "Landmark North Carolina Death Penalty Study Finds Dramatic Racial Bias," http://www.deathpenalty info.org (accessed November 1, 2003).

14. See summary of studies in Robert M. Bohm, Deathquest: *An Introduction to the Theory and Practice of Capital Punishment in the United States.*

15. Thomas P. Bonczar and Tracy L. Snell, *Capital Punishment, 2002*, p. 1.

16. Ibid., p. 13.

17. J. Weisberg, "This Is Your Death," *The New Republic,* July 1, 1991.

18. George Lombardi, Richard D. Sluder, and Donald Wallace, "The Management of Death-Sentenced Inmates: Issues, Realities, and Innovative Strategies," paper presented at the annual meeting of the Academy of Criminal Justice Sciences, Las Vegas, Nevada, March 1996.

19. Robert Johnson, "Under Sentence of Death, The Psychology of Death Row Confinement," *Law and Psychology Review,* vol. 5 (Fall 1979), pp. 141–192.

20. As quoted in Bonnie Bartel Latino and Bob Vale, "Welcome to Death Row," *The Birmingham News,* January 16, 2000, pp. 1C, 4C.

21. Thomas J. Reidy, Mark D. Cunningham, and Jon R. Sorensen, "From Death to Life: Prison Behavior of Former Death Row Inmates in Indiana," *Criminal Justice and Behavior,* vol. 28, no. 1 (February 2001), pp. 62–82.

22. Mark Costanzo, *Just Revenge: Costs and Consequences of the Death Penalty* (New York: St. Martin's Press, 1997), p. 51.

23. As quoted in John Ortiz Smykla, "The Human Impact of Capital Punishment," *Journal of Criminal Justice,* vol. 15, no. 4 (1987), pp. 331–347.

24. Summaries of recent poll findings can be found on the Website of the Death Penalty Information Center, http://www.deathpenaltyinfo.org (accessed November 1, 2003). See also Gallup Poll Organization, Poll Topics and Trends: Death Penalty. http://www.gallup.com/poll/topics.

25. Brenda L. Vogel, "Support for Life in Prison Without the Possibility of Parole Among Death Penalty Proponents," *American Journal of Criminal Justice,* vol. 27, no. 2 (Spring 2003), pp. 263–275.

26. As cited in Robert M. Bohm, "The Future of Capital Punishment in the United States," *ACJS Today,* vol. 22, no. 4 (November/December 2000), p. 4.

27. *Washington Post,* December 25, 1998.

28. *Callins v. Collins,* 510 U.S. 1141 (1994).

29. *Furman v. Georgia,* 408 U.S. 238 (1972).

30. *Woodson v. North Carolina,* 428 U.S. 280 (1976); *Roberts v. Louisiana,* 428 U.S. 325 (1976); *Gregg v. Georgia,* 428

U.S. 153 (1976); *Jurek v. Texas,* 428 U.S. 262 (1976); and *Proffitt v. Florida* 428 U.S. 242 (1976).

31. *Ring v. Arizona,* 122 U.S. 2428 (2002).

32. James Liebman, Jeffrey Fagan, and Valerie West, *A Broken System: Error Rates in Capital Cases, 1973–1995* (New York: Columbia University School of Law, 2000), p. i.

33. Ibid. See also Timothy G. Poveda, "Estimating Wrongful Convictions," *Justice Quarterly,* vol. 18, no. 3 (September 2001), pp. 689–708 and Talia Roitberg Harmon, "Predictors of Miscarriages of Justice in Capital Cases," *Justice Quarterly,* vol. 18, no. 4 (December 2001), pp. 949–968.

34. http://www.deathpenaltyinfo.org (accessed January 10, 2004).

35. Liebman, Fagan, and West, *A Broken System: Error Rates in Capital Cases, 1973–1995,* p. 18.

36. http://www.deathpenaltyinfo.org (accessed November 1, 2003).

37. James S. Liebman, Jeffrey Fagan, Andrew Gelman, Valerie West, Garth Davies, and Alexander Kiss, *A Broken System, Part II: Why There Is So Much Error in Capital Cases, and What Can Be Done About It* (New York: Columbia University School of Law, 2002), pp. 391–428.

38. M. Watt Espy and John Ortiz Smykla, "Executions in the U.S., 1608–2003: The Espy File."

39. Does not include Jose High, executed November 6, 2001, in Georgia. He may have been 17 years old at the time of the crime. Records concerning his age are disputed.

40. http://www.gallup.com/poll (accessed November 1, 2003).

41. Deborah Yurgelun-Todd, "Functional Magnetic Resonance Imaging of Facial Affect Recognition in Children and Adolescents," *American Academy of Child and Adolescent Psychiatry,* vol. 38 (1999), pp. 195–199.

42. *Atkins v. Virginia,* 536 U.S. (2002).

43. *Patterson v. Texas,* 536 U.S. (2002).

44. Ibid., pp. 1–2.

45. *In re Stanford,* 537 U.S. (2002).

46. Ibid., p. 6.

47. *Atkins v. Virginia,* p. 11.

48. Chris Kahn, "Inmate in Retardation Case Remains on Death Row," *The Birmingham News,* Novemeber 29, 2003, p. 8A.

49. Ibid.

50. Gennaro F. Vito, "Presidential Address. Research and Relevance: Role of the Academy of Criminal Justice Sciences," *Justice Quarterly,* vol. 16, no. 1 (March 1999), pp. 10–13.

Chapter 16

1. Tom Sheehan, "Buddy Testifies Teen Didn't Like His Stepmother," *The Columbus Dispatch,* February 2, 2000, p. 1B.

2. "Teen Admits Killing Father, Stepmother," *The Cincinnati Enquirer,* Tristate Digest, March 25, 2000, http://enquirer.com/editions/2000/03/25/loc_tristate_digest.html (accessed June 13, 2003).

3. Ken Wooden, *Weeping in the Playtime of Others* (New York: McGraw-Hill, 1976), pp. 23–24.

4. *People ex rel. O'Connell v. Turner,* 55 Ill.280, 8 Am. Rep. 645.

5. R. M. Mennel, *Thorns and Thistles: Juvenile Delinquency in the United States, 1825–1940* (Hanover, NH: University Press of New England, 1973), p. 131.

6. *Kent v. United States,* 383 U.S. 541 (1966).

7. *In re Gault,* 387 U.S. 1, 55 (1967).
8. *In re Winship,* 397 U.S. 358 (1970).
9. *McKeiver* v. *Pennsylvania,* 403 U.S. 528 (1971).
10. *Breed* v. *Jones,* 421 U.S. 519 (1975).
11. Melissa Sickmund, *Juveniles in Court* (Washington, DC: Office of Juvenile Justice and Delinquency Prevention, June 2003), p. 5.
12. FBI, *Uniform Crime Reports: Crime in the United States, 2002* (Washington, DC: U.S. Government Printing Office, 2003).
13. Charles Puzzanchera, Anne L. Stahl, Terrence A. Finnegan, Nancy Tierney, and Howard N. Snyder, *Juvenile Court Statistics 1998* (Washington, DC: Office of Juvenile Justice and Delinquency Prevention, June 2003).
14. Sickmund, *Juveniles in Court.*
15. Ibid., p. 2.
16. Anne L. Stahl, Melissa Sickmund, Terrence A. Finnegan, Howard N. Snyder, Rowen S. Poole, and Nancy Tierney, *Juvenile Court Statistics 1996* (Washington, DC: U.S. Department of Justice, Office of Juvenile Justice and Delinquency Prevention, July 1999), p. 9.
17. Ibid.
18. Howard N. Snyder and Melissa Sickmund, *Juvenile Offenders and Victims: 1999 National Report* (Washington, DC: Office of Juvenile Justice and Delinquency Prevention, September 1999).
19. American Correctional Association, *1997 Directory, Juvenile and Adult Correctional Departments, Institutions, Agencies, and Paroling Authorities* (Lanham, MD: ACA, 1997), p. 39.
20. Melissa Sickmund, Howard N. Snyder, and Eileen Poe-Yamagata, *Juvenile Offenders and Victims: 1997 Update on Violence* (Washington, DC: Office of Juvenile Justice and Delinquency Prevention, 1997).
21. Gerald Bayens, *Assessing the Impact of Judicial Waiver Laws in Kansas: Implications for Correctional Policy* (Ann Arbor, MI: University Microfilms International, 1998).
22. Charles M. Puzzanchera, *Delinquency Cases Waived to Criminal Court, 1989–1998* (Washington, DC: Office of Juvenile Justice and Delinquency Prevention, September 2001).
23. Tammy Hawkins, personal communication, September 21, 1998.
24. Jeffrey A. Butts and Janeen Buck, *Teen Courts: A Focus on Research* (Washington, DC: Office of Juvenile Justice and Delinquency Prevention, October 2000).
25. Tammy Hawkins, personal communication, September 21, 1998.
26. *1999 National Youth Gang Survey* (Washington, DC: Office of Juvenile Justice and Delinquency Prevention, 2003).
27. James H. Burch and Betty M. Chemers, *A Comprehensive Response to America's Youth Gang Problem* (Washington, DC: Office of Juvenile Justice and Delinquency Prevention, 1997).
28. Federal Bureau of Investigation, Kids Crime Prevention Page, www.fbi.gov, 2002 (accessed June 20, 2003).
29. Candice M. Kane, *Prosecutor: Technical Assistance Manual* (Washington, DC: OJJDP, 1992).
30. Ibid.
31. Office of Juvenile Justice and Delinquency Prevention, *1998 National Youth Gang Survey* (U.S. Department of Justice, Washington, DC, November 2000).
32. Jeff Ferrell, "Criminological Verstehen: Inside the Immediacy of Crime," *Justice Quarterly,* vol. 14, no. 1, 1997, pp. 3–23.
33. James Turpin, "Juvenile Justice in the Spotlight," *Corrections Today,* vol. 59, no. 3 (1997), p. 124.
34. *Briefing Paper: Prosecuting Juveniles in Adult Court* (Washington, DC: The Sentencing Project, 1999).

Appendix A

1. John Barker and Jim Kellen, *Career Planning: A Developmental Approach* (Upper Saddle River, NJ: Merrill, 1998).
2. Ibid., p. 75.
3. Tom Jackson, *The Perfect Resume* (New York: Doubleday, 1990).

Glossary

Numbers in parentheses indicate the chapters in which the terms are defined.

A

absconding Fleeing without permission of the jurisdiction in which the offender is required to stay. (149)

accreditation Process through which correctional facilities and agencies can measure themselves against nationally adopted standards and through which they can receive formal recognition and accredited status. (230)

adjudication The process by which a court arrives at a final decision in a case; or the second stage of the juvenile justice process in which the court decides whether the offender is formally responsible for (guilty of) the alleged offense. (19)

administrative officers Those who control keys and weapons and sometimes oversee visitation. (339)

aggravating circumstances Factors that may increase the culpability of the offender. (556)

AIDS (acquired immunodeficiency syndrome) A disease of the human immune system that is characterized cytologically, especially by reduction in the numbers of CD4-bearing helper T cells to 20 percent or less of normal, rendering a person highly vulnerable to life threatening conditions. The disease is caused by infection with HIV commonly transmitted in infected blood and bodily secretions (as semen), especially during sexual intercourse and intravenous drug use. (428)

Americans with Disabilities Act (ADA) Public Law 101-336, enacted July 26, 1990, which prohibits discrimination and ensures equal opportunity for people with disabilities in employment, state and local government services, public accommodations, commercial facilities, and transportation. It also mandates the establishment of TDD/telephone relay services. (450)

arraignment An appearance in court prior to trial in a criminal proceeding. (19)

Auburn system The second historical phase of prison discipline. It followed the Pennsylvania system and allowed inmates to work silently together during the day but were isolated at night. Implemented at New York's Auburn prison in 1815, eventually sleeping cells became congregate and restrictions against talking were removed. (241)

average daily population (ADP) The number of people confined on a specific day. (203)

B

back-end programs Sanctions that move offenders from higher levels of control to lower ones for the final phase of their sentences. (160)

balancing test A method the U.S. Supreme Court uses to decide prisoners' rights cases, weighing the rights claimed by inmates against the legitimate needs of prisoners. (401)

best efforts standard A standard that made the federal law weaker than many states victims' rights laws in which provision for victims' rights and services is mandatory. (506)

bifurcated trial Two separate hearings for different issues in a trial, one for guilt and the other for punishment. (555)

blended sentencing A two-part (juvenile and adult) sentence in which the adult sentence may be waived if the offender complies with all provisions of the juvenile sentence. (593)

block officers Those responsible for supervising inmates in housing areas. (339)

boot camp A short institutional term of confinement that includes a physical regimen designed to develop self-discipline, respect for authority, responsibility, and a sense of accomplishment. (186)

bridewell A workhouse. The word came from the name of the first workhouse in England. (53)

C

capital crime A crime for which the death penalty may but need not necessarily be imposed. (539)

capital punishment Lawful imposition of the death penalty. (537)

certification A credentialing process, usually involving testing and career development assessment, through which the skills, knowledge, and abilities of correctional personnel can be formally recognized. (31)

chlamydia The most common sexually transmitted disease. Caused by the bacteria *Chlamydia trachomatis*, it can affect the eyes, lungs, or urogenital (urinary-genital) area, depending on the age of the person infected and how the infection is transmitted. (449)

chronological resume A resume that organizes information in reverse time sequence and emphasizes work history. (A-7)

citation A type of nonfinancial pretrial release similar to a traffic ticket. It binds the defendant to appear in court on a future date. (226)

civil liability A legal obligation to another person to do, pay, or make good something. (391)

classification The process of subdividing the inmate population into meaningful categories to match offender needs with correctional resources. (254)

clemency Kindness, mercy, forgiveness, or leniency, usually relating to criminal acts. (545)

client-specific plan (CSP) A privately prepared presentence report that supplements the PSR prepared by the probation department. (153)

cocorrections The incarceration and interaction of female and male offenders under a single institutional administration. (381)

coed prison A prison housing both female and male offenders. (381)

community corrections A philosophy of correctional treatment that embraces (1) decentralization of authority, (2) citizen participation, (3) redefinition of the population of offenders for whom incarceration is most appropriate, and (4) emphasis on rehabilitation through community programs. (159)

community corrections acts (CCAs) State laws that give economic grants to local communities to establish community corrections goals and policies and to develop and operate community corrections programs. (193)

community notification Notification to the community of the release or pending release of convicted offenders. (516)

community service A sentence to serve a specified number of hours working in unpaid positions with nonprofit or tax-supported agencies. (174)

commutation A change of a legal penalty to a lesser one; e.g., from death to life imprisonment. (545)

compensatory damages Money a court may award as payment for actual losses suffered by a plaintiff, including out-of-pocket expenses incurred in filing the suit, other forms of monetary or material loss, and pain, suffering, and mental anguish. (393)

concurrent sentences Sentences served together. (86)

conditional diversion Diversion in which charges are dismissed if the defendant satisfactorily completes treatment, counseling, or other programs ordered by the justice system. (118)

conditional release Pretrial release under minimum or moderately restrictive conditions with little monitoring or compliance. It includes ROR, supervised pretrial release, and third-party release. (226)

consecutive sentences Sentences served one after the other. (86)

consent decree A written compact, sanctioned by a court, between parties in a civil case, specifying how disagreements between them are to be resolved. (408)

constitutional rights The personal and due process rights guaranteed to individuals by the U.S. Constitution and its amendments, especially the first 10 amendments, known as the Bill of Rights. Constitutional rights are the basis of most inmate rights. (391)

contract system A system of prison industry in which the prison advertised for bids for the employment of prisoners, whose labor was sold to the highest bidder. (244)

convict lease system A system of prison industry in which a prison temporarily relinquished supervision of its prisoners to a lessee. The lessee either employed the prisoners within the institution or transported them to work elsewhere in the state. (245)

corporal punishments Physical punishments, or those involving the body. (42)

correctional clients Prison inmates, probationers, parolees, offenders assigned to alternative sentencing programs, and those held in jails. (4)

correctional econometrics The study of the cost-effectiveness of various correctional programs and related reductions in the incidence of crime. (78)

correctional officer personalities The distinctive personal characteristics of correctional officers including behavioral, emotional, and social traits. (336)

corrections All the various aspects of the pretrial and postconviction management of individuals accused or convicted of crimes. (21)

corrections professional A dedicated person of high moral character and personal integrity who is employed in the field of corrections and takes professionalism to heart. (30)

counter performance The defendant's participation, in exchange for diversion, in a treatment, counseling, or educational program aimed at changing his or her behavior. (114)

crime A violation of the criminal law. (4)

crime index An annual statistical tally of major crimes known to law enforcement agencies in the United States. (10)

crime rate The number of index offenses reported for each unit of population. (10)

criminal justice The process of achieving justice through the application of the criminal law and through the workings of the criminal justice system. Also, the study of the field of criminal justice. (14)

criminal justice system The collection of all the agencies that perform criminal justice functions, whether these are operations or administration or technical support. The basic divisions of the criminal justice system are police, courts, and corrections. (14)

criminal law (also called *penal law*) That portion of the law that defines crimes and specifies criminal punishments. (24)

cruel and unusual punishment A penalty that is grossly disproportionate to the offense or that violates today's broad and idealistic concepts of dignity, civilized standards, humanity, and decency (*Estelle* v. *Gamble*, 1976, and *Hutto* v. *Finney*, 1978). In the area of capital punishment, cruel and unusual punishments are those that involve torture, a lingering death, or unnecessary pain. (408)

custodial staff Those staff members most directly involved in managing the inmate population. (329)

customer model In this model, a company hires a correctional institution to provide a finished product at an agreed-upon price. The correctional institution owns and operates the business that employs the inmate workforce. (263)

D

day fine A financial penalty scaled both to the defendant's ability to pay and to the seriousness of the crime. (170)

day reporting center (DRC) A community correctional center to which an offender reports each day to file a daily schedule with a supervision officer, showing how each hour will be spent. (178)

death row A prison area housing inmates who have been sentenced to death. (548)

deliberate indifference Intentional and willful indifference. Within the field of correctional practice, the term refers to calculated inattention to unconstitutional conditions of confinement. (409)

delinquent offenses Acts committed by juveniles that, if committed by adults, could result in criminal prosecution. (585)

deprivation theory The belief that inmate subcultures develop in response to the deprivations in prison life. (363)

deserts See **just deserts.**

design capacity The number of inmates that planners or architects intend for the facility. (271)

detention hearing A judicial review of the intake officer's detention decision. (588)

determinate sentence (also called *fixed sentence*) A sentence of a fixed term of incarceration, which can be reduced by good time. (88)

deterrence The discouragement or prevention of crimes through the fear of punishment. (75)

direct file provisions Provisions under which the prosecutor determines whether to initiate a case against a juvenile in juvenile court or in adult criminal court. (594)

direct-supervision jail See **third-generation jail.**

discretionary release Early release based on the paroling authority's assessment of eligibility. (289)

disposition The third stage of the juvenile justice process in which the court decides the disposition (sentence) for a juvenile case. (589)

disturbance An altercation involving three or more inmates, resulting in official action beyond summary sanctions and for which there is an institutional record. (470)

diversion Formal efforts to use alternatives to processing a person through the justice system, including the referral of defendants to non–criminal justice agencies; "the halting or suspension, before conviction, of formal criminal proceedings against a person, conditioned on some form of counter performance by the defendant"; or a nonjudicial juvenile sanction. (113)

drug court A special court that is given responsibility to treat, sanction, and reward drug offenders with punishment more restrictive than regular probation but less severe than incarceration. (165)

due process A right guaranteed by the Fifth, Sixth, and Fourteenth Amendments to the U.S. Constitution and generally understood, in legal contexts, to mean the expected course of legal proceedings according to the rules and forms established for the protection of persons' rights. (411)

E

employer model The most common approach to private business partnerships with prisons. The prison provides a company space in which to operate and a labor pool to hire. The company supervises its inmate employees and makes all decisions. (263)

end-of-life programs Formalized measures to assist terminally ill inmates through their passing. (437)

equity The sentencing principle that similar crimes and similar criminals should be treated alike. (102)

exchange rates An approach to sentencing that emphasizes interchangeability of punishments; for example, three days under house arrest might be considered equal to one day of incarceration. (465)

external classification Interinstitutional placement of an inmate that determines an inmate's security level. (255)

F

fair sentencing Sentencing practices that incorporate fairness for both victims and offenders. Fairness is said to be achieved by implementing principles of proportionality, equity, social debt, and truth in sentencing. (101)

Federal Prison Industries (FPI) A federal, paid inmate work program and self-supporting corporation. (264)

felony A serious criminal offense; specifically, one punishable by death or by incarceration in a prison facility for more than a year. (9)

fine A financial penalty used as a criminal sanction. (169)

first-generation jail Jail with multiple-occupancy cells or dormitories that line corridors arranged like spokes. Inmate supervision is intermittent; staff must patrol the corridors to observe inmates in their cells. (208).

flat sentences Those that specify a given amount of time to be served in custody and allow little or no variation from the time specified. (86)

folkways Time-honored ways of doing things. Although they carry the force of tradition, their violation is unlikely to threaten the survival of the social group. (24)

frivolous lawsuits Lawsuits with no foundation in fact. They are generally brought for publicity, political, or other reasons not related to law. (414)

front-end programs Punishment options for initial sentences more restrictive than traditional probation but less restrictive than jail or prison. (160)

functional resume A resume that emphasizes abilities over work history, organizing information according to skills, results, contributions, or functions. (A-10)

G

gain time Time taken off an inmate's sentence for participating in certain activities such as going to school, learning a trade, and working in prison. (331)

gang A criminal enterprise having an organizational structure, acting as a continuing criminal conspiracy, that employs violence and any other criminal activity to sustain itself. (595)

general deterrence The use of the example of individual punishment to dissuade others from committing crimes. (76)

genital herpes A sexually transmitted disease caused by the herpes simplex virus or HSV. It is one of the most common STDs in the United States. (449)

good time The number of days or months prison authorities deduct from a sentence for good behavior and for other reasons. (87)

gonorrhea The second most common sexually transmitted disease. Often called *the clap*, gonorrhea is caused by the *Neisseria gonorrhea* bacteria found in moist areas of the body. Infection occurs with contact to any of these areas. (449)

group home A nonsecure residential facility for juveniles. (590)

guardian *ad litem* A person appointed by the juvenile court, often defense counsel, to serve as a special guardian for the youth being processed through the juvenile justice system. (589)

guided discretion Decision making bounded by general guidelines, rules, or laws. (555)

H

habitual offender status A law that (1) allows a person's criminal history to be considered at sentencing or (2) makes it possible for a person convicted of a given offense and previously convicted of another specified offense to receive a more severe penalty than that for the current offense alone. (98)

hands-off doctrine An historical policy of the American courts not to intervene in prison management. Courts tended to follow the doctrine until the late 1960s. (388)

hedonistic calculus The idea that people are motivated by pleasure and pain and that the proper amount of punishment can deter crime. (60)

HIV (human immunodeficiency syndrome) Any of a group of retroviruses that infect and destroy helper T cells of the immune system, causing the marked reduction in their numbers that is diagnostic of AIDS. (428)

HIV-positive inmate An incarcerated individual infected with HIV. (428)

hospice An interdisciplinary, comfort-oriented care facility that helps seriously ill patients to die with dignity and humanity in an environment that facilitates mental and spiritual preparation for the natural process of dying. (438)

I

importation theory The belief that inmate subcultures are brought into prison from the outside world. (363)

incapacitation The use of imprisonment or other means to reduce an offender's capability to commit future offenses. (76)

indeterminate sentence A sentence in which a judge specifies a maximum length and a minimum length, and an administrative agency, generally a parole board, determines the actual time of release. (86)

industrial shop and school officers Those who ensure efficient use of training and educational resources within the prison. (339)

informational interviewing Talking to people who are currently employed in a career field of interest. (A-3)

infraction A minor violation of state statute or local ordinance punishable by a fine or other penalty but not by incarceration, or by a specified, usually very short term of incarceration. (9)

injunction A judicial order to do or refrain from doing a particular act. (393)

inmate roles Prison lifestyles; also, forms of ongoing social accommodations to prison life. (365)

inmate subculture (also *prisoner subculture*) The habits, customs, mores, values, beliefs, or superstitions of the body of inmates incarcerated in correctional institutions; also, the inmate social world. (361)

institutional corrections That aspect of the correctional enterprise that "involves the incarceration and rehabilitation of adults and juveniles convicted of offenses against the law, and the confinement of persons suspected of a crime awaiting trial and adjudication." (20)

institutional needs Prison administration interests recognized by the courts as justifying some restrictions on the constitutional rights of prisoners. Those interests are maintenance of institutional *order,* maintenance of institutional *security, safety* of prison inmates and staff, and *rehabilitation* of inmates. (391)

intake The first stage of the juvenile justice process. A court-appointed officer reviews the case and recommends a course of action—dismissal, informal disposition, formal disposition, or transfer to adult criminal court. (586)

intangible losses Costs such as fear, pain, suffering, and reduced quality of life that accrue to victims as a result of their victimization. (510)

integration model A combination of importation theory and deprivation theory. The belief that, in childhood, some inmates acquired, usually from peers, values that support law-violating behavior but that the norms and standards in prison also affect inmates. (363)

intensive supervision probation (ISP) Control of offenders in the community under strict conditions, by means of frequent reporting to a probation officer whose caseload is generally limited to 30 offenders. (164)

intermediate sanctions New punishment options developed to fill the gap between traditional probation and traditional jail or prison sentences and to better match the severity of punishment to the seriousness of the crime. (158)

internal classification Intrainstitutional placement that determines, through review of an inmate's background, assignment to housing units or cellblocks, work, and programming based on the inmate's risk, needs, and time to serve. (255)

J

jail accreditation Formal approval of a jail by the American Correctional Association (ACA) and the Commission on Accreditation. (230)

jails Locally operated correctional facilities that confine people before or after conviction. (203)

job interview A meeting with a prospective employer in which a job applicant projects his or her most impressive qualities. (A-14)

jurisdiction The power, right, or authority of a court to interpret and apply the law. (394)

just deserts Punishment deserved. A just-deserts perspective on criminal sentencing holds that criminal offenders are morally blameworthy and are therefore *deserving* of punishment. (74)

juvenile court Any court that has jurisdiction over matters involving juveniles. (589)

juvenile detention facility A facility for keeping juvenile offenders in secure custody, as necessary, through various stages of the juvenile justice process. (588)

L

legitimate penological objectives The realistic concerns that correctional officers and administrators have for the integrity and security of the correctional institution and the safety of staff and inmates. (401)

M

mandatory death penalty A death sentence that the legislature has required to be imposed upon people convicted of certain offenses. (555)

mandatory minimum sentencing The imposition of sentences required by statute for those convicted of a particular crime or a particular crime with specific circumstances, such as robbery with a firearm or selling drugs to a minor within 1,000 feet of a school, or for those with a particular type of criminal history. (95)

mandatory release Early release after a time period specified by law. (289)

mandatory sentences Those that are required by law under certain circumstances—such as conviction of a specified crime or of a series of offenses of a specified type. (85)

manpower model An approach to private business partnerships with prisons in which the prison's role is similar to that of a temporary personnel service. (263)

maximum- or close/high-security prison A prison designed, organized, and staffed to confine the most dangerous offenders for long periods. It has a highly secure perimeter, barred cells, and a high staff-to-inmate ratio. It imposes strict controls on the movement of inmates and visitors, and it offers few programs, amenities, or privileges. (274)

medical model A philosophy of prisoner reform in which criminal behavior is regarded as a disease to be treated with appropriate therapy. (246)

medium-security prison A prison that confines offenders considered less dangerous than those in maximum security, for both short and long periods. It places fewer controls on inmates' and visitors' freedom of movement than does a maximum-security facility. It has barred cells and a fortified perimeter. The staff-to-inmate ratio is generally lower than that in a maximum-security facility, and the level of amenities and privileges is slightly higher. (274)

minimization of penetration A form of diversion that keeps an offender from going further into the system. (114)

minimum-security prison A prison that confines the least dangerous offenders for both short and long periods. It allows as much freedom of movement and as many privileges and amenities as are consistent with the goals of the facility. It may have dormitory housing, and the staff-to-inmate ratio is relatively low. (274)

misdemeanor A relatively minor violation of the criminal law, such as petty theft or simple assault, punishable by confinement for one year or less. (9)

mitigating circumstances Factors that, although not justifying or excusing an action, may reduce the culpability of the offender. (555)

model of criminal sentencing A strategy or system for imposing criminal sanctions. (86)

mores Cultural restrictions on behavior that forbid serious violations—such as murder, rape, and robbery—or a group's values. (24)

N

net widening Increasing the number of offenders sentenced to a higher level of restriction. It results in sentencing offenders to more restrictive sanctions than their offenses and characteristics warrant. (160)

networking Meeting new people who can give you information about careers, the job market, and specific positions. It is often done through people you know. (A-2)

new offense violation Arrest and prosecution for the commission of a new crime by someone on parole or probation. (150)

no frills prisons and jails Correctional institutions that take away prisoner amenities and privileges. (481)

nolo contendere A plea of "no contest." A no-contest plea may be used by a defendant who does not wish to contest conviction. Because the plea does not admit guilt, it cannot provide the basis for later civil suits. (19)

nominal damages Small amounts of money a court may award when inmates have sustained no actual damages, but there is clear evidence that their rights have been violated. (393)

noninstitutional corrections (also *community corrections*) That aspect of the correctional enterprise that includes "pardon, probation, and miscellaneous [activities] not directly related to institutional care." (21)

O

open institution A minimum-security facility that has no fences or walls surrounding it. (274)

operational capacity The number of inmates that a facility's staff, existing programs, and services can accommodate. (271)

P

pains of imprisonment Major problems that inmates face, such as loss of liberty and personal autonomy, lack of material possessions, loss of heterosexual relationships, and reduced personal security. (362)

pardon An executive act that legally excuses a convicted offender from a criminal penalty. (289)

parens patriae A Latin term that refers to the state as guardian of minors and incompetent people. (579)

parole The conditional release of a prisoner, prior to completion of the imposed sentence, under the supervision of a parole officer. (288)

parole eligibility date The earliest date on which an inmate might be paroled. (293)

parolee A person who is conditionally released from prison to community supervision. (300)

paroling authority A person or correctional agency (often called a *parole board* or *parole commission*) that has the authority to grant parole, revoke parole, and discharge from parole. (297)

penal law See **criminal law**. (24)

penitentiary The earliest form of large-scale incarceration, it punished criminals by isolating them so that they could reflect on their misdeeds, repent, and reform. (241)

Pennsylvania system The first historical phase of prison discipline involving solitary confinement in silence instead of corporal punishment. Conceived by the American Quakers in 1790 and implemented at the Walnut Street Jail. (241)

perimeter security officers Those assigned to security (or gun) towers, wall posts, and perimeter patrols. These officers are charged with preventing escapes and detecting and preventing intrusions. (339)

pleasure-pain principle The idea that actions are motivated primarily by a desire to experience pleasure and avoid pain. (76)

policy-centered approach A method of thinking about and planning for intermediate sanctions that draws together key stakeholders from inside and outside the corrections agency that will implement the sanction. (190)

precedent A previous judicial decision that judges should consider in deciding future cases. (401)

predisposition report A report that documents (1) a juvenile's background; (2) the juvenile's educational history; (3) information gathered from interviews with the juvenile, family members, and others; (4) available placement options; and (5) recommended dispositions. (589)

presentence report (PSR) A report prepared by the probation department of a court that provides a social and personal history as well as an evaluation of a defendant as an aid to the court in determining a sentence. (85)

principle of least eligibility The requirement that prison conditions—including the delivery of health care—must be a step below those of the working class and people on welfare. (271)

prison A state or federal confinement facility that has custodial authority over adults sentenced to confinement. (4)

prison argot The special language of the inmate subculture. (364)

prison code A set of norms and values among prison inmates. It is generally antagonistic to the official administration and rehabilitation programs of the prison. (363)

prisoners' rights Constitutional guarantees of free speech, religious practice, due process, and other private and personal rights as well as constitutional protections against cruel and unusual punishments made applicable to prison inmates by the federal courts. (390)

prisonization The process by which inmates adapt to prison society; the taking on of the ways, mores, customs, and general culture of the penitentiary. (361)

privatization A contract process that shifts public functions, responsibilities, and capital assets, in whole or in part, from the public sector to the private sector. (222)

probation The conditional release of a convicted offender into the community, under the supervision of a probation officer. It is conditional because it can be revoked if certain conditions are not met. (119)

profession An occupation granted high-social status by virtue of the personal integrity of its members. (25)

professional associations Organizations of like-minded individuals who work to enhance the professional status of members of their professional group. (30)

program-centered approach A method of planning intermediate sanctions in which planning for a program is usually undertaken by a single agency, which develops and funds the program. (191)

program staff Those staff members concerned with encouraging prisoners to participate in educational, vocational, and treatment programs. (329)

property crime Burglary, larceny, automobile theft, and arson as reported by the FBI's Uniform Crime Reports. (10)

proportionality The sentencing principle that the severity of punishment should match the seriousness of the crime for which the sentence is imposed. (102)

pseudofamilies Familylike structures, common in women's prisons, in which inmates assume roles similar to those of family members in free society. (375)

public accounts system The earliest form of prison industry, in which the warden was responsible for purchasing materials and equipment and for overseeing the manufacture, marketing, and sale of prison-made items. (244)

public works system A system of prison industry in which prisoners were employed in the construction of public buildings, roads, and parks. (246)

punitive damages Money a court may award to punish a wrongdoer when a wrongful act was intentional and malicious or was done with reckless disregard for the rights of the victim. (393)

R

rabble management Control of people whose noncriminal behavior is offensive to their communities. (207)

racism Social practices that explicitly or implicitly attribute merits or allocate value to individuals solely because of their race. (33)

rated capacity The number of beds or inmates a rating official assigns to a correctional facility. (217)

recidivism The repetition of criminal behavior; generally defined as rearrest. It is the primary outcome measure for probation, as it is for all corrections programs. (129)

reentry court A court that manages the return to the community of individuals released from prison. (309)

reform school A penal institution to which especially young or first-time offenders are committed for training and reformation. (580)

rehabilitation The changing of criminal lifestyles into law-abiding ones by "correcting" the behavior of offenders through treatment, education, and training. (79)

reintegration The process of making the offender a productive member of the community. (79)

release on bail The release of a person upon that person's financial guarantee to appear in court. (225)

release on own recognizance (ROR) Pretrial release on the defendant's promise to appear for trial. It requires no cash guarantee. (225)

relief officers Experienced correctional officers who know and can perform almost any custody role within the institution, used to temporarily replace officers who are sick or on vacation or to meet staffing shortages. (341)

remote-location monitoring Technologies, including global positioning system (GPS) devices and electronic monitoring (EM), that probation and parole officers use to monitor remotely the physical location of an offender. (179)

residential community center (RCC) A medium-security correctional setting that resident offenders are permitted to leave regularly—unaccompanied by staff—for work, for education or vocational programs, or for treatment in the community. (183)

residential treatment center A residential facility that provides intensive treatment services to juveniles. (590)

restitution The practice of requiring an offender to repay the victim or the community in money or through the providing of services for the harm caused. Also the payments made by a criminal offender to his or her victim (or to the court, which then turns them over to the victim) as compensation for the harm caused by the offense. (84)

restoration The process of returning to their previous condition all those involved in or affected by crime—including victims, offenders, and society. (80)

restorative justice A systemic response to wrongdoing that emphasizes healing the wounds of victims, offenders, and communities caused or revealed by crime. (80)

resume A list of your job and other related experiences and education. (A-6)

retribution A sentencing goal that involves retaliation against a criminal perpetrator. (74)

revenge Punishment as vengeance. An emotional response to real or imagined injury or insult. (74)

revocation The formal termination of an offender's conditional freedom. (147)

revocation hearing An administrative review to determine whether a violation of the conditions of probation or parole warrants removal from the community. (147)

right of allocution A statutory provision permitting crime victims to speak at the sentencing of convicted offenders. A federal right of allocution was established for victims of federal violent and sex crimes under the Violent Crime Control and Law Enforcement Act of 1994. (525)

riot Any action by a group of inmates that constitutes a forcible attempt to gain control of a facility or area within a facility. (470)

roles The normal patterns of behavior expected of those holding particular social positions. (328)

S

salient factor score (SFS) A scale, developed from a risk-screening instrument, used to predict parole outcome. (298)

second-generation jail Jail where staff remain in a secure control booth surrounded by inmate housing areas called *pods* and surveillance is remote. (208)

security threat groups (STGs) The current term for prison gangs. (466)

self-assessment Learning who you are and what you can and want to do by evaluating your interests, skills, and values. (A-0)

sentence The penalty a court imposes on a person convicted of a crime. (72)

sentencing The imposition of a criminal sanction by a sentencing authority, such as a judge. (72)

sentencing commission A group assigned to create a schedule of sentences that reflect the gravity of the offenses committed and the prior record of the criminal offender. (88)

sentencing enhancements Legislatively approved provisions that mandate longer prison terms for specific criminal offenses committed under certain circumstances (such as a murder committed because of the victim's race or a drug sale near a school) or because of an offender's past criminal record. (94)

serious error Error that substantially undermines the reliability of the guilt finding or death sentence imposed at trial. (560)

social debt The sentencing principle that the severity of punishment should take into account the offender's prior criminal behavior. (103)

social order The smooth functioning of social institutions, the existence of positive and productive relations among individual members of society, and the orderly functioning of society as a whole. (73)

special master A person appointed by the court to act as its representative to oversee remedy of a violation and provide regular progress reports. (481)

special-needs inmates Incarcerated individuals who require special treatment because they suffer from mental illness, chemical dependency (drug or alcohol), communicable diseases (such as HIV/AIDS and tuberculosis), or general problems of the elderly. (426)

specific deterrence The deterrence of the individual being punished from committing additional crimes. (75)

staff roles The normal patterns of behavior expected of correctional staff members in particular jobs. (328)

staff subculture The beliefs, values, and behavior of staff. They differ greatly from those of the inmate subculture. (333)

state use system A system of prison industry that employs prisoners to manufacture products consumed by state governments and their agencies, departments, and institutions. (245)

status offenses Acts that are law violations only for juveniles such as running away, truancy, or ungovernability (sometimes referred to as *incorrigibility* or *being beyond parental control*). (585)

statutory exclusion provisions Provisions under which adult criminal court jurisdiction for certain juvenile cases is established by state law. (594)

stress Tension in a person's body or mind, resulting from physical, chemical, or emotional factors. (341)

street gang An organized group of people on the street often engaged in significant illegitimate or criminal activity. (597)

structured conflict The tensions between prison staff members and inmates that arise out of the correctional setting. (332)

structured sentencing A set of guidelines for determining an offender's sentence. (465)

subculture The beliefs, values, behavior, and material objects shared by a particular group of people within a larger society. (333)

substance-abusing inmate An incarcerated individual suffering from dependency on one or more substances including alcohol and a wide range of drugs. (427)

supermax housing A free-standing facility, or a distinct unit within a facility, that provides for management and secure control of inmates who have been officially designated as exhibiting violent or serious and disruptive behavior while incarcerated. (476)

supervised pretrial release Nonfinancial pretrial release with more restrictive conditions (for example, participating in therapeutic or rehabilitative programs, reporting to a pretrial officer, and checking in regularly). (235)

supervision The second major role of probation officers, consisting of intervention, surveillance, and enforcement. (142)

syphilis A sexually transmitted disease caused by the bacteria *Treponema pallidum*. If left untreated syphilis can cause serious heart abnormalities, mental disorders, blindness, other neurological problems, and death. Syphilis is transmitted when infected lesions come in contact with the soft skin of the mucous membrane. (449)

T

tangible losses Costs such as medical expenses, lost wages, and property losses that accrue to crime victims as a result of their victimization. (510)

technical violation A failure to comply with the conditions of probation or parole. (149)

teen courts Courts in which youths adjudicate and impose disposition for a juvenile offense. (594)

therapeutic community (TC) A residential treatment program in which substance-abuse inmates are housed in a separate unit within a prison or jail facility. (442)

third-generation jail Sometimes called **direct-supervision jail,** a jail where inmates are housed in small groups, or pods, staffed 24 hours a day by specifically trained officers. Officers interact with inmates to help change behavior. Bars and metal doors are absent, reducing noise and dehumanization. (209)

tort A civil wrong, a wrongful act, or a wrongful breach of duty, other than a breach of contract, whether intentional or accidental, from which injury to another occurs. (392)

total admission The total number of people admitted to jail each year. (203)

total institution A place where the same people work, play, eat, sleep, and recreate together on a continuous basis. The term was developed by the sociologist Erving Goffman to describe prisons and other facilities. (360)

totality of conditions A standard to be used in evaluating whether prison conditions are cruel and unusual. (409)

true diversion A form of diversion that keeps an offender out of the system and helps him or her avoid formal prosecution and labeling. (114)

truth in sentencing The sentencing principle that requires an offender to serve a substantial portion of the sentence and reduces the discrepancy between the sentence imposed and actual time spent in prison. (103)

tuberculosis A highly variable communicable disease that is characterized by toxic symptoms or allergic manifestations that in humans primarily affect the lungs. (435)

U

unconditional diversion The termination of criminal processing at any point before adjudication with no threat of later prosecution. Treatment, counseling, and other services are offered and use is voluntary. (118)

UNICOR The trade name of Federal Prison Industries. UNICOR provides such products as U.S. military uniforms, electronic cable assemblies, and modular furniture. (264)

unit management system A method of controlling prisoners in self-contained living areas and making inmates and staff (unit manager, case manager, correctional counselor, and unit secretary) accessible to each other. (260)

utilitarianism The principle that the highest objective of public policy is the greatest happiness for the largest number of people. (60)

V

victim Someone who suffers direct or threatened physical, emotional, or financial harm as the result of the commission of a crime. The term *victim* also includes the immediate family of a minor or homicide victim. (504)

victim assistance program An organized program that offers services to victims of crime in the areas of crisis intervention and follow-up counseling and that helps victims secure their rights under the law. (524)

victim compensation A form of victim assistance in which state-funded payments are made to victims to help them recover financial losses due to crime. (519)

victim-impact statement A description prepared by victims or friends and relatives of the loss, trauma, and suffering that a crime has caused them. The judge considers it when sentencing the offender. (80)

victim notification Notification to victims of the release or pending release of convicted offenders who have harmed them. (513)

victims' rights The fundamental rights of victims to be represented equitably throughout the criminal justice process. (505)

violent crime Interpersonal crime that involves the use of force by offenders or results in injury or death to victims. In the FBI's Uniform Crime Reports, violent crimes are murder, forcible rape, robbery, and aggravated assault. (10)

W

waiver provisions Provisions under which the juvenile court orders transfer of the case to adult criminal court. (593)

work detail supervisors Those who oversee the work of individual inmates and inmate work crews. (339)

writ of *certiorari* A writ issued by an appellate court to obtain from a lower court the record of its proceedings in a particular case. (20)

writ of *habeas corpus* An order that directs the person detaining a prisoner to bring him or her before a judge, who will determine the lawfulness of the imprisonment. (392)

Y

yard officers Those who supervise inmates in the prison yard. (339)

youth gang A gang whose membership is generally comprised of people between the ages of 12 and 24. (597)

▶ Credits

Case Index

Subject Index

LEHIGH COUNTY DEPARTMENT OF CORRECTIONS

CORRECTIONS SHERIFF'S OFFICE MOBILE, ALABAMA

DEPARTMENT OF JUSTICE ★ FEDERAL BUREAU OF PRISONS

OHIO DEPARTMENT OF REHABILITATION & CORRECTION

GEORGIA STATE OF GEORGIA 1776 CORRECTIONS

DEPARTMENT OF CORRECTIONS · MICHIGAN ·

CORRECTIONS CORPORATION ★★★ CCA OF AMERICA

COOS COUNTY SHERIFF'S OFFICE

DEPARTMENT OF JUVENILE JUSTICE DJJ STATE OF FLORIDA

INDIANA DEPARTMENT OF CORRECTION

WASHINGTON STATE DEPARTMENT of CORRECTIONS

DEPARTMENT OF THE STATE OF TEXAS CRIMINAL JUSTICE

NEW YORK STATE EXCELSIOR CORRECTIONAL SERVICES

DEPARTMENT OF CORRECTIONS STATE OF KANSAS

SOUTH CAROLINA DEPARTMENT OF CORRECTIONS

Tuscolameta, inc. Walnut Grove Youth Correctional Facility

OFFICE OF SHERIFF The Bold New City of the South JACKSONVILLE CORRECTIONS

DEPARTMENT OF XVI TENNESSEE COMMERCE CORRECTION